Londinium and Beyond

Essays on Roman London and its hinterland
for Harvey Sheldon

List of tables

List of principal contributors

Nick Bateman: Museum of London Archaeology Service, Mortimer Wheeler House, 46 Eagle Wharf Road, Hackney, London N1 7ED

David Bird: 14 King's Road, Guildford, Surrey GU1 4JW

Joanna Bird: 14 King's Road, Guildford, Surrey GU1 4JW

Colin Bowlt: Ruislip, Northwood and Eastcote Local History Society, 7 Croft Gardens, Ruislip, Middlesex HA4 8EY

Gary Brown: Pre-Construct Archaeology Ltd, Unit 54, Brockley Cross Business Centre, Endwell Road, London SE4 2PD

Tony Brown: Nether Hall, Church Street, North Kilworth, Leicestershire LE17 6EZ

John Clark: Department of Early London History and Collections, Museum of London, London Wall, London EC2Y 5HN

Jonathan Cotton: Department of Early London History and Collections, Museum of London, London Wall, London EC2Y 5HN

Carrie Cowan: English Heritage, 1 Waterhouse Square, 138–142 Holborn, London EC1N 2ST

Robert Cowie: Museum of London Archaeology Service, Mortimer Wheeler House, 46 Eagle Wharf Road, Hackney, London N1 7ED

Nina Crummy: 2 Hall Road, Copford, Colchester CO6 1BN

Martin J Dearne: 9 Junction Road, Edmonton, Middlesex N9 7JS

Michael Fulford: Department of Archaeology, University of Reading, Whiteknights, PO Box 227, Reading RG6 6AB

Francis Grew: Department of Early London History and Collections, Museum of London, London Wall, London EC2Y 5HN

Jenny Hall: Department of Early London History and Collections, Museum of London, London Wall, London EC2Y 5HN

Mark Hassall: c/o Institute of Archaeology, University College London, 31–34 Gordon Square, London WC1H 0PY

Ian Haynes: School of Historical Studies, Armstrong Building, University of Newcastle upon Tyne NE1 7RU

Martin Henig: Wolfson College, Oxford OX2 6UD

Peter Hinton: Institute of Field Archaeologists, SHES, University of Reading, Whiteknights, PO Box 227, Reading RG6 6AB

Ralph Jackson: Prehistory and Early Europe, British Museum, Russell Square, London WC1B 3DG

Fiona Macdonell: Department of Community and Audience Development, Museum of London, London Wall, London EC2Y 5HN

Nick Merriman: President of the CBA and Director, Manchester Museum, University of Manchester, Oxford Road, Manchester M13 9PL

Gwladys Monteil: 21 Wilberforce Road, Wisbech PE13 2EX

Jude Plouviez: Suffolk County Council Archaeology Service, Shire Hall, Bury St Edmunds, Suffolk IP33 2AR

Christie Pohl: c/o Department of Conservation and Collections Care, Museum of London, London Wall, London EC2Y 5HN

Louise Rayner: Archaeology South-East, Centre for Applied Archaeology, University College London, 31–34 Gordon Square, London WC1H 0PY

Richard Reece: The Apple Loft, The Waterloo, Cirencester GL7 2PU

Peter Rowsome: 105 Winston Road, London N16 9LN

Laura Schaaf: c/o Department of Early London History and Collections, Museum of London, London Wall, London EC2Y 5HN

Fiona Seeley: Museum of London Specialist Services, Mortimer Wheeler House, 46 Eagle Wharf Road, Hackney, London N1 7ED

John Shepherd: 12 Finchingfield Avenue, Woodford Green, Essex 1G8 7JW

Roz Sherris: Department of Early London History and Collections, Museum of London, London Wall, London EC2Y 5HN

Jane Sidell: English Heritage, 1 Waterhouse Square, 138–142 High Holborn, London EC1N 2ST

Barney Sloane: English Heritage, 1 Waterhouse Square, 138–142 Holborn, London EC1N 2ST

Hedley Swain: Museums, Libraries and Archives, Victoria House, 7th Floor (North), Southampton Row, London WC1B 4EA

Chris Thomas: Museum of London Archaeology Service, Mortimer Wheeler House, 46 Eagle Wharf Road, Hackney, London N1 7ED

Ian Tyers: 65 Crimicar Drive, Fulwood, Sheffield S10 4EF

Angela Wardle: Museum of London Specialist Services, Mortimer Wheeler House, 46 Eagle Wharf Road, Hackney, London N1 7ED

Tim Williams: Institute of Archaeology, University College London, 31–34 Gordon Square, London WC1H 0PY

Notes

Abbreviations

BM P&E – British Museum, Department of Prehistory and Early Europe
CIL – *Corpus Inscriptionum Latinarum*
CoLAT – City of London Archaeological Trust
EH – English Heritage
LAARC – London Archaeological Archive and Research Centre, Museum of London
LAMAS – London and Middlesex Archaeology Society
MoL – Museum of London
MoLAS – Museum of London Archaeology Service
RIB – Roman Inscriptions of Britain
SLAEC – Southwark and Lambeth Archaeological Excavation Committee

Other notes

All illustrations are © MoL unless otherwise stated

All accession numbers are MoL unless otherwise stated

Archaeological accession numbers are usually of the form: Site Code/date [context] <finds number>, see Tables 1 and 2 for lists of principal sites mentioned in text

Summary

Despite now being one of the most extensively and intensively explored Romano-British towns, Londinium does not always figure prominently in wider synthetic studies of the Roman province of Britain or of the Roman empire. In part this is due to the sheer complexity of the evidence, in part to the rate at which it is being excavated, and in part to the inevitable delays in organising the resources required to assemble, study and disseminate it. The essays contained in this volume attempt to bring some of this detailed evidence to wider notice. The contributors include many of those directly involved in the fieldwork and the finds study currently going forward in the capital. Moreover, a deliberate attempt has been made to examine Londinium 'in the round', placing Southwark and the Greater London hinterland firmly centre-stage alongside the walled city itself.

The volume has been organised into four more-or-less equal sections, each of which addresses specific 'Framework objectives' set out in the relevant chapters of the *Research Framework for London Archaeology* (Nixon *et al* 2002). The Framework was intended 'to guide but not prescribe the direction of archaeological research in London' (Nixon *et al*, x), and was aimed squarely at 'the people of Greater London, for those who manage and curate the archaeological resource ... and for anyone with an interest in Greater London ... at whatever level' (Nixon *et al*, 2–3). While we trust that the present volume speaks to this 'home' audience, we also hope that it will inform students of both Roman Britain and the wider Roman Empire beyond.

The first of the four sections sets the scene by examining the development, purpose and chronology of the Roman city itself. Introductory papers by Clark ('Fanciful ichnography') and Sloane ('Images of Empire') remind us that modern studies of Londinium are part of a continuing evolution of understanding that stretches back centuries. Rowsome ('Mapping Roman London') draws on the many excavations that have now taken place within the Roman urban area on both banks of the river to review the physical evidence for the town's layout and infrastructure – an undertaking greatly aided by the advent of Geographic Information Systems (GIS). Swain and Williams ('The population of Roman London') make the first detailed attempt in over 80 years to estimate the population of the Roman city. Using population density models they have come up with rather lower estimates than hitherto: *c* 10,000 for the mid-1st-century town and *c* 25,000–30,000 for its early 2nd-century heyday, with a similar or slightly lower figure for *c* AD 200. Fulford ('*Imperium Galliarum, Imperium Britanniarum*') and Reece ('Satellite, parasite, or just London?') remind us that there was a wider Roman world beyond Londinium and its immediate hinterland. Finally Cowie ('Descent into darkness') explores the early Saxon period within Greater London, while Tony Brown ('Was there a Saxon Southwark?') reviews the evidence for a Saxon *burh* south of the river.

The contributions to the second section explore the landscape and environment of the Roman city and its hinterland. This holistic approach is made manifest in the papers by Sidell ('Londinium's landscape') and Tyers ('Tree-ring dates from Roman London'). Both draw attention to the nature of the later prehistoric landscape in which Londinium was situated, while the latter's paper provides an independent chronology for the foundation and subsequent development of the town. Cowan and Hinton ('The Roman garden in London') develop this landscape theme and offer a pioneering attempt to identify the evidence for gardens within Londinium.

Alongside the quays and wharves of the Roman riverside the road network was a vital component of the infrastructure that served the town. Much work has now been conducted on the various routes that radiated away from it, and Gary Brown ('The London to Colchester road') provides a detailed glimpse of the work that his team, and others, have adduced for one of the major roads. The road theme underpins two further papers as Dearne ('Roman Enfield') and Thomas ('Roman Westminster') review the evidence for two important settlements on the road network. The papers by David Bird ('Further speculation about the Shadwell "Tower"'), and Bowlt ('A possible extension to Grim's Dyke'), furnish timely reassessments of much-debated sites. Bird finds a military function for Shadwell compelling, while Bowlt follows Mortimer Wheeler in arguing for a Saxon origin for the linear earthwork that runs to the north of Londinium.

The third section takes us beyond the physical remains of Roman London and its hinterland to consider the intellectual and spiritual context within which its people lived their lives. Using documentary, literary and epigraphic sources Hassall ('London: Britain's first "university"?') suggests that there would have been a centre for higher education within the province and that it was most likely to have been situated in London. Merrifield and Hall ('The nature of the Walbrook stream valley') focus on more spiritual matters in reviewing finds from the Walbrook stream. Haynes ('Sharing secrets?

The material culture of mystery cults') focuses on the occurrence of vessels of 'Camulodunum 306' form, and points out that an artefact's meaning is defined as much by its context as its form. Joanna Bird ('A samian bowl by Crucuro') notes the evidence for the popularity of Hercules as a household god among Roman Londoners, which expresses the essential *'Romanitas'* of their beliefs.

The last three papers in this section celebrate the diversity of Londinium's transpontine quarter, Southwark. Grew ('Who was Mars Camulus?') deals with the remarkable marble dedicatory plaque to Mars Camulus recovered from the temple complex at Tabard Square and traces the god's origins back to Gallia Belgica and the *civitas* Remorum. Cotton ('Harper Road revisited') reviews a burial first published over 25 years ago whose unusual features hint at the cosmopolitan nature of society in early Londinium, while Bateman ('Death, women and the afterlife') uses a *bustum* burial identified in the popular press as a 'female gladiator' as the starting point for a discussion of the wider role of the amphitheatre and the games in Roman culture.

The fourth section considers the practical aspects of finds research and acts as a taster for the proposed establishment of an online database of finds assemblages held in public collections from across Londinium. Plouviez ('Counting brooches') focuses on brooches as a means of exploring regionality and touches on the social meaning of artefacts, a point developed by Crummy ('Small toilet instruments from London'), who seeks to identify latent tribal influences within Londinium. Monteil ('The distribution and use of samian inkwells') demonstrates that the town's fortunes can be traced by the use and distribution of inkwells and suggests that pen and ink records were the domain of the mercantile classes, while Rayner and Seeley ('The Southwark pottery type-series') review developments in local pottery studies since the formative work of Geoff Marsh and Paul Tyers a generation ago.

Jackson ('Imagining health-care in Roman London') discusses the evidence for health-care with regard to the surgical instruments recovered from the Walbrook stream and elsewhere, while Wardle ('Bathing in Roman London') rounds up the distinctive artefactual evidence for bathing in the form of glass oil flasks (*aryballoi*) and strigils. The widespread distribution of such items across the city suggests that bathing was something indulged in by many of its inhabitants. The final two papers explore the luxury end of material culture. Henig ('Intaglios from Roman London') has compiled a catalogue of intaglios and in so doing opened a 'fascinating window on London life and aspirations', while Shepherd ('Luxury colourless glass vessels in Flavian London') draws attention to a significant corpus of fine glassware. Pliny was of the opinion that such vessels were superior to those made of silver and gold and Roman Londoners perhaps felt the same.

Wide though the range of contributions in all four sections is, it but scratches the surface of the available evidence – more of which will eventually be disseminated through the various research and online database programmes to be developed by the Museum of London and the London Archaeological Archive and Research Centre in Hackney. In the meantime, we hope that the papers gathered together here provide a taste of the good things to come. They are offered in tribute to Harvey Sheldon, a friend and respected colleague who has toiled long and hard to record London's Roman past.

Sommaire

Londinium, bien quelle soit une des villes d'époque romano-britannique étudiée de manière extrêmement intensive et extensive, ne figure pas toujours de façon prééminente dans les études de synthèse sur la province romaine de Grande-Bretagne (*Britannia*) ou dans celles dédiées à l'empire romain. Cet état d'affaires est dû en partie à la complexité des données, en partie au rythme de promulgation de ces dernières, et en partie au délai inévitable que l'organisation, la collection, l'analyse et la dissémination de ces données entraîne. Les études contenues dans ce volume ont pour objectif d'attirer un public plus large vers ces données. Y contribuent des spécialistes directement engagés sur le terrain et dans l'analyse du mobilier en cours dans la capitale britannique. De plus, cette collection d'études a le but explicite d'examiner Londinium dans son ensemble, en plaçant le Southwark et les environs de Londres (Greater London) côte à côte avec la ville *intra muros*.

La volume contient quatre sections plus ou moins égales, chacune dédiée à un thème exposé dans les chapitres respectifs des 'Thèmes de recherche pour l'archéologie de Londres' (Research Framework for London Archaeology (Nixon *et al* 2002)). Ce document avait pour but de 'guider et non pas prescrire la direction de la recherche archéologique à Londres' (Nixon *et al*, x), et s'adressait de manière directe 'à la population de Londres, à ceux engagés dans la gestion et la mise en valeur de ses ressources archéologiques … et à tous ceux qui s'intéressent à Londres … à n'importe quel niveau' (Nixon *et al*, 2–3). Le volume présenté ici s'adresse à un public 'autochtone' mais nous espérons également qu'il trouvera un public auprès de chercheurs engagés dans l'étude de la province romaine britannique, de l'empire romain et au-delà.

La première section décrit le cadre, en brossant un tableau de l'évolution, de la raison d'être et de la chronologie de la ville. Les articles d'introduction de Clark ('Une iconographie fantaisiste') et de Sloane ('Images de l'empire') nous rappellent que les études modernes sur Londinium s'inscrivent dans une continuité qui remonte à des siècles. Rowsome ('Cartographie de Londres romaine') se base sur les nombreux chantiers de fouilles complétés à ce jour à l'intérieur du tissu urbain des deux côtés de la Tamise dans une mise au point sur le plan de la ville et de son infrastructure – un travail qui a énormément bénéficié de l'apport de Systèmes d'Information Géographique (SIG). Swain et Williams (' La population de Londres romaine') s'attachent, pour la première fois en 80 ans, à la question de la taille de la population de la ville romaine. Sur la base de modèles de densité démographique, ils arrivent à un chiffre plutôt inférieur à celui estimé jusqu'à présent: environ 10 000 habitants au milieu du 1er siècle apr. J.-C., environ 25 000 à 30 000 habitants pour son apogée au début du 2nd siècle, et un chiffre semblable ou un peu inférieur pour les alentours de 200 apr. J.-C. Fulford (*Imperium Galliarum, Imperium Britanniarum*) et Reece ('Satellite, parasite, ou juste Londres ?') nous rappellent qu'il existe un monde au-delà de Londinium et de ses environs immédiats. Enfin Cowie ('Descente dans les ténèbres') explore la période saxonne à Londres et dans ses environs, alors que Tony Brown ('Le Southwark existe-t-il à l'époque saxonne ?') examine les preuves d'existence d'un *burgh* saxon au sud de la Tamise.

Les contributions à la seconde section s'intéressent au paysage et à l'environnement de la ville romaine et de ses alentours. Une approche holistique est manifeste dans les articles de Sidell ('Le paysage de Londinium') et de Tyers ('Datation dendrochronologique de Londres romaine'). Tous deux attirent l'attention sur le paysage protohistorique dans lequel Londinium s'est implanté; le second article propose aussi une chronologie élaborée indépendamment pour la fondation de la ville et son évolution. Cowan et Hinton ('Le jardin romain à Londres') développent ce thème de paysage et font œuvre de pionniers en proposant des jardins à l'intérieur de Londinium.

En dehors des quais et des entrepôts longeant la Tamise à l'époque romaine, le réseau routier était une composante essentielle de l'infrastructure de la ville. Grâce à une série de travaux exécutés sur les artères rayonnant à partir de Londinium, Gary Brown et son équipe ('La voie de Londres à Colchester') a pu donner une image détaillée de l'une de ces artères. Le thème routier est également au cœur de deux autres articles: Dearne ('Enfield à l'époque romaine') et Thomas ('Westminster romain') présentent deux importants postes sur ce réseau routier. Les articles de David Bird ('Encore quelques spéculations sur la 'tour' de Shadwell') et de Bowlt ('Un prolongement possible de la Grim's Dyke') revoient les données fournies par deux sites controversés. Bird interprète Shadwell comme établissement militaire, tandis que Bowlt suit Mortimer Wheeler en proposant une origine saxonne pour le tracé linéaire d'une levée construite au nord de Londres.

La troisième section délaisse les vestiges physiques de Londres et de ses environs, pour nous amener à considérer le contexte intellectuel et spirituel de ses habitants. Hassall (dans 'Londres: première université de Grande-Bretagne ?') suggère, sur la base de documents littéraires et épigraphiques, qu'un un centre d'éducation supérieure aurait existé dans la province et qu'il était probablement situé à Londres. Merrifield et Hall ('Le caractère de la vallée du Walbrook') examinent l'aspect spirituel du mobilier récupéré dans le ruisseau. Haynes ('Secrets partagés ?: la culture matérielle des cultes de mystère') se penche sur un type de vaisselle, la forme 'Camulodumum 306' pour proposer que le sens d'un objet se définit autant par son contexte que par sa forme. Joanna Bird ('Une coupe en terre sigillée de Crucuro') souligne la popularité d'Hercule comme dieu domestique auprès des Londoniens, trait qui exprime la '*Romanitas*' de leurs croyances.

Les trois derniers articles de cette section célèbrent le quartier outre-rivière de Londinium, le Southwark, dans toute sa diversité. Grew ('Qui était Mars Camulus ?') examine une remarquable plaque en marbre dédiée à Mars Camulus retrouvée dans le temple de Tabard Square et retrace les origines de ce dieu en Gaule Belge, dans la *civitas* des Rèmes. Cotton ('Harper Road revisitée') réexamine une sépulture publiée il y a 25 ans: certains traits insolites laissent entrevoir une société cosmopolite au début de l'époque romaine à Londres. Bateman ('La mort, les femmes et l'au-delà') prend pour exemple une sépulture que la presse populaire avait décrite comme sépulture de 'femme-gladiateur' pour se pencher sur le rôle des amphithéâtres et des jeux dans la culture romaine.

La quatrième section a pour thème les aspects pratiques de l'analyse du mobilier; elle sert également à introduire une base de données numérique qui cataloguera toutes les collections d'objets des musées publics de la zone londonienne. Plouviez ('Comptons les fibules') se penche sur les problèmes d'identification régionale au moyen de fibules et émet quelques hypothèses sur la signification des objets; ce thème est développé par Crummy ('Petits instruments de toilette provenant de Londres') qui cherche à identifier des influences tribales sousjacentes au sein de Londinium. Monteil ('La répartition et l'usage des encriers en terre sigillée') démontre l'utilité des encriers pour documenter les vicissitudes subies par la ville et suggère que la maîtrise de l'écriture était l'apanage de la classe marchande; enfin Rayner et Seeley ('Typologie de la céramique provenant du Southwark') offrent une mise au point des analyses de céramique locale élaborées depuis l'étude de base de Geoff Marsh et de Paul Tyers il y a une génération. Jackson ('Imaginons le service de santé à Londres à l'époque romaine') examine la santé à travers les instruments de chirurgie retrouvés dans le ruisseau du Walbrook et ailleurs, tandis que Wardle ('Les bains à Londres à l'époque romaine') résume les données relatives à cette activité sous forme de flacons d'huile en verre (*aryballoi*) et de strigiles. L'étendue de la répartition de ces objets suggère qu'une partie importante de la population pouvait s'y adonner. Henig ('Intaglios [gemmes taillées] provenant de Londres romaine') présente un catalogue de ces objets et, ce faisant 'ouvre une fenêtre fascinante sur la vie londonienne et ses aspirations'. Enfin, John Shepherd ('La vaisselle de luxe en verre de couleur à Londres à l'époque flavienne') attire l'attention sur une importante collection de verrerie fine. Pline était d'avis que la vaisselle en verre était supérieure à celle en argent ou en or; peut-être les Londoniens étaient-ils du même avis.

Quoique chaque section contienne un large éventail de sujets, ces contributions ne font qu'égratigner la surface – une série de programmes de recherche et de bases de données en cours de développement au Musée de Londres, aux Archives Archéologiques de Londres et au Centre de Recherches de Hackney s'attacheront à la dissémination de ces nouvelles données. En attendant, nous espérons que les articles présentés ici alimenteront l'appétit. Ils sont offerts en hommage à Harvey Sheldon, ami et collègue respecté qui a œuvré durement et longuement pour le passé romain de Londres.

Zusammenfassung

Obwohl Londinium zu einer der ausführlichsten und intensiv erforschten romano-britischen Städte zählt, hält es oft keine prominente Stellung bei breitangelegten Synthesestudien der römischen Provinz Britanniens oder des Römischen Kaiserreiches. Das ist zum Teil durch die schiere Komplexität der Beweismaterialien begründet, zum Teil liegt am zeitlichen Abstand zwischen Forschungsarbeit und Veröffentlichung, und zum Teil durch die Zeitrahmen, die bei der Organisation der Sammlungen notwendig sind, um diese zu erweitern, zu erforschen und zu disseminieren. Die Beiträge in diesem Band versuchen einige der detaillierten Studienergebnisse an eine allgemeine Hörerschaft zu bringen. Die Autoren bestehen aus Forschern, die oft direkt mit den Ausgrabungen und den aktuellen Fundauswertungen, die zur Zeit in der Hauptstadt durchgeführt werden, beteiligt sind. Außerdem wurde ein bewußter Versuch gemacht, ein umfassendes Bild von Londinium zu präsentieren, wobei Southwark und das Londoner Umfeld mit der Stadt innerhalb der Stadtmauern gleichgestellt werden sollen.

Dieser Band ist so organisiert, daß er in vier, ungefähr gleich lange Abschnitte aufgeteilt ist. Jeder davon befasst sich mit bestimmten 'Rahmenzielen', die in den entsprechenden Kapiteln der 'Leitfaden für die archäologische Forschung Londons' (Nixon et al. 2002) enthalten sind. Dieser Forschungsrahmen 'soll ein Lcitfaden sein, aber nicht die archäologische Forschungsrichtung in London verordnen'. (Nixon et al., x), und war direkt an die Zuhörerschaft

im Großraum London gerichtet, an die Manager und Kuratoren des archäologischen Bestands. ... und für jeden der ein Interesse an der Londoner Archäologie hegt. ... egal auf welchem Niveau (Nixon et al., 2–3). Wir vertrauen darauf, daß der vorliegende Band sich an die heimische Leserschaft wendet, wir hoffen aber auch, daß es eine Informationsquelle bietet für Studenten des römischen Großbritanniens, aber auch über diese Grenzen hinaus für das römische Kaiserreich.

Der erste der vier Abschnitte bestimmt den Schauplatz, indem er die Entwicklung, den Zweck und die chronologische Geschichte der römischen Stadt untersucht. Die einleitenden Abhandlungen von Clark (Phantasievolle Ichnographien) und Sloane (Bilder des Kaiserreiches') erinnern uns daran, daß die aktuellen Londoner Forschungsarbeiten Teil einer kontinuierlichen Entwicklung sind, die schon Jahrhunderte zurück liegt. Rowsome ('Die Kartierung des römischen Londons'), stützt sich auf Informationen aus den vielen Ausgrabungen, die bisher innerhalb der römischen Stadtgrenze auf beiden Seiten des Flußufers stattgefunden haben, um die Ruinen der Stadtanlage und Infrastruktur zu untersuchen - ein Vorhaben, daß durch die Einführung von Geographischen Informationssystemen (GIS) unterstützt wird. Swain und Williams (Die Bevölkerung Londons in der Römerzeit) machen den ersten detaillierten Versuch seit 80 Jahren, die Bevölkerungszahl der römischen Stadt zu schätzen. Bisherige Modelle der Bevölkerungsdichte kamen bisher auf niedrigere Schätzungen: ca. 10.000 für die Stadtbevölkerung im mittleren 1. Jahrhundert, und ca. 25.000-30.000 während der Blütezeit im 2. Jahrhundert, mit einer ähnlichen, oder etwas geringeren Schätzung für das Jahr um 200 AD. Fulford ('Imperium Galliarum, Imerium Britanniarum') und Reece ('Satellit, Parasit oder einfach London?') erinnern uns daran, daß über Londinium und seinem unmittelbaren Hinterland hinaus eine weitere römische Welt existierte. Zuletzt untersucht Cowie ('Abstieg ins Dunkel) untersucht die Sächsische Periode im Großraum London, während Tony Brown ('Gab es ein sächsisches Southwark?') erläutert Hinweise auf eine sächsische Burh südlich des Flusses.

Die Beiträge des zweiten Abschnittes untersuchen die Landschaft und Umwelt der römischen Stadt und ihrem Hinterland. Ein holistischen Denkansatz wird in den Beiträgen von Sidell ('Londiniums Landschaft') und Tyres ('Jahresring Datierung im römischen London') offenkundig. Beide lenken die Aufmerksamkeit auf die Beschaffenheit der späten prähistorischen Landschaft um Londinium, während der letztere Beitrag eine eigenständige Chronologie der Stadtgründung und nachfolgender Stadtentwicklung erstellt. Cowan und Hinton (' Der römische Garten in London') entwickeln das Landschaftsthema weiter und haben eine Pionierarbeit bei der Interpretation der Überreste von Gärten innerhalb Londiniums geleistet.

Neben den Kais und Landestellen entlang des römischen Flußufers war das Straßennetz ein lebenswichtiger Teil der Infrastruktur die zur Versorgung der Stadt diente. Viel Arbeit wurde bislang an verschiedenen Routen geleistet, die von der Stadt strahlenförmig ausgehen, und Gary Brown ('Die Straße von London zur Colchester Road') vermittelt einen detaillierten Eindruck auf die Arbeit, die sein Team und andere an einer der wichtigsten Verkehrslinien geleistet haben. Zwei weitere Beiträge werden vom Straßenthema geprägt, in denen besprechen Dearne ('Das römische Enfield') und Thomas ('Das römische Westminster') die Spuren von zwei wichtigen Siedlungen entlang dem Straßennetz. Die Beiträge von David Bird ('Weitere Spekulationen über den "Turm" von Shadwell') und Bowlt ('Eine mutmaßliche Verlängerung des Grim's Deichs') erstellen eine zeitgerechte Neubewertung der mehrseitig debattierten Ausgrabungsorte. Bird argumentiert für eine militärische Funktion des Shadwell Turms, wogegen Bowlt sich Mortimer Wheeler anschließt, in dem er für einen sächsischen Ursprung der geradlinigen, nördlich aus London ausgerichteten Erdarbeiten, argumentiert.

Der dritte Abschnitt geleitet uns über die physischen Überreste des römischen Londons hinaus in sein Hinterland, um sich dem intellektuellen und geistlichen Kontext zu widmen, in dem die Bewohner lebten. Anhand dokumentarischen, literarischen und epigraphischen Quellen deutet Hassall ('London: Großbritanniens erste "Universität"?') darauf hin, daß es ein höheres Bildungszentrum innerhalb der Provinz gegeben haben muß, und das war am wahrscheinlichsten in London zu finden. Merrifield und Hall ('Die Beschaffenheit des Walbrook Tals') richten ihre Aufmerksamkeit auf geistigere Inhalte, indem sie die Funde aus dem Walbrook Bach besprechen. Haynes ('Geheimnisse Teilen? Die materielle Kultur der Mysterienkulte') konzentriert seine Arbeit auf das Auftreten von Gefäßen der 'Camulodunum 306' Form, und macht darauf aufmerksam, daß die Bedeutung eines Artefaktes sowohl durch seinen Kontext definiert ist, als auch durch seine Form. Joanna Bird ('Eine terra sigilata Schüssel von Crucuro') verzeichnet Nachweise für die Popularität von Herkules als Hausgott der Londoner römischen Bevölkerung, was den grundlegenden 'Romanitas' ihres Glaubens zum Ausdruck bringt.

Die letzten drei Beiträge aus diesem Abschnitt feiern die Vielfältigkeit des Stadtviertels Southwark südlich der Themse. Grew ('Wer war Mars Camulus?') befasst sich mit einer außergewöhnlichen Marmortafel mit einer Widmung an Mars Camulus, die aus dem Tempelkomplex in Tabard Platz geborgen wurde, und verfolgt die Herkunft dieses Gottes nach Galliea Belgica und die Civitas Remorum

zurück. Cotton ('Ein Wiedersehen mit Harper Road') hält eine Rückschau auf ein Begräbnis, das vor über 25 Jahren zum ersten Mal veröffentlicht wurde, und dessen ungewöhnliche Merkmale auf den weltoffenen Charakter der Gesellschaft im frühen Londinium deuten. Bateman dagegen, ('Tod, Frauen und das Jenseits') benutzt eine bustum (=Scheiterhaufen) Bestattung, die von der Presse als 'weiblicher Gladiator' identifiziert wurde, als einen Startpunkt für eine Diskussion über die weitgreifendere Rolle des Amphitheaters und der Spiele in der römischen Kultur.

Der vierte Abschnitt betrachtet die praktischen Aspekte der Funduntersuchungen und agiert als eine Kostprobe auf die geplante Einrichtung einer Online-Datenbank der Funde, die in öffentlichen Sammlungen im gesamten Raum Londiniums enthalten sind. Plouviez ('Broschen zählen') setzt den Fokus auf Broschen als Mittel zur Erforschung regionaler Unterschiede, und bespricht kurz die soziale Bedeutung von Artefakten, eine Frage, die von Crummy ('Kleine Toiletteninstrumente aus London') weiter auserarbeitet wird, und der den Versuch macht, latente Stammeseinflüsse innerhalb Londiniums zu identifizierten. Monteil ('Die Verbreitung und der Gebrauch von Tintenfässern aus Terra Sigilata') veranschaulicht, wie die Entwicklung des Wohlstands in der Stadt durch den Gebrauch und die Verbreitung von Tintenfässern verfolgt werden kann, und schlägt vor, daß der Gebrauch von Feder und Tinte bei Schriftgütern in den kaufmännischen Klassen verbreitet war. Rayner und Seeley ('Die Keramiktypen von Southwark') besprechen die Entwicklung der regionalen Keramikforschung seit den eine Generation zurückliegenden, wegweisenden Forschungsarbeiten von Geoff Marsh und Paul Tyers.

Jackson ('Ein Studie des Gesundheitssystems im römischen London') diskutiert die Beweismaterialien für ein Gesundheitssystem anhand von chirurgischen Instrumenten, die unter anderem aus dem Walbrook Bach geborgen wurden. Wardle ('Die Badekultur im römischen London') trägt charakteristische Beweisfunde zusammen, die mit dem Baden in Verbindung stehen, wie zum Beispiel die Form von Ölflaschen aus Glas (Aryballoi) und Schabern (Strigilis). Die Fundstreuung über die ganze Stadt deutet darauf hin, daß Baden für viele Einwohner eine Leidenschaft war. Die letzten beiden Arbeiten untersuchen Luxusartikel. Henig ('Intaglios aus dem römischen London') hat einen Katalog von Intaglios zusammengestellt und öffnet damit einen faszinierenden Einblick in den Londoner Alltag und die Zukunftshoffnungen der Einwohner. Shepherd ('Luxusgefäße aus durchsichtigem Glas im flavischen London') lenkt die Aufmerksamkeit auf eine bedeutsame Sammlung von Glaswaren. Pliny war der Meinung, daß solche Gefäße denen aus Silber und Gold überlegen waren, und vielleicht haben auch die Römer in London das auch so empfunden.

Obgleich Palette der Beiträge aus den vier Abschnitten breitgefächert ist, werden die zur Verfügung stehenden archäologischen Beweise nur oberflächlich erfasst - es wird erhofft, daß in Zukunft Informationen mit Hilfe von diversen Forschungsprojekten und Online-Datenbanken ausgetauscht werden können, die vom Museum of London und dem Londoner Archäologischen Archiv und Forschungszentrum in Hackney erarbeitet werden. Bis dahin hoffen wir, daß die Beiträge, die hier zusammengetragen wurden, einen Vorgeschmack auf zukünftige Entwicklungen geben. Sie sollen unsere Anerkennung für Harvey Sheldon ausdrücken, ein Freund und respektierter Kollege, der lange und mühsam gearbeitet hat, um die römische Geschichte Londons aufzuzeichnen.

Editors' introduction   *John Clark, Jonathan Cotton, Jenny Hall, Roz Sherris, Hedley Swain*

This volume has two principal aims: to honour Harvey Sheldon and to celebrate Roman Londinium. Both aims deserve explanation.

The genesis of the project was the suggestion, first voiced by Martin Henig, to offer a volume of essays to Harvey in recognition of his long devotion to London's archaeology. From his early days excavating Roman pottery kilns in Highgate Wood and Roman roads in Bow, to his leadership of the Southwark team, to directing the Museum of London's Department of Greater London Archaeology, to reaching a new generation of students through his teaching at Birkbeck College, Harvey has been – and remains – a doughty and principled champion of London's buried heritage.

He also has a happy knack of inspiring people to work with him, and of generating fierce loyalty to the cause. The widespread affection and respect in which he is held created its own challenge, however: how to keep any volume of dedicated essays to manageable proportions? The solution adopted by the editorial team was to focus hard on one of Harvey's driving interests, the archaeology of Roman London and its immediate hinterland, and to impose a tight word limit on individual contributions.

As the offers of papers flowed in from friends and colleagues it quickly became apparent that we had an excellent opportunity to do more than simply present Harvey with a series of 'party pieces' appropriate to the occasion. We had the wherewithal to address a substantial number of the 'Framework objectives' outlined in the recently published *Research Framework for London Archaeology* too (Nixon *et al* 2002, 30–43). In this way we could not only honour an admired colleague but also, as he himself would wish, we could continue to move the subject forward. As far as this latter aim is concerned a contribution from Harvey is one of the most obvious and significant omissions from the volume!

The volume itself is divided into four equal sections, each of which is preceded by a short introduction that links it explicitly to the relevant parts of the London research framework document. The first of the four sections deals with the development of Roman London, its historical study, demography and chronology. The second section widens the perspective to take in the town's landscape setting, environment and hinterland. The third focuses on people, through an exploration of education and spirituality, while the fourth examines people from the standpoints of self-image, health and trade. A final, fifth, section offers an illustrated biography of Harvey, together with a list of his published work.

Furthermore, in order to help readers unfamiliar with the London scene, we have listed the principal sites mentioned (Tables 1 and 2) and located them on two maps. The first (Fig 1) shows Greater London and the Roman road network. The second (Fig 2) focuses on the central area. All references are quoted in the Harvard style and contained in a consolidated bibliography at the end of the volume, along with a listing of suggested modern editions for classical references.

It remains our pleasant duty to thank a number of individuals and institutions. Firstly we are grateful to the contributors, for adhering to the various parameters we imposed on them; to the President of the CBA, Nick Merriman (an old London hand himself), for providing a Preface; and also to Jane Thorniley-Walker, Catrina Appleby and Frances Mee of the CBA for smoothing our way throughout.

The look of the volume has been vastly improved by the collective skills of Pete Hart-Allison, Carlos Lemos, Jeannette McLeish and Faith Vardy of the Museum of London Archaeology Service's Drawing Office, and the photographic expertise of John Chase, Torla Evans and Richard Stroud of the Museum of London and Andy Chopping and Maggie Cox of MoLAS. Jackie Keily kindly brought a fresh pair of eyes to the texts after they had been assembled. Particular thanks are due to our referee, Martin Millett, for his contribution and insights at what was for him an especially busy time. Susannah Barford remained an ever-present source of inspiration. Any remaining errors or inconsistencies are the responsibility of the editors.

This volume could not have been contemplated without the financial support of a number of sponsoring bodies, and we should like to acknowledge the following: the London and Middlesex Archaeological Society (LAMAS) and the Council for British Archaeology (CBA); the Museum of London; Southwark and Lambeth Archaeological Excavation Committee (SLAEC); the City of London Archaeological Trust (COLAT) and the Standing Conference on London Archaeology (SCOLA). Finally, we would also like to thank Barney Sloane and English Heritage (EH) for sanctioning the use by LAMAS of monies raised from the sale of EH special papers (London).

Table 1 Key for Figure 1: principal archaeological sites in Greater London mentioned in the text

Site code	Address	Grid reference	This volume
AGH90	72A Armagh Road, 91–93 Parnell Road E3	TQ36848351	2.4
BAQ90	B&Q, Old Kent Road SE1	TQ34307789	4.7
BEG92	Bramcote Grove, Bermondsey SE16	TQ35057813	2.1
BLA87	Bricklayers' Arms Railway Depot Site, Rolls Road SE1	TQ33807850	2.1
BOD91	Ranwell East Estate II, Armagh Road, Libra Road (between), Bow E3	TQ36718350	2.4
BSF87	Beddington Sewage Farm, Beddington Lane, Croydon CR0/SM6	TQ29796576	2.1
CAW91	Canada Water, Jubilee Line Ext 22, Surrey Quays Road, Rotherhithe SE16	TQ35507950	2.1
CGW05	Cromwell Green, Westminster SW1	TQ30177955	2.1
DAC03	Crown Wharf Ironworks (former), Dace Road E3	TQ37298391	2.4
ELR76	Lincoln Road, Enfield EN1	TQ34089607	2.5
GD79	Grim's Dyke, Harrow Weald Common, Old Redding HA3	TQ14169288	2.8
GM450	County Hall Ship, Belvedere Road SE1	TQ30697979	1.2, 2.2, 2.6
GVE01	108–110 The Grove, Stratford E15	TQ39058451	2.4
HGA02	172–176 The Highway, Shadwell E1	TQ34848070	2.2, 2.6
HL81	Holloway Lane, Harmondsworth, West Drayton UB7	TQ06707810	2.1
HOO88	Hooper Street, Back Church Lane E1	TQ34208100	4.2, 4.8
HW70	Highgate Wood, Muswell Hill Road N6/N10	TQ28208900	1.2, 5.1
HW-AL94	Angel Lane, Stratford E15	TQ39808437	2.4
LCN04	22–24 Lincoln Road, Enfield EN1	TQ33309607	2.5
LD74	London Docks, The Highway, Shadwell E1	TQ35008070	2.6
LD76	London Docks, The Highway, Shadwell E1	TQ34958074	2.6, 4.3
LEK95	271–321 Lefevre Walk Estate, Parnell Road, Bow E3	TQ37008355	2.4, 4.7
LFR69	Lefevre Road E3	TQ37048360	2.4
MAK94	St Mary Abbot's Hospital, Marloes Road W8	TQ25687920	2.1
MIP04	27b St Martin's Approach, Ruislip HA4	TQ09108790	2.8
MFEB88	Mayfield Farm, Stanwell Road, East Bedfont TW14	TQ07507360	2.1
MGP98	63 Main Road, Gidea Park, Romford RM2	TQ52318981	2.4
MNF03	69 Main Road, Gidea Park, Romford RM2	TQ52378983	2.4
NAG87	National Gallery Extension (Hampton Site), St Martin's Street, Whitcomb Street WC2	TQ29898051	2.7
NPY73	New Palace Yard, Parliament Square, Westminster SW1	TQ30247963	2.1
PLQ95	Parliment Square (south-east corner) SW1	TQ30147961	2.7
PRB95	91–93 Parnell Road, Bow E3	TQ36928356	2.4
PSW93	Gas main diversion, Parliament Square, Parliament Street SW1	TQ30147968	2.7
PWC92	Palace of Westminster (St Stephen's Crypt Chapel Undercroft), St Margaret Street SW1	TQ30247950	2.1
RBW03	510–518 Roman Road E3	TQ36618331	2.4
RGC02	Romford Golf Course, Gidea Park, Main Road RM2	TQ52629027	2.4
ROB05	568A Roman Road E3	TQ36788340	2.4
RO-SN92	St Neot's Playground, Colchester Road, Harold Hill RM3?	TQ54839134	2.4
SFG98	Safeway site, The Grove, Stratford E15	TQ39208465	2.4
SGT94	Storey's Gate, Horseguards Road, Birdcage Walk SW1	TQ29877972	2.1
SMD01	St Martin-in-the-Fields Church, 12 Adelaide Street WC2	TQ30128051	2.7
SPD85	Stockley Park, Dawley Road, Hayes, Middlesex UB3	TQ08308080	2.1
SWY97	Summerton Way, Thamesmead SE28	TQ48008128	2.1
TOC02	Tobacco Dock, 130–162 The Highway, Shadwell E1	TQ34758070	2.2
WCG78	Cromwell Green, Parliament Square, St Margaret Street, Westminster SW1	TQ30187953	2.1
WGF79	Wall Garden Farm, Sipson Lane, Harlington, West Drayton UB7	TQ07707820	2.1
WST86	Westminster Abbey, Undercroft Museum, Broad Sanctuary SW1	TQ30087942	2.7
W-RR86	30 Romford Road, Stratford E15	TQ39208440	2.4

Fig 1 Map of Greater London showing the location of principal sites mentioned in text

Table 2 Key for Figure 2: principal archaeological sites in Londinium and Southwark mentioned in the text

Site code	Address	Grid reference	This vol
1STS74	1–7 St Thomas Street SE1	TQ32738019	2.3, 4.6, 4.7, 4.8
2SSBS85	2 Southwark Street, 1A Bedale Street SE1	TQ32688020	1.8, 2.2
4STS82	4–26 St Thomas Street, SE1	TQ32748016	4.8
15SKS80	Calverts Buildings, 15–23 Southwark Street SE1	TQ32528011	2.2, 4.6, 4.8
52SOS89	52–54 Southwark Street SE1	TQ32328016	2.2, 4.6, 4.2
64BHS74	64–70 Borough High Street SE1	TQ32568006	2.1
93BHS74	93–95 Borough High Street SE1	TQ32618008	4.5
106BHS73	106–114 Borough High Street SE1	TQ32527996	4.6
107BHS81	107–115 Borough High Street	TQ32598005	3.3
120BHS89	120–124 Borough High Street SE1	TQ32517994	2.2
170BHS79	170–194 Borough High Street SE1	TQ32447982	2.2
175BHS76	175–177 Borough High Street, SE1	TQ32537990	4.8
179BHS89	179–191 Borough High Street, Southwark SE1	TQ32557985	2.2, 2.3, 4.2, 4.5, 4.7, 4.8
199BHS74	199 Borough High Street SE1	TQ32527984	4.6
201BHS75	201–205 Borough High Street SE1	TQ32517983	4.6, 4.5
207BHS72	207–211 Borough High Street SE1	TQ32517983	4.6, 4.5
AB78	Arcadia Buildings, Great Dover Street SE1	TQ32577966	4.7
ABS86	St Albans House, 124 Wood Street EC2	TQ32288150	4.6
ANT88	9–10 Angel Court EC2	TQ32788133	2.2
AST87	22–25 Austin Friars EC2	TQ32898137	2.2, 4.6
AUT01	Minster House, 12 Arthur Street EC4	TQ32778076	2.1, 2.2, 2.3
BA84	Bermondsey Abbey, Abbey Street SE1	TQ33407935	4.6
BAZ05	35 Basinghall Street EC2	TQ32558148	4.5
BBH87	Billingsgate Bath House, 100 Lower Thames Street EC3	TQ33108069	2.2
BC75	Baynards House, Queen Victoria Street EC4	TQ31948091	2.2
BGB98	Broadgate, 201 Bishopsgate (phases 12–13), 31–37 Norton Folgate E1	TQ33348198	4.3
BGE98	288 Bishopsgate EC2 & E1	TQ33408190	2.2
BGG01	116–126 Borough High Street SE1	TQ32507994	4.7
BGH95	Main Ticket Hall, Borough High Street SE1	TQ32698020	4.2, 4.5, 4.6, 4.7
BHB00	117–136 Borough High Street SE1	TQ32618000	2.2
BIG82	Billingsgate Market Lorry Park, Lower Thames Street EC3	TQ32988065	2.2, 4.2
BII00	5 Billiter Street EC3	TQ33288110	4.8
BIP88	Palmerston House, 41–63 Bishopsgate EC2	TQ33118134	4.6
BKT01	Borough Market, Stoney Street SE1	TQ32598023	4.8
BOS87	274–306 Bishopsgate EC2	TQ33418187	4.2, 4.5
BPL95	Monument House, 30–35 Botolph Lane EC3	TQ33028074	2.2, 4.2
BRL87	19–25 Birchin Lane, Bengal Court, 1–3 Castle Court EC3	TQ32908106	4.2
BTBHS91	BT shaft, Borough High Street SE1	TQ32608009	2.2
BUC87	DLR shaft, Bucklersbury EC4	TQ32598107	2.2, 4.2, 4.5
CAO96	Gateway House, 25 Cannon street EC4	TQ32218107	4.2
CAP86	Capel House, 54–62 New Broad Street EC2	TQ33048150	4.7
CASS72	Sir John Cass School, 20–30 Aldgate E1	TQ33528116	4.6
CAT86	52–54 Carter Lane EC4	TQ31828109	4.2
CCP04	Cannon Place EC4	TQ32628085	2.3
CDP04	120 Cheapside EC2	TQ32328124	4.7
CH75	Chaucer House, Tabard Street, Southwark SE1	TQ32667962	4.7, 4.8
CHWH83	Chamberlain's Wharf, Tooley Street SE1	TQ32948033	2.2
CID90	72–80 Cheapside EC2/EC4	TQ32498112	2.2, 2.3, 4.2, 4.7, 4.8
CKL88	8–9 Cloak Lane EC4	TQ32538089	4.2
CNL81	68–73 Cornhill EC3	TQ32998114	4.8
CO88	Courage Brewery, Park Street SE1	TQ32448026	4.6, 2.2, 4.5
CO89	Courage Brewery, 3 Redcross Way SE1	TQ32458020	4.2
COSE84	Courage Brewery (south-east), Park Street SE1	TQ32448026	2.2, 4.2, 4.3, 4.5, 4.6
COV87	10–12 Copthall Avenue EC2	TQ32798142	2.2, 4.5, 4.6
CSW85	Courage Brewery (south-west), Park Street SE1	TQ32308023	2.2
CUS73	Custom House, Lower Thames Street EC3	TQ33298059	2.1, 2.2
DGH86	Dowgate Hill House, 14–16 Dowgate Hill EC4	TQ32548081	2.2, 3.2, 4.7
DMT88	Dominant House, 85 Queen Victoria Street EC4	TQ32238089	4.5
DUK77	St James's Passage subway, 2–7 Duke's Place EC3	TQ33528119	4.2
EAE01	41 Eastcheap, 16–18 Rood Lane EC3	TQ33108083	4.8
EAG87	Eagle House, 90–96 Cannon Street EC4	TQ32718087	4.2
ELD88	Liverpool House, 15–17 Eldon Street EC2	TQ32988165	4.6
EST83	27–29 Eastcheap, 14–15 Philpot Lane EC3	TQ33058084	4.7
ETA89	7–11 Bishopsgate EC2	TQ33028119	4.2
FCC95	Lloyd's Register of Shipping, 68–71 Fenchurch Street EC3	TQ33398098	4.2, 4.3, 4.5
FCS87	107 Fenchurch Street EC3	TQ33388104	4.6
FEH95	168 Fenchurch Street EC3	TQ33048097	4.2
FEN83	5–12 Fenchurch Street, 1 Philpot Lane EC3	TQ33038092	4.2, 4.5
FER97	Plantation Place, 26–38 Fenchurch Street EC3	TQ33188087	1.3, 2.3, 4.2, 4.5, 4.8
FMO85	37–40 Fish Street Hill, 16–20 Monument Street EC3	TQ32928073	4.2
FNE01	60–63 Fenchurch Street, EC3	TQ33368098	2.1
FOT01	11–12 Foster Lane, 1–4 Carey Lane EC2	TQ32208133	4.2, 4.5
FRE78	1–6 Lower Thames Street EC3	TQ32948064	2.2
FSE76	160–162 Fenchurch Street, 22–23 Lime Street EC3	TQ33058096	4.2, 4.8
FSS96	51–53 Southwark Street SE1	TQ32408015	2.2

Table 2 Continued

Site code	Address	Grid reference	This vol
FW84	Fenning's Wharf, 1 London Bridge SE1	TQ32868037	2.1, 2.2
GAG87	Guildhall Art Gallery, Guildhall Yard EC2	TQ32518136	2.2
GDV96	Great Dover Street, Southwark SE1	TQ32687946	3.7
GHL89	Guy's Hospital, St Thomas Street SE1	TQ32928003	2.2
GHT00	Blossom's Inn, 30 Gresham Street EC2	TQ32418125	1.3, 2.1; 2.2, 2.3, 4.2, 4.5, 4.7, 4.8
GM9	52 Aldgate High Street (Aldgate East underground station) E1	TQ33718123	2.4
GM29	Cannon Street Station	TQ32678088	2.3
GM37	Sun Life Assurance, 110–116 Cheapside EC2	TQ32418127	4.5
GM96	Lloyd's Site, 41–51 Lime Street, Billiter Street EC3	TQ33198106	4.8
GM111	Billingsgate Roman Bath House, 100 Lower Thames Street EC3	TQ33118068	4.2, 4.5
GM131	Central Criminal Court, Old Bailey, Warwick Square EC4	TQ31818130	2.3
GM133	Price Waterhouse, 27–34 Old Jewry EC2	TQ32558121	4.2
GM156	Walbrook Wharf, Upper Thames Street EC4	TQ32618097	4.2
GM157	Temple of Mithras site, Bucklersbury House EC4	TQ32598099	1.2, 2.1,2.3, 3.2, 3.3, 4.2
GM158	St Swithin's House, 30–37 Walbrook EC4	TQ32638100	4.8
GM182	Blackfriars Wreck, 1 Coffer Dam EC4	TQ31698082	2.2
GM219	11 Ironmonger Lane EC2	TQ32538124	4.8
GM318	GPO, St Martin le Grand EC2	TQ32168131	1.2
GPO75	GPO, 81 Newgate Street EC1	TQ32058135	4.2, 4.6, 4.7, 4.8
GRL88	21–26 Garlick Hill EC4	TQ32388090	2.2
GSM97	10 [formerly 2–12] Gresham Street EC2	TQ32288123	1.3, 4.2, 4.5, 4.7, 4.8
GYE92	Guildhall Art Gallery, Guildhall Yard East Site EC2	TQ32518136	1.3, 2.1, 2.2, 4.2, 4.5, 4.7, 4.8
HHO97	Hunt's House, Great Maze Pond SE1	TQ32757995	1.8, 2.1, 2.2, 4.3
HIB79	Hibernia Wharf, Montague Close SE1	TQ32748040	1.8, 4.8
HR79	Harper Road SE1	TQ32467930	3.6
ILA79	Miles Lane EC4	TQ32808074	2.2, 4.2, 4.7, 4.8
IME83	27–30 Lime Street EC3	TQ33108098	4.2, 4.5
IRO80	24–25 Ironmonger Lane, 9–12 King Street EC2	TQ32508122	4.6
ISH88	166–170 Bishopsgate, 14–15 New Street EC2	TQ33308157	4.6
JOA91	Joan Street SE1	TQ31618003	2.1
KEW98	King Edward Buildings (GPO site), 102–105 Newgate Street	TQ31948137	2.3
KEY83	15–35 Copthall Avenue EC2	TQ32778150	2.2, 4.2
KNG85	36–37 King Street EC2	TQ32458121	4.5
KWS94	Regis House, 39–46 King William Street EC4	TQ32888074	1.3, 2.1, 2.2, 2.3, 4.2, 4.8
LBI95	London Bridge site 8, Escalator Shaft/Ticket Hall SE1	TQ32818027	4.2
LCT84	Leadenhall Court, 2–6 Leadenhall Street EC3	TQ33068109	2.3, 4.2, 4.3, 4.5, 4.6, 4.8
LDL88	Albion House, 34–35 Leadenhall Street EC3	TQ33278111	4.6
LEA84	71–77 Leadenhall Street/ 32–40 Mitre Street EC3	TQ33458115	4.6
LEN89	145–146 Leadenhall Street EC3	TQ33118115	4.6
LGK99	5–27 Long Lane SE1	TQ32577976	2.2
LGM02	211 Long Lane, Morocco Street SE1	TQ33157960	2.1
LLS02	Tabard Square SE1	TQ32567965	1.3, 3.5, 4.8
LOW88	52–63 London Wall, 20–56 Copthall Avenue EC2	TQ32828147	2.2, 4.5, 4.6, 4.8
LTU03	52–56 Lant Street SE1	TQ32257970	4.3
LYD88	Cannon Street Station (N), Upper Thames Street EC4	TQ32608083	4.6, 4.7, 2.2
LYS01	55 Leroy Street SE1	TQ33167905	2.1
MGT87	55–61 Moorgate, 75–9 Coleman Street EC2	TQ32688149	4.6
MLK76	1–6 Milk Street EC2	TQ32388127	2.2, 4.2, 4.7
MOG86	49–53 Moorgate, 72–74 Coleman Street EC2	TQ32678147	4.5
MRG95	Northgate House, 20–28 Moorgate EC2	TQ32728142	1.2, 2.2, 3.2, 4.2, 4.3, 4.8
MSL87	49–55 Mansell Street E1	TQ33808110	4.7, 4.8
NEB87	35–45 New Broad Street EC2	TQ33038153	4.2
NFW74	2–6 Lower Thames Street EC3	TQ32958066	2.2
NHA86	9 Northumberland Alley EC3	TQ33478104	4.2
NHG98	Northern House, 19–29 Gresham Street EC2	TQ32248144	4.7
OBL97	Britannia House, 16–18 Old Bailey EC4	TQ31738130	4.7
ONE94	1 Poultry EC2/EC4	TQ32588110	1.3, 1.4, 2.1, 2.2, 2.3, 3.2, 3.4, 3.7, 4.2, 4.7
OPT81	2–3 Cross Keys Court, Copthall Avenue EC2	TQ32758149	2.1, 2.2, 2.3, 4.3, 4.5, 4.6
ORG86	St Martin Orgar churchyard, 24–32 King William Street EC4	TQ32828082	4.5
PDN81	11–11A Pudding Lane, 121–127 Lower Thames Street EC3	TQ32928071	2.1, 2.2, 4.2, 4.5
PEN79	Peninsular House, 112–116 Lower Thames Street EC3	TQ32978070	2.2
PEP89	Colchester House/ Woodruffe House, Pepys Street EC3	TQ33258083	4.6
PET81	St Peter's Hill & 223–5 Upper Thames Street EC4	TQ32048092	2.2
PNS01	Charterhouse Buildings, 1 Paternoster Row EC2	TQ32078123	4.2
POM79	GPO middle area, Newgate Street EC1	TQ32068138	4.6
PUB80	The George Public House, 86 Fenchurch Street EC3	TQ33498109	4.6
QUV01	Salvation Army, 99–101 Queen Victoria Street EC4	TQ32108091	2.2
RAG82	1–12 Rangoon Street EC3	TQ33508102	2.3, 4.6, 4.8
RWG94	Redcross Way, Southwark SE1	TQ32478011	2.2
SBH88	Southbridge House (site of Rose Theatre), 2–10 Southwark Bridge Road SE1	TQ32288042	5.1
SCS83	9 St Clare Street EC3	TQ33728106	4.5
SFO03	Stamford House, 1 Stamford Street SE1	TQ31618045	2.1
SH74	Seal House, 106–108 Upper Thames Street EC4	TQ32788070	2.2

Table 2 Continued

Site code	Address	Grid reference	This vol
SHI95	19 St Mary at Hill EC3	TQ33068068	2.2
SLO82	Beaver House, Sugar Loaf Court, 71 Queen Victoria Street EC4	TQ32348087	4.2
SM75	2–6 Lower Thames Street EC3	TQ32938065	2.2
SRP98	Spitalfields (ramp), Spital Square, 280 Bishopsgate E1	TQ33468189	4.7
STE95	Steward Street car park, 250 Bishopsgate E1	TQ33438180	4.7
SUF94	Suffolk House, 154–156 Upper Thames Street EC4	TQ32718077	2.1, 2.2, 4.2, 4.6
SUN86	Sunlight Wharf, Upper Thames Street EC4	TQ32128082	2.2
SWA81	Swan Lane Car Park, 95–103 Upper Thames Street EC4	TQ32728068	2.2, 4.2
SWN98	Sorting Office (former), Swan Street SE1	TQ32457965	4.3
TEA98	41–53 Threadneedle Street, 1–17 Old Broad Street EC2	TQ32958125	4.2, 4.8
TEX88	Thames Exchange Buildings, 78 Upper Thames Street EC4	TQ32458075	2.2, 3.4, 4.7
TGM99	8–10 Throgmorton Avenue EC2	TQ32878144	4.2, 4.5
THL78b	Tower Hill EC3	TQ33608070	4.6, 4.8
THY01	6–8 Tokenhouse Yard EC2	TQ32768132	2.2
TOL79–84	Tower of London EC3	TQ33648046	2.2
TR74	Triangle, 101–110 Lower Thames Street EC3	TQ33018068	2.2, 4.3
TST78	GPO Tunnel, Upper Thames Street EC4	TQ32388084	2.2
TW70	Topping's Wharf, Tooley Street SE1	TQ32868034	2.1
TYT98	London Bridge City, Tooley Street SE1	TQ33118021	2.2
UNE03	27–29 Union Street SE1	TQ32448000	4.8
UNS91	206 Union Street (Jubilee Line Extn, Site 13) SE1	TQ31788001	2.1
UPT90	66–67 Upper Thames Street EC4	TQ32348082	2.2
USA88	10–18 Union Street, SE1	TQ32458002	4.2
USB88	10–18 Union Street	TQ32458002	4.2
UTA87	Cannon Street Station (S), Upper Thames Street EC4	TQ32578073	2.2
VAL88	Fleet Valley between Blackfriars and Holborn Viaduct stations EC4	TQ31678092	2.2, 4.6
VRY89	Vintry House, 68–9 Upper Thames Street EC4	TQ32378081	2.2
WAT78	Watling Court EC4	TQ32358104	2.1, 2.2, 4.2, 4.5, 4.8
WEL79	5–10, 12A–13 Well Court, 44–48 Bow Lane EC4	TQ32418109	3.4, 4.2
WFG3	Windsor Court & Castle Street, 38–40 Monkwell Street EC2	TQ32288159	4.2
WFG9	31–32 Noble Street (south-west turret) EC2	TQ32228147	4.7
WFG22	St Albans' Church, Wood Street EC2	TQ32358146	4.2
WFG41	Blossom's Inn/ Lawrence Lane EC2	TQ32438123	4.6
WFG44/45	Temple of Mithras site, Bucklersbury House EC4	TQ32598099	1.2, 2.1,2.3, 3.2, 3.3, 4.2
WFG48	St Swithun London Stone, 111 Cannon Street EC4	TQ32678092	4.2
WIV88	1–7 Whittington Avenue EC3	TQ33118109	2.3, 4.2
WP83	Winchester Palace, Clink Street SE1	TQ32608035	1.3, 2.1, 2.2, 2.3, 2.6, 4.8, 5.1
WTN84	West Tenter Street E1	TQ33908101	4.7
WWB95	Walbrook Wharf, Upper Thames Street EC4	TQ32518076	4.2

Fig 2 Map of the City and Southwark showing the location of principal sites mentioned in text

Preface _Nick Merriman_

Incredible though it seems, Harvey Sheldon has already been involved in the archaeology of London for over four decades and is still going strong. This volume pays tribute to his enormous contribution through essays by many of his colleagues and friends on subjects close to Harvey's heart.

There is a piece by Laura Schaaf _et al_ at the end of this volume on Harvey the man, so here is not the place to indulge in personal anecdotes (of which each contributor will have many) relating to Harvey's humour, dress sense, fondness for turf accountants' premises, general informality and 'matiness', all of which have made such an impression on generations of London archaeologists, professional and voluntary. I will instead confine myself to a very brief personal overview of something of Harvey's career within the context of the archaeology of London.

One of the early highlights was the work he and Tony Brown undertook at Highgate Wood pottery kilns, in which volunteers uncovered evidence of some of the earliest Roman pottery production in the London area. This was followed by his long-standing association with the archaeology of Southwark and Lambeth through the Southwark (and later Southwark and Lambeth) Archaeological Excavation Committee (S[L]AEC), working particularly around the area of Borough High Street, revealing crucial evidence of the development of London's first suburb.

A major step was taken in 1975 with the creation by the newly formed Museum of London of the Department of Greater London Archaeology (DGLA) comprising the two archaeologists of the former London Museum who worked outside the city. Harvey was the first archaeology officer of the DGLA, and used his now-famous campaigning skills to help bring about the creation in 1983 of a Greater London Archaeological Service which ensured for the first time comprehensive archaeological coverage of the whole London area.

As Head of a seemingly ever-expanding DGLA in the middle to late 1980s, Harvey's work was increasingly of a strategic nature. These were amazing, even slightly surreal times, especially with the financial and building boom which saw unprecedented archaeological activity in London. At its height in the late 1980s, the Museum of London was employing over 400 field archaeologists, rumoured at the time to be more than half the archaeologists in the country.

Although the boom, inevitably, eventually turned to bust, the legacy of this period of activity, both in the city and across the rest of Greater London, was a profound deepening of our understanding of the archaeology of London. Although the pace of activity was intense, the professionalism of the work undertaken meant that a highly successful publication programme ensued, covering most aspects of London's past, from prehistoric to post-medieval times. As a result of this work, for the first time it became possible to synthesise some of the broad themes in the development of London, and eventually to develop a research framework within which to conduct future investigations (Nixon _et al_ 2002).

The late 1980s and early 1990s were a time of enormous change within archaeology, and much of the impetus for that change came from developments within London. One episode in particular stands out: the campaign to save the Rose Theatre from complete destruction following its discovery and excavation in 1989. The huge outcry amongst members of the acting profession and the general public about the prospect of its destruction – leading to its subsequent rescue – had a significant impact on the implementation of Planning Policy Guidance Note 16 (PPG16) in 1990, which in turn revolutionised archaeological practice in the country. Needless to say, Harvey has played a major role in the subsequent preservation and display of the Rose, and continues to be involved in the campaign to make it permanently accessible to the public.

Following his departure from the Museum of London in 1991, Harvey's main centre of activity became Birkbeck College where he was, and still is, an Associate Lecturer in the Faculty of Continuing Education. In many ways this has been a return to his roots in volunteer archaeology. Here, he has inspired a further generation of people to study archaeology for sheer interest's sake, or possibly to pursue a career in the subject. The tutors of the many courses on offer read as a roster of Harvey's friends and colleagues of many years' standing. Of particular note have been the training excavations he has instigated in various parts of London, from Southwark to Syon House to Ewell, which have provided much-needed practical fieldwork experience for non-professionals.

The four decades of Harvey's involvement in London's archaeology have seen profound change, from a situation in which archaeology was almost entirely led by volunteers operating on shoestring budgets, to one where hundreds of professionally trained archaeologists work in the area in an enterprise fundamentally linked to development, and substantially paid for by the private sector. In terms of the discovery of new knowledge, huge strides have been made. An exemplary string of publications has been produced, and material is now freely accessible to all those who wish to use it at the London Archaeological Archive and Research Centre (LAARC).

Nevertheless, much still remains to be done. Strategically, archaeology in London is far more fragmented than it should be, and archaeologists find it difficult to speak with one voice, which hinders advocacy efforts. At the time of writing, moves are being made to establish a single CBA group for London, and if this is successful, let us hope that it will provide a point around which to unite London's disparate archaeological voices.

In particular, a great deal more could be done in relation to public engagement with London's archaeology. We still lack up-to-date and accessible overviews of many periods; and the vast majority of Londoners are excluded from most aspects of archaeology, apart from occasional museum visits or perhaps participation in National Archaeology Week. London, because of its densely urban nature and the diverse nature of its population, poses particular challenges in terms of community archaeology. Nevertheless, these challenges must be grasped if archaeology is to continue to thrive. Most pressingly, archaeology needs to find ways of engaging those Londoners who come from more recent diaspora communities.

And it is through his gift for engaging people, alongside his substantial archaeological fieldwork and writing, that Harvey has perhaps made his greatest contribution. The loyalty, affection and enthusiasm which he has inspired through his love for archaeology over such a long period, and his ability to encourage people to follow and develop their own interests, mark him out as a unique figure in London archaeology.

1 Development – chronology and cartography

Discovery of the Bucklersbury mosaic. Illustrated London News, *1869*

Introduction *Hedley Swain*

As outlined in the general introduction above, the volume is divided into four equal sections, each of which addresses a number of the 'Framework objectives' contained within the *Research Framework for London Archaeology* (Nixon *et al* 2002). This first section, which focuses on Roman London's chronology and cartography, explores some wide-ranging themes that establish a broad context for some of what follows in Sections 2–4. Several of the papers, such as that by Hedley Swain and Tim Williams, and that by Robert Cowie, address individual Framework objectives head on. Others, such as those by Michael Fulford and Richard Reece, are relevant to a broad range. Those by John Clark and Barney Sloane fall outside the strict remit of the *Research Framework*, but form a suitable introduction. For ease of reference, the following 'Framework objectives' are addressed in this opening section:

R1 Framework objectives
- Exploring the nuances of civic status and governance: of private, public and military life;
- Examining the reasons for and characteristics of contraction, decline and abandonment of the urban settlement.

R3 Framework objectives
- Identifying the factors influencing structural change, from single events such as fires to long-term trends such as late Roman economic contraction;
- Comparing Roman London's development with other major Roman towns in Britain and on the Continent, particularly western provincial capitals.

R6 Framework objectives
- Comparing Londinium's public building provision with other major Roman towns.

R8 Framework objectives
- Estimating population size, character and composition, and changes over time including evidence for settled and transient populations;
- Examining population density and household size.

S1 Framework objectives
- Studying the transition between late Roman and early Saxon, including the reasons and implications for shifting settlement patterns.

S4 Framework objectives
- Studying data from Southwark, in order to be able to characterise the nature of the settlement there.

The papers of John Clark and Barney Sloane are reminders that modern studies of Londinium have a place in a continuing evolution of understanding, that has seen major paradigm shifts through time. Peter Rowsome's paper maps out the present understanding of the town's development based on the slow methodological piecing together of the many hundreds of excavations that have now taken place. It makes real the old adage that London is one big site that is being dug in lots of very small pieces. Hedley Swain and Tim Williams make the first detailed attempt in over 80 years to estimate the population of Roman London, showing how many variables are involved but that reasonable estimations are possible. Richard Reece and Michael Fulford use their many years of experience studying Roman Britain and its towns to offer overviews of Londinium's economic and political place in south-east England and how it changes in relation to other towns. They offer a valuable reminder to London's often inward-looking archaeological community that Londinium sits within a wider Roman world. Finally Robert Cowie explores the evidence for the end of Roman London and Tony Brown looks explicitly at evidence for the rebirth of Southwark in the Saxon period.

What the papers confirm is that, at the macro level, Londinium remains one of the best understood towns of the North-West provinces, an understanding that has grown through over 30 years of methodical professional excavation building on several centuries of antiquarian enquiry. There are, though, still many unknowns and open questions. The vagaries of development mean that some questions will now never be answered, although recent excavations have shown the capacity for the crowded city landscape to continue to throw up amazing discoveries, as at Drapers' Gardens (DGT06; Hawkins, Brown and Butler 2008). However, as the *Research Framework* makes clear it may well be the synthesis and study of the incredible resource that is the Museum of London's London Archaeological Archive and Research Centre (LAARC) that will reveal most new evidence in the future.

1.1 'Fanciful ichnography': William Stukeley's maps of (?) Roman London John Clark

Introduction

Dr William Stukeley (1687–1765) (Fig 1.1.1), characterised by Stuart Piggott (1950, xi) as 'the eighteenth-century antiquary larger than life-size', lived in London from 1717 until 1726, during which time he was also Secretary of the fledgling Society of Antiquaries. Although over 40 unpublished drawings by Stukeley of sites in London and Middlesex survive (Celoria and Spencer 1968, 30 note 7), his published writings betray little interest in the history and antiquities of London. His Commonplace Book (Stukeley 1717–, but henceforth simply 'Commonplace Book'), now in the library of the Wiltshire Archaeological and Natural History Society, Devizes (Hatchwell and Burl 1998), has three pages of notes about London (fols 25–6), but these are largely unattributed summaries of others' discoveries and theories.

However, this Commonplace Book contains (fol 40, page 71 in the original pagination) an extraordinary map (Fig 1.1.2). It has been described as a map of Roman London (Piggott 1950, 216; Hatchwell 2005, 58), although Stukeley nowhere names it as such. Hatchwell identifies it as the basis of Stukeley's later engraved map of 'Londinium Augusta', which is discussed below (Fig 1.1.3). This is debatable, as comparison of the two figures will show, and I hope to demonstrate that the maps represent two entirely different conceptions of London's past.

Londinium – or Trinovantum?

The Commonplace Book map is in ink and grey wash, with some preliminary pencil drawing. It is unfinished – a building in the north-east of the city is merely sketched in. It can be dated with some confidence to 1719, for the next page contains a plan of Avebury and an account of Stukeley's visit there on 19 May 1719.

As well as the Thames (strangely labelled in Greek 'ΠΟΤΑΜΟC', 'river') the map shows two tributaries, *River of Wells* (the Fleet) and *Wallbrook*, and two smaller streams feeding into these, *Heolbourn* and *Langbourn*. This underlying topography is derived from John Stow, who in his *Survey of London* in 1598 traced the early use of the name River of Wells (Stow 1908, **1**, 12–13) and mistakenly identified the nature and locations of the 'Oldborne' and 'Longborne' streams (Stow 1908, **1**, 14–15). For the first, rather than a stream running down Holborn Hill as Stow believed and Stukeley shows it, is a name for the Fleet itself (Barton 1962, 29 and fn 1), and the latter is a myth inspired by the name of Langbourne Ward (Stow 1908, **2**, 307).

Instead of the irregular polygon of the line of the city wall, familiar from any modern map purporting to show Roman (or medieval) London, Stukeley shows a wall running in a curve. Dotted lines outside it suggest that he envisaged a later rebuilding of the wall that produced the more angular plan. Four gates are shown, two named in Latin – 'Gate of Mercury' and 'Gate of Mars'. The latter leads to the *Campus Martius*. This presumably is the 'Field of Mars' described by a contemporary of Stukeley's, John Bagford (1715, lxi–lxii), where the Romans 'train'd up and exercised their Young Souldiers'. Bagford identifies this with the later Artillery Ground, Bishopsgate Street – Stukeley seems to place it further to the west.

Bagford (c 1650–1716), a self-educated book dealer and bibliographer with strong (if occasionally eccentric) antiquarian interests (Gatch 1986), supplied John Strype with information on antiquities found after the Great Fire, which Strype incorporated in a chapter in his revised edition of

Fig 1.1.1 William Stukeley. Engraving by John Smith, 1721, after a portrait by Sir Godfrey Kneller, Bt (National Portrait Gallery, London)

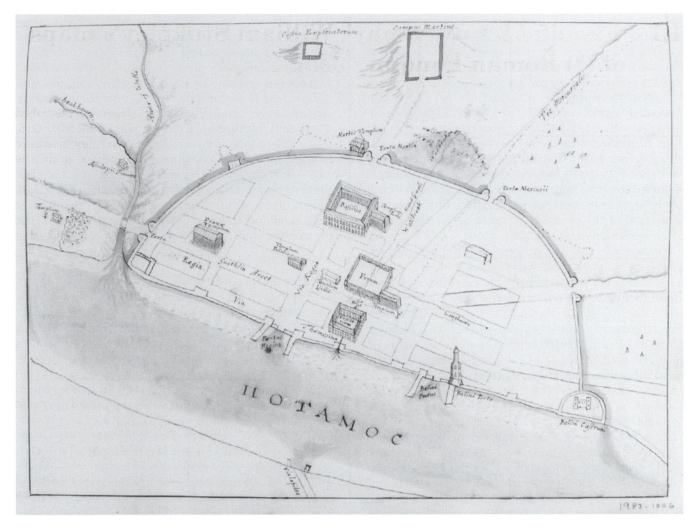

Fig 1.1.2 Plan of early London, drawn by William Stukeley in his Commonplace Book, 1719 (Wiltshire Archaeological and Natural History Society: Wiltshire Heritage Library)

John Stow's *Survey of London* (Stow 1720, **2**, app, 23). Bagford himself published two short but valuable accounts of archaeological discoveries in London (Bagford 1710, 114–18; 1715). A passage in the second of these explains the appearance on Stukeley's map, south of the river, of a road labelled *Via Lapidea* ('stony street') – not Roman Stane Street, but Stoney Street, Bankside:

[the Roman military way] led along Kent-street [ie the Old Kent Road/Tabard Street, Southwark (Gover *et al* 1934, 31–2)] ... and pointed directly to Dowgate, now so call'd, through an Arch built by the Bishop of Winchester at his Stayres, which to this Day is called Stone-street, and came directly out of Surrey. 'Twas at this very place (as I take it) that the Roman Legions forded over the River of Thames ... (Bagford 1715, lix).

Within the city wall Stukeley marks a number of temples, a *Basilica*, a *Forum* and a *Praetorium*. The *Praetorium* is placed where building works after the Great Fire in the area of Bush Lane, Cannon Street, had uncovered remains of a large building with tessellated floors (Aubrey 1980, 500, 505 and 508;

Wren 1750, 265–6; Stow 1720, **2**, app, 23). John Bagford (1715, lx) considered it the headquarters established by the general leading the invading Roman forces. Both will be recognised as precursors of the later identification of this building as the 'governor's palace' (Merrifield 1969, 78–81).

Between the *Praetorium* and the *Forum* is a dot labelled *Milliare*. This is London Stone, that surviving monument of mysterious reputation that was widely identified at the time as a Roman central milestone, from which measurements were taken: 'I take [it] to be a *Milliarie*, or *Milemarke*' (Camden 1610, 423); 'a Pillar in the Manner of the *Milliarium Aureum* at *Rome*' (Wren 1750, 265 – although Wren did not agree with this identification); and a '*lapis milliaris* from which distances are reckon'd' (Stukeley 1724, 112).

However, a number of features suggest that the map shows not Roman Londinium at all but a supposed earlier British town. Beside the river is a pharos-like tower, with below it the names *Belini Porta* and *Belini Portus*. This is the tower, with a gate (*porta*) below and a landing-place for ships (*portus*), that the 12th-century arch-confabulator Geoffrey of Monmouth (1966, 100), playing with the etymology of Billingsgate, attributed to his legendary British king Belinus. Stukeley also labels as *Belini Castrum* what is clearly the Tower of London. There was indeed some confusion over whether Belinus's 'tower' was a separate structure or (as Geoffrey probably intended) the original of the Tower of London itself (Tatlock 1950, 31); Stukeley seems to allow for both interpretations.

In the western corner of the city is a walled enclosure, presumably the later Norman fortress of Baynard's Castle. Beside it, an erased word is followed by the adjective *Regia* 'royal'. In 1758 Stukeley was to write 'the first palace of the British kings was at the south-west corner of the city, where afterwards Baynard's Castle stood' (1776, **2**, 16). Stukeley attributes this knowledge to 'the historians'. The source may be Gervase of Tilbury, writing in about 1215, who certainly claimed that the first British king, Brutus, had built Baynard's Castle (Gervase of Tilbury 2002, 400–1). Also marked are *Via Regia* and *Portus Regius*, which would have no place in Roman London (and were no doubt inspired by later King Street and Queenhithe). Significantly, also, alongside the name *Wallbrook* appears *Nant Gual.* – 'Nantgallim', the 'British' name invented by Geoffrey of Monmouth for the stream (1966, 130; Tatlock 1950, 31).

This is London in the time of the British kings.

As we shall see, Stukeley was convinced that there had existed a London before Roman Londinium. This seems to be his first attempt to map it: Trinovantum or New Troy, the legendary city founded by the Trojan settlers led by Brutus to the land of Albion, as described by Geoffrey of Monmouth (1966, 73–4; see Clark 1981).

Londinium Augusta

Best known of Stukeley's published works is the *Itinerarium Curiosum* of 1724. The fifth of the antiquarian excursions described in this volume, the *Iter Romanum*, would have brought him to London, but he notes 'According to method I should speak of *Londinium* here, but because the great deal that may be said thereupon, will make a discourse by its self; we content our selves at present with giving the plan of it as we suppose it might appear in the time of the *Romans*' (Stukeley 1724, 112).

This, his plate 57, is one of several plans of Roman towns and sites included in the *Itinerarium*, such as Silchester (pl 61) and Verulamium (pl 95). Much later Stukeley provided some comments on his map, in an essay (written in 1758) on The Brill, St Pancras, and other sites around London that he identified as 'Caesar's camps' (Stukeley 1776, **2**, 1–16). Although these clarify some obscurities in the map he had drawn over 30 years earlier, there are not surprisingly some inconsistencies.

In this later paper, Stukeley's chief concern was with *pre-Roman* London: 'London, then called *Trinobantum*, was a considerable *emporium* in British times, and before Caesar's arrival here' (Stukeley 1776, **2**, 1). Although he does not accept Geoffrey of Monmouth's account of the coming of Trojan settlers to London, he uses Geoffrey's work, as we have seen in the Commonplace Book map, as a source for the geography of the pre-Roman town.

Stukeley's London map is headed 'LONDINIUM Augusta' (Fig 1.1.3). Later, he was to state that it was under Constantine the Great that 'the title of *Londinium Augusta* commenced', and the city walls were built (1776, **2**, 16), and we must assume that that is the supposed period of most of the features shown on the map. The map is dated 7 November 1722, and dedicated to Stukeley's friend the Earl of Pembroke.

Rivers, walls and roads

The map is orientated with west towards the top. It shows the same rivers as the Commonplace Book map, and several wells and pools also listed in John Stow's chapter on 'Auncient and present Rivers . . .' (Stow 1908, **1**, 11–19).

The course of the city wall is prominently marked, much as it existed in Stukeley's own time and was shown on John Strype's map of 1720, printed for his edition of Stow's *Survey*. But Stow (1908, **1**, 9) had made it clear that it was only in 1282 that the wall was extended westwards from Ludgate to the Fleet, and that it had previously run straight from Ludgate to the Thames – and this is how Stukeley shows it. Stow also (1908, **1**, 8) explains that the wall was originally continuous along the riverside – quoting William FitzStephen's 1173 description of London as proof – so Stukeley shows a riverside wall.

Outside the north-west corner of the city Stukeley marks the site of a supposed Roman fortification: *Castrum Exploratorum Barbican*. This had already appeared, although without the identification as the Barbican, on his Commonplace Book map. Sadly, he does not enlarge on the nature of this *castrum*. John Bagford (1715, lxii) is more forthcoming. There was 'another old Building of the Romans, which was a Watch-Tower, then and now called Barbican . . . Here they kept Cohorts of Soldiers in continual Service . . .'. John Stow (1908, **1**, 70 and 302), with some rather shaky etymology, had identified 'Barbican' as meaning 'watch-tower', but hazarded no guess as to its antiquity. Bagford admits 'nothing remains of this antique Building except the Name' (1715, lxii), yet to him and Stukeley it was without doubt a Roman fortification.

Stukeley marks only four gates in the city wall on the landward side – Ludgate, Newgate, Bishopsgate and Aldgate – leading to what he took to be the main Roman roads. The road from Bishopsgate is labelled both *Via Militaris* and *Hermen* [Ermine] *Street* – Stukeley has distorted the traditional name of this Roman road to suit his derivation of it from a supposed 'Saxon' word meaning 'warrior', and its translation into Latin as *Via Militaris* (1724, 73).

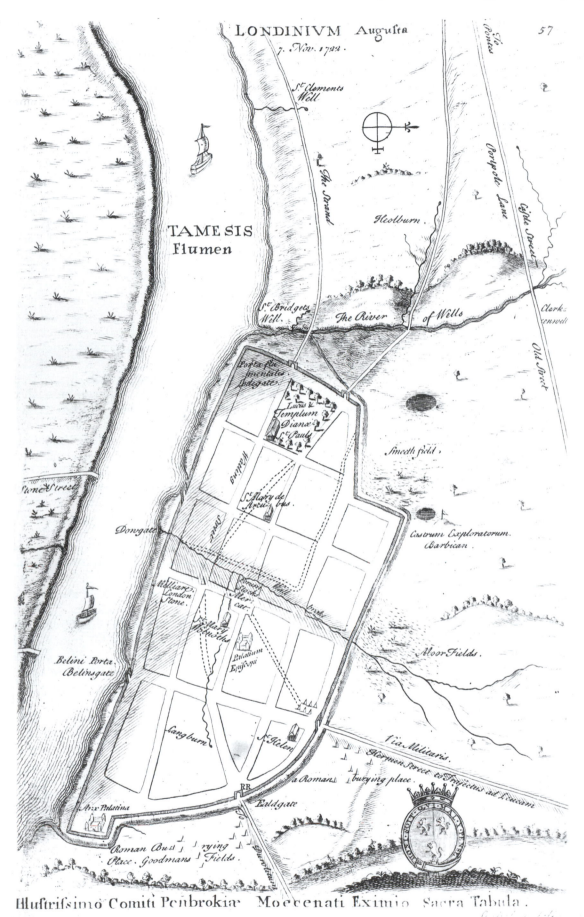

Fig 1.1.3 'Londinium Augusta': William Stukeley's map of Roman London dated 7 November 1722, Plate 57 in his Itinerarium Curiosum, *1724*

Two gates are marked in the riverside wall. One is labelled *Belini Porta Belinsgate*. The evidence of the Commonplace Book map suggests that Stukeley indeed considered it was named after the legendary British king. By 1758 he has reconsidered, and suggests (Stukeley 1776, **2**, 9) that it may be derived from the name of Cunobelinus (who, one might add, has the advantage of having existed!). Another gate is shown further west, between today's Dowgate and Queenhithe. A jetty opposite on the Southwark shore leads to a road labelled *Stone Street*. This, misplaced to the west, is Stoney Street, Bankside, seen already on the Commonplace Book map.

Streets, temples, churches and palaces

A grid of streets within the city walls looks promisingly Roman. But Stukeley explains its inspiration: 'By collecting several old maps I discern there were four principal streets running from west to east' (1776, **2**, 12). These are represented by Gresham Street, Cheapside, *Watling Street* (named on the map) and Thames Street. Although he was aware of Wren's discovery of a Roman 'causeway' by St Mary le Bow church in Cheapside (Wren 1750, 265), it is the regularity of the medieval street plan of London that Stukeley takes as his source.

Near the centre of the town there is a small obelisk labelled, as on the Commonplace Book map, *Milliare London Stone* – the '*lapis milliaris* from which distances are reckon'd' (Stukeley 1724, 112). Nearby, on the banks of the Walbrook, is *Forum Stocks Mercat* – presumably the coincidence of the central position and the existence here of the medieval Stocks Market suggested this identification. The *Forum* on the Commonplace Book map was also in this location.

Prominent in the western part of the map is a gabled building set amid trees and labelled *Lucus & Templum Dianae St Pauls* – the same temple appeared on the Commonplace Book map. The concept that St Paul's cathedral stood on the site of a temple dedicated to Diana had been familiar since the time of William Camden (Camden 1610, 426; Clark 1996). Unconvinced, Christopher Wren had noted that he had found no trace of such a temple during the works for his new cathedral (Wren 1750, 266 and 296); but Stukeley has no doubt of the temple's existence, and goes on to surround it with a 'grove', presumably inspired by the famous sacred grove of Nemi (Cary *et al* 1949, 274).

Stukeley marks three Christian churches: St Mary le Bow (*St Mary de Arcubus*), St Mary Woolnoth, and St Helen (Bishopsgate). The first of these at least has a solid (if mistaken) archaeological basis, for it was here, during the clearance of the remains of the medieval church prior to rebuilding after the Great Fire, that Christopher Wren uncovered the walls and floor of 'a Temple, or Church of Roman Workmanship' (Wren 1750, 265). Sadly, there is nothing to support Wren's identification of

'Roman workmanship', and this is surely a reference to the Norman crypt that underlay the medieval church (Schofield 1994, 118–19).

Archaeological discoveries were also made on the site of St Mary Woolnoth in 1716. John Strype (Stow 1720, **2**, app, 24) describes the finding of masses of broken Roman pottery and a tessellated floor, and records that Dr John Harwood of Doctors Commons considered that the Temple of Concord (another of Geoffrey of Monmouth's conceits (1966, 90)) stood on or near this site.

The 'Roman' origin of St Helen's is more problematical. Although modern gazetteers (Page 1909, 86–146; RCHM(E) 1928; Merrifield 1965, 189–325) record no early Roman discoveries from the site of the church, there *were* reportedly finds made in the 18th century – 'urns, paterae and other remains of Roman antiquities . . . and a vault arched over with equilateral Roman bricks, fourteen feet deep, and within it two skeletons' (Brayley 1829, **1**, 35) – and even a note in the Society of Antiquaries Minutes that Stukeley himself had seen a Roman grave on the site (Brayley 1829, **1**, 35). Yet if Brayley is right, these discoveries were made in 1725 and 1726 respectively – too late to have been incorporated into Stukeley's map of November 1722!

Perhaps Stukeley took the church's unusual dedication to Helena, mother of the Emperor Constantine and supposedly the daughter of the legendary King Coel of Colchester (Kightly 1982, 59–83), to be sufficient evidence of its early origin. The 'myth' that the church was built by Constantine as a memorial to his mother proved a hardy one (Cox 1876, 4).

More surprising, perhaps, is the *omission* from the map of the one church that claimed for itself a foundation date in the Roman period. Already in 1417 the parishioners of St Peter's upon Cornhill were claiming that their church was the oldest in London, founded as a cathedral by the first British king to accept Christianity, King Lucius (Riley 1868, 651–2) – while John Stow noted the presence in the church of a brass plate dating its foundation to AD 179 (Stow 1908, **1**, 194). Whatever might lie behind this strongly held local belief (Smith 1979, 30), perhaps it provides the rationale for the *Palatium Episcopi* – 'bishop's palace' – that Stukeley marks in this vicinity.

Stukeley labels the Tower of London *Arx Palatina* (the 'palatine citadel'), the term used by William FitzStephen in his 12th-century account of London, which Stukeley would have found printed in Stow's *Survey* (1908, **2**, 219–29). A four-square structure with corner turrets is shown: the White Tower. In 1758 Stukeley dated its construction to the same period as the city wall – as we shall see below, to the time of Constantine – 'then it was that the Tower was built, an *armamentarium* [armoury or arsenal], as the castle of Colchester' (1776, **2**, 13). Its identification as an armoury is surely an imaginative backdating of its later medieval function. Its identification as Roman has a longer pedigree.

In late medieval and Tudor literature the Tower had been attributed to Julius Caesar. The idea was mooted in a poem *The Parlement of the Three Ages* in 1370, dismissed by Polydore Vergil in 1534, but asserted in Richard Grafton's *Chronicle* in 1569, and twice by Shakespeare (Nearing 1948). John Stow gave reasons why he believed this could not be true, and traced documentary evidence for its building in the reign of William I (1908, **1**, 44–5). But its antedating remained popular. The White Tower was clearly of great age, 'perhaps as ancient as any Building now amongst us' (Bagford 1715, lxi). Attribution to the Romans remained an attractive proposition – as it was for other great stone castles like Chepstow and Caerphilly (Hunter 1975, 185). The presence of the Tower of London on Stukeley's map is only to be expected.

London before Londinium

Two unambiguously Roman sites *are* marked by Stukeley: cemeteries outside Bishopsgate and in *Goodmans Fields* outside Aldgate. Discoveries from the first of these, made in 1576, were recorded from personal observation by John Stow (1908, **1**, 168–71). Of the second, John Bagford (1715, lxi) notes 'in digging the Foundations for building of Houses in or about the Year 1678/9 there were found many Urns, together with the Ashes and Bones of the Dead'. A further 'burying place', identified on the site of St Paul's by Sir Christopher Wren (1750, 266), is ignored by Stukeley – deliberately, for the presence of burials here would argue against Stukeley's claim that the earliest Roman town lay between Ludgate and the Walbrook (below).

Stukeley marks the cemeteries with a scattering of small 'obelisks', and places a cluster of six of these symbols *inside* the city wall at Bishopsgate. These reflect discoveries made in April 1707 in Camomile Street – but displaced from east to west of Bishopsgate. Dr John Woodward of Gresham College recorded the constructional details of the city wall revealed during the building of new houses here (Woodward 1723, 15–19), and noted the presence of cremation burials *inside* the wall; and since the Roman custom was to bury the dead outside the limits of a town, he had no doubt that 'the Wall must have been built since the Urns were reposited there' (Woodward 1723, 36).

Woodward states that 'burning fell into general Disuse towards the latter End of the Times of the Antonines'; but bones had also been found – so the cemetery had gone on in use, and the date when the wall was built must be 'very high' (Woodward 1723, 40–1). He comes to no conclusion but notes (Woodward 1723, 16) the common belief, shared by Camden (1610, 423), Stukeley (1776, **2**, 13) and Bagford (1715, lxxi), that the city wall was built by Constantine the Great. Camden says this was 'at the request of his mother Helena', and Stukeley allows the alternative – that it was built by Empress Helena 'our countrywoman' herself. Attribution to Constantine seems to be an antiquarian rationalisation of the longstanding medieval tradition that Helena built the walls of London and Colchester. Whatever its origin, this story appears to have first been popularised among historians by Henry of Huntingdon, writing in 1133: 'Now Helena, the high-born daughter of Britain, is said to have encircled London with a wall, which is still there, and to have furnished Colchester with fortifications' (Henry of Huntingdon 1996, 62–3).

The concept that the wall marked a late extension of the city boundary was common to both Wren (1750, 265–6) and Stukeley. On Stukeley's map a rectangular area in the western half of the city is bordered by double dotted lines. He explains its significance, and its pre-Roman date, in 1758 '. . . we discern, the original ground-plot of the oldest city is comprehended, in length, from Ludgate to the present Walbrook; in breadth, from Maiden-lane, Lad-lane, Cateaton-street [now united as Gresham Street], to the Thames' (Stukeley 1776, **2**, 12).

The eastern boundary he places on the Walbrook because it was there, *outside* the town, that a battle took place in the 3rd century, in the time of Allectus (Stukeley 1776, **2**, 16). Sadly, the evidence for this battle beside the Walbrook is solely in the fictions of Geoffrey of Monmouth (1966, 129–30) – who in any case makes it clear that the battle and the imagined slaughter of a Roman legion by the Walbrook took place *inside* the city.

Double dotted lines extending from the Walbrook to Aldgate and to Bishopsgate mark the routes of original roads: 'when the city was enlarged and encompassed with new walls, the three roads beyond the east gate were converted into streets, as at present, Threadneedle-street, Cornhill and Lombard-street' (Stukeley 1776, **2**, 16).

We must give Stukeley credit for recognising that the street plan was a palimpsest, preserving patterns of an earlier date, and for attempting to interpret its history. He has effectively combined in this map two phases in the development of London from pre-Roman beginnings in what he conceived of as 'Trinobantum' to the Augusta of the 4th century. Yet both depend more on imagination and received opinion than on archaeological evidence.

Conclusion

The Great Fire of 1666 ushered in the first great period of archaeological discovery in the City of London. In his capacity as Secretary of the Society of Antiquaries William Stukeley had access to records of recent London discoveries and the latest theories. Yet little of this new knowledge was reflected in his map of '*Londinium Augusta*'. His plans of Silchester and Verulamium, for example, were clearly the result of site survey, and portray the then surviving features of these two important Roman towns. His Londinium map, by contrast, is a product of the library.

Stukeley was locked into a tradition that identified the Tower of London as Roman, assigned the city wall to Constantine (or Helena) and placed a Temple of Diana under St Paul's. As we have seen, the explanation of features on his maps can usually be found in the thought of his contemporaries like John Bagford and John Woodward, or predecessors like John Aubrey, William Camden and John Stow.

Even scholars of the Enlightenment tended to regard the durability of a tradition as evidence of its truth. And some of the traditions they depended on date back to early medieval authors like Henry of Huntingdon and Gervase of Tilbury – and (particularly in the case of Stukeley's Commonplace Book map) to that most unreliable of all, Geoffrey of Monmouth.

In his approach to early London, Stukeley was no great innovator. His maps reflect a dependence on 'authority' that is not unknown today. They do not advance our knowledge of Roman London's topography; rather they shed light on antiquarian thought in the 17th and 18th centuries. The later antiquary Richard Gough's dismissal of the published map as 'a fanciful ichnography [plan] of London as under the Romans' (1780, **1**, 744) is well founded, and, with a change of wording to 'under the Britons', is even more apt for the untitled Commonplace Book map.

Acknowledgements

I am grateful to the Wiltshire Heritage Museum, Devizes (Wiltshire Archaeological and Natural History Society) and the Sandell Librarian and Archivist Dr Lorna Haycock for the opportunity to study Stukeley's Commonplace Book. This case-study of the perils, for even the most eminent of archaeologists, of relying too much on 'authority' or believing too readily the currently accepted view is offered here to Harvey Sheldon, one who has throughout his archaeological career understood the pre-eminence of practical, personal investigation of London's archaeology, in recognition of a long friendship.

1.2 Images of Empire: illustrating the fabric of Roman London *Barney Sloane*

In 1969 and 1970, Harvey Sheldon was involved in the excavation and recording of an important Roman kiln site at Highgate Woods in Middlesex, north of London. Almost three centuries earlier, in 1672, the London apothecary and antiquary John Conyers was also intent on revealing the detail of a remarkably well-preserved Roman pottery kiln, this time in part of the churchyard of St Paul's, disturbed for the foundations of London's great new cathedral. Conyers produced a small working sketch in the margins of his notes (Fig 1.2.1), not to be seen by the interested public until the publication of the Victoria County History for London in 1909 (Page 1909, 124, fig 1). Harvey's team and the staff of the Horniman Museum, on the other hand, conserved, lifted and arranged for the display of the kiln in that museum (see Butterworth 1969). The development of imaging and display in the period separating these two archaeologists is, effectively, the story of the presentation of archaeological discovery, and as such lies far beyond the bounds of this work, but a selective, primarily pictorial, essay on how generations of Londoners (and the rest of the world)

have been introduced to what Roman London originally looked like keeps this important issue alive and at the same time provides a handsome look at some of the key Roman sites in London. It should be noted that all of these discoveries are placed in their archaeological context within such seminal studies as the Victoria County History of London (vol 1; Page 1909) and the Royal Commission's volume on Roman London (RCHM(E) 1928), and subsequent extensive studies on the Roman city and surroundings, from which the summaries presented here are drawn.

Conyers was no professional draughtsman, displaying little command of perspective in his cutaway of the St Paul's kiln, but at least he made a record. From the late 17th century there would be little attempt for nearly 100 years to record by illustration any Roman structures in London. One of the earliest was published in *Archaeologia* (Gough 1787, 117, pl 5) concerning discoveries revealed by extensive digging for sewers in Birchin Lane and Lombard Street in 1785 and brought to the attention of antiquary Richard Gough, who had

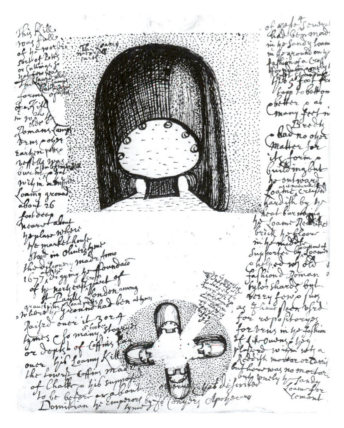

Fig 1.2.1 Conyers 1672. Cutaway sketch of a Roman pottery kiln found in St Paul's churchyard. Ink on paper. British Museum Sloane MSS 958 fol 105 (courtesy British Museum)

Fig 1.2.2 Anon 1786. Piece of Roman mosaic found in Birchin Lane. Watercolour on paper (maximum dimension 0.42m) (Guildhall Library Print Room Pr.73/BIR © Corporation of London)

11

himself made a sketch of Bastion 7 of the City Wall in 1763 (RCHM(E) 1928, 107, pl 28). The plan of the various structures is most interesting, since, although not produced to scale, each element was located by annotating the 'modern' house number adjacent to it. This plan is important as it thus represents the earliest 'site location' plan for Roman London. Among wall bases and fragments of wall plaster was found the corner of a fine polychrome mosaic. A watercolour dated 1786 survives in the Guildhall (Fig 1.2.2) and is notable in that it appears to be the earliest surviving colour rendition

of a part of Roman London, albeit a highly fragmentary one. It was a detailed work, and cannot be far off a 1:1 scale.

The beauty and complexity of such remarkable remains ensured their place in the wider public consciousness when at least three very well-preserved mosaics were discovered during developments on Leadenhall Street, and at the Bank of England, in the early 1800s. Thomas Fisher (1781–1836) was the artist who captured both, and also ensured their publication in the *Gentleman's Magazine* (Fisher 1804; Fisher 1807).

Fig 1.2.3 Fisher 1804. Roman tessellated pavement, discovered in Leadenhall Street, London, in December, 1803. Engraving (by J Basire) on paper (maximum dimension 0.54m) (Guildhall Library Print Room Pr.345/LEA © Corporation of London)

The Leadenhall Street example, found in 1803 and dated to the 1st or 2nd century, shows Bacchus riding a tiger, and formed the central square in a large room over 20ft (6m) square (RCHM(E) 1928, 127) (Fig 1.2.3). The Bank of England floor was a more stylised acanthus-leaf design in a smaller room, 11ft (3.3m) square. The Leadenhall Street floor was lifted in sections after recording, but its condition deteriorated through storage in open-air conditions. The pavement was transferred to the British Museum in 1880 and restored.

The Bank of England example (Fig 1.2.4) was found in 1805, and dates to the 3rd century. The Bank's Governor gifted it to the British Museum and it has been on display there ever since.

Both pavements were rendered in colour and engraved with a very high degree of accuracy. Their life-like colouring, combined with the very high degree of preservation thus provided to members of the public their first real sense of eminent Roman Londoners' use of space. It is interesting to note that in its 1800-year existence, the Bank of England

Fig 1.2.4 Fisher 1806. Roman tessellated pavement discovered under the south [sic: north] west angle of the Bank of England in 1805. Engraving on paper (maximum dimension 0.36m) (Guildhall Library Print Room Pr.44/BAN © Corporation of London)

Fig 1.2.5 Anon 1848. Remains of the Roman villa, on the site of the new Coal Exchange. Watercolour on paper (maximum dimension 0.3m) (Guildhall Library Print Room Pr.156/ COA (1) © Corporation of London)

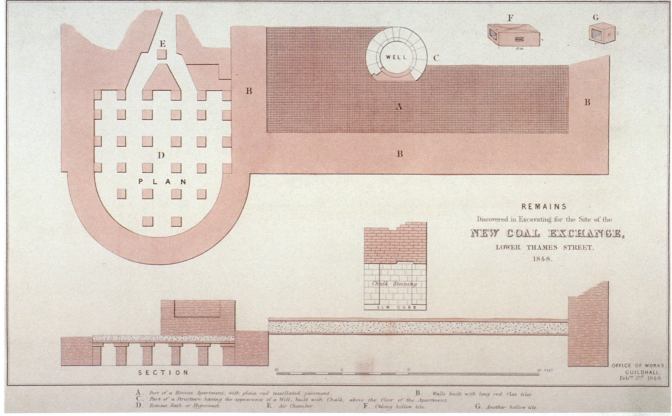

Fig 1.2.6 Anon 1848. Ground plan and section of the Roman remains discovered while digging the foundations for the new Coal Exchange. Lithograph on paper (maximum dimension 0.3m) (Guildhall Library Print Room Pr.156/COA(1) © Corporation of London)

pavement has now been an exhibit for at least as long as it functioned as a floor.

Numerous discoveries, particularly in the city, but also in Southwark and the suburbs, were made and illustrated over the next half-century, including a notable measured section through a Roman 'road' with retaining walls, found in Eastcheap in 1831, published in the *Gentleman's Magazine* for 1836 (RCHM(E) 1928, 117). Perhaps the most significant development in illustrative technique took place in the 1840s, exemplified by discoveries at the new Coal Exchange on Lower Thames Street in 1848. The remains of what was thought to be a Roman villa formed part of a bath house attached to a winged town house (see Fig. 1.2.7), the whole probably dating from the late 2nd through the 3rd centuries. The preservation of the complex was an early decision, which permitted the survival and viewing of the remains. Indeed, following the Ancient Monuments Act in 1882, it was one of the first sites to be scheduled in London. However, the representation of the site in 1848 was the key development. Illustration took two distinct forms: a realistic watercolour of the excavations themselves, showing the disposition of the site and remains (Fig 1.2.5), and a technical illustration displaying scaled plan, sectional and elevational elements (Fig 1.2.6). Technical drawings such as these (and also seen at the Roman house found at St Thomas Hospital,

Southwark, in 1840; RCHM(E) 1928, 50, pl 46) witness a profound development towards an ability to appreciate ancient structures in three dimensions accurately (compare with photograph in 2003, Fig 1.2.7). Additional to this was the innovation of identifying sub-components on the plan and providing an accompanying key: effectively archaeological feature identification had arrived. In parallel, the watercolours of the 'site view' provided the (educated) public with a sense of archaeology as process, and allowed them to share in the discovery itself, not just the artefacts.

In 1859, one of London's most active antiquaries, Charles Roach Smith, printed for subscribers his *Illustrations of Roman London*. This was the first coherent attempt to provide readers with a view of the Roman city's fabric and artefacts, drawing together many of the more important discoveries of the previous century. Ten years later, the public thirst for such antiquities was amply demonstrated on the occasion of the excavation of the famous Bucklersbury pavement. This superb mosaic, from a late 3rd- or 4th-century town house was excavated and recorded by members of the London and Middlesex Archaeological Society in 1869, and was on temporary display to the public while still *in situ*. A staggering 50,000 people saw it in three days (Fig. 1.2.8). It was then lifted in sections to be displayed in the Guildhall Museum. In 1976 it was

Fig 1.2.7 MoLAS 2003. View of hypocaust arrangement for bath house at Lower Thames Street

ROMAN PAVEMENT FOUND IN THE POULTRY, NEAR THE MANSION HOUSE.—SEE PAGE 550.

Fig 1.2.8 Illustrated London News 1869. Crowds flocked to see the mosaic pavement discovered in Bucklersbury

relaid in the Museum of London. The records include beautiful and accurate watercolours of both the pavement itself, recalling the approaches of the early 1800s, and the technical analysis of the sub-structure as at the Coal Exchange (Figs 1.2.9 and 1.2.10).

In the second half of the 19th century, a new form of illustrative medium arrived – the photograph. Henry Fox Talbot had published his 'Pencil of Nature' in 1844, showing that photographs could be published, and over the succeeding decades, interest in the new art form expanded at a remarkable rate. Use of photographs to display Roman remains was not immediate as far as we can tell, and it does not begin to appear with any frequency until the 1880s. The clarity and contrast achieved in the display of the archaeological features in these early images mixes powerfully with the sense of immediacy intro-duced by the often 'industrial' feel to the surround-ings and the apparently oblivious (although surely posed) labourers often visible. A classic example is that of the city defensive wall at Trinity Place, with foreman and labourers alongside a beautifully cleaned-up section of Roman masonry and tile (Fig 1.2.11). Two decades later, this rather brutal, industrialistic feel is enhanced on the photograph of the same defensive wall towards its western end by the scaffolding and demolition rubble surrounding the ancient structure (Fig 1.2.12).

The drawn archaeological record of Roman London had continued to develop over the second half of the century with examples of highly detailed records such as those by Philip Norman in 1884 at Bastion 9 of the wall (RCHM(E) 1928, pls 31–2) showing the reused Roman architectural fragments, and by Henry Hodge at around the same time where coloured phasing was used to distinguish between the Roman and medieval structures at Leadenhall Market (Guildhall Print Room La.Pr.343/LEA). It was, however, a highly unusual discovery of the re-mains of a large Roman ship under County Hall on the south side of the Thames in 1910 that, arguably, provided the need for a new, more detailed approach (Fig 1.2.13). Strictly speaking, a ship does not form a physical part of the structure of Roman London, but the size of the vessel and the importance of the Roman port permits some leeway.

The ship, built entirely of oak, and dated to *c* AD 300, was represented by the bottom and part of one side of the hull, measuring as found some 13m by 5.5m. It was carvel-built locally, but in a fashion typical of the Mediterranean method of Roman shipbuilding. The entire surviving part was lifted, conserved and displayed. It was also meticulously recorded, and it was this aspect that perhaps represented the greatest advance in archaeological depiction of Roman London. The numbered timbers, their careful drawing, the noting of specific details

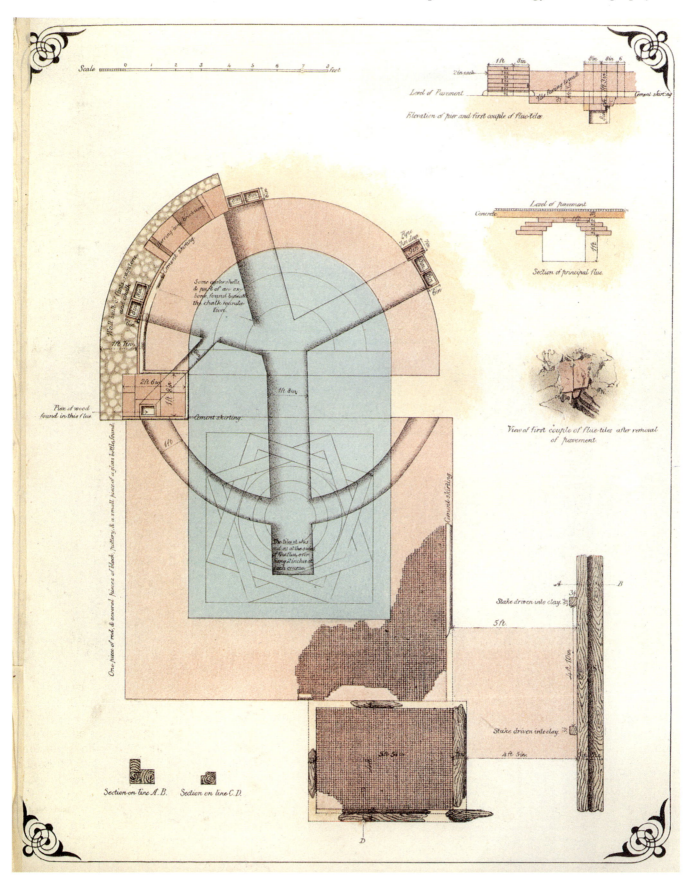

Fig 1.2.9 Emslie, J P, 1869. Plans, section and details of the Roman hypocaust found in Bucklersbury. Watercolour on paper (maximum dimension 0.74m) (Guildhall Library Print Room La.Pr.113/BUC © Corporation of London)

Fig 1.2.10 Anon 1870 after H R Payne, 1869. Roman mosaic pavement dating from AD 300, found in Bucklersbury. Chromolithograph showing the mosaic as recorded

Fig 1.2.11 Anon 1882. View of part of the Roman city wall at Trinity Place, during its demolition to make way for the Circle Line (English Heritage, National Monument Record PEN02/02 AL0147-49)

such as nail locations, all combined to produce what must be the very earliest timber-by-timber recording and analysis of a *wooden* Roman structure in London (Fig. 1.2.14). Such detailed recording proved its worth, since the vessel deteriorated while on display and was for the most part eventually lost.

Whether or not the County Hall ship had an immediate impact on approaches to illustrating other Roman sites in London is not clear. However, within just a few years, redevelopment of the General Post Office on St Martin le Grand (GM318) had permitted an archaeological investigation. Instead of accurate visual images, the approach adopted was a simple line-drawn affair (probably reflecting the piecemeal nature of the discoveries) involving outline plots of the individual 'pot-holes' (pits, postholes, ditches etc). What sets this particular work apart from preceding investigations is the combination of codings to show the dates of each feature on the plan. This represents the first known attempt to display 'spot-dating' of individual features (as opposed to broad phasing) and although modest-looking in comparison with earlier works of art, must be seen as a development of considerable archaeological significance (Fig 1.2.15).

Between World Wars One and Two, numerous sites were investigated (usually as watching briefs, occasionally as more detailed recording exercises). Combinations of plan, section, pen-and-ink illustrations and photographs made up the repertoire, but there is nothing particular to help develop the thread

of this paper until the middle of the 20th century, and the arrival of film and television. The famous *Animal, Vegetable, Mineral* television programme (started 1952) had made archaeology (and archaeologists) very popular with those who had access to the TV, and Mortimer Wheeler and Glyn Daniel had become household names. The discovery of the 3rd-century Mithraic temple near Walbrook in 1954 was highly newsworthy (Fig 1.2.16), and the site became a *cause célèbre*. The sense of archaeological discovery, held in 19th-century watercolours, then monochrome photographs, could now be transmitted to a mass market, providing the next best thing to actually being there. The temple was dismantled in its entirety and moved to a new location where continuing public access was guaranteed.

Harvey Sheldon was a nipper at the time of the discovery, and while history does not relate whether he saw the news items or visited the excavations in 1954–55, it was to be only another fourteen years before his own efforts resulted in the successful lifting and display of the Highgate Roman kiln introduced at the start of this paper (Fig 1.2.17). While modest in comparison with the temple, it was a further significant development, since the kiln, by its very nature, was composed of degraded tile, clay and soil blocks – a very different conservation proposition to Kentish ragstone and mortar.

Behind these successful experiments in public display of excavated structures, providing visitors

Fig 1.2.12 Anon 1903. View of the excavations at Newgate, showing a portion of the Roman defensive wall. Photograph to paper (maximum dimension 0.29m) (Guildhall Library Print Room La.Pr.446/OLD(1) © Corporation of London)

Fig 1.2.13 1912. Photograph of the so-called County Hall Roman ship excavated in 1910 (Riley and Gomme 1912)

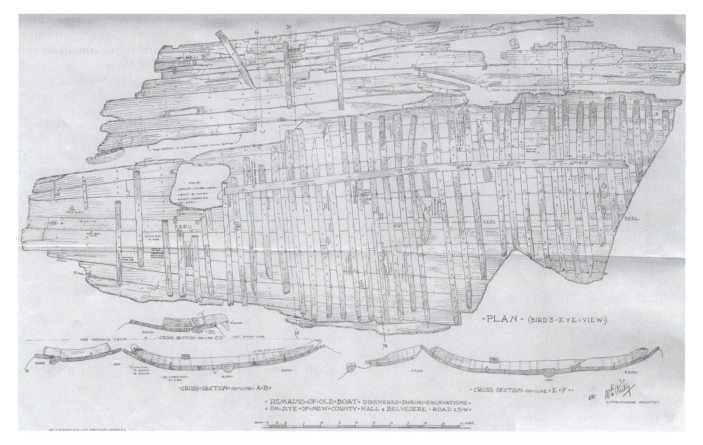

Fig 1.2.14 1912. Drawn record of the ship timbers (Riley and Gomme 1912)

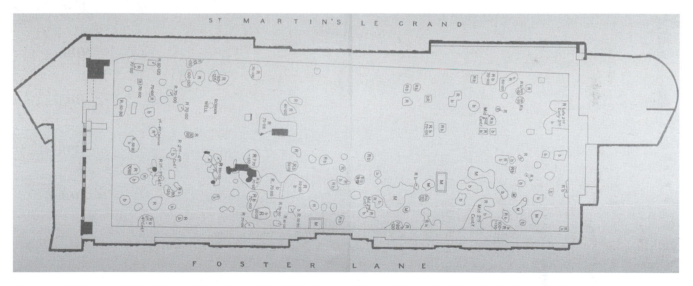

Fig 1.2.15 Anon 1914. Plan of the site of the Old General Post Office, St Martin le Grand (GM318), showing the excavated pot-holes [sic] and giving approximate dates of the objects found. Ink on paper (maximum dimension 0.6m) (Guildhall Library Print Room Pr.252/GEN © Corporation of London)

a chance to get up close to the three-dimensional entities themselves, the recording of archaeological features through plans, sections, photographs and videos continued to develop and change in the later 20th century. Drawing on the key developments of the numbered 'context' (the smallest identifiable element of the archaeological sequence – so a pit fill, or a posthole, a single length of wall, or a single ship's timber), systems were developed that ensured plans of such contexts were separated out and described individually, permitting the detailed reconstruction of the exact developmental sequence of a site in order to integrate artefactual and environmental data. The site plan is now rendered most often in 6H pencil drawings on durable drawing film, gridded for ease of accuracy, and interpreted by sketches by the archaeologist to accompany specific comments on each context.

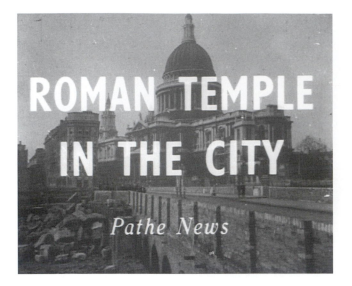

Fig 1.2.16 Pathe Newsreel title shot from a film on the discovery of the temple of Mithras near Walbrook (© British Pathe Limited, by permission)

Colour and monochrome transparencies or digital photographs provide the accompanying visual record. A case in point is the excavation at Northgate House (MRG95), conducted by the Museum of London Archaeology Service in 1995, which revealed a Roman pottery workshop (Fig 1.2.18). Here, we can see the formal outline archive plan and the interpretative sketches.

Archaeology in London is moving rapidly into the digital age: digital photographs are now commonplace and capture of spatial data through laser technology and digital, satellite-linked survey equipment is becoming so. Digital software packages allow for detailed site records to be assimilated into 'fly-through' virtual three-dimensional reconstructions of objects and structures, and the Internet is placing such resources at the hands of an ever-increasing market of all ages. The means of communicating images of the Roman Empire in London look set to change again, and the future will bring some very exciting results, I am sure.

But to conclude this paper, I wish to return to the 'bread-and-butter' of imaging the Empire. Specifically, to the archive drawings from such sites as Northgate House, for I believe it will be a good while yet before we abandon completely the need for such archives. These kinds of drawings, as works of art, cannot stand shoulder to shoulder with the wonderful watercolours of the 19th century, or with the entrancing virtual realities of the 21st century. It is, however, without doubt that they contain the essence of modern archaeological work. The

Fig 1.2.17 Roman pottery kiln at Highgate Wood; one of those found was lifted, conserved and displayed at the Horniman Museum

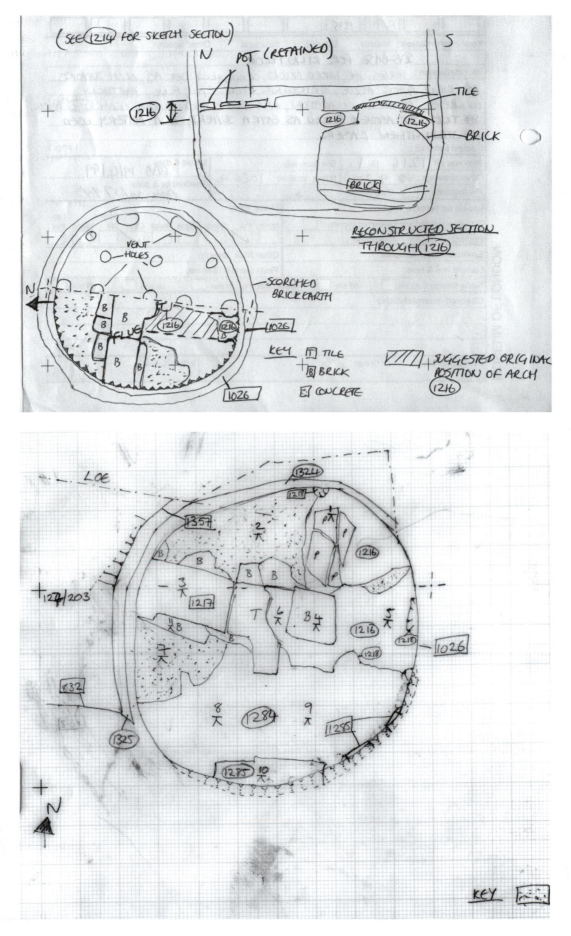

Fig 1.2.18 Northgate House, Moorgate (MRG95), excavated in 1995. Context 1216 (kiln) scale 1:20 plan, annotated sketches on descriptive sheet (see Seeley and Drummond-Murray 2005)

mud-smears on the permatrace recording 'kiln 1216' are real, the hurried nature of the sketch-plans defines the lot of today's contracting excavator, and yet in the clarity of archaeology presented for the photographs it is evident where the real archaeological effort has gone. Understanding the fact that just the same attention to detail has been exercised as for a grand watercolour is sufficient to transmit the wonder of the discovery to those who want to learn about archaeology. John Conyers started this paper and, comparing 1672 with 1995, I believe it is entirely appropriate that we finish on such an example to find that, while methods have changed, the language remains essentially the same.

1.3   Mapping Roman London: identifying its urban patterns and interpreting their meaning

Peter Rowsome

'*... it cannot be supposed that men would go by a crooked line, where they could arrive by a straight one*' Sir William Chambers, architect 1723–96.

Introduction

This paper reviews work on interpreting Londinium's layout and presenting it as a new map, updating the *Ordnance Survey map of Roman London* (Museum of London 1983) for the urban area on the north bank of the Thames whilst finally including the islands of North Southwark. Understanding the physical evidence for the town's street pattern, land use and building layout also requires interpretation of the urban processes that were at work, the character of the settlement and differences between its districts. The ability to use map data as an analytical tool has been greatly enhanced by the advent of Geographic Information Systems (GIS). The area eventually enclosed by the defences on the north bank of the Thames occupied 135 hectares, with the two main islands of Southwark extended through reclamation to cover a further 36 hectares. Roman London's total area is greater than many continental provincial capitals and a huge amount of archaeological evidence has been recorded in a detailed and consistent manner, providing excellent potential for digital mapping-related research.

In theory there are two kinds of towns, the systematically planned and the organic, but in fact no city, however arbitrary its form may appear to us, is truly unplanned (Kostof 1991, 52). To understand the morphology of Roman London we first need to build up a detailed plan of its physical parts. Archaeological work has always depended on the accurate recording of discoveries, their interpretation, and conjecture into unexplored areas. This archaeological groundwork has been going on for centuries, with London's antiquity commented on by Bede and visible in the physical remains of the Roman city's defensive wall. The 17th and 18th centuries witnessed a growth in the careful recording of finds, allowing William Stukeley to produce his map of Roman London in 1724 (Clark, this volume, Fig 1.1.3). By the 1960s there was an extensive archive of archaeological recording by antiquaries and the first professional archaeologists (Merrifield 1965). In the 40 years since then the record has grown massively, as archaeological units have gained formal access to sites and developed standardised recording methods, placing Roman London amongst the best-known towns in the Empire (Millett 1998, 8).

A river ran through it – siting and form of the first settlement

We tend to assume that most Roman towns were strictly gridded, but topography is a common cause of irregularities in their plans. The site chosen for Londinium included hills, streams and islands but was dominated by the Thames. In planning terms Roman London can be described as a riverine settlement (Kostof 1991, 54), and the river and surrounding landscape were major factors in the town's evolving plan.

Roman development began with the establishment of a river-crossing at the lowest bridgeable point on the Thames that was also suitable for port facilities (Watson *et al* 2001). The bridgehead road was built across the tidal mudflats south of the river and up Cornhill to the north of the Thames, where it intersected with an east–west road leading west towards Calleva (Silchester) and Verulamium (St Albans), dated to AD 47 by a timber drain at 1 Poultry (ONE94; Hill and Rowsome forthcoming; Tyers, this volume). South of the river the main road is dated to between AD 50–55 on the basis of pottery and coins (Sheldon 1978, 27). The precise sequence of road construction may have been from north to south after an initial crossing at Westminster and a survey of the north bank, or outwards from a base established on the river itself. In any case, Londinium's position ensured that it would quickly become the major port and focus of the road system for the new province.

It would be difficult to overestimate the role of the Roman port in determining the layout of the first settlement (Brigham 1990b; Milne 1985). The main settlement to the north of the Thames was built on two hills whilst its major suburb to the south lay on a series of low islands, but it was the navigable river which made the contrasting banks an ideal pairing (Fig 1.3.1).

London's town plan also had as a focus the high ground on Cornhill, where the two main roads met in a T-junction on the south side of the chosen site of the forum, a common pattern of town foundation (Perring 1991b). The crest of Cornhill was probably the site of the first settlement away from the docks (Perring 1991a, 1–75), identifiable by its grid of early streets.

The street grid offered a simple system for measuring out and distributing land, creating an orthogonal pattern of right-angled junctions lending itself to the organisation of trade, defence and administrative functions. A flexible plan could be achieved by combining independent patches of street

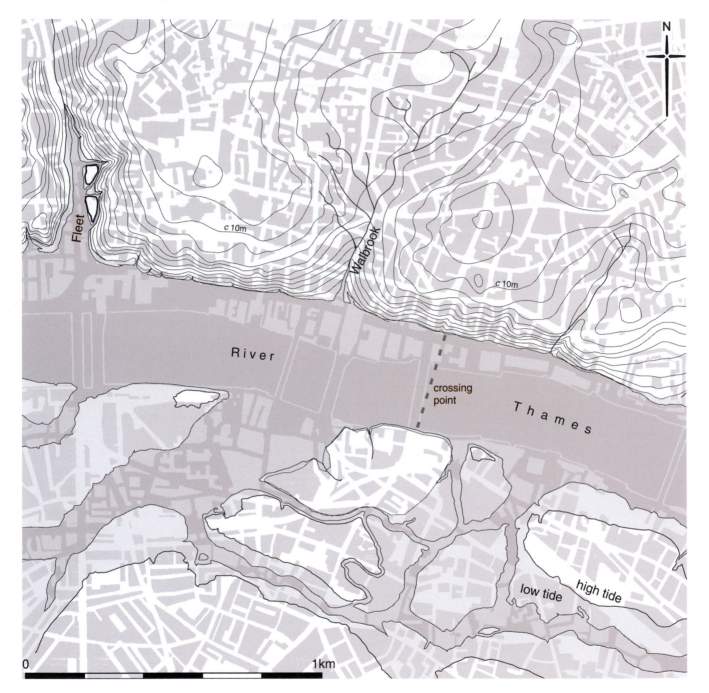

Fig 1.3.1 The natural topography of the site of Londinium. Based on David Bentley's interpretation of an 1841 survey of surface relief in the City of London with contours at 3ft intervals (Museum of London 1983) and the conjectural extent of tidal mudflats and land above 1m OD in North Southwark (Yule 2005). The Roman bridging point is shown for reference. Recent work on surface deposit modelling for the area north of the Thames has generated a more detailed topography (see Jamieson 2002)

grid at different alignments, creating a best fit with topographical features or social needs (Kostof 1991, 96). Even Manhattan, which originated as a small riverside settlement, first expanded as a patchwork of grids set at various angles, before a single grid was imposed on the remainder of the island in 1811 (Kostof 1991, 121). A classic example of a Roman grid is Timgad in North Africa, founded in *c* AD 100, but the settlement includes both a strictly orthogonal central area and more organic surrounding development (Fig 1.3.2).

Roman London grew quickly, powered by the economic engines of port and road traffic. The topography of the northern bridgehead was modified with new terraces along the riverbank, and from AD 52 the lowest of these was progressively protected by timber revetments both up- and downriver from the crossing (Brigham *et al* 1996; Brigham and Watson 1996). The southern bridgehead was very low-lying and would have required immediate protection, although the earliest revetted embankments are apparently post-Boudican (Yule 2005).

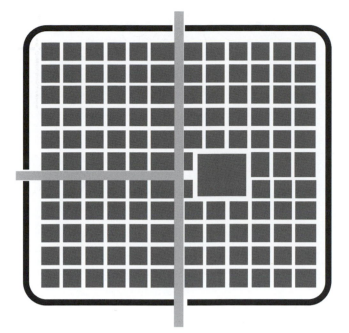

Fig 1.3.2 Diagram of Timgad's regular grid and central T-junction in front of the forum, a similar plan to that adopted on Roman London's Cornhill and at many other towns in the North-West provinces

Several topographical factors may have influenced the road pattern away from Cornhill. The main east–west road crossed both the Walbrook stream and Fleet River at the optimum bridging points near their tidal heads (see Merrifield and Hall, this volume). To the east of Cornhill the main east–west road turned north-eastwards towards Aldgate, skirting a minor stream valley to the south-east (Bluer *et al* 2006). The main roads were a focus for radial development (Hill and Woodger 1999) and to the west of the Walbrook this generated the beginnings of a secondary road system (Hill and Rowsome forthcoming), creating a built-up corridor *c* 100m wide that stretched nearly to the Fleet valley. To the east of the Walbrook expansion along the main roads east to Aldgate and north to Bishopsgate may have been less pronounced.

Extensive early activity also took place near the southern bridgehead, with intensive quarrying along the roadsides giving way to ranges of strip buildings, some separated by alleyways (Drummond-Murray *et al* 2002, 36). The shape of the islands was a fundamental constraint on the physical layout of the settlement south of the Thames (Cowan *et al* forthcoming), but within these limits the Southwark settlement was systematically laid out over a large area, respecting the line of the main road or the riverfront. The evidence for early boundaries suggests that land division was strongly influenced by the parcelling out of the riverfront (Cowan *et al* forthcoming).

Although secondary roads west of the Walbrook and in Southwark were often set at odd angles and irregular spacings, early development throughout the settlement was orderly – roads were straight and the first external activity typically supplanted by carefully set-out roadside properties. Topographic factors certainly seem to have held greater sway away from Cornhill, perhaps indicating that the initial status of these areas was suburban, but it may also be the case that the rate of expansion simply outstripped the authorities' ability to keep pace (Figs 1.3.3 and 1.3.4).

Post-Boudican expansion: questions of planning and status

Reconstruction following the Boudican revolt was hesitant, with most of the decade passing before residential properties were rebuilt at many sites (Perring 1991a, 22). Infrastructure was re-established more quickly and the military may have played a prominent role in reopening roads and other work. Post-Boudican reconstruction of the waterfront around the north end of the bridgehead took place in *c* AD 64, with evidence of military work gangs found at Regis House (KWS94; Brigham 1998, 25–7). At Plantation Place, just to the south-east of the intended site of the forum, a double ditch and palisade defining a military enclosure (*fossa fastigata*) was constructed in the years following the Boudican revolt (FER97; Dunwoodie *et al* forthcoming). The enclosure, which may have occupied two or more *insulae*, was located at what was perhaps the settlement's most strategic point, commanding the high ground adjacent to the junction of the two main roads and overlooking the northern end of the bridgehead. This and the subsequent development of the forum confirmed the gridded street layout of the district on Londinium's eastern hill. Securing a reliable water supply was also of prime importance to post-Boudican recovery, and recent work has identified unusually large, deep wells and sophisticated water-lifting equipment at 30 Gresham Street, the first dated to AD 63 (GHT00; Blair *et al* forthcoming). Capable of supplying the water requirements of several thousand people, this high-volume water extraction zone lay to the north of the main east–west road to the west of the Walbrook, indicating that the western hill may have been officially earmarked for extensive development (Fig. 1.3.5).

After AD 70 development accelerated and expansion of the street system was accompanied by private building. Secondary roads to the west of the Walbrook were extended south and north from the main road, providing access to the waterfront and previously undeveloped areas to the north-west and in the Upper Walbrook valley (Perring *et al* 1991; Hill and Rowsome forthcoming; Maloney and de Moulins 1990; Seeley and Drummond-Murray 2005) (Fig. 1.3.6).

Growth included an ambitious public building programme, although the overall area set aside for public buildings may have been smaller than that at

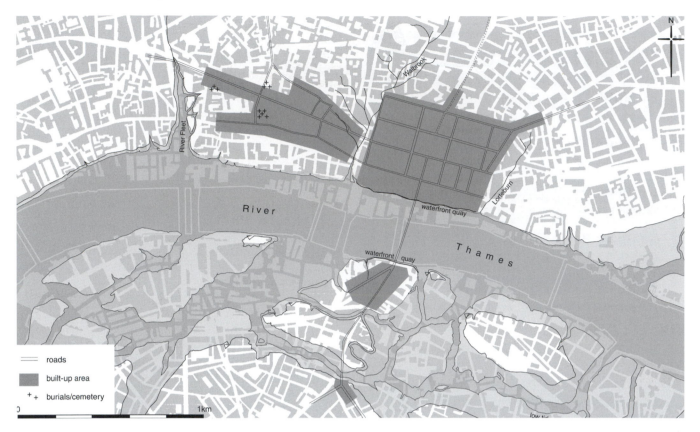

Fig 1.3.3 The pre-Boudican settlement's street pattern and principal features suggest three distinct districts: a gridded core on Cornhill, radial suburban development along the main road to the west and occupation to the south of the bridgehead on the islands of north Southwark

Fig 1.3.4 Reconstruction view of the early settlement (Peter Froste)

continental provincial capitals (Millett 1998, 12). Londinium's administrative status remains uncertain and it may not have included a governor's residence, but the procurator's office was based here. Many of the major new public facilities, such as the

Huggin Hill baths, temples and the amphitheatre, were established in peripheral locations west of the Walbrook shortly after AD 70, away from the main settlement on the eastern hill (Rowsome 1998). This may indicate differences in status between

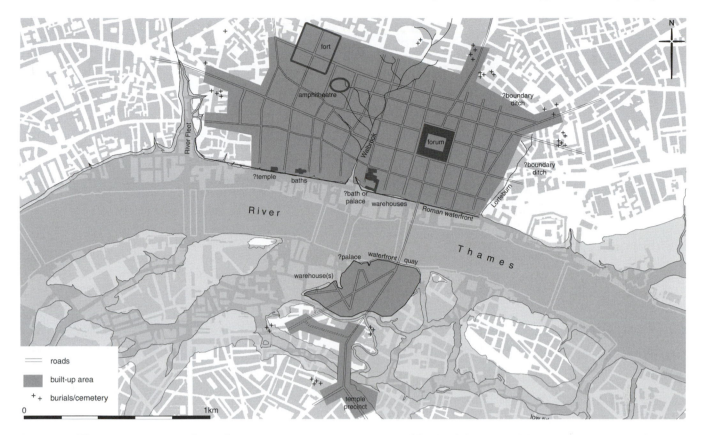

Fig 1.3.5 The expanding early 2nd-century town: new streets, public buildings and boundaries help define the extent of the settlement and point to intriguing differences in the morphology and possibly the status of the districts east and west of the Walbrook and south of the Thames

the town's main districts or an intention to develop public amenities as separate foci for the urban area (MacDonald 1986), but is more likely to reflect a pragmatic selection of unused land for building. Post-Boudican development on the islands of Southwark followed a similar pattern, with secondary roads extended into previously undeveloped areas, and roadside buildings and facilities established (Cowan 2003; Yule 2005).

Identifying the boundaries of the expanding settlement is difficult. In Southwark both the north and south islands were largely settled by the end of the 1st century. To the north of the Thames boundary ditches provide tentative evidence for the extent of the Flavian town. An east–west ditch established along what later became the south wall of the fort may have been the Flavian *pomerium* marking the northern edge of the settlement (Howe and Lakin 2004), and late 1st-century boundaries have also been recorded across the north side of Cornhill (Howe 2002). The western boundary of the Flavian settlement may be indicated by the distribution of burials across the crest of the western hill, as burial within a settlement was prohibited by Roman law (Williams 1993, 33–5), whilst Romano-British circular houses recorded at 10 Gresham Street might represent an unsanctioned development at or outside the town's early western boundary (GSM97; Casson *et al* forthcoming).

While the timber amphitheatre was located in an unoccupied area on the fringe of the Walbrook valley (Bateman 1997; Bateman *et al* forthcoming), the higher ground to the west at Cripplegate was initially used for small-scale residential and industrial activity, with no evidence that the amphitheatre was paired with a 1st-century fortress. The amphitheatre was largely rebuilt, partly in masonry, not long after AD 120, and it was only then that the fort seems to have been established. Early 2nd-century expansion of public building facilities also took place on the eastern hill, where the second forum and basilica, constructed between AD 100 and 130 (Brigham 1990a; Dunwoodie 2004), was the largest building in Roman Britain.

The late 1st century saw a 30-year programme of quay construction which was at least as important as the development away from the waterfront. New wharves were built in *c* 130m-long sections, beginning upstream from the bridge on the north bank, and by AD 90 three further sections had been completed, one downstream of the bridge, and the final two on either side of the Walbrook, creating a balanced wharf with the bridge and the Walbrook as twin foci (Brigham 1998). Waterfront warehouses formed an integral part of the wharfside and may have been publicly built. London's port dealt with substantial quantities of goods and cargo was handled along the entire wharf; it included a public

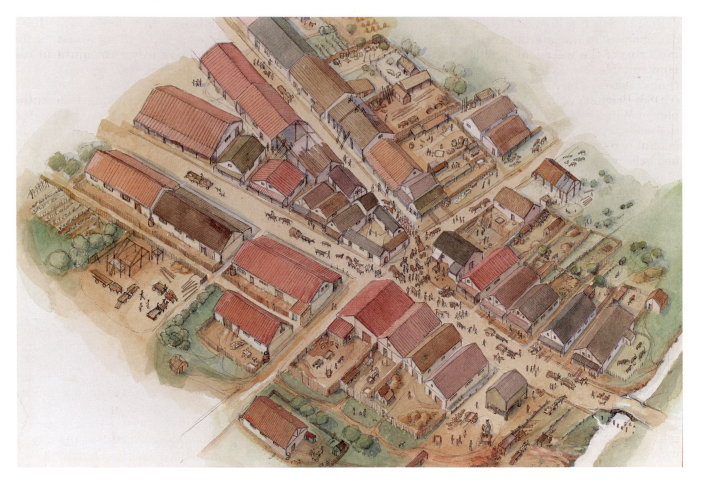

Fig 1.3.6 Reconstruction view of roadside development at the Walbrook crossing emphasises the commercial character of the town (Judith Dobie)

riparian thoroughfare 4m wide and similar to the main streets (Brigham 1998).

Falling sea levels after AD 50 had encouraged waterfront reclamation and construction of new quays, exerting a strong influence on the way the town developed. In the 120s the waterfront downstream of the Walbrook was rebuilt to a line considerably further out into the river. Reclamation and new revetment construction followed a similar pattern in Southwark, with much of the north island's river and creek frontage converted into usable waterfront (Cowan 2003; Yule 2005).

The spatial and chronological development of Londinium would have been influenced not only by its topography, but by its role as an officially sanctioned entrepôt or privately initiated trading community, complex civil and military inter-relationships and administrative arrangements that may have flowed from its status. A bipartite division between a military centre west of the Walbrook and a civilian centre at Cornhill has been suggested (Grimes 1968, 38–9), but the distribution of military finds is inconclusive. Southwark was much more than a suburb, but it remains uncertain how a tripartite settlement would have functioned, though the area south of the river could have been a community of non-citizens (Millett 1994).

Adjustments to the town plan and the construction of defences

Fire destroyed most of the city in *c* AD 125 and recovery may have been less vigorous than before due to changing economic circumstances and a decline in trade (Perring 1991a). It is true that many areas have revealed little in the way of domestic building beyond the mid-2nd century, but sites such as 1 Poultry provide evidence for continuity in property use into the 3rd century and later (Rowsome 2000). The absence of post-Hadrianic occupation levels in some areas may be the result of later truncation and soil formation processes resulting in dark earth (Yule 1990), meaning that the argument for settlement contraction has been overstated. Renewed public building also saw completion of the forum-basilica, amphitheatre and fort, with the disruption caused by the fire perhaps an opportunity to reorganise hitherto scattered billeting arrangements for soldiers. Post-Hadrianic reconstruction included repair of the existing street plan and its extension northwards into areas such as Cripplegate (Casson *et al* forthcoming). The waterfront also continued to expand, with new revetments constructed between AD 140 and 160 and in about AD 180.

Roman Southwark was the subject of continued development in the later 2nd century, with increasing areas of the intertidal mudflats converted into land suitable for development, such as the AD 152 timber warehouse recorded at Courage's Brewery (CO88; Brigham *et al* 1995), and the building complex at Winchester Palace (Yule 2005). In *c* AD 160 the eastern side of the main island was reclaimed behind a revetment, and other revetments continued to be maintained to protect the low-lying fringes of Roman Southwark. At Tabard Square a religious complex, complete with temples and a guest house within a precinct or *temenos*, was established in the mid-2nd century next to Watling Street and just to the south of Roman Southwark's islands, providing more evidence for the importance of the Southwark settlement (LLS02; Pre-Construct Archaeology 2003).

North of the river, construction of the landward defensive wall took place between *c* AD 190 and 230 (Perring 1991a, 92) and this had a significant impact on the town's layout (Fig 1.3.7). Some built-up areas, particularly radial development along the main roads at Newgate and elsewhere, were left outside the wall line (Lyon forthcoming). The Cripplegate fort was incorporated into the defensive circuit and other public buildings were enclosed inside the new wall line, which defined a large area that included some open ground. Areas now immediately outside the town walls were given over primarily to burial (Barber and Bowsher 2000; Hall 1996; Watson 2003). Major public buildings such as the forum-basilica and amphitheatre remained in use until about the end of the 3rd century.

In about AD 200 an effort was made to restore a unified river frontage by constructing substantial new quays along the north bank of the Thames, but declining trade and falling river levels combined to hasten the end of the port, and between AD 250 and 270 the wharf was dismantled. The process was complete before construction of the riverside defensive wall in *c* AD 275, which separated the town from the river (Hill *et al* 1980). Port facilities may have continued in use in Southwark or moved downstream to the vicinity of Shadwell, where significant Roman activity has been recorded (Lakin *et al* 2002; Bird, this volume) and work by Pre-Construct Archaeology in 2002 uncovered evidence of extensive occupation and a public bath building dating from the mid-3rd century (HGA02; Douglas 2004). Despite all these changes, Southwark continued to flourish outside the 'defended' area (Fig 1.3.8).

Building and investment continued even in the late 4th century, as a series of bastions were added to the eastern side of the city wall in *c* AD 351–75 (Maloney 1983) and a major stone building was constructed in the south-eastern corner of the city at about the same time (Sankey 1998). Overall though it may be that at any one time there was money for

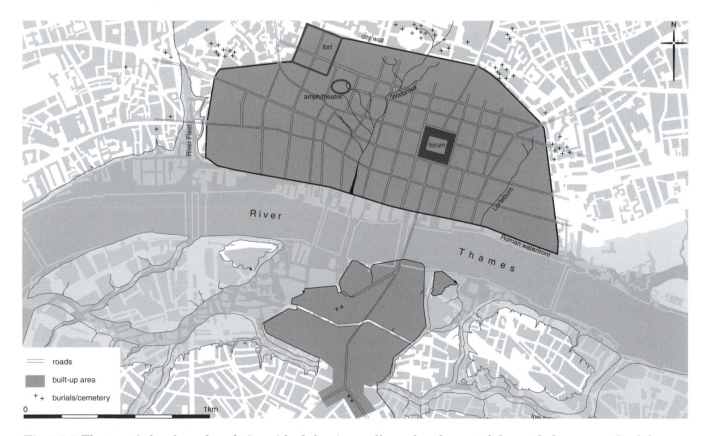

roads

built-up area

+ + burials/cemetery

0   1km

Fig 1.3.7 The town's landward and riverside defensive walls enclosed most of the settled area north of the Thames as well as some undeveloped areas of open ground but separated the town from its waterfront; although left outside the defences, the overall impact on Roman Southwark may have been beneficial

Fig 1.3.8 Reconstruction view of the late Roman town enclosed by its defensive walls (Peter Froste)

public buildings or defensive structures, but not for both. The expensive campaigns of defensive work may have been a response to perceived threats and uncertainty, although some see it as an example of competitive civic munificence (Millett 1990, 139).

Many aspects of the late Roman town remain poorly understood, as do changes to the town plan as the population declined. Some properties fell out of use, as did peripheral areas and elements of the street system, though this is difficult to quantify or map due to the extent of truncation at many sites. Demolition of several of the town's principal public buildings left areas apparently underutilised within the walled area, but do not necessarily represent overall decline (Wacher 1995, 96).

Future research directions

The interrogation of map data as part of a GIS may reveal unsuspected patterns in the evolving provision of streets, public buildings and other physical features of the town plan and we can now quantify the town's built-up area at various points in time. Detailed analysis of land use across Roman London's 170+ hectares might also be used to study aspects of the urban environment, such as the changing proportion of occupied versus open land, plot size and building density, and relate these data to hypotheses about population size and economic activity. The overall population of the settlement is difficult to estimate, but figures of about 10,000 on the eve of the Boudican revolt and over 20,000 in the 2nd century have been suggested (Rowsome 2000, 33), whilst a fascinating new review of models for estimating ancient urban populations (Swain and Williams, this volume) suggests a peak of up to 30,000 Roman Londoners. We know a lot about Roman London but some interesting research still remains to be done.

Acknowledgements

We are deeply indebted to the late David Bentley for his work on Roman London's topographical development and his enthusiasm for the subject, which we hope to honour with a new Roman map, kindly funded by CoLAT, LAMAS and SLAEC. Thanks also go to Mark Burch for his work on interpreting and digitising map data, and to many others at MoLAS, the Museum of London and elsewhere for their input and interest in continued research into Roman London's layout. Warm thanks are also due English Heritage for their funding of the Greater London publication programme, and to the many other clients who have funded work on individual sites mentioned here.

1.4 The Population of Roman London
Hedley Swain and Tim Williams

Introduction

One of the most frequent questions from the public concerning Roman London is 'what size was its population?' Most accounts of Londinium, however, decline to discuss population figures. When figures are given they normally derive from the estimates developed by Gordon Home, in 1925, and Ralph Merrifield, in 1969, both of whom suggested a population of around 45,000 people for the town at its peak.

This paper examines a number of models for estimating ancient urban populations, and suggests ranges of population for Roman London at three points in time: immediately prior to the Boudican revolt, in *c* AD 60/1; at its height, in the early 2nd century; and after the construction of the city walls, in the early 3rd century. We recognise, however, that these estimates are open to considerable debate.

Previous estimates

The earliest attempt at an estimate of the town's population was made by Gordon Home in his 1925 book *Roman London*, when he adopted the model of estimating population density (per acre) and multiplying this by the city area (Home 1925, 94). He revised his estimates slightly in the 1948 edition of his book, in which he estimated that the area enclosed by the later city walls was 326 acres (132 ha); suggested that Roman military camps had about 170 people per acre; that Roman town streets were rather narrow; that the houses were generally two storeys; and that there were fewer open spaces than in modern times (Home 1948, 80). He suggested a population for the walled area of 45,000, taking into account the Walbrook and unoccupied land, and a conservative estimate of 140 people per acre. To this would be added those in the 'transriverine quarter' and 'such suburbs as existed', plus 'the considerable floating population due to the presence of visitors, ships' crews and perhaps small military details', and he concluded that 'the population of Londinium between AD 200 and 280 may be reckoned at not less than the figure stated [45,000]; it may have been more, but can hardly have been less' (Home 1948, 80).

A similar figure was proposed by Ralph Merrifield in 1969. Taking Tacitus's figure of 70,000 casualties during the Boudican revolt he suggested a division of 15,000 each for St Albans and Colchester, 30,000 for London and 10,000 for exaggeration (Merrifield 1969, 147). He went on to suggest that the increased scale of the later town might suggest that the population rose to about 45,000 (Merrifield 1969, 147).

More recently Dominic Perring, using the same criteria of those slain by Boudica, also suggested that Londinium of AD 60 had a population of 30,000, or probably less (Perring 1991a, 16). He also suggested that later 1st-century London was 'a very crowded place' and that 'comparison is difficult but it was quite possibly twice as populous as the city destroyed in AD 60' (Perring 1991a, 70), again inferring a population of perhaps *c* 50,000.

Others have shied away from specific population estimates, although many have suggested dramatically changing population levels through time. Peter Marsden and Barbara West (1992), for example, used the quantity of domestic rubbish, the number of wells, and the quantity of animal bone, to suggest that there was a marked decline in the population after the mid-2nd century, although they state that absolute population estimates are impossible on the present evidence (Marsden and West 1992, 138).

The size and density of cemeteries are difficult to estimate from. As Bruno Barber and Dave Bowsher state, in their account of the eastern cemetery, 'in the light of the uncertainty regarding the calculation of the cemetery population, and in the absence of similar data for other burial areas of the settlement, there is no justification for moving towards estimates of population numbers for the town at any given period' (Barber and Bowsher 2000, 311).

So can we develop new estimates for the population of Roman London? Perhaps the most obvious line of enquiry is based upon the same method as Home (above), modelling population densities, drawn from a variety of historical and ethnographic comparisons, coupled with our improved archaeological knowledge of the extent of built-up areas within the city and its suburbs.

The area and density of urban settlement in Roman London

There are two key issues that we might take into consideration when considering the scale of the urban area:

1   A simple estimate of the total area/extent of the settlement;
2   The density of settlement within that area: specifically estimating the scale of residential buildings, as opposed to non-residential buildings and non-built space.

The extent of the settlement over time

Recent excavations have developed a more detailed understanding of the changing scale of settlement in the city and Southwark over time: while we cannot precisely identify the position of the town boundary at all times, we can make reasonable estimates of extent at certain stages in the life of the settlements. The scale of excavation has also given us some indication of the extent of the built-up area, although there are notable gaps in our understanding. Perhaps the best periods for study are:

- Immediately before the Boudican revolt *c* AD 60/61: well preserved and archaeologically recognisable because of the fire. At this time occupation was focused on the eastern hill (Cornhill), but with some occupation on the western hill and in Southwark (Fig 1.4.1).
- The early 2nd century, *c* AD 100/120: extensive residential occupation on both hills and extending into the valley systems; developed waterfront zones; Southwark extensively occupied (Fig 1.4.2).
- At the time of the construction of the town walls, *c* AD 200: extensive occupation within the walled

area, although with less developed areas, and in Southwark (MoLAS 2000, map 8) (Fig 1.4.3).

In simple terms, therefore, we can suggest the area of settlement (see Table 1.4.1).

The density of occupation

While we cannot be precise about the intensity of occupation within these boundaries we can make some suggestions, based on the numerous excavations within the town.

For the later 1st and early 2nd centuries the occupation revealed by excavation is relatively similar across the townscape: a rough grid of rectangular city blocks, with strip-buildings (rectangular clay and timber buildings, short end facing onto a street), often with yard areas to the rear, and town houses. However, the nature of the built space does vary, from perhaps the more common shop/workshop and associated domestic residence (eg

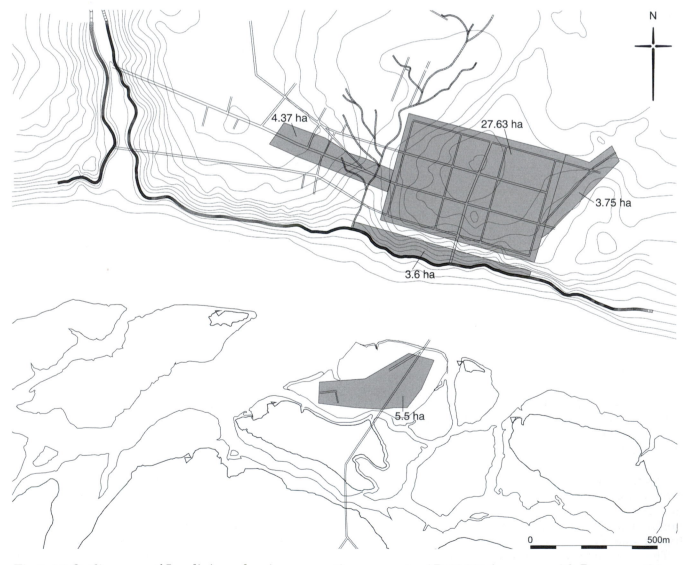

Fig 1.4.1 Outline map of Londinium showing occupation areas at c AD 60/61 (compare with Rowsome, this volume, Fig 1.3.3)

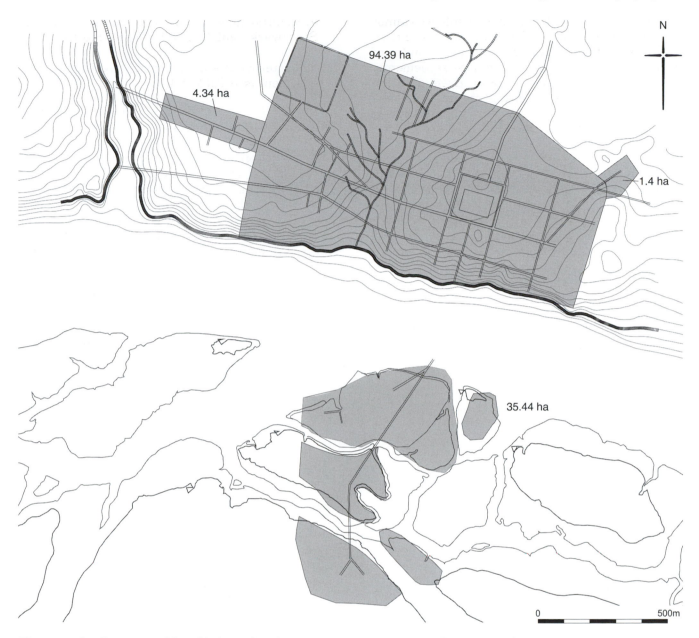

Fig 1.4.2 Outline map of Londinium showing occupation areas at c *AD 100/120 (compare with Rowsome, this volume, Fig 1.3.5)*

Perring *et al* 1991, 102–4; Perring 2002, 55–60), to buildings with rooms designed to be let out as separate tenancies (Perring *et al* 1991, 104; Perring 2002, 60, 193), and a variety of town house structures (Perring 2002, 64–72).

In addition, the presence of servile kin and household slaves further complicates the issue, with potential for sleeping space in workshops and shops, and higher density usage of space. These differing functional spaces and social groups reflect potentially different estimates of the number/density of occupants within any given structure (see below), although perhaps the presence of small rooms and densely packed buildings, as evidenced in London, might suggest that the estimates should be on the higher side (Perring 2002, 193).

These residential and commercial blocks are punctuated by several large public building complexes, including the forum and basilica, and the amphitheatre, and numerous smaller complexes such as public baths, commercial buildings (such as *macella*), and temples.

Major topographic features are also likely to have influenced the scale and density of occupation, and can be used to divide the city into zones as follows (and approximate to those used in Section 4 of this volume, Fig 4.0.1):

- *The Walbrook valley:* this marks the western edge of the early city and divides the later town in two. The lower part of the valley was occupied from an early stage in the life of the Roman town, whereas the upper valley had large amounts of open space in the 1st century (Maloney and de Moulins 1990, 119–20) but as drainage was controlled, by *c* 120, new buildings were constructed (Maloney and de Moulins 1990, 121). While the buildings were extensively used for small-scale

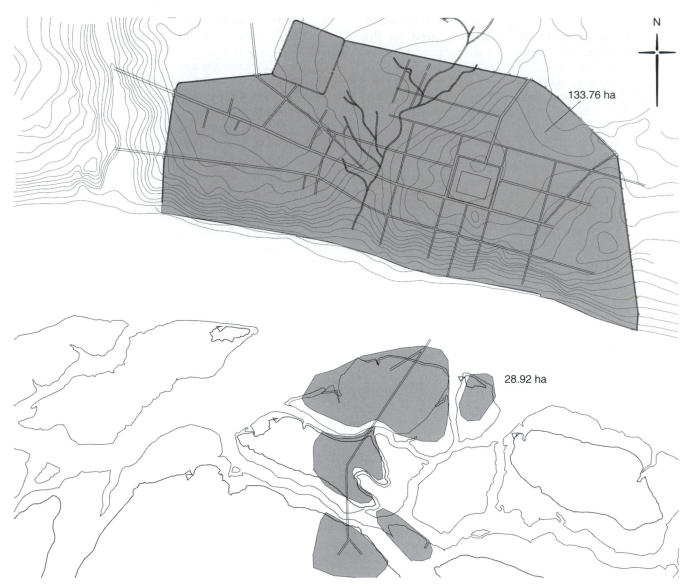

Fig 1.4.3 Outline map of Londinium showing occupation areas at c AD 200 (compare with Rowsome, this volume, Fig 1.3.7)

industrial processes and workshops, people would also have lived in these structures (Maloney and de Moulins 1990, 122), although the density of occupation was less than in the core 'residential' areas.

• *The eastern valley:* a broad valley system in the east of the town (Bentley 1984), probably outside the boundary of the pre-Boudican town, encroached upon by the early 2nd century, and enclosed by the later walls. Much of the valley was probably used for animal enclosures, although some later housing extended into the area (Williams forthcoming).

• *The southern hillsides of the western city:* the hillside from the two hills down to the Thames was relatively steep, particularly in the south-west quarter of the later town, and it is probable that the difficulty of the terrain led to very restricted domestic occupation. The area was also used for public building complexes (Williams 1993).

• *The waterfront, east of the Walbrook:* warehouses and commercial facilities suggest that there may have been reduced domestic occupation in this area of the city (in Section 4, this forms part of the East of Walbrook zone).

• *The western extension to the city at c AD 200:* with the construction of the landward city wall in *c* AD 200 a substantial additional area of the western hill was enclosed, probably to enable the more effective siting of the wall at the top of the Fleet Valley. This enclosed a large area of land that was probably never extensively developed.

• *Southwark islands and creeks:* while the area was extensively occupied, low-lying wetland areas and channels would have restricted the overall density of the settlement.

Calculating the residential area

Given the above, the approach taken was to:

a Calculate the total occupied area for each study period (calculating the main city area on the north bank, its western and eastern suburbs, and the settlement in Southwark). This relatively crude measure of urban scale (*sub-total (a) in Table 1.4.1*) can be used for the broader urban population calculations discussed below.

To establish an estimate of the total residential area, we subtracted from the above:

Table 1.4.1 Estimated areas of Roman London at c AD 60/61, c AD 100/120 and c AD 200

Pre-Boudican c AD 60/61			
a Total settlement area		Ha	Ha
Core area of city		27.63	
West of Walbrook suburb		4.37	
Eastern suburb		3.75	
Southwark		5.50	
Waterfront		3.60	
	Sub-total (a)	*44.85*	
b Non-residential areas			
Central piazza/forum			0.37
	Sub-total (b)		*0.37*
c Lower density housing			
Waterfront	3.60 @ 75%		2.70
Southwark marshes & creeks	5.50 @ 50%		2.75
Walbrook valley, Eastern valley & Southern hillsides			n/a
	Sub-total (c)		*5.45*
	Total	**39.03**	
c AD 100/120			
a Total settlement area		Ha	Ha
Main city		94.39	
West suburbs		4.34	
Eastern suburbs		1.40	
Southwark		35.44	
	Sub-total (a)	*135.57*	
b Non-residential areas			
Forum/basilica			2.85
Amphitheatre			0.75
Huggin Hill baths			1.05
Temples in SW			1.16
	Sub-total (b)		*5.81*
c Lower density housing			
Walbrook valley	10.29ha @ 50%		5.15
Waterfront	4.55ha @ 50%		2.28
Eastern valley	4.83ha @ 75%		3.62
Southwark marshes & creeks	35.44ha @ 50%		17.72
	Sub-total (c)		*28.77*
	Total	**100.99**	
c AD 200			
a Total settlement area		Ha	Ha
Main city		133.76	
West suburbs		0.00	
Eastern suburbs		0.00	
Southwark		28.92	
	Sub-total (a)	*162.68*	
b Non-residential areas			
Forum/basilica			2.85
Amphitheatre			0.75
Huggin Hill baths			1.05
Temples in SW			1.16
	Sub-total (b)		*5.81*
c Lower density housing			
Walbrook valley	10.29ha @ 50%		5.15
Waterfront	4.55ha @ 50%		2.28
Eastern valley	10.37ha @ 75%		7.78
Western extension	8.00ha @ 75%		6.00
Southern hillsides	3.78ha @ 75%		2.84
Southwark marshes & creeks	28.92ha @ 50%		14.46
	Sub-total (c)		*38.51*
	Total	**118.36**	

b Areas of known non-residential space, such as the forum and the amphitheatre (*sub-total (b) in Table 1.4.1*).
c An allowance for areas of less dense residential settlement (see above). These areas have been reduced by a percentage to reflect this (*sub-total (c) in Table 1.4.1*):
• Walbrook valley reduced by 50% to allow for channels, and less densely packed settlement;
• Waterfront (east of the Walbrook) reduced by 50% to reflect commercial and administrative areas and the steep hillside behind;
• Eastern valley reduced by 75% to reflect sparse occupation outside of animal enclosures;
• Southern hillside of the western city reduced by 75% as there was little domestic settlement in the area;
• Southwark reduced by 50% to allow for the channels and low-lying areas.

Population density models

There are two methods that have commonly been used for estimating population density:

1 Estimates of the number of people per property, combined with property size (including the number of building storeys), leading to models for the density of people per square metre of residential areas;
2 Historic and ethnographic parallels of urban populations, commonly leading to estimates of population per hectare.

The number of people per property

People per square metre
Andrew Wallace-Hadrill (1994) developed a model based on the idea that Pompeii might have had a population of *c* 10,000, which with an average property size of 271m^2 would suggest an average of between 6–8 people inhabiting each house, and give an average density of one person per 34–45m^2 (Wallace-Hadrill 1994, 99). Alston (2002) suggested a slightly smaller figure of between 5.4 and 5.52 people per house for the classical city, while estimates of early modern pre-industrial cities include Dingwall (1994) who suggested an average of 4.5 people per house for 17th-century Edinburgh, and Galley (1998) who postulated an average of 6.1 people per house for 16th- and 17th-century York.

Millett and Graham (1986, 154) came up with a similar calculation based on the Roman small town at Neatham, where they estimated a total of 21 buildings within the excavated area of 0.37 hectares and thus a suggested density of 57 buildings per hectare. They estimated five people per building

(Millett and Graham 1986, 154), which equates to 285 people per hectare or a density of one person per 35m², very similar to Wallace-Hadrill's upper estimate.

Between 1994 and 1996 MoLAS excavated 1 Poultry (ONE94), in the centre of Roman London (Rowsome 2000). This gave the largest and best-preserved section of residential Roman London excavated to date and formed the basis for the exhibition *High Street Londinium* at the Museum of London in 2000–01, which reconstructed three of the buildings from the site (Hall and Swain 2000). The excavation area for *c* AD 100 included ten buildings, within an excavation area of *c* 3,318m². Allowing for streets, etc, the average property was *c* 282m², similar to the Pompeian example. The East of the Walbrook project (Williams forthcoming) examined evidence for about 200 domestic buildings in the eastern Roman city, and estimated that they occupied an average area that was somewhat smaller, at *c* 240m², also close to the Pompeian case. So perhaps the Pompeian model of one person per 34–45m² might be reasonable to apply to London.

Number of people per room
Wallace-Hadrill also explored an alternative model based on the ratio of people to rooms, suggesting one-to-one as a possible scale for ground floors, based on ethnographic and historical parallels. This gave a similar estimate for the population of Pompeii of *c* 10,000 (Wallace-Hadrill 1994, 100). He notes, however, that second storeys might have a higher ratio – perhaps two per room – and that if this is added to the model the population density would increase dramatically (Wallace-Hadrill 1994, 100).

Alston (2002, 59) argued, in his Mediterranean case studies, that buildings ranged between one and four storeys, with occasional examples as high as seven storeys. He suggested the average house had two storeys. Hobson (1985, 217), studying Karanis, documented three one-storey houses, six two-storey houses, and three three-storey houses, again suggesting an average of two storeys per houses.

For Roman London, it seems unlikely that there were many multi-storey structures, and perhaps it might be more reasonable to suggest that only 50% of houses had second storeys, and perhaps that each of those upper storeys would only have been about half the size of the ground floor. This would, however, still increase the estimate based on ground floors alone by 50%.

If we adopt the one-person-per-room model for the ground floor, the number of rooms observed at 1 Poultry would suggest that each property housed *c* 6–8 people. We do not know if any of these structures had second storeys, but adding 50% would give a revised estimate of *c* 9–12 people. This would suggest between 60 and 120 people living in the area (3,318m²) and thus a density of one person per 28–55m².

Historic and ethnographic parallels

Old quarters of Middle Eastern towns
Fekri Hassan (1981) developed Robert Adams' arguments to use population densities in the old quarters of Middle Eastern towns to develop a model for ancient cities. In this, densities of between 137 and 216 people per hectare were postulated. Martin Millett drew upon this work to make estimates about the total population of Roman Britain (Millett 1990, 182).

Later populations of London
Can known later populations of London be of any help in identifying the population of Roman London? The same criteria we have used above must apply: what was the populated area and what was population density? A simple observation is that the later we get in time the more accurate are the figures for population, but the less relevant they are as a comparison with Roman London as the area occupied grows and the type of urban living changes.

Derek Keene (1989) has suggested that the population in 1100 was *c* 25,000, at a time when the medieval city was perhaps closest to Roman London in size. However, it was probably already very different in terms of its living conditions, with the introduction of churches and monastic precincts being the most obvious factors.

Pasciuti (2002), building on Finlay's work (1981), summarises the historical data for 17th-century London and suggests an overall density of people per hectare of 214 (in 1600), 204 (in 1650) and 226 (in 1700), averaging 215 people per hectare.

Paul Bairoch's estimates
Bairoch undertook a careful analysis of urban populations, especially in the Indus valley, suggesting a density of *c* 150 people per hectare (Bairoch 1988).

Comparison with research in other Roman towns
Work has been done, using the above models, on estimating the population of Gallic towns, which has been summarised and discussed by Greg Woolf (Woolf 1998, 137–8). He summarises a number of estimates for the density of population per hectare for Roman towns (Table 1.4.2).

Table 1.4.2 Estimates for provincial Roman population density (Woolf 1998)

Town	People per hectare	Average
Saturnia, Etruria	50–100	75
Pompeii	123–187	155
Gallo-Roman general	150 max	[<]150
St Roman-en-Gal	100–120	110
Upper limit suggested	350	350
Preferred average	100	100

The estimates

So we have two rather different estimating models. The first is based upon calculations of the numbers of people per hectare within residential areas: for example, based on the number of people per room. The model is calculated on the basis of *the estimate of people per hectare of residential space multiplied by the estimate of total residential space only*.

The second is based on a more general estimate of urban populations, and already takes into account non-residential space. The model is therefore calculated on the basis of *the estimate of people per hectare multiplied by the estimate of total urban space*.

The models of population densities, and the estimates of urban space and residential densities, are summarised in Table 1.4.3.

Conclusions

Pre-Boudican London

Merrifield's estimate of 30,000 people (above) for the pre-Boudican city seems very high in comparison to the other models. The models we are using group around the 9,300 people estimate (range 7,300–11,500). It is noticeable that the Group 2 broader estimate models tend to suggest a lower population (averaging *c* 8,000) compared to the average of *c* 10,500 for the Group 1 models. This is perhaps because the former are not as responsive to the densely packed pre-Boudican built landscape, with relatively fewer open spaces, public buildings, etc, and the latter is perhaps a better model for this period. So we might suggest a population in the immediate pre-Boudican period of *c* 10,000.

The population in *c* AD 100/120 and *c* AD 200

Home's and Merrifield's estimates of a population of *c* 45,000 at the peak of the city would also seem to be rather high. The average of all the models suggests a population of around 26,000 in *c* AD 100/120, and 30,500 in *c* AD 200. It is perhaps interesting to note that Home's estimate of 140 people per acre (or 346 people per hectare) is well above the suggested upper limit for population density suggested by Greg Woolf (see Table 1.4.2), and also well above any of the other models used in this paper (Table 1.4.3).

The notion that Roman London is more populous in AD 200 than it was a century before is perhaps a little misleading. We are concerned that the enlarged area of the settlement, as reflected by the city walls, has somewhat skewed this figure, and while both groups of models take into account non-residential space, the large almost unoccupied areas are perhaps not fully reflected in this. Also, detailed work on properties in the eastern town (Williams forthcoming) might also suggest that property density was falling in the mid- to late 2nd century, with increased areas of unbuilt space. If one applied a figure of perhaps 25% unbuilt space to the core area of the city at *c* AD 200, it would reduce the average Group 1 model result (the most responsive to changes in residential areas) to 24,894, or slightly less than the Group 1 model for AD 100/120 of 27,217, which might be a more accurate reflection of the trend.

The quality of the models

There are clearly problems with all the models. There is a lack of clarity in many of the models as developed as to the definition of residential space

Table 1.4.3 Population models for Roman London at *c* AD 60/61, *c* AD 100/120 and *c* AD 200

	Model			c AD 60/61			c AD 100/120			c AD 200		
	(people per hectare)			Residential area 39 ha Total area 45 ha			Residential area 101 ha Total area 136 ha			Residential area 118 ha Total area 163 ha		
	Low	*Ave*	*High*	*Low*	*Average*	*High*	*Low*	*Average*	*High*	*Low*	*Average*	*High*
Holme (1925/1948)		346									45,665	
Merrifield (1969)					30,000						45,000	
Group 1 Models	These are calculated on residential areas only											
Wallace-Hadrill Pompeii	*222*	254	*286*	*8,673*	9,912	*11,151*	*22,444*	25,650	*28,856*	*26,306*	30,064	*33,822*
Millett & Graham: Neatham		285			11,123			28,784			33,738	
1 Poultry: people per room	*182*	269	*357*	*7,096*	10,517	*13,938*	*18,363*	27,217	*36,071*	*21,523*	31,900	*42,278*
Group 2 Models	These allow for non-residential areas and are calculated on total settlement area											
Middle eastern town model	*137*	177	*216*	*6,144*	7,916	*9,687*	*18,573*	23,928	*29,283*	*22,287*	28,713	*35,139*
Bairoch		150			6,727			20,336			24,402	
Pre-industrial London		215			9,642			29,148			34,976	
AVERAGES: overall				*7,304*	9,306	*11,592*	*19,793*	25,844	*31,403*	*23,372*	30,632	*37,080*
Group 1				*7,884*	10,517	*12,544*	*20,404*	27,217	*32,463*	*23,915*	31,901	*38,050*
Group 2				*6,144*	8,095	*9,687*	*18,573*	24,470	*29,283*	*22,287*	29,364	*35,139*

Note: Averages are based on the total Model 1 and Model 2 data (but not the Holme or Merrifield data)

and the calculation of property size: do the estimates include only internal floor space or yards and courtyards? Many of the calculations simply divide the number of buildings into excavated area, and thus include public spaces such as roads.

The models based on residential area (Group 1), rather than gross urban area (Group 2), seem to suggest slightly higher population sizes. However, they are more responsive to increasing archaeological information about property densities, and as we refine our understanding of different zones of the town, we could also devise more sophisticated estimates of the scale of unbuilt space in different parts of the town, moving from the fairly crude 50% or 75% estimates to ones based on detailed observations.

As Wallace-Hadrill (1994, 100–1) emphasises, it is perhaps more interesting to consider the size of households and the complexity of family, kin and slave relationships than simply conjecturing on overall population size. Certainly the larger average property size in Roman London as opposed to the Roman small town of Neatham (about two-thirds of the size, see above) is interesting. Does this mean smaller households at Neatham than London (as Millett and Graham suggest, 5 per building, compared with Wallace-Hadrill's 6–8 people in Pompeii or 1 Poultry's suggested 6–12 people), perhaps with greater kin/slave numbers in a major urban context, or are we looking at the same groups of people accommodated in smaller spaces?

Overall, we would not suggest that we can establish an accurate population figure for Roman London, but rather that we can try to refine some hypotheses based on the excavated data. Our work would suggest that the currently used figures of 30,000 for the pre-Boudican town, and 45,000 for the town in its heyday, might be reasonably revised downwards to perhaps *c* 10,000 people at the time of the Boudican sack, *c* 25,000–30,000 at its peak in the early 2nd century, and perhaps a similar, or slightly reduced figure by *c* AD 200.

1.5 *Imperium Galliarum, Imperium Britanniarum.* Developing new ideologies and settling old scores: abandonments, demolitions and new building in south-east Britain, *c* AD 250–300
Michael Fulford

As his contribution to a timely study of the western provinces of the Roman Empire in the 3rd century (King and Henig 1981) Harvey Sheldon wrote about the evidence for changes in the pattern of settlement in town and country in London and the south-east of Britain (Sheldon 1981). Across the region, north and south of the Thames, he found a remarkable consistency in the evidence both for breaks or cessations of occupation between the late 2nd and the early to mid-3rd century and in commencements or recommencements of occupation in the latter part of the 3rd century. This picture was based on evidence derived from pottery and coins, categories of material that introduce a possible element of circularity. As coins of the second and third quarters of the 3rd century up to the Gallic Empire are rare as site finds, so there is correspondingly little pottery that is associated with, and seen to be typical of, this period. While there is abundant evidence for, and incidence of, new pottery forms that can be attributed to the later 2nd century, or late 2nd/early 3rd century, thereafter there is a dearth of comparable evidence until the last quarter or third of the 3rd century when coins are once more abundant in the archaeological record. The favoured explanation was that a combination of social and economic difficulties, perhaps including the politically motivated confiscation of estates, accounted for the dislocations observed in the archaeological record (Sheldon 1981, 378–9).

In the 25 years or so since that paper much has happened, especially in London, which makes a re-examination timely of the pattern of breaks, or cessations in occupation of sites across the south-east of Britain in the 3rd century. To celebrate Harvey's contribution to the development of the archaeology of London and the south-east, the purpose of this essay is to examine a little more closely the corresponding evidence from public buildings and monuments in London and the south-east for their destruction and abandonment at this time, and to set it in the context of his important paper. Much of the evidence was not available in 1981.

Unlike in Gaul and elsewhere in the Empire where there is a considerable amount of evidence for the destruction of public buildings and burial monuments to provide material for the construction of city walls in the 3rd century (Johnson 1983), the corresponding situation in Britain is quite different. Where Roman material is commonly incorporated in town defences, it is in the medieval period, as has been noted in Bath (Collingwood and Wright 1965, 161–71) and London (Collingwood and Wright 1965, 112), for example.

London, however, also provides clear evidence for the inclusion of monumental material in the riverside defences constructed in the third quarter of the 3rd century as a later addition to the land-facing wall. Not only does this project include relatively portable items like dedicatory altars, but also carved blocks derived from at least two other large public monuments – a monumental arch and a screen of gods, presumably originally located close to their position in the city wall in the south-west quarter (Hill *et al* 1980). These monuments were probably less than a hundred years old at the time of their destruction. Reused but undecorated blocks of monumental masonry were also discovered in the foundations of the monumental building at St Peter's Hill, also in the south-west quarter, for which a *terminus post quem* of AD 293–94 is provided by dendrochronology (Williams 1993; *cf* Millett 1994, 431–2). Not long before, as the altar dedicated by the deputy imperial propraetorian legate, Marcus Martiannus Pulcher (reckoned to have been governor of Britannia Superior in the 250s), attests, restoration work was being ordered on the Temple of Isis (Hassall 1980). A second altar, not independently dated, but probably contemporary, also refers to the restoration of a second temple, possibly to Jupiter (Hassall 1980). In mid-3rd-century London effort was being made to restore temples, probably situated in the south-west quarter; within a few decades associated monuments, if not these very temples, were being destroyed to improve London's defences and to provide a new monumental building, arguably for the usurper emperor Allectus.

In this south-west quarter of London we can see both the destruction of public monuments and their reuse in new projects. In the centre of the city we have evidence for the destruction at the end of the 3rd century of at least the basilica, if not the whole forum and basilica, a vast construction and the principal public building of the town, and the largest of the entire province from the time of its construction in the early 2nd century. The excavators concluded 'that the Basilica was razed following a period of abandonment around the end of the 3rd century' (Brigham 1990a, 82). Unlike the monuments in the south-west quarter we have no clue as to where the vast amounts of rubble from the demolition of the building were deployed. The same is true of the material from the amphitheatre in the north-west quarter. Here there is evidence for the demolition of the Period 5 arena and entrance walls around the mid-3rd century, only to be followed by rebuilding within a decade or two of AD 250, but with a narrower width of wall on the existing foundations (Bateman *et al* forthcoming).

The fate of the London basilica recalls that of the Silchester forum basilica where recent excavation has demonstrated that the basilica was used for metalworking (iron, copper alloy, pewter) from the late 3rd century onwards (Fulford and Timby 2000). Unlike London, there is no evidence for the destruction or demolition of the building at this time, but the appearance of the basilica floor in the late 3rd century suggested that the building, whose construction was commenced in the early to mid-2nd century, was not necessarily completed by the time the decision was taken to turn it into a metalworkers' hall. Limited excavation, both of the range of rooms forming the west side of the basilica, and of the forum, suggests that the industrial activity was confined to the basilica. At Caistor St Edmunds, Norfolk, Frere published the excavations of Atkinson on the site of the forum basilica, which were undertaken between 1929 and 1935 (Frere 1971). The original, 2nd-century forum basilica produced evidence of two phases of burning, the second of which is assumed to lie in the 3rd century. The fact that the forum was rebuilt without using the foundations of its predecessor suggests that the latter was 'totally obliterated' (Frere 1971, 11). No evidence was found for a new basilica, but the arrangements of the west side of the new forum in the late Roman period remain unclear. Such evidence as there was for dating suggested a *terminus post quem* for the second forum of *c* AD 270–90 (Frere 1971, 25–6). Earlier (1924–27), Atkinson had excavated the forum basilica at Wroxeter where he discovered that, though reconstructed following a fire in the late 2nd century, it was not further, comprehensively rebuilt following destruction which he dated towards the end of the 3rd century (Atkinson 1942). It has to be admitted that the evidence for both the date and the totality of the second destruction is far from clear; in particular that from the basilica and the associated west range of rooms. Moreover there is patchy evidence from across the forum basilica as a whole for a further phase, or phases, of occupation ('The Latest Period') (Atkinson 1942, 108–13). From the evidence of three, possibly four, forum basilicas it might be inferred that such buildings, particularly the basilica element, as at Caistor, London and Silchester, were considered redundant to public administration. While we lack clarity as to the fate or use of the forum, rather than the basilica, at London and Silchester in the late Roman period, at Caistor there is positive evidence for its restoration. While the forum is generally associated with market trading, as the evidence from the Wroxeter forum suggests, the basilica is associated with the administration of justice. In these three or four towns this function must have been carried on elsewhere than in the forum basilica in the later 3rd and 4th centuries.

Not all towns took the same view as to the use and purpose of their forum basilica. At Caerwent in south-east Wales there is considerable evidence for a major programme of rebuilding of the forum basilica in the late 3rd century, which then continued in use as a civic building until towards the mid-4th century (Brewer 1993; 1997, 52). Similarly at Cirencester, although the extent of modern investigation is limited, there is evidence for the maintenance of the forum basilica through to the post-Roman period (Holbrook 1998, 99–121). Indeed there is disputed evidence for a major reconstruction in the late 4th century (Holbrook 1998, 107–8). So, while two forum basilicas in the west reveal evidence for not just the continuity of their use as public buildings, but significant reinvestment in their fabric in the late 3rd and 4th century, three towns in the east produce completely contradictory evidence. But for the equivocal evidence from Wroxeter, it could be suggested that there was a simple east–west split across southern Britain in the regard that civic leaders paid to what had been the principal public building of their towns in the 2nd century. While at Caistor and London the evidence suggests a deliberate obliteration of the 2nd-century basilica by demolition, at Silchester the shell of the building continued to be used. As we have seen the situation at Wroxeter is not entirely clear. In London destruction was not just focused on the forum basilica; there is also the evidence from the south-west and north-west of the city for the demolition of public monuments in the second half of the 3rd century. In the one area we have exceptionally good evidence for a *terminus ante quem* of AD 293/94.

The iconoclastic approach to great monuments of the past, even of the recent past, was not just confined to the towns, particularly London. In the course of the second half of the 3rd century one of the great monuments of Roman Britain, that located at the port of Richborough, Kent, and believed to celebrate the Claudian conquest, was totally destroyed. Situated at the entrance to Britain, the start of Watling Street, the road to London, this quadrifrons monument had been constructed in the late 1st century using large quantities of marble imported specifically for the project from Italy. Perhaps initiated by Vespasian, but completed by Domitian (Strong 1968; Shotter 2004), Strong concluded 'The detail, it is true, is strikingly plain with no hint of the rich ornamental detail associated with Flavian building enterprises in Italy, but in scale the building rivals all the great monumental arches constructed in the Roman world and its massive severity must have been as effective and impressive a piece of imperial propaganda as one could find throughout the Roman

Empire' (Strong 1968, 73). By the late 3rd century, when it is thought that it served as a look-out post, the monument had been enclosed by three ditches and a rampart. Precisely when this happened in the 3rd century is not clear, but the final filling of the ditches gives a *terminus ante quem* of *c* AD 280. 'The function of the fort as a look-out post and signal station to warn the coast of impending raids seems certain' (Cunliffe 1968, 244). It is the filling of the ditches which contained Carausian coins which gave Bushe-Fox a Carausian date for the construction of the rectangular 'Saxon shore fort', though this has been challenged, with the Carausian coins associated with the initial occupation, and a date under the emperor Probus (AD 276–82) preferred (Cunliffe 1968, 245–9; Johnson 1970; Pearson 2002, 58). It is not clear how, if at all, the fabric of the monument was affected by the construction of the earlier fortlet (which may possibly have been designed in part to preserve the monument). However, unequivocal evidence for its demolition by the late 3rd century comes from the inclusion of fragments of its masonry and marble casing in the walls of the shore fort (Strong 1968, 52).

The demolition of major structures in the 3rd century is not just confined to public buildings and monuments but also embraces military establishments. Just to the south of Richborough at Dover we have evidence for the demolition of the *classis Britannica* fort and its subsequent replacement by a 'new style' shore fort. In this case the demolition of the first fort has been dated early in the 3rd century, perhaps about AD 210 according to Philp (1981, 94), when it was followed by the development of a fine soil over 50 years or so before the construction of the later fort, probably after AD 275–80 (Wilkinson 1994). The apparently long interval between demolition and rebuilding is puzzling, and the evidence for it not strong, given the presumed continued importance of Dover as a fort, and port of entry to Britain, and for the continuation of the *classis Britannica* until up to at least the mid-3rd century (Cunliffe 1968, 261). Across the Channel at Boulogne the *classis Britannica* fort met a similar fate, but with evidence for a shorter interval between demolition and new construction. Here destruction of the early fleet base took place after AD 269 and the construction of the replacement 'shore fort' after the early AD 270s, but attributed by Seillier to Carausius (Brulet 1989, 62–72).

In the case of civil building in town and country the picture has not moved on substantively since Harvey's survey of 1981. However, the counties to the south of the Thames have been subjected to a thorough survey, such that a division can be made between south-eastern villas completely abandoned in the second half of the 3rd century and those where major rebuilding only followed after demolition of the pre-existing structure, eg Farningham I and East Cliff, Folkestone (Kent), and Beddington and Walton-on-the-Hill (Surrey) (Black 1987, 37–42, fig 19; Howell 2005). Whereas economic factors may

well explain the desertion of a site, the building anew on the site of a demolished villa may suggest other explanations, such as a new owner, but also recalls the rebuilding of the London amphitheatre on its original foundations. As Black points out, 'Normal practice would be for an owner simply to add rooms or blocks of rooms onto a standing structure' (1987, 39). The dating evidence from the rural sites, often derived from early excavations, is poor and can seldom be given much precision and it is possible, as has been suggested at Dover, that rebuilding followed after a gap in occupation.

One town in the south-east also gives evidence of radical change at the end of the 3rd century. Recent and continuing excavations of insula ix at Silchester have produced evidence for the total demolition of a substantial town house (House 1) in the second half of the 3rd century followed by the re-allotment of the internal space of the block and rebuilding by the beginning of the 4th century. Whereas the demolished house represents the end of a succession of developments laid out on an alignment whose origin lies in the late pre-Roman Iron Age, the reconfiguration of the insula and the rebuilding all conform to the orientation of the Roman street grid, laid out on the cardinal points and itself dating back to the mid-1st century. The change represents a real break in tradition. A reconsideration of the evidence from all the insulae in the north-west quarter of the town suggests a comprehensive replanning and rebuilding of the area. While town houses had been a feature of the early Roman occupation in this area, the later layout has a more artisanal flavour with narrow-fronted shops-cum-workshops dominating the insulae (Fulford *et al* 2006). Though the evidence is much less conclusive, other areas of the town may have changed in a similar way.

Our dating evidence for demolitions and abandonments is good in only a handful of examples. In south-west London we have evidence on the one hand for the restoration of temples around the mid-3rd century, on the other for the construction of a monumental palace building after AD 294. At Richborough we can be reasonably certain that the monumental arch still existed in some form until the construction of the shore fort in the late AD 270s or early 280s. The argument that all such demolition of public buildings was not necessarily confined to the second half of the 3rd century is raised in London by the demolition of the Huggin Hill public baths, also in the south-west quarter of the town, which Marsden attributed to the late 2nd century (Marsden 1976), and by the Dover fort. The dating evidence for Huggin Hill is derived from material dumped with clay and gravel over the remains of the building. The date range of the pottery is Flavian to mid-2nd century, strongly suggesting that it was a redeposition of material derived wholesale from another project (Marsden 1976, 55–7). The true date of demolition may well turn out to be later.

In contextualising his study of nine counties of the south-east Harvey chose to sample the north, an area extending as far south as Cheshire, Derbyshire and Lincolnshire. He noted that 'The figures appear to suggest that the phenomenon [of early 3rd-century cessation and later 3rd-century revivals] is apparent but less marked in the North' (Sheldon 1981, 377). That there is a particular south-eastern focus to the pattern of desertions and recommencements is brought out by the evidence collected together by the former RCHM(E) for the Cotswolds (1976), where the evidence is not of cessations and recommencements, but of continuities through the 3rd century and of commencements from the later 3rd century. Although as yet undefined regional factors in economic activity may need to be taken into account, it is difficult to explain such different patterns of behaviour in the east and in the west of a territory as small as the south of Britain.

The purpose of this essay has been to introduce the evidence from public buildings and monuments, most of it the result of new work unavailable to Harvey at the beginning of the 1980s, into the discussion of settlement behaviour in the second half of the 3rd century. Can it, however, help us understand this behaviour any better? The construction in the south-west quarter of London of the monumental building complex employing timbers felled in the winter of AD 293/94 has given us one close context for the demolition of existing public buildings and it is hard not to attribute the work to the usurper Allectus. The recovery of new dating evidence from the foundations of the shore fort at Pevensey, East Sussex, which pointed to a date after AD 293, once again raised the possibility of attribution of all the late 3rd-century shore forts with the new architecture of massive walls and projecting bastions to the reigns of the usurper emperors Carausius and Allectus (Fulford and Tyers 1995). It has long been recognised that the coinage of the usurpers introduces elements of a new ideology (*cf* Williams 2004, 60–73 and appendices), both reassuring in its reference to ancient literary giants such as Virgil ('*Expectate veni*'; see Hassall, this volume) and challenging in its commemorations of legions not otherwise known to have been part of the British military establishment, and its assertion of equal identity with the 'established' rulers, Diocletian and Maximian ('*Carausius et fratres sui*').

Another approach to the establishment of a new identity was to challenge the status quo through the construction of new public architecture, in this case evidenced by the London 'monumental building' and the new shore forts. Whether the erasure of existing monuments was part of the strategy to build a new identity or the consequence of a very practical need to find building materials is impossible to say. It is likely that the temples and altars which provided material for the Allectan palace were located close by and their destruction could have been driven by economic necessity. In the case of the basilica, however, we have no idea of the destination of the building material, and the same is true of the basilica at Caistor-by-Norwich. Is it possible that

the destruction or, in the case of Silchester, the conversion of these monuments, such archetypes of the early empire, was driven by ideological motives? We cannot begin to know how dilapidated the great monument at Richborough had become by the late 3rd century, for it may, as has been suggested, have been converted into a watch-tower, but was it essential for its foundations to be at the heart of the new shore fort and its materials incorporated into its walls? There were other locations to place a fort, but perhaps it was necessary to assert its symbolism of opposition at the entry to Britain and the start of Watling Street, and at the expense of the early imperial arch which commemorated a conquest which the new rulers did not want to see repeated. Similar ideological necessities may have driven the destruction of the imperial fleet bases at nearby Dover and Boulogne.

There were other contexts in the second half of the 3rd century when public buildings might have suffered in the assertion of new ideologies associated with a new regime. One such may have been the British response to the *Imperium Galliarum* from Postumus's rebellion from AD 259 and the quantities of regular and 'barbarous' imitations of the Gallic Empire found within the basilica at Silchester do suggest that it had become dedicated to metal-working by the AD 260s. The find of a coin-mould for producing *antoniniani* of Tetricus II hints at the possibility that the great hall continued to be used for official purposes (Fulford and Timby 2000, 576–8). With the London basilica the evidence is less clear: 'the Basilica was destroyed some time after AD 250, since there were no pottery types necessarily later than that date, and certainly none from the 4th century' (Brigham 1990a, 82). There is little clarity for the date of the demolition of the Forum IB basilica at Caistor, nor for by how much it predated the construction of Forum II dated after *c* AD 270–90 (Frere 1971, 26).

Public buildings of the early empire are unlikely to have been a target of Constantius following his retaking of Britain in AD 296, nor of Aurelian following the collapse of the Gallic Empire in AD 274. We do not know what view either took of the supporters of, respectively the Gallic Empire and of Carausius and Allectus, but it would not be unreasonable to suppose that purges followed and estates were confiscated (as Harvey Sheldon had argued for Severus at the beginning of the 3rd century (1981, 378–9)). Equally Carausius and his successor may have had to use force to assert their authority, perhaps at the expense of estate owners loyal to the legitimate emperor in the 'home' territory of the south-east. The conscious erasure of the buildings associated with a disgraced elite offers a possible explanation for those villas where there is evidence of extensive demolition prior to late 3rd-/early 4th-century rebuild. Interestingly, while good, close evidence for the dates of abandonment is largely absent across the countryside of the south-east, the destruction (without further rebuild) of one great house, the villa at Fishbourne, can be dated to the very end of the 3rd century, certainly after AD 271–73 (Cunliffe 1971, 220). Though the work of raiding pirates cannot be ruled out (and one other south coast villa at Preston, Brighton, may have been destroyed by fire at this time (Black 1987, 38)), the temptation to connect the destruction of a great house associated with an *ancien régime* with the power struggles of the late 3rd century is very great.

Whether occasioned by the politics of the Gallic Empire, the usurpation of Carausius and Allectus and the development of a new ideology, or the recapture of Britain by Constantius Chlorus, the evidence for disturbance and change is concentrated in the south-east of Britain. Indeed the contrast with the south-west is striking in yielding neither a picture of 3rd-century cessations of occupation, nor of destructions of public buildings. It is tempting to associate the changes in the south-east with the end of the domination of the affairs of Britannia by an old elite whose ancestry can be traced back through the history of its town houses and villas to the 1st century, and its replacement with the '*nouveau riche*' of the south-west. The former had its origins in the politics of the kingdoms of the late Iron Age and the conquest period, while the latter were associated perhaps with the families of those who made up the leading men of the Roman army of Britain, and who lived within easy reach of the spa-town of Bath and the *colonia* at Gloucester. But this takes us into a subject best pursued in another context.

1.6 Satellite, parasite, or just London?
Richard Reece

London seems to have been untypical throughout its existence. A non-place for most of prehistory, a non-*civitas* capital in the Roman period, an empty property in the early Saxon period, and then the royal ruling-place from thereon. Perhaps it is right that it should have had an untypical archaeologist to guard and guide much of its archaeological fortunes in the recent past. But first London, and then Harvey.

The search for pre-Roman London has been quite intensive over the years and has had some success, but even now it probably has to be admitted that the city and Westminster were not focal places in the sense of concentrated population or practical human activities before the middle of the 1st century. It could be that this was because the area was in some way sacred, a focus of occasional cult activity, but the evidence, apart from deposits in the local rivers, is thin. Ritual is often the refuge of the despairing archaeologist.

So why did this muddy estuary suddenly spring to commercial life? Perhaps the way to investigate this is to look at who wanted to get in touch with us Britons, and why. Earlier links with mainland Europe were with Brittany and central north France to the south coast, then with Gallia Belgica to Essex. This perhaps means that the focus of communication moved to the Rhine and thence to a base in Britain suitable for striking out to all points of the compass. Trade was overtaken by political expedience, communication by conquest.

The blueprint for making Britain a Roman province: set up centres through which Roman authority could get at the natives and construct means of communication to reach them. The Thames foreshore was therefore the end of the cross-channel route; London was the means of getting at Britain. From London roads spreading out to a number of designated tribal *foci* and *civitas* capitals were conceived. London was not a *civitas* capital; it was the base from which to get at all the *civitates*. The *civitas foci* were the means of getting at the tribal natives.

This explains my first two descriptions: London as an offshore satellite from which to get at the natives of Britain, and London as a foreign growth in the body of Britain, without visible means of support, a parasite. It also summarises many published attitudes to London, though the satellite image, not surprisingly, has been given preference. This has automatically meant that London has been mainly studied as a Roman implant – if the key is Roman-shaped, then the lock into which it is to fit must obviously also be Roman-shaped. This accords well with the establishment view of Roman Britain, which is in fact the logical view: we study those aspects of Britain in the first four centuries AD that had Roman origins – the study of Roman Britain rather than the study of Britain in a period that happens to be politically Roman.

If only the natives had also taken this view all would have been well. But it has become increasingly obvious as the archaeology of London has been revealed that all was not well. The thriving, Romanising, centre of trade and cultural activity of the early years of the 2nd century seems to have become a much less bustling and thriving focus of official administration in the 4th century: an administrative enclave rather than a thriving town with an administrative centre. To be fair, this change is seen widely throughout the empire, is almost a commentary on the urban life of parts of the empire. But it is not a commentary on the burgeoning life in the countryside of Britain.

The contrast between the archaeology of Britain and the archaeology of London (and other towns) has caused something of a 'British backlash' and a wish to understand Britain in its own terms rather than in purely Romanising terms. Yes, there were Roman aspects to life in Britain in the first four centuries AD but there was a basic British way of life, which formed the substructure on to which Roman aspects were added.

On the other hand there was not a British way of life in the area to become Londinium – or if there was it was fragmentary and in no condition to form the basic British way of life in the town-to-be. The balance of foreigner and native in the early years of London can only be guessed, but it must have been heavily influenced by the influx of traders, most of whom would have been foreign. They needed servants and workers, and those would presumably be mostly Britons (male) displaced from the countryside. Though of course in a concentration of men there were the usual job opportunities for women as well, and they were presumably also British. The person hoisting the packages out of the hold, or off the deck of the ship was foreign, the person on the dock guiding the packages down to the ground was probably British. The society that developed was very mixed.

At a higher level London presumably became the port of entry for those who represented authority. It may well be that several decades passed before they were based in London, but conditions had to be right to receive them. Roman authority would expect a Roman welcome. At this stage of development a reception of welcome would need to provide decent wine and Apician nibbles. Mead, offered with comment 'We drink the British drink mead here, Excellency', would be dashed to the ground with the curt response 'Well I don't'.

I assume that these two aspects of life continued through the 2nd century with the satellite image in the ascendant, logistically and economically supported by substantial trade. The trade presumably supplied dues and taxes, as well as actual food to eat, goods to buy, fashions to adopt and religions to savour so the administrative enclave was surrounded by a thriving town. This is the town depicted brilliantly by John Morris (1982). Yes, it has lots of mad ideas in it, and many had been cut out before it was published, but it brings the whole of his knowledge of the sources and the material of the Empire to bear on the Roman aspects of London. Rome-on-Thames in fact. Of course it needs to be read with Ralph Merrifield's *London* (1983) because that gives the accurate material background against which Morris's classically informed flights of fancy have to be set.

Thus far a model for London as a satellite in the sense of a space station seems helpful. It was moored in the northern sea as a point of entry to 'get at' the natives and resources of Britain. The traveller could dock there, in a Romanised atmosphere, and the fortunate ones could do all their necessary business in a Romanised setting without leaving the satellite for the wild country beyond. The less fortunate would have to put on special clothing to cope with almost extra-terrestrial conditions of fog, wind and rain. Very often, of course, they would find their stay little different from a tour of duty in the Alps, the Balkans or Brittany.

But any satellite has inherent problems. Maintenance is needed, wear and tear has to be repaired to high standards, and this can be a constant drain on resources. We do not know whether Britain, regarded as an Imperial Enterprise, ever turned a profit or whether the remarkably heavy garrisons, added to the administration, made it for ever a financial liability. We do not even know whether the empire had the techniques and information to construct a notional balance sheet for a province.

At this point, when the downturn in inter-provincial trade started late in the 2nd century, and then more obviously in the 3rd century, the model of London as a parasite might become more attractive. When the riverside wall was built, when trade through the city declined, and revenues declined in tandem, London had to be financially supported by the home base in Rome or by the province.

My reasoning here is something that many people either cannot, or do not, want to admit. My view is that a concentration of population such that it is unable to feed itself off the immediately surrounding countryside – call it a town, a city, or an administrative enclave – has to have some reason for its existence. If that reason lies in the inhabitants then they will willingly shoulder the burdens of organisation and administration that the concentration of people brings with it. So the tribal *foci* or *civitas* capitals of Britain were encouraged by Roman authority to make themselves in the image of Rome. The people who moved in to those centres apparently saw enough advantages to such nucleation to shoulder the burdens nucleation brought with it, at least until the early 3rd century. The profits that supported the town came from a circulation of goods and services to and from the tribal area, the *civitas*, or probably very soon, the convenient market area. Goods came in, were locally taxed, sold, and used in the town or moved out again to the countryside or beyond. Services joined in the same circulation. London, on the other hand, since it was not at the centre of a *civitas*, and seems to have had a fairly sparse surrounding population, perhaps because of the poor quality of the land, depended on trade passing through from the empire to the province.

When trade declined, and the surrounding population was too sparse to 'want' a town, the reason for London evaporated – from a British point of view, that is. Authority however apparently wanted to keep its foothold, its point of entry. Either it has to make the British inhabitants somehow responsible for authority's entry point, or it had to pay up itself. Either way, London became a parasite, an organism that could not live without a host to sustain it. Elsewhere in Britain my view is that as larger blots on the landscape lost their superiority, their reasons for existence, settlements evened out in size and all became more or less equal administrative agro-villages.

Harvey has never been happy with my apparently flippant view of his heartland in Southwark as demoted in the later 3rd century to be the market garden to supply the administrative enclave that was late London. Yet with its abundant black earth and only a fair sprinkling of desirable out-of-town-residences that does fit the material picture as far as I know it. What is still missing, on this model, is the reduced area of the enclave of London, surrounded by fortifications within the old city. There is extra walling around the Tower of London, but returns through the old built-up area to the west and north have still to be found.

So much for London the satellite and London the parasite; what about Just London? This might appear to be the proper way to study and think about London. Calling it a satellite, a parasite, or anything else shows an individual throwing his prejudices at an archaeological site that cannot fight back. Why not be objective about it and let London speak for itself? We don't want personal opinions, we want facts.

The excavations at St Peter in the Thicket took place from 15 July to 17 August. The site was 30m by 40m and two trenches were excavated, both 20m square. Complete open plan excavation was impossible due to foundations. In trench 1 a concrete cellar floor was removed by machine and immediately below was a dark layer (colour chart 77B) in which the following material was found ...

If I reproduced the full (imaginary) list of facts all readers would soon switch off and a number would shout – 'Yes, all very well, but what does it all MEAN?' And of course the answer is that I cannot give you any meaning because you asked for facts, and meanings are matters of interpreting facts. Even worse, we can only interpret facts together, and reach an intelligible conclusion, if we share a common language. Not so much English or French, but a framework into which to fit the facts, a framework which is widely intelligible even if some regard it as nonsense. Like satellites, or parasites, or any other type of model.

I don't think that it is possible to write about Just London because every single observation or material piece of evidence has to be interpreted by analogy with other sites, other material, and probably other times. So the idea of the satellite could be more acceptably rephrased to ask 'Is London more like major Roman cities nearby on the mainland of the Empire, or other towns in Britain?'. The parasite idea could be rephrased as 'What is the market area to which late Roman London distributes goods and the area from which it absorbs produce?'. Both of these are major research projects, and the main difficulty with both is that they are not under the control of London.

A project to consider the kilns providing pottery to later Roman London is possible because it depends mainly on an examination of material which is under London control and which has been more or less standardised. A project to compare and contrast London and Trier and London and Cirencester is much more difficult to set up because it depends on circumstances beyond London's control. It is not so much a matter of troublesome individuals but the fact that London and Cirencester, or Trier, have been excavated by completely different teams and methods. The areas excavated are different, the sites themselves are very different, and so the problems multiply. The projects are not impossible, but they do pose major logistical difficulties.

It is much easier, and therefore probably more potentially productive, to set out a model – early

London was a satellite – to find material ways in which this can be tested, supported or falsified, and to work with the provisional results. At this point the obvious thing for me, as a coins person, to do would be to provide a short summary of how coins from London and other sites support or falsify the ideas of comparison, satellites and parasites. I would very much like to do this, and I look forward to doing it one day. London is unusual in British archaeology because it is the only large settlement for which we do not have reliable full coin lists, which, due to a combination of past financial shortfalls and ill-judged policies, means that we can say very little about coin use in London compared with either the rest of Britain or the mainland of the empire. Coins could provide a very good method of testing ideas about satellites and parasites, and lots of other models, and we can only encourage any plans to remedy this in the future.

But let's think positive. I ended my modelling by returning to earth and to material. It is now time to pick up my earlier suggestion that an untypical site, like London, needs an untypical archaeologist like Harvey. He has not often indulged in modelling – I can almost hear him saying that there are more than enough airy-fairy-modelling types in certain places in London anyway – but he has usually engaged with the models floated and he has done his part by providing the material against which models can be tested. When I was involved with the Southwark and Lambeth Excavation Committee he and I sometimes differed on the amount of resources that should be given to publication and further excavation. The reason that I gave in without major scuffles was that the records of past excavations were at least present and in good order and it would have been absolute physical torture for Harvey to be chained to a desk knowing that sites were being destroyed, unexcavated, around him. He has been a major force in the development of archaeology in London and has been personally responsible for a major part of the material record created. Which makes us academic and administrative types look rather small.

1.7 Descent into darkness: London in the 5th and 6th centuries   *Robert Cowie*

Introduction

The two centuries following the end of Roman provincial rule are the most poorly understood of London's historic past. This period is also the most contentious, and has for generations provoked arguments among historians and archaeologists alike. Arguably the most fiercely debated questions relating to this period are those concerning 'continuity' of Roman life after the end of imperial rule and the nature and magnitude of Anglo-Saxon settlement in eastern England (see Hills 2003). These particularly difficult but related topics should be addressed at both national and regional level, and are duly listed in the current research framework for the region (Nixon *et al* 2002, 46, 52, 88). For the purposes of this paper the London region (hereafter 'the region') is defined as the area roughly corresponding to modern Greater London.

At present battle lines are drawn between those who consider that Roman life, or *Romanitas*, in eastern England came to an end in the first two or three decades of the 5th century and those who believe that it persisted for much longer. Discussion of this subject has often been hindered by a failure to define terms. To obviate this Faulkner and Reece (2002, 64–5) compiled a list of diagnostically Roman features that should be visible in the archaeological record if continuity is to be proved. In brief, they include evidence for administrative towns, centralised authority (manifested by public buildings and infrastructure and regular town plans), villas, masonry buildings, domestic and monumental architecture and luxury items reflecting Graeco-Roman Mediterranean taste, long-distance trade and communication networks, and mass-produced goods.

There is similar polarisation of opinion about the mechanisms for the widespread switch to 'Germanic' material culture and language that apparently occurred in eastern England during the 5th and 6th centuries. Some take the traditional standpoint that this change was due (at least in part) to a mass influx of migrants from the Continent. However, the more fashionable view is that change occurred due to the influence of a 'Germanic' warrior elite that arrived in post-Roman Britain in relatively small numbers. Its exponents regard, perhaps with some justification, the use of ethnic labels such as Celtic, British and Anglo-Saxon as unhelpful and potentially misleading.

Problems of chronology

Research about the region in the 5th and 6th centuries is seriously hampered by the scarcity of evidence. The lack of contemporary historical sources is particularly striking, for there are no reliable references to London between about AD 400, when it is listed in the *Notitia Dignatum*, and AD 601, when Pope Gregory wrote to Augustine expressing his wish that London should become the primary see (Bede *Ecclesiastical History*, 1.29; Milne 1995, 18–19; Coates 1998, 204–5). Stephen of Byzantium briefly mentions London and its inhabitants in his geographical dictionary, probably written in the early 6th century, although he presumably derived this information from earlier classical authors for archaeological evidence suggests that the settlement was long abandoned by this time.

The *Anglo-Saxon Chronicle*, compiled in the late 9th century, alludes to 5th-century London only once. It states that in AD 456 Britons fled to London after the Jutish war-leader Hengest and his son Æsc or Oisc routed them at Cregcanford (traditionally identified as Crayford) (Garmondsway 1953, 13). This entry, however, should be regarded as highly suspect for a number of reasons. First, the original source for the events of AD 456 is unknown, although in all likelihood the account is an amalgam of various oral traditions. Secondly, there is no archaeological evidence that London existed as a settlement or defensive centre at this time, although the chronicler might have meant the *site* of London. Thirdly, the historicity of Hengest and his son is doubtful.

Similarly the relative paucity of archaeological data for this period has frustrated attempts to construct a well-defined chronological sequence for the major social, economic and cultural transformation that the region (and indeed the rest of Britain) underwent at this time. The problem begins in the second half of the 4th century with the collapse of industries engaged in mass production, and the breakdown of long-distance trade and the monetary economy, so that from this time the number of closely datable and diagnostically Roman artefacts entering the archaeological record rapidly diminishes. Anglo-Saxon material culture of the 5th and 6th centuries is generally less well understood, and in London the assemblages of artefacts recovered from settlement sites of this period are small. While considerable progress has been made in developing a pottery chronology based on typology and fabric (Blackmore forthcoming), this has not been tested by absolute dating techniques. Indeed, the few radiocarbon dates that have been obtained from Early Saxon sites are not suitable for this purpose (see Cowie and Blackmore 2008, table 72).

An urban myth

For much of the 20th century it was commonly thought that the walled area of the Roman city was never completely abandoned (Wheeler 1934, 290; Biddle *et al* 1973, 18). However, the cumulative results of numerous rescue excavations undertaken in the city and Southwark over the past 30 years tell a different story. They suggest that the Roman town began to decline in the second half of the 2nd century. This was a slow and complex process punctuated by at least one period of modest revival in the late 3rd and early 4th century. The general trend, however, is clearly evident from the marked reduction in the number of buildings, pits and wells dated to about AD 150–400, and in a decline in the standard of road maintenance from about AD 300 (Milne 1995, 81–9; Marsden and West 1992). Similarly, in Southwark the presence of late Roman burials in once occupied areas show that by the late 4th century the settlement had shrunk to a small area around the southern bridgehead (Sheldon 2000, 144; Cowan 2003, 87–8).

Contraction of occupied areas in the City and in Southwark is also indicated by the presence of so-called 'dark earth' covering the latest Roman occupation levels. This rather vague term, first used in London in 1977, is now often applied to strata comprising homogeneous dark loam sealing the latest occupation levels of Roman and later settlements at sites in the United Kingdom and on the Continent. In central London dark earth was once interpreted as imported material laid down to prepare ground for cultivation, and therefore to represent urban land that had been converted for agriculture and/or gardening (Merrifield 1983, 143; Roskams 1991). For various reasons this interpretation is now considered extremely unlikely (Yule 1990; Watson 1998a, 102–6). Analyses of dark earth at several sites in London now suggests that it mainly comprises soil formed by various processes, including weathering, root action, burrowing animals and reworking by soil fauna especially *Enchytraeidae* (Macphail 1988a; 2003). Moreover, pollen and phytoliths recovered from dark earth are consistent with grassland or urban wasteland rather than cultivated land. Thus in most cases its presence seems to indicate the abandonment of either entire settlements or localised areas within them.

Occupation of Londinium apparently ceased altogether either at the time of Roman withdrawal or soon after (Milne 1995, 89; Perring 1991a, 128), presumably because its role as an imperial administrative and military centre had ended. The evidence for urban decay and desertion supporting this conclusion is now overwhelming, for decades of excavations have failed to uncover any post-Roman features of 5th- or 6th-century date in the city. The old explanation that such remains may have been destroyed by later activity (Wheeler 1934, 297; Biddle *et al* 1973, 16) is scarcely credible, for such truncation would not have been universal. In any case, if town life had continued, the survival of deep rubbish pits and wells might at least be expected.

The archaeological evidence is entirely consistent with the complete dereliction of the settlement, so that by the middle of the 5th century the walls enclosed a crumbling ghost town partly concealed by scrub vegetation. Low-lying and poorly drained areas of the town were gradually buried beneath hillwash and flood deposits. Indeed, as the Roman drainage system failed some areas would have become uninhabitable due to wet and boggy conditions. Such areas have been identified behind the riverside wall, along Walbrook and its tributaries and on the site of the former amphitheatre (Horsman *et al* 1988, 16–17; Maloney and de Moulins 1990, 79–81; Millett 1980, 14; Porter 1997, 148). Nevertheless, ruinous buildings would still have been clearly visible, as would the eroded and overgrown banks and arena of the amphitheatre. Indeed, some intramural Roman structures survived long enough to influence the topography of parts of Late Saxon and medieval London, but far too few to affect significantly the development of these later townscapes (Horsman *et al* 1988, 110–11).

There is very little archaeological evidence for activity of any kind during the Early Saxon period either within the city walls or along the adjacent waterfront. The only stratified post-Roman artefact from this area that may be confidently dated to the 5th century is a saucer brooch that was found among fallen roof tiles lying in the *frigidarium* of a ruined Roman bath house at Billingsgate (Cook 1969; Marsden 1980, 185–6; Welch 1975, 91). The brooch is of a type dated to the mid-5th century and is paralleled in late 5th-century burials at Mitcham and Guildown (Welch 1975; Wheeler 1935, 119; Vince 1990, 7). A single potsherd found nearby might be contemporaneous with the brooch or date to later in the Early or Middle Saxon periods. The fabric of the sherd suggests a provenance in the Charnwood region, north-west of Leicester, or Scandinavia (Symonds *et al* 1991, 62).

Evidence for 6th-century activity is almost as sparse and is only indicated by a handful of artefacts, most of which are of uncertain provenance. They include fragments of a bracteate (a disc-shaped pendant) from the foreshore at Queenhithe (British Museum acc no 2941. 1996,0605.1), buckles from the Guildhall (Egan 2007, 447, <S1>), Custom House and possibly the Barbican, and a spearhead from Poultry (Wheeler 1935, 148, 167, 187). Three Frankish pots dated to the late 6th or early 7th century, comprising two biconical greyware jars and a dish, were supposedly found in the city, although their recorded find spots may not be genuine (Wheeler 1935, 156, 187; Vince 1990, 11–12; Vince and Jenner 1991, 113). Several residual sherds of chaff-tempered pottery from four sites to the south of St Paul's might be roughly contemporaneous with these imports or date to the Middle Saxon period (Cowie 2001, 196). The rarity of such finds suggests that they represent only a transient presence in the city, and that they were probably lost by occasional visitors scavenging among the ruins.

Sub-Roman hinterland?

In the surrounding countryside principal roads were perhaps the only major elements of the Roman infrastructure to survive relatively intact through the 5th and 6th centuries, although these do not appear to have been maintained or extensively used for long-distance communication until the Middle and Late Saxon periods. Locally, topographic features such as large earthworks and elements of field systems would have survived from the prehistoric and Roman periods.

Archaeological evidence suggests that very few villas or Romano-British farmsteads in the region survived into the late 4th century, and none seems to have continued to operate beyond the early 5th century. As yet no culturally distinct sub-Roman settlement sites have been identified in the region. Either such sites are virtually invisible to the archaeologist or they are so few that they have eluded detection. The lack of mass-produced durable items and the possible use of timber-frame construction methods might explain invisibility, as might the possible adoption by sub-Roman communities of Anglo-Saxon material culture and customs (see Halsall 1999). Alternatively the evidence might reflect a decrease in the local population at this time. Such a decline might account for the possible regeneration of woodland during the Early Saxon period (Greig 1992, 79–80, 84–5; Tyers *et al* 1994, 20–1).

Various factors could have caused population decline in Britain at this time including plague, warfare and agrarian recession due to climate change (Higham 1992, 77–80). In the Lower Thames Valley the abandonment of Londinium would probably have had a detrimental impact on the rural economy. However, the breakdown of a 'protected social order' following the end of imperial rule must have been particularly important in determining the region's settlement pattern and population level. Under these circumstances some inhabitants may have moved away from the exposed Thames corridor to the relative safety of surviving British enclaves and the protection of an emergent warrior elite (see Garwood 1989). Such an enclave is thought to have existed in the Chilterns, and Grim's Dyke in north-west London may have been modified early in the post-Roman period to serve as its boundary (Castle 1975; Vince 1990, 51–2). However, Wheeler's (1935, 54–5) contention that there remained a sub-Roman community in London powerful enough to exclude 'the German yokels' from a territory extending out between 5 and 10 miles from the city walls must now be discounted (Cowie 2000, 181).

Nevertheless, it seems likely that during the early stages of the migration period a distinct British presence persisted in some parts of the region. This may account for the few place-names in the region with possible Celtic or Latin elements. The latter include *camp* (Latin *campus*, meaning field) as in Addiscombe, *funta* (Latin *fontana*, meaning spring) as in Bedfont, Cheshunt and Wansunt, and *wīchām*

(possibly derived from *vicus*) as in West Wickham (Gelling 1977). With one or two exceptions, such as Penge, all Celtic names in the region are of rivers (Mills 2001, xvi). For example, the Brent and Lea may respectively derive from the Celtic words *Brigantia* (probably high or holy river) and *lug* (bright) (Gover *et al* 1942, 1, 4). The Old English name Lunden comes from the Roman name for London, which in turn derives from Celtic or possibly pre-Celtic names (Coates 1998).

Several place-names in the region contain the Old English word *Wealh* (foreigner, Welshman or slave) that came to be applied by the English to the Britons. They include Walbrook, Wallington, Walworth and the field names Waleport (Wallpits) and Walhulle in Kingston (Cameron 1980, 28; Gover *et al* 1934, 27; Mills 2001, xvi; Wakeford 1984, 251–6). Such place-names might, therefore, allude to surviving British communities or to sites that they were known to have occupied.

Place-name evidence, the presence of late Roman metalwork and artefacts with quoit brooch style decoration at Croydon, and the proximity of Croydon and Mitcham to Roman roads might also indicate a lingering British presence on the upper reaches of the River Wandle in the early to mid-5th century (Hines 2004, 92, 97–8). The recent discovery at an Early Saxon cemetery in Croydon of a burial in a chalk-lined coffin prompted speculation that the site may have been used by sub-Roman and Saxon communities (McKinley 2003, 12–13, 111). Its radiocarbon date of cal AD 340–640 (NZ14468; 1571 ±70 BP) might bear this out, although chalk or 'plaster' burials have been often found in the Roman cemeteries around Londinium and those in the eastern cemetery commonly date to the late 3rd and 4th century (Barber and Bowsher 2000, 103–4).

Culture change

In the second or third quarter of the 5th century rural settlements characterised by a new type of building, the *Grubenhaus* (pit-house) (Tipper 2004), and Germanic-style artefacts began to develop along the valleys of the Thames and its tributaries, such as the Cray, the Effra, and the Wandle. At the same time Germanic-style grave goods and burial practices were introduced to the region. Settlement dating to this phase is represented by occupation sites at Ham, Mucking, St Mary Cray and Tulse Hill (Hamerow 1993, 93; Cowie and Blackmore 2008), and by cemeteries at Croydon, Guildown, Mitcham, Orpington and possibly Beddington (Bidder and Morris 1959; Morris 1959; Poulton 1987, 199; Tester 1968; 1970). The early date and strategic positions of the sites at Mucking, Mitcham and Croydon, on important land or river routes to London, prompted speculation that *foederati* may have been stationed at these sites to guard the approaches to the city (Morris 1959, 152; Welch 1997; McKinley 2003, 110). However, as Roman

London (and possibly its bridge) had probably ceased to exist before any of these settlements were established this seems unlikely.

Settlement later in the 5th century is indicated by occupation sites at Clerkenwell, Darenth, Hammersmith, Harmondsworth, Keston, Kingston and Mortlake (Cowie and Blackmore 2008) and a cemetery at Shepperton (Longley and Poulton 1982). A cemetery and putative settlement at Hanwell also probably dates to this phase (Wheeler 1935, 136–9). Radiocarbon dates suggest that the intriguing timber structure recently discovered in a former channel of the River Lea at Edmonton may also date to the 5th century, or possibly slightly later (GVV04; Ron Humphrey, AOC Archaeology Group, pers comm). The structure might form part of a bridge or jetty, although it is currently thought more likely to be the foundations of an artificial island or crannog (Stephenson 2006).

The evidence from Clerkenwell, comprising a cluster of eight pits containing pottery dated to about AD 450–550, is particularly significant given its location some 800m to the north-west of the former Roman city (Sloane and Malcolm 2004, 21–3). Finds from nearby sites include two sherds of similar pottery from St Bride's Church (Blackmore with Williams 1997, 54–6), a sherd of 5th-century glass vessel from St Bartholomew's Medical College (Barber and Thomas 2002, 8–9) and four sherds of 5th- or 6th-century pottery from the Saxo-Norman city ditch at Aldersgate (Jarrett 2001, 65–6). Together they suggest scattered settlement along the lower reaches of the Fleet Valley. Another area of possible Early Saxon occupation has been identified on the river terraces overlooking the Strand, where pits containing finds of this date have been found at three sites (Blackmore *et al* 2004; Cowie and Blackmore forthcoming). It is also thought that three undated inhumation burials found nearby at the Inner Temple might be of Early Saxon date, for one was accompanied by two objects, respectively of iron and bronze (Butler 2005, 16–18). The iron object, possibly a sword or spearhead, had been placed parallel to the body.

The distribution of Roman and Early Saxon settlement in the region appears to have been determined mainly by local geology, topography and drainage, for in both periods gravel terraces in river valleys were favoured locations (Cowie 2000, 181; MoLAS 2000, 178–9 and map 7; Sheldon and Schaaf 1978, 60). Early Saxon settlement sites have been found among Roman field systems at Dagenham, Harmondsworth, Kingston, Mitcham, Mortlake, Mucking, South Hornchurch, Rainham and St Mary Cray, and others have been found at or near villa sites such as Beddington, Darenth,

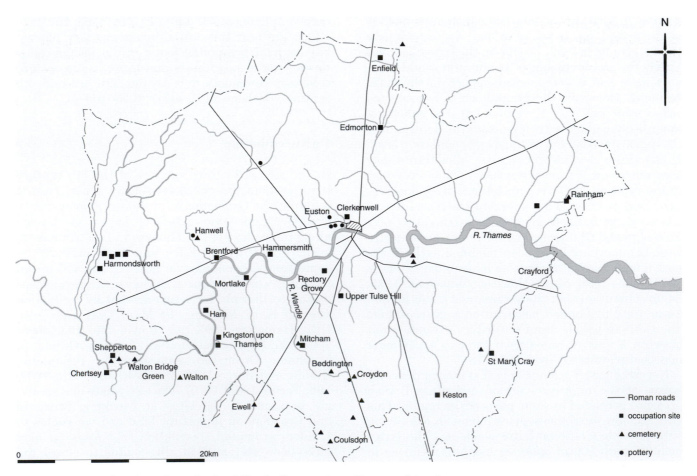

Fig 1.7.1 Map showing the principal Early Saxon sites discussed in the text

Keston, Orpington and Rivenhall. Occasionally the conjunction of Late Roman and Early Saxon settlements has prompted suggestions that occupation was continuous or that Roman farms were 'taken on as going concerns' by Anglo-Saxon settlers. This may have been so, but unfortunately current dating evidence is simply not accurate enough to substantiate such claims. On the other hand site sequences at St Mary Cray and Mortlake clearly show that the *Grubenhäuser* found there were built after Roman ditches had silted up (Hart 1984; Cowie and Blackmore 2008).

Conclusions

There is absolutely no physical evidence for the survival of any aspect of Roman life in the region after the first quarter of the 5th century. Londinium was probably abandoned in the second decade of the 5th century or soon after, by which time most Roman rural settlements in the region appear to have been long deserted. The walled circuit of the town and major Roman roads across the region were substantial enough to survive relatively intact, but these do not appear to have been maintained in the Early Saxon period. The significance of the few Celtic and Latin place-names is unclear, although they raise the possibility that isolated British communities survived into the Early Saxon period.

From the middle of the 5th century only Anglo-Saxon material culture (the occasional exotic import excepted) is evident in the archaeological record of the region. This would accord with documentary evidence, which suggests that by the 440s 'the Saxons were a major force in Britain' (Sims-Williams 1983, 12), and with the overwhelming dominance of English place-names in the region. How this cultural transformation came about is uncertain; either the indigenous population adopted Germanic culture wholesale or Anglo-Saxon settlers substantially replaced the British inhabitants of the region. On the face of it, the limited evidence seems to point to the latter, but more information is needed to resolve this question. Discussions and arguments concerning written sources and place-name evidence for this period are well rehearsed and are unlikely to provide fresh insights. Archaeological data, on the other hand, is steadily accumulating and offers the best hope of resolving the issues discussed here. The recovery of archaeological evidence for this period must be a priority. Particular emphasis should be placed on dating sites and their artefactual assemblages as accurately as possible by radiocarbon assay and other means of absolute dating. The recovery of environmental data to reconstruct the vegetational history of the region during this period should be another priority. This may provide information about changes in climate, the extent and nature of human interaction with the environment, the ratio of farmland to woodland and possibly population level. By these means light may at last be shed on London's 'Dark Age'.

Acknowledgements

The author is indebted to Lyn Blackmore, John Clark and Lesley Hannigan for commenting on the text, and is also grateful to Ron Humphrey formerly of AOC for information about the site at Edmonton.

1.8 After the Romans: was there a Saxon Southwark? *Tony Brown*

'Across the river Anglo-Saxon Southwark still seems oddly elusive' (Clark 2000, 218). This situation has arisen because the historical and archaeological sources about Saxon Southwark seem not to be in particularly good agreement; it is the purpose of this contribution, after a brief look at the immediate post-Roman phases, to attempt reconciliation.

The 4th century saw a gradual reduction in the intensity of occupation in Roman Southwark, with the concentration of activity, particularly metal-working, in a zone around the bridgehead (Hammer 2003; Cowan 2003). Excavations along the eastern side of the northern island at Hunt's House (HHO97) have shown that fields were laid out in the 5th century; there was also the large-scale dumping of earth and building materials to maintain as much dry land as possible in the face of water levels which had been rising since *c* AD 350. This material could well have been derived from the robbing of disused buildings close by (another robbing phase began in the late Saxon period), and deposits associated with it produced a little pottery of 5th- to 6th-century date. This phase of very late activity, perhaps animal husbandry, came to an end when the rising water flooded the area. Drainage only began again in the 14th century (Taylor-Wilson 2002). The pattern of the medieval or later reclamation of land that had been occupied during the Roman period has been repeatedly seen in numerous archaeological excavations in Southwark (in addition to the above, Cowan 1992, 76, and many sites in LAARC archive). Also commonly found are layers of 'dark earth', a type of deposit which can form at any time in an area left open to the elements and which is now understood to be the result of the decay and intermixture of building materials, domestic and industrial rubbish, and organic materials of all kinds (Macphail 2003). What it means at Southwark is dereliction.

There are a few items of the 6th and 7th centuries, for example a coin of Justinian of AD 537 from King's Head Yard, and a gold thrysma from the foreshore between Southwark and Blackfriars Bridges, but these are casual losses, not indicators of actual occupation (MoLAS 2000, 187; Watson *et al* 2001, 56). However, given the position of the northern-most of the Southwark islands as the land on the south bank closest to London, it might be considered odd if it had not retained some significance as a route for anyone from Surrey, Sussex or Kent who wanted to get to the old walled area or indeed the trading centre of Lundenwic, even if a ford at Lambeth was now favoured (Watson *et al* 2001, 52). Clearly the 'public way' referred to in the boundary clause of a Chertsey charter of the sub-king Frithuwald of AD 672–74 cannot have been south of

the Thames given the location of the 'the port of London where ships come to land' along the Strand; this road might have been what is now Oxford Street considering the size of the grant and a comparison with the bounds of a much smaller estate granted to Westminster Abbey by Edgar in AD 959 (Gelling 1953; Dyson 1980; Blackmore 1997). Just when Roman London Bridge ceased to exist is unknown; on the evidence of the date-range of coins thrown off it as offerings a date as early as *c* AD 330–48 has been suggested but the coins from the approach road on the Southwark side go down to the 370s at least (Watson *et al* 2001, 36; Drummond-Murray *et al* 2002, 144). The well-built bridge piers would have survived, but cannot have represented an impediment to traffic up the river when Lundenwic flourished in the 7th to 9th centuries.

There could therefore have been a ferry from Southwark to the north bank. The legend of a ferry and the subsequent foundation of a nunnery (picked up by John Stow from Bartholomew Linstead, the last Prior of St Mary's) lacks substance, as Stow's contemporary and friend William Lambarde thought (Stow 1908, **1**, 21; **2**, 56, 273); it does not figure in *The Annals of Southwark* (Tyson 1925). But there is a suggestion in the plan of Southwark that at an early date a north–south route did exist across the islands. In general the main medieval approach roads to and through Southwark did not follow their Roman predecessors exactly; in places dark earth covered the road leading to the Roman bridge. The medieval road does not make for London Bridge directly; it gets to the bridge by having to turn slightly to the north-east at a point south of the site of St Margaret's church and what could have been its original course continues almost due north, with its apparent destination St Mary Overy dock, which in the 17th and 18th centuries was longer than it is now (Yule 2005, 10). Could this have been the starting point for a ferry? What does look likely is that whatever importance this road had pre-dated the full development of the High Street. It is possible to suggest this because properties that were set at right-angles to the High Street extended towards the north-west in a way that distorted the line of the dock approach road (Fig 1.8.1).

Southwark's revival is usually thought of as beginning with the creation of a *burh* or fortification during the campaigns of King Alfred against Viking war bands during the later 9th century. The evidence for this comes from the Burghal Hidage, a document of (probably) the earlier years of Alfred's son and successor Edward the Elder, which lists 31 such forts in Wessex, with the hidage assessments for the maintenance of each of them (Rumble 1996). One version of this document has a calculation

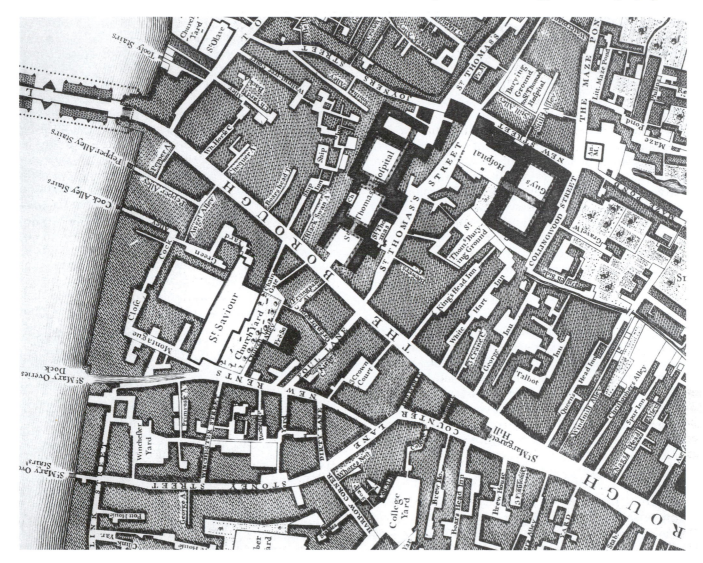

Fig 1.8.1 Extract from John Rocque's map of 1746 to show how the medieval High Street ('The Borough') veers to the north-east at St Margaret's Hill to get to London Bridge. Counter Lane and New Rents share the same alignment towards St Mary Overy dock, but this is interrupted by a block of buildings (Crown Court) with a frontage on the High Street

which explains how the hidages were related to the length of the defensive circuit of each fort, at the rate of four hides per pole of 16ft 6in (5.3m). The list is systematically arranged; it begins on the south coast, works its way westwards to Devon, turns eastward and ends, after Eashing in Surrey, with *Suthringageweorche*. Since the days of the great historian F W Maitland (1897) this, which means 'the defensive work of the men of Surrey,' has been taken to refer to Southwark (Dodgson 1996). The number of hides assigned to it is 1800, giving a circuit of 7425 feet (2263m); only Winchester and Wallingford had longer ones. No trace of this important fortification has yet been found.

The significance of this entry requires some appreciation of what the Viking threat was in the lower Thames area in the AD 880s. The attacks had drawn the kingdoms of Wessex and Mercia together and numismatic evidence suggests that at various times Alfred may actually have controlled London, for many years a Mercian centre. The Danish army,

which now occupied East Anglia, had for a time been neutralised by Alfred's victory at Edington in AD 878, but another apparently independent group arrived in AD 879 and set up a base at Fulham; there was no London Bridge to stop them. This band left for Ghent in AD 880, but in AD 883 there seems to have been further fighting involving something which in certain versions of *The Anglo-Saxon Chronicle* sounds like a siege ('the English encamped against the Danes at London') (Keynes 1998, 21–2; Keene 2003, 241–2). In AD 885 a portion of the Fulham group returned to attack Rochester, this time helped by the East Anglians. Alfred drove them off, but it would have been the sense of the possibility of further trouble in the south-east which in AD 886, according to his biographer Asser, made Alfred 'restore the city of London splendidly – after so many towns had been burned and so many people slaughtered – and make it habitable again; he entrusted it to the care of Aethelred, ealdorman of the Mercians' (Keynes and Lapidge 1983, 97–8). In his

Latin translation of the *Anglo-Saxon Chronicle*, produced almost a century later, Aethelred's role is explained by Aethelweard as being 'to guard the citadel after the ranks of the garrison had been strengthened' (Dyson 1990, 99).

The dominant factors in Alfred's actions were military, and specifically the maintenance of security, without which nothing, including the development of trade and certainly habitability, would have been possible. In military terms Alfred's initiative paid off; the *burhware* (garrison) of London successfully attacked the fort set up by another manifestation of the Fulham Vikings at Benfleet in AD 894 (but failed near Hertford in 896) (Swanton 1996, 86, 89).

But what did 'restoration' actually mean? The repair of the walls and gates, including the 3rd-century riverside wall, can reasonably be assumed. But for an idea of what else Alfred may well have done we have to turn to what was happening at the same time in the Frankish Empire. In AD 885 the Fulham Vikings, having sacked Rouen, made their way up the Seine, only to find their passage blocked by the defences of Paris. The town itself lay on the Île de la Cité and was linked to the banks by a pair of fortified bridges, which prevented the Vikings from moving their ships upstream. The result was an eleven-month siege beginning in November AD 885 during which the people of Paris endured numerous assaults, including an attempt to burn down the principal bridge by floating fireships against it and attacks by covered battering rams and missile-throwing engines. An account of the siege was written in flowery verse by an eye witness, Abbo, a monk of the Abbey of St Germain des Pres. It seems clear from his account that the defences were relatively simple. Each bridge had a tower (*turris*) at the end of it, with a ditch in front. The latter would, one imagines, normally have been considered encumbrances to traffic and were quite possibly temporary features in anticipation of an attack, since we know that the defenders of Paris, Odo, count of Paris and its bishop Gozelin, were forewarned enough to be able to make preparations. The towers, like the superstructure of the bridges, were of wood; after the initial assault the Parisians were able to more or less double in a night the height of the tower at the end of the *Grand Pont* (where the *Pont au Change* now is), and when the central section of the *Petit Pont* leading to the south bank was carried away by the river, isolating its tower, the Vikings set fire to it and killed the dozen men of the garrison when they tried to escape (Boyer 1976; *Annales Vedastini*; Pavels 1984). Now Alfred would certainly have known about the siege of Paris. It is referred to by Asser (Keynes and Lapidge 1983, 97) and the movements of this particular force of Vikings is followed with great assiduity in the *Anglo-Saxon Chronicle* (Swanton 1996, 81–3); it may indeed have been the case that the events at Paris prompted his occupation of London at that particular time because they made abundantly clear

how effective river defences could be. It can therefore be suggested that an essential element of Alfred's restoration of London would have been a new London Bridge.

There is no historical evidence that stands in the way of the notion of an Alfredian bridge. The raid of the Danes 'up along the Thames until they reached the Severn' in AD 894 was a horsed affair along the Thames Valley, not involving ships. The *Anglo-Saxon Chronicle* makes it clear that one of the components of this force arrived from Boulogne with its horses in AD 893; they went through the Weald 'in gangs and mounted groups' in AD 894 and ended by eating most of their animals when besieged at Buttington later in the year (Swanton 1996, 84–7). There is nothing to suggest that this force penetrated the defences of Wessex. It is quite possible that the existence of London Bridge forced the Vikings to take their ships (necessary if they were to establish another base) up the Lea in AD 896 (Hassall and Hill 1970).

It is during the reign of Aethelred II that the first specific references to London Bridge are to be found in historical sources. The *Chronicle* shows how London stood out as the one fortified town the Danes could not take, unlike Wallingford, Oxford, Exeter, Watchet and other places that had figured in the Burghal Hidage. In AD 993 Olaf Tryggvason and Swein 'came to London town with 94 ships and ... wanted to set it on fire, but there they suffered more harm and injury than they ever imagined that any town dwellers would do to them'. In 1009 the *Chronicle* recorded that despite frequent attacks, London stood 'sound, and (the Danes) always fared badly there'. In 1016 they 'besieged the town, and attacked it fiercely both by water and by land, but the Almighty God rescued it' (Swanton 1996, 127–9, 139, 149–50). Anyone who managed to get past the bridge, either by digging a channel around its southern end (Cnut in 1016) or by skilfully managing the tides (Godwine in 1052), was considered to have achieved something remarkable.

There is no archaeological evidence for Alfred's bridge. The earliest structural timbers recovered from the southern abutment area of the medieval bridge, two pieces of oak cut from the same tree, from respectively a foreshore fluvial deposit and reused in the foundations of the medieval bridge, have felling dates *c* AD 987–1032. There is abundant evidence for determined attempts to stabilise the south bank upstream of the bridge with wooden revetments from *c* 1000, which is in accord with statements in the *Anglo-Saxon Chronicle* about damaging tides at this time (Watson *et al* 2001). But Alfred might have been able to make use of the surviving piers of the old Roman bridge, as one might expect given Asser's emphasis on restoration; it was a Roman city that was being re-established. It is possible that these proved unable to withstand the erosive force of tides and river, particularly on the south where the erosion was greatest, and the southern abutment of the bridge was relocated 40m to the east in the late 10th century.

If this is accepted, then the implications for late Saxon Southwark are considerable. The southern defences of Alfred's bridge, as those of its immediate successors, could have been simply a wooden version of the stone ones put up by Peter of Colechurch between *c* 1176 and 1209 and a large defended enclosure as apparently required by the Burghal Hidage need not be expected. London and Southwark together need not therefore be thought of as an Alfredian double *burh*, as is sometimes the case (Peddie 1999). In origin these defences were not like the fortified bridges built by the Emperor Charles the Bald during the period AD 862–*c* AD 877 to block the Seine and Loire (Coupland 1991). The best known of these, *Pont de l'Arche* near Rouen, had a fortified enclosure (*castellum*) at each end. The earthworks of the northernmost of these, *Le Fort*, survive and show that it had an internal area of about 6 ha. But this bridge was not attached to a town, lying instead in the countryside near the palace (*villa*) of Pitres; not only were workmen specially drafted in to build it, but they were to be settled there to act as a garrison of military colonists (Gillmor 1989; 1997). The double *burhs* of Edward the Elder were also different, since unlike London they formed part of an offensive strategy involving the establishment of garrisons close to or within potentially hostile territory. The one example of which anything remains, Bedford, consisted of a semi-circular enclosure of 12ha to the south of an earlier rectangular enclosure.

It is therefore possible to read the Burghal Hidage entry for Southwark in a different way. *Suthringageweorche* is unique in that it is not the name of a specific place. Also *geweorche* does not have to mean 'defensive' or 'military' work; it can signify 'work' in the sense of 'labour' or 'doing'. Thus the heading of the early 11th-century document which sets out in detail the obligations of the various estates of the lathe of Aylesford for the maintenance of the bridge at Rochester ('This is the labour-service (*geweorc*) for the bridge at Rochester') is probably a better guide to the real significance of our Burghal Hidage entry (Brooks 2000, 232). This is what the Burghal Hidage could have meant in relation to Surrey; it was a statement of the number of hides from which bridgework could be demanded for London. It is not a coincidence that the number of hides in Surrey set out in Domesday Book before various relatively recent reductions was 1800, the same as the *Suthringageweorche* figure. In this regard Surrey resembled Cheshire, which at the time of Domesday had to provide one man from every hide for the repair of the city wall and bridge (Morgan 1978, 262).

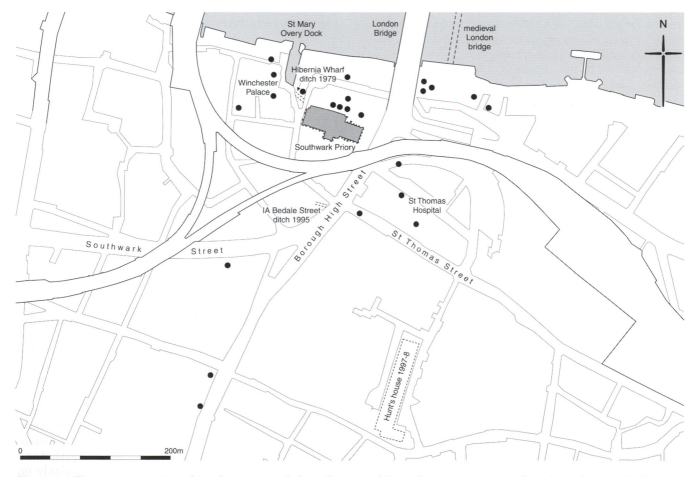

Fig 1.8.2 Features mentioned in the text, and distribution of Late Saxon pottery in Southwark, mainly Late Saxon Shelly Ware, used during the period c 850–1050 (Sources: LAARC summaries, summaries in Medieval Archaeology *and* London Archaeologist*)*

The place-name Southwark, the 'south work' in relation to London Bridge, first appears on coins in the reign of Aethelred II; there was a mint from some point in the period *c* AD 988–97 (Gover *et al* 1934, 29–30; North 1963, 116; Metcalf 1978, 161). Now the area on the south side of the bridge was participating in the economic expansion well attested archaeologically in London itself *c* 1000, where there is evidence for the construction of waterfront facilities downstream of the bridge, the creation of more streets, the expansion of the built-up area and increased foreign trade (Keene 2000, 190–3). The results of this at Southwark can be seen in Domesday: there was a minster (*monasterium,* now the Cathedral), a dock (*acque fluctum,* St Mary Overy dock), a trading shore (*strand*), and at least 51 tenements belonging to manors in Surrey; also quite probably a market attached to the *monasterium* (Carlin 1996, 201). So an appropriate name would have been required for this new and developing London suburb.

But did this settlement have defences? During excavations at Hibernia Wharf in 1979 a length of ditch 4m wide, dated to the late 10th or early 11th century, was found running from St Mary Overy dock towards the Cathedral (Fig 1.8.2) (HIB79; Webster and Cherry 1980, 228); it contained a remarkable ship's paddle blade. This ditch has not been traced further to the east, but the possibility has to be considered that it had formed part of a ditch in front of the southern end of the bridge. The existence of defences, perhaps temporary ones, is clearly set out in the account (perhaps exaggerated) of the attack on London Bridge by Aethelred II's commander Olaf in 1014: 'on the other side of the river there was a great market town called Southwark and there the Danes had a great host

fitted out; they had dug dykes and within they had set up a wall of trees and stones and turf' (Carlin 1996, 14; Hagland and Watson 2005). No indication is given of how close to the bridge these defences were. Later on, during a period of civil war in Henry III's reign, there were evidently temporary fortifications: in 1266 'all the fortifications, the barbican and the covered way, which had been made around Suwerk his lordship the king caused to be destroyed and levelled, even so, that the place where they were is no longer to be seen' (Riley 1863, 100). There are references to ditches made in time of war in the cartulary of St Thomas's Hospital at about this time (Riley 1863, 100; Drucker 1932, 29). Perhaps the medieval ditch 8m wide running north-west/south-east found at 1A Bedale Street in 1985 (255BS85; Youngs *et al* 1986, 143) could belong to this episode. Yet when the army of Duke William arrived in 1066 it apparently had no difficulty in burning Southwark; it was London Bridge itself that prevented it from crossing the Thames (Mills 1996). Maybe Southwark was provided with defences when they were required and when there was sufficient organisation and will to set them up.

In any event, the search for defences at Southwark should go on, but not for those of a large Alfredian *burh*.

Acknowledgements

For help with information, to David Bird, Surrey County Council; Emily Brants, Surrey SMR Officer; Chris Chandler and Liz Gawith, NMR; Barry Taylor, Greater London Historic Buildings SMR; John Mills, West Sussex County Council; Cath Maloney, LAARC.

2 Landscape, environment and hinterland

Modern coppice in Sussex (photo: Jane Sidell)

Introduction *Jonathan Cotton*

The papers within this section touch on a wide range of issues connected with the landscape, environment and overall setting of Roman Londinium. Given the broad remit, it is no surprise that there are a number of Framework objectives relevant to these topics contained within the *Research Framework for London Archaeology* (Nixon *et al* 2002), as follows:

R2 Framework objectives
- Defining the relationships between the landscape, river and settlement;
- Studying the impact of settlement on the environment.

R3 Framework objectives
- Further refining our understanding of the foundation of London, and the functioning and management of the countryside up to and during the period of the Boudican revolt;
- Elucidating the relationship of the central core to nucleated settlements and villas, or agricultural settlements; did people gradually drift into the roadside settlements and the city itself?

R4 Framework objective
- Analysing the nature and reasons for the evolution of the road system, river crossings and internal street layouts and their importance as engines of development and change.

R8 Framework objective
- Identifying regional models for studying population size and character of roadside settlements.

R10 Framework objective
- Refining our understanding of the ... extramural evidence of defensive or military structures.

R13 Framework objective
- Investigating the relationship between the urban centre, its hinterland and other settlements in the supply of raw materials, using consumption as a key indicator.

As such, the *Research Framework* recognises the growing awareness of an holistic approach to the study of Londinium. Following the earlier leads provided by Harvey Sheldon and Laura Schaaf (1978) and Ralph Merrifield (1983, 115–39), it is now no longer enough to study the town in isolation from the countryside that surrounded it, and which helped sustain it through the provision of produce and people. The importance of the hinterland can be expected to come still more significantly into focus in the next few years as the campaigns of fieldwork conducted on the gravels east, west and south of the capital are published.

This also comes across clearly in a number of the contributions in this section, but most especially in those of Jane Sidell and Ian Tyers. Both rightly draw attention to the nature of the later prehistoric landscape into which Londinium was inserted, while the latter's paper also provides an objective independent chronology for the founding and subsequent development of the town. Carrie Cowan and Peter Hinton's joint paper offers a pioneering attempt to identify evidence for the direct transposition of the countryside into the town in the form of garden cultivation.

Along with the quays and wharfs of the riverside the road network was clearly a vital component of the infrastructure that served Londinium. Much work in recent years has been conducted on the various routes that radiated away from the town, and Gary Brown provides a detailed glimpse of the archaeological evidence that his team, and others, have adduced for the major road that linked London with Colchester. This road theme underpins two other contributions: that of Martin Dearne, who rounds up information relating to the small roadside settlement at Enfield on Roman Watling Street (north); and Chris Thomas, who provides a similar assessment of the evidence on and around Thorney Island, Westminster.

The final papers in this section deal with the siting and military potential of two much-debated sites: David Bird re-examines the stone building at Shadwell and finds a military (as opposed to a funerary) function compelling; while Colin Bowlt reassesses the alignment, function and dating of the Middlesex Grim's Dyke earthwork and follows Wheeler in reasserting a Saxon origin. It is clear that both sites will repay further study: Grim's Dyke in particular finds a place in the prehistoric, Roman and Saxon chapters of the *Research Framework*, for instance!

2.1 Londinium's landscape *Jane Sidell*

Introduction

This paper endeavours to draw together some of the information regarding palaeoecology and human influence at the Iron Age/Romano-British transition in the London region. An often overlooked question, because of its simplicity, is *'what did the landscape look like?'* There need be no scholarly embarrassment at posing such a simple question: transitional periods between different cultures and social systems are moments fraught with interest. At these moments in time, basic questions can have great validity. From knowing *what?*, one can hope to move on to the *how?* and finally *why?*

Could there have been ecological, hydrological or geomorphological reasons for the positioning of Londinium, or was it chosen for its position on an apparently blank canvas of encircling Iron Age tribal zones? Did the new population undertake significant modification to tame the landscape? Were new plants introduced?

Unfortunately, information on these points is scarce; the majority languishes in grey literature, unused and unsynthesised. Botanical remains are notoriously fragile, and often overlooked by archaeologists who naturally enough are more enraptured by artefacts and structural remains. Yet without landscape context, we would be interpreting the creation of the city in a lifeless and colourless void, so the effort is worth making and indeed is highlighted in the *Research Framework*, under Roman theme R2: *defining the relationships between landscape, river and environment and examining the impact of settlement upon the landscape* (Nixon *et al* 2002, 31). Further research objectives relevant to this paper come under the theme of Topography and Landscape, specifically: to synthesise evidence of ancient woodland (Nixon *et al* 2002, 79).

Vegetation cover – outer London

Evidence for the Late Iron Age is in short supply in London; sites are difficult to date accurately, are rare anyway and often situated on gravel, which is not conducive to the preservation of botanical remains. West Heath, Hampstead, is a rare example in the north, where the pollen spectrum assigned to the Iron Age shows an increase in tree pollen suggesting some woodland regeneration from earlier deforestation and a contraction of the heathland (Greig 1992), perhaps resulting from earlier overgrazing.

To the west, more sites exist, and show evidence of a farmed landscape, which was largely (but not entirely) cleared of deciduous woodland cover in the Neolithic and Bronze Age. Grassland and arable cultivation dominate the vegetation cover, with evidence for the cultivation of emmer or spelt wheat at Stockley Park (SPD85; Nick Elsden and Dominique de Moulins pers comm). Mayfield Farm (MFEB88) and Holloway Lane (HL81) also have Late Iron Age farming settlements, growing barley, spelt and emmer wheat. Farming persists at these sites into the Roman period (Elsden and Giorgi pers comm). Wall Garden Farm also has an early Romano-British farming settlement, growing einkorn (generally considered to be an imported item; Gill Campbell pers comm), barley and wheat. There is also Roman evidence for presumably relatively local woodland stands, including oak coppice, as shown in the rungs of an oak ladder found in a well (WGF79; MoLAS 2000, 124; Fig 2.1.1), although this could have been transported from some distance. The same context contained ash and alder wood, and may indicate deciduous woodland nearby, possibly being managed from the farmsteads, perhaps for their own use and also for selling onto the city.

Tentative pollen evidence from Chelsea also shows this combination of open grassland with some

Fig 2.1.1 An oak ladder with coppiced rungs emerges from a Roman waterhole or gravel quarry at Wall Garden Farm, Sipson (WGF79) in west London

oak-dominated woodland in the Iron Age/Romano-British period (Scaife 2001a). Moving further east, at St Mary Abbot's Hospital, Kensington, another transitional site, shows arable cultivation through the plant macrofossil evidence with barley and oat (MAK94; Howe 1998). Similarly, to the south, at Beddington, the Late Iron Age enclosure and settlement has provided charred grains of wheat. Cultivation seems to extend into the Early Roman period to include barley and oats, potentially for animal fodder (BSF87; de Moulins 2005, 103–4).

Staying south of the river, in Wandsworth, pollen studies have shown a combination again of woodland and wet grassland. In the Roman levels from the Arndale Centre (Scaife no date) wet sedge and grassland, and pine, oak and hazel reflect local cover, subsequently denuded, whilst cereal-type pollen may reflect local arable cultivation. Close by at Point Pleasant (Scaife 1998) pollen from the Roman levels shows local woodland, grassland and also saltmarsh. Cereal-type pollen is again present, as well as rye which may provide firmer evidence of arable cultivation.

To the east, pollen analysis of several sites shows both Iron Age grassland and woodland, for instance White Hart Triangle, Thamesmead (Scaife 2003c), and Silvertown (Wilkinson *et al* 2000). They also show local marshland components, particularly alder carr (Fig 2.1.2) and saltmarsh. This is fairly ubiquitous in the early Iron Age before the floodplain becomes submerged under estuarine muds (Sidell 2003).

A rare record from south-east London comes from Caesar's Camp, Keston – with evidence for Iron Age woodland cover, including oak, hazel, birch and holly but also clear evidence for local arable cultivation (Piercey Fox 1969). There is also, of course, the five-acre wood Verlucionium in the canton of the Cantiaci, which was the subject of an early 2nd-century dispute recorded on a wooden writing tablet from Throgmorton Avenue (TRM86; Tomlin 1996).

Vegetation cover – the City, Southwark and Westminster

The city

Preservation of suitable deposits in the city itself is rare. However, Iron Age deposits in the Walbrook

Fig 2.1.2 Modern alder carr, Scotland; environment of a type common along the margins of the Thames in the early Iron Age (photo: Jane Sidell)

Valley indicate that the Walbrook ran clean and clear, but not particularly fast (de Moulins 1990, 89) with marshy vegetation on the riverbanks. Recent evidence from 1 Poultry provides more information about the pre-Roman Walbrook (ONE94; Scaife forthcoming). Alder, rush and sedges fringed the stream, with areas of bracken, rough grassland and some trees, including lime, oak and hazel, with rather less birch, elm, holly, willow and beech, presumably on and above the valley sides. There is also some evidence for pre-Roman arable cultivation in the vicinity. In the first few decades of Roman occupation, little had changed at the water's edge, but rubbish was being dumped in and beside the stream, notably cereal. Pollen evidence from below the Walbrook Mithraeum (Scaife 1982) and plant macro-fossil analysis from Broadgate (Jones 1986) confirm the picture of wet marshy fringes to the Walbrook with meadowland nearby (perhaps managed meadow to supply hay to the town), and limited tree cover in the hinterland which was further reduced following colonisation.

Mid- to Late Iron Age evidence from the waterfront at Suffolk House shows a marshy foreshore with alder carr, and pre-Roman deforestation in the hinterland (SUF94; Sidell 2001, 77). Similarly, Arthur Street (AUT01; Scaife 2003a) also has evidence for Iron Age oak and hazel woodland remaining following clearance (particularly of lime) in the Bronze Age. There is more evidence for wet sedge marshland, presumably close to the river edge, which expands in the Roman period.

Away from the waterfront, 1st-century pollen from Blossom's Inn (GHT00; Scaife 2004) shows the area to be largely denuded of tree cover, with grassland and some marsh present in the vicinity. Roman or earlier land surfaces at Fenchurch Street (FNE01; Scaife 2003b) show evidence largely of grassland, with some suggestions of arable cultivation, and only very limited tree cover, possibly isolated tree clumps, mainly oak and hazel with a little beech and alder.

Southwark

Coverage for Southwark is quite good: pollen from Joan Street (JOA91) and Union Street (UNS91) indicates low-lying marsh during the later Iron Age, with evidence for grassland and deciduous woodland presumably to the south (with arable cultivation, including oats) (Sidell *et al* 2000, 88, 117). Slightly further to the west, at Stamford House, Iron Age grassland with cereal type and rye were found, along with evidence for oak woodland and alder carr.

In eastern Southwark, several sites at the Bricklayers' Arms show Iron Age marsh again with alder carr (BLA87; Branch no date), grassland including cereal type and ribwort plantain, a more convincing piece of evidence for localised cultivation. Once again oak-dominated woodland (including lime) was present locally. Nearby Bramcote Grove (BEG92;

Thomas and Rackham 1996) has Iron Age alder carr bog with some oak woodland in the vicinity. Leroy Street (LYS01; Scaife 2001b) again confirms the Iron Age picture of north-east Southwark consisting of extensive marsh, including reedmace (*Typha*) with oak and lime woodland further from the river and localised cereal. Canada Water (CAW91; Sidell *et al* 2000, 96–97) shows deforestation in the vicinity, but on site, once again, boggy conditions in the Iron Age with sedge and rush swamp, but also evidence for cultivation, including rye and perhaps oats (Sidell *et al* 2000, 117). There is also evidence for woodland clearance carrying on into the Roman period, concurrent with arable cultivation, again including rye. By the Roman period at the Bricklayers' Arms and Leroy Street, woodland has also been reduced, with a continuation of grassland, but the addition of hemp and exotic species such as walnut (Scaife 2001b).

Recent work on Long Lane (LGM02; Allen *et al* 2005) has shown the later Iron Age environment to be a boggy channel side environment supporting some poor sedge fen adjacent to mudflats. Further from the river, wetland species such as meadowsweet and marsh marigold were growing, with alder and willow in the vicinity. The area dried out somewhat following the Roman incursion, with drier grassland and also some trees, mainly oak and hazel, as seen elsewhere.

To the south, at the Elephant and Castle, pollen in Roman deposits (Tyers 1988) confirms more woodland, including oak, ash and hazel. There is also evidence for cereal cultivation, and a marsh element, even this far south, including alder and iris.

In central Southwark, the evidence shows similarities with the outer margins, suggesting a reasonably consistent landscape in the later Iron Age. The Winchester Palace waterfront was marshy with sedge and rushes but also a bushy element, including apple/pear, elder and alder. Moving into the Early Roman period, burnt and dumped crop processing waste appears in the marsh, including wheat and barley, alongside exotic introductions such as fig (Giorgi 2005, 171–2). Similarly at the Courage Brewery, up to the end of the 1st century there are signs of a boggy water edge, again with dumped barley and spelt wheat (Davis 2003, 188). Early Roman 199 and 64–70 Borough High Street consisted of boggy, seasonally flooded grassland, and dumped cereal (199BHS74; 64BHS74; Tyers 1988, 458, 463). The Borough High Street group of sites recently excavated for the Jubilee Line (Drummond-Murray *et al* 2002) shows a similar pattern of pre-Roman scrub and marshy environment with some tree cover. The boggy note is maintained during the construction of the settlement, with the appearance of economic plants, presumably from the marketplace rather than cultivated (very little cereal chaff is present, and the non-cereal species are exotics), eg wheat, barley, oat, fig, lentil and stone pine. Cereal remains were also found at Hunt's

House (HHO97; Carruthers 2002, 61), but appear to represent the processing of spelt wheat, and it has been suggested that the assemblage may have been a by-product of malting.

Westminster

Only limited information is available for Westminster; at New Palace Yard (NPY73; Greig 1992), oak, lime and elm woodland was still present during the Late Iron Age along with marsh and scrub. From Cromwell Green (WCG78; Greig 1992), the Iron Age woodland is once again reflected in the pollen record, with oak, hazel, lime and pine but also alder carr, presumably reflecting Thames- and Tyburn-side marsh. Cereal-type pollen and ribwort plantain suggests cultivation of the landscape at this point. Hemp and hop were present but could have been growing wild. An unusual record comes from Storey's Gate (SGT94; Sidell *et al* 2000, 34), with fir in the Iron Age woodland alongside the more common oak, hazel, beech and holly. The fir pollen may be derived from long distance rather than being a true local component. There is also evidence here for arable cultivation (Sidell *et al* 2000, 34).

Less data exist for the Roman period, largely owing to a hiatus in the sedimentary sequence around Thorney Island between the Iron Age and medieval period. However, the area was taken into cultivation once again: at New Palace Yard, Greig (1992) found Roman (although not well dated) pollen indicative of a rising water table (similarly at St Stephen's East (PWC92; Sidell *et al* 2000, 115)) leading to freshwater swamp and less woodland relative to the Late Iron Age. Cereal was present, perhaps representing continuation of tradition from the earlier farming communities seen at Storey's Gate, or perhaps this was a new initiative associated with Londinium itself.

The introduction of exotic species

With a relatively limited taxonomic diversity in the new province of Britannia, what new plant species were imported (see Willcox 1977)? The evidence suggests imports were designed to increase diversity of basic foodstuffs with fruit, vegetables and nuts, and herbs and spices to add flavour. There is further evidence for new plant species being used for novel decorative and ritual purposes, some new, some native species, such as stone pine and box; leaves of the latter were found in Copthall Avenue (OPT81; Armitage *et al* 1983; Fig 2.1.3). This brief summary cleaves to the Early Roman evidence to continue the theme of what plants early Londoners would have seen in the markets rather than growing native.

Fruit was imported in quantity, presumably dried or otherwise preserved. Fig is present extensively across London, including Early Roman levels in Southwark (Tyers 1988), New Fresh Wharf (NFW74;

Fig 2.1.3 Box leaves, of the sort shown here, have been found at Copthall Avenue (OPT81) in the city (photo: Jane Sidell)

Willcox 1977) and early 2nd-century levels at Suffolk House (Gray-Rees 2001, 111). Grapes or raisins are also seen extensively across Londinium, with early examples from Southwark (Tyers 1988) and New Fresh Wharf (Willcox 1977). Mulberry has been found in 1st-century levels at the Triangle (TR74) and New Fresh Wharf (Willcox 1977; Campbell and Hall 2004), and possibly was grown here, unlike pomegranate, found in a Boudican fire horizon at 1 Poultry (Davis forthcoming a) and likely to have been imported in preserved form. Date, presumably dried, has been found from a 1st- to 2nd-century *bustum* burial in Southwark (GDV96; Giorgi 2000, 65; Bateman, this volume). Cucumber has been recovered from the 2nd-century deposits in Southwark and the city waterfront (Willcox 1977) and olive also from the 2nd-century city waterfront (Gray-Rees 2001, 111) and elsewhere in London (Tomlinson and Hall 1996).

Herbs and spices include coriander from 1st-century 64–70 Borough High Street (Tyers 1988), the Triangle, New Fresh Wharf (Willcox 1977) and Watling Court (WAT78; Armitage *et al* 1983), and also 2nd-century Suffolk House (Gray-Rees 2001, 111). Black cumin has been found in 1st-century levels at 1 Poultry (Davis forthcoming a) and black pepper is present in the eastern Roman cemetery, but poorly dated (Davis and de Moulins 2000). Dill was found in early levels in Southwark (Giorgi 2005, 171–2) and the Triangle (Willcox 1977), with fennel at 1st-century 64–70 Borough High Street (Tyers 1988).

Several species of nut were imported; walnut is also thought to have been cultivated, as pollen has been found as well as shell fragments. Sites include Suffolk House, the Walbrook Mithraeum and 1 Poultry (Scaife forthcoming; Tomlinson and Hall 1996). Almond was recovered from the *bustum* burial in Southwark (Giorgi 2000, 12; Bateman, this volume). A waterlogged post of sweet chestnut has also been found, in London Wall (Nayling 1991; Smith 2002), suggesting the tree might well have been growing locally.

Imports of more staple items include spelt wheat, einkorn and lentil from the Boudican fire horizons in the Forum (the spelt here is thought to be imported although it is present earlier in Britain; see Straker 1984). Other cereals stored in the Forum (but not necessarily imported) included wheat, barley, oats and rye (Armitage *et al* 1983; MoLAS 2000, 153). Lentils were also found in graves in the eastern cemetery (Davis and de Moulins 2000, 369) and so are considered to have a ritual significance as well as a culinary one. This is also the case with stone pine: whole cones have been found at 1 Poultry, Regis House (KWS94) and the Walbrook Mithraeum (Scaife forthcoming; Brigham *et al* 1996; Brigham and Watson 1996; Scaife 1982). The wood has been found at the amphitheatre (Bateman 2000, 36), whilst the pine nuts were found in 1st-century levels at New Fresh Wharf (Armitage *et al* 1983) and in the *bustum* burial in Southwark (Giorgi 2000, 12; Bateman, this volume).

The river

The Thames has an enduring centrality to London and Londoners that is manifested in many ways: from the riverside camps of the hunter-foragers, the deposition of Bronze Age metalwork (York 2002) through to the current use for New Year and Diwali festivals (Burdon 2004). Yet, the ancient river was very different to the canal we see today, so, what is known of the river in the Late Iron Age and did this change with the advent of the Roman city?

By the Late Bronze Age the Thames was tidal beyond Thorney Island (Sidell *et al* 2000, 110). However, the microfossil record in Westminster and Southwark shows that the tidal signal declines, and it would appear that the location of the tidal head gradually shifted downstream throughout the Iron Age. At Union Street the microfossils indicate this was not uniform and that either storm surges or a reversal in the downstream progression of the tidal head occurred at *c* 900 cal BC (–0.72m OD) and *c* 1 AD (–0.45m OD) (Sidell *et al* 2000, 110).

There is only a very limited amount of useful Roman material in the floodplain outside central London. Summerton Way in Thamesmead (SWY97; Lakin *et al* 1999) is a useful indicator of apparently dropping and then rising river levels in that the stratigraphy demonstrates a transition from alder carr (*c* –1.6m OD) to freshwater muds (–0.7m OD) and then mid-Roman terrestrial deposits forming on the earlier foreshore, subsequently sealed by Late Roman estuarine muds at –0.4m OD. Further upstream at New Palace Yard, Westminster, mollusc samples show freshwater conditions (Evans no date), with indications of large flood events. Evans suggests that by the Roman period the influence of the tidal Thames was less than in the Late Iron Age, based on reconstruction of a still-water environment in which reed swamp was able to take hold. He suggests that this may have been due to a shift in the course of the river or to a drop in river levels, as seen further downstream (see below).

Roman data from the city and Southwark provide more precise indicators for the Thames levels. It is likely that the initial Roman constructions had been undertaken before detailed observations of the tidal problems were available, and that they were not always sited to best effect as a result. With the exception of the first quays, it should be safe to assume that the waterfront is generally situated at approximately highest astronomical tide (HAT) to minimise flooding of the working surface.

Southwark provides useful data owing to the low-lying nature of the eyots that were initially colonised by the Roman settlers. There are some issues caused by reclamation and river defences protecting areas below mean high water (MHW). In the Late Iron Age, river deposits had overtopped Fenning's Wharf (FW84), Topping's Wharf (TW70; Sheldon 1974), the Courage Brewery and Park Street (CO88; COSE84; Cowan 2003, 11) to above 1.0m OD and indeed much of north Southwark (Yule 1988). This appears to have been the level settled and reveted by the Romans, as much artefactual debris from the mid-1st century is present in the upper levels of the river silts, thought to have formed at HAT in the Late Iron Age (Watson *et al* 2001). This is also the case at Topping's Wharf (Sheldon 1974), where a gravel embankment reconstructed to possibly 2.0m OD was found on the AD 50–80 Roman foreshore (Watson *et al* 2001, 12). Furthermore, a series of early Roman roads were built at *c* 1.5m OD, crossing Southwark and heading for the bridgehead (Milne 1985, 81) with no signs of having been flooded. Other early revetments at 64–70 Borough High Street (Graham 1978) have been reconstructed up to 1.75m OD. Signs indicating a subsequent drop in river levels come from the Courage Brewery wooden warehouse, built over intertidal deposits in AD 152 at 0.5m OD, and thought to be below MHW (CO88; Brigham *et al* 1995; Fig 2.1.4).

The earliest evidence for the waterfront in the city is from Regis House (Brigham *et al* 1996), with a very rough revetment dating to AD 52 along a terrace between 2.0 and 2.5m OD. This was replaced shortly after spring AD 63 with a more robust quay with the upper surface at 1.6m OD. This quay is almost certainly related to the 1st-century quay from Pudding Lane, dated to AD 59–74 (probably AD 60–65) (PDN81; Bateman and Milne 1983).

Fig 2.1.4 The wooden warehouse at Courage Brewery, Southwark (CO88), under excavation

Another structure of this date comes from Billingsgate dating to AD 70–100 at 1.6m OD but is not thought to be quite complete. Foreshore samples collected in association with the Pudding Lane quay were rich in the brackish diatom *Cyclotella striata*, demonstrating the tidal nature of the 1st-century Thames (Bateman and Milne 1983). A second revetment at Billingsgate was built shortly after, between AD 100 and 125, 3m to the south. Again this did not survive to the full height, but it is notable that it is built significantly downslope of the first revetment with the base below OD whilst the base of the first revetment is at +0.5m OD. A third revetment was built between AD 125 and 160, 5m to the south with the base projected at -0.75m OD and the top at +1.5m OD. Similarly, the Regis House waterfront was rebuilt to the south in AD 102, again on a line with the AD 95–100 waterfront at Pudding Lane (Bateman and Milne 1983; Watson *et al* 2001, 31), but at a decreased height from the Neronian quay, at *c* 1.38m OD. Following the Hadrianic fire, the waterfront was once more moved south. This consistent southward movement and reduction in altitude strongly suggests that river levels were dropping and if the waterfront was to function, it had to be periodically relocated.

At Custom House (CUS73; Tatton-Brown 1974) Late Iron Age river levels were identified at > −1.5m OD. Limited environmental data indicate the Thames was fresh here in the Roman period, but this is not supported elsewhere (Bateman and Milne 1983; Wilkinson 1998). Two waterfronts were recovered: an early 2nd-century (AD 140–43; Fletcher 1982) revetment at below 0.5m OD and a later 2nd-century (probably AD 180–90) box structure, 6m to the south of the first quay. The later 2nd-century MHW is estimated to be at OD, with MLW below -1.6m OD (base of the box structure) on the basis of the quay heights (Fig 2.1.5).

Concluding thoughts

The information concerning landscape cover across London in the Late Iron Age is patchy, but provides a picture suggesting that woodland had certainly not been entirely cleared, and in fact was regenerating following large-scale clearance in the Middle Bronze Age. Woodland composition was dominated by oak and hazel, with ash, beech, birch and holly, and some lime and elm persisting. The evidence also shows a moderately swampy riverside beside

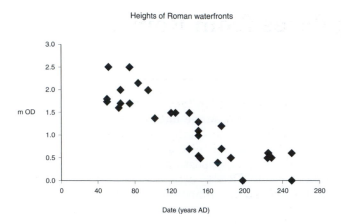

Fig 2.1.5 Heights of the Roman waterfronts, from Sidell 2003

the Thames and in the tributary valleys, with alder carr, sedges and rushes fringing the waterside. Open grassland was widely present, with arable cultivation, apparently of wheat, barley, oats and rye, occurring across the region. There may be issues associated with pollen taphonomy that could be making this seem more prominent than was the case; however, it seems possible that London was not as underused as has been previously thought. The pre-Roman city seems to have been lightly wooded, with grassland and local arable cultivation and marshy fringes to the tributary streams and the Thames itself. Fairly rapid clearance of trees occurred, as would be expected during new town construction, but the marshy fringes persisted in the valleys (apparently used as dumping grounds) and on the Southwark island margins. A wide range of food plants were imported following the Roman conquest, with exotic fruits, spices and nuts – some of which were cultivated locally.

The river was still tidal within the central area when Londinium was founded, but only weakly. It may well be that the position of the tidal head was viewed as the limit of navigation and one of the reasons for locating the town here; another may have been the relatively unforested environment needing only limited clearance before building. It was perhaps an unexpected consequence of placing the town that the waterfront required relocation on several occasions. On the south side, the marshy riverside was occupied but remained relatively natural for longer. Certainly revetments were constructed, but the picture seems to be of a more informal response to the changing Thames. This means that whilst the river was considerably built up on the north side, the south side was relatively unconstrained, and therefore would not have changed the river regime at all.

Whilst pointing out gaps in our knowledge, this takes us someway towards a clearer image of Londinium's landscape. Dating at this transitional period is poor – there are many more botanical reports that could be useful, if only tighter dating were available. The Late Iron Age could certainly bear closer scrutiny in terms of the amount of cereal cultivation potentially taking place. With regard to sites, the Fleet Valley is one source that should provide more data in future, along with the northern limits of the Roman city and Westminster.

Acknowledgements

Particular thanks go to James Rackham, Rob Scaife and Ian Tyers for all their assistance, past and present. To Jon Cotton, for giving me the opportunity to write this paper, to Gill Campbell, Dominique de Moulins, Yvonne Edwards, Nick Elsden, John Giorgi and Barry Taylor for providing me with information and assistance. And finally, to Harvey, for all the help, advice, tea and cake.

2.2 A gazetteer of tree-ring dates from Roman London   *Ian Tyers*

Introduction

In 1983 Harvey Sheldon and I wrote an article in *London Archaeologist* that listed tree-ring dates from Roman sites in Southwark (Sheldon and Tyers 1983). Two years earlier the tree-ring sequences from Roman London had been successfully linked to those from continental Europe. This had produced absolute dates for tree-ring chronologies from Roman sites in London, and indeed for the UK, for the first time (Fletcher 1981; Hillam and Morgan 1981). This linkage was a crucial step towards the production of a multi-millennial absolutely dated tree-ring chronology intended for radiocarbon calibration purposes, since the newly dated London Roman data itself dated Carlisle Roman data, which in its turn dated a long sequence of bog-oak data from Belfast. A combined chronology complete to 5289 BC was produced by 1984 (Pilcher *et al* 1984). Our 1983 article raised the total number of dated Roman oak timbers from London from 57 to 102, derived from a dozen sites. At the time of preparing this paper the total number of dated Roman oak timbers from London stood at 994 from 70 sites. The detailed evidence for the majority of these is of course as yet unpublished.

This paper therefore constitutes an attempt to provide a gazetteer (Table 2.2.1) of the dated Roman oak timbers from London, along with summary information about the dates of some of the structures from which it derives. This is combined with a brief discussion of the macro-characteristics of the dataset as a whole. Readers should refer to the *London Archaeological Gazetteer* volumes (Schofield and Maloney 1998; Thompson *et al* 1998), and on the London Archaeological Archive and Resource Centre (LAARC) online catalogue <http://www.museumoflondon.org.uk/laarc> for site summaries.

Overview

Datable Roman oak timbers have been excavated at 70 sites in London (Fig 2.2.1), whilst the LAARC lists *c* 5000 sites. It is thus self-evident that such material is far from being ubiquitous and is therefore a valuable though relatively rare resource. The sites include twelve that have each produced only a single datable timber, whilst at the other end of the scale seven have produced 40 or more datable Roman timbers. The chronological extents of the data are listed for each site as a composite, with the exception of the thirteen sites that produced non-contiguous tree-ring data for which both sequences are listed. The summary interpretation of the structures dated on the site is given; this

summary is simpler for the smaller sites, which often had only a single datable structure, than for some of the complex multi-structure sites. The level of detail provided is also to some extent still dependent on ongoing post-excavation or publication programmes. Due to taphonomic and preservation issues only some timbers are complete to bark-edge. Such material, where dated, produced interpretations that were precise to the felling year of the material. Dates of this type are given for all the sites from which such material was obtained. However the vast majority of the timbers dated do not have bark-edge and these, depending on whether sapwood is present produced either range dates, or *terminus post quem* dates. In Table 2.2.1 these are grouped together wherever it is appropriate and this ignores any material likely to be of the same date as timber of precisely known date. A number of results where poorly preserved timbers give *tpq* dates in the BC period are excluded.

The tree-ring data is of highly uneven chronological distribution. Timber is more likely to have survived in the lower and earlier Roman deposits, as these are more likely to have remained waterlogged. Higher and later timbers are obviously also more vulnerable to disturbance by later structures. Later Roman structural timber has rarely survived intact, and what has survived is primarily derived from sunken pile groups and wells. The overall effect is that the composite tree-ring data from London is heavily biased to the 1st and earlier 2nd centuries AD.

The source of the material

Figure 2.2.1 maps the 70 sites: 46 of these are located within the city of London, 20 within the Borough of Southwark, with one in Lambeth and three in Tower Hamlets (the entire area in Fig 2.2.1 is bounded by a rectangle *c* 4km by 2km). The larger individual assemblages come primarily from sites located along Upper and Lower Thames Streets and the western Walbrook. The London assemblage constitutes 59% of the dated Roman timbers from England and Wales; the only area which yielded a similar concentration of material is the pre-Hadrianic fort at Carlisle which has produced another 396 dated Roman oak timbers (a further 23.5% of the present total, in that instance derived from an area *c* 1km^2). The rest of the country combined has, so far, yielded a further 296 datable Roman timbers, over half of which are from further 1st-century sites in the northern frontier area. Such a disjointed distribution prevents any serious investigation of the movements of timbers into

Table 2.2.1 Dated Roman oak timbers from London

The summary interpretation is given as a single date if the timber or timbers retained bark-edge, with season given where known, or ? where bark edge uncertain. If there was some sapwood the summary interpretation of the timber or timbers is given as a range date, with ? where sapwood edge uncertain, all ranges calculated using 10–46 sapwood estimate. If the timber or timbers were entirely heartwood with no indication of sapwood the summary interpretation is given with *tpq*, these can be significantly earlier than the archaeological date of usage, calculated using 10 years minimum sapwood.

Site code	Site name	Analysed by	Date analysed	Number of dated timbers	Sequence dates	Summary interpretation	Major publication of site
	City of London						
ANT88	9–10 Angel Court EC2	Tyers	1988	1	AD 77–191	AD 191?	
AST87	22–25 Austin Friars EC2	Nayling	1990	4	142 BC–AD 68	AD 68–78	
AUT01	12 Arthur Street EC4	Tyers	2002	26	143 BC–AD 193	AD 54; AD 55; AD 61–97; AD 203 *tpq*	
BBH87	Billingsgate Bath House, 100 Lower Thames Street EC3	Hibberd	1992	5	66 BC–AD 47	AD 57 *tpq*	
BC75	Baynards House, Queen Victoria Street EC4	Morgan	c 1975	6	AD 140–249	AD 253–270	Morgan 1980a, 88–94
BGE98	288 Bishopsgate EC2 & E1	Tyers	1999	5	162 BC–AD 59	AD 69–105?	
BIG82	Billingsgate Lorry Park, Lower Thames Street EC3	Groves & Hillam	1986	12	AD 24–239	AD 188–217; AD 239–269	Hillam 1990, 164–70
BPL95	30–35 Botolph Lane EC3	Tyers	1999	1	AD 106–175	AD 176–212	
BUC87	DLR shaft, Bucklersbury EC4	Nayling & Tyers	1988–90	54	211 BC–AD 79; AD 165–225	AD 79; AD 235–271?	
CID90	72–80 Cheapside EC2/EC4	Tyers	1992	22	205 BC–AD 63	AD 52; AD 53; AD 60; AD 63	Hill and Woodger 1999
COV87	10–12 Copthall Ave EC2	Tyers	1988	2	AD 2–97	AD 107 *tpq*	
CUS73	Custom House, Lower Thames Street EC3	Fletcher	1973	1	130 BC–AD 48	AD 58 *tpq*	
DGH86	14–16 Dowgate Hill EC4	Tyers	1986	4	68 BC–AD 101	AD 47–83; AD 111–147	
GAG87	Guildhall Art Gallery, Guildhall Yard EC2	Tyers & Nayling	1988–2001	34	368 BC–AD 135; AD 181–242	AD 54; AD 89; AD 122–158; AD 252 *tpq* total of 18 structure groups	
GHT00	Blossom's Inn, 30 Gresham Street EC2	Crone & Tyers	2002	72	165 BC–AD 153	AD 69; AD 104; AD 153 total of 12 structure groups	
GM182	Blackfriars Wreck 1, Coffer Dam EC4	Tyers	1989	11	49 BC–AD 118	AD 128–164?	Tyers 1994, 204
GRL88	21–26 Garlick Hill EC4	Tyers	1988	6	16 BC–AD 138	AD 138–162	
GYE92	Guildhall Art Gallery, Guildhall Yard EC2	Tyers	1993–2001	58	282 BC–AD 139; AD 170–243	AD 70; AD 79; AD 88; AD 243; AD 103–135; AD 144–180 total of 20 structure groups	

Table 2.2.1 Continued

Site code	Site name	Analysed by	Date analysed	Number of dated timbers	Sequence dates	Summary interpretation	Major publication of site
ILA79	Miles Lane EC4	Hillam	1982	47	169 BC–AD 105	AD 48–84; AD 105–132; AD 55 *tpq*	
KEY83	15–35 Copthall Avenue EC2	Hillam	1987	1	72 BC–AD 59	AD 69 *tpq*	
KWS94	Regis House, 39–46 King William Street EC4	Tyers	1995–96	127	202 BC–AD 107	AD 52; AD 63; AD 68; AD 101; AD 117–153 multiple structures	
LOW88	52–63 London Wall & 20–56 Copthall Ave EC2	Nayling	1990	6	39 BC–AD 135	AD 145 *tpq*	
LYD88	Cannon Street Station, Upper Thames Street EC4	Hillam & Nayling	1989	10	136 BC–AD 64	AD 74–107	
MLK76	1–6 Milk Street EC2	Hillam	1980	1	90 BC–AD 15	AD 25 *tpq*	
MRG95	20–28 Moorgate EC2	Tyers	2001	4	105 BC–AD 64	AD 74 *tpq*	
NFW74 (SM75 FRE78)	2–6 Lower Thames Street EC3	Morgan & Hillam	1976–78	17	53 BC–AD 241	AD 209–235; AD 251 *tpq*	Hillam and Morgan 1986, 75–85
ONE94	1 Poultry EC2 & EC4	Tyers	1994–2000	96	307 BC–AD 290	AD 47; AD 48; AD 51; AD 55; AD 61; AD 77; AD 181; AD 225; AD 252; AD 112–148; AD 223–236; AD 302–334 total of 37 structure groups	
OPT81	2–3 Cross Keys Court, Copthall Avenue EC2	Hillam	1986	8	45 BC–AD 86	AD 86 *tpq*	
PDN81	11–11A Pudding Lane & 121–127 Lower Thames Street EC3	Hillam	1983	52	173 BC–AD 86	AD 59; AD 86	
PEN79	Peninsular House, 112–116 Lower Thames Street EC3	Hillam	1981	20	252 BC–AD 70	AD 80 *tpq*	
PET81	St Peter's Hill & 223–225 Upper Thames Street EC4	Hillam	1987	7	119 BC–AD 25; AD 191–294	AD 294 spring	Hillam 1993, 95–9
QUV01	Salvation Army, 99–101 Queen Victoria Street EC4	Tyers	2001–03	19	185 BC–AD 293	AD 165?; AD 293 spring; AD 294 spring; AD 205–232	
SH74	Seal House, 106–108 Upper Thames Street EC4	Morgan	?1976	3	73 BC–AD 171	AD 181 *tpq*	Hillam 1990, 164–70
SHI95	19 St Mary at Hill EC3	Tyers	1995	2	AD 55–174	AD 174	
SUF94	Suffolk House, 154–156 Upper Thames Street EC4	Boswijk	1996	18	170 BC–AD 128	AD 84 spring; AD 128;	Brigham and Woodger 2001
SUN86	Sunlight Wharf, Upper Thames Street EC4	Hillam	1987	7	AD 225–293	AD 90–112	Hillam 1993, 95–9
SWA81	Swan Lane, 95–103 Upper Thames Street EC4	Groves	1986	6	56 BC–AD 169	AD 293 winter; AD 179 *tpq*	Hillam 1990, 168–9
TEX88	Thames Exchange Buildings, 78 Upper Thames Street EC4	Nayling	1990	1	47 BC–AD 182	AD 192–228	

Table 2.2.1 Continued

Site code	Site name	Analysed by	Date analysed	Number of dated timbers	Sequence dates	Summary interpretation	Major publication of site
THY01	6–8 Tokenhouse Yard EC2	Tyers	2003	22	199 BC–AD 84	AD 85 spring; 6 other later 1st century structures	
TR74	101–110 Lower Thames Street EC3	Morgan	c 1974	2	107 BC–AD 14	AD 24 *tpq*	Morgan 1980b, 28–32
TST78	GPO Tunnel, Upper Thames Street EC4	Hillam	1981	11	159 BC–AD 39	AD 39–71	
UPT90	66–67 Upper Thames Street EC4	Nayling	1991	1	49 BC–AD 191	AD 191–222	
UTA87	Cannon Street Station, Upper Thames Street EC4	Nayling	1990	3	32 BC–AD 175	AD 169–189; AD 185 *tpq*	
VAL88	Blackfriars to Holborn Viaduct Stations EC4	Nayling, Tyers & Hibberd	1990–92	15	131 BC–AD 158	AD 116 winter; AD 74–94; AD 158–185	
VRY89	Vintry House, 68–9 Upper Thames Street EC4	Hibberd & Tyers	1991–94	4	49 BC–AD 197	AD 192?; AD 197?	
WAT78	Watling Court EC4	Hillam	1980	4	110 BC–AD 57	AD 60–96	
Lambeth							
GM450	County Hall Ship, Belvedere Road SE1	Tyers	1988–91	10	AD 95–277	AD 287 *tpq*	Tyers 1994, 205
Southwark							
120BHS89	120–124 Borough High Street SE1	Tyers	1989	1	45 BC–AD 34	AD 44–80?	
15SKS80	Calverts, 15–23 Southwark Street SE1	Tyers	1982	33	144 BC–AD 74	AD 72; AD 74; AD 60 *tpq*	
170BHS79	170–194 Borough High Street SE1	Tyers	1983	1	170 BC–39 BC	29 BC *tpq*	
179BHS89	179–191 Borough High Street SE1	Tyers	1990–97	10	109 BC–AD 47; AD 53–151	AD 120 winter; AD 151–187; AD 57 *tpq*	
2SSBS85	2 Southwark Street & 1A Bedale Street SE1	Tyers	1986	1	44 BC–AD 24	AD 34 *tpq*	
52SOS89	52–54 Southwark Street SE1	Tyers	1994	4	64 BC–AD 34	AD 44–65	
BHB00	117–136 Borough High Street SE1	Tyers	2003	2	180 BC–AD 58	AD 68 *tpq*	Cowan 2003
BTBHS91	BT shaft, Borough High Street SE1	Tyers	1991	6	118 BC–AD 38	AD 48–84	
CHWH83	Chamberlain's Wharf, Tooley Street SE1	Tyers	1983	4	AD 117–231	AD 231	
CO88	Courage Brewery, Park Street SE1	Tyers	1988–94	6	125 BC–34 BC; AD 60–152	AD 152 winter	Brigham *et al* 1995, 63–69
COSE84	Courage Brewery, Park Street SE1	Tyers	1984	9	52 BC–AD 39; AD 104–175	AD 49 *tpq*; AD 185 *tpq*	Cowan 2003
CSW85	Courage Brewery, Park Street SE1	Tyers	1985	1	100 BC–AD 86	AD 96 *tpq*;	Cowan 2003
FSS96	51–53 Southwark Street SE1	Nayling	1998	5	109 BC–AD 72	AD 72?; AD 78–114	
FW84	Fennings Wharf, 1 London Bridge SE1	Tyers	1984	4	19 BC–AD 122	AD 132 *tpq*	Tyers 2001, 180–5
GHL89	Guy's Hospital, St Thomas Street SE1	Tyers	1990–96	26	236 BC–AD 163; AD 173–241	AD 161/2; AD 241 winter	
HHO97	Hunt's House, Great Maze Pond, SE1	Tyers	1999	3	129 BC–AD 51	AD 61 *tpq*	Taylor-Wilson 2002
LGK99	5–27 Long Lane SE1	Tyers	2001	3	129 BC–AD 30	AD 40–53?	
RWG94	Redcross Way SE1	Tyers	1994	3	AD 33–121	AD 131 *tpq*	
TYT98	London Bridge City, Tooley Street SE1	Tyers	1999	4	AD 139–232	AD 211?; AD 232 spring	
WP83	Winchester Palace SE1	Tyers	1983	10	104 BC–AD 69	AD 69–89	Yule 2005
Tower Hamlets							
HGA02	172–176 The Highway, Shadwell E1	Tyers	2006	1	AD 175–232	AD 232–262	
TOC02	Tobacco Dock, 130–162 The Highway, Shadwell E1	Tyers	2006	3	AD 160–227	AD 228 spring	
TOL79–84	Tower of London, Tower Hamlets EC3	Hillam	1980	2	AD 166–241	AD 251–287	
[BGE98]	See above under City sites, but partly in Tower Hamlets]						

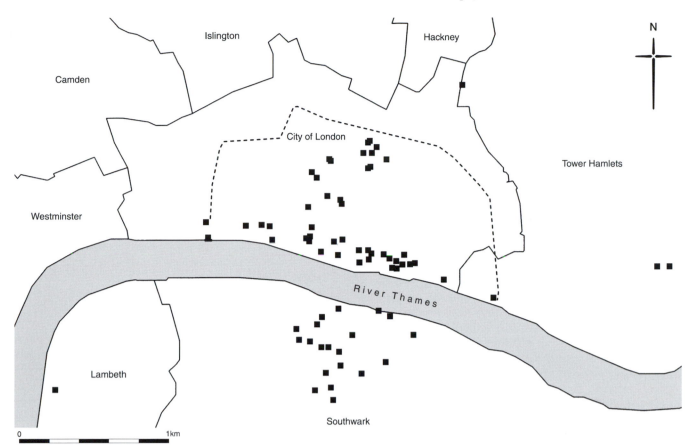

Fig 2.2.1 Location map of the 70 sites listed in Table 2.2.1, with the outline of Roman Londinium (dotted) and the modern boundaries of the City of London and encircling London boroughs

Londinium. At present there is no internal statistical evidence to suggest any one London site used timbers primarily sourced any significant distance from those used on any other site. This observation is not meant to imply that no imported timber was present in Londinium. There is evidence of the widespread presence of silver fir wood (*Abies alba*), which was used particularly in barrels and writing tablets, and this material was clearly imported since it grows naturally no nearer than eastern France, eastern Germany and Switzerland.

Earliest date for activity in Londinium

The ability of dendrochronological dating techniques to yield results of annual resolution clearly makes the technique applicable to the question of the date of the founding of Londinium. The favoured foundation date is *c* AD 50 in most modern reviews (for example Merrifield and Perring 1997). There have been a number of attempts to extract datable material from the Roman road under Borough High Street, in Southwark. However success here has been thwarted by the use of scrubby oaks and alders, presumably derived from the immediate vicinity. The 1 Poultry site (ONE94) produced the currently earliest Roman datable oak; one drain used a timber felled in the winter of AD 47/48, whilst another used a timber felled in the spring or

summer of AD 48. Whilst we can never entirely eliminate the possibility that these timbers are not reused in later structures, the presence of two samples felled in AD 47–48 on one site is evidence for some activity at this date in the vicinity. This material pushes back activity in London to within five years of the invasion in AD 43. The tree-ring evidence continues to support the notion that the founding of Londinium occurred during the governorship of Scapula (AD 47–52), although if this is correct it must be at the start of his period as governor. The earliest tree-ring evidence from Roman Britain is from a timber from a fortress on the Fosse Way that was felled in AD 43/44 (Sauer 2000).

Late material

The general paucity of later Roman waterlogged structural timber has resulted in a failure thus far to date any Roman structures later than the early 4th century. The 1 Poultry site also provides the current latest Roman tree-ring dated structure from London; a building there has a felling date range of AD 302–34. The latest precisely dated structure from London is the structure at Sunlight Wharf (SUN86), St Peter's Hill (PET81), and more recently the Salvation Army (QUV01) site where most material was felled in the spring of AD 294.

Landscape and economic implications

Although all of these timbers were used during the Roman era they provide some insights into the pre-Roman landscape. Consider a 200-year-old oak felled for the post-Boudican reconstruction, for example in late AD 63; the tree-ring sequence in such a tree would run from 137 BC–AD 63 inclusive, covering 20 years of the Roman period, and 180 years of the pre-Roman Iron Age. This results in significantly greater quantities of pre-Roman tree-ring data, rather than Roman tree-ring data, being obtained from most Roman sites.

There are a number of observations concerning this material that can be made. These appear most likely to reflect aspects of the landscape at the time of the Roman invasion, and may also eventually indicate changes in landscape and resource availability during the period of the Roman presence. Exploitation of a landscape inevitably changes the age composition of the standing woodland, and typically any opening up of a landscape produces trees that grow faster than hitherto. This response may imply that the frequency with which long-lived slower-growing trees are utilised in any period is likely to be higher if more of the landscape contained relatively unexploited woodland with dense canopies. The tree-ring data sets allow us to compare both the average or extreme ages of the trees used, and the average growth rates of different groups of timber utilised at different periods, and in different parts of the country. As an example of this we can consider the current oldest trees known to have been used in 1st-century AD structures in London and Carlisle. The chronology from Roman London includes only fourteen trees (that is just over 1% of the total) that started growing before 200 BC. This strongly contrasts with the assemblage from Carlisle, which has produced 40 (slightly over 10% of the total). In addition the average growth rate of the oldest London trees rises from *c* 1.0mm/year before *c* 200 BC to a figure of *c* 2.5mm/year by *c* 150 BC. In contrast the Carlisle trees continue to grow at *c* 1.0 mm/year until the later 1st century AD. This marked difference between the two areas perhaps hints that the form and content of the woodlands subsequently supplying Londinium had changed significantly during the early 2nd century BC. The extent of the hinterland required to supply Londinium with sufficient building timber and fuel for heating and cooking would have been determined by population size and the percentage of the landscape occupied by woodland as well as the form of the trees occupying those woodlands. Whilst the tree-ring evidence from Londinium is probably derived from a more restricted area than is the case for the medieval city, it is probably representative of a significant part of the lower Thames valley.

Conclusion

It is a quarter of a century since tree-ring analysis of Roman timbers from London began to produce absolute dates. During the intervening period a range of results from pre-Boudican to early 4th-century date have been obtained from 70 sites. This material provides primary dating evidence for the sites themselves, and allows us to address questions such as 'when was Londinium founded?'. In addition it has the potential to provide insights into the nature of the landscape of the Thames valley that the Romans found when they arrived, and subsequent changes to it. This potential has to be tempered by the fact that the excavated resource is but a small, and quite probably heavily biased, assemblage of the structural timber that was supplied to London over the succeeding centuries.

Acknowledgements

My thanks to Pete Rowsome for giving permission to utilise the results from MoLAS, DGLA, DUA, SLAEC, and Guildhall Museum excavation sites, and Frank Meddens for giving permission to utilise the results from PCA excavations. I thank the currently active specialists who have worked on London material; Gretel Boswijk, Anne Crone, Cathy Groves and Nigel Nayling for allowing me to summarise data in this paper.

2.3 The Roman garden in London
Carrie Cowan with Peter Hinton

Introduction

The Roman city of London has probably been excavated more extensively than any comparable urban centre of the Roman world (MoLAS 2000, 122). While over 450 gardens have been revealed at Pompeii, we have virtually no evidence for gardens in Londinium – ignorance that should be a matter of concern (Perring 2002, 179). In fact, the Roman garden does not even appear as a research priority in the recent *Research Framework for London Archaeology* (Nixon *et al* 2002, 29–44).

The main purpose of this survey is to provide a review of the archaeological information presently available in order to stimulate suggestions towards a research agenda for Roman garden archaeology in London.

The Roman garden

The possession of a garden was a status symbol. Gardens offered a representation of nature and greenery subject to Roman order, countryside brought tamed into the city (Farrar 1998, 189–90). Gardens were there to be seen, an extension to the house. They provided a public reception space (Hoadley 1996, 6), not a private retreat. They were a place for study, exercise, leisure and contemplation, and had health-giving properties (Farrar 1998, 189–90). A sense of space could be created with backdrops and *trompe l'oeil,* effectively making the garden into an extra room, for working, relaxing or outdoor dining. Just as the house extended into the garden, in turn the garden allowed light and fragrance into the house as well as providing fruit (from espaliered trees), vegetables, herbs and pond fish for the kitchen, and perhaps medicinal herbs.

Most houses of significance from the 2nd century onwards enjoyed some kind of enclosed garden or yard. It was set off by the house, and views were framed by porticos and porches (Perring 2002, 179). In Pompeii the majority of houses, including relatively small ones, had a peristyle or courtyard garden reached from the street by passing through a front door and atrium; and some had two. The size varied, the smallest measuring less than 0.5m by 2.0m; so did the shape, including square, rectangular and L-shaped (Jashemski 1981, 41). Plant beds and paths were arranged in a symmetrical manner with the paths and sight lines leading to a focal point of an architectural nature such as an *aedicula* or *nymphaeum* on a rear wall, as at Pompeii and Ostia (Farrar 1998, 30, 42). At Pompeii, a tree was found in each corner in the peristyle garden of the House of the Ship Europa and in the garden of the House of Polybius were five trees forming an inner ring (Jashemski 1979, 29, 31, 53).

The formal garden was primarily a green garden with, for example, clipped box; flowers played a minor role (Jashemski 1994, 16), although they were important for garlands and wreaths and at festivals, weddings, games and funerals (Jashemski 1979, 267). There are wall paintings that depict flower dealers. Roses, lilies and violets were the main flowers for garlands listed by Pliny.

In addition to the gardens of town houses, market gardens were located on the outskirts of the city, or at Pompeii in a less dense area of housing within the city walls (Farrar 1998, 176). One market garden at the House of the Ship Europa had two areas of bedding trenches or furrows that Jashemski (1979, 233–42, fig 346) interpreted as vegetable plots. A fruit orchard was also found within the city walls (Jashemski 1979, 251–65).

In Britain the archaeological evidence for Roman gardens is limited, with the majority of the information coming from villas such as Frocester Court (Gloucestershire), Gorhambury (Hertfordshire), and Bancroft and Latimer (both Buckinghamshire); or from the famous garden of the palace at Fishbourne (Currie 2005, 9). The garden at Bancroft villa contained a rectangular pond with water supplied by drains from the house. At Fishbourne fragments of four ornamental basins were found into which fountains might once have played (Cunliffe 1971, 131), and part of the masonry water tank which served them (Cunliffe 1998, pl 17). Paths were for circulation and divided the area into beds: the garden at Frocester Court had a path of limestone cobbling and rectangular beds cut into a gravelled area.

Dickson (1994, 49–50) describes the remains of possible garden plants found in pits and wells at Silchester and Caerwent, or in Roman forts such as York (Dickson 1994, 54). Perring (2002, 153–4, fig 59) refers to garden porches on houses at Verulamium and Silchester. Farrar (1998, 176) also draws attention to non-residential gardens at *mansios,* such as the garden at Wall furnished with a demi-lune water basin. Evidence for purely decorative plants is slight in Roman Britain (Dickson 1994, 58).

The London evidence

London was the largest and most significant town in the Roman province. London's late 1st- and 2nd-century town houses were among the finest in Britain: only Fishbourne and villas on the Sussex coast have produced mosaics of comparable quality from this period (MoLAS 2000, 159). If it was simply status and affluence that created or served the desire for gardens in Roman Britain, and considerations of the value and availability of urban space did not preclude them, one might reasonably expect gardens to have been present in Londinium.

Declaring features or plants to be unequivocally related to Roman gardening is a risky business, and even garden tools and planters can have non-horticultural uses. Ambiguity is our greatest problem, and so our evidence tends to be circumstantial. But that body of evidence is growing.

Garden features

Peter Marsden (1969, 7 and fig 2) interpreted spade marks at Warwick Square near Newgate as the edge of a garden bed (GM131; Figs 2.3.1 and 2.3.2). Within an area enclosed by Roman walls, a row of shallow angular cuts parallel with one wall were cut into the natural brickearth. Root holes were more numerous on one side of the spade marks, suggesting that this was the planted area. There was no dating evidence but one wall cut through a pit containing late 2nd-century pottery.

Marsden also discovered a 'Great Pool' of Farrar Type C (Farrar 1998, 75) at Cannon Street Station on the site known as the 'Roman governor's palace'. It had a smaller apsidal pool on one side with a pier base in the centre, perhaps as a base for a decorative feature (Marsden 1975, 31–3). A recent evaluation at Cannon Place, Cannon Street Station, revealed Roman walls of the mid-1st to mid-2nd century; one of these may have been part of the 'Great Pool', lying in a garden court, measuring about 31m long and

Fig 2.3.2 Martin Henig showing how the spade marks were dug at Warwick Square

10m wide (internally) and 1.8m deep. Two adjoining curved walls were found, both sloping towards the base; rather than one small pool, it seems likely that there were three adjoining pools alongside the larger one (Taylor 2004).

Recent work has disproved the 'palace' hypothesis, as the buildings were not structurally integrated and the lines of symmetry do not accord with Marsden's interpretation of a palace building with wings. Milne and Perring suggest that some of the 'palace' buildings might have been part of a bath house (Milne 1996, 50; Perring 1991a, 30–4). *Palaestrae* associated with baths were sometimes planted as gardens, for example the Forum baths at Pompeii (Jashemski 1979, 163–4), but there is little evidence for a garden at Cannon Street aside from the pool.

One building at 1 Poultry (ONE94) was extended in AD 223–36 by a new suite of rooms. It was a large residential property located close to the junction of two roads, and had a hypocaust. The extent to which the grounds around the building were landscaped is unclear but within an external area were many scattered stakeholes and larger postholes perhaps indicating fences (Hill and Rowsome forthcoming, fig 241). They are not closely dated, being sandwiched between Hadrianic fire debris (AD 120) and post-Roman dumping, but some pottery recovered from the posthole fills suggests a date of *c* AD 250–70. This was contemporary with what may have been a hedge some 12m to the south of the postholes: the adjacent road gravels contained leaves and short stems from box (*Buxus sempervirens*), apparently clippings, and a smaller number of fragmented, needle-shaped leaves from a coniferous tree or shrub, possibly juniper (*Juniperus communis*) (Davis forthcoming a). It is possible that the remains

Fig 2.3.1 Warwick Square (GM131) spade marks

fell from trees or shrubs growing beside the road, but it is tempting to postulate a box and possibly juniper hedge in a garden or landscaped area next to the large house. Elsewhere on the Poultry site were oak split-pale fences, some at least head-high, dividing the yards of many houses (Goodburn forthcoming) – no doubt the yards had many uses, of which one may have been as gardens as the presence of manure may indicate (Peter Rowsome pers comm).

Brian Yule (2005, 86) has interpreted a large prestigious building complex on the Southwark waterfront at Winchester Palace as a public building. Here several small pits and gullies or slots may indicate elements of a garden, though little formal pattern is apparent (WP83; Yule 2005, 54, 74, fig 40). The small pits could mark the positions of small trees or shrubs, and broad, shallow gullies may have been bedding trenches. A gully with closely spaced stakeholes along it adjoined the corner of the building, and presumably held a fence or screen. The open area here is interpreted as a garden area contemporary with buildings dating to the 2nd–3rd century (Yule 2005, 74). Unfortunately botanical samples from the area failed to produce supporting evidence, but analysis of dark earth suggests the possibility of accretion through gardening (Macphail 2005, 90).

Two fragments of painted wall plaster from the same site show part of a garden scene (Yule 2005, fig 94, 134–5 and Fig 2.3.3). The main decorative element was a cross-strut fence, painted in two shades of yellow against a green background. Further embellishments of dark red ochre may represent plant tendrils. The fencing is reminiscent of scenes found on plaster from Pompeii, showing luxuriant gardens and vistas beyond. Such schemes were also used as a way of enlarging space in an actual garden (Ling 1991, 152) and the plaster, although not *in situ*, came from one of the gullies (Yule 2005, fig 40) in the area interpreted as a garden. The wall plaster from Winchester Palace, Southwark, is unusual as it appears to be the only London example to show garden elements (Ian Betts pers comm).

Evidence for cultivation has been found at 1–7 Whittington Avenue near Leadenhall Street, interpreted as a field or market garden (WIV88; Brown 1988). At the beginning of the sequence, the naturally sloping ground surface was levelled with dumps of brickearth and a road was laid out lined with buildings. These burnt down, possibly in the Boudican revolt. The two sides of the road then developed differently. To the west, cultivation was followed by use as a rubbish tip; to the east buildings were constructed. After the fire, a plot measuring at least 9.00m by 3.50m was delineated by ditches. In it were a number of shallow U- or V-shaped linear grooves 80–200mm wide and

Fig 2.3.3 Wall plaster from Winchester Palace (WP83) showing a fence, perhaps part of a garden scene (approximate overall dimensions: W 100mm; H 65mm)

60–200mm deep. They were thought to be too insubstantial to have been made with an ard or plough and were thought to have been caused by digging with a spade or similar. Micromorphological analysis showed that the grooves had been lined with humified organic matter or manure (Macphail 1988b). Pottery dating from overlying dumps was dated to the late 1st century/early 2nd century when the basilica was constructed. There was no coherent pattern although north–south and east–west alignments were visible. Contemporary with the cultivated plot were buildings at the Leadenhall Court excavations thought to have been part of a farm (LCT84; Milne and Wardle 1993, 30–2). A number of tree holes contained grassland and arable weeds which may indicate farming-related activities (Davis 1993, 66).

Some sections within the walled area of Londinium were sparsely occupied, particularly the south-west and south-east corners, and it is likely that these were cultivated. Ditches and banks which probably formed field systems and stock enclosures have been identified in peripheral locations near major routes into the early city, for example at Rangoon Street near Aldgate, and at Aldersgate and Bishopsgate (RAG82; MoLAS 2000, 145).

Enclosures surrounding theatres or temples might contain a garden. So too might cemeteries: tomb monuments were set in a formally planted garden outside Rome (Jashemski 1979, 144, 149), but disappointingly there is little archaeological evidence for a garden from the well-studied East London cemeteries (Barber and Bowsher 2000). Similarly Dickson identifies gardens by the root and stalk of a cabbage *(Brassica* sp) at Chesterholm fort on Hadrian's Wall and summer savory (*Satureja hortensis*) found at York fort (Dickson 1994, 54), but no gardens have been identified in the London fort.

Garden and food plants

It is very difficult to establish whether particular species represented in the archaeobotanical record were used as medicinal, food or ornamental plants, or merely grew naturally in Londinium. High seed frequency of individual plants and assemblages with low species diversity are the best indicators of exploitation, and possibly of local cultivation.

Some food plants may have been grown in gardens within the town. Many of the herbs found in botanical samples in London are very likely to have been cultivated in town gardens for culinary and medicinal purposes, along with green vegetables. Seeds of the *Brassica/Sinapis* group (which includes cabbage, swede and rape) have been found in low numbers at several sites in Roman Southwark and in the city, as has summer savory. With these seeds, however, it is difficult to distinguish cultivated species from their wild relatives. The same is true for carrot (*Daucus carota*), represented by seeds at 179 Borough High Street (179BHS89; Giorgi

forthcoming), and also for a number of plants such as parsnip (*Pastinaca sativa*).

Often plants such as hazel, sloe and blackberry were collected from the wild (Dickson 1994, 48). Cucumber (*Cucumis sativus*) is a definite cultivar, and cucumber seeds were found in a timber-lined pit at 1–7 St Thomas Street (1STS74; Willcox 1978, 412); but the cucumbers could have been imported as luxury items along with fig (*Ficus carica*), olive (*Olea europea*) and grape (MoLAS 2000, 144). Grape pollen (*Vitis vinifera*), such as that found recently found at 1 Poultry (ONE94), may derive from local viticulture on the valley side of the Walbrook (Scaife forthcoming).

Remains of several decorative plants were found at 1 Poultry, including rose, hop, box and holly (Davis forthcoming a). It is difficult if not impossible to differentiate between plants deliberately grown as flowers and those occurring wild (John Giorgi pers comm). We cannot be sure that any of these plants were cultivated in London – though box is a strong contender. Box (*Buxus sempervirens*) is a native species in beech woods on chalk and limestone in southern England, but was also commonly planted by the Romans for hedges. Box does grow close to London on the North Downs (eg Box Hill, Surrey), but it is unlikely to occur naturally in London itself (Anne Davis pers comm). Its leaves have been found at Copthall Avenue near London Wall (OPT81; de Moulins 1990, 85), at Blossom's Inn (GHT00; 30 Gresham Street) near the Guildhall (Davis forthcoming c), and on several London waterfront sites near modern Upper Thames Street with good waterlogged preservation, including in 2nd-century drain fills at 132–7 Upper Thames Street (Davis forthcoming b). At Regis House near Monument (KWS94; Davis forthcoming d) box leaves were preserved in two samples from an early 2nd-century occupation layer and a late 2nd- to 4th-century well fill. Dumping behind a 2nd-century quay at Minster House, 12 Arthur Street, contained leaf fragments, including some from box (AUT01; Roberts forthcoming). The presence of leaves in these waterfront deposits suggests that box was being used as a hedging or ornamental plant in the waterfront area during the 2nd century.

Seeds of marigold (*Calendula* sp) were also recovered from one of the large wells at Blossom's Inn. Marigold was an introduced plant used decoratively in gardens (Davies forthcoming c). Walnut tree pollen has been found at the Temple of Mithras (Murphy and Scaife 1991, 93) and 1 Poultry (Scaife forthcoming). Apple, cherry, wild strawberry, coriander, fennel and dill have also been identified from Roman London, but whether they are food or garden waste is impossible to tell (Anne Davis pers comm).

Plant pots

Early 2nd-century material dumped into a channel at 179 Borough High Street, Southwark, included

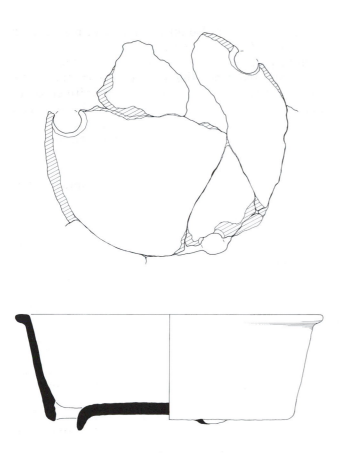

Fig 2.3.4 The plant pot from 179 Borough High Street (179BHS89[181]) (approximate diameter 380mm)

a shell-tempered, straight-walled bowl with three large holes in the base close to the wall junction (Fig 2.3.4). The holes (each *c* 25mm in diameter) had been perforated before firing, but the undersides had not been smoothed or carefully finished, which suggests that the vessel did not sit flat on a surface but was suspended or embedded whilst in use. It is likely that the Southwark vessel was a plant pot: 28 similar vessels were found in Pompeii in the House of the Ship Europa, buried slightly below the surface of the earth (Jashemski 1979, 239–40, fig 350). Jashemski suggests that they were used for starting seedling trees before replanting or for propagating trees or shrubs by layering. Layering involves pinning a branch down against the soil to encourage it to form roots; once roots are developed the branch can be separated from the parent plant and lifted in its pot without disturbance to be planted elsewhere. More of these pots were found in the Garden of Hercules, which was interpreted as a commercial flower garden on account of the many perfume bottles found there (Jashemski 1979, 287). Several plant pots were also found at Fishbourne (Cunliffe 1998, 104; Farrar 1998, 163; Ryley 1998, 4, 9).

Other possible examples of purpose-made plant pots are found amongst the kiln material from Eccles, where jars with triangular cut holes in the wall and base were manufactured (Detsicas 1981,
441–5). These jars are also noted for having bases 'which are neither smooth nor quite flat, as if the vessels were not intended to stand on their base' (Detsicas 1974, 305). Two of these, dated AD 50–65, were found in the City of London and one is published (Davies *et al* 1994, 36–7 and fig 28, 122). Pliny refers to similar pots with breathing holes for roots being used to transport trees such as lemons (*Naturalis Historia*, 12.16), and the pots manufactured at Eccles kiln site may have had a similar packaging/transporting role. Bowe suggests that the holes were for root pruning to improve fruit production (2004, 50).

Garden tools

As well as more obviously agricultural tools, there are pitchforks, hoes, sickles and spades, all of which could have been equally well used in arable farming or in orchards or vineyards. In the Museum of London collections there are about twenty iron rakes, one of which (from Copthall Court, Throgmorton Street) had at least seventeen tines. Most of these tools are from the Walbrook valley, largely because the metal is well preserved there and the area became popular with antiquarian collectors. Other examples come from the earlier excavations of Roman London, including an iron hoe from the Walbrook at Bucklersbury House (Temple of Mithras site). The hoe has a triangular blade at one end and two prongs at the other in the manner of a modern mattock.

The single tine of a rake from 72–75 Cheapside (CID90) is an extremely early example (Wardle forthcoming b). Other rake tines come from post-Roman contexts, eg at Plantation House, Fenchurch Street, and from a 16th-century context from Merton Priory – the latter probably originally derived from activity associated with the Roman road and pits there. An antler rake pierced with an iron nail from King Edward Buildings, 102–5 Newgate Street, was found in the medieval city ditch and could have been of medieval date.

An oak spade, complete with iron sheath, was found in a Roman roadside ditch at 1 Poultry. Such an implement could have been used for the spade-cuts at Warwick Square (see above) but this spade was as likely to have been used for digging and clearing mud and silt from ditches (Wardle forthcoming b). Seven spuds have been found in London, one in the River Wandle; these are used normally as weeding implements (Zeepvat 1991, 59, fig 5.5).

Explaining the paucity of London evidence

One explanation for the lack of London evidence is that there were not many gardens in the 1st and early part of the 2nd centuries. Fashions in building form have a significant effect on the amount of private and public green space in a city, particularly when there is increasing urban density – for example, the creation of shared gardens in London's terraced Georgian squares, le Corbusier-style landscapes around the post-war estates in slum-cleared areas, and the late 20th-century proposals of Richard Rogers (Urban Task Force 1999). Densely occupied 'strip buildings' were common in the early Roman city; these narrow structures had commercial areas on the street frontage, with workshops behind and residential quarters at the back with little room for a garden (Perring *et al* 1991). At Borough High Street in Southwark, where there was room at the back, open areas with hearths, pits and wells were found but there was no evidence for gardens (Drummond-Murray *et al* 2002, 36–7, 68–9, figs 31, 56).

A second reason why evidence for gardens is limited probably concerns the truncation of ground surfaces. The London sites have many layers of occupation and later cut features obscure or remove earlier evidence. When a garden is abandoned it soon becomes overgrown, the beds disturbed by roots and the processes that form dark earth; similarly the turning over of garden soils introduces oxygen and plant macrofossils decay. Our best comparator, Pompeii, was sealed by volcanic ash and debris, preventing the disturbance or truncation by later features, arresting the processes of change. Here, Jashemski had the opportunity to compare casts of root cavities with modern root shapes, and was able to distinguish plants such as fig and olive (Jashemski 1979, 196, 246; 1981, 35).

A third explanation arises from London's history of relatively small plots of property and the continuity of medieval and later property boundaries, which normally determine the scale and nature of development in modern London, and thus limit areas of excavation. There are many fragments of Roman buildings but few complete plans.

Fourthly, it may be that our techniques and research designs are not as well suited to the identification of gardens as they should be. In London's earlier excavations it was not commonplace to take suitable samples for archaeobotanical analysis, especially not from the uninspiringly named 'open areas'.

Refining the search for Londinium's gardens

The main hard landscaping elements to be expected in London are peristyles, low walls and balustrades, fences, trellises and paths. Water features such as ornamental pools and *piscinae*, with pipes and drains, are also to be expected, as are seats and tables, altars, shrines and statues, and of course bedding trenches. There could also be evidence of tree-holes and cordon fruit trees in a row alongside a wall and planting beds (eg at Warwick Square), or decorative bedding trenches (eg Fishbourne).

Garden history must be of an interdisciplinary character. Much of what we find is fragmentary and inconclusive, and it is essential to use all the evidence (stratigraphic, structural, environmental, artefactual) contained within the garden to facilitate the understanding of the function of the sampled feature/area. The best way of distinguishing garden remains from non-horticultural elements is through several (one or two could be food waste) good assemblages of food, medicinal or ornamental plants with low species diversity.

The identification of other plant parts, such as leaf and stem epidermis and charred roots and tuber fragments, should be pursued in order to broaden our base for evidence of food plants beyond that represented simply by fruits and seeds (Giorgi forthcoming); for example, leaf epidermis of leek (*Allium porrum*) has been identified from Nantwich and York (Dickson 1994, 55). Murphy and Scaife (1991, 93) also list the macrofossils of wild fauna, such as insects and molluscs, that are capable of yielding information on the structure and species of garden vegetation. Micromorphological analysis has been invaluable in understanding the Whittington Avenue and Winchester Palace sites (Macphail 1988b; 2005).

The future for Roman gardens in London is brighter. As well as the recent data from sites such as 1 Poultry and Winchester Palace, new evidence is being assembled. In the Londinium Assessment project (Wardle 2005), research has been proposed to provide an opportunity to examine Roman plant foods in London – the chronological and spatial distribution of all foods, including cereals, legumes, fruits, nuts, vegetables and flavourings. Exotic species such as olive, stone-pine, cucumber and introduced food plants and semi-exotics like mulberry, walnut, grape, fig and lentil, will be studied, and compared with the more common home-grown and wild foods (Davis forthcoming b), though in the case of exotics this research is unlikely to demonstrate local cultivation.

The use of a category of horticultural and agricultural tools on the MoL database has allowed for a search facility for easier access to information that would otherwise have been hidden (Angela Wardle pers comm). The use of ceramic vessels in horticulture has been discussed recently in relation to the pot from 179 Borough High Street (Rayner and Seeley forthcoming). There are over 200 vessels with holes in the MoLAS Oracle database; while many may be strainers, wine coolers or colanders there is potential to review those vessels in the London database with single or multiple pre-firing holes in their bases and/or lower halves to identify those of horticultural use.

The plotting of gardens might tell us more about the distribution of social classes and wealth, and the extent of Romanisation of different parts of London. Future excavations should question – in the field – the uses to which open areas might be put, and apply excavation techniques that look for typical garden features and ensure adequate environmental sampling. Roman gardens now need to be included in the London research framework, as it is possible that we have overlooked an important social, economic and environmental dimension to Roman London.

Acknowledgements

The authors are grateful to Ian Betts, Gary Brown, Anne Davis, Madeline Edmead, John Giorgi, Jenny Hall, Julian Hill, Peter Rowsome, Fiona Seeley, Jeremy Taylor and Angela Wardle who provided much information and to Andy Chopping and Faith Vardy for the illustrations.

2.4 Archaeological evidence for the Roman London to Colchester road between Aldgate and Harold Hill *Gary Brown*

Introduction

In the *Research Framework for London Archaeology* a single research objective relating to Roman roads in the London region was established (Nixon *et al* 2002, 34, Framework objective R4). Much of the discussion in the document naturally centred on the settlement at Londinium, although it was acknowledged that:

> an accurate chronology for roads, including their prehistoric antecedents, will help to foster a clearer understanding of the relationship between settlements and their economic development. The nature and chronology of radial development along the main roads leading from the urban area has received relatively little attention and is under represented in the archaeological record (Nixon *et al* 2002, 33).

However, archaeologists have sought to establish both the precise routes and chronologies of the road system for years. Within modern urban areas this can be both difficult and frustrating, and it is now largely dependent upon commercial archaeology and the unsequenced availability of sites.

There have been advances in our understanding of all the major Roman arterial roads, even if these have lacked a synthetic approach to reporting. Codrington (1928) laid the base, and Margary (1973) and Merrifield (1965; 1969; 1983) ably built upon it, though the most recent of the latter's work was published over 20 years ago. Since then, however, qualitative information has been obtained for Ermine Street (Gentry *et al* 1977), Stane Street (Maloney and Gostick 1998), Watling Street North (Bowsher 1995), Watling Street South (Rogers 1990), the London–Silchester route (Parnum and Cotton 1983), and of course the London to Colchester road (Sheldon 1971; 1972; Mills 1984; Brown *et al* forthcoming). This paper examines the evidence, positive and negative, for the latter route within the metropolitan boundaries, the extremities of the study being Aldgate in the west and Harold Hill in the east.

The London to Colchester road

The doyen of the Roman road system, Ivan Margary, like Codrington before him, had determined the general orientation of this road, primarily relying on historic and cartographic evidence for the route. But of course a road linking Londinium with Camulodunum was well known, appearing on the Antonine Itinerary as both *Iter V* and *Iter IX* (Hull 1963a, 24). Margary confidently wrote that the road extended from Aldgate to Old Ford while lamenting that 'remains of it have not yet been traced' (1973, 246). He went on to describe its postulated route from Old Ford where it crossed the river Lea extending north-east to Stratford, on to Forest Gate, Manor Park, where it crossed a second river, the Roding, and noted that from then on its 'course through Ilford and Seven Kings to Chadwell Heath is remarkably well preserved' (Margary 1973, 246).

Margary was commenting on the usually accepted route, not on physical evidence for the road itself. He also suggested that the route from Chadwell Heath to Romford was uncontested but not confirmed between Romford and Gallows Corner, and that from this point to Brentwood via Harold's Wood the route was fairly fixed. Although the distance between Aldgate and Brentwood is 30km (18.6 miles), Margary did not, with one exception, use archaeological evidence to confirm this hypothesis. The lack of physical evidence had already concerned archaeologists. As early as 1910 Reginald Smith noted that no evidence for the road between Romford and London existed, and that 'this part of the route is rapidly being covered with houses' which made it important to 'collect and preserve any indication of the line while there is yet a chance of testing conjecture by the spade' (Smith 1909–11, 230). Half a century later Hull still bemoaned of the road that 'neither its metalling ... nor its ditches have anywhere been seen' (1963a, 24). Less than a decade later Harvey Sheldon cut his first sections across the road at Old Ford (Sheldon 1971).

It would be satisfying to state that archaeological investigations have significantly increased our understanding of the road, but this is only partly true. The section west of the River Lea is located entirely within Tower Hamlets, and relatively frequent investigations in this borough have not significantly advanced Sheldon's findings of 1969–70 or Merrifield's assessment of the road (1983, 123–4). There is even less to celebrate east of the Lea, but cumulatively **all** of the investigations on, or in the vicinity of, the Roman road assist in our understanding of its alignment and idiosyncrasies (Fig 2.4.1).

There can be little doubt that the road had, initially at least, a strategic function. Indeed, Davies (2002, 148 and fig 60) has suggested that the road pre-dated the foundation of Londinium itself as the road does not conform with the grid-like street pattern of the later 1st-century town, but cuts diagonally from the *decumanus maximus* after

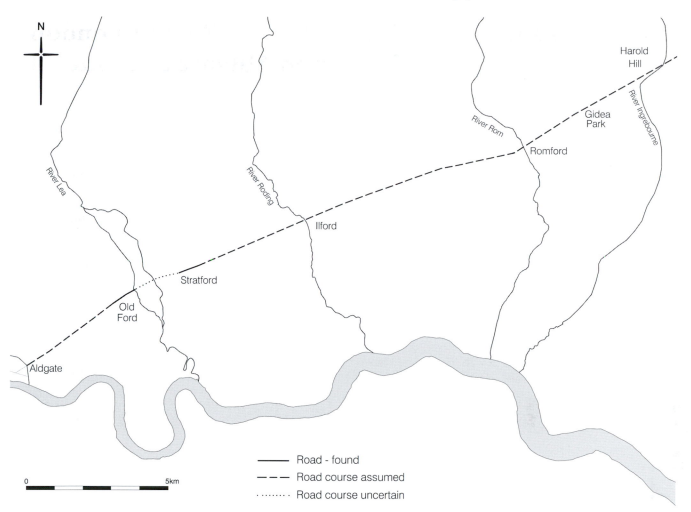

Fig 2.4.1 Roman road between Aldgate and Harold Hill. Scale 1:12,500 (Pre-Construct Archaeology Ltd)

crossing the Thames. More questionable is his inter-pretation for the existence of an early non-metalled track of 2.6m width at Old Ford (Davies 2002, 118) used tactically by the army to penetrate into hostile territory in the early months and years of occupa-tion. Such a feature was not observed by Sheldon or in any of the subsequent extensive excavations (see below) and must have represented a very local construction variation. In succeeding centuries the road continued to maintain its importance, as dem-onstrated by its regular modifications and repairs, presumably for commercial and administrative rather than military reasons.

Aldgate to Old Ford

For our purposes the starting point of the road is taken as the Roman gate at Aldgate, although the road also extends south-west from this point, roughly on the line of Fenchurch Street (Merrifield 1983, 123). A 65m-length of the road was recorded in plan and section at Old Ford in 1995–96, incorpo-rating the areas investigated by Sheldon and Mills (Sheldon 1971; 1972; Mills 1984; Brown *et al* forthcoming), and provides an accurate fix up to the

edge of the Lea valley. Assuming that the road was *actually* straight between Aldgate and Old Ford the distance between the gate and river was approximately 4.6km.

The first stretch of the road is mirrored by Aldgate High Street and Whitechapel Road before the latter turns slightly to the south close to the junction at Greatorex Street, presumably reflecting medieval priorities. Excavations in 1938 for the Aldgate East Underground station exposed gravels, interpreted as part of the road to the east of the gate, at a depth of 10ft (3.03m) (Merrifield 1965, 298). East of this Codrington (1928, 181) reported that 'five road sur-faces were met with, the lowest one of large flints set close together and very difficult to break through' during the construction of a railway at Whitechapel High Street. While it is possible that these were of Roman origin, there was no conclusive proof, and these may equally have been of medieval date. Hereafter there is no firm evidence for the location of the road until Old Ford, although the Inner London Archaeological Unit made a game attempt to locate it when a 100m-long trench at Davenant Street, between Old Montague Street and White-chapel Road, was excavated in 1977 (Richardson 1978).

Between Davenant Street and Old Ford there is no physical proof for the course of the road, and a recent evaluation on the projected course of the road, close to Meath Gardens, also failed to locate it (Sankey 2005). The most westerly recorded fragment in Old Ford was at the rear of 510–18 Roman Road, where portions of the central section of the road were recorded, but they were too limited in extent to determine the structure in any detail (RBW03; Boyer 2003). The maximum area available east to west was only 5.3m and there were no delineating features present. However, a shallow hollow filled with sandy gravels is similar to that found to the east and underlying the central *agger* (see below), therefore allowing the road's approximate position to be established. It was sealed by bedding layers and rammed gravel surfaces of the road proper, all presumably associated with the central carriageway.

A number of interventions have taken place along Roman Road in Old Ford between number 490 and the Lefevre Walk Estate, location of Sheldon's and subsequent discoveries (Fig 2.4.2). However, these have been almost invariably located on the north side of the road (for example the Ranwell East Estate (BOD91; Pitt 1991) and 91–93 Parnell Road (AGH90; PRB95; Pitt 1990; 1995)), and it is now clear that the Roman road lay to the south. Roman features have been found across this area and included an unsuspected enclosed cemetery at Ranwell East Estate (Pitt 1991), isolated burials (Owen *et al* 1973), structures at 91–93 Parnell Road (Pitt 1990), and field and other boundaries elsewhere (eg McIsaac *et al* 1979). One evaluation on the south side, at 568A Roman Road, recorded no evidence for the road or roadside ditches (ROB05; Vuolteenaho 2005). However, a row of postholes at the north of the site on a general east–west alignment with a north–south return suggests a building parallel to and in close proximity with the road. The broader interpretation of the Roman landscape at Old Ford is covered in greater detail in Brown *et al* forthcoming.

Lefevre Walk Estate, Old Ford

Major excavations were conducted at Lefevre Road Estate by Pre-Construct Archaeology in 1995–96 (LEK95; Brown *et al* forthcoming; Fig 2.4.3), incorporating areas previously examined by Sheldon (1970; 1971) and the former Inner London Archaeological Unit (Mills 1984). The traces of the road found here can be assumed to be representative of

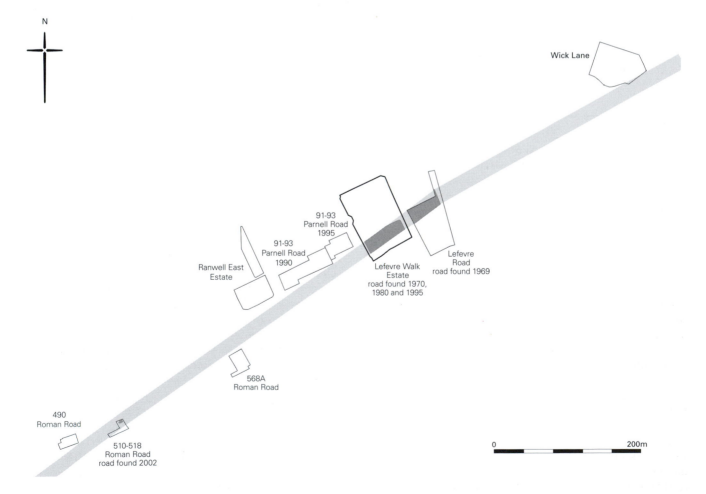

Fig 2.4.2 Archaeological investigations at Old Ford in the vicinity of the Roman road, including negative evidence. Scale 1:5000 (Pre-Construct Archaeology Ltd)

Fig 2.4.3 London to Colchester road at Lefevre Road Estate, Old Ford (LEK95), looking west towards Londinium (Pre-Construct Archaeology Ltd)

its general characteristics. Initially a broad scoop was cut down through the natural brickearth to the top of the natural gravels, as also observed at 510–18 Roman Road to the west (Fig 2.4.4). The scoop defined the line of the road *agger*. The northern and southern limits of the road were marked with relatively shallow and narrow boundary ditches, with an upcast bank on the outer edge. The distance between the centres of the boundary ditches was *c* 25.5m (83–84 feet) establishing it as a 'first class highway' using Margary's definition (Margary 1973, 16; see also Davies 2002, 33). On both sides of the road boundary ditches were construction quarry pits. The scoop was infilled with redeposited brickearth that was moulded into an upstanding ridge up to 0.5m thick and between 10.50m and 11.20m wide. The domed surface formed the road's substructure and was capped with the central carriageway's primary surface of rammed gravels, typically 4.60m wide.

On both the north and south sides of the central *agger* were metalled side or auxiliary tracks, interpreted as being for foot traffic and livestock. In its earliest form the south track was 3.5–4.5m wide, and the north track 5.5m wide, and both up to 0.6m lower than the central *agger*. It is probable that the road was constructed shortly after the conquest. The

best dating evidence was recovered during Sheldon's investigations although a quarter stater of the late Iron Age king Cunobelin (died *c* AD 40) was recovered from beneath the south track during the 1995–96 work. After the southern boundary ditch was infilled a thin layer of pebbles extended from the track and into the ditch depression creating a shallow metalled ditch base or hollow-way. It is possible that this feature was restricted to the approach to the River Lea as it was only found at the east but not the west of the site.

In the late 1st or early 2nd century the north track was raised and remetalled; the modified track was *c* 0.20m higher and flatter that the original. The southern hollow-way was resurfaced, probably at the same time, and extended for several metres beyond the road itself in the east, possibly as hardstanding for livestock. In the mid- to late 2nd century the north track was resurfaced for a second time, before this track was abandoned. It was during this period that the road was transformed from a three-lane highway into a dual carriageway by raising the south track to the level of the central carriageway. The width of the carriageway was at least 6.0m in the west of the area, widening to 8.5m at the east. Sheldon recorded the track as being 10.0m wide at the extreme eastern limits of

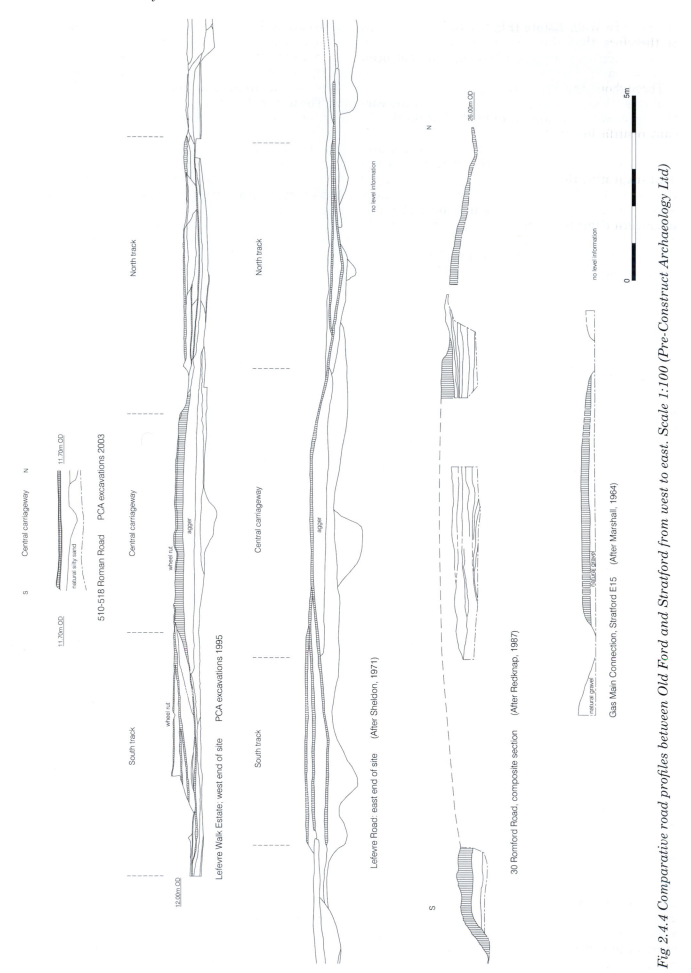

Fig 2.4.4 Comparative road profiles between Old Ford and Stratford from west to east. Scale 1:100 (Pre-Construct Archaeology Ltd)

the Lefevre Walk Estate (Fig 2.4.4). The inference is therefore that the road widened towards the river crossing, although for how far has not been established.

Throughout the remainder of the 2nd and 3rd centuries there were no major changes to the carriageway. Minor repairs were made, but no significant resurfacing episodes are recorded. In the 4th century the 'south track' zone was resurfaced and was elevated slightly above the central carriage area suggesting that the road had moved slightly to the south. The dual carriageway was at least 9.0m wide, although the evidence is not conclusive due to modern damage to the road at this level. It also appears that during the 4th century only limited maintenance occurred to the road with wind-blown detritus accumulating along the southern edge, although domestic activity at the road edges, first recorded in the mid-3rd century, continued. The central carriageway demonstrated frequent and relatively deep ruts (Fig 2.4.4), indicating the continued use of wheeled transport. In the later 4th century the road zone was being increasingly encroached upon.

It is likely that the road continued to be used, if not effectively maintained, into the medieval era. Queen Matilda's splash into the Lea suggests the road was functioning in the 12th century, although it is also possible that she and her retinue used the more northerly route now marked by Old Ford Road and which is also likely to have had Roman antecedents (Margary 1973, 57).

The 1995–96 excavations recorded a 65m-length of the road to which may be added a further 52m investigated by Sheldon up to the former railway line that marks the housing estate's eastern boundary. Including the fragment of the road recorded at 510–18 Roman Road, we now have positive identification of its course for over 550m to the edge of the Lea valley (Fig 2.4.2). A similar sequence has been recorded close to the road's terminus in Colchester (Hall 1942) and one of the larger questions is whether the road maintains this three- then two-carriageway profile along its complete course or whether there are variations along the way.

Crossing the Lea

The question of the river crossing place continues to vex. The traditional view has been for a ford, the location being close to Iceland Wharf where, in 1906, fragments of an *opus spicatum* (herringbone) tile floor were dredged from the Lea, the small bricks supposedly forming the ford's surface. This seems improbable; more likely they derived from a villa or other significant building close to the river. To date there is neither proof of the location nor type of crossing across the shallow but relatively wide valley floor. It is more probable that the road traversed the valley by a series of bridges and gravel causeways connecting small gravel islands, thus

avoiding the inconvenience of diurnal and seasonal flooding. If the place-name evidence is anything to go by, the majority of the river crossings along the route may have been marked by fords, as at Stratford, Ilford and Romford, but as Hull put it, 'These are English names for post-Roman conditions; the Romans would have had bridges' (Hull 1963a, 24).

It has been suggested that the western edge of the notional 'bridge' may have been located close to the fording point indicated on 19th-century maps where a short length of road off Wick Lane may represent a vestigial tail of the Roman road's course. Although archaeological investigations in the vicinity of the putative crossing point (eg Holden 2002) have revealed no conclusive proof, other sites in the vicinity are likely to become available for development in the near future as part of the 2012 Olympic Games or its aftermath.

One final point for consideration: Davies suggests that the three-carriage road might be a local variation and that the 'Three parallel lanes ... were used individually in a complex sequence, often with lanes going out of use for a period, during which they were blocked. One interpretation may be that the three roads each provide, in turn, an approach for a timber bridge. Such bridges needed to be replaced from time to time, often with a new version being built alongside one which needed changing, the new structure being founded on the remains of an earlier bridge' (Davies 2002 106). Whilst worthy of consideration it should be remembered that the road was used and modified between the 1st and 4th centuries and it is possible that on such an important road timber bridges were replaced in stone. A three-lane carriageway was located close to the west gate at Colchester away from a watercourse, indicating that this was the form of the road throughout.

A short distance to the north of this conjectured crossing point, at the former Crown Iron Works, Dace Road, significant worked timbers of Roman date have been recorded. These comprised more than 40 driven piles of varying size and shape and two large vertical posts set on substantial base plates, making several possible north-west/south-east alignments (DAC03; Alexander and Stephenson 2004). Although these may represent elements of a bridge they appear too far north from existing conjectured lines and were probably part of a wharf or jetty structure.

The Lea valley is, in its current form, generally shallow and relatively wide. However, a recent assessment of the palaeotopography indicates that in the vicinity of Old Ford the pre-Holocene valley profile was at its deepest with a relatively narrow valley floor at least 1.6km wide along the postulated route of the road (Burton *et al* 2004, 214, fig 58, map 2). By the Roman era the valley had infilled somewhat with sands and alluvia, and it is suggested that the river may have been tidal as far upstream as Old Ford (Burton *et al* 2004).

In February and March 2005 a combined team from Pre-Construct Archaeology and the Museum of London Archaeology Service investigated two sites between Carpenters Road and the Waterworks River in advance of work associated with a new Aquatics Centre for the 2012 Olympic Games. In total the area of investigation measured 640m north–south and overlapping trenches were set out to intercept the projected line of the road. The road was not located but investigations at the time of writing have yet to be completed. As suggested above it is possible that the course was not direct and by the shortest route but rather – as with the bridge-head road in Southwark – irregular and dictated by eyots or high points in the valley floor. It is possible that the crossing was achieved by a combination of causeway and bridges.

East from Stratford

At Stratford the line of the Roman road is thought to approximate to that of the Romford Road and it is at this location that there have been several proba-ble, but not conclusive recordings. The closest, at 30 Romford Road, was approximately 1.8km east of the valley. Here, a composite section across the road indicated that it was *c* 30m wide, with up to '9 successive deposits of sand and gravel' (W-RR86; Redknap 1987, 294) and with a possible auxiliary track at a lower level on the north. However, dating was very poor, and restricted to two fragments of possible Roman tile. A previous investigation 430m to the east in 1963 during utility works was limited in extent and recorded in section only but revealed two metalled surfaces separated by a 'stratum of dirty gravels'. The lower of these was up to 0.4m thick, but only 4.8m wide with ditches on either side (Marshall 1964, 208–12). It is possible that this was not part of the London to Colchester road at all, but a smaller and more local route in the vicinity. Furthermore, Marshall interpreted a sequence of overlying gravels as being of medieval date, and it is possible that both surfaces were also post-Roman.

During investigations at The Grove, Stratford, a length of the north side of the road and roadside ditch was recorded towards the south of the develop-ment, close to Romford Road (SFG98; Green 2001). Unfortunately the manuscript report lacks detail, and despite claiming that this was 'the first firm evidence from the Stratford area' (for the road), no further information is given. Gravel spreads recorded at Angel Lane, Stratford, are interpreted as being on the line of the Roman road, but the investigations were limited in extent and the interpretation is open (HW-AL94; Greenwood and Maloney 1995, 346).

Beyond Stratford archaeological evidence for the road is non-existent and its line is based more on historical conjecture than hard evidence. Margary reports that it continued on to Forest Gate and Manor Park, and that its course 'appears to be slightly distorted from the true line' (1973, 246). This is essentially the same route as the modern A118 road to the crossing of the River Roding at Ilford, presumably via a bridge. However, the Greater London Sites and Monuments Record has a note of an aerial photograph to the west of the river at the Cottons Recreation Ground that recorded a 'white mark across field ... possible Roman road being on the alignment of the Roman road' (GLSMR 061129).

East of the River Rom

East of the Rom a more determined effort has been made to look for the road. Here Margary states that 'at Romford the present road deviates a little to the south of the true line and the course of the Roman road is uncertain' (1973, 246). Between 1998 and 2004 three investigations were undertaken in the vicinity of Gidea Park adjacent to the north of Main Road (in the grounds of 63, 63A, 69 Main Road: MGP98, Gadd 1998; MNF03, Anon 2003a; Barker 2004). No evidence for the road was found. An alter-native course has been proposed to the north of these investigations in an area that is now part of the Romford Golf Course, but originally within the grounds of Gidea Hall. The hall itself was in exis-tence by 1250, underwent many transformations and was finally demolished in 1930 (Bluer 2002, 9). Historic maps (eg Ordnance Survey 1862) show a roadway leading from the hall and linking up with the 'Roman Road' (A12), and the feature was evident in the ground in recent times.

A recent project noted that 'running on an east–west orientation across the lush fairways of the Romford Golf Club is a pronounced ridge of 3–4m width. Its continuous linear aspect, plus the relative thinness of the grass on it, leaves little doubt that it represents a metalled thoroughfare of some sort' (RGC02; Bluer 2002). Indeed so important is this stretch of 'Roman' road that it has been designated as a Scheduled Ancient Monument (County Monu-ment #109). That notwithstanding, trenching at three points across the ridge demonstrated that the feature was only 4.0m wide and associated with at least one sherd of post-medieval pottery. The report concluded that the 'Roman' road was in fact 'proba-bly constructed to provide access to Gidea Hall for traffic from the Chelmsford direction' (Bluer 2002).

Further east still, in the vicinity of Harold Hill, two more investigations were undertaken, one close to the junction of Spilsby Road and Colchester Road and the other 0.5km down the road at the St Neots Sports Ground (RO-SN92). Both failed to record any evidence of the road (Beasley 1993; Anon 1992). The cumulative negative evidence from the Main Road/Colchester Road investigations indicates that the Roman road lies beneath or to the south of the present roads (A118/A12).

Conclusions

Despite the course of the Aldgate to Colchester road being apparently well established, particularly through evidence shown on post-medieval maps and the Antonine Itinerary, only in the vicinity of Old Ford and more particularly between Parnell Road and the eastern boundary of the former Lefevre Walk Estate is there any certainty regarding the road's orientation, constructional phasing and date. The reality is that between the edge of Londinium and Harold Hill (a distance of 24km or 14.9 miles) we are certain only of a 125m length. With the findings at 510–18 Roman Road it is possible to extend this to 550m or approximately 2.25% of the length between these two points. As the paper has demonstrated, the limitations on our knowledge are not because the course of the road has not been looked for. In some cases, especially Old Ford and to a lesser extent Gidea Park, the fact that the road was not found contributes significantly to our understanding of where the road should be. In Stratford the situation is somewhat different. Here several fragments of a road or roads have been located, but there is no conclusive evidence that any of them are a continuation of the Old Ford road.

Elsewhere there are huge gaps in our knowledge including the locations of all the river crossing points, the exact route between Aldgate and Old Ford and much of the route east of Stratford. Where the modern road and the Roman road are coincident there may be little proactive work that can be undertaken, but targeted investigations of development sites at the road margins should be prioritised. In this way roadside features such as ditches or building lines (for example as at 590 Roman Road) may at least confirm an approximate date and orientation for the roadway. Where there are major civil engineering works on or close to the putative road, for example for drainage, road widening or realignment works connected with the 2012 Olympic Games, for example, archaeological investigations should be dovetailed into development proposals. There are also plenty of opportunities for local societies. These might include geophysical investigations in green spaces such as Meath Gardens in Globe Town or Cottons Recreation Ground, Romford, or even small interventions in private gardens or other public or private open spaces along the route.

Recognising the limitations in our knowledge of this individual road it is worth considering the following statement by Hugh Davies (2002, 150): 'roads which were eventually built radiate from London and were sometimes of substantial size, built of gravel, sometimes with cobbles or flints as a foundation. Water was usually dealt with by timber bridges, corduroys, drains or culverts'. We still have some way to go to achieve even this level of detail for the main London to Colchester road within our area.

Acknowledgements

In order to prepare this paper I required access to a number of unpublished documents and I would like to thank in particular David Divers, Greater London Archaeology Advisory Service, and Nick Bateman and Kieron Tyler, Museum of London Archaeology Service, for assistance in this matter. Victoria Ridgeway and Josephine Brown have made positive suggestions on drafts of the text and the latter is to be thanked especially for the illustrations. Finally, thanks to the Sites and Monuments Records for providing me with the base data upon which I could start the survey.

pits, metalled surfaces and finally two successive corn dryers (suggesting the 'backyard' of a property). On site 16 an Antonine beam slot was superseded by a cobbled surface, then a smaller expanse of cobbling at one end of the large 4th-century ditch noted above, both overlain by a thick occupation and rubbish deposit. On a third site (9) the 'road zone' ditch was succeeded by abandonment/cultivation and rubbish pits and then in the later 2nd century by a postpad-constructed building, which gave way to a ditch on the same alignment and again a general occupation deposit.

Although some settlement shrinkage after the 2nd century in the south is possible, activity continued well into the 4th century, the final phase at site 4 having late or sub-Roman gravel spreads/post bases (Gentry *et al* 1977, 125) and a ditch that produced a Germanic buckle (Gentry *et al* 1977, 169, no 18) perhaps of *c* AD 360–400 (cf Böhme 1986, 485–6, ill 14 and nos 33–4), evidently unknown to Knight (1998, 40–2, type C), but seen as Middle Saxon by Going (1987). Though the coins on site 4 suggest decline after *c* AD 380 and the latest issues are of the House of Theodosius (Hammerson and Coxshall 1977, 161) there are also hints of possible Saxon activity on sites 14 and 20. The evidence generally suggests only a moderate degree of prosperity with unexceptional levels of mainly low-value coin loss (as well as a hoard of *c* AD 334 (Kent 1977, 168–9)), samian and other fine wares, fairly utilitarian vessel glass and virtually no window glass.

Thus, the settlement appears to have conformed broadly to a class of small undefended roadside settlements typified by, for example, Camerton or Hibaldstow (Burnham and Wacher 1990, 292–6 and 300–4). At Camerton ditches running parallel to the road were also superseded by properties incorporating strip buildings set at right angles to the road. Furthermore there was evidence for a network of metalled paths, some form of industrial function(s) in and after the 1st century, and early agricultural activity. Like Enfield, these settlements show evidence of 2nd-century expansion, some 3rd-century decline but often a continuance of occupation through and even beyond the 4th century.

The context and economy of the settlement

The Bush Hill Park settlement might be assumed to have acted as the first *mansio* north of Londinium, with cobblers, smiths, brewers, inns, stables and provisions merchants. Oddments of post-1st-century military equipment could identify one group amongst the clientele. But this assumption is too easily made and relies on the notion that because a settlement is next to a road it must be there primarily to serve travellers along that road. As Burnham and Wacher (1990, 5) have recognised, however, all small towns also provided 'some level of manufacturing capacity not only for their own communities, but also frequently for the surrounding countryside' and 'many also acted as centres for groups of villas and peasant settlements' (eg as a pool of seasonal agricultural labour). Others such as Hingley (1989, 111–20) have gone further and see all southern British quasi-urban settlements as principally 'local centres', local markets serving a restricted (static) catchment area.

We need to remember though that roads run both past and from settlements. People stop at settlements while travelling along roads. But people also find them convenient points to join roads and to begin or continue journeys, transit points providing services where B road meets motorway or cart track meets Ermine Street. Whatever the determinant of the precise location of the settlement (say the siting of a *mansio*) we should consider, along with traveller services and those for rural consumers, whether roadside settlements provided services to rural producers too.

The western edge of the Bush Hill Park settlement is probably marked by cremation burials on the Lincoln Road site (Gentry *et al* 1977, 110), with another surely implied here by a complete glass jug (Price 1977, 155 no 2), and more by complete vessels found at Landseer Road in 1902 (Fig 2.5.1). Just south of it there are limited records of burials including a stone coffin at Trinity Avenue (Gillam 1973, 21) (Fig 2.5.2). Yet well to the west of the settlement, antiquarian finds indicate the presence of other, often high-status, burial groups clearly not directly connected to it (Fig 2.5.2). The nearest, still 0.5km away, was a stone coffin found at Wellington Road (EAS 1967; Gillam 1973, 20 and pl 3), perhaps an outlier from a burial group found 150m further west at Private Road (Whitaker 1911, 16–19; Sharpe 1932, 113; Gillam 1973, 19–20 and pl 1). Here an inhumation and several cremations in/accompanied by glass and ceramic vessels and a coin of Vespasian were under an artificial chalk mound on a slight hill. Some 350m to the north-east a probably separate burial group, of possible 3rd-century date, at Burleigh Road comprised an adult 'in a deposit of lime' within a highly decorated lead coffin and two cremations (one possibly a child) in lead *ossuriae* in a *tegulae* cist covered by a flint dump (*Illustrated London News*, 8 October 1902; *Daily Graphic*, 10 December 1905; Smith 1902–03).

Some or all of these burials seem likely to relate to finds made in a gravel pit 150m north-west again of Private Road, '. . . in one part of which workmen invariably find human remains . . . bones, large iron nails and coins and small earthen pots . . . . [A tenant] once found a hearth set in brickwork . . . [and] in 1816 several Roman urns and coins were found . . . and some skeletons' (Robinson 1823, 57). The details are sketchy but seem to imply more than just further burials. Indeed, it is apparent that the Bush Hill Park settlement formed part of a landscape that included several possible occupation sites (see Sheldon and Schaaf 1978, fig 4). Another stone coffin burial with a glass jar in the vicinity of further ceramic flagon finds at Raglan School

Fig 2.5.2 The environs of the Bush Hill Park settlement

(Sturges 1938, 5; Gillam 1973, 20–1), over 600m south-west of the settlement, might imply one, for example. The location is *c* 200m north of Salmons Brook, an east-flowing tributary of the River Lea in Edmonton, along which further possible Romano-British burial evidence has been recorded (EAS 1959; Gillam 1973, 24 and pl 8; CBA 1960, 27).

Also north of Salmons Brook and 300m west of Ermine Street substantial evidence of a settlement at Churchfields has been recorded since the 1920s (Collingwood and Taylor 1931, 240; Sturges 1938, 2–5, 7 and 35; Gillam 1953; Geoffrey Gillam pers comm). Though badly damaged by quarrying, a mainly 3rd- to 4th-century settlement existed on land sloping down to the brook. A dense pattern of roof tile finds is known, and an early find was almost certainly a 3m² timber-lined well approached by a flint cobbled track or road with a nearby inhumation. Ditches on one site might represent water management adjacent to a timber structure, plausibly interpreted as a large sunken tank with a wooden lid. Early interpretations of the site as a tilery are to be treated with caution and there is some reason to believe that the tiles derived from a (possibly hypocausted) structure, especially as window glass, *tesserae* and possibly tufa have been recovered. The finds assemblage seems to imply domestic occupation but an industrial element is possible and the presence of a well so near to a brook and of a large tank might be suggestive of something such as a tannery.

Thus, the roadside settlement existed as part of a settled landscape possibly with industrial as well as presumably agricultural *foci* (possible field boundaries have been identified on site 17 (Fig 2.5.1) and in the vicinity of the Wellington Road burial (LCN04; Densem 2004 and pers comm)). Some of the agricultural *foci* were apparently prosperous enough to generate burials of the status one might expect from villas, and the roadside settlement can hardly have existed in a vacuum from them. Servicing such settlements could have been a bonus on top of servicing any *mansio* and travellers along the road. The likelihood that the settlement expanded gradually does seem to be more consistent with serving incrementally expanding enterprises, not the consistent level of demand one might envisage a *mansio* and casual travellers to represent.

As Burnham and Wacher (1990, 44) observed, the largest concentrations of 'first class' villas cluster around the larger 'small towns' not more major settlements, though other studies (such as Hingley 1989, 118–20) have come to a different conclusion, which might hint at particularly close connections between the two. The precise location of the settlement need not have been economically determined by the road itself at all. Any *mansio*, provided by local *civitas* authorities, may have stimulated an initial settlement agglomeration that drew in additional settlers. Furthermore, the status of the land bordering the road may have made it more conducive for settlement than that elsewhere. Settlement could even have been officially encouraged or sanctioned. Indeed, the often-noted absence of villas in the environs of Londinium may be relevant here. The distance from Enfield to Londinium is reasonable for a *mansio* location. But its location could have been determined by tenurial factors as well. If the hinterland of Londinium was an imperial estate devoid of private villas their possible appearance in Enfield might mark its northern edge (broadly a day's travel north of the city). If so the Enfield settlement could have grown round an official establishment (be it *mansio* or not) as much intended for administrators touring the boundaries of the estate as longer distance travellers.

However, if the road was an economic determinant of settlement location, as well as servicing any *mansio* and/or acting as a centre for the rural community to acquire 'consumables' (as the Hingley (1989) model would suggest), a potential factor in its primary economic role might well have been the redistribution of rural production. If the settlement existed in a villa landscape the villas would presumably have an agricultural surplus to market, quite probably to Londinium via Ermine Street, and it ought to be considered whether the settlement had a role in assembling loads and facilitating their transport. This could have encompassed the processing and forwarding of a range of animal and arable products (eg meat, hides, wool and beer as well as grain) and the settlement could even have served as a base for middlemen sourcing bulk supplies. Indeed, as it is the possible villas not roadside settlement that display the most obvious signs of wealth, were they 'operating' parts of it as an adjunct to farming, both as redistribution centre and roadside services including for example an inn, as Varro (*Rerum Rusticarum* 1.2.23) advised in the late 1st century BC? This is distinct from Hingley's (1989, 114–16) suggested parallels with the medieval situation, which envisage private enterprise as developing a hierarchy of 'local markets' at regular intervals determined by central place concepts.

Conclusion

Of course these speculations are not all new (eg Hingley 1989, 116–20; Salway 1981, 596–7). But the intention here has been to highlight 'commercial' redistribution as one possible element in the varied origins and economies of small roadside towns near major urban centres. Equating roadside location with reliance on passing travellers (or regarding rural consumers as the main economic base) is too simplistic. Even if a settlement had a primary function unconnected to servicing travellers or rural consumers and would have grown up anyway – whether or not it was developed as a way of diversifying a villa estate – the economic 'multiplier' effect of a roadside location is likely to have been a key determinant. Such a settlement could not fail to tap a transient market on its doorstep and naturally would accrue some local market centre functions. But like Churchfields (near enough to Ermine Street to suggest that it may have played a part in its location yet far enough away to rule it out as serving travellers) the Enfield settlement could have had, primary or subsidiary to its economy, a role in a mechanism of supply that led from a rural production zone via processing and redistribution centres, on to Ermine Street and thence to Londinium.

Ultimately few 'local centres' like that at Enfield are well-enough known for their role to be gauged other than by the application of various economic models reliant on assumptions about the fundamental nature of the Roman economy, assumptions that beg questions about levels of commercialisation, balance of governmental and private influence, and degree of mobility of resources. Therefore the recovery of archaeological evidence will be the key to making progress beyond the theoretical in studying the relationship of Londinium to those settlements that existed in its hinterland.

Acknowledgements

Harvey Sheldon's contribution to the archaeology of the city of London and Southwark is considerable, but his support for the investigation of its hinterland, the relationship of whose nucleated, villa and other settlements to Londinium is a Research Agenda priority, has also been important and he has long been the President of the Enfield Archaeological Society (EAS), so it is a pleasure here to present to him a provisional discussion of the results of over 40 years of work on Roman Enfield and Edmonton.

A full account of the Roman archaeology of Enfield and Edmonton is in preparation by the author who is grateful to the late Geoffrey Gillam, Les Whitmore, Roger Dormer and Mike Dewbrey of the EAS for making available site records and other archives drawn on there and here. The ideas contained herein grew out of and have benefited greatly from discussions with all of them but responsibility for any errors or opinions expressed rests solely with the author, who is also grateful to Jenny Hall for arranging access to records and artefacts held by the Museum of London, and to Les Whitmore for permission to use the illustration on which Figure 2.5.1 is based.

2.6 'The rest to some faint meaning make pretence, but Shadwell never deviates into sense' (further speculation about the Shadwell 'tower')
David Bird

Introduction

The title, quoting two lines from John Dryden (*Mac Flecknoe*), actually refers to one Thomas Shadwell, but seems to sum up both archaeological sites as a whole and the difficulties of making any sense of the discoveries at Shadwell. The Shadwell 'tower' caused great interest when it was first found in 1974, and for several years its initial interpretation as a signal station or watch tower (LD74; Johnson 1975, 280) was generally accepted (for example by no less a scholar than Ralph Merrifield: 1983, 192–4). In 1976 another excavation close by (LD76) found further evidence for Roman-period features. These excavations have only recently been published by David Lakin (Lakin *et al* 2002), to whom we owe a considerable debt for the achievement. He not only had to struggle with old records but for the tower part of the site had little in the way of records at all and few of the original finds, although fortunately some of the finds reports had survived. That it is possible to offer a different interpretation here should be seen as a tribute to his work, not a criticism.

The publication necessarily concentrated on making available the results of the excavations, but it also offered the opportunity for reconsideration of the purpose of the tower. It was suggested that this was more likely to have been a mausoleum, although the possibility of it being a temple *cella* was also explored (Lakin *et al* 2002, 25–6). The recent discovery of the bath house and other features just down the slope from the tower (HGA02) has led to further suggestions about the function of the Shadwell site as a whole (Anon 2003b; Anon 2004). This paper speculates further about the purpose of the tower, and will argue that a military link should not yet be dismissed.

The evidence

The tower was built near the edge of a terrace, south of which the ground sloped down to the Thames, which is now around 500m away (Lakin *et al* 2002, 7; the Roman river frontage is as yet unrecorded). It had foundations of mortared flint and chalk approximately 1.9m wide and was about 9m square externally. What little of the walls survived above foundation level suggests that they were built of the same material as the foundations and flint-faced with tile courses that did not penetrate the full width of the wall. It is likely that ragstone from

later layers and features on the site came from the bath house (see below). Internally there was a floor level, or make-up for a floor, of sand over a deposit of sand and clay, with a fragmentary pot dating to after AD 150 (Lakin *et al* 2002, 10), the most obvious origin of which would be a disturbed burial: a fragment of a Nene Valley colour coat vessel was noted from one cremation group to the east (Lakin *et al* 2002, 8). The foundations were apparently only c 450mm deep, but as they were very wide and probably founded on gravel quite a tall structure may have been possible (the immediate subsoil was probably brickearth, but the site ditches were said to cut sand and gravel; Lakin et al 2002, 7 and 15). It is quite possible that there was a timber-framed upper structure, although the buttresses on the southern side (above the slope) may suggest that at least the ground floor of the tower was stone built with tile levelling courses.

As well as the tower, various other features were found, but there is some difficulty in phasing them because of lack of records (Lakin *et al* 2002, 10). Pottery indicates three main periods of activity: late 1st–early 2nd century, the middle of the 3rd century and the mid- to late 4th century (Seeley 2002, 31). The sequence probably begins with some brickearth quarrying in the 1st century and occasional use for cremation burials, perhaps mostly in the mid-2nd century (although much of the pottery is earlier, many of the vessels may have already been damaged or worn when buried and some are specifically dated to AD 150 or later; Lakin *et al* 2002, 8–9 and 13). It is possible that two inhumations known from the site also belong to this phase of use (Lakin *et al* 2002, 24), and this simpler interpretation is perhaps to be preferred to the idea of a late Roman return to burying at this location. Later dress items thought to be possibly related to burials (Lakin *et al* 2002, 27) can now be explained as linked in some way to the finds from the building north of the bath house (Anon 2004, 25). The site was, therefore, probably not part of the major eastern London cemetery where nearest known burials are c 500m to the west (Lakin *et al* 2002, 2).

The site may then have been little used until the mid-3rd century. The majority of the pottery dates to this period (Seeley 2002, 31), and it is perhaps most likely that the tower was constructed at this time. It has no obvious relationship to the burials whereas it is in alignment with several features probably of this date: a large ditch, several shallow pits and a narrow timber building about 4m wide

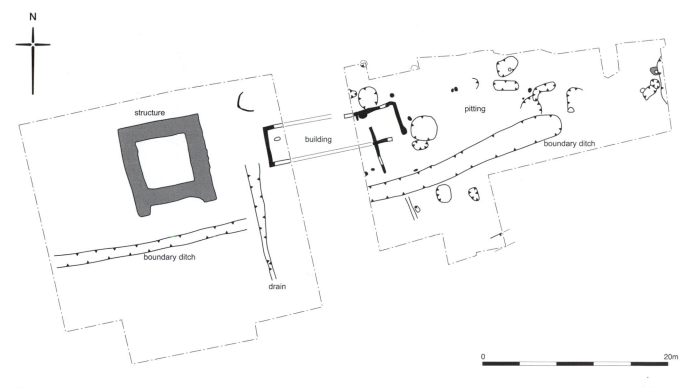

Fig 2.6.1 The tower and possibly related mid-3rd-century features (after Lakin et al 2002, figs 7–9)

and 15m in length, apparently with its long southern side partly open (Fig 2.6.1). Later excavations suggest that the ditch continued for more than 50m to the west (Anon 2004, 23). A timber-lined drain ran at right angles to the ditch, starting from between the tower and the timber building. These features could also be contemporary with the construction of the bath house and other structures to the south. The fill of the ditch near the tower 'contained nearly half the pottery (by EVEs) from the site and in general differs from much of the rest of the pottery: the average sherd size is larger and less abraded, and there are a substantial number of complete profiles'; there were also two nearly complete glass vessels (Lakin *et al* 2002, 19). The pottery is dated up to about AD 270 or a little later and there were coins of AD 270–90 and AD 324–34. The latter seem out of place and may be intrusive, perhaps from the later gullies that cut across the ditch or from slumping of later layers (Lakin *et al* 2002, 16 and 20). It seems reasonable to interpret the evidence as an organised site clearance at some point near the end of the 3rd century, or, if the later coins are not intrusive, clearance after a period of abandonment before the next use of the site.

Again there seems to have been a hiatus in use of the site, until around the mid-4th century, when some sort of industrial use is possible, with one or two timber-lined 'tanks' and drains. Various gullies may also date to this phase as some at least are stratigraphically later than earlier features such as the main ditch and the timber building, their fills include some much later finds and they have a rather random pattern. Although the main 'drain' appears to cut the line of one of the gullies, a site photograph suggests that this area was much disturbed and it is noticeable that the other features whose line should have crossed the same area were not recorded here (Lakin *et al* 2002, 11, fig 6; 16, fig 9; 20, fig 10; Merrifield 1983, 191, fig 30; 193, pl 48). The gullies were filled with demolition material, mostly from timber buildings but including stone, perhaps indicating initial site clearance before the final phase when a large spread of rubble including ragstone/limestone, chalk, mortar, roof tile, flue tiles and *opus signinum* suggests activity associated with the demolition of a major building, which was probably the bath house (Lakin *et al* 2002, 23–4; Anon 2004, 24). Pottery and coins associated with the fill of the gullies and with the rubble layer suggest that this activity was taking place in or after AD 365, and coins indicate that any remnants of the tower were also robbed at this time (Lakin *et al* 2002, 20, 23 and 24). It is not clear if the tower was still standing; there may only have been stub walls surviving by then, particularly if the structure was partly timber framed, as suggested above.

The explanations

Four explanations have been proposed for the tower, not necessarily mutually exclusive: a mausoleum; a temple; a structure related in some way to the bath house or a new port; a signal station or watch tower.

Could the tower have been a mausoleum? This suggestion was made because of the nearby cremations, but there is little or no evidence from the tower itself (Lakin *et al* 2002, 24). The cremations are mostly in two small groups and hardly seem to relate to the tower in any way; in contrast, the latter *is* related to several other features, as noted above. The structure would also be large for a mausoleum, with unusually wide walls (Lakin *et al* 2002, 26), and the latter objection applies even more to interpretation as a cemetery enclosure. The cremations pre-date later structures and by the mid-3rd-century activity on the tower site is surely too extensive to be associated with a local burial ground (for which there is no contemporary evidence). On balance, interpretation as a mausoleum is unlikely.

Could the structure have been a temple *cella*? Lack of an ambulatory or of an entrance on the east does not necessarily exclude it, but it would certainly be on the large side (Lakin *et al* 2002, 10). The coins from the site could be offerings (Hammerson 2002, 54) but none of the other finds suggests a religious interpretation and the samian seems unlikely in this context. It is perhaps also unlikely that the finds would bunch in three main periods. The site would be quite good for a temple: it would be prominently placed for those coming up river, and the place-name perhaps indicates a noted spring – 'shallow well or spring' (Gover *et al* 1942, 151). A healing shrine would fit well with the bath house and the jewellery and other female-related objects (Lakin *et al* 2002, 27; Anon 2004, 25), but given the scale of the baths we would expect an altogether more elaborate central shrine. On balance, interpretation as a temple is unlikely.

Could the tower be linked in some way to the bath house or other nearby buildings? One rather curious suggestion was use as a 'water tower' (Anon 2003b), but in the absence of any parallels (except settling tanks on raised aqueducts like that at Segovia) this is unlikely. As well as the bath house several other contemporary buildings are now known on the slope below the tower, and divided from it by the main ditch (Anon 2004, 26). Although quite a large area has been subject to examination these buildings are quite scattered, but the whole area has been subject to a great deal of later disturbance. The known buildings all seem to be timber-framed and align roughly east–west, in line with the tower (Anon 2004, 23). It has been suggested that the buildings were part of new port facilities, replacing those in London because construction of the riverside wall cut them off from the city (Anon 2004, 22). This raises the extraordinary spectacle of goods being unloaded downstream at an undefended port so as to be taken by road to the defended city through gates in the landward wall because the city authorities had not thought to provide gates in the riverside wall.

The idea of a new port is based in part on the suggestion that falling river levels led to the need to move the port facilities downstream (eg Brigham 1990b, 159–60). The evidence is not, however, conclusive and probably too much is made of the absence of later dated waterfronts on certain specific sites in London and of the need to use the tidal

flow to reach the city. New arrangements for the waterfronts would have been required as a result of the building of the riverside wall and the disuse of some, as at New Fresh Wharf, is probably closer in date to the construction of the riverside wall than is sometimes allowed. There may be some evidence for new arrangements in London (Perring 1991a, 108), which coupled with the use of lighters (Brigham 1990b, 147) might well have been sufficient for the port to continue. A probable seagoing ship dated to the end of the 3rd century (or later) is known from the County Hall site (Merrifield 1983, 201–2), and the dramatisation depicted on the Arras medallion of Constantius rescuing London in AD 296 implies that he arrived by ship (eg Merrifield 1983, 201, fig 49). The building of the riverside wall strongly implies a fear that the city could be attacked by raiders sailing up the river. No evidence for port facilities or a new road network has so far been found at Shadwell.

Could the original idea of a signal station or watch tower be correct? Unfortunately we have few parallels for the date or the location. The Yorkshire coast 'signal stations' are later and set in very different circumstances (Lakin *et al* 2002, 25; see now Hind 2005). Signal towers on the German *limes* show that such structures could be timber-framed (eg Baatz 1993, 43 fig 26), but they too were intended for use in different circumstances. It is generally accepted that the great monument at Richborough was used as a signal station or watch tower at some point in the 3rd century before the Carausian period (Cunliffe 1968, 244), which suggests that we might be unwise to seek a standard type. If the tower was originally a mausoleum it would therefore be acceptable to postulate that it was reused. Such things would hardly cause a problem for people who were now regularly using tombstones and broken-up religious monuments to build city walls. A signalling line to Richborough and/or along the Thames would certainly make sense (Fig. 2.6.2), perhaps comparable to the line of watch towers now thought to have existed along parts of the lower Rhine (Wilson and Creighton 1999, 28). It may be noted that Cohors I Baetasiorum, the garrison of the shore fort at Reculver at some point in the late 2nd or early 3rd century, probably had Maryport as its previous posting (Philp 2005, 225), where it is likely to have had good experience of working with signalling towers (Woolliscroft 2001, 88–9, 95–6). Of course this may not have been relevant by the mid-3rd century, and there is currently no archaeological evidence for a signalling line from Richborough or Reculver or along the Thames, although it is intriguing to note that a cemetery at Mucking has produced several samian vessels of a similar date to those at Shadwell (Bird 1993, 4, 8 and 10). The strategic importance of this site on a higher river terrace has long been recognised (Jones 1968, 212; Myres 1968, 226–7).

A signal station at Shadwell may be unlikely, at least on present evidence, but a watch tower would not be out of place. The Shadwell site would give a

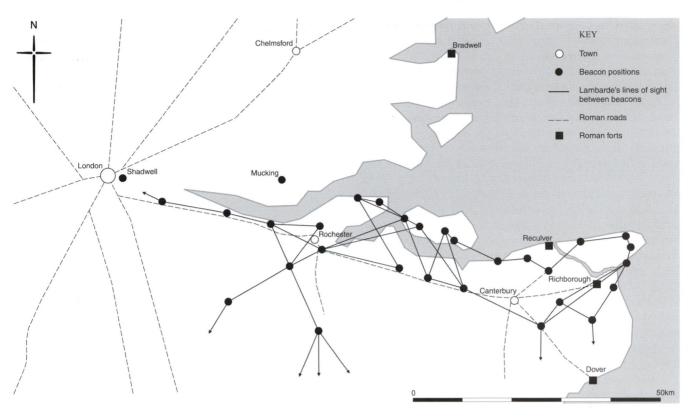

Fig 2.6.2 Shadwell in its setting from London to the east coast, with Roman roads and sites mentioned in the text. Kentish beacon positions and their lines of sight recorded by Lambarde in 1585 are shown as an indication of the options for workable beacon chains on the southern side of the Thames (after William Lambarde's map printed in Rodríguez-Salgado et al 1988, 148, fig 7.69)

good view of danger approaching from some distance down river. It is also well placed to act as the end of a beacon chain, which would be of particular value to warn of a threat at night (Woolliscroft 2001, 25 and 30). The use of beacons has also been identified in a later Saxon context (Reynolds 1999, 95–6, with some reference to the situation along the Thames east of London). If the tower was part of a military establishment, mounted messengers could quickly carry information on to the city. A 'noticeably high proportion of horse bone', thought not to be intended for human consumption, came from the main ditch associated with the mid-3rd-century phases (Lakin *et al* 2002, 18), and the only definite military item from the site is a piece of horse harness (Lakin *et al* 2002, 26; Wardle 2002a, 53). Could the open-fronted building alongside the tower have served as a stable, making use of the adjacent drain?

Discussion

An important aspect of the first excavations was the comparatively large amount of late samian ware dated to AD 225–50 (Bird 2002, 31). The high proportion of late East Gaulish wares is very unusual, particularly for a non-urban site, and is best paralleled in a military context (Bird 2002, 35). This type of material is often found on later

military sites, such as South Shields, Piercebridge, Brancaster, Caister-on-Sea, Richborough, Reculver and Dover (Bird 1993, *passim* and pers comm). Its presence at Shadwell as part of a trade consignment (eg Brigham 1990b, 160) does not square with the evidence of the pottery itself (Bird 2002, 35). It is considered likely, however, that the late samian reached the site at about the same time, which would suggest that it was either provided in response to a specific demand or brought in by a particular group or high-ranking individual.

Much of the rest of the pottery matches the samian in date and to some extent in quality (Lakin *et al* 2002, 16–18). Most of the glass vessels are of generally good quality and are likely to date to the 3rd century; a flask from the main ditch seems to be a rare find in a British context although well known on the Continent (Shepherd 2002, 50–1). The sudden leap in numbers of coins from the site dated after AD 250 is not unusual, but Hammerson notes (2002, 54) that 'some form of activity on the site during the 250s is suggested by the three coins of Maximinus I [AD 235–38], Trebonianus Gallus [AD 251–53]) and Volusian [also AD 251–53], the first showing some wear and the others only slight wear'. The two later coins are unusual as site finds (Richard Reece pers comm), as are two coins of Aurelian (AD 269–75), two of Tacitus (AD 275–76) and one of Probus (AD 276–82). Also notable was an unusually high proportion (in total 39) of coins of Carausius and Allectus (AD 287–93 and 293–96) (Hammerson 2002, 55).

Taken all together, the finds from Shadwell indicate a high-status site established around AD 250 or later. At this time and in this location, outside and downstream from the defended centre, it is logical to assume that the site had an official, military purpose. It is not clear whether there might have been other possible military objects in addition to the solitary harness fitting (itself known only from an archive drawing) from the site (Wardle 2002a, 53). The animal bone associated with the mid-3rd-century use of the site probably indicates on-site butchery, with a high proportion of cattle bones indicating a beef diet (Rielly and Ainsley 2002, 63), both aspects characteristic of urban and military sites. A large proportion (82%) of the coins of Carausius and Allectus were found in the trench that included the tower (Hammerson 2002, 57), so it is unfortunate that the 1974 material from that particular area was not available for study (Wardle 2002a, 51).

The construction of the bath house can apparently also be dated to the mid-3rd century (Anon 2004, 22). Its unusually good survival makes it appear special, but in fact it would not be out of place in a military context. Reasonable parallels in scale and layout of rooms can be seen associated with forts in Germany and beyond (eg Baatz 1993, 28, fig 19; 147, fig 78; 286, fig 133) and much nearer home it might be noted that the baths on the Winchester Palace site in Southwark have a military connection (Sheldon 2000, 133–4). Military bath houses were usually outside forts, often found among buildings similar to the others now known at Shadwell. On the other hand what is known of the 3rd-century shore forts indicates that we should not expect much of the old military regularity of buildings by this date. The female accessories from a building near the bath house (Anon 2004, 25) would also not be out of place in or near a later military establishment, indicating families associated with the soldiers. For instance, finds from the Caerleon bath house suggest regular female use (Bidwell 1997, 82) and many hairpins were found at Reculver (Chenery 2005, 162–5).

The mid-3rd century was a time of considerable upheaval, with coastal raids, frequent trouble on the Rhine and Danube frontiers, and even more frequent changes of emperor (Frere 1987, 172–5). In consequence, troops were often moved around, including British detachments, such as those Gallienus took with him to the Danube in the later 250s (Frere 1987, 173). Others travelled in the opposite direction. Two of the legions listed on coins of Carausius (IIII Flavia and VII Claudia) were based on the Danube and to explain this it has been suggested that vexillations may have found their way to a base that came to be within his 'empire' (Williams 2004, 69). It has recently been shown that a unit, with its women and children, based at the northern fort of Brougham within the period AD 220–300, probably

originated in the Danube area. Related finds also showed a strong Rhenish component including late East Gaulish samian (Cool 2004, 463–6). In this context, two coins of Aemilian and Trajan Decius of the period AD 250–53 from the shore fort at Reculver are noteworthy because they are very unusual in Britain. The simplest explanation is in terms of the movement of people, such as a troop movement from the Danube (Reece 2005, 103). The coins are likely to have been removed from circulation by AD 280. A probably 3rd-century intaglio of Jupiter Optimus Maximus from Reculver without direct British parallels but identical to ones from Bonn and Cologne may also be noted (Henig 2005, 182). These finds provide an interesting context for the unusual coins of about AD 250–80 at Shadwell, together with the samian and glass, and other imported material such as the Moselkeramik, Cologne colour coat and Rhineland white ware vessels (Lakin *et al* 2002, 16).

If there was a military establishment at Shadwell in the mid-3rd century, what would it be? London merchants involved in a Rhine-Thames trade axis would be very conscious of the dangers posed by seaborne raids and therefore concerned about attacks up the river to London. Arguments that such raiding was not possible in the later Roman period (Cotterill 1993, 228) seriously underrate earlier seafaring abilities (Gifford and Gifford 2002; Mason 2003, 164–7; Haywood 2005). The forts at Reculver, Brancaster and Caister-on-Sea were possibly built by the end of the 2nd century (Philp 2005, 225–6) and other shore forts were added throughout the 3rd century and later. The only reasonable explanation for them is coastal protection of some sort. The London riverside wall must have been built in anticipation of raids up the river, and seems to have been started not long after the mid-3rd century (Perring 1991a, 107). A fleet based to protect London would therefore be likely, particularly while the wall was being built. Flotilla bases were increasingly sited in rivers or estuaries in the later Roman period; possible sites at Rouen and near Bordeaux would make good parallels for London (Johnson 1976, 77 and 83). In the early 11th century ships were stationed at Greenwich to protect London in just this way (Hagland and Watson 2005, 329); Shadwell is in a similar loop of the river. Although the *Classis Britannica* was still in existence around the mid-3rd century (Cunliffe 1968, 261), no bases are known after the fort at Dover was given up at the beginning of the century (Philp 2005, 229). The later fleet is usually thought to have been divided between different locations, and, for instance, associated with shore forts (Mason 2003, 140–3).

Carausian activity at Shadwell is suggested by the comparatively large number of coins of this period. Coins were required to pay officials and troops (Reece 2002, 49), so a military (and perhaps fleet base?) link again suggests itself. Carausius must have been well informed (he knew of the intention to remove him from his command) and well known in British and other military circles (he would not have been accepted as emperor otherwise; cf Frere 1987, 326). It is not difficult to imagine the fleet commander wanting a well-placed and comfortable base near London. The British 'empire' came to an end with the defeat of Allectus in AD 296. There are no coins of AD 296–310 at Shadwell and although this could be the result of a 'period of stability' (Hammerson 2002, 54) when coin loss is usually comparatively low (Reece 2002, 57), the pottery evidence suggests a hiatus (Seeley 2002, 31). There was probably a defensive reorganisation after Allectus (Frere 1987, 331) and it is tempting to suggest that the apparent site clearance at Shadwell at the end of the 3rd century is connected. Indeed, throwing away samian and more or less complete glass vessels, when evidence suggests that it was usual to look after such material, may indicate that something dramatic happened at the site. Evidence from both the 'tower' part of the site and the more recent excavations (Anon 2004, 24–6) suggests that activity was thereafter much reduced.

Conclusions

Clearly a firm conclusion about the purpose of the Shadwell tower is impossible with the current state of our knowledge. The nature of our dating evidence for all features in the area is such that even where they can be reasonably well dated we cannot say that any of them are truly contemporary, and the tower itself could be many years earlier. But it is evident that a great deal started to happen at Shadwell around the middle of the 3rd century, and on the tower site it continued to the end of the century with at least implied Carausian period activity. It seems most logical to place an unusual tower-like structure at the time when unusual things were happening on site. In such a location and with such quality and oddity of finds, a military establishment makes most sense and therefore interpretation of the structure as a watch tower associated with such an establishment should not yet be dismissed.

Acknowledgements

It is a great pleasure to offer a paper to Harvey, whose friendship I have valued over many years (even if he has never quite forgiven me for once beating him at table football). I hope he will enjoy this rather speculative paper and that it will stimulate further discussion.

I have had a great deal of assistance from my wife, Joanna, by no means only resulting from her extensive knowledge of samian ware. Richard Reece has also been very helpful, as have the editors. Finally, it is appropriate to thank David Lakin and his specialists, without whose hard work this paper would not have been possible.

2.7 Roman Westminster: fact or fiction?
Chris Thomas

Introduction

Westminster has not generally proved to be a productive hunting ground for archaeologists interested in the Roman period, and yet there is tantalising evidence of more to be discovered there than might appear at first glance (Fig 2.7.1). This article seeks to review some of what is known about Roman Westminster, which is defined here as the area to the west of the modern City of London and south of the line of the old Roman road beneath the modern Oxford Street. Thorney Island, where so much of the centre of later English and British history lies, provides a focus.

Much of the debate on Roman Westminster has centred on those crucial first few years after the Roman invasion before the founding of Londinium in c AD 50. As we shall see, this debate is focused to a significant extent on the layout of the Roman roads and their relationship to the city of Londinium itself. However, even the road network is very much a matter of supposition and is often hotly disputed. What is generally agreed is that, by the later Roman period, there were two routes westward out of Londinium: one following the line of Holborn and Oxford Street out of Newgate, the other following the line of Fleet Street and the Strand out of Ludgate. What is disputed is the layout of the roads prior to the foundation of Londinium.

After the foundation of the town, the lands immediately west of Newgate were used for burial and it is not intended to review the copious evidence for that here (but see Hall 1996, 58–64). But what of the environs of Covent Garden, the Island of Thorney and the lands west where Piccadilly, the West End and the Royal Parks now lie?

The invasion years: AD 43–50

Our knowledge of the tactics of the invading Roman armies in AD 43 with regard to the London area is sketchy at best, with Dio Cassius's oft quoted passage on the invading armies chasing the local tribes through the marshes the only real evidence. He states that:

> The Britons retreated to the River Thames in the area where it empties into the Ocean and at flood-tide forms a lake. They crossed it without difficulty, as they had accurate knowledge of the firm ground and the places where movement was possible. But the Romans in attempting to follow them went astray in the area. However, the Germans again swam across, and another group crossed someway upstream by a bridge. Then they attacked the barbarians from several sides at once and cut down many of them. But they pursued the rest somewhat incautiously and fell into marshes from which it was difficult to extricate themselves and they lost a large number of men.
>
> Togodomnus had died about this time, but the Britons, far from yielding, joined together all the more firmly to avenge his death. Because of this, and because of the losses encountered at the Thames, Plautius took alarm and advanced no further. Instead he proceeded to guard what had already been won and sent for Claudius; this is what he had been ordered to do if there was any particularly stubborn resistance.
> (Hind 1989)

This then is the historical evidence but it raises at least as many questions as it answers. Where exactly did the Britons cross? Where was this bridge by which the Romans crossed? Where exactly did the battle take place? Was that the real reason that

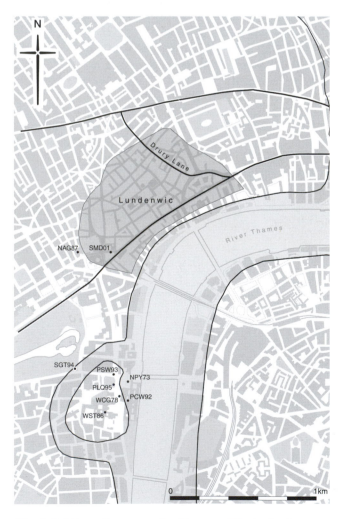

Fig 2.7.1 Location map for Roman Westminster, with road network, finds spots and extended river

Claudius came over to join his armies? To take the last of these questions first, surely it is much more plausible that the victory 'triumph' was deliberately delayed until Claudius could arrive to take the credit as a political gesture.

The most important element of Dio Cassius's description is that the Britons crossed the river at the point where the tide met the flowing river and that when the tide went out it left 'a lake' where it was possible to ford the river.

Recent work has demonstrated that the Thames was tidal at Westminster during the Bronze Age (Sidell *et al* 2000, 109–10; Thomas *et al* 2006, 13–14; Fig 2.7.2). The recovery in 1910 from County Hall of a Roman ship that would seem to have required tidal waters in which to operate (Marsden 1994, 109–29) suggests that stretch of the river was still tidal in the Roman period, although there does seem to be evidence of a move downstream of the tidal head in the late Roman period (see Milne *et al* 1983; Brigham 1990b; Sidell *et al* 2000, 110; and Sidell, this volume). How much further upstream the river was tidal is unclear but we should certainly be looking for a crossing point between Westminster and perhaps Battersea. However, the area from Thorney Island to Victoria is mostly low-lying, due to the delta formed by the tributaries of the Tyburn and

Westbourne, and a most unsuitable site for fording the Thames. Traditionally, the crossing point has been given as Westminster but it is important to point out that there is no archaeological evidence for this (Sloane *et al* 1995) despite various definitive assertions that the crossing was there. This does not mean that the crossing was not at Westminster, merely that there is no archaeological evidence for it.

So where was this bridge and how did the Romans get to the crossing point? We have no evidence for a bridge of this date, nor were any of the roads laid out prior to AD 50. Various road alignments in Southwark have been postulated from archaeological evidence as pointing towards a junction with a putative Watling Street but these are based on short lengths of minor roads and, in any case, the topography does not allow the traditional straight alignment for the roads. As we know, the low-lying areas of Southwark and Lambeth provide a particularly difficult terrain upon which to build settlements and roads, and it is now clear that the Romans settled the higher eyots and then 'island hopped', jumping from island to island across the shortest possible route. Thus, an analysis of the topography is the starting point from which we should make a judgement about any routes the invading armies might have taken.

Fig 2.7.2 Thorney Island lay at the confluence of the Thames (foreground) and Tyburn (top) in the Bronze Age (modern buildings have been left in to give an impression of scale!)

It is generally assumed that the Romans set up camp somewhere on the London fringes although even this has been disputed (Bird 1994), with Elephant and Castle and even Mayfair put forward as potential locations (Fuentes 1985; Sole 1993). Again, archaeological evidence is entirely lacking and, indeed, the lack of even a smattering of finds from the SMR suggests the idea of a 'metropolis in Mayfair' is somewhat far fetched. It has been argued that a temporary encampment might leave little in the archaeological record but Caesar's *de bello Gallico* tells us that even the most short-lived encampment was a remarkable piece of engineering that would have left plenty for the archaeologist to find. So where do we get concentrations of Roman artefacts from the 1st century? The only concentration of Roman material known in the Westminster area is at Thorney Island, and this is all post-1st century in date.

It seems plausible that the Roman armies came to London along the line of Watling Street, even if it did not exist as a major thoroughfare at the time, coming down from the high ground in Greenwich before picking their way across the Thames floodplain. It is difficult to imagine a point downstream where they might have forded the Thames so it seems likely that they crossed at some point from Westminster upstream, and we do at least have concentrations of Roman material at Thorney Island, Westminster, even if they are 2nd century and later in date. We should therefore accept that, while at present we do not have sufficient archaeological information upon which to put forward strong hypotheses, we might try to concentrate our efforts on the high ground at Thorney Island to see if there is any evidence for a fording point, an encampment, or even a battle. Environmental sampling and topographic modelling may also be critical to our understanding of the tidal reach of the Thames in the 1st century and this may help to focus our attention.

Roman Westminster after the establishment of Londinium

Covent Garden

The large number of sarcophagi found in the vicinity of St Martin-in-the-Fields in the past suggests that the area was used for burial, and the recent discovery of another (Fig 2.7.3) seems to confirm this, but there have also been persistent suggestions of other Roman activity there. Recent excavations have uncovered a late Roman tile kiln beneath the crypts of the church, adding a rather confusing industrial nature to the activities in the area (SMD01; Gordon Malcolm pers comm). The presence of a tile kiln would imply brickearth quarrying in the area during the late Roman period but the largest quarries excavated were found beneath the National Gallery extension and have been dated to

Fig 2.7.3 Stone sarcophagus found in 2006 during excavations at St Martin-in-the-Fields (SMD01). It contained the skeleton of a man in his late 30s or early 40s who had probably died between c AD 390 and 430

the Middle Saxon period (NAG87; Whytehead *et al* 1989, 60–5). Elsewhere in the Covent Garden area, the excavations have focused on the nationally important discoveries of the Saxon town of Lundenwic, and the low levels of residual Roman artefactual material; lack of accompanying features or stratigraphy suggests any Roman activity there was light, quite possibly agricultural.

The West End

Evidence for Roman activity west of the land later occupied by Saxon Lundenwic is even more difficult to find. However, what discoveries have been made conform to what one might expect. A review of the road system combined with topographic information immediately suggests that some revisions to current thinking should be made. Firstly, there seems little reason to doubt that the line of the Oxford Street road continued eastwards as what is now modern-day Bayswater Road, and that the Strand road continued westwards as Piccadilly – although not surprisingly there is no archaeological evidence for either. It also seems clear that the line of Whitehall and the now demolished King Street led to Thorney Island and that Tothill Street might also have existed in the Roman period. If so, it must have crossed the River Tyburn twice, first when it left Thorney Island and then again somewhere in the vicinity of Buckingham Palace where it would have continued and joined Piccadilly around Hyde Park Corner. This area could perhaps be of greater importance and warrant closer examination, as the points at which the roads crossed the Tyburn and Westbourne rivers might be sites at which some form of settlement occurred. It has also long been considered that Watling Street continued north-wards along the line of Park Lane to join the line of Oxford Street but despite investigations in the area no evidence for the road has been uncovered.

There seems no reason not to suppose that the Roman road continued westwards along the line of Kensington Gore and Kensington High Street as these seem to follow the higher ground away from the Thames floodplain. The discovery of Roman buildings and ditches in this area in 1994 (MAK94; Howe 1998) suggests that the area was farmland in the hinterland of Londinium and that the structures might have been part of a small farmstead. Indeed, there is some evidence for continuity of use of this site from the Iron Age.

Thorney Island

On Thorney Island itself there are numerous antiquarian observations of Roman features and artefacts but relatively few from modern archaeo-logical work. The earliest was the discovery of a stone sarcophagus immediately north of Westmin-ster Abbey nave in 1851 (Poole 1870). This was thought to have had a later Saxon cross inscribed into it and is then thought to have been reused after the realigning of the nave in the 12th and 13th centuries (Thomas *et al* 2006).

Other antiquarian observations include the discovery of a wall, thought to be of Roman date, running at an oblique angle to the nave, part of a hypocaust, found when the grave of George Gilbert Scott was dug in 1866 (Westlake 1923, 2), *opus signinum* floors beneath the cloister buildings (RCHM(E) 1928, 148) and Roman tile courses in the walls of the nave and apse of Edward the Confessor's abbey church (Robinson 1910, 99–100; Tanner and Clapham 1933, 233). Analysis of the levels at which the *opus signinum* floors were found clearly indicates that they were not *in situ* Roman floors but reused building material placed on top of a flood silt laid down in the mid-11th century (Thomas *et al* 2006, 38). The reuse of Roman building material on Thorney Island was clearly widespread.

More recent archaeological discoveries include the recovery of Roman ceramics from a mid-11th-century ditch beneath the undercroft of the east range of the abbey cloister (WST86; Goffin 1995, 97),

opus signinum and ceramic tiles in the robber trenches of a 12th-century building in the south-east corner of Parliament Square, and one robbed out wall and two drystone walls of probable Roman date beneath Parliament Square (PSW93; PLQ95; Thomas *et al* 2006, 35–9). Other sites have also produced Roman artefacts, although it is perhaps significant that these become fewer the further the excavations are from the highest point of the island, beneath the abbey. These include a Roman brick seen in the foundations of St Stephen's Chapel and Roman stone and brick from New Palace Yard.

Finally, pits of Roman date were also excavated beneath the Treasury Buildings in the 1960s, immediately to the north of Thorney Island adjacent to the northern branch of the Tyburn.

Conclusions

So what are we to make of this limited data? Can we characterise the nature of the settlement, and can we put it into a chronological framework?

It seems clear that the West End and much of Covent Garden was agricultural land run as small-holdings, comprising ditched enclosures serviced by the typical range of small farm buildings as evidenced by the occupation found in Kensington. Large areas of what is now dry land, not only by the Thames but in the Tyburn and Westbourne deltas, were part of the river system – either under water or prone to flooding. Nevertheless, settlements may have built up around river crossings, for instance around Hyde Park Corner where the road lines crossed the Tyburn and Westbourne, and to the north, where the Oxford Street road crossed the Tyburn. There may have been a Roman cemetery in the region of St Martin-in-the-Fields but it is by no means certain that the sarcophagi were not brought from elsewhere for reuse in the Saxon period. The recent discovery of industrial activity adds a new and intriguing element to our understanding of the area. It may represent no more than local makers exploiting the available resources, but it is still hard to rationalise brickearth quarrying and tile making within a cemetery.

There seems to be clear evidence of occupation on Thorney Island. Whilst the number of attributable features is low, the finds *corpora*, and in particular the building material, indicate that there must have been Roman structures there. It seems scarcely credible that the builders of the 11th-century abbey, the 13th-century St Stephen's Chapel, or the other main abbey and palace buildings, would have gone to the trouble of recovering Roman bricks, tiles and *opus signinum* from the City of London a mile down-stream simply to add to the large quantities of new medieval building stone that were being used in the construction of those buildings. Nor does it seem likely that anyone would have bothered dragging a large stone sarcophagus from the environs of the city or even from the environs of St Martin-in-the-Fields for reuse after accidentally discovering it. The Roman boat found on the opposite bank in 1910 must also have been going somewhere upstream of the city.

There is no evidence either way to indicate whether the Romans initially forded the Thames at Westminster. We do know there was substantial settlement on Thorney Island in the Neolithic and Bronze Age periods but there is only meagre evidence for the Iron Age (Thomas *et al* 2006, 30–2). What there is seems mostly to come from the highest ground beneath the abbey, much like the Roman material, suggesting that the river level may have been higher at that time, making the lower-lying areas liable to flooding. So perhaps we should be looking for evidence of Roman (and indeed Iron Age) occupation of Thorney Island on gravel that lies above 1m OD (or even at above 1.5m OD) – the river certainly exceeded that level to the east in the city (Milne 1985, 84). Then there is the movement of the tidal head to consider. Westminster was certainly tidal in the Bronze Age and it was certainly not tidal there in the late Roman period, but it is unclear whether it was tidal in the early Roman period. Thus it may well have been the late Roman sea-level regression that took the tidal head downstream of Westminster.

A quick glance at the location map (Fig 2.7.1) shows clearly that we should be looking for Roman Westminster underneath what is now the abbey and perhaps Parliament Square – precisely where the most compelling evidence lies.

So what should we make of the dating evidence? Although meagre, the finds seem to date from at least the 2nd century to the end of the Roman period, suggesting that Thorney Island was occupied from quite early and was then in use throughout. We are, however, seriously lacking in well-dated features.

It is in the character of the settlement that we have the most interesting evidence. There have been no observations of clay and timber buildings, no evidence for streets, no large assemblages of ceramics and other finds *corpora*, no deeply stratified building sequences; in short nothing that symbolises urban occupation. The evidence is, in fact, of high-status masonry buildings with *opus signinum* floors and hypocausts, situated on the highest ground beneath Westminster Abbey. Even the evidence for Roman structures beneath Parliament Square (Thomas *et al* 2006, 35–8) indicates that they were of masonry.

Thus we have high-status masonry buildings situated on high ground on an island a mile or so upstream of Londinium. They must have been serviced by roads, so versions of the medieval Whitehall and King Street (destroyed in the 19th century) to the north and Tothill Street to the west seem likely to have existed in the Roman period, in which case the Romans must also have bridged the Tyburn. We cannot say at this juncture whether the buildings were public but their distance from the city might suggest that they were not. If private they would seem to be fairly substantial and might be indicative of a large residence for a wealthy and important member of the Roman community. Alternatively, and with a nice sense of continuity, might the complex have been religious? Perhaps the monks' account of the abbey being founded on a Temple of Diana wasn't a fictitious attempt to keep up with St Paul's after all – they must surely have been aware of the large quantities of Roman material being uncovered and sometimes reused every time a deep foundation was dug. The Romans may even have been deliberately using an important prehistoric religious site as is well attested elsewhere.

For the future, archaeologists must avail themselves of every opportunity to examine areas in and around the abbey if we are ever to develop our understanding of what was clearly an important site in the Roman and prehistoric periods, not just the medieval and later.

2.8 A possible extension to Grim's Dyke
Colin Bowlt

Introduction

Writing in LAMAS *Transactions* Hugh Braun (1936, 379) said 'The problem of Grim's Dyke [Middlesex] is one which has been tantalising antiquaries for several centuries'. In spite of archaeological investigations since then, the date and purpose of this earthwork are still tantalisingly unclear.

Stone (1935) published a detailed field survey, with six maps based on the OS 6 inch (1:10,560) 1897 map, of the several sections of Grim's Dyke still extant in his time. It is, or was, a large earthwork, and appears to have been at least 4 to 5 miles (6.5–8km) long. Stone noted, however, that it had been much mutilated in recent years, and this process has continued since then. His survey, from Cuckoo Hill/Pinner Green in the west to Harrow Weald Common in the east, with the sections still visible, is shown superimposed on a modern street map in Figure 2.8.1. Stone noted that the condition of the earthwork was very often indistinct, the ditch having completely disappeared in some places – but that in the grounds of Grim's Dyke House (now a hotel) 'considerate treatment has preserved a very important section of the earthwork, which must have suffered little damage from man or time' (1935, 286).

A note in the *Antiquaries Journal* of 1923 (Anon 1923, 66) claimed that the line of the Dyke had been picked up westward of Cuckoo Hill with remnants preserved in gardens, hedges and wooded areas as far as the River Colne, Uxbridge, and possibly as far as Langley Church. This is one of several such reported field observations of supposed extensions of the Dyke both eastward and westward which have never been substantiated. More recently Castle (1975) published results of excavations of an earthwork at Pear Wood, Brockley Hill, and pointed out that these, plus documentary evidence, suggest it to be an eastern continuation of the Harrow and Pinner Grim's Dyke. It is the purpose of this paper to summarise the archaeological findings to date, and then to show that an archaeological investigation of an earthwork at Ruislip suggests that it may be a western extension of Grim's Dyke (Fig 2.8.2).

All commentators have agreed that Grim's Dyke was a significant earthwork, but actual recorded measurements are few. Even those given are often not sufficiently precise to enable strict comparisons. Meaningful measurements of ancient earthworks are difficult, due to natural erosion and human disturbance. This can produce different measured dimensions even for closely spaced sections, as shown by the excavations at Pear Wood (Castle 1975). In addition, where constructed on non-level ground, the exact edges of ditch and bank can be

difficult to determine. This is the case with the Ruislip earthwork where the southern edge of the ditch is level with the top of the bank on the north side due to the descending northward slope.

Wheeler (1935, 62–3) pointed out that in all sections of the earthwork the ditch was invariably on the more southerly side and the bank on the northerly side. Both Stone and Wheeler concluded from this that the structure was the handiwork of a community living to the north-west of the earthwork (ie away from the Thames and the London area). However Stone (1935, 299–300) noted that it was constructed without the least concern for the most elementary military requirements (eg for considerable lengths it is commanded by higher ground). Wheeler thought that the earthwork more probably marked a boundary. Without any excavated archaeological evidence available at that time, he concluded (Wheeler 1935, 72–3) that the most likely date for its construction was some period in the 5th–6th century (ie pagan Saxon period). In this connection, Clarke (2004) has pointed out that, perhaps surprisingly, Grim's Dyke is not referred to in any Anglo-Saxon deeds or charters associated with Pinner/Harrow – 'Any significance it may once have had in this respect had obviously passed'.

Excavations

There have been only a few actual excavations of the earthworks, and these are briefly covered below in chronological order (see Fig 2.8.2 for site locations).

1 In 1957 excavations at Pinner Green by the North Middlesex Archaeological Research Committee (see Castle 1975, 275 and footnote 28) showed that the earthwork there consisted of a wide low bank with a relatively small ditch on its south side. It was reported that quantities of Belgic pottery were recorded from the ditch, and sherds of handmade jars of Iron Age type A from the bank itself. These finds unfortunately are now lost. Castle suggested that the small quantity of Iron Age pottery recorded from the bank and ditch was residual.

2 A rescue excavation undertaken nearby on the Mill Farm Housing site, Pinner Green, in 1962 by the North Middlesex Archaeological Research Committee (see Castle, 1975, footnote 28) indicated that the ditch here was probably 30ft (9.1m) wide and 8ft (2.4m) deep, but no dating evidence was found.

During 1948–73 a series of excavations was carried out along a ditch and bank earthwork at Pear

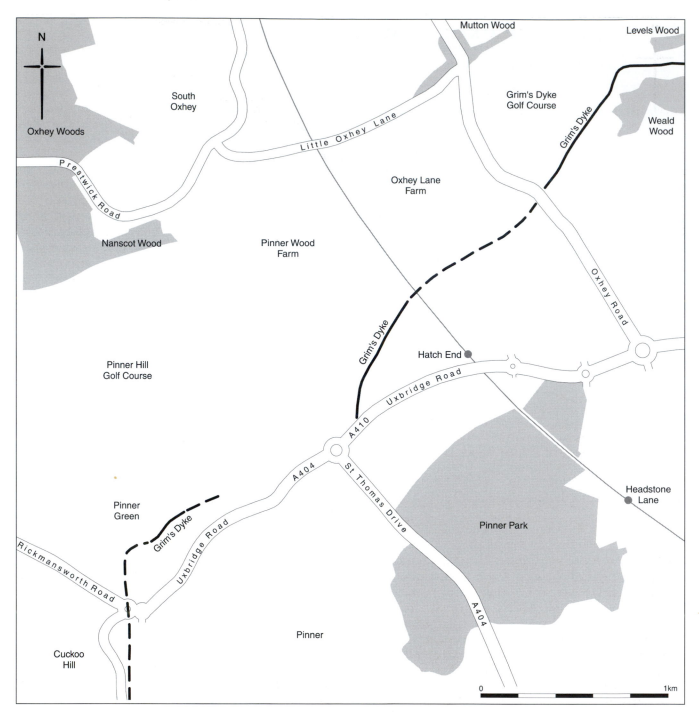

Fig 2.8.1 Course of Grim's Dyke. Continuous line indicates sections still visible

Wood, Brockley Hill (Castle 1975, 268–72) with the following findings:

3   Site A: from ditch – coarseware pottery and coin (Roman), sherds of native ware; from bank – one sherd 'Iron Age 'A' type'.

4   Site B: ditch 14ft (4.3m) wide by at least 5ft 6in (1.7m) deep.

5   Site C: ditch 14ft (4.3m) wide by 5ft 6in (1.7m) deep; from the upper ditch silts – coarse Roman ware, tile and iron spearhead (Roman).

6   Site D: from ditch – native ware, 1st- to 2nd-century coarse Roman ware; from bank – single sherd of native ware.

7   Site G: from ditch – sherds of native and Roman ware, two 1st- to 2nd-century Roman coins.

8   Site H: from outer bank – native and Roman sherds.

9   Site J: his was the best recorded excavation. A V-shaped ditch 23ft (7.0m) wide by 5ft 4in (1.6m) deep was revealed, with a north bank 4ft (1.2m) wide, and a minor bank on the south side 15ft 6in (4.6m) wide, and 8in (0.2m) high. Roman pottery, nails glass, etc (3rd–4th century). It was noted that the north bank contained more material than could have been derived from the ditch.

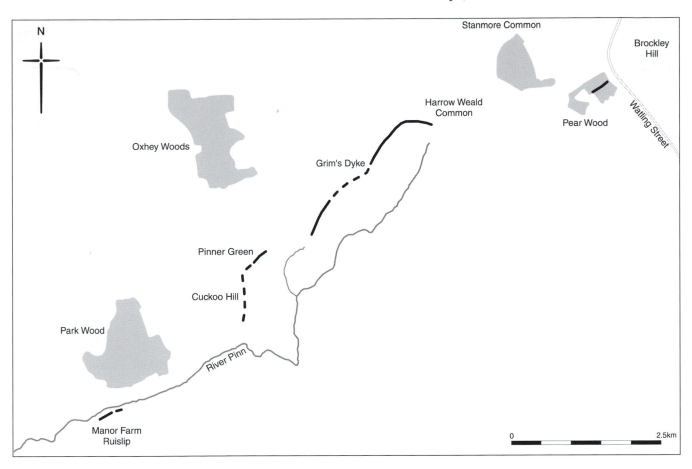

Fig 2.8.2 Course of Grim's Dyke, with possible eastern extension at Pear Wood, Brockley Hill (Castle 1975), and western extension at Manor Farm, Ruislip

Additional excavations showed that the earthwork terminated at the eastern side of Pear Wood, and did not recommence beyond that, on the other side of the nearby Watling Street. Castle concluded that the native and Roman finds were clearly residual, and that excavation J, in particular, showed that the earthwork could not be earlier than late Roman. It was noted that the Pear Wood earthwork was similar in size and construction to the Pinner Grim's Dyke. Recent commentators (eg MoLAS 2000, 127) have referred to them as the Grim's Dyke/Pear Wood earthwork.

10 In 1979 a limited rescue excavation was conducted in the central section of Grim's Dyke in advance of construction of a new entrance way to the Grim's Dyke Hotel, by the then Inner London Archaeological Unit (GD79; Ellis 1982, 176). There were signs of more recent disturbance at this point. The only pottery recovered comprised two abraded sherds of probable Iron Age date. However the excavator reported finding within the bank the remains of a small fire which 'appeared to be in situ'. A ^{14}C dating of the associated charcoal gave a date of 50+/– 80 AD (recently reassessed as cal AD 60–340 (HAR-3747, 1900, +/– 80 BP) using OxCal v 3.10

and the INTCAL 04 curve). The author pointed out that this was a single determination and should be treated with caution.

The Ruislip (Middlesex) earthwork

Ruislip has a number of earthworks centred on the Manor Farm site close to St Martin's parish church. The old manor house is on a moated site, which has the characteristics of a motte-and-bailey. The Domesday Survey for Ruislip recorded a 'park for wild beasts' (*parcus ferarum*; Morris 1975, 129d). The moated site is in the extreme south-west corner of the bank and ditch which enclosed the 138 ha of the park. This earthwork was still fully traceable until the 1930s (Braun 1933, 102–3; 1936, 375–6). The southern section has been built upon since then, but the northern section of the Park bank and ditch still exists within Park Wood and the rear of some nearby gardens.

Eighty metres north of the Manor Farm moated site, where the ground drops rapidly to the floodplain of the River Pinn, there is a large ditch and bank running east–west for 190m. The bank is on the north side of the ditch. It is terminated at its western end by Bury Street, and by a garden in

St Martin's Approach at its eastern end (MIP04). The 1866 OS 25in (1:25,000) map shows that it continued, at that time, for another 200m eastward but this is now built over. Although nothing is really known about the structure, Braun (1933, 107 and fig 5) claimed it to have been part of a defensive work surrounding Ruislip village in Saxon times. There is no real evidence for such a supposition, and the fact that the bank is on the opposite side of the ditch away from the village rules it out as a defensive work.

In 1976 the Ruislip, Northwood and Eastcote Local History Society excavated a trench across the ditch and into the bank as far as the centre (Fig 2.8.3) (Bedford and Bowlt 1977). The earthwork was 13m wide from the southern edge to the top of the bank on the northern side. The ditch was 2.2m deep relative to the edge on the southern side. The bank itself is on the north side of the ditch (as also at Grim's Dyke and Pear Wood) with its top 1.7m above the floodplain on the River Pinn side. At the time of the excavation in April 1976 the water table was close to the surface of the bottom of the ditch,

which greatly hampered work. Digging here was continued until a stony layer was struck which was assumed to be undisturbed stratum. The skeleton of a piglet (modern) and some sherds of unglazed red ware (possibly Tudor) were recorded from the waterlogged clay at the bottom of the ditch.

Excavation of the bank showed four distinct strata. The top layer of brownish clay contained white Roman sherds and a few animal teeth. The pottery was unglazed coarseware and was identified by the then Department of Urban Archaeology (DUA) as deriving from the Roman potteries at Brockley Hill, Stanmore. The third layer down contained some worked flints and sherds of Roman coarse grey ware identified by Harvey Sheldon and Clive Orton (pers comm). The rim of a mortarium was considered by Mrs K F Hartley (pers comm) to have been made in the Verulamium region *c* AD 90–130. Three small pieces of indistinguishable rusted iron were also recovered. Some pieces of fired daub occurred sporadically throughout this layer with a distinct band 0.27m thick at a depth of 1.06m from the top of the bank. Some of the daub

Fig 2.8.3 Excavation by the Ruislip, Northwood and Eastcote Local History Society across the ditch and bank at Manor Farm, Ruislip, in 1976, looking north towards the River Pinn

had impressions of wattle. The flints showed Mesolithic/Neolithic affinities. All the finds were clearly residual.

Discussion

The abraded sherds of Roman ware found within the bank of the Ruislip earthwork show that the structure is no earlier than 2nd century. There are a number of features which make this earthwork an enigma. It is a massive earthwork with no obvious purpose. It does not appear to have any relationship to the other earthworks at Ruislip. As already pointed out the position of the large bank on the north side of the ditch away from the Manor Farm site and the village shows that it was not intended for defence.

There are, however, a number of similarities with the several sections of the Pinner Grim's Dyke and the Pear Wood earthwork.

1 All are large earthworks which seem to be entirely unsuitable for defence.
2 All have their banks on the north or north-west side of their ditches (ie facing away from the Thames and London). Wheeler (1935) laid great emphasis on this point in comparing Grim's Dyke with Offa's Dyke in the Chilterns.
3 The latest finds within the bank at Ruislip were of Roman date, as at Pear Wood.
4 The dimensions of the Ruislip earthwork are similar to those recorded for Grim's Dyke/Pear Wood earthworks, in so far as they can now be determined with any accuracy.

The accepted Grim's Dyke in the Harrow Weald/Pinner area exists in several sections wending a curious east–west course along no obvious boundary (Stone 1935; Wheeler 1935). Whether it ever consisted of a single continuous structure is unknown, but it is difficult to think of a use for a disjointed series of relatively short sections of a massive bank and ditch.

It has been suggested (Castle 1975) that the Pear Wood earthwork is an easterly section of Grim's Dyke at a distance of 2.7km (direct) from its eastern end. The accepted western section at Cuckoo Hill where it begins to run in a more southerly direction is also about 2.7km distance direct from the large Ruislip earthwork.

A recent research framework objective (Nixon *et al* 2002, 27) was 'Assessing stretches of linear earthworks such as Grim's Dyke which remain poorly dated or understood. It is possible that further earthworks lie unrecognised in the wooded clay lands of the northern heights'. The purpose of this paper is to draw attention to the similarities between Grim's Dyke proper, the Pear Wood earthwork and that at Ruislip in the hope that it might stimulate further consideration of these puzzling constructions.

Dating of Grim's Dyke

The problem of the date of construction of the several sections remains. The 'Belgic' pottery found at Cuckoo Hill was considered by Castle (1975) to be residual. The ^{14}C date of cal AD 60–340 from apparently *in situ* charcoal within the bank at Grim's Dyke was from a single measurement and caution was urged in using this date (Ellis 1982). The Pear Wood excavations showed that that structure could not be earlier than 3rd/4th century, whilst the Ruislip earthwork must be later than the 2nd century.

If the several sections are all part of a single undertaking (but perhaps spread over several years of construction) then a post-3rd-/4th-century date is indicated. It cannot be later than 1306 when it is mentioned in a rental of the Priory of St Bartholomew the Great (Castle 1975). Clarke's observation (2004) that it is not referred to in the Anglo-Saxon deeds and charters of Harrow might not be of significance since it is not clear to which area they refer, nor do they give a perambulation.

All in all, the excavated evidence to date does not seem to alter Wheeler's (1935, 72) conclusion of a pagan Saxon construction date for Grim's Dyke.

Acknowledgements

More than 30 years ago Harvey Sheldon helped the Ruislip, Northwood and Eastcote Local History Society to date finds from the excavation at Ruislip on which this paper is based. I should like to dedicate it to Harvey in recognition of all his continuing help in matters archaeological.

I should also like to thank all those members of the Ruislip, Northwood and Eastcote Local History Society, alas some now dead, who helped with the excavation.

3 This world and beyond: mind and spirit

Copper-alloy statuette of Hercules (A9632)

Introduction   *John Clark*

This group of papers takes us beyond the physical nature of Roman London and its hinterland to consider the intellectual and spiritual context within which its people lived their lives. Much of what is contained in the essays that follow contributes quite naturally under a single heading of the published *Research Framework for London Archaeology* (Nixon *et al* 2002).

R11 Framework objectives
- Identifying religious sites and buildings, their chronology and use;
- Examining the role and diversity of religion in society, and how it changed over time.

Two of the papers, however, those by Joanna Bird and Nick Bateman, remind us of the dangers of imposing too strict a modern categorisation upon an ancient culture. They both consider aspects of religious belief that impinged upon the Roman games – the *Research Framework* includes the Roman games only under 'Recreation'.

R9 Framework objectives
- Investigating the role of leisure and recreation in daily life, both within the household and through public amenities;
- Examining the changing provision of public and private facilities such as the baths and games, and the social and economic implications.

Meanwhile, in examining the evidence for the way Roman classical education, an education that supported the social and political structure of the Roman Empire, must have been provided in Britain, Mark Hassall takes us into the field of 'Society'.

R7 Framework objectives
- Finding evidence of the exercise of social and political power in society.

Perring and Brigham (in MoLAS 2000, 120) have stressed that 'the potential of the site [Londinium] to contribute to our understanding of the ancient world has, however, been poorly realised ... London is infrequently mentioned in works of broader synthesis on the character of Roman provincial society'. And quite rightly our authors travel far 'beyond Londinium' for their evidence.

In the first paper in this section Mark Hassall uses documentary, literary and epigraphic sources to show that the full range of Roman education must have been available in Roman Britain. He suggests that there would have been a centre of higher education and that it was most likely to have been in Londinium.

The *Research Framework* drew particular notice to the evidence for 'ritual activity' along the Walbrook valley and concluded 'The religious significance of the Thames, Walbrook, Fleet and other rivers needs further consideration and synthesis'(Nixon *et al* 2002, 39–40). Our next paper re-examines the evidence from the Walbrook stream. This was a topic to which the late Ralph Merrifield devoted a great deal of thought, and we are very pleased to be able to include here an unpublished paper by him, brought up to date and expanded by Jenny Hall, in which they clarify the nature of the famous 'Walbrook deposits'.

Ian Haynes's paper notes the presence in apparent ritual contexts not only of such obvious 'sacred ceramics' as vessels decorated with frogs or snakes – as found in Walbrook excavations – but of the bell-shaped bowls usually known in Britain as 'Camulodunum 306' – a reminder, as he points out, that an artefact's meaning is defined by its context, not by its form. He argues that evidence from sites elsewhere can inform our understanding of the context of the London Mithraeum and the relationship between the different mystery cults of the Roman world.

Joanna Bird discusses a samian bowl, showing the figure of Hercules armed as a gladiator and perhaps mirroring representations of Hercules's labours and combats staged in Roman amphitheatres. She notes the evidence of images and artefacts for the popularity of Hercules as a household god among Roman Londoners; in this Londoners followed fashions found elsewhere in the Roman empire and expressed the essential *'Romanitas'* of their beliefs.

The last three papers in this section revisit Harvey Sheldon's old stamping ground of Southwark to consider finds from the area east and south of the church of St George the Martyr. This is an area from which Roman burials have long been known, but whose wider significance has been highlighted by the Tabard Square excavations (Durrani 2004) which revealed what has been termed a Roman 'ritual landscape'.

One item from the Tabard Square site that caught the attention of both the archaeological world and the press is the remarkable marble dedicatory plaque, the first to spell out the name of Londinium – or rather *Londinienses*, 'Londoners'. Francis Grew considers the god 'Mars Camulus' to whom it was dedicated and brings together epigraphic evidence from Britain and elsewhere in the Roman world to identify the origins of this god.

The next two papers discuss the nature and implications of two unusual female burials in Southwark, excavated in 1979 and 1996 respectively. Jonathan Cotton reviews a burial first published in brief over 25 years ago. He convincingly reunites with it two samian plates found in the fill of a Victorian pit, confirming that the burial dates very early in the life of Roman Londinium. Its unusual features hint at the cosmopolitan nature of Londinium from its earliest years.

Finally Nick Bateman takes the Southwark burial that the popular press identified as a 'female gladiator' as the starting point for a discussion of the wider role of the amphitheatre and the games in Roman culture. He sees both the imagery associated with the Great Dover Street burial and the gladiatorial combats of London's amphitheatre as representative of Roman attitudes to death and resurrection.

3.1 London: Britain's first 'university'? Education in Roman Britain *Mark Hassall*

Introduction

I take as my starting point an imperial rescript of 376 (*Codex Theodosianus*, 13.3.11; Pharr *et al* 1952, 389) to the Prefect of the Gauls saying that *rhetores* (literally rhetoricians or orators) and *grammatici* (grammarians) of the Attic and Roman learning should be established in each metropolis, that is the capital of each of the provinces in his prefecture – a vast administrative fief which included the diocese of Britain. London was not only the metropolis of the province of Maxima Caesariensis, it was also the capital of the diocese of Britain (Hassall 1996) and it would be good to put 'London University' in the same league as, say, Trier, which besides being an imperial capital, was the metropolis of Belgica Prima, and had two *grammatici* (one Latin and one Greek – though the latter post was not always filled) and two or three *rhetores* (*Codex Theodosianus*, 13.3.11; Pharr *et al* 1952, 389), or Bordeaux, the metropolis of *Aquitanica Secunda* with its six *grammatici* and four *rhetores* so pithily described by the poet Ausonius in the *Professores*. And what applies to London should also apply to the other capitals of the constituent provinces of the British diocese, York and Lincoln, as well as Cirencester and, perhaps, Carlisle (Hassall 1976).

So much for the claims of the so called 'older Universities' such as the parvenu Oxford with its spurious claims to a foundation by King Alfred, or, even more ridiculous, the apocryphal King Mempric (Morris 1978, 7; Rous 1745, 21)! But intention is one thing and compliance is another. Were the terms of the rescript ever enforced? Nor does the rescript of 379 necessarily imply that there were not *grammatici* and *rhetores* operating from centres like London at a period before that date. It is time to look at the evidence, such as it is, for 'University Education' in Roman Britain – or indeed the evidence for education of any kind in Britain during the Roman period.

The background

Over 80 years ago Theodore Haarhoff of the University of Cape Town produced a study of pagan and Christian education in Gaul in the last century of the western empire (Haarhoff 1920). Haarhoff distinguished three levels of education. First is the teaching of the basic skill of reading. The teacher of such skills was known as a *litterator,* that is the one who taught the child his *litterae*, letters. Secondly there was the teacher of the literary classics of Greece and Rome, foremost among which were the works of Virgil. The teaching of the classics was entrusted to a *grammaticus* – or, as one might call him, a grammar school teacher. Thirdly, there was *rhetor*, the teacher of rhetoric, the nearest equivalent to a university professor. Educational establishments like those at Bordeaux, the famous Maeniana at Autun or the imperial capital at Trier had on their establishments both *grammatici* and *rhetores*.

Primary education – the role of the *litterator*

There is both indirect and, surprisingly, direct evidence for the activities of the *litterator* in Roman Britain. The former consists of the widespread evidence for literacy in the province in the scratching of the names of owners on pottery vessels and other graffiti. Direct evidence for the work of the *litterator* and their pupils comes at both ends of the social scale. At the lower end are the graffiti on tiles scrawled by workers before the clay had become too hard (Tomlin 1979; Frere and Tomlin 1993, 2491.1–229). Some at least of these appear to have been informal writing exercises performed by the 'students' of unofficial *litteratores* 'during the lunch break'. They include alphabets, in some cases copied out a couple of times (Frere and Tomlin 1993, 2491.135 and 142). Another probable example is the personal name Bellicianus four times repeated on tile found at Caerwent (Frere and Tomlin 1993, 2491.80).

A tile from Silchester (Frere and Tomlin 1993, 2491.148) is inscribed with four (or five) personal names followed by the words *conticuere omnes*. These words are part of the line, *Conticuere omnes intentique ora tenebant* . . . 'They all fell silent and steadfast held their gaze' found at the beginning of the second book of the *Aeneid* (2.1), and describe Dido and her court, when Aeneas begins to tell the tale of his escape from Troy. This Virgilian tag is echoed by another from a later book of the epic poem, also used as a writing exercise, but from a very different social milieu. It was found at Vindolanda where the medium employed for writing was ink used with pens on wooden tablets and here the *litterator* was no workman, but a member of the household of Flavius Cerealis, the equestrian commander of the Cohors IX Batavorum at Vindolanda, and the pupil, the tribune's young son. The child has copied out the beginning of a line *Interea pavidam volitans pinnata (per) u(r)bem* . . . 'meanwhile winged (rumour) fluttering through the trembling city . . .' (*Aeneid* 9.473), in capitals on a wooden tablet (Bowman and Thomas 1994, no 118) and the *litterator* has written *segn(iter)* . . . 'sloppy', against it.

Secondary education – the role of the *grammaticus*

The purpose of secondary education was to acquaint the student with a knowledge of the literary classics, especially the works of Virgil, the foremost of Latin poets. If direct evidence for *grammatici* themselves in Roman Britain is problematical (see below), the fruits of their labours are well attested especially among the wealthy villa-owning class of the 4th-century diocese of Britain (Barrett 1978). As young men in their teens the 'landed gentry' acquired a lasting love of the classics. Proof of this comes from the decoration of the walls and floors of the villas, which were adorned with scenes drawn from classical mythology and literary epic. In fact, of course, the evidence from the walls has almost entirely disappeared and it is only through meticulous excavation and restoration that the frescoes which once adorned the walls of such establishments is now coming to light (Davey and Ling 1982). However, the words ... *Bina manu l* (... 'with two (or both) hands ...' (referring to a warrior grasping a spear) painted on a wall at the Roman villa at Otford, Kent, shows what might have been, for these are the first two words (and part of a third) of a line *bina manu lato crispans hastilia ferro* 'brandishing in his hands two spears of broad head', which occurs twice in the *Aeneid*, once (1.313) describing Achates, and the other (12.165) the Italian King Turnus. Appropriately enough nearby were found fragments of painted plaster depicting a figure holding a spear as well as other fragments of letters and human figures. As Frere and Tomlin reasonably conclude, 'it seems probable that a corridor was decorated with scenes from the *Aeneid* with appropriate quotations as captions' (1992, 2447.9).

The sort of scenes that would have been depicted are shown on the famous mosaics from villas at Low Ham in Somerset (eg Henig 1995, pls 9 and 10) and Frampton in Dorset (eg Henig 1995, pl 11). The former shows in strip cartoon fashion the arrival of Aeneas at Carthage and his reception by Queen Dido, as recounted in *Aeneid* Book 1; the latter Aeneas plucking the golden bough before his descent to the Underworld as described in *Aeneid* Book 6 (Barrett 1977). It has been suggested (Henig 1995, 126) that the illustrations in the Low Ham and Frampton pavements derive from illuminated manuscripts of the Aeneid like the two examples in the Vatican library (Toynbee 1962, pls 260–1) – manuscripts that were perhaps even produced in Britain. Even if this last were not correct, the mere existence of such pavements shows the high level of literary appreciation in Britain in the late Roman period, an aspect of the sort of literary culture fostered by the *grammatici*. A mosaic from a third villa, Lullingstone, Kent, has a scene showing the rape of Europa as described by, among others, Ovid (*Metamorphoses* 2.839), but where there is an accompanying couplet which alludes to the *Aeneid* (1.50–2). This passage is discussed in the following section.

Tertiary education – the *rhetores*

The first point to make is that while primary education was very much an *ad hoc* affair, and stood on its own, secondary and tertiary education went together. Where *rhetores* were to be found, there also one found *grammatici*. The second point is that just as it is possible to suggest the existence of *grammatici* in Britain by pointing to the influence that they had on the villa culture of 4th-century Britain, so it may be possible to point to the influence of *rhetores* by a similar line of reasoning. What, however, was the role of the *rhetor*? His primary function was, as his name implies, to teach dialectic (Haarhoff 1920, 68–93). The student of rhetoric was set various tasks by his professor that appear to the modern mind academic, artificial and sterile. Thus the young Augustine was given the task (*negotium*) of paraphrasing the words of Juno (Virgil *Aeneid* 1, 37–49) in her anger and grief at not being able to turn Aeneas aside from Italy (*Confessiones* 1.17). Or the student might be required to invent an entire speech, such as the words of Dido when she saw the departure of Aeneas (Ennodius 1885, *Dictiones* 28). More elaborate exercises might be undertaken such as those described by the Greek rhetorician Aphthonius of Antioch in the later 4th century.

Aphthonius was the author of the *Progymnasmata* ('Preparatory Exercises'), in which chapter 3 is devoted to Refutation (ἀνασκευή). Its opening section is summarised by Haarhoff (1920, 74–5), thus: 'The *first* step is to attack your opponent, the *next* to give a statement of his case, the *third* to refute this statement under the following heads: (1) *Obscurity*, (2) *Incredibility*, (3) *Impossibility*, (4) *Illogicality*, (5) *Impropriety*, (6) *Inexpediency*'. There follows an example – the story of Apollo and Daphne – a story incidentally probably shown on one of the mosaics from Brading on the Isle of Wight (eg Witt 2005, 37 and pl 16) and the recently discovered mosaic at Dinnington in Somerset (Cosh and Neal 2005). This myth is subjected to minute analysis under the heads listed, and the irrefutable conclusion is given in the closing *peroration* 'All poets are fools – avoid them!' It might be suggested that the story of Juno going to Aeolus to request him to raise a storm and thus prevent Aeneas and the Trojan fleet from reaching Carthage (*Aeneid*, 1.50–2) could have been the object of a similar *negotium*, and that this is the origin of the couplet attached to the depiction of Europa and the Bull on the Lullingstone Mosaic. Juno's request to Aeolus was certainly *inappropriate* (5), and she would have had greater justification in seeking the wind god's aid if she had been trying to prevent the rape of Europa from Crete by the Bull – the disguise adopted by her unfaithful husband Jupiter: *Invida si tauri vidisset Iuno natatus | Iustius Aeolias isset adusque domos ...*' 'If jealous Juno had thus seen the swimming of the bull, with greater justice would she have gone to the halls of Aeolus' (Frere and Tomlin 1992, 2448.6). On the other hand Barrett (1978) argues convincingly that the couplet can be best explained as an Ovidian pastiche – not only in its language and metre, but in its general form, since the poet often says that 'if a certain figure of myth or legend had acted in a certain way, a certain result would have ensued' (Barrett 1978, 312, with four examples). There can however be little doubt that in general terms the composition of the couplet was the product of the rather precious literary milieu of the rhetorical school.

Did such dry and academic exercises have any relevance to the real world? Was this the training of those who were set on a career in the law? Surprisingly – or perhaps not surprisingly – no. The budding advocate went on to Rome as Pelagius – the first attested alumnus of a British 'University' – went from Britain in the late 4th or early 5th century. And yet on occasion there was scope for the rhetorician. Some of the foremost exponents of this genre of literary writing were the orators from Gaul, such as Eumenius of Augustodunum (Autun), and the products of their oeuvre are preserved in collection known as the *Panegyrici Latini Veteres*. Several of the panegyrics were addressed to the Caesar Constantius, both as patron of the Maeniana at Autun, but also as the tetrarch entrusted to wrest Britain back from the control of the usurpers Carausius and Allectus at the end of the 3rd century. *Panegyric* 8 (=5) addressed to Constantius described the joy of the citizens of London when the Caesar entered London in triumph; 'at last they were free, at last Romans, at last restored afresh by the true light of the empire' (*tandem liberi, tandem Romani, tandemque vera imperii luce recreati*) (*Pan Lat* 8 (=5), 19.2). The language is echoed by the commemorative golden medallion found at Arras (Sutherland 1967, 167, Trier 34), which shows the emperor on horseback welcomed by a female figure, the personification of London, kneeling before him at the gates of the city. Around the rim of the medallion flanking the emperor is the legend *Redditor Lucis Aeternae* – 'Restorer of the Eternal Light'.

But Carausius, the great rival of Constantius in Britain, had not been averse himself to using the brief messages cut on the dies used to produce coinage in his name for propaganda purposes. Remarkably two coins of the British usurper refer to the works of Virgil and imply familiarity with the works of the poet on the part of those who designed the coins (de la Bédoyère 1998): *Expectate veni* 'Come, O long expected one' – ie Carausius (Webb 1933, 439–40 and 510 nos 554–8). This is a quotation from the *Aeneid* (2.282–5) which reads in full:

Quae tantae tenuere morae? Quibus Hector ab oris
Expectate venis? ut te post multa tuorum
Funera, post varios hominumque urbisque labores
Defessi adspicimus!

(What delays detain you? From what shores do you come, Hector, O long expected one? So that we may look upon you, depleted after the deaths of so many of your friends and worn out after the manifold labours of your people and of your city!).

Another legend on coins of Carausius, including many of those cited above, is the letters RSR found in the exergue, while the letters INPCDA are also found in the exergue of a unique medallion of this emperor (de la Bédoyère 1998, 81). These two legends have been brilliantly interpreted by de la Bédoyère (1998) as *R(edeunt) S(aturnia) R(egna)* and *I(am) N(ova) P(rogenies) C(aelo) D(emittitur) A(lto)*. Taken together these two tags mean 'The golden age is back! Now a new generation is let down from heaven above' and are a quotation from Virgil's *Eclogues* (4, 6–7):

Iam redit at virgo, redeunt saturnia regna,
Iam nova progenies coelo demittitur alto

(Now the virgin returns, the golden age is back! Now a new generation is sent down from heaven above).

We shall never know the precise circumstances under which the dies for producing these coins were designed. What we can say is that the designers were familiar with the works of Virgil and that it is familiarity that will have come from their school days when they sat at the feet of *grammatici*. Whether one could go further and suggest that the Virgilian echoes were transmitted not directly but through the works of some rhetorician, a London-based orator who wrote panegyrics on Carausius just as the anonymous Gallic writer – but he *could* have been British too! – wrote a panegyric on Carausius' rival, the Caesar Constantius (*Pan Lat* 8 (=5)), whose language found an echo in the legend on the Arras medallion.

Conclusion

It is time now to turn to the direct evidence such as it is for 'grammarians' and 'rhetoricians' in Britain. Here not only the most important reference but also the earliest one is found in the pages of the life written by Tacitus of his father-in-law, Agricola. Agricola, as Tacitus tells us (*Agricola* 4), was born at Forum Julii (Fréjus) in Gallia Narbonensis, and, as a young boy had as to (*parvulus*), had had as the *alma mater* of his studies (literally *sedes ac magistram studiorum* 'seat and mistress of his studies') Massilia (Marseilles). The Greek city of Massilia was the oldest and at the time the most prestigious centre of education in Gaul. It was here that Tacitus recalls his father-in-law told him that he would have 'imbibed the study of philosophy more deeply' than was appropriate for a Roman and a senator had not his mother prudently steered him towards a career in public service. Nevertheless given his early enthusiasm for the life of an academic, it is not surprising that in AD 79, two years after his arrival in Britain as governor, Agricola set about introducing the Britons to the fruits of civilisation as he understood it, not only encouraging the Britons to build 'temples, market places and town houses' (*templa, fora, domos*) but also 'educating the sons of the chieftains in the liberal arts' (*principum filios liberalibus artibus erudire*) (*Agricola* 21). In this context Tacitus recalls that he 'rated the natural talents of the Britons above the trained skills of the Gauls' (*et ingenia Britannorum studiis Gallorum anteferre* (*Agricola* 21). Is this simply a literary topos? Is Tacitus merely attributing to Agricola the sort of actions that the conscientious governor would take? Or are we justified in taking the implication of Tacitus' words literally? In the case of the *fora* we know that it was indeed literally true, for as a famous inscription tells us, the dedication of the forum/basilica complex at Verulamium took place in *precisely* this year – AD 79 (Wright 1956, 146–7). But what of the 'schools for the sons of chiefs'?

The case for the establishment of a centre for higher education in Britain could be said to be proved if we could accept the statement of A R Burn (1969, 48) that 'Plutarch in his essay On the Cessation of Oracles (*de defectu oraculorum* 410 A) mentions how he had met at Delphi in AD 83, a Greek teacher of rhetoric (recte *grammatikos*) named Demetrius who just come back from lecturing in Britain'. In fact, extremely interesting though the Plutarch passage is, there is no mention of Demetrius having fulfilled the function of *grammatikos* – let alone *rhetor* – while in Britain. On his own account (*de defectu oraculorum* 419 E) he would appear to have been acting on imperial orders as a 'scientific observer' attached to the Classis Britannica operating off the west coast of Scotland, having been seconded from Agricola's staff (cf Collingwood and Wright 1965, 662–3, two bronze plaques found in York one of which is dedicated to the 'deities of the governor's headquarters' by a certain Demetrius). Yet the establishment of some sort of

school at this period to provide young British aristocrats with a grounding in Latin (if not Greek) literature, rhetoric and allied disciplines, is not unlikely, and there is a hint that this may indeed have been so. Martial writing about AD 96 reports (*Epigrams* 11, 3,5) that 'it is said that Britain declaims our verses' (*dicitur et nostros cantare Britannia*). On the other hand, for what it is worth, it was not until the reign of Hadrian that the satirist Juvenal (15, 112–13) says that 'Eloquent Gaul has been teaching British lawyers. Thule now talks of hiring a rhetorician'. As it happens the first really direct evidence for a teacher of any kind, comes from the 3rd century and then relates probably to a humble *litterator*, rather than a *grammaticus* or *rhetor*, for we read in the biography of Bonosus, a usurper under the emperor Probus, that he was the son of a British schoolmaster (*paedagogus litterarius*) (*Scrip Hist Aug* 3: *Bonosus* 16, 1). Though the historical reality of Bonosus has been doubted (Birley 2005, 367), intriguingly the name Bonosus occurs as a maker's stamp appropriately enough on an iron stylus found in London (Frere and Tomlin 1991, 2428.9).

This then is the sum of the evidence. And yet, I seem to recall years ago seeing a pot sherd in the stores of the Museum of London with the word *rhetor* scored as a graffito. It is time to start excavating the Museum of London's stores and Archaeological Archive (LAARC) at Mortimer Wheeler House.

Acknowledgements

Harvey Sheldon has devoted his working life to the study of Roman London, partly as the doyen of practical excavators and more recently in the academic field, as a lecturer in the archaeology of London based at Birkbeck. It is appropriate therefore that the subject of this tribute should deal with some aspect of Roman London and some aspect too of education.

3.2   In its depths, what treasures – the nature of the Walbrook stream valley and the Roman metalwork found therein   *†Ralph Merrifield and Jenny Hall*

Introduction

In recent years a number of publications of excavations, past and present, have given us a clearer picture of the Walbrook valley in Roman times. One publication dealt with the upper Walbrook, the area north of the Bank of England within and without the walled city (Maloney and de Moulins 1990). Another on the middle Walbrook valley dealt with excavations and observations between 1927 and 1960 (Wilmott 1991). Here there has only been one controlled excavation of a section through the valley itself, that by W F Grimes intermittently between 1951 and 1954 on the site of Bucklersbury House, summarised by Grimes (1968) and published in full by Shepherd (1998). There has, however, been a great deal of observation variably recorded on nearby sites and a huge mass of metalwork collected, mainly on four large building sites in the middle Walbrook – the Bank of England in 1928–34, the National Safe Deposit Company site in 1872–73 (Puleston and Price 1873), Bucklersbury House in 1954–55 and more recently at 1 Poultry (ONE94, Hill and Rowsome forthcoming). This paper reviews past evidence, updates the present and looks to the future.

The upper Walbrook

This part of the valley (Fig 3.2.1) was originally marshy, intersected by a number of tributary brooks, none of which can be identified as the main stream but which collected into a basin before forming the single watercourse of the middle Walbrook (Wilmott 1991, 15). Maloney and de Moulins (1990) were able to trace the history of the upper Walbrook valley in a series of dated phases. It was reclaimed for occupation in *c* AD 90–120 by channelling the brooks between raised banks. The building of timber workshops and houses began almost at once and continued through the 2nd and 3rd centuries, with some of the later houses built of masonry on higher ground. The area seems to have been intended mainly for industrial purposes from the beginning, providing evidence for leather-, wood- and bone-working and also of smithing, more so than elsewhere in the town (Hall 2005, 135–6). There is now also extensive evidence for glass working (Keily and Shepherd 2005) and pottery production, with kilns at Northgate House showing a wide variety of vessel types (MRG95; Seeley and Drummond-Murray 2005).

Quite early in the 2nd century the drainage system failed and there was flooding, a frequently repeated cycle identified by: erosion of the dumped material that made up the banks, leading to rapid silting up of the channels and their overflowing, followed by more dumps to raise the bank beside new or recut drainage ditches making the system in the upper Walbrook wholly artificial. The area became increasingly wet and is thought to have been abandoned in the latter part of the 4th century, although recent evidence from Drapers' Gardens (DGT06) shows that a wood-lined well near to a section of revetted stream was constructed as late as AD 330. In the fill, a collection of copper-alloy vessels suggest ritual closure of the well in about AD 380 (Hawkins, Brown and Butler 2008).

The lower Walbrook

There have been few excavations in this area and records lack detailed sections through the lower Walbrook valley, between the Thames itself and the area south of Bucklersbury House (Fig 3.2.1). The stream was observed in section in 1958 north of Upper Thames Street and appeared to be up to 6m wide (Merrifield 1965, Gazetteer 260) and excavations at Dowgate Hill House (DGH86, unpublished but summarised in Brigham 1990b, 129–31) revealed the mouth of the Walbrook which resembled a tidal creek (Shepherd 1998, 216–17) and which was lined with quays that extended back from the waterfront quays (Fig 3.2.2b; MoLAS 2000, 132 and see Sidell, this volume). The mouth of the stream was truncated by terracing which created an artificial basin in the late 1st or early 2nd century. A clay bank and revetment formed a new north side of the Walbrook basin and a drainage ditch was constructed behind the bank, probably to drain the east side of the valley, while the main stream probably flowed to the west, entering the basin at a separate point (Fig 3.2.2c; Brigham 1990b, 130). The combined reclamation and drainage schemes tried to relieve marshy land conditions and localised flooding in the lower Walbrook, a problem which was reversed by a subsequent fall in the level of the Thames. Construction of the riverside wall again restricted drainage and led to a return to waterlogged conditions in the 4th century (Fig 3.2.2f; Brigham 1990b, 148).

A number of building programmes on the Thames waterfront were initiated in response to the

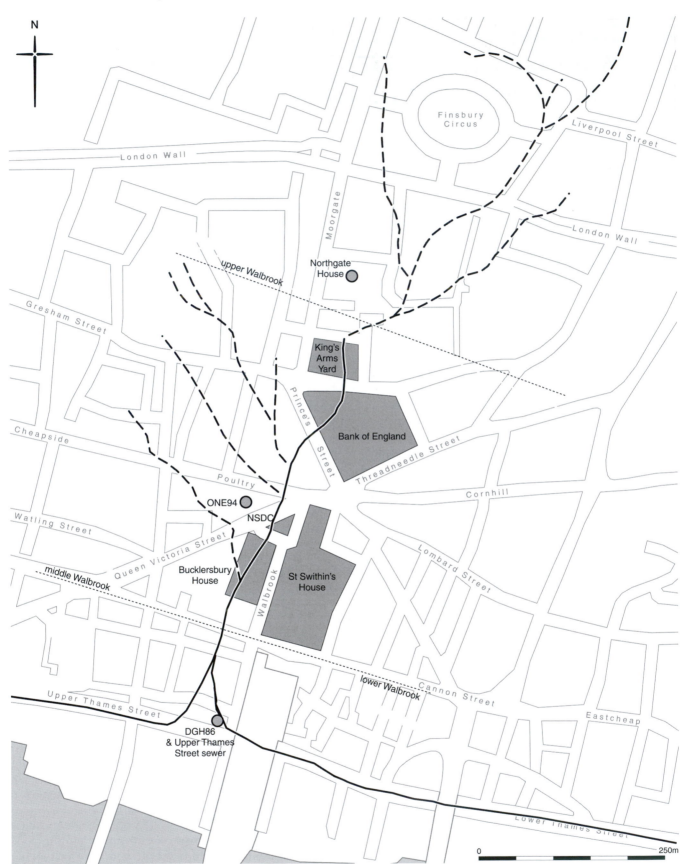

Fig 3.2.1 The Walbrook stream valley, showing the course of the stream and the nominal divisions into upper, middle and lower Walbrook with those sites mentioned in the text

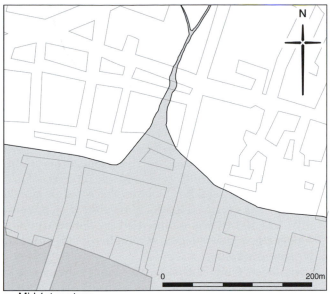

a. Mid-1st century

b. Late 1st century

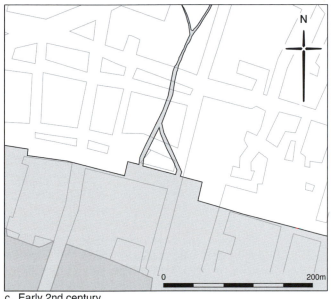

c. Early 2nd century

d. Mid-2nd century

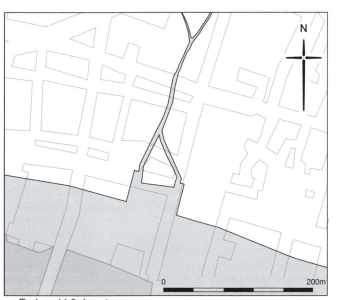

e. Early–mid-3rd century

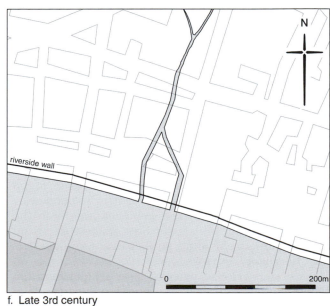

f. Late 3rd century

Fig 3.2.2 The course of the lower Walbrook stream and the phases of waterfront development at the mouth of the stream (after Brigham 1990b)

long-term fluctuations in the tidal range of the Thames (Brigham 1990b, 143–5 and Milne 1985, 79–86). There was a substantial fall (of about 1.5m) in the tidal levels between the end of the 1st and the mid-3rd century. During the 1st and 2nd centuries the profile of the natural Walbrook valley fell within the tidal range of the Thames and at high tide, water would have flowed up the stream. It has been possible to suggest, therefore, that during the pre-Roman and early Roman period, the level of the water in the Walbrook valley was influenced by the tides reaching as far north as Bucklersbury House (Shepherd 1998, 217, cutting F), if not slightly beyond – perhaps as far as Poultry (Hill and Rowsome forthcoming).

The middle Walbrook

In the middle reaches, between the Bank of England and Bucklersbury House, the stream flowed in a single channel that in all probability followed its prehistoric course (Fig 3.2.1). At Bucklersbury House, the Walbrook valley consisted of a broad, shallow depression, about 91.5m wide. With the fluctuations of the tides, the width of the actual stream could have varied from 3m to 13m (Shepherd 1998, 216 and fig 241). The tidal range in the Walbrook valley, therefore, would have had a major effect upon the initial layout and planning of the Roman town, in particular the position of the main east–west Roman road running parallel with the Thames, sited as it was beyond a series of tributaries joining the main stream to the north and the tidal reach to the south. The stream itself, however, had been approachable from an early date where it was crossed by this major road between the sites of the National Safe Deposit Company and Bucklersbury House. Just to the west of these sites at 1 Poultry, a long stretch of the road has been dated to AD 47 and the area around the Walbrook crossing soon became established as both commercial and residential in character (Rowsome 2000, 18–21; Hill and Rowsome forthcoming).

From an early date, therefore, the banks of the Walbrook were raised to provide dry ground for occupation and to create a close approach to the stream itself. Wilmott pointed out that the peak of coin loss at both the Bank of England and Bucklersbury House was in the early Flavian period, possibly marking a period of intense activity in the area (1991, 178), as the Flavian town started expanding some 20 years earlier than the first occupation of the upper Walbrook valley which in turn expanded as space was needed. For the same reasons as in the upper Walbrook, the stream was subject to silting and its banks to flooding, so that again and again it was necessary to raise the banks by dumping. At Bucklersbury House, where a 100m-stretch of revetted stream was traced, the width of the revetted channel varied from 2.43m in the north to 4.26m in the south. The only archaeological section through

the valley itself, however, was recorded by W F Grimes on the same site (1968, 93–8) and discussed in detail by Shepherd (1998, 36–43) (Figs 3.2.3 and 3.2.4). It shows that the dumps were mainly of clean clay, but sometimes of gravel, interspersed with black peaty organic layers, varying in thickness. Elsewhere, however, the organic layers have been found to be much thicker. They consisted partly of organic refuse in a waterlogged condition, partly of silt, and in the past have been described as 'peat' or 'black silt', according to the proportions of the organic and inorganic contents in the make up of the banks. This make up provided a succession of surfaces for occupation, each serving this purpose until in time it was submerged by floodwater and replaced by a new surface at a higher level, provided by more dumping.

Evidence from the same Grimes section shows that revetting on the west bank began in the Flavian period. Any evidence for a matching revetment on the east bank, if there was one at this early date, had been destroyed by modern foundations (Shepherd 1998, fig 40). In the late 1st or early 2nd century, however, evidence shows that the east bank of the northern section of the stream at Bucklersbury House was revetted and deliberately stepped eastwards, increasing the width of the channel to

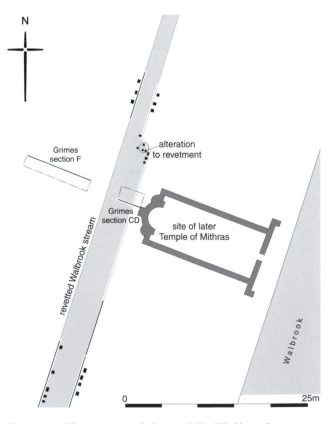

Fig 3.2.3 The course of the middle Walbrook stream showing the alteration to the revetment at Bucklersbury House in the late 1st or early 2nd century, the position of Grimes's section (F) through the stream valley (see Fig 3.2.4) and the later position of the Temple of Mithras (after Wilmott 1991)

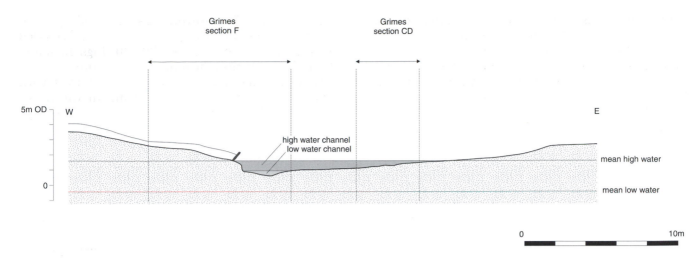

Fig 3.2.4 Grimes's work has provided the only archaeological section through the Walbrook valley which showed the effect of the tides on the Walbrook valley at this point in the late 1st century (after Shepherd 1998)

4.26m (Revetment 2, Wilmott 1991, 19 and figs 7 and 8) (Fig 3.2.3). The alignment of piles at right angles to the stream-bed may have been intended as a breakwater, allowing stream water flowing down from the north and tidal water from the south to meet without causing damage and flooding.

As in the upper Walbrook, there is evidence for industrial activity on both banks in the later 1st and 2nd centuries, with wooden buildings, timber-framed wells and plank-gutters. The buildings mostly seem to have been workshops and some areas probably remained open. Nevertheless it is clear that by the mid-2nd century the efforts of Roman engineers had achieved sufficient stability to make areas of the middle Walbrook valley more desirable for residential areas. Upgraded timber and new stone-built houses with mosaic floors began to be constructed mainly north of the main highway (Rowsome 2000, 40; Wilmott 1991, 145–6). The extensive continuous sequence of coins from the stream-bed of the Walbrook was cut short at AD 155–56 (Merrifield 1962, 38–52). Wilmott suggested that this marked the end of industrial activity and the completion of drainage and reclamation work in the middle Walbrook valley, after which greater stability was achieved, allowing more permanent buildings to be constructed on the banks (Wilmott 1991, 178–80). This cut-off point may now seem artificial.

In publishing the Grimes section where higher levels remained, Shepherd has shown that occupation on the west bank continued as before with timber platforms and buildings (1998, 219). It is clear, however, that silting continued and the revetted bank collapsed later in the 2nd or 3rd century, so that when the Mithraeum was built on the eastern bank in *c* AD 240, the stream flowed in a runnel through silt at a considerably higher level. The coin series from Bucklersbury House ceased during the mid-2nd century at a time also interpreted as the end of the industrial activity. In

1954–55, the excavations at Bucklersbury House consisted of Grimes's systematic excavations of trenches across the site, while Ivor Noël Hume for the Guildhall Museum was excavating other areas in what can only be regarded as a rescue excavation (Wilmott 1991; Noël Hume 1978, 18–21). The deposits published by Merrifield and Wilmott were truncated, caused by on-site machining. Contrary to previously held beliefs, therefore, that there was a marked cut-off date for activity on both banks of the stream, the evidence from the Grimes excavation shows that occupation continued on both sides of the stream until the end of the Roman period. The character and function of the west bank, with substantial timber buildings, remained the same. It was on the east bank, however, that there was a marked change in use prior to the construction of the Mithraeum, with various structures including a large chalk and flint wall running parallel with the course of the stream, rather than timber buildings and dumps (Shepherd 1998, 219). However, did the deposition of metalwork indeed come to an end at this date?

The evidence from Grimes's section (F) shows a period when management of the channel ceased, resulting in it rapidly silting up. From ceramic evidence, this phase of silting would seem to have taken place in the late 2nd to early 3rd century (Shepherd 1998, 219, Phase V). Few metal objects, however, were recorded by Grimes as having come from these later phases except for two tin-alloy plates from Phase V (Shepherd 1998, 136 and fig 158, nos 34 and 35; Jones 1983, 54 and fig 6, nos 8 and 9) dated as 1st or 2nd century on the strength of similar high tin-alloy material from the Walbrook, although pottery evidence shows the phase to be late 2nd to later 3rd century in date. No metal objects in later phases matched the quantity and quality of the rest of the middle Walbrook material and the cessation of the deposition of finely preserved metalwork from the Walbrook occurred before or coincided approximately with the beginning of the lack of concerted management of the channel in the late 2nd century or later.

Roman metalwork from the stream

An analysis of finds by material for the middle Walbrook sites of the Bank of England, King's Arms Yard and Bucklersbury House shows a remarkable similarity, where objects of copper alloy and iron predominate, in contrast with upper Walbrook and waterfront sites, where glass and leather are predominant (Merrifield 1995, 33–43). Similarly, analysis of finds by function shows no significant difference between stream and bank deposits, but with a strong preponderance of dress and personal ornaments in all middle Walbrook groups (Wilmott 1991, 168–71, and see Crummy, this volume).

The metalwork from the bank dumps of organic material, however, resembles that from the stream-bed in both composition and condition. Copper alloys come from both in untarnished condition and iron uncorroded, indicating that they had always remained in anaerobic waterlogged conditions. The bank dumps were often described as black silt and were formerly identified as part of the stream-bed, giving rise to the false impression that the Walbrook was a wide stream navigable up to the site of the Bank of England. The middle Walbrook's single channel had the same tendency to be choked by silting and refuse-dumping as the upper channels, probably even to a much greater extent because it was readily accessible to more people. It would be surprising if the remedial efforts of the middle reaches of the valley as in the upper did not include regularly clearing the channel as well as raising the banks. Wilmott identified that clearance must have taken place at least once. The earliest stratified level within the stream-bed was pebbly, indicating a swift-flowing stream, and contained material of the Claudian-Flavian period (Wilmott 1991, 68, ER268E). Above this, with its base at a low level within the revetments, was a fine layer of gravelly silt, from which came most of the stratified stream-bed finds. This evidence is consistent with the hypothesis of a clearance (or clearances) during the first half of the 2nd century, which removed much of the silting of the later 1st and early 2nd century, and left the channel in a reasonably healthy state in the mid-2nd century, with a slow but free-flowing stream.

Grimes's Bucklersbury House section also shows a gap in the stratigraphy of successive stream-beds between the earliest and the first above the revetted channel, the space being occupied by a confused stratigraphy of mixed silts, as might be expected if a massive clearance had taken place. If this material was deposited on the banks, as strict processual logic suggests it must have been, before it could dry out, it would have been covered with clean clays brought to the valley, thus preserving the anaerobic conditions that protected the metalwork, and producing the interleaved effect shown in Grimes's section (Shepherd 1998, 38–9 and fig 36).

If this interpretation is correct, no distinction can be made between the metalwork from the organic dumps in the banks and that from the stream-bed from which it must have been removed. Both were uncorroded; both included a large number of objects that appear, superficially at least, to be still serviceable. Indeed, the proportion of these seems to be somewhat higher in the bank deposits than in the stream-bed. This may, however, be accounted for by the survival in the stream-bed of the latest deposits of metalwork intact. These belong to the period when some artificers were leaving their workshops and may have found it expedient to dump their scrap-metal and perhaps also to deposit large quantities of metal artefacts (Merrifield 1962, 47; 1995, 40–2). We can be reasonably sure that any metal artefact found embedded in waterlogged silt used to make up the banks had originally been deposited in the stream itself.

It should also be noted that certain types of material may be under-represented from these middle Walbrook sites. Wilmott commented that the middle Walbrook assemblages may have been selected by on-site workmen with an emphasis on what was recognisably uncorroded (1991, 61–7). In addition, Wardle points out that very little organic material, such as leather, was retrieved from the Bank of England, Bucklersbury House and King's Arms Yard sites, although the excavators noted that there were large dumps of leather footwear and waste which were not collected. By comparison, more recent controlled sites record leather as the largest single category, shown clearly by the finds from Poultry where certain areas of the site also revealed material that can be identified as coming from silts thrown up from the stream-bed (Wardle forthcoming b).

Conclusions

Some idea of the concentration and quality (with special reference to serviceability) of the middle Walbrook metalwork has been obtained by comparing the finds from waterfront sites and those in the middle Walbrook valley. The difficult question of the possible role of ritual as a contributory factor to the deposition of metalwork in the stream of the Walbrook and the subject of religious activity in the valley has also been examined in detail elsewhere (Merrifield 1995, 33–43) and, although some artefacts had been bent or broken prior to deposition, a sign of ritual 'killing', not all can be regarded as votive. Accidental loss in the process of regulating the stream and raising its banks must have been a contributing factor, and casual losses from passing crowds must be taken into account, particularly at the National Safe Deposit site, where the main road crossed the stream. It should be noted that the classes of object most abundant on this site are small implements likely to be carried on the person. Craftsmen's tools, that would be more commonly kept in workshops, were abundant on both the Bank of England and Bucklersbury House sites, the two sites immediately upstream and downstream, but were conspicuously scarce on the National Safe Deposit Company's site where the road crossed the stream. Industrial activity was presumably kept at a distance from the central highway.

Structural evidence at Bucklersbury House reveals the possibility of the area being religious in nature. The charred remains of arcaded and moulded timber panelling and the deposition of a face urn indicated possible shrines (Wilmott 1991, 29, feature 8 and fig 17), although evidence for shrines can also be postulated along the upper and middle reaches of the Walbrook (Merrifield 1995, 40). It has often been suggested, therefore, that this area of the middle Walbrook held a particular religious significance, with numerous shrines along its bank and with objects being ritually deposited in the stream long before the construction of the Mithraeum in the mid-3rd century. Henig suggests a shrine of the Dioscuri from the evidence of a sculpture of either Castor or Pollux found in the vicinity of the Mithraeum (Shepherd 1998, 182–3 and fig 214; Henig 1998, 232) and also cult shrines to Bacchus and Sabazios (Bird 1996, 125–6). If, as it would seem, this was regarded as a sacred area, why then was this part of the Walbrook particularly venerated?

We have seen in the pre-Roman period that the Thames was a place for ritual deposits of metalwork (Fitzpatrick 1984, fig 12.1), a practice which continued into the Roman period (Creighton 2006, 95) and that coins thrown from the Roman bridge into the Thames were perhaps votive offerings at shrines to the deities of the bridge or the river (Rhodes 1991b, 183). Could it also be that the middle Walbrook area with its surrounding wetland (see also Crummy, this volume) was venerated because, confined as it was by two major bridged roads to the north and south and affected by tidal water regularly increasing the volume of stream water in the 1st–2nd century, there was a need to placate local water deities? As the tidal flow receded, the volume of Walbrook water decreased and the cleansing properties of the daily tides were no longer at hand, so physical veneration of the area ceased. The recognition of the area as religious continued, however, for the construction of such later temples as that dedicated to Mithras, later to Bacchus and with a possible temple at 1 Poultry (Rowsome 2000, 40).

The differences between these middle Walbrook sites suggest that the metalwork from the stream and its banks may after all tell us something about the activities on those banks. Further work is required on the untarnished and uncorroded metal objects from all middle Walbrook sites held in both the Museum of London, the London Archaeological Archive and Research Centre (LAARC) and the British Museum, and comparisons sought elsewhere for places of worship where the landscape or waterscape underwent radical changes. An assessment has been made of the quantities of Roman material from the town by function in these institutions prior to work beginning on a catalogue of London material (Wardle 2005). It is hoped that when such work begins, we can again review the enigmatic nature of all the metalwork from the Walbrook stream, whether from the stream-bed itself or from those dumps of silts that came from the clearing of the Walbrook channel, to see whether any more tales can be told about those treasures from the depths of the Walbrook.

Postscript

In 1992/93, following the publication of two reviews of the upper and middle reaches of the Walbrook (Maloney and de Moulins 1990; Wilmott 1991), Ralph Merrifield wrote this exposition on the topographical and archaeological background of the Walbrook valley when studying the significance of the Roman metalwork found there. He was keen to dispel the argument that material found in the Walbrook had been dumped there from elsewhere in the city and to propose instead that it was redeposited silt cleared out from the Walbrook stream-bed itself. He was also of the opinion that certain types of material had been deliberately chosen and ritually deposited in this part of the Walbrook valley, which was used as a religious area as opposed to the industrial zone of the upper Walbrook. This previously unpublished article formed the prelude to Merrifield's main exposition, given as the Hugh Chapman Memorial lecture in 1994 and which was published by the London and Middlesex Archaeological Society in 1995 (Merrifield 1995).

Acknowledgements

Jenny Hall's grateful thanks go to Mrs Lysbeth Merrifield, for allowing her to offer this abridged and updated paper under joint authorship to Harvey Sheldon from two 'old' friends, and also to John Shepherd and Angela Wardle for commenting on a draft of this paper.

3.3 Sharing secrets? The material culture of mystery cults from Londinium, Apulum and beyond

Ian Haynes

Introduction

One of the singular delights of the archaeology of the Roman Empire is the opportunity it affords for comparative study. Discoveries in widely differing regions can illuminate one another and, in so doing, advance our understanding of wider cultural patterns within the Empire. At a local level, this understanding in turn facilitates identification of religious sites, simultaneously advancing our knowledge of their chronology and use. Comparative studies are thus invaluable when addressing the *Research Framework for London Archaeology* Framework objectives for the study of belief in Roman London (Nixon *et al* 2002, 38). To explore this dimension, this paper therefore reviews new research on two excavations, the Walbrook Mithraeum site in Londinium and the Liber Pater sanctuary in Apulum (modern Alba Iulia, Romania). The Walbrook Mithraeum was famously excavated by Professor Grimes in the 1950s and then very ably written up by John Shepherd (1998), while the Apulum sanctuary was excavated by the author in collaboration with Alexandru Diaconescu and Alfred Shafer. This paper concentrates on artefacts and contexts of deposition rather than structures because the role of both these elements in identifying ritual activity and in illuminating exchange between cults is often neglected.

Up until relatively recently, study and understanding of the so-called Mystery Cults has focused on literary sources, epigraphy, art and architecture.[1] This focus has ensured that while the cults are discussed together as communities distinguished by secret knowledge, actual similarities of practice can be neglected. Attention to pottery, small finds and to the context of votive deposition is redressing this imbalance.[2]

Cult compared

The site of London's Walbrook Mithraeum and the newly excavated sanctuary of Liber Pater (Bacchus) in colonia Aurelia Apulensis, Dacia, offer an interesting comparison, but as with any such study, care is required.[3] Not only does some of the material recovered at the Walbrook site and discussed here pre-date the founding of the Mithraeum in the mid-3rd century, other elements post-date 4th-century changes in the building's structure. Whether this rebuilding marked a change in focus is open to question. Henig (1998, 230–2) suggests that the site was reused as a *bacchium* or *sacrarium* dedicated to Bacchus in the 4th century. If this is correct, it would render the comparison with Apulum still more interesting, though Schäfer (2004, 125–31) has recently challenged this interpretation and I do not believe it is necessary to understand the remains in this way. Whatever the later cult use of the site, surviving statuary demonstrates that the Walbrook site housed Bacchic images during its use. The Apulum sanctuary, in use throughout the first half of the 3rd century, was for its part primarily focused on Liber Pater, as the discovery of parts of five statues and a dedicatory plaque indicates. Nevertheless, excavations also yielded Mithraic material including a neighbouring Mithraeum and, within the complex, two disturbed fragments of relief/sculpture that could be linked to Mithraism. At one level this is unsurprising; even in the case of mystery cults the principal deities were far from the only ones to be represented. Both the Walbrook and Apulum sites have, for example, produced representations of Mercury and Serapis.[4]

In what follows, four elements associated with both sites are considered. The first is the presence of pots with applied animals. The next element is the use of an altogether less striking range of pottery vessels, Camulodunum type 306 (CAM 306), a form that is nevertheless of intense importance to students of cult (Symonds and Fiedler 2004). Comparative commentary on votive pits at the two sites follows, emphasising the need for further study. The paper closes with further reflection on votive deposition within pits, focusing especially on the fragmentation of statuary.

Sacred ceramics

Vessels decorated with applied animals are among the most conspicuous forms of cult pottery. They have received extensive academic attention (for example Amand 1984; Gassner 1990; Schmid 1991). These vessels may be divided into two groups: pots with a range of animals and symbols, and pots with snakes only. Some of the earliest examples in the former category date from the first half of the 1st century AD (Filtzinger 1972, pl 44, 4 and pl 45, 8–9); they were therefore an established feature of cult devotion before the surge in popularity of mystery cults that took place in the late 1st and 2nd century AD. Bird offers an excellent commentary which places the examples recovered in the Walbrook excavations in a wider context (Bird 1996). These examples, which appear to pre-date the Mithraeum, include a fragment with a frog and another example decorated with a crested snake. Apulum, for its part, provided an excellent opportunity for the study of cult pottery generally (Höpken 2004; Fiedler 2005;

and the work of both in Haynes *et al* forthcoming) and vessels with appliqué animals in particular. Snake pot fragments were also discovered at the Apulum Liber Pater sanctuary (Bolindeţ 1999; Höpken 2004, 244–5) while snake pots and a vessel with an appliqué lizard were found at the Liber Pater shrine in Cosa, Italy (Collins-Clinton 1977, 30–7). The occurrence of this exotic and distinctive pottery at such different sites is interesting in itself. Early studies of these vessels argued that they were linked to either Mithras (Swoboda 1937) or Sabazius (Staehelin 1948), but it is clear that both types were used across different mystery cults and even beyond (Bird 1996). While the use of snakes in some mysteries may have inspired their development and adoption, it is evident that snake pots and related vessels became a more widespread feature of mystery cult material culture. Whatever the unique features even of these mystery cults, it is clear that complex ideas about cult objects passed between them. It is likely that the agents of this transfer were the cult members themselves; we know that worshippers frequently offered devotions to a range of deities (Turcan 1996, 9). However individual cult communities understood these vessels, the pots' sheer exoticism may have made them tempting targets for replication further afield.

Altogether less conspicuous are the humble CAM 306 pots (Fig 3.3.1). As the name suggests these vessels were first identified at Colchester (Camulodunum) (Hull 1958). Similar vessel types have been described as Bell-Shaped Bowls and traced to the Rhineland (Swann and Macbridge 2002). Symonds and Fiedler (2004) focus on examples from Britain, Bordeaux and Romania. They are overwhelmingly associated with 3rd- and 4th-century contexts. Plain, undecorated and normally produced in a simple grey fabric, these vessels might not at first appear to have any special significance, but work in both Britain and Romania has demonstrated that they did (Symonds and Fiedler 2004). The discovery of CAM 306s in structured deposits at the Apulum Liber Pater site helped prove the hypothesis, first developed in the study of British material, that these mundane objects had particular cult significance. Not only did CAM 306s predominate in key contexts within the sanctuary, notably votive pits in the north range of the cult complex, they also appear to have been treated in a special way. One large group was, for example, carefully placed at the bottom of a pit and then shattered by stones thrown at them from above (Fig 3.3.1; Fiedler 2005, 97–100). From the condition of the vessels and the location of the stones it was clear that fragmentation was not a by-product of the pit's backfilling, but rather a deliberate act.

It was particularly fortunate that Dr Robin Symonds was present with the Apulum team at the time of these excavations. While previously reviewing finds from both Colchester and London, he had reached the conclusion that the CAM 306 form had cult significance. Symonds and fellow Apulum Project member Dr Manuel Fiedler were therefore able to draw on insights from both the London and the Transylvanian excavations in offering a valuable, but unpublished paper on the topic to the 24th International Congress of *Rei Cretariae Romanae Fautores* in Namur, Belgium (Symonds and Fiedler 2004). CAM 306 was not found evenly across Colchester, appearing in quantity only in two buildings, structures interpreted as a Mithraeum and a church, and within the Butt Road Cemetery (Symonds and Fiedler 2004). In London, CAM 306 is known from five published excavations (Symonds

Fig 3.3.1 Photo of Pit 1 at Apulum, showing deliberately smashed CAM 306s, with inset of CAM 306 pot

and Fielder 2004). Recent work by Pre-Construct Archaeology at Tabard Square in Southwark has also revealed small numbers of the vessels (Malcolm Lyne pers comm). Significantly the Tabard Square site was clearly a focus for cult activity in the Roman period (Durrani 2004). Martin Millett has kindly also drawn the author's attention to the 'type 79 jar' from Neatham, Hampshire, a form clearly derived from CAM 306, which he notes is also strongly associated with special deposits (Millett and Graham 1986, 78, 85 and fig 61). For our purposes the most important of these vessels come from the Walbrook Mithraeum (Shepherd 1998, 156, 162, 185 and 194; Henig 1998, 230–1) but it is worth noting that each of the other finds may be explained as linked to votive deposition. Of particular interest is that fact that all of the London and Colchester examples are represented by fragments rather than complete vessels, a phenomenon that may perhaps be explained by the practice of ritual destruction observed at Apulum.

The picture that emerges from this combination of evidence is extremely important. In suggesting that CAM 306 vessels played a special role in cult activity, it invites reconsideration of those contexts in which it has been identified. It reinforces the suspicion, for example, that deposits such as the distinctive well assemblage recovered at 107–15 Borough High Street in Southwark have votive significance (107BHS81; Yule 1982). In future, we may come to see CAM 306 as as strong an indicator of cult as statues, inscriptions and architectural forms. Certainly, colleagues encountering this ostensibly unremarkable vessel form should pay special attention for signs of structured deposition. The importance of this association operates, however, at a still higher level.

As I have repeatedly emphasised there is nothing especially remarkable about the CAM 306. While the exotic forms of snake and animal pots naturally make a strong impression on the viewer, inciting perhaps emulation from one cult setting to another, the CAM 306 appears decidedly humdrum. Yet we see here that it was nonetheless used by different cult communities. This may arguably be seen in the evidence from the Walbrook Mithraeum alone, where it is notable that the vessels are found in both 3rd- and 4th-century contexts, before and after, therefore, the complex was substantially remodelled. It becomes clearer, however, when the pottery assemblages of the 3rd-century phases of the Mithraeum are compared with the 3rd-century Transylvanian shrine of Liber Pater. That such a humble artefact could become so widespread suggests a depth of interplay between cult communities that we have only begun to examine. Crucially too, the distribution of CAM 306s underscores the extent to which ideas of proper form travelled across space. While thus far CAM 306s have been identified only at sites in Britain, France and Romania, growing interest in the vessel form may increase the number of identified examples dramatically over the next few years (Symonds and Fiedler 2004). It is to be hoped that this will also help us ascertain with which other forms the vessel was associated.

Structured deposition

No less important than the association of artefacts within structured deposits are the contexts of the deposits themselves. Some of the most remarkable finds from the Walbrook Mithraeum were recovered from a pit interpreted as a *favissa* in the final report (Shepherd 1998, 161, 167–70; Henig 1998, 230). At Apulum we also found this term offered a useful shorthand for what was clearly a complex process. Pits were dug during the temple's active life to accommodate objects used in cult practice that were no longer required. Such objects could not be treated as mere rubbish, however, and therefore had to be interred on sacred ground. Both the Romanian and London discoveries provide the opportunity for further reflection on the term *favissa* and the particular issues linked to studying votive deposits.

The word *favissa* is so widely used in archaeological literature that it is easy to take it for granted. In fact, though it is generally taken to refer to a repository into which cult material was placed at the end of its life, it is more widely applied and often abused (Holban forthcoming). Some scholars have found *favissa* a convenient formulation when trying, for example, to describe deposits found in Bronze Age sites of the Near East or in the temples of Pharaonic Egypt. While this at least reflects the fact that patterns of votive deposition found within the Roman Empire originated out of multiple established regional practices, it remains problematic. There is little in such deposits to recall the depositional practices of the Etruscans with whom the term originated. Part of the difficulty with the term lies in attempting to reconcile an evolving diversity of depositional practices with a handful of ancient references. The best known and most frequently cited ancient reference to *favissae* is that of Gellius in *Noctes Atticae* (2.10). Yet it is clear that Gellius was referring specifically to rooms and chambers on the Capitol in Rome.

Ordinarily one might expect that the archaeology of Roman London would furnish students of cult with superb examples of votive deposition. Awareness of the complexity and diversity of structured deposition is well established within the archaeological community (Merrifield 1987). Furthermore, the widely respected single context planning recording methods developed by the Museum of London are well suited to precise documentation of such deposits.[5] Given that many votive depositions are only recognised for what they are at a late stage in their excavation, or indeed after they have been excavated, a consistently high standard of site recording is vital to ensure that information is properly preserved. It is therefore no surprise that the London data have generated a range of interesting discussions about the diversity of ritual behaviour and the challenge of its identification (Merrifield 1987; Haynes 2000). Merrifield's intriguing study of the Walbrook Valley, for example, argued that the stream itself was a ritual focus specially selected for the deposition of styli and brooches (Merrifield 1995; *contra* Maloney and de Moulins 1990, 24; Wilmott 1991, 177; and see Merrifield and Hall, this volume). Yet because so few temple sites have been unearthed within Londinium proper, there has been little opportunity to study actual temple deposits.

It is ironic therefore that it was the application of these methods in Romania that enabled us to characterise votive pits within the sanctuary of Liber Pater (Fiedler 2005; Haynes *et al* forthcoming). By studying the individual contexts associated with each pit, the complex rituals that lay behind them could be identified. The most important group of pits lay in the north range of the cult complex adjacent to a walled and partially covered garden. Here the team identified four pits. The first two, running east to west, were approximately 6.5m long and 1.5m deep, the third, which was only partially excavated, appears to have been the same, while the fourth, 1.5m long, 1m wide and 0.5m deep, was markedly smaller because it had to avoid both the earlier pits and the presence of other cult buildings. There were significant variations in the activities associated with individual pits, all of which will be discussed in the final report, but the case of pit 1, the first and easternmost in the sequence rewards discussion here (Fig 3.3.1; Fiedler 2005, 97–110).

Careful excavation of the pit demonstrated that a clear point of access was built up on the eastern side. This is significant, for it demonstrates that it was not considered sufficient just to dump material into the pit; rather the objects had to be carried in and placed on the bottom. The first objects into the pit were CAM 306s and plates. These vessels were then smashed. Rather than being smashed with a stick or bar, or simply dropped from a great height, however, the vessels were clearly broken by having stones thrown at them from the edges of the pit. This was not a particularly efficient method so some vessels were more badly damaged than others, but it may have been chosen to facilitate the participation of a larger group of individuals in the process. Other items found within this layer suggest that damaged artefacts of other types were deposited while it was still open. Thereafter a series of fills are discernible, suggesting that the pit was evenly backfilled in stages. Within these fills the team found coins, lamps, terracottas, animal bones, nails and a fragment of broken statue. The pit was then covered over and a fire lit on its northern side. Traces of similar fires were discovered in the same discrete location over two of the other pits, suggesting that fire-lighting formed part of a ritual act of closure.

Unfortunately, despite the likelihood that others once existed, only one pit fill found within the Walbrook Mithraeum site has been advanced as of votive character. This deposit consists of statuary fragments associated with an upturned pot and has been explained by Henig as a *favissa* (Henig 1998, 230). If this is correct, the Apulum finds might suggest that there was other detail of importance that was not recorded. Perhaps the difficult conditions of excavation and modern disturbance in the immediate area of the find obscured important detail (Shepherd 1998, 54–5). Certainly recent studies of Mithraea have yielded considerable evidence for structured deposition (Martens 2004).

If, however, it is therefore difficult to identify similarities and differences in votive pits, there is one example linked to the deposition of cult material that may prove significant. In an important recent study, Croxford (2003) has drawn our attention to the fact that there is a statistically significant variation in the parts of Roman statuary recovered across Britain. Heads are strikingly over-represented as a proportion of all surviving fragments, while hands are under-represented (Croxford 2003, 86–8). While factors such as identification and retention by those who discovered the fragments may have contributed to this, ancient votive practice must also be considered. Both the pits of the Liber Pater sanctuary and the Walbrook statuary that Henig believes was deposited in a *favissa* reinforce the view that ancient selection was at work.

At Apulum the team discovered part of a statue in one of the pits. Though the fragment was small it was sufficient to identify the deity with which it was associated, for it depicted a hand holding a distinctive double-handled drinking vessel, a *cantharos*. This vessel is an attribute of Liber Pater. It might be argued that the hand simply found its way into the pit because it was ritual rubbish. Hands and arms were particularly susceptible to breakage. Yet it is interesting that only one other fragment of statuary was recovered from the pit. This was an altogether smaller nondescript piece. Perhaps therefore the fragment with hand and *cantharos* was a significant choice. It is certainly possible to suggest, on the basis of votive deposits found elsewhere, that diagnostic fragments were deliberately selected to represent whole statues and deities.

A suggestion that this might have been the case comes from the Walbrook Mithraeum. The three pieces of statuary identified within Henig's putative *favissa* include a hand clasping a knife (Toynbee 1986, 21–3; Shepherd 1998, 170). The other two, a head of Serapis and a figure of Mercury, need not detain us here (Shepherd 1998, 167–70). As with the Apulum fragment, though, the hand would have instantly conveyed the identity of the deity with which it was associated. In this case, hand and knife instantly recall Mithras's slaying of the celestial bull, the act that lay at the very heart of Mithraism (Croxford 2003, 92). Perhaps the deposition of part of a sword at the Tienen Mithraeum underneath a platform where the bull-killing relief had been displayed (Martens 2004, 337) reflects a similar intention.

With the ongoing work of the Arts and Humanities Research Council (AHRC)-funded Favissa Project, launched to examine aspects of votive deposition in the Roman world, it is hoped that it will prove possible to demonstrate whether these diagnostic fragments do form an aspect of cult practice, or whether their presence is simply coincidental. The project, directed by the author and based originally at Birkbeck, University of London, now at Newcastle University, has been expanded to study broader patterns of votive deposition in the ancient world (Haynes 2006). It incorporates an advanced database to facilitate a comparison not just of assemblages, but also of the archaeologically discernible processes linked to such rites. For the moment though it is worth reflecting on another aspect of statuary deposition, which touches on both sites. This is the suggestion that special significance was attached to an entirely different part of the divine anatomy.

Reviewing the evidence from the Walbrook, Henig sees in the presence of two broken torsos of Bacchus a further element of selectivity. He argues that 'They are so similar that it is tempting to think that breakage in this manner, preserving the generative parts of the image, was no coincidence. Perhaps the answer lies not in iconoclasm but in Bacchic myth and ritual' (Henig 1998, 230). Drawing on evidence from across Roman Britain Croxford (2003) also suggests that we need to question the degree to which iconoclasm was responsible for much of the damage on statues. In offering another explanation for fragmentation, Henig and Croxford help move us away from notions of actions and aesthetics that are partially framed by later Christian thinking. In this case, however, neither the sanctuary of Liber Pater at Apulum nor any other temple of Bacchus is able to offer a parallel. Certainly none of the Bacchic images recovered at the Romanian shrine exhibit the same pattern of breakage.

Conclusion

Scholars have long appreciated that similar cult objects were used by the worshippers of different deities within the Roman Empire. The power of polytheism to facilitate syncretism and the exchange of ideas is extensively attested. It is clear that the two sites examined here, though miles apart, were similarly exposed to such currents.

Yet this simple comparison of the two sites raises further questions. In both cases, as arguably at Cosa in Italy where it may have affected the layout of the Liber Pater shrine (Collins-Clinton 1977, 23), the juxtaposition of Mithraic and Bacchic elements is striking. This is interesting as such a connection has attracted relatively little attention in studies of either deity. It is striking that in his comprehensive and widely acclaimed study of Mithras, Clauss (1990), for example, discusses Mithras and other gods without really mentioning Liber Pater/Bacchus. I hope that future research will examine the relationship further.

When it comes to votive deposition, both sites demonstrate that we have much more to do to appreciate the range of ancient practice. Understanding the precise motives behind the deposition may be beyond us, but patterns of behaviour and norms of practice may yet emerge from further scrutiny. Clearly, diverse cults were affected by wider imperial norms of 'proper form'; rules for the correct disposal of objects belonging to the gods were obviously widespread. The need to inter such artefacts on holy ground was shared by a diverse range of religious communities, including those that taught different mysteries.

More interesting, however, is the way in which the humblest of artefacts are found to spread between both cults and provinces. That so humble a vessel as the CAM 306 can be found in cult sites so far apart testifies eloquently to the depth of association that could take place. Somehow, the CAM 306 became part of how 3rd- and 4th-century worshippers as far removed from one another as London and Transylvania experienced the divine. They illuminate in a small way the processes by which diverse parts of the Empire could share in particular ideas about the sacred.

Do the connections really amount to sharing secret knowledge? Here we need to reflect carefully on the changing nature of the sites, the character of material culture and the use of meaning in mystery cults. As my good friend and colleague, Harvey Sheldon, would stress, it is central to any understanding of material culture that an artefact's meaning is defined by its context. While snake pots and CAM 306s seem to have been used in similar ways in the different locations, we still know little of precisely when they were used, what they contained and who used them. They could have been invested with different meaning and importance in different communities. All we can say with confidence is that they became part of the manifestation of cult at a time when the so-called mystery beliefs were at their height. Yet even for this to happen, individuals of influence had to move between cults that we often imagine as secretive and obscure. The whole picture therefore contributes to our understanding of the ties that bound the Empire together, helping us to appreciate the nature of an empire that once embraced Londinium, Apulum and beyond.

Acknowledgements

In preparing this paper I have benefited enormously from the expertise of many colleagues. Dr Alexandru Diaconescu and Dr Alfred Schäfer, my co-directors on the Apulum Project, have shared many conversations about cult and classical culture. Drs Manuel Fiedler, Constanze Höpken, Robin Symonds and Mihaela Ciaucescu, whose understanding of cult pottery far exceeds mine, have been enormously generous with their time and advice throughout my preparation of this paper. Dr

Symonds' insight with the CAM 306 vessels at Apulum was one of the Project highlights. Doru Bogdan, who spent more time working on the actual excavation of the Apulum pits than any of us, has kindly talked through the deposits with me many a time. As with any field project, the directors' debts are to the whole project team, too many to name individually, but all vital to the growth in our understanding that accompanied the excavations. I offer here my thanks again for all their contributions. I also greatly appreciated Ben Croxford's insightful comments on this paper. Finally, it is a pleasure to thank the AHRC, which funded both the Apulum Project and the Favissa Project that made this paper possible.

Notes

1 For a similar observation and similar recommendations see the excellent paper by Martens (2004, 333). I follow Henig (1984b, 119) here in classing some forms of Bacchic Cult with the so-called Mystery religions. Nevertheless, I thank Alfred Schäfer, for the welcome reminder that that name is often too readily applied to cults.

2 Though it is invidious to select a few works from the wide range of studies now available, I would single out the papers that arose from an excellent conference 'Roman Mithraism: the Evidence of Small Finds' (Martens and de Boe 2004) as an example of the kind of approaches that are now transforming our understanding. Appropriately this volume also includes a paper on material from the Liber Pater sanctuary at Apulum by Constanze Höpken (Höpken 2004).

3 See Shepherd (1998) for the Walbrook Mithraeum site. For the Apulum site see Schäfer and Diaconescu (1997), Diaconescu *et al* (2001) and Haynes *et al* (forthcoming).

4 Walbrook Serapis (Toynbee 1986, 13–18; Shepherd 1998, 167–9), Walbrook Mercury (Toynbee 1986, 18–21), Apulum Serapis (Haynes *et al* forthcoming), Apulum Mercury (Höpken 2004, 252).

5 Though at Apulum I adapted single context planning to incorporate 3D small finds recording and, when excavating the cult pits, supplemented this by dividing contexts into smaller units for higher resolution documentation. The latter innovation was introduced at the suggestion of Dr Fiedler.

3.4 A samian bowl by Crucuro and the cult of Hercules in London   *Joanna Bird*

Introduction

The bowl that forms the main subject of this paper came from excavations carried out during 1979–80 at Well Court in the City of London (WEL79), by the then Department of Urban Archaeology of the Museum of London (Richardson 1980, 384; 1981, 45). It was a residual find in a context of Hadrianic to early Antonine date (Roberta Tomber pers comm), but its main interest lies in its iconography and in what it can tell us about the sources of imagery on samian ware in the late 1st century. It also provides a starting point for considering the cult of Hercules in London.

The Crucuro bowl

This hemispherical bowl is of Dragendorff form 37, and just over half the decorative scheme survives (Fig 3.4.1). The potter's stamp [CR]VCVRO is partially present and comes from die 2b of the potter identified in the Leeds Index of Samian Makers' Names as Crucuro i (Brenda Dickinson pers comm;

Hartley and Dickinson forthcoming); he worked at La Graufesenque in South Gaul during the period *c* AD 75–100. The decoration consists of an ovolo border above panels, of which two are almost complete and three only partially present. The first and fifth are divided horizontally into two, with figures above diagonal wavy lines and imbrication; the fifth panel held two figures, of which only a robed Apollo carrying a lyre can now be identified. The second and fourth are also divided, with an animal, of which only a hare survives, above a saltire with buds and leaves, somewhat smaller and narrower in the second panel than the fourth. Apart from the figure of Apollo (Hermet 1934, pl 18, no 3), these motifs have all been previously recorded on mould-stamped Crucuro bowls (cf Mees 1995, pl 52, 1, pl 53, 2, pl 54, 1, and pl 57, 1 and 5). The other half of the bowl probably repeated the animal/saltire panels and held another large figured scene comparable to the third.

The third and largest panel shows a naked man armed with helmet, shield and club, about to strike at a monstrous serpent rearing above a tree stump; he stands on a pair of small arcades, probably

Fig 3.4.1 Crucuro bowl from Well Court, London (WEL79[211]). Scale 1:1

134

representing rocks. The monster has a single body and a large head with a mass of smaller necks and heads, and is clearly the Hydra of Lerna, one of the creatures the hero Hercules had to overcome during his Twelve Labours. Despite the anomalous armour, two other Crucuro bowls show that Hercules is intended here. A bowl from a cemetery at Reims (Fig 3.4.2, 1) has five surviving panels, of which two have the same figure, one attacking a similar but not identical Hydra. The others show a slightly different armed figure with arm padding and a short sword, attacking a lion; a figure wearing a light cloak and armed with a short sword, attacking a boar; and a large eagle. Three of the panels have ERCVLE inscribed in reverse into the mould beside the figures, and this identifies the scenes as three of the Labours: Hercules fighting the Hydra, the Nemean lion and the Erymanthian boar (Mees 1995, pl 58, 1; Hermet 1934, pl 109, 1). Hedan and Vernhet suggest that here the eagle probably represents a fourth Labour, that of the Stymphalian birds (1977, 292). The second bowl, from the kiln-site at La Graufesenque (Fig 3.4.2, 2), has three surviving panels, two with the figure on the Well Court bowl; one has him armed with a spear and fighting a lion, as on a Dragendorff 30 mould from La Graufesenque (Mees 1995, pl 55, 1), and Hedan and Vernhet note that Crucuro varied the image by adding different weapons to the same figure (1977, 288). The central panel has the cloaked figure of the Reims bowl fighting a boar, with the inscription AC[TA E]-RCVLENTIS in reverse above (Mees 1995, pl 58, 2; Hermet 1934, pl 109, 2). Both bowls have a row of small arcades, variously containing the potter's stamp, spirals and, at least on the Reims bowl, rows of imbrication, in place of the ovolo border. A more fragmentary bowl (Fig 3.4.2, 3), also from La Graufesenque, with Crucuro's mould-stamp but no further inscription, shows the Well Court figure, probably originally armed with a club, attacking a large snake rearing up beside a grape-vine, with a boar beyond. This is likely to be another Hercules bowl, showing the Erymanthian boar and a further Labour, the slaying of the dragon Ladon and the theft of the golden apples from the Garden of the Hesperides (Mees 1995, pl 55, 5; Hermet 1934, pl 89, 5).

Crucuro's figures of Hercules are exceptional in showing him armed and wielding weapons other than his club. Images of Hercules occur regularly in a wide variety of media, including sculpture, wall painting, mosaic, terracottas, gemstones and coins (eg Ramage and Ramage 1995, fig 8.32; Strong 1976, pl 172 and 203; Bailey 1983, fig 159; Henig 1974, pl 14, 427–38; Reece 1983, fig 146, c), as well as other samian (see below), and these invariably show him carrying out his feats naked apart from his tutelary lionskin and armed only with his club, or occasionally a bow, as recounted in the myths (Graves 1960, **2**, 100–206). Grenier (1940, 636–40) suggests that Crucuro's figures may have come from the arena, where the helmet, round shield, short sword and arm padding were regularly in use (cf Köhne and

Ewigleben 2000, fig 36), and it is precisely during Crucuro's working life that large arena scenes appear on South Gaulish samian ware (Bird forthcoming a). The Twelve Labours would have made an impressive spectacle; although there is apparently no mention of their performance in the ancient texts, Martial records seeing a man dressed as Hercules carried heavenwards on the back of a bull (*Liber spectaculorum* 16, 1–2), while Tertullian describes a criminal burnt alive in the role of Hercules, either wearing an inflammable shirt resembling the poisoned shirt given to Hercules by Nessus, or re-enacting his pyre on Mount Oeta (*Apologeticum* 15, 4; Coleman 1990, 60–1). The weapons and fighting methods shown demonstrate a degree of adaptation appropriate to a confrontation between a professional *venator* and a wild beast, since in the legends the Nemean lion was wrestled to death after arrows, sword and club proved ineffective, while the Erymanthian boar was bound and carried away alive on Hercules' shoulders. It would certainly not have been beyond the ingenuity of the presenters to devise a Hydra or Ladon using stage props or even live snakes (*cf* Coleman 1990, 68). The helmeted 'Hercules' appears on another Crucuro bowl from Moers-Asberg on the Lower Rhine, fighting a lion with fallen figures below. This may be a conventional arena scene, but could also be another fight with the Nemean lion, with condemned prisoners acting the role of the lion's victims (Mees 1995, pl 57, 1; pl 57, 2, from London, is probably from the same or a similar mould). If this 'theatrical' interpretation of the scenes is correct, the arcades replacing the ovolo bands on the two inscribed bowls may represent the arches of the amphitheatre.

The evidence for the cult of Hercules in London

Hercules was a popular image on samian ware, with 65 figure-types in Oswald's catalogue (1936–37, types 746–799A), but on most bowls he is only one element in the decoration, appearing with a variety of gods and other figures, animals, foliage and decorative motifs. The Crucuro bowls, on the other hand, show him as the subject of large narrative panels, suggesting that the buyers would have chosen these bowls deliberately for their imagery and therefore probably held Hercules in some veneration. While no altars or inscriptions that might indicate a temple dedicated to Hercules have so far been found in London, this is an appropriate point to consider the other evidence for his cult in the city.

The largest and most public image is that on the monumental arch, pieces of which were found reused in the Roman riverside wall (BC75). Three discrete blocks, showing a shoulder, a forearm and burly torso, and part of a club, enable the identification of one of the fragmentary figures as Hercules; he would probably have been wearing his lionskin, as shown in the reconstruction (Blagg 1980, figs

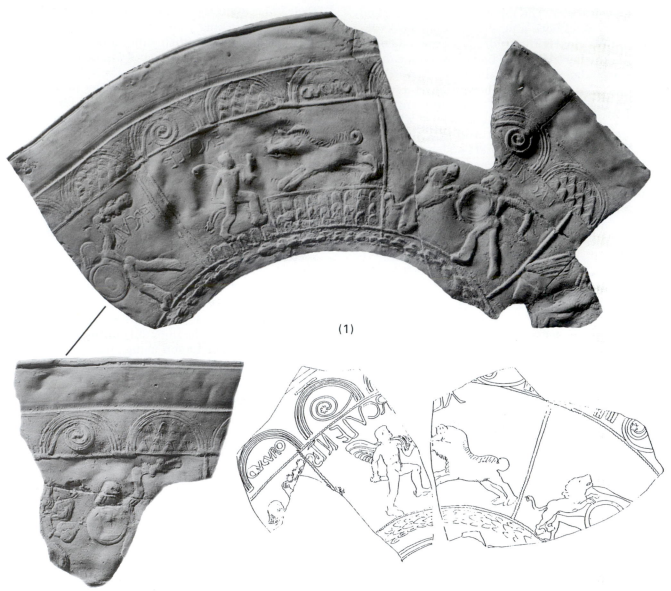

(1)

(2)

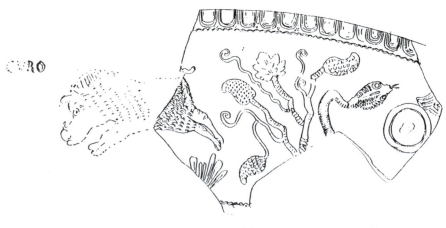

(3)

Fig 3.4.2 Crucuro bowls showing the Labours of Hercules: 1 – Reims; 2 and 3 – La Graufesenque. Scale 1:2 (drawings after Hermet 1934; illustrations courtesy of Allard Mees)

70–2 and 84). The arch, which is probably of late Antonine or Severan date, would have been a major monument in the south-western part of the city, and Blagg suggests that it may have formed the entrance to a religious precinct (1980, 175–8). The only other stone image recorded is part of a statue that was found reused in the city wall just north of Ludgate in 1806 (Figs 3.4.3 and 3.4.4; RCHM(E) 1928, pl 9, top right, and pl 62, left). The surviving piece is some 630mm tall and lacks the head, the right arm, and most of the legs; the body is naked, apart from the lionskin lying over the left shoulder and draped over the left arm, and the left hand grips the top of the club. Its reuse in the wall suggests that it was standing in the open, probably as part of a funerary monument similar to the inscribed pedestal found with it (Fig 3.4.4; Collingwood and Wright 1965, no 21).

Two joining fragments of wall plaster showing a small and finely painted image of Hercules wrestling with the Nemean lion on a plain red background (Fig 3.4.5) were found with other demolished wall plaster in a large building in Redcross Way, Southwark (RWT93; Drummond-Murray *et al* 2002, 128–33). The building is dated after the middle of the 2nd century, and the plaster probably came from more than one room; the decorative scheme apparently included an elaborate dado painted in imitation of coloured marbles and a large red area with floral decoration. The image of Hercules may have formed part of this scheme, perhaps similar to the 1st-century painting showing a small figure set within a large red panel in the House of the Vestals at Pompeii (Ling 2005, pl 15), and it is possible that other Labours were depicted in the same room. The nature of the building, whether official or an opulent private residence, is unfortunately unknown.

A number of small copper-alloy statuettes of Hercules have been found in London, mostly with no closer provenance. The statuettes shown in Figure 3.4.6 are all nude and beardless with short straight 'Celtic' hair, measure between 75 and 125mm in height, and are the sort of simple castings that would have been bought to furnish domestic and workplace shrines or to give as votive offerings. The commonest type holds his club in his raised right hand and has the lionskin over his left arm. There are two complete examples, and two more are probably the same but now lack the right hand; one of these has a squareish integral loop below the feet to attach it to a stand (Fig 3.4.6, 1, 2, 5 and 6). A fifth, found at Grocers' Hall Court so perhaps from the Walbrook, now lacks both the club and an object once held in the left hand (Fig 3.4.6, 3; Wheeler 1930, pl 19, 3); here the lion's mask and paws are shown in more detail than usual. A variation on this type has the club in his left hand and a handled bowl or cup in the right (Fig 3.4.6, 7), while a separate club with a tang to secure it to the hand of a somewhat larger figure was found east of the city at Whitechapel (Fig 3.4.6, 8). A statuette from the Royal Exchange has the lionskin over his left arm and holds the stump of a stick-like object in each hand; these may have been the snakes that attacked Hercules in his cradle (Fig 3.4.6, 4).

A more classical figurine comes from a probable votive deposit of mid-1st-century date at Swan Street, Southwark (SWN98, Beasley *et al* 2006, fig 9.11); it is bearded and long haired, nude apart from a lionskin draped over the shoulders and left arm, and now lacks the right hand and lower left leg (Fig 3.4.7). The posture of the figure, with the right leg bent up and the arms outstretched, suggests movement, and a peg projecting from the back may have attached it to a support or to another figure or figures in a group. A taller statuette, some 277mm high, was found in Queen Street, Cheapside, in 1842; it shows a naked bearded archer straining to draw a powerful bow which is now missing, and may represent Hercules shooting the Stymphalian birds. It is much more sophisticated in style than the other London figures, with the eyes inlaid with silver, and Henig suggests that it reflects a Greek original (Henig 1978c, 118–19, fig 9; 2000a, 68; British Museum acc no 1882.0518.1). A figurine from St Paul's Churchyard may also be Hercules: it is nude and beardless and has a diadem, a probable lionskin over the left arm and an object, now lost, in the left hand (Reynolds 2000), while a seated figure found in contractors' spoil from the Billingsgate

Fig 3.4.3 Part of a stone statue of Hercules found near Ludgate in 1806; height 630mm (3365/2)

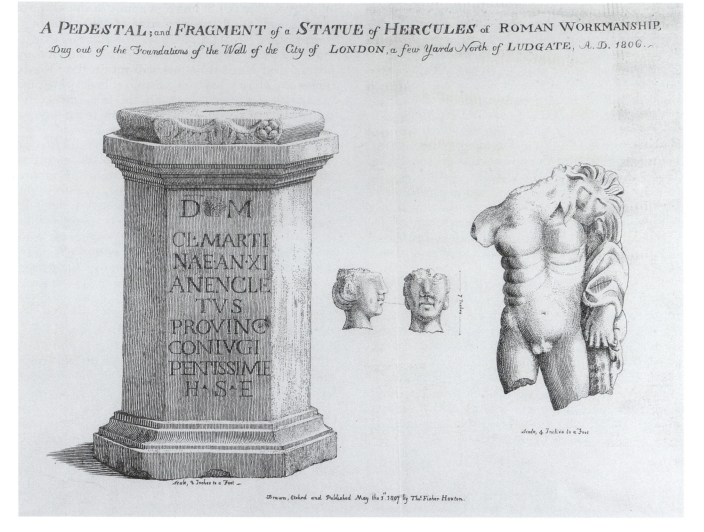

A PEDESTAL; and FRAGMENT of a STATUE of HERCULES of ROMAN WORKMANSHIP.
Dug out of the Foundations of the Wall of the City of LONDON, a few Yards North of LUDGATE, A.D. 1806.

D·M
CL·MARTI
NAE·AN·XI
A·NENCLE
TVS
PROVINC
CONIVGI
PENTISSIME
H·S·E

Scale, 2 Inches to a Foot.

7 Inches

Scale, 4 Inches to a Foot

Drawn, Etched and Published May the 1st 1807 by Thos Fisher Hoxton.

Fig 3.4.4 Etching by Thomas Fisher dated 1807 (A24560), showing the carved stones found near Ludgate in 1806 including the Hercules statue (right)

Lorry Park site (BWB83), with a wineskin in the right hand and a cup in the left, may represent Hercules or a satyr (Museum of London acc no 85.276).

Pottery finds from London that show Hercules or related themes consist of lamps and samian ware.[1] Eckardt notes that Hercules was popular on British lamps, accounting for almost 16% of the images of deities, and that he is usually shown as a bust wearing the lionskin (2002, 130, 371–4). This is the image on a lamp in Lyon ware from Leadenhall Court (LCT84; Milne and Wardle 1993, fig 49, 79; Eckardt 2002, no 1326). Only two other relevant lamps have apparently been recorded from London: the first, found at the Bank of England in 1928–34, so probably from the Walbrook, has three cupids lifting Hercules' club; the second, found outside the city at Charing Cross in 1862, seems to show the infant Hercules strangling the snakes (Eckardt 2002, nos 2363 and 2381, fig 73; Museum of London acc nos 14004 and P185).

Samian bowls which include Hercules among the decoration are much more numerous, but, as noted above, he is normally only one figure among several,

and so the deliberate choice of a bowl for any specific association with him is less likely than for the Crucuro bowls or the lamps. Several London bowls showing Hercules have been published; they range in date from the middle of the 1st century to the first half of the 3rd and were produced at all the main kiln-sites. One of the earliest is a South Gaulish Dragendorff 30 from the pottery shop at 1 Poultry (ONE94) which was destroyed in the Boudican revolt of AD 60/61 (Bird forthcoming b, no 52). Stanfield and Simpson illustrate Central Gaulish bowls from Les Martres-de-Veyre, dated c AD 100–125, including the styles of Drusus I and several anonymous potters (1958, pl 5, 57, pl 10, 121, pl 34, 402 and 410, pl 40, 468, and pl 46, 534), and from Lezoux, c AD 125–200, including mould-marked bowls of Criciro and Cinnamus and a bowl in the style of Banvus (1958, pl 117, 10, pl 140, 14, pl 161, 53). The latest piece is probably a bowl from the Walbrook, which has a mould-stamp of Firmus II of Rheinzabern and dates from the first half of the 3rd century (Bird 1998, fig 165, 31).

A small number of other London finds are associated with Hercules. A gold ear-ring from the

Fig 3.4.5 Wall painting from Redcross Way, Southwark, showing Hercules and the Nemean lion (RWT93[265]<65>). Overall height 220mm

Walbrook (Fig 3.4.8) has a pendant in the shape of a stylised club, a tapering cone of gold sheet with horizontal lines of applied gold wire, finished at the base with a plain gold plate; the knots of the club are outlined in wire and a few still retain their brown glass or enamel setting. Such a jewel probably had talismanic as well as ornamental value (Johns 1996c, 129–30, 199). There are two intaglio gemstones whose owners would have associated themselves with Hercules via their personal seal. An iron ring from Miles Lane has a brown paste setting showing Hercules fighting a giant (Henig 1974, pl 14, 434; Wheeler 1930, fig 30, 16), and a carnelian from Thames Exchange (TEX88) shows Hercules carrying a large animal, probably the Cretan bull, on his back (Henig 2000a, 73; see also Martin Henig, this volume, cat nos 36 and 37). A bronze medallion from Paternoster Row shows a bearded bust, the hair bound by a fillet, and may represent Hercules; it was probably originally applied to a larger object such as a vessel, a box, or an ornate leather strap (Wheeler 1930, fig 37, 3). Finally, a number of coins showing Hercules are held in the Museum of London, and it is possible that some of these were kept as lucky amulets by their owners.

Conclusion

The finds from London demonstrate that the cult of Hercules had a firm place in the religious life of the city. The various features of his legend gave him a wide appeal, and he was venerated both as hero

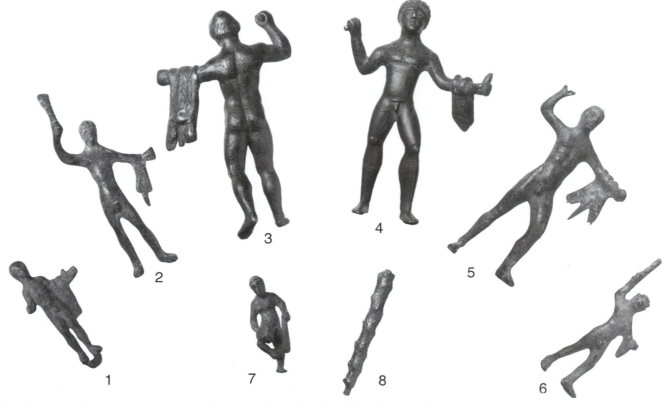

Fig 3.4.6 1–8 Bronze statuettes of Hercules from London. Height of tallest statuette 125mm. 1, 23129; 2, 22143; 3, A9632; 4, A17713; 5, 2062; 6, 22142; 7, 59.94/39; 8, 2086

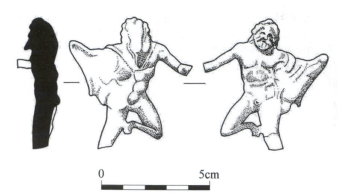

Fig 3.4.7 Bronze statuette of Hercules from Swan Street, Southwark (SWN98[1431]<70>). (Pre-Construct Archaeology Ltd)

Fig 3.4.8 Gold ear-ring in the shape of Hercules's club, from the Walbrook; overall height 38mm (British Museum, P&E 1934.12.10.2; photo: Ralph Jackson)

and as god. This double nature, together with his great strength and superhuman feats, made him particularly popular with men, notably with the army (Henig 1974, 43–4), while emperors such as Commodus and Caracalla associated themselves

with his imagery. Many of his feats were also beneficial to mankind in general, and he had a chthonic aspect which accounts for his funerary associations: his Labours included the subjection of the three-headed dog Cerberus, guardian of the Underworld, and he rescued Theseus and Alcestis from Hades, as well as ultimately achieving immortality and divinity himself. In the Celtic world particularly he also acquired healing powers (Green 1976, 25), and these various aspects made him a protector of women and children as well as men. Apart from the monumental arch and perhaps the Southwark wall painting, the evidence from London is very much of a personal nature: the statue from Ludgate may have belonged with a grave, the Southwark statuette and at least some of the finds from the Walbrook were probably votive offerings (*cf* Merrifield 1995; see also Merrifield and Hall, this volume), and other statuettes would have furnished private shrines. This is in line with the evidence from Pompeii and elsewhere, where it has been noted that Hercules was one of the most popular domestic gods (Ling 2005, 107), and emphasises the 'Roman' nature of belief among many Roman Londoners.

Acknowledgements

It is a great pleasure to offer this paper to Harvey Sheldon, who has been both a friend and a colleague since I first started to work on London pottery, and who was the first to entrust me with a specialist samian report. I owe a special debt to Jenny Hall for information on London finds and for arranging photographs, and I would also like to thank David Bird, who has read and commented on the text, Alain Vernhet for discussing Hercules on samian and for several references, Angela Wardle for information on the Southwark statuette, Martin Henig for information on the gemstones, and Geoffrey Dannell for his comments on the dating and affiliations of Crucuro. I am also grateful to Roberta Tomber who drew the bowl to my attention, to Brenda Dickinson for the stamp identification, to Allard Mees and Ralph Jackson for illustrations, to Frank Meddens of Pre-Construct Archaeology for permission to include the Southwark statuette, and to Fiona Seeley, Roy Stephenson and Paul Tyers for additional information.

Note

1   Since this paper was completed, Paul Tyers has kindly drawn my attention to a sherd from Harvey Sheldon's excavations at Highgate Wood (HW.T32.F1) which shows part of another of Hercules's Labours, the capture of the Ceryneian hind. The image was identified by Kevin Greene and is close to one on an applied medallion from a Rhône Valley flagon (Déchelette 1904,

2, 265, no 5). Armand Desbat identified the fabric as 'terre sigillée claire B', made in the Rhône Valley, and considered that it came from a large moulded jar or bowl. It is possible that a sherd from such a rare import may have been valued for the amuletic property of its image and perceived as giving protection to the potters and their kilns.

3.5 Who was Mars Camulus? *Francis Grew*

Introduction

A marble dedication plaque discovered in 2002 at a site on Tabard Street SE1 (LLS02) is the latest in a series of important inscriptions to have been excavated in the former Roman settlement south of the Thames. What a contrast to the situation just 40 years ago! *The Roman Inscriptions of Britain*, first published in 1965 (Collingwood and Wright 1965), records no inscribed stones at all from Southwark, compared with 36 from north of the river and three from Greenwich. The plaque (Fig 3.5.1) reads:

NVM(inibus) AVGG(ustorum) | DEOMARTICA | MVLO TIBERINI | VSCELERIANVS | C(ivis) BELL(ovacus) | MORITIX | LONDINIENSI | VM | [pr]IMVS [. . .
'To the Divinities of the Emperors (and) to the god Mars Camulus. Tiberinius Celerianus, a citizen of the Bellovaci, moritix, of Londoners the first [. . .' (Hassall and Tomlin 2003, 364–5).

Marcus Aurelius (AD 161–80) was the first emperor to co-rule with a colleague, and so the reference to a *pair* of emperors ('AVGG') makes his reign the earliest possible occasion for the dedication. The years AD 161–69 (joint rule with Lucius Verus) or AD 177–80 (with Commodus) are possibilities that are consistent with the lettering style (Hassall and Tomlin 2003, 365 note 12), though the double 'G' notation is in fact more characteristic of the Severan period or later (Fishwick 1994, 128–9).

Dating apart, most discussions have focused on the meaning of the word *moritix*. While the etymology is reasonably certain – it derives from a 'Celtic' root meaning 'seafarer' or 'sea traveller' (compare Latin *mare*, 'sea') – there are too few instances of its usage to reveal what the word would have meant to a contemporary Roman. Alongside literal meanings of 'ship's captain' or 'trader', more metaphorical meanings related to leadership of a guild or municipal organisation cannot be excluded (Corcoran *et al* 2002; Adams 2003). But what of the god, Mars Camulus, to whom the plaque was dedicated? He has largely escaped comment. To champions of Colchester's archaeology, of course, the meaning has been clear from the start. Here was the old British war god, patron of the *colonia* of Camulodunum, exerting his authority in the new town of Londinium.

The god Mars

De his eandem fere, quam reliquae gentes, habent opinionem . . . Martem bella regere (Caesar, *de bello Gallico*, 6.17)

'[The Gauls]', says Caesar, 'have roughly the same belief about these [gods] as other peoples have . . . Mars controls wars.' Numerous images of the war god, resplendent in full armour, have been found throughout the Roman empire and echo this description. But Caesar, the general and politician, was simplifying in an effort to show how comprehensive his victory had been, how united Gaul had become. Other characteristics of Mars go unmentioned. Cato, over a century earlier, had advised farmers to propitiate Mars by sacrificing a pig, ram and bull. The animals must be 'driven or carried round (*sive circumagi sive circumferenda*) as much of the farm or lands as requires purification' (Cato, *de agricultura*, 161.1) – presumably so as to make the boundaries of the estate and all its parts known to the god. Mars's role as the farmer's patron explains why, in Roman Britain, sculptural reliefs of him are as common in rural Gloucestershire (Toynbee 1964, 154) as in the military areas of the province. Neither should we forget that Mars had a special place in the official religion of the Roman state, being the legendary father of the city's founders, Romulus and Remus. To some people god and hero could easily be conflated. So Gulioepius, a man of 'Celtic' extraction who wished to demonstrate his loyalty to the empire, dedicated to Romulus a plaque that shows the hero quite clearly in the guise of Mars (Henig 1993, 21, no 60).

One measure of Mars's importance in Britannia is the number of votive altars that were dedicated to

Fig 3.5.1 Photograph of London inscription after cleaning

him. The votive altar, a public and comparatively costly form of offering, was made to repay the god for granting a favour that had previously been requested (Derks 1995, 115–17, 122). Mars has over 60 to his name and is surpassed only by Jupiter, who has over 120. None of the other deities – including Mercury, who was regularly venerated for his association with commerce as well as the other world – has as many as 20. Eleven of the dedications to Mars explicitly link him with Victory and so were probably made in gratitude for a battle won or for survival from a tour of duty. But in more instances (nearly 30) – as on the Southwark plaque – he is assimilated to 'Celtic' or north European deities. In Britain (though not in Gaul) this is another characteristic that is not much shared with other Roman gods: Apollo Maponus (three votive altars) and Sulis Minerva (two) are the only other regular assimilations.

Is the 'assimilated' Mars the god who controls battles, the god who watches over the farmer's interests, or the god who fathered the legendary founder of Rome? If we follow Caesar, it will have been exclusively the first. Many times during the conquest of Gaul and Britain chieftains turned tribes to fight alongside the Romans against their neighbours, and so it is quite plausible that their gods should have followed suit. Cocidius, for example, worshipped with Mars by men of the Second Augustan Legion on Hadrian's Wall (Collingwood *et al* 1995, 2024), may have been a British war god who changed sides and fought with the Romans. The geographical distribution of the dedications, however, suggests that this is only a partial explanation. Even when allowance is made for the random nature of discovery, or differences caused by the availability of stone, dedications to the 'assimilated' Mars fall into two groups: those that cluster almost exclusively in one region, and those that may have local clusters but are also scattered widely across Britain, Gaul and Germany.

Mars Belatucadrus has an exclusively local distribution (Table 3.5.1; Fig 3.5.2). Five dedications to the 'assimilated' gods, alongside a further 21 to Belatucadrus alone, cluster at the western end of Hadrian's Wall and in the hinterland to the south. Mars Cocidius (five 'assimilated' dedications, eighteen to Cocidius alone or associated with gods

Table 3.5.1 Dedications to Belatucadrus on votive altars

Location	Form of dedication	Dedicator (and status, if known)	Type of monument	References
Dedications to Mars-Belatucadrus				
Old Penrith	Marti Belatucadro et numinib(us) Aug(ustorum)	Iulius Augustalis, *actor Iuli Lupi pr(a)ef(ecti)* ('agent' of Iulius Lupus, the prefect)	Altar	RIB 918
Burgh-by-Sands	Marti Belatucad(ro)	illegible	Altar	RIB 2044
Carlisle	Marti Belatucadro	missing	Altar	RIB 948
Carvoran	Marti Belatucairo	none	Altar	RIB 1784
Netherby	Marti Belatucadro	reading uncertain	Altar	RIB 970
Dedications to Belatucadrus alone				
Old Penrith	Bel[a]tuca(dro)	none	Altar	RIB 914
Old Penrith	Balatocadro	none	Altar	Hassall & Tomlin 1978, 474 no 7
Old Penrith	Belatucairo	none	Altar	Hassall & Tomlin 1978, 474 no 8
Brougham	B[a[latu(cadro)	name illegible, but someone from a military unit, *ex cune(o)*	Altar? (much damaged)	RIB 772
Brougham	Balatucairo	Baculo *pro se et suis* ('for himself and his family')	Altar	RIB 773
Brougham	Blatucairo	Audagus	Altar	RIB 774
Brougham	Belatu[ca]dro	Iulianus	Altar	RIB 775
Brougham	Belatuca[i]ro	missing (or none originally)	Statue base or altar	RIB 777; Collingwood *et al* 1995, 773
Kirkby Thore	Belatucadro	illegible	Altar	RIB 759
Maryport	Belatucadro	Iul(ius) Civilis, *optio* (second-in-command of a century)	Altar	RIB 809
Old Carlisle	Belatucadro	Aur(elius) Tasulus, *vet(eranus)* (ex-soldier)	Altar	RIB 887
Old Carlisle	Belatucadro	Aurelius Diatus	Altar	RIB 888; Collingwood *et al* 1995, 775
Old Carlisle	Belatucauro	illegible or none	Altar	RIB 889
Bowness-on-Solway	Belatocairo	Peisius M(arcus)	Altar	RIB 2056
Burgh-by-Sands	Belatuca(dro)	none	Altar	RIB 2038
Burgh-by-Sands	Belatocadro	Antr(onius) Auf(idianus)	Altar	RIB 2039
Castlesteads	Belatugagro	Minervalis	Altar	RIB 1976
Castlesteads	Belatuca[d]ro	Ullinus or [.]ullinus (eg Iullinus)	Altar	RIB 1977; Collingwood *et al* 1995, 793
Carvoran	Baliticauro	none	Altar	RIB 1775
Carvoran	Blatucadro	none	Altar	RIB 1776
Carrawburgh	Belleticauro	Lunaris	Altar	RIB 1521

Table 3.5.2 Dedications to Cocidius on votive altars

Location	Form of dedication	Dedicator (and status, if known)	Type of monument	References
Dedications to Mars-Cocidius				
Lancaster	Marti Cocidio	Vibenius Lucius b(ene)f(iciarius) co(n)s(ularis) (a soldier seconded to the provincial governor's staff	Altar	RIB 602
Cumbria, exact location unknown	I(ovi) O(ptimo) M(aximo) et | [...] M(arti) | Coc(idio) (reading of first two lines uncertain)	Vita(lis) (reading uncertain)	Altar	RIB 1017; Collingwood et al 1995, 777
Hadrian's Wall, between Castlesteads and Stanwix	Marti [C]ocidio (jointly with the Genius of, almost certainly, Carlisle, Genio [Lugu]vali)	Martius [... c]oh(ortis) I Ba[tavorum] (soldier of unspecified rank in the First Cohort of Batavians)	Altar	RIB 2015; Rivet & Smith 1979, 402
Hadrian's Wall, between Castlesteads and Stanwix	Marti Cocidio)	'Soldiers of the Second Legion Augusta – the Sanctian century and Secundinus's century – discharged their vow under the direction of Aelianus, a centurion. Felix, an optio, was in charge.' (m(ilites) leg(ionis) II Aug(ustae) c(enturia) Sanctiana c(enturia) Secundini d(ono) sol(uerunt) sub cura Aeliani c(enturionis) cura(vit) Oppius [F]elix optio)	Altar	RIB 2024
Bewcastle	Ma[rt]i Cocid(io)	Aeliu[s] Vitalianus	Altar	RIB 993
Dedications to Cocidius alone and to Cocidius paired with gods other than Mars				
Ebchester	Vernostono Cocidio (Vernostonus, otherwise unattested, was presumably another god – native either to Britain or to the dedicator's homeland)	Virilis Ger(?manus), 'a ?German'	Altar	RIB 1102
Hadrian's Wall, between Castlesteads and Stanwix	Cocidio	Soldiers of the Sixth Legion (milites leg(ionis) VI Vic(tricis))	Altar	RIB 2020
Hadrian's Wall, between Birdoswald and Castlesteads	Cocidio	Soldiers of the Second Legion Augusta (milites l[eg(ionis)] II Aug(ustae))	Altar	RIB 1955
Hadrian's Wall, between Birdoswald and Castlesteads	Cocidio	Soldiers of the Twentieth Legion Valeria Victrix (milites legi(onis) XX V(aleriae) V(ictricis))	Altar. Bears a consular date, probably mid-3rd century	RIB 1956
Hadrian's Wall, between Birdoswald and Castlesteads	Cocid[io]	Vexillation (special detachment) of the Sixth Legion Victix (text can be restored with tolerable certainly: vexil[latio] leg(ionis) VI V[ictricis])	Altar	RIB 1961
Hadrian's Wall, between Birdoswald and Castlesteads	Co[cidio]	missing	Altar	RIB 1963
Birdoswald	Cocidio	Soldiers of the First Cohort of Dacians, commanded by Valerianus (coh(ors) I Aelia [... c(ui) p(raeest) ...] Valerianus	Probably an altar	RIB 1872
Birdoswald	Cocidio	illegible	Altar (later overwritten with dedication to Jupiter)	RIB 1885
Chesterholm	Cocidio	Decimus Caerellius Victor, pr(aefectus) coh(ortis) II Ner(viorum) (commanding officer of the Second Cohort of Tungri)	Altar	RIB 1683

Table 3.5.2 Continued

Location	Form of dedication	Dedicator (and status, if known)	Type of monument	References
Hadrian's Wall, between Housesteads and Great Chesters	Cocidio	Vabrius	Altar	RIB 1633
Housesteads	Cocidio [et] Genio Pr[ae]sidi ('to Cocidius and the Spirit of the Garrison')	Valerius, m(iles) l[e]g(ionis) VI V(ictricis) (soldier of the Sixth Legion Victorious)	Altar	RIB 1577
Housesteads	Silvano Cocidio	Q(uintus) Florius Maternus, praef(ectus) coh(ortis) I Tung(rorum) (commanding officer of the First Cohort of Tungri)	Altar	RIB 1578
Housesteads	I(ovi) O(ptimo) M(aximo) et deo Cocidio Genioq(ue) hui(u)s loci ('to Jupiter Best and Greatest, and to the god Cocidius, and to the Spirit of this place')	Soldiers of the Second Legion Augusta (mil(ites) leg(ionis) II Aug(ustae))	Altar	RIB 1583
Netherby	Cocidio	Paternius Maternus tribunus coh(ortis) I Nervan(a)e ex evocato Palatino (commander of the First Nervan Cohort (of Germans), formerly one of the emperor's Praetorian Guardsmen)	Altar	RIB 966
Bewcastle Bewcastle	Cocidio Cocideo	Annius Victor centu[r](io) legioni[s] (a legionary centurion) Aurunc(eius) Felicessimus tribun(us) ex evocato (commander of an auxiliary unit, probably a former Praetorian Guardsman – though evocatus is not elaborated with Palatinus, as on the previous altar, or with the Praetorian cohort number as on RIB 1896)	Altar Altar	RIB 985 RIB 988
Bewcastle	Cocidio	Q(uintus) Peltrasi[u]s Maximus tribu(unus) ex corniculario praefe(ctorum) praetorio (auxiliary unit commander, formerly adjutant to the commanders of the emperor's Praetorian Guard)	Altar	RIB 989
Risingham	Cocidio et	[... (A relief above the inscription shows a hunter god, and Phillips and RIB read SIL[... in the second line (though this is not clear on the photograph). The dedication may thus have been to Cocidius and Silvanus; compare the Housesteads altar above.)	illegible	Altar	RIB 1207; Phillips 1977, 84–5 no 234 and pl 63

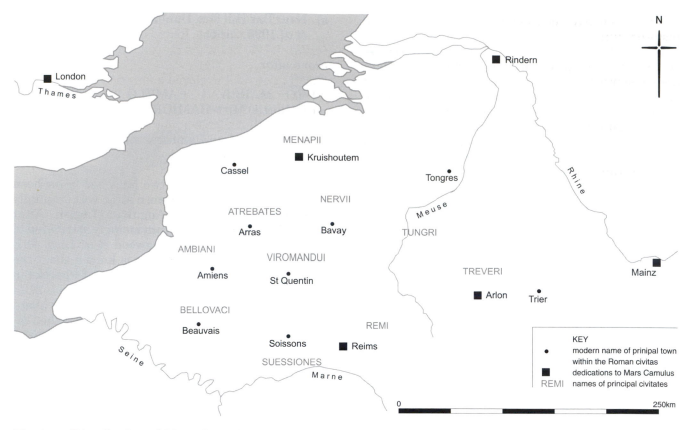

Fig 3.5.3 Distribution of Mars Camulus inscriptions in Gaul and Germany

d) Kruishoutem, Belgium (Rogge *et al* 1995, 205–6 and fig 9)

Bronze plinth for a figurine

DEO MARTI CAMVLO | VERECVNDVS FRVC-
TI | V(otum) S(olvit) L(ibens) M(erito)
'To the god Mars Camulus, Verecundus son of Fructus willingly and deservedly fulfilled his vow'

The figurine is missing, but the plinth was found in association with twenty bronze figurines of Mars, six of Minerva and one of Victory. Thirty brooches and 50 coins (mid- to late imperial) were also found. This seems to have been the site of a rural sanctuary in the northern part of Gallia Belgica, overlooking the river Schelde and probably in the territory of the Menapii.

e) Rindern, Germany (CIL 13.2 8701)

Stone block, either part of an altar or a statue base (Fig 3.5.4)

(front) MARTI CAMVLO | SACRUM PRO | SALVTE {TIBERII} | CLAVDI CAESARIS | AVG(usti) GERMANICI IMP(eratoris) | CIVES REMI QVI | TEMPLVM CONSTITV | ERVNT
'To Mars Camulus a sacred offering for the safety of {Tiberius} Claudius Caesar Augustus Germanicus Imperator, the citizens, Remi, who founded the temple'

(back) O(b) C(ives) S(ervatos) (in an oak wreath)
'For saving the citizens'

This block, which has long been a treasured possession of the people of Rindern and which serves today as an altar in the church of St Willibrord, may have been brought in medieval times from nearby Xanten (Horn 1987, 458–9). The name 'TIBERII' is secondary: the other names are nonsensical in terms of the titulature of the emperor Tiberius, and an earlier

Fig 3.5.4 Statue base now in St Willibrord's Church, Rindern (photo: Rainer Hoymann)

name has clearly been erased. That name can be restored unequivocally as 'NERONIS', 'of Nero'. The dedication may well have been made in AD 65–66 to give thanks for the emperor's escape from the conspiracy led by Calpurnius Piso, which had involved the provincial governor of Germany (*l'Année épigraphique* 1981, 176–7, no 690; *pace* Rüger 1981, 334–5, who connects the dedication with Vindex's rebellion in March AD 68). A second inscription from Xanten, on an altar dedicated to Mars Cicollius by *cives* Lingones, has very similar wording and almost certainly commemorates the same event (Rüger 1981). The communities of Remi and Lingones – probably trading delegations – who lived in the civil settlement that had grown up alongside the legionary fortress will have come under the jurisdiction of the Roman authorities, but evidently maintained their cultural integrity. The Remi perhaps regarded the new temple of Mars Camulus as their official cult centre.

f)   Reims, France (Wuilleumier 1963, 351)

Stone plaque

[IN] HONOR[EM ?D(omus) ?D(ivinae)] | [?ARAM] MARTIS CAM[VLI] | [. . .] T(itus) IVCVNDINIV[S] | [LAVRENTI]VM LAVINAT[IVM]
'In honour of the Divine Household, ?an altar of Mars Camulus, Titus Iucundinius, (member of) the Laurentes Lavinates, (gave it)'

The first line – a dedication to the Emperor's Household (*domus divina*) – can be restored by analogy with many other Rhineland inscriptions and, fortunately, the central section of the plaque is undamaged, allowing us to reconstruct the sense but not the exact phrasing of the remainder. Iucundinius, who made an offering to Mars Camulus, was evidently one of the Laurentes Lavinates, a religious community associated with the Italian town of Lavinium (modern Practica di Mare, 30km south of Rome). Despite its small size, this was a place of immense importance. According to tradition, it had been founded by Aeneas and so was the ancestral home of his remote descendant, Romulus, the legendary founder of Rome itself. Every year newly elected Roman magistrates processed there to make offerings to the household gods of Rome (Derks 1998, 109–10).

Conclusion

The surviving inscriptions thus link Mars Camulus primarily with Gallia Belgica and the *civitas* Remorum in particular. His influence also appears to have extended westwards and northwards, and the dedications from Britain have, in one case, a certain and, in the other, a possible link with the same area. Like the London plaque, which opens with a dedication to the emperors, items (e) and (f) are strong expressions of loyalty to the imperial regime and Roman ancestral values. Loyalty to Rome was ingrained in the politics of the Remi. Caesar says (*de bello Gallico* 6.12) that when he arrived in Gaul the tribe was not a powerful one; but it sided with him immediately and acquired a new position of authority (*novam et repente conlectam auctoritatem*), second only to the Aedui. During the revolt of Vercingetorix in 52 BC the Remi remained loyal (7.63), doubtless usurping the place of the Aedui as Rome's principal allies after that tribe had been defeated. In AD 21, the Remi seem to have stood firm when Julius Florus led their neighbours, the Treveri, in rebellion; and it was in Reims itself that the leaders of the Gallic *civitates* met in AD 70 (Tacitus *Historiae* 4.69), issued a declaration supporting Rome and Vespasian, and so caused the revolt of Civilis to dwindle away.

If Camulus protected the lands of the Remi, assimilating him with Mars would add a link with the very origins of Rome. But suppose the leaders of the Remi wished to make the connection more explicit, to prove that the legendary origins of their tribe and of Rome coincided? After all, could it be by chance that they should carry the name of Romulus's twin brother? On the monumental arch that served as a gateway to Reims, the designers seem to have given a prominent position to scenes showing Romulus and Remus, Venus and Aeneas, Rhea Silvia and Mars (Derks 1998, 105–10). In the early 1st century AD searching for origin myths was a popular pastime. It was actively encouraged by Augustus and Claudius, who wished to secure their regime by recalling ancient values and giving places outside Rome a sense of importance. So it was that at Lavinium, which had been abandoned for centuries and whose 6th-century BC altars had fallen into disrepair, a *religiosa civitas* – the Laurentes Lavinates – was established (Saulnier 1984), together with a new priesthood to superintend the cult of Rome's household gods (Beard *et al* 1998, **1**, 323–4; **2**, 12–13). Any rituals were probably not 'revived' so much as 'reinvented'. The Laurentes, who were required to attend ceremonies in Lavinium only once a year and so did not live in the town, have left over 70 inscriptions across the empire. All were of equestrian rank and many were patrons of cities. Why should one of them, Iucundinius – whether a visitor to Reims or a resident – have chosen to honour Mars Camulus? Was he an antiquary, intrigued by the name Remi, who enjoyed erudite speculation about legend in the congenial surroundings of an elite dining-club?

Epilogue

When Tiberinius Celerianus, a citizen of the Bellovaci, dedicated his plaque in London, he was honouring a god whose influence was strongly felt in his homeland – a god who, because of the political history of the Remi, symbolised the Roman achievement in Gaul. And what of Camulodunum? Personal names such as Camulius, borne by a man from

Turin who died in Chester (Collingwood *et al* 1995, 524) – not to mention the existence of a second Camulodunum and of a Camulosessa in north Britain – show that Camulus spread far, but there may have been a particular reason for applying his name to Colchester. It first appears on coins of Cunobelin (Rivet and Smith 1979, 294–5). The motifs on that ruler's coinage, as Creighton has demonstrated (2000, 101–25, 174–88), were carefully chosen with an eye to the images that Augustus himself was using to promote a manifesto uniting present victories with destiny, tradition and promises of a Golden Age. Imagine Cunobelin crossing the Channel, finding congenial company among the Remi, and then deciding to declare his allegiance to their values by naming his headquarters after their patron. On this reading, Camulus would be no British war god but a thoroughly Romanised immigrant. No wonder Boudica sacked the place that bore his name.

Acknowledgements

The discovery of this plaque can reasonably be regarded as a fruit of the efforts of Harvey Sheldon, who for some 40 years has championed the cause of Roman Southwark, demanding that archaeology here should be put on an equal footing with archaeology in the city. How fitting it is that this, the first monumental inscription to name London – or, to be accurate, 'Londoners' – should come from south of the Thames, not from the north.

The plaque was found at Tabard Square, 34–70 Long Lane, 31–47 Tabard Street SE1 (LLS02[1566]), and is on display at the Museum of London. The excavation was carried out by Pre-Construct Archaeology (PCA) and was financed by Berkeley Homes (South-East London) Ltd. For help in studying and publishing the find, I am especially grateful to Gary Brown and Frank Meddens (PCA), Nansi Rosenberg (archaeological consultant), Jenny Hall, Susan Walker, and, especially, Roger Tomlin.

3.6 Harper Road, Southwark: an early Roman burial revisited *Jonathan Cotton*

Prologue: *An ending ... and some beginnings*

It was the ululating wail of the hired mourner at the head of the small procession that first caught the attention of the idlers by the cookshop on the road running south from the river. That and the diminutive pipe-player, whose reedy discordant notes added to the cacophony.

Behind the bier strode a red-eyed elderly man, felt cap tightly balled in one hand. His quick glance missed little and he nodded curtly to the ox-cart driver and the muleteers who had drawn aside to let his wife's body pass.

From his vantage point atop the cart the driver gazed down into the open wooden coffin as it swayed past and took in the dead woman's juniper-wreathed grey hair and carefully depilated, starkly-painted face – testimony to the undertaker's practised artifice.

Had he cared to look closer he might have pondered too on the strangeness of the woman's garb, and would certainly have made a quick mental calculation as to the worth of the mirror and the curious neck-ring glinting at her slippered feet.

But he'd been on the road since first light and hunger had the last word. His eyes flickered instead to the rest of the funeral party who carried with them the makings of a modest feast: joints of ready-roasted pork, plates of pastries and a heavy flagon of sweetened Gaulish wine.

Having walked from the far side of the settlement on the opposite bank of the swollen river the bearers of the feast were hungry too, and anxious to reach the appointed burying ground in the herb-scented, hawk-haunted pastures further south.

Besides, few of them were more than casual acquaintances of the dead woman and her husband. And in this thrusting nascent town time was money and friendships easily won were just as easily lost – especially when fresh opportunity swirled in on every tide ...

Introduction

The burial considered here was briefly published over 25 years ago (Dean and Hammerson 1980) and has been mentioned in passing a number of times in the literature since (eg Perring 1991a, 3 and fig 1; Philpott 1991, 183, 355; Hall 1996, 79, S25; Barber and Bowsher 2000, 134, 300; Sheldon 2000, 142; Bird 2004, 135). Elements of it are due to be incorporated in a forthcoming Southwark publication (Cowan *et al* forthcoming).

However, conservation and research carried out prior to and following its display in the Museum of London's *London before London* gallery in 2002 suggests that the grave group familiar in the literature is incomplete. The opportunity has therefore been taken here to reconstruct and publish it in full for the first time. The concluding discussion focuses on the messages contained within the burial itself, and on the wider creation of identity within the newly founded Londinium.

The excavation

Two seasons of student training excavations were carried out at Harper Road in 1977 (HR77) and 1979 (HR79) by Martin Dean under the aegis of the Southwark and Lambeth Archaeological Excavation Committee (SLAEC). Initially four areas were trial trenched by machine in the area bounded by Dickens Square, Merrick Square, Falmouth Road and Harper Road, Southwark (Fig 3.6.1; Dean 1977). All produced useful topographic information, but further work only proceeded in three hand-dug trenches (numbered II–IV) on that portion of the site lying to the rear of Merrick Square (HR79). Overall the work revealed a series of mainly late Roman features in the form of linear ditches and two human inhumation burials, one early and one late. It is the early burial that concerns us here.

Harper Road is situated around 1.1km south of the present Thames on the 'higher' ground beyond the projected junction of two Roman roads, Watling Street and Stane Street, on the southern outskirts of the known Southwark settlement. The line of Watling Street runs 150m or so to the north-east and the supposed line of Stane Street somewhat further to the west (see Sheldon 2000, 130, for discussion of this point). The underlying geology comprises Upper Floodplain gravels (of Kempton Park/East Tilbury Marshes type) variably capped with 'brickearths' (Langley Silts).

The early burial

The early inhumation lay within Trench III, which was sited in the former rear gardens of 18–19 Dickens Square, the latter backing onto the garden of 19 Merrick Square (Fig 3.6.1, inset). The grave cut [310] was aligned north-east/south-west and had been dug into the Langley Silts. Its base lay at +1.55m OD, and the top of the identifiable cut lay at +1.69m OD. Though therefore shallow and somewhat difficult to define, the cut was at least 2.3m × 1.0m in extent. The extended skeleton of a woman lay on its floor, and rather to one side, with her head to the south-west and arms by her sides. A number of iron nails within the grave backfill suggested

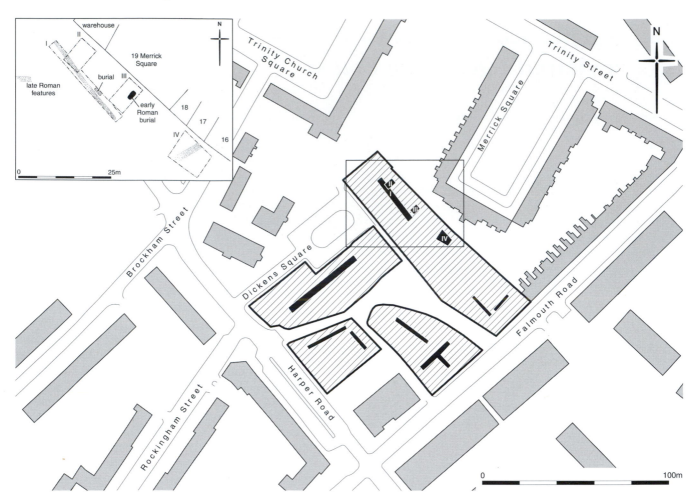

Fig 3.6.1 Harper Road, site location; the early burial lay within Trench III (inset)

to the excavator that she may have been interred within a wooden coffin.

The skeleton was accompanied by a range of grave goods outlined in the initial publication of the discovery (Dean and Hammerson 1980, 20). These comprised: a complete ceramic flagon placed at the right side of the head; a bronze neck-ring just above the right ankle; and a rectangular bronze mirror over the right foot (Fig 3.6.2).

Recent work has identified further objects that almost certainly formed part of the original grave assemblage. These included two samian plates dumped in the backfill of a 19th-century pit [304] that had removed the bones of the skeleton's left foot. (A small rim sherd of samian recovered from the grave cut itself belongs to the more complete of the two vessels.) Furthermore, bones comprising the left forelimb of a pig were identified during the re-examination of the human remains. These were clearly recovered from the grave cut, although their position was not located on the plan.

The grave contents

The contents of the grave are summarised in Table 3.6.1 (and see Fig 3.6.3).

Discussion

The Harper Road burial

Following recent conservation and research a fuller reconstruction of the Harper Road burial is now possible. Firstly, we can be clear that the deceased herself was somewhat taller and older than previously thought. At 5ft 4in (1.63m) she falls well within the upper end of the expected height range for women of the period. Moreover, with an age at death of 45+ she was within the top 10.5% of the population in terms of longevity (Hall and Conheeney 1998, 38). Unfortunately, chemical isotope analyses carried out on her teeth in an attempt to determine her place of childhood residence gave conflicting results, although the strontium (Sr) and lead (Pb) data were generally consistent with a UK or northern continental origin. It is clear that the woman had been exposed to a high concentration of lead (Budd 2002, 8), possibly through drinking water channelled through lead pipes or perhaps through the ingestion of smoke-borne residues from metal-working or other processes.

The obvious explanation for the iron nails recovered from the grave fill is that they were used

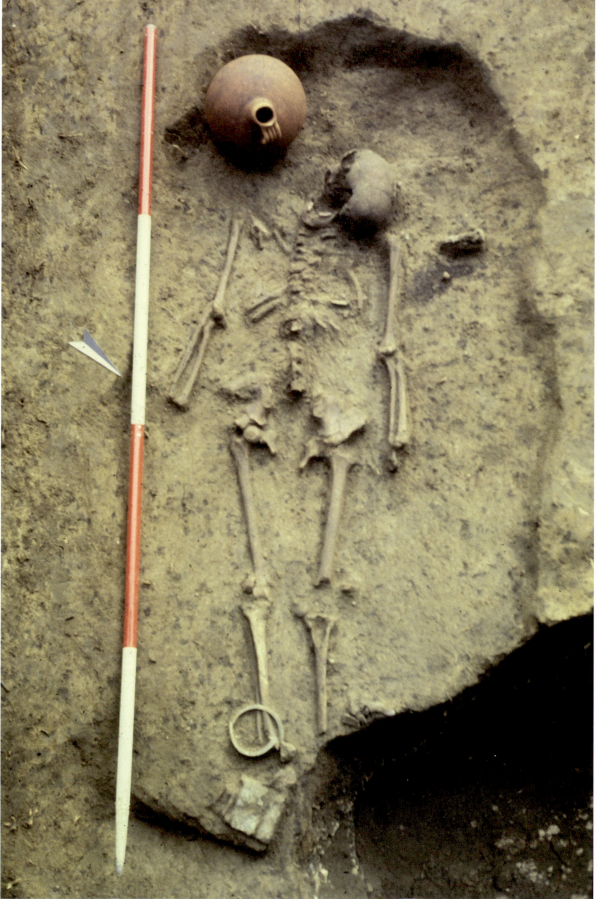

Fig 3.6.2 The early burial, as excavated. Note the presence of a Victorian pit which has cut away the skeleton's left foot

Table 3.6.1 Harper Road burial: summary of grave contents (Fig 3.6.3)

Acc No	Object	Description	Position	Dimensions	Date
HR79 [310]	Human skeleton	The skeleton was poorly preserved. Only an estimated 40% of the bones survived, and these were in a friable condition. Many of the smaller bones, a majority of the ribs, and the bones of the left foot were missing. Based on features of the skull and pelvis, the bones could be identified as those of a woman with a biological age at death of 45+ (probably within the range 45–49) (Brian Connell pers comm). There were no obvious signs of injury in the form of healed fractures, though she had suffered from mild osteoarthritis. Also, mechanical changes in the form of flattened facets or 'squatting' facets were present on her shin and ankle bones. Given her relatively advanced age her teeth were in reasonable condition, though one had a deposit of calculus (tartar) on its surface indicative of poor oral hygiene.	Off-centre within grave	H: 1.63m (5ft 4in)	
HR79 [310]	Pig foreleg	Six fragments of an adult pig (*Sus*) left elbow were identified amongst the human bones (Brian Connell pers comm): five fragments of distal humerus and one of proximal ulna, presumably originally articulated. The elbow joint (trochlea) had been chopped through.	Unknown, recovered from grave fill		
HR79 [310] <80>	Iron nails	Two, possibly three, nails.	Grave fill	Most complete nail L >37mm, with square head 14mm Longest nail L 101mm, with square head 25mm L 25–42mm with square heads 12–15mm and square shanks 3mm	
HR79 [310] <85>	Iron nails	Two nails	Grave fill		
HR79 [310] <86>	Iron nails	At least nine nails or fragments	Grave fill		
HR79 [310]	Ceramic flagon	Complete collared flagon of 'Hofheim' form, which is the predominant type in use during the pre-Flavian period. Fiona Seeley writes: Because of its completeness it has not been possible to examine the fabric in fresh fracture at x20 magnification. However, the pink colour of the surfaces and soft and powdery surfaces suggest one of two attributions. The first is Hoo ware (HOO) which is a light red fabric with a white slip. The slip tends to be friable and may only survive in the grooves of the handle, collar or foot ring of the vessel. However, no slip was identified on this example. Furthermore, the distinctive rim form of the present flagon is not found on any published examples identified as Hoo ware (Davies *et al* 1994, 38–40, fig 30, nos 130–3). The second and more likely option is that it is one of the fabrics grouped under the common name North French/South East English oxidised wares (NFSE) (for full discussion of these fabrics see Davies *et al* 1994, 62–67). In particular the fabric NFSE-2667, which is present in the earliest Roman assemblages in London (ibid, 62). This fabric can be pink in colour and is powdery to the touch and can have an abraded appearance. The collared flagons in this fabric have a 'distinctive groove or undercutting of the rim' and published examples are not unlike the Harper Road vessel (ibid, 63, fig 52, 288–90).	Placed at the right side of the head and tilted at a slight angle from the vertical, with the handle towards the head.	H: 300mm Capacity: 9 pints (5.1 litres)	AD 50–70

Table 3.6.1 Continued

Acc No	Object	Description	Position	Dimensions	Date
HR79 [310] <83>	Bronze neck-ring	Complete bronze neck-ring, now in two pieces, and twisted out of true. The ring is of flat penannular form with a rectangular cross-section and gently expanded terminals. Its small size suggests that it was intended for a slender neck. SEM analysis indicates that it was cut from a hammered sheet of high-tin bronze. Semi-quantitative data of the elemental composition of the metal alloy utilised showed that it comprised: Cu 47.72%, Sn 31.98% and Pb 8.93% (Christie Pohl pers comm). Decoration is confined to the upper surface and is composed of a symmetrical arrangement of more-or-less crisply punched and engraved motifs. These comprise three transverse rows of punched dots asymmetrically arranged at either terminal as a single row and a pair (the latter worked so as to produce a raised 'beaded' effect); a pair of flamboyant 'feather' motifs (one slightly botched), made up of a combination of short tooled linear strokes and ring-and-dot impressions; and four saltire motifs of short linear strokes punctuated by ring-and-dot impressions arranged quincunx fashion. A pair of these saltires has been placed side by side directly opposite the terminals, with two single opposed examples spaced midway between. The 'feather' motifs on the neck-ring offer further points of interest and are here suggested to represent the tail feathers of the male peacock (Fig 3.6.4). This iconography would have been wholly appropriate in a funerary context, for peacocks, originally from India, had supposedly incorruptible flesh which made them obvious symbols of immortality. The birds were linked with the goddess Juno (Toynbee 1973, 251) and the 'eyes' in the tail feathers of the male peacock (economically schematised on the present piece by ring-and-dot impressions) were likened to the stars in the night sky. Moreover, Juno was the patroness of female fertility and of marriage and, as Juno Lucina, goddess of childbirth, so the peacock may have had a particular resonance for women. Toynbee (1973, 252) notes that the bird was also appropriated as the badge of empresses and other ladies of the imperial house. Two late Roman inhumation burials (one male? and the other female) in the eastern cemetery of Londinium were accompanied by coins portraying empresses ascending to heaven on the backs of peacocks (Barber and Bowsher 2000, B202 and B291, 156 and 168–9). The neck-ring has been subjected to a twisting motion which has bent the metal out of true in the horizontal plane. This appears to have happened prior to burial, either in life or, conceivably perhaps, in the act of putting on or removing the ring from the neck of the corpse during the funerary obsequies. The crispness of the decoration and the lack of any obvious wear around the inner edge of the ring itself – together with its small size – rather suggests that it was specifically made for display and/or burial. This raises a further question: when was the neck-ring broken – prior to burial or in the ground afterwards? The SEM analysis provided no definitive answer (Christie Pohl pers comm). There are still no close parallels (Dean and Hammerson 1980, 20, footnote 6) which might strengthen the notion suggested above, that it was a special one-off piece commissioned as a funerary gift. Few other neck-rings have been found in London. However, a copper-alloy necklet of twisted wire from which was suspended a separate pendant was worn by a mature female in the Atlantic House cemetery (ATL89 and ATC97; Watson 2003, Burial 12, 42–3), while a solid copper-alloy torc with knobbed terminals (MoL 18661) was recovered from the Walbrook at St Swithin's House (Wilmott 1991, no 270, 114).	Placed over the right ankle	Diam (internal): 110mm; W (terminal): 10mm; Wt: 36.92g	

Table 3.6.1 Continued

Acc No	Object	Description	Position	Dimensions	Date
HR79 [310] <84>	Bronze mirror	Bronze mirror, nearly complete. Recent conservation has confirmed that this is of rectangular (not square) form with plain bevelled edges. It is likely that it was originally protected by a wooden frame or case. SEM and XRF analyses have revealed that the mirror is of high-tin bronze and probably chill cast (Meg Wang pers comm; see Meeks 1988). Differential cooling rates might explain why the centre of the mirror is less well preserved than the edges. Quantitative XRF analysis showed that the metal comprised Cu 56.2%, Sn 30.7% and Pb 5.5%. This is broadly comparable to that of the neck-ring (see above). Lloyd-Morgan (1981, 3, Group A) notes that the origins of this type of mirror are uncertain, though 'by the first century AD it was one of the most popular forms, with examples coming from virtually all provinces of the empire.' In the original publication (Dean and Hammerson 1980, 20, footnote 7) she suggested that the Harper Road piece probably originated in a North Italian workshop. However, given the large number of mirrors of this form found with burials at Nijmegen, Holland, a production centre may have existed there too (Lloyd-Morgan 1981). Over 100 complete or fragmentary mirrors of various forms have now been recovered from the London area (Angela Wardle pers comm), some associated with burials. These include several circular mirrors found with cremation burials in Deverell Street (Kempe 1836, 467) a little way to the south-east of Harper Road. Group A rectangular mirrors are known from the cemetery at West Tenter Street (WTN83 and WTN84; Whytehead 1986, 91 and fig 38 no 2) and from Cheapside (CID90 [922] <1333>), Moorfields Marsh (Cuming Museum acc no C912), St Martin Orgar (ORG86 [1043] <40>), London Wall (LOW88 [391] <1336>), Paternoster Square (PNS01 [320] <200>) and the GPO site, Newgate Street (GPO75 [9487] <4394>).	Placed over the right foot	120mm x 90mm in area and >1mm thick	1st cent AD
HR79 [310]	Samian sherd	Rim sherd of South Gaulish samian plate, Drag 18 form, which belongs with the more complete samian plate from [304] (below).	Grave fill		AD 45–65
HR79 [304]	Samian plate	Samian plate of Drag 18 form, around 65% complete, with a lustrous sealing-wax red slip characteristic of La Graufesenque. It has a slight step at the junction of the wall and floor. The floor rises in the centre and bears a small complete name-stamp reading OFVITALIS (Joanna Bird and Brenda Dickinson pers comm). The base of the (complete) footring is worn, as is the outside of the beaded rim.	Found in the fill of a Victorian pit which had removed the skeleton's lower left leg and foot.	Diam: 188mm	AD 45–65
HR79 [304]	Samian plate	Samian plate of Drag 18 form, around 50% complete. It appears generally more worn than its more complete fellow. The floor rises slightly in the centre and has been pierced deliberately by punching through a name-stamp reading O . . . TALIS (Joanna Bird and Brenda Dickinson pers comm). The base of the (complete) footring is worn.	Found in the fill of a Victorian pit which had removed the skeleton's lower left leg and foot.	Diam: 180mm	AD 45–65

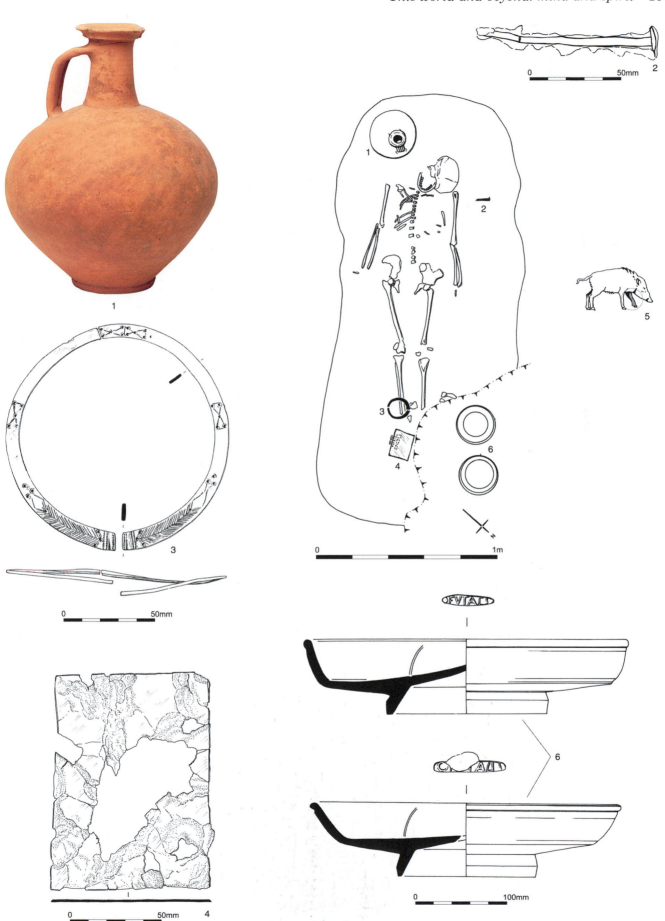

Fig 3.6.3 The burial and accompanying grave goods, various scales. The flagon is 300mm in height. The exact position of the pig forelimb (5) within the grave is unknown

to secure the planks of a wooden coffin (as Watson 2003, 33–4), although the length of the longest nail (101mm) in particular seems extravagant for the task. Such was the level of root and other disturbance within the grave, however, that no meaningful pattern in their distribution could be discerned. Furthermore, 16% of adult inhumations in the rural cemetery at Chantambre, Essonne in France, contained deposits of loose nails thought to possess magical symbolism (Murail and Girard 2000, 107), and it is conceivable that something similar lay behind the incorporation of the nails at Harper Road. The enormous quantities of nails recovered

from the Walbrook stream may bear much the same sort of interpretation (eg Merrifield 1995, 41–2).

The present study has confirmed the burial's 'unusually early date'. Hitherto, this attribution has rested squarely on the collared flagon, which is certainly of pre-Flavian and probably pre-Boudican date (Fiona Seeley pers comm). This dating is now supported by the pair of samian plates recovered from the Victorian pit [304], and presumably originally placed close to the left foot of the deceased (Figs 3.6.4 and 3.6.5). Both plates are products of Vitalis i, whose output at La Graufesenque spanned the period AD 45–65 (Joanna Bird and

Fig 3.6.4 Close up of the decoration at the terminals of the neck-ring, here interpreted as schematised representations of peacock tail feathers (photo: Meriel Jeater)

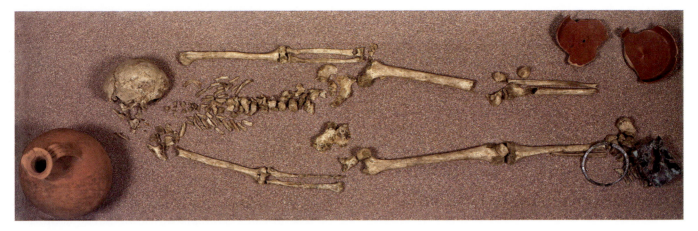

Fig 3.6.5 The burial as displayed in the Museum of London

Brenda Dickinson pers comm). Drag 18 plates are, along with Drag 27 cups, the most popular products of this early period although Willis (1998, 118) notes the rarity of samian in early burials, which he ascribes to 'cultural factors operating in the mid-first century AD ... amongst the indigenous community in Britain'. The worn nature of both plates, and indeed the flagon, suggests that the vessels were withdrawn from everyday use rather than bought specially for burial. This phenomenon has been noted elsewhere (eg in the later Roman cemeteries east of Londinium; Barber and Bowsher 2000, 122), but is not considered here to carry any implications affecting the early dating of the burial itself. Presumably, the samian plates and the capacious flagon originally held food and drink for a graveside feast and/or offerings to accompany the deceased, though examination of the interior of the flagon by fibre-optic endoscope showed no obvious traces of residues.

This leaves the foreleg of pork as the only direct evidence of a consumable to survive in the ground. Animal remains, both burnt and unburnt, are widely found in graves in London and beyond (eg Sidell and Rielly 1998; Philpott 1991, 195–208). Choice of animal species and selection of a particular joint of meat may also have been circumscribed by the age and sex of the deceased. Pig was particularly popular and was the most common animal represented, for example, in adult burials within the late Iron Age and early Roman cremation cemetery at King Harry Lane, St Albans (Stead and Rigby 1989, 250). A little later, pig bones were equally well represented in the midden deposits at Leadenhall Court (LCT84) in the heart of Londinium (Milne and Wardle 1993, 67–70), and Hilary Cool (pers comm) has suggested that here as elsewhere the consumption of pork may have formed part of a cultural package closely associated with notions of 'being Roman'. There is space in the Harper Road grave for other perishable organic remains to have been deposited too. These could have included fillets of meat, bread/grain, flowers and textiles.

As far as the other surviving grave goods are concerned, it is conceivable that the high-tin bronze neck-ring is an early example of a special funerary commission – perhaps made to order in one of the local metal-shops such as that located at Arcadia Buildings a little to the north (AB78; Dean 1980, 369). Other later commissions, of bone fittings and miniature ceramic vessels, have been identified within the eastern cemetery (Barber and Bowsher 2000, 331–2). The general form of the neck-ring is also likely to nod to the gender and possibly even the ethnicity of the deceased (but see below), although the 'peacock-feather' motif itself – here suggested to symbolise immortality – appears wholly classicising (Fig 3.6.4). Copper-alloy torcs were commonly worn by women in La Tène II inhumation cemeteries on the continent (eg Flouest and Stead 1979, 22–4), but in Britain such objects – often made of precious metals – were more usually deposited in hoards (eg Stead 1991; Jope 2000, 80–91 and 148–50). It may be possible to regard the Harper Road piece as a 'pidgin' artefact, to use Carr's term (2003, 116), that is, a unique item representing a single creative response to a particular situation at the very beginning of Roman contact.

The placement of the Harper Road neck-ring towards the feet of the deceased is an obvious inversion of its position as worn in life and further distinguishes it as a special artefact. Moreover, its physical breakage, if deliberate, was probably intended to transfer the metaphysical essence of the object to the realms of the shades. (Was this inversion and possible breakage also intended to symbolise a clean break with a 'non-Roman' life lived prior to the woman's arrival in Londinium?) With the hole punched through its name-stamp one of the two samian plates shows more definitive evidence of ritual 'killing', while Joanna Bird and Jenny Hall have suggested (pers comm) that these products of Vitalis i may even have been specially chosen as a play on the Latin words 'VITA' (life) or VITALIS ('of life' or 'vital'). (In this context, a bowl of Vitalis ii was incorporated in the second of two Flavian cremation burials from Grange Road, Winchester;

Biddle 1967, 234 and fig 7, no 3). The rectangular mirror too may carry other messages beyond the obvious ones connected with gender, appearance and prestige. It is possible to regard it as a dangerously personal object in which the face of the deceased had been reflected in life, and which was thus best buried with its original owner (see Barber and Bowsher 2000, 322 and 325).

Topographic context

The general impression gained from work carried out in this area of Southwark is that it was given over early to agriculture and scattered settlement, thereafter to burial and religious activity, before finally reverting to agriculture and burial in the later Roman period. As such it appears to have occupied a distinctly liminal position beyond the approach roads to the main southern settlement – the latter seemingly focused on the north and south sand islands. Topographically the locality was somewhat more elevated here and, lying at +1.55m OD, the base of the Harper Road grave cut appears to have been deliberately sited to keep it out of the reach of contemporary flooding. Furthermore, on present evidence, the grave appears to have been placed at some distance from either of the two major roads, possibly within fields or, perhaps more likely, within an enclosure oriented on the nearer of the two, Watling Street. The north-east/south-west alignment of the grave itself may reflect this same posited orientation. It is possible that early burial plots were served by narrow gravel tracks similar to that recorded at Arcadia Buildings (Dean 1980, fig 4).

While none of the other burials so far recorded from this southern zone is as early (eg RCHM(E) 1928, 167; Hall 1996, table 9.4; Mackinder 2000; and Bateman, this volume), mid-1st-century activity with distinctly non-utilitarian overtones is present at Swan Street (SWN98) a little to the northwest. Wide linear ditches may have served to mark the southern limit of the settled area and a series of wells or shafts beyond incorporated a range of arguably placed objects including, in their later phases, a number of 'killed' flagons (Beasley *et al* 2006). The temple complex at Tabard Square (LLS02) on the east side of Watling Street is later in date, though it is preceded by a sequence of early clay and timber buildings (Durrani 2004) which must have lain adjacent to the pre-Flavian structures recorded at Arcadia Buildings (Dean 1980, 369).

The creation of identity

This peripheral siting would have afforded any funeral procession ample opportunity to make an eye-catching statement as it wound its way south out of the settled area. The scenario imagined at the start of this contribution assumed a creolised but aspirationally 'Roman' approach to the funerary ceremonies. Can we make such an assumption? Put another way, the early dating suggests that the burial is almost certainly that of a first-generation Londoner, but is it possible to say where she might have come from?

Given its unusual features, it is tempting to regard the burial rite – and by extension the deceased herself – as intrusive to the area, and indeed this has been suggested previously (eg Dean and Hammerson 1980; Philpott 1991, 183). The lack of any obvious pre-existing local burial tradition (eg Whimster 1981), the early dating, the decision to inhume rather than cremate, and the idiosyncratic combination of grave goods (including the curious neck-ring), are all suggestive here; it is unfortunate that the chemical isotope analysis gave conflicting results as to the deceased's place of childhood origin. Yet modern researchers have become increasingly coy about making definitive statements regarding the 'provenance' or 'biological and cultural distance' of individuals on the basis of material culture alone, conscious of the fact that identities can be assumed and changed at will (eg Hill 2001, 12) and that, by its very nature, burial is a transformation rather than a direct reflection of an individual's identity (eg Pearce 2000, 8). In any case, as ancient writers make clear, it was the ostentation of the funeral procession itself, the route taken, and the number and status of the attendant mourners that made the greatest public impact, not necessarily the objects buried with the deceased. Furthermore, as Creighton has pointed out (2006, 100), such public assertion of identity is likely to have been especially important in a newly founded settlement with a largely transient and cosmopolitan population.

While we might therefore be well advised not to attempt to 'read off' the woman's ethnicity from the grave goods buried with her, we are on firmer ground in suggesting that they were likely to reflect her age and gender, and probably her class – as well as the tastes and vanities of her mourners. But if her 'cultural provenance' must perforce be left open, then the messages embedded within her grave surely underline the complexity of the wider social forces in play around the newly founded Londinium in the middle of the 1st century – a phenomenon with which 21st-century Londoners will be equally familiar.

Epilogue: *'The mystery of difference . . .'*

Venture south from London Bridge today – out beyond Peter Ackroyd's foetid Dickensian Borough – and another more suburban Southwark presents itself. Here, post-war high-rises jostle for position with elegant early 19th-century town houses set in discreet well-tended squares.

On the south side of Harper Road sits Ellington House, a solid brick-built block of post-war vintage whose parade of shops reflects entrepreneurial zeal and cultural diversity in equal measure. Rezwana ('Sarees and Suits'), the Bangla Store and Deshi Fish ('supplier of quality Bangladeshi and Afro-Caribbean fish') all vie for custom alongside the Total Care laundry and The William pub.

Directly opposite, astonishingly, is a slice of inner city wildscape administered by the Rockingham Estate Play Association (aim: to provide 'safe and challenging play opportunities for all local 5–16 year olds'). A riot of bird song assails the senses, and dappling light lances the secluded site of our early Roman grave.

Nearly 80 generations of Londoners have come and gone since its occupant was interred (and another generation since she was disinterred . . .). The area has passed from woods and fields to horsefair to tenter-ground to housing and back again.

Change defines London, and the need for a fresh start may have been what drew our woman here in the first place – as so many since. But it is tempting to think too that she would still recognise something of her own world in this modern melting pot of manners, meanings and memories a mile or so south of the busy bridge, and the still-swirling river . . .

Acknowledgements

Archaeologists often seek to detect patterns in the past by studying and manipulating whole populations of data. However, this process inevitably downplays the importance of individual human actions and motivations which are certain, as here, to have been richly complex and contingent, and not susceptible to easy decoding. This contribution is offered with gratitude to Harvey Sheldon, friend and colleague – and long-time student of such foibles, past as well as present!

Other thanks are due too: firstly to Martin Dean, the original excavator of the site, for taking the time and trouble to discuss the burial with me; to Cath Maloney and Steve Tucker in LAARC for access to the original archives held in their care; to Conservators Jill Barnard, Christie Pohl and Meg Wang for their patience and expertise; and to Lindsay Allason-Jones, David Bird, Joanna Bird, Paul Budd, Brian Connell, Hilary Cool, Nina Crummy, Brenda Dickinson, Thomas Grane, Jenny Hall, Martin Henig, Fiona Seeley, Ian Stead, Angela Wardle and Bill White for help and advice. Particular thanks are due to Fiona Seeley for supplying the report on the ceramic flagon incorporated in the table, and to Christie Pohl and Meg Wang for undertaking the metal analyses of the neck-ring and mirror.

3.7   Death, women, and the afterlife: some thoughts on a burial in Southwark   *Nick Bateman*

An unusual funeral

Excavations at Great Dover Street in Southwark in 1996 (GDV96) revealed an early 2nd- to mid-3rd-century Roman roadside cemetery with several phases of inhumations and cremations. Some burials were accompanied by grave goods, the largest group coming from a single cremation pit, of probably early 2nd-century date, which contained eight ceramic lamps and eight undecorated tazze (Mackinder 2000, 9–12, 33–7; Rayner and Seeley, this volume, Fig 4.3.5, 30 a–b) (Fig 3.7.1). The burial was in a *bustum* – a pit over which the body had been burnt on a pyre, the remains collapsing eventually into the pit which was then backfilled. *Busta* are very rare in Britain: they occur usually at military sites and it is generally felt that they represent an intrusive custom, brought here perhaps by eastern auxiliaries (Struck 1993a; see also Philpott 1991, 48–9).

Burial with lamps was also probably a Roman introduction to Britain (see Eckardt 2002, 98–115). At first the rite was associated with military sites, but by the end of the 1st century it is known even in small towns and rural areas. Tazze are also often found in conjunction with lamps in cremations, and have often been interpreted as vessels for burning incense (Philpott 1991, 191–3). The lamps and tazze at Great Dover Street were carefully chosen to accompany the burial rite. Four of the lamps are undecorated and all of the same type; the rest are 'volute lamps', and the choice of decorative subject appears to have been deliberate. One shows a fallen gladiator, a Samnite/*secutor* wearing a helmet, a relatively common figure type on the Continent though less so in Britain. The other three show jackal-headed Anubis, the Egyptian god (Mackinder 2000, 33–4; Eckardt 2002, 106).

All the ceramics were unburnt and had been placed carefully on the top of the cremation fill. They do not appear to have been used and this may suggest that they were acquired specifically for the ceremony, and intended to provide symbolic light in the underworld. Other elements of a complex funerary ritual include molten glass and gold thread (possibly from a textile), the presence of burnt pine cones and nuts (incense?), and the remains of a ceremonial meal including a chicken, bread, dates,

Fig 3.7.1 The Great Dover Street 'Gladiator' grave group

figs and almonds (Mackinder 2000, 12–13 and 37; see also Philpott 1991, 192).

Grave goods imagery

Gladiator images are relatively rare on lamps in Britain, though there is an identical version of the form from Poultry and another from Lombard Street (Mackinder 2000, 33). The type is more common on the Continent, for example at Vindonissa and Trier.

Anubis, the Egyptian god who controlled entry to the underworld in the Isis cult, was also a rare subject for imagery in Britain. Anubis was linked, in the Roman assimilation of deities, with Hermes/Mercury Psychopompus, the conveyor of souls to the underworld. The god's Greek name, Hermanubis, reflects this. Anubis symbolised victory of Life over Death, leading the dead to their resurrection (Plutarch *Isis and Osiris,* 12–20). Witt suggests (1971, 208) that to someone taking part in Isiac rituals following a death Anubis/Mercury was as familiar as an undertaker would be in Christian communities. The cult of Isis spread throughout the Roman empire and was of particular appeal to women (see Heyob 1975; Turcan 1996, 95–104). A flagon from Tooley Street, Southwark, bears an inscription referring to an *Iseum* in London (Harris and Harris 1965, 79–80), and an inscription records the restoration of what may be the same temple (Hassall 1980, 196–8). Other objects suggesting the presence of the cult in London have also been recognised (Johns 1996a; Henig 1984b, 113). As Wardle (2000, 27–8) suggested, 'It is therefore possible that in this burial we have further indirect evidence, certainly for the rites of an eastern cult, perhaps for that of Isis'.

A fallen gladiator?

What then of the gladiator image? The presence of a lamp with the image of a gladiator gave rise to some speculation that the burial was that of a dead gladiator, a professional buried with due ceremony. The fact that the burial lay towards the periphery of the area excavated appeared to support this, in view of the well-attested marginal status of gladiators (see Greenidge 1894). Wardle (2000, 28) concluded that while 'interpretation of the cremation burial as that of a ... gladiator can only be speculative ... it is certainly possible'.[1]

Certainly the use of a *bustum* has a resonance with the world of the amphitheatre. Gladiatorial games had their origins in funeral games for warriors in the 4th and 3rd centuries BC. The term used by the Romans for gladiatorial games was *munera* – the singular, *munus,* with an original meaning of duty, as in duties offered to the dead. Although eventually *munera* might take place months after the death they were celebrating,

they were originally supposed to happen when the body was placed on the funerary *bustum*. From this derived the word *bustuarius*, a colloquial term of abuse for a gladiator (Daremberg and Saglio 1877, 1564–5).

Further suggestion of a link between gladiators and Hermes/Anubis lies in one of the god's very specific roles. Contemporary Roman writers reported that, when a gladiator was killed, slaves entered the arena dressed as Dis Pater and/or Mercury/Hermes Psychopompus to bring the body out (Tertullian *ad nationes* 1, 10.47; *Apologeticum* 15; Dio *Roman History*, 72, 19.4; and Wiedemann 1992, 30). As Coleman (1990, 67) says 'The outcome of fatal encounters in the amphitheatre was ... ritualised in terms of the transition to the underworld: 'Larvae' [ghosts] ... hounded cowardly recruits, 'Mercury' prodded corpses with a brand to test their lifelessness, and 'Pluto' accompanied the bodies out of the arena.' The primary role of the Dis Pater/Hermes figures was to verify death. After this, if they had been professionals who had fought bravely their bodies were carried out on a stretcher; if they had been *noxii* they were dragged out with hooks. The bodies were removed through the Porta Libitina (a goddess associated with corpses), laid out in an antechamber of the amphitheatre, and there ritually stripped. Bodies of *noxii* were thrown into great pits along with dead animals; those of dead professionals were also placed in mass graves unless collected by a spouse or funeral group (Pearson 1973, 21; Daremberg and Saglio 1877, 1596; Grant 1967, 76; see also Clavel-Lévêque 1984, 75).

So could this burial have been that of a professional gladiator? No burial in London has been identified as being that of someone who died in the amphitheatre.[2] Indeed until recently this was true for the entire Roman Empire (see however Kühnen 2000, 126–8, on excavations of gladiator burials at Trier). Some have suggested that the cloak of *infamia* which surrounded gladiators was so extreme that all trace of them was completely obliterated even after death. Donald Kyle has argued (1998, 213–27) that in Rome the Tiber was extensively used for the ritual disposal of 'polluted' corpses, including those ritually exorcised as enemies of the state, *noxii*, and 'unredeemed' victims of the arena. Roman society distanced itself from arena deaths by killing the victims in a disassociative way (Dis Pater/Mercury), removal by hooks to avoid pollution, and ritual disposal (Auguet 1972, 55; Kyle 1998, 213–27). However, Kyle argues (*cf* also Barton 1989) that though failed, 'unredeemed', gladiators were effectively reduced to the status of *noxii*, with accompanying denial of rites, entertaining and 'co-operative' professionals who fought and died well got decent treatment and burial. It was performance and not legal status (ie whether slave or free) which determined burial (Kyle 1998, 268).

However, one further factor needs to be taken into account with the Dover Street burial: despite it being a cremation there was sufficient osteological evidence to prove that this was the grave of a woman.

Women as gladiators?

There is little or no evidence of women fighting as gladiators under the Republic, but things changed rapidly between the building of the first proper amphitheatre at Pompeii under the dictator Sulla in *c* 80 BC, and the opening of the Colosseum under the Emperor Titus in *c* AD 80. An inscription at Ostia (1st century) records the *editor* of a *munus* boasting that he was the first to put on a show with women fighting (Wiedemann 1992, 10 and n24).

From the time of Augustus onwards, emperors frequently found themselves in an ambiguous position regarding what was permitted in the arena. On the one hand, many desired to be seen as the upholders of tradition and morality, and in this capacity many emperors legislated on who could not appear in the arena. On the other hand every emperor was effectively in competition with predecessors (and rivals) to provide ever more spectacular shows (Wiedemann 1992, 112). Commonly this took the form of quantity (for example, 300 gladiators instead of 30); but emperors also encouraged 'exoticism' – the search for spectacles never witnessed before. The provision of women to fight in the arena is generally viewed within this context.[3]

The so-called Maastricht relief is said to show two female gladiators, and a monument from the eastern Mediterranean in the British Museum shows two women gladiators called Amazonia and Achillia (Wiedemann 1992, 53 n117, fig 11 and fig 16). Roman historians gave numerous instances, for example: Cassius Dio and Tacitus mention shows given by Nero at which women fought (Dio *Roman History* 62, 17.3–4; Tacitus *Annals* 15.32; also Wiedemann 1992, 112); Titus's dedication games for the Colosseum involved women *bestiarii* (Dio *Roman History* 66, 25.1–5); Domitian encouraged fights between dwarfs and women (Dio *Roman History* 67, 8.3–4). As late as AD 200 a troop of women gladiators was causing such a stir in Rome that Severus issued an edict to forbid the recruitment of women fighters (Daremberg and Saglio 1877, 1577; Dio *Roman History* 76, 16.1). Echion in the *Satyricon* (Petronius 1953, 45) gives the voice of the people: 'And now we are about to have a first class three day show by gladiators ... Titus ... has already procured as many toughs as you like, a woman to fight from a chariot ...'.

So, women gladiators certainly existed. Perhaps though, the Dover Street woman was merely a keen follower of the arena?

Women as fans?

With the exception of the very rich, women were normally not encouraged to attend either the theatre or the amphitheatre. However, in the anarchic last days of the Republic, restrictions on women in the audience had become mild or non-existent (Plutarch 1958, Sulla 35). Laws restricting women to the uppermost tier of amphitheatre seating have been ascribed to Domitian but probably came in under the Julio-Claudians (Wiedemann 1992, 131). Augustus's reforms of morals after the civil wars included prescriptions for behaviour and seating in public venues: '... whereas men and women had hitherto always sat together, Augustus confined women to the back rows even at gladiatorial shows ...' (Suetonius 1957, 76). Populist emperors, such as Caligula or Domitian, on the other hand, frequently reversed these rules, allowing anyone to sit anywhere – men with women, free with slaves, with only the emperor set above them (Veyne 1990, 415; Clavel-Lévêque 1984, 158).

The numbers of women in audiences fluctuated, therefore, according to the prevailing moral climate. But, as is often the case when things are proscribed, the existence of repeated legislation against mixed seating probably indicates its continued popularity. The extent to which legislation was followed in provincial towns is debatable, but a cosmopolitan place such as Londinium, without a strong indigenous base, may well have taken its lead from the prevailing situation in Rome.

'Theatres of terror'

One thing that is quite clear is that Romans did not view death in the arena in ways shared by modern people. Watching the deaths of professional gladiators was fundamentally different to watching the execution of *noxii*, however. Shows involving the latter were concerned with displaying Roman power and the punishment of those cast outside Roman society (see Bauman 1996, especially 77–91 on *utilitas publica*). *Noxii*, of whatever type or origin, were essentially less than human. By contrast, the gladiatorial *munera* were concerned with the way humans faced Death (Kyle 1998 269; Plass 1995, 21; Brown 1992, 208).

A number of contemporary writers located the value of the arena in what might be called 'moral education' rather than entertainment. Livy (*History of Rome* 28, 21) said that the fact that gladiators were free men allowed their *virtus* to be the more demonstrated. Cicero (*Tusc Disput* 17.41–2) thought the *munera* cruel and brutal – but also that 'there could be no better schooling against pain and death'. Pliny (*Panegyricus* 33.1) said that citizens were inspired to 'face honourable wounds and look scornfully upon death'. One of the authors of the *Scriptores Historiae Augustae* concluded that Romans wanted to look at fighting and wounds so that they would not be frightened by the real thing – war (*Scrip Hist Aug* 2, Maximius and Balbinus 8.7). Tertullian (*de spectaculis* 12) said of the audiences at the arena that 'they found comfort for death in murder' (*cf* also Burkert 1983, 53). However, it was not the moment of death but the 'moment of truth' that most images relating to the arena show: the point at which the defeated gladiator waits bravely for his fate – death or *missio*, the chance of another life. It appears to have been the way one faced this moment, rather than killing per se, which fascinated audiences (Barton 1989, 13).

A modern interpretation might add that gladiatorial combats provided a psychological and political safety valve for the teeming urban poor: a platform perhaps – as perhaps media news provides nowadays? – for the mutual sharing of violence and tragedy, with reassurance for the spectators that they themselves were safe and unaffected. Whatever happened in the arena, the spectators were always on the winning side. In the face of Death spectators shared, equally and collectively, the 'voluptuousness of living' (Hopkins 1983, 29–30; Maurin 1984, 107).

Maurin elaborated Tertullian's assertion that arena shows were essentially offerings to the dead, and developed his parallel between *munera* and *funera*. Both celebrations are liminal liturgies – rituals conducted at a threshold – and the amphitheatre can be deconstructed as a sacred meeting place surrounding a threshold between this world and the next (Maurin 1984, 109). Roman society was in fact permeated with 'a cultural consciousness that interpreted the amphitheatre as the threshold of the underworld' (Coleman 1990, 67). In the arena, ('below') lay Barbarism, Nature and Death. Above, and at the same eye level, was ranged the citizen body facing itself. The Romans had a highly developed and theatrical sense of public ceremony: in words that could have been written about the *munera*, Wells (1986, 277) described Roman funeral ceremonies as forming part of a 'theatre of terror . . . a lesson on pain and death, in the uncertainly of life, in the stratification of society, and the arbitrariness of power'.

It is no accident that the only two regular *munera* in Rome were 22–24 December and 19–23 March. Like the festivals of Christmas and Easter which replaced them, they were clearly associated with the winter solstice and the spring equinox, age-old celebrations of the conquest of Death, of rebirth and renewal. Paradoxically, despite the bloodiness, the *munera* offered a vision of the overcoming of Death, of being granted another life. They were in a sense a metaphor for Resurrection. Indeed, Wiedemann concluded that 'it was not the element of death or suffering in a gladiatorial performance that Christians found impossible to come to terms with, but the possibility of resurrection' (Wiedemann 1992, 92 and 155). The *munera* were a fundamental expression of Roman belief that a person who was *infamis* might be redeemed (saved) and prove his *virtus*. This was an essential contradiction to the central tenets of Christianity, within which redemption is only possible through God's Grace, not individual acts. Strangely, this may be why *venationes* were able to continue for several centuries after the

munera were banned – because in these the Will of God could find its way through the aleatory unpredictability of beasts (Wiedemann 1992, 155–6).

The pagan military ritual of *devotio*, the gladiators' oath, and Christian martyrdom, were all equally rooted in ideology centred on benevolent god(s) who find satisfaction in transformational death. The idea of 'contractual self-sacrifice' or 'contractual suffering' provided 'an alternative to, and a radical transformation of, the despair felt at . . . the arbitrary hostility of the gods or Fortune' (Barton 1989, 20). The central point here is, however, voluntariness: cowardly death was unseemly within the *munera* precisely because it exposed the possibility that those who died were mere victims (Plass 1995, 21).

The figure of the gladiator therefore became a potent symbol for resurrection, the overcoming of death. In magic and certain cults the best media are frequently those who have died prematurely or violently. By-products of the amphitheatre therefore acquired a potent role within contemporary Roman 'magic'. For example, gladiators' blood was a prize ingredient for charms; the rite of 'aspersion' of the statue of Jupiter – by a priest or the emperor – involved the blood of a man killed by a gladiator; images of gladiators were used to ward off the evil eye; epileptics were encouraged to drink gladiators' blood as a cure (Apuleius *Metamorphoses* 3, 17.5; le Glay 1990, 222; Clavel-Lévêque 1984, 66; Daremberg and Saglio 1877, 1592; Pliny *Naturalis Historia* 28, 3.1; Tertullian *Apologeticum* 9; Maurin 1984, 111).

Conclusions

Considering the imagery associated with the Great Dover Street burial we are left with at least two possible interpretations. Firstly, that it relates directly to the life experience of the person buried: in which case the burial may be that of a female gladiator. The second, and to be honest more justifiable interpretation, follows deconstruction of the images as religious iconography – in which case what we are witness to is a complex ritual based on belief in the afterlife and the possibility of resurrection. The rites of this burial illustrate a particular characteristic of Roman spiritual experience in general: the dense interweaving of different strands of belief and ritual – Greek, Egyptian and Latin – in a complicated dialectic. Whatever the meaning for the individual woman buried here, or her mourners, the resultant pattern provides a fascinating context within which to view the existence of London's amphitheatre, the activities which took place within it over more than 200 years, and the ways in which those activities themselves modified beliefs prevalent in Londinium.

It is surely grossly mistaken to imagine that spectacles involving so much human struggle, pain and death could ever truly have been just 'entertainment'. As Wiedmann (1992, 93) points out, although the skills with which gladiators *avoided* death were obviously of interest to contemporary peoples, 'scholars are imposing their own moral preference when they imagine that the audience came simply to watch a dangerous sport like motor racing. They came to see how men faced the necessity of dying'.

Notes

1   On 14 May 2001 Channel 4 television broadcast a documentary called 'Gladiator Girls', which championed an interpretation of the Great Dover Street burial as being of a female gladiator. Many archaeologists (including the present author), experts and historians were quoted in the programme. All agreed that the burial was highly unusual, though no-one went as far as the programme itself in the extent of the speculative conclusion.

2   Londinium's amphitheatre was in use from *c* AD 70 till at least AD 270/280 – and possibly later. It is unlikely that those colonists, traders, soldiers, officials, money-lenders, artisans and other foreign immigrants who made up Londinium did not seek the same entertainments that they were accustomed to elsewhere in the Empire. The logical conclusion of this is that, for over 200 years, people were dying in Londinium's amphitheatre – presumably with some frequency or there would hardly have been sufficient justification to maintain an amphitheatre.

3   There was a parallel increase in the use of women in the theatre throughout the imperial period (from the Julio-Claudian period drama was probably only read in an auditorium. In the immense theatres constructed after the 1st century BC audiences would never have been able follow intricacies of plot or poetry). Tragedy was replaced by 'pantomime', often based on myth, and involving extensive use of stereotypes. Comedy degenerated into 'mime' (low-status farce): no masks or symbols were used, women were played by women, and the subject matter was domestic, ribald, and coarse caricature. Tertullian (*de spectaculis, 17*), commenting on mime in particular, said that 'its supreme charm is above all things contrived by filth'. Lactantius (2003, 6, 20.9–14) said that all spectacles destroyed the ability to act rationally – but that the sexual titillation of the theatre was the worst for morals (see Carcopino 1941, 223–31; Roueché 1993, 15–26; Wiedemann 1992, 148).

4 Living in a material world

Banded agate intaglio of Pegasus (EST83[399]<60>)

Introduction *Jenny Hall*

This final section considers the practical aspects of finds research and shows the benefit of the basic catalogue. The following contributions are welcome additions to the planned series of finds research projects that come under the banner of Londinium – a series of proposals for publications and an online database, submitted to English Heritage (Wardle 2005) – intended to bring together all of Londinium's collections, whether held in the Museum of London, either in the permanent reserve collections, or the London Archaeological Archive and Research Centre (LAARC), the British Museum or elsewhere.

It is to be hoped that the Londinium series will attempt to answer some of the important questions about life in London, as posed in the *Research Framework for London Archaeology*, where it was noted that earlier studies of Londinium had concentrated on buildings and chronology to the detriment of finds research (Nixon *et al* 2002, 30). This was often due to the sheer quantity and wealth of material which needed a formulated strategy (and funding) to be able to deal with it. This lacuna has so far prevented the examination of the wider social, cultural and economic issues relating to Londinium.

However, we have to learn to walk before we can run and basic catalogues are the first steps in the process. Where possible, material from both the Museum of London and British Museum have been included in the catalogues here. The following objectives from the *Research Framework* are considered in this section:

R7 Framework objective
- Identifying Roman Londoners through the archaeological record and the evidence of their possessions;
- Examining the social meaning of artefacts.

R13 Framework objective
- Considering the evidence for Roman London's role as a port and centre of trade;
- Refining theories of trade specialisation over time, shifting zonation within the main settlement and peripheral areas.

As part of the proposed Londinium assessment project, Angela Wardle (2005) points out the benefit of looking at material on a regional and provincial basis but it is necessary to start by studying objects at a more local level. It will be possible to utilise the contextual dating from more recent excavations in order to provide closer dates for much of the material in the reserve collections of the Museum of London. It is also clear that certain areas can be identified as finds 'hotspots', for example the Walbrook stream area. The Londinium project will look at zones of occupation from the material culture standpoint. The catalogues included in this section (apart from in Henig, where too many provenances were imprecise) have also included these zones, based on the geographical siting of the city and its evolution, as peripheral suburbs became subsumed into the rapidly expanding city. The main explanation for these zones can be found in Figure 4.0.1.

Having established this basic foundation, the interpretation and understanding of London's position in the province and beyond can only be achieved by looking at the broader picture. Jude Plouviez's summary of brooch types pinpoints the way forward looking at regional types, while Nina Crummy shows that detailed research of particular types of finds, in her case toilet implements and especially nail-cleaners, can now begin to flag up regional differences and even tribal influences within the city itself (a formula demonstrated in Crummy and Eckardt 2004). Gwladys Monteil also demonstrates that the development and economic growth of the city can be traced by the use and distribution of samian inkwells which suggest that, perhaps, pen and ink records were the domain of the mercantile classes.

Harvey Sheldon has always emphasised the importance of the settlement in Southwark. The evidence from post-war rescue excavations in Southwark by Kathleen Kenyon was later enhanced by the excavations of the Department of Greater London Archaeology (DGLA), finally putting Southwark on the map, not as a mere suburb to the city on the northern bank but significant in its own right. Recent excavations and finds have testified to the importance of Southwark and the formative work by Geoff Marsh and Paul Tyers on a pottery type-series for Southwark (Marsh and Tyers 1978) is now reviewed by Louise Rayner and Fiona Seeley in the light of a further 30 years of ceramic studies.

Pertinent to the physical well-being of Roman Londoners, Ralph Jackson discusses the evidence for health-care in London, using some of the material evidence for surgical implements preserved so well in the Walbrook stream. Associated with health-care are the requisites for bathing, a very Roman habit as discussed by Angela Wardle, and then toilet implements including nail-cleaners that reflect, as indicated by Nina Crummy, a more native fashion and are more commonly to be found in small towns and minor settlements, rather than in such large towns as Londinium. Her conclusions raise questions in terms of production, supply and identity.

The final two papers look at the luxury end of the market. For many years Martin Henig (who first suggested this tribute to Harvey Sheldon) has wanted to publish a catalogue of London's Roman intaglios and review the evidence for their content. His findings show a splendid cache, providing, as

However they may also carry messages about the wearer's social position (particularly in the late Roman period), perhaps about their tribal origin in the early period and perhaps about religious affiliations.

Defining and visualising brooch groups

The key elements of Roman assemblages found by metal detectorists are coins and brooches: for example, in 2004 a total 10,390 Roman objects recorded by the Portable Antiquities Scheme included 7,568 single coins and 1,485 brooches (Worrell 2005, 449). These provide a complementary picture of the chronology of a site as the majority of coins are late Roman losses whereas the brooches are predominantly early. But while for coins the 'normal' pattern of loss has been quantified and illustrated, most particularly by Richard Reece and John Casey (eg Reece 2002, 148), there have only been a few attempts to provide inter-site comparisons for brooch assemblages. For example, John Creighton used a similar approach on four sites in North Lincolnshire (Creighton 1990).

Faced with publishing an assemblage of 211 brooches from the 1970s excavations, including metal detecting, on a large Roman settlement at Hacheston, Suffolk, it seemed sensible to attempt some comparison of the assemblages from other sites in the region. The data were presented as numbers and percentages of types in a table for eight assemblages and showed chronological and regional variations (Plouviez 2004, 87–9). Definition of the types quantified drew heavily on studies by Mackreth (1981; 1986; 1991; 1996) and could be related to the terms used in the detailed catalogue of the Hacheston brooches (Plouviez 2004, 89–107). Recently, brooch studies have seen the publication of a major corpus, the Richborough assemblage, placed in the context of general Romano-British brooch use (Bayley and Butcher 2004). This provides an account of the development of the various brooch types related to the comprehensive type-series developed but not published by M R Hull (Simpson *et al* forthcoming) while taking into account the important work of Donald Mackreth, whose 'Big Book' on brooches is also still a work in progress. Bayley and Butcher also provide a digital copy of the metal analysis results for all Roman brooches examined by the Ancient Monuments Laboratory between the 1970s and 2000 (available as a CD within Bayley and Butcher 2004 and downloadable from the Archaeological Data Service), in all, almost 3500 brooches classified by Hull type and listed by site. These data, although only a tiny proportion of the total available material, provide a starting point for establishing what the 'normal' brooch assemblage might be in Britain.

The late Iron Age and Roman brooches found in Britain include both native and imported types, and there is also regional variability which sometimes reflects local production of specific types, sometimes chronological factors and sometimes

a restricted function or market for the types. In Bayley and Butcher this is illustrated by mapping the distribution of particular published types comparable to the Richborough assemblage. For example, the Polden Hill types are shown as mainly present on sites in the western half of Britain, around the Severn Valley (Bayley and Butcher 2004, 196, fig 172) in contrast to the broadly contemporary two-piece Colchester brooches which are present on sites in the east midlands, East Anglia and south-east England (Bayley and Butcher 2004, 194, fig 170). However the problem with mapping occurrence by site is illustrated by the inclusion of one East Anglian site, Saham Toney (Brown 1986) where the 'western' Polden Hill spot represents only four individual brooches from a total assemblage of 185 (nine of which are the two-piece Colchester brooches and a further 37 are related Colchester-derivative types). As the number of large assemblages for which data are available increases, the distribution map will have to be modified to show quantities rather than simple presence and absence – a problem already apparent to anyone attempting to use the Portable Antiquities Scheme database.

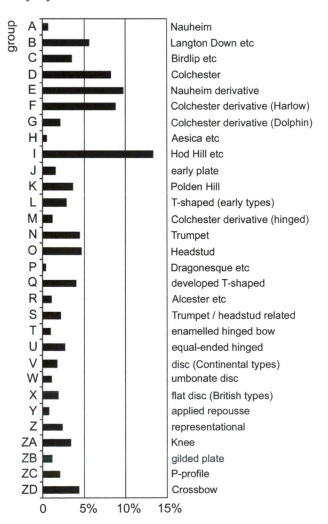

Fig 4.1.1 Brooch groups diagram for all data (from Bayley and Butcher 2004)

Rather than simply presenting brooch assemblage data in tables it seems sensible to convert the numbers into simple graphical representations, which is now easily done with a spreadsheet program. My preference is to use percentages (but always with actual totals clearly shown) and a bar chart format, similar to the original Reece coin loss diagrams but turned sideways. The choice of groups and types included is based on Bayley and

Butcher's grouping of the Hull types as shown in Table 4.1.1. These are arranged in an approximately chronological order for the graph. This is more broadly applicable beyond eastern England than my Hacheston groups but there are still gaps and biases. In particular, the penannular brooches are excluded, because of the difficulties of separating early and later types within the current classifications.

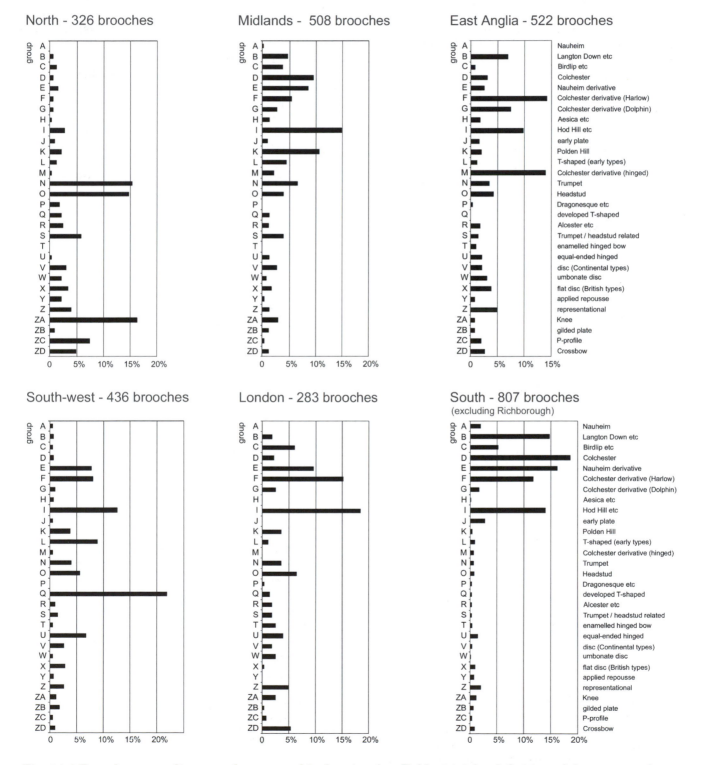

Fig 4.1.2 Brooch groups diagrams by geographical region (see Table 4.1.2 for definition of the areas and numbers of assemblages)

The first graph (Fig 4.1.1) shows the complete data set from Bayley and Butcher (2004), giving us a preliminary picture of the British norm. This clearly shows the early peak, with over half the total number made before the end of the 1st century (groups A to L), dropping to around 10% produced in the 3rd and 4th centuries (groups ZA to ZD). In the earliest groups the forms are predominantly bow brooches, presumably functioning as a safety pin type of fastener, with less than 2% of the overall total in the early plate brooch group (J). Between the late 1st and early 3rd centuries there is a more even spread of types, although the predominantly British-produced bow brooches remain more common than the plate types. Amongst the plate brooch types the probable imports (groups U, V) are nearly as common as the mainly British types (groups W, X, Y), though this excludes the figurative types (group Z) which is a mixture of native and imported types. In the late period the bow brooches are again in the majority, and we have the often-cited pictorial evidence of Stilicho shown wearing a crossbow brooch to hold his cloak on his right shoulder (Salway 1993, 293); however the 3rd-century British plate brooches (group ZB) remain a significant element at just under 10% of the late groups.

When the data are subdivided into regional groups (Fig 4.1.2; Table 4.1.2) it is very clear that the strong 1st-century pattern of brooch use is restricted to lowland Britain. Two factors are at work here. Firstly, in the period before AD 43 the common brooch types (Langton Down, Rosette, Colchester) form part of the cultural assemblages loosely described as 'Belgic', typified by the King Harry Lane cemetery at St Albans (Stead and Rigby 1989). These early bow brooch groups (B, C, D) are very scarce in both the south-western and the northern graphs. Secondly, the chronology of the conquest which brought new types (the Hod Hill, ie most of group I, and the early plate types, J) initially to the south-east. The Claudio-Neronian period also sees the proliferation of locally produced bow brooches, particularly the Colchester derivatives (groups F, G) and the simple one piece (Nauheim derivatives, group E). All of these occur in significant numbers in the areas brought under Roman rule – thus in the south-west groups E, F and I make up 28% of the overall total – whereas brooch use in the north seems to reflect the arrival of the army late in the 1st century. The graph for the north also makes the point that later bow brooch types (groups ZA, ZC, ZD) relate, though not exclusively, to the army – many of these types are also common on the Rhine frontier.

The separation into geographic groups also shows the predicted regional production of certain types – in the south-west the early and later T-shaped groups (L, Q), in the south the two-piece type of Colchester derivative (Group F), in East Anglia the wider range of Colchester derivative types (F, G, M) and in the midlands the Polden Hill (group K). The

Trumpet and headstud groups (N, O, R, S) look strong in the north but generally widespread, and the discussion and redefinition of the Trumpet series in Bayley and Butcher (2004, 160–4) suggests that these groups need subdivision to pick up the separate workshop areas. We can also see localisation of some of the smaller groups on the graphs – the dragonesque brooches (group P) which are traditionally ascribed to the north (Snape 1993, 26) are not common elsewhere, and the Aesica and its variants (group H) are shown to be mainly found in the midlands and East Anglia.

Urban assemblages

Having established that this representation of the selected brooch type groups does show the broad chronological pattern and differences between regions of Britain it seems reasonable to examine and compare individual large assemblages including London. An obvious urban comparison is with nearby Verulamium; Figure 4.1.3 shows the late Iron Age cemetery at King Harry Lane and the assemblage from Frere's excavations in the town (Frere 1972; 1984). Although a small group at 65 brooches, the Frere material contrasts well with King Harry Lane where cremation burial had ceased by around AD 60 if not earlier. A more rural picture within Hertfordshire is provided by the small town at Baldock where the late Iron Age is again strongly represented and the 1st century includes an extraordinarily large group of Nauheim derivatives (Group E) – despite evidence for on-site

Table 4.1.2 Counties included in the regional diagrams

Region	pre-1974 Counties (brooch nos)
North: 21 assemblages (326 brooches)	Cheshire (2), Cumberland (51), Durham (35), Lancashire (2), Northumberland (40), Scotland (14), Westmorland (3), Yorkshire (179).
Midlands: 22 assemblages (508 brooches)	Derbyshire (29), Huntingdonshire (1), Leicestershire (9), Lincolnshire (73), Northamptonshire (165), Nottinghamshire (2), Rutland (62), Shropshire (59), Warwickshire (76), Worcestershire (32).
East Anglia*: 7 assemblages (522 brooches)	Cambridgeshire (101), Norfolk (86), Suffolk (335).
South West: 23 assemblages (436 brooches)	Cornwall (16), Devon (3), Dorset (55), Gloucestershire (47), Isles of Scilly (129), Somerset (64), Wiltshire (122).
South (excluding Richborough): 24 assemblages (807 brooches):	Bedfordshire (46), Berkshire (1), Buckinghamshire (16), Essex (175), Hampshire (136), Hertfordshire (396), Kent (26), Oxfordshire (1), Sussex (10).

* East Anglia is the only region where extra data were added to that from Bayley and Butcher 2004 – additional published groups are from Stonea (Mackreth 1996), Hacheston (Plouviez 2004) and an unpublished surface metal-detected group from a probable temple site at Charsfield, Suffolk.

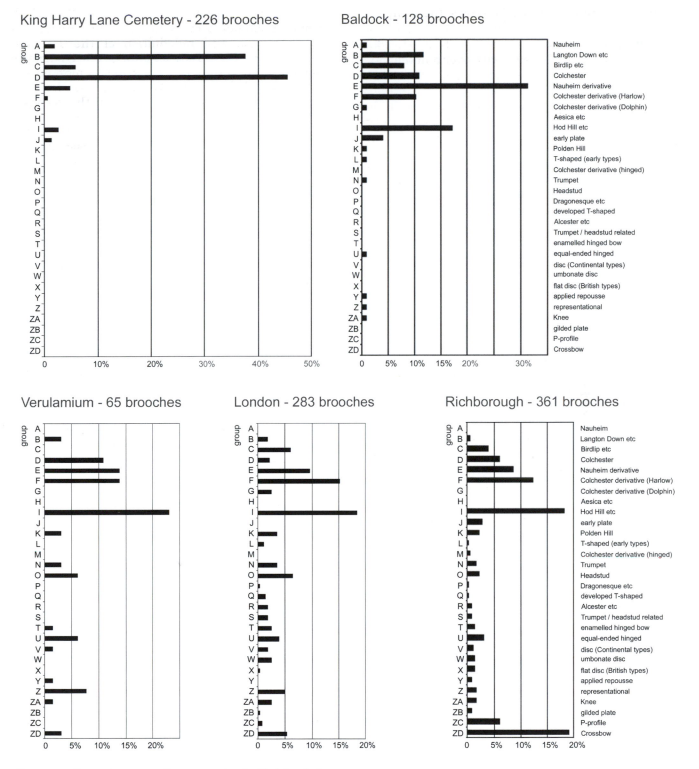

Fig 4.1.3 Brooch group diagrams for individual sites

manufacture of Colchester (group D) types (Stead and Rigby 1986, 122–3). Richborough provides a unique mixture of military and urban activity in southern Britain; the relatively huge number of crossbow brooches (group ZD), more even than in the northern British graph, correlates with the very high deposition of Theodosian coins identified by Reece at Richborough (Reece 1991, 27).

The London diagram is based on the data in Bayley and Butcher (2004), described as 'various sites' rather than the (fewer) published brooches or a complete assessment of the available material; it probably represents a viable sample of the potential total for Greater London. It compares well with the Verulamium and Richborough groups but with even fewer of the late Iron Age types of groups B and D, reflecting Londinium's creation around AD 50. Group C is here mainly continental types (Eye, Kräftig-profilierte), perhaps arriving with the army in Britain, whereas other types within group C reflect pre-conquest imports and native types. The strong showing of the Colchester derivatives (group F) correlates with their regional distribution in the south-east seen in Figure 4.1.2. But during the same 1st-century period London shares a high proportion of Hod Hill types (group I) with Richborough and Verulamium. As Mackreth suggests at Stonea (Mackreth 1996, 299), where he contrasts 46% of Hod Hill types in the assemblage from within Stonea Camp with only 14% for the wider Stonea settlement area group, these may suggest an army presence. Other East Anglian sites where a 1st-century fort is known have 15–20% Hod Hill types, compared with less than 10% elsewhere (Plouviez 2004, 88). It seems likely that these represent a commodity which arrives in Britain as part of the military supply system and then finds a wider market within the province. Similarly in the 4th century the presence of soldiers and government officials in Londinium generates a peak of crossbow types (group ZD) contrasting with the general pattern in the south but also visible at Verulamium. The overall spread of brooch types from London suggests that it drew on a wide range of sources and styles throughout the Roman period. For example, the mainly continental imports in groups T, U and V are well represented, as well as virtually all groups from all parts of Britain being present. The figurative plate brooches (group Z) are common in London, and also in Verulamium and in East Anglia. In the case of the East Anglian assemblages this peak derives from several locations where temples or shrines are known or suspected. It may be that a more detailed examination will show some correlation in the major urban sites with areas where brooches were being manufactured, sold or deposited for votive purposes.

Not surprisingly this generalised view of London's brooches reflects the cosmopolitan nature of the town in the Roman period, but within a general southern British background. The broad groups tend to conceal unique treasures, such as the representation of a boat from 1 Poultry (ONE94; Wardle 1998, 84) or the pair of silver tutuli type showing that a German woman was buried in the Eastern cemetery (Barber and Bowsher 2000, 183–4). However, it is to be hoped that this method for looking at brooches will prove a useful basis for comparing groups both within different areas of the city and beyond.

Acknowledgements

This piece should really have been about glazed poppy beakers – but sadly I know even less about these unusual vessels now than I did shortly after leaving London in the late 1970s, when I got regular phone calls from Harvey Sheldon about the possible whereabouts of the Southwark example. This was shortly after a formative period working for Harvey Sheldon in various parts of London. So instead, I have offered a method for looking at brooches which may suggest new questions for future research in London, with many thanks to Harvey for his help, encouragement and friendship over the years.

4.2 The distribution and use of samian inkwells in Londinium *Gwladys Monteil*

Introduction

Samian inkwells are linked with the use of carbon ink on wooden leaf tablets, a writing technology cheaper and probably more accessible than others (Bowman 1991, 128; Bowman 1994, 83–4). Because of soil conditions, few wooden ink tablets survive from London, but some are known (eg Turner and Skutsch 1960, 108–11; Wilmott 1991, 148). Metal pens for ink writing are also rare (Hanson and Conolly 2002, 155) but several examples have been recognised from London (Guildhall Museum 1908, 42–3; Wheeler 1930, 58). Samian inkwells are by far the most common type of inkwells (Willis 2005, 63 and 112) and they form a good body of evidence for ink writing because they are less dependent on conditions of preservation than wood and metal. They are relatively common artefacts in Londinium and they offer the potential for an assessment of the extent of literacy and contexts for ink writing.

The data used in this survey derive from a dataset gathered during a PhD thesis and the details of the methodology can be found there (Monteil 2005). Samian data from well-dated Roman contexts were distributed chronologically using the method developed by Willis (1998, 94–5) and the values tabulated to create phases. A total of 154 entries for samian inkwells were analysed in this way and the results have been plotted on maps of Roman London at three periods (Figs 4.2.1–4.2.3). A full list of the sites can be found in Table 1 at the front of this volume, but Table 4.2.1 provides a concordance to the figures.

The pre-Flavian period (AD 50–69)

Only 27 inkwells are recorded for the pre-Flavian period, a relatively small number, but their distribution in the city is centred on the eastern core

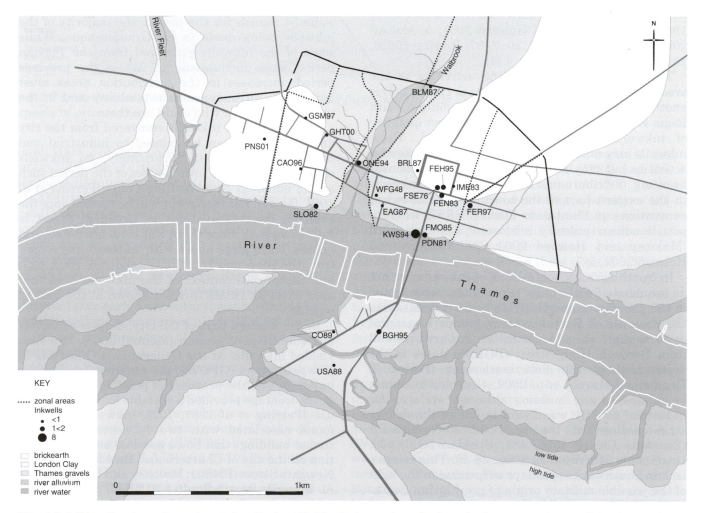

Fig 4.2.1 Distribution of samian inkwells in AD 50–69 (note that the late 2nd-century city wall is shown for purposes of orientation)

177

irrefutable evidence for a variety of industrial activities in the area (Maloney and de Moulins 1990, 124; Wilmott 1991). Inkwells recorded from Throgmorton Avenue (TGM99; Maloney and Holroyd 2000, 42), Blomfield House and 35–45 New Broad Street (BLM87 and NEB87; Maloney and de Moulins 1990, 46) may have been associated with these activities (as may fragments of wooden writing tablets and an iron stylus recovered from another upper Walbrook site, 15–35 Copthall Avenue (KEY83; Groves 1990, 82)). Alternatively, the inkwells could have been dumped as domestic rubbish (Millett 1994, 429). Only a single inkwell, found at 8–9 Cloak Lane (CKL88), is known from the lower Walbrook.

Recorded findspots of inkwells are not confined to inside the city. Sherds have been recovered in the area of the eastern cemetery (HOO88), although the occurrence of inkwells in this area is slightly earlier than the traditional dating of the establishment of the cemetery to the 'end of the 1st or beginning of the 2nd century' (Barber *et al* 1990, 4). Stained and burnt sherds could have resulted from feasting and/or offerings made during the cremation (Barber *et al* 1990; Barber and Bowsher 2000, 76–81; MoLAS 2000, 148). It is tempting to imagine such inkwells as a personal offering on the pyre.

The number of inkwells in Southwark increases dramatically in the later 1st century and most date to the period of reconstruction of the settlement (Period 4; Drummond-Murray *et al* 2002). The inkwells at Borough High Street (BGH95) come from open areas but several commercial strip-buildings with possible baker's and butcher's shops and a substantial building identified as a market hall were excavated nearby (Drummond-Murray *et al* 2002, 54). In addition, an inkwell from London Bridge Street (LBI95) came from a large masonry structure used for trade and storage (Building 2, Period 4; Drummond-Murray *et al* 2002, 71–9) and later as 'the small workshop of a local craftsman' (Period 5; Drummond-Murray *et al* 2002, 94). On the Courage Brewery site, areas for iron-smithing and copper-alloy casting were established by the early Flavian period (Westman 1998, 63; Sheldon 2000, 141; Cowan 2003, 86) but inkwells from Redcross Way, also part of the brewery site (CO89; Cowan 2003, site G), came from buildings identified as residential (Cowan 2003, 87). An unstratified iron stylus was also recovered from the residential area of the site (Wardle 2003, 167). At 52–4 Southwark Street (52SOS89), inkwells came from the development of 1st-century waterfronts (Cowan 2003, 17–19).

The Hadrianic-Antonine period (AD 120–199)

There are 53 inkwells recorded for the period (Fig 4.2.3) and, while the fabric of some remains unidentified, the majority are South Gaulish and potentially residual. Although some come from redeposited refuse, others are from more reliably dated contexts. Little is known, however, about how long samian inkwells remained in use. The sample for the present study seems to confirm that some South Gaulish examples might have lasted longer than domestic vessels. There are generally fewer samian inkwells produced in the 2nd century and it has been suggested by Willis (2005) that this could correspond to a decrease in the 'popularity' of ink writing.

Small quantities of samian inkwells found in the Cripplegate fort corresponded to the period of its construction (Howe and Lakin 2004, 25–41). The two entries in the database, from Grimes' excavations on the western wall (WFG03; Grimes 1968, 28 and 17–19) and in the *praetentura* (WFG22; Grimes 1968, 28 and 36), are South Gaulish and hence residual so it is difficult to relate them with any certainty to the life of the fort itself. They could even relate to earlier industrial activities noticed in recent excavations (Howe and Lakin 2004, 23–4). Unfortunately, no inkwells were recorded in any of the modern excavations in the area to help clarify the context of their use. There was also a complete absence of other types of writing equipment recovered from recent work in the fort (Keily 2004, 118–22) but this may be due to the soil conditions. At Plantation Place masonry structures succeeded the military occupation (Maloney and Holroyd 2001, 70), but there were still large quantities of inkwells. Most are South Gaulish and were part of the residual material redeposited in the clearance following the Hadrianic fire.

Three sites in the middle Walbrook valley had inkwells from dated contexts (BUC87; GM156; ONE94). This area of the Walbrook seems to have not only a strong commercial and industrial profile in both this and the previous period, particularly for leather-working (Grimes 1968, 97; Wilmott 1991) and blacksmithing (Rhodes 1991a, 132–8) but also a religious significance (see Haynes 2000, 96–7; Merrifield and Hall, this volume). Due to waterlogged conditions, writing tablets have also survived better here than in other parts of London (Wheeler 1930, 54–7; Richmond 1953, 206–8; Groves 1990, 82–3; Wilmott 1991, 117–18; Shepherd 1998, 113–14; Tomlin 1996, 209–15; Tomlin 2003, 41–51; Tomlin and Hassall 2003, 373–5). A South Gaulish inkwell came from 1 Poultry but may be residual.

The inkwell from Bucklersbury (BUC87) comes from the same context as a stock of unused but burnt vessels from Les Martres-de-Veyre found in material dumped to raise the ground level following the Hadrianic fire (Davies 1991). It is burnt and could have been either part of the stock or used by the shopkeeper. An inkwell from the lower Walbrook valley at Walbrook Wharf, Upper Thames Street (GM156), is part of a large samian group dated to the Antonine period. As mentioned above, very little published information is available about the context of the inkwell from 8–9 Cloak Lane (CKL88).

Further north in the upper Walbrook valley, during excavations of pottery kilns at Northgate House (MRG95), South Gaulish inkwell sherds were

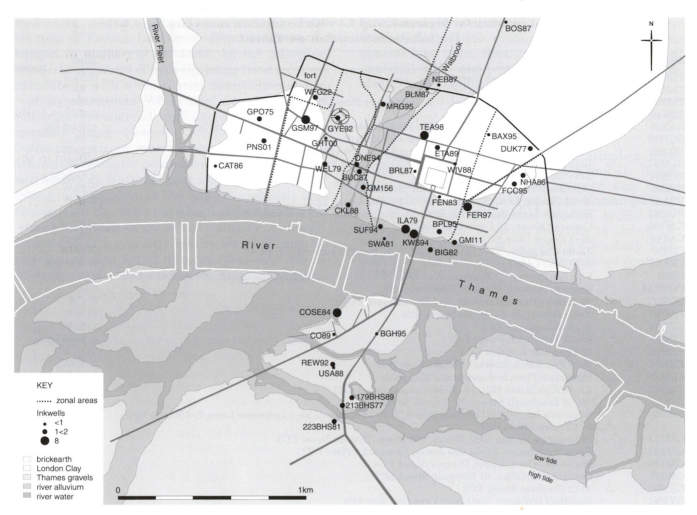

Fig 4.2.3 Distribution of samian inkwells in AD 120–199 (note that the late 2nd-century city wall is shown for purposes of orientation)

found in contexts contemporary with a stock of discarded Central Gaulish samian (Seeley and Drummond-Murray 2005; Maloney and Holroyd 2000, 41). On the eastern fringes at 68–71 Fenchurch Street (FCC95) an inkwell was associated with large but dispersed quantities of Montans' stamped vessels, explained as a possible shop stock despite the lack of a secure context (Fiona Seeley pers comm).

At Courage Brewery in Southwark, there was evidence of mixed occupation with industrial, residential and warehousing activity (Cowan 2003, 38–58; MoLAS 2000, 133). The three entries for inkwells (COSE84) are all South Gaulish and unfortunately it has not been possible to relate the inkwells to industrial or residential activity. The presence of samian inkwells in this area is nevertheless interesting since commerce and trade was a strong 2nd-century feature (Cowan 2003, 56–67). On Southwark's southern island, little published information is available for the inkwells at 179 Borough High Street (179BHS89). Although a timber jetty was uncovered there (Sheldon 2000, 140), the pottery group from the same context is mixed and seems to have been part of a series of dumped material to fill the inlet channel (Fiona Seeley pers comm).

The context for inkwells on six northern waterfront sites has proved problematic. While examples from Regis House, Miles Lane (ILA79), Swan Lane (SWA81) and Billingsgate Lorry Park (BIG82) can be associated with wharves and warehousing, the other sites are not so straightforward. Both Suffolk House (SUF94) and Billingsgate (GM111) had evidence for high-status town houses. Both, however, revealed mixed occupation, with waterfront reclamation at Suffolk House (Esmonde Cleary 1997, 436–7; Symonds 1998, 342) and earlier waterfront activity prior to the construction of the Billingsgate house and baths (Richardson 1991, 61). The samian assemblages from other houses within the town, for example from Milk Street (MLK76; Perring *et al* 1991, 49), lack any inkwells for the period, a feature reminiscent of the town house at Watling Court in the Flavian-Trajanic period. When fabric identification is available, most of the inkwells from the waterfront area are South Gaulish and are probably redeposited as part of the ongoing construction and maintenance of the waterfront.

The Central Gaulish inkwell from the amphitheatre (GYE92) is associated with the masonry rebuild of the amphitheatre (Bateman 1997, 67) where architects and possibly the military would have been

4.3 The Southwark pottery type-series: 30 years on
Louise Rayner and Fiona Seeley

Introduction

In 1978 *The Roman Pottery from Southwark* was published, providing an overview of potteries supplying London and a classification of coarseware pottery in use in Southwark during the 1st and 2nd centuries. Integral to the article was the presentation of a form type-series which had been 'designed to facilitate the analysis of pottery from current and future excavations' (Marsh and Tyers 1978, 533). That this form type-series remains the basis of typological classification in use across Greater London over 25 years later is testament to its success in achieving this aim.

The original form type-series excluded imported and specialised wares, such as amphorae, colour-coated fine wares and mortaria, and did not extend into the 3rd and 4th centuries due to a lack of such dated excavated deposits in Southwark at that time. The excavations that have since taken place in both Southwark and the City of London have required and enabled the type-series to be extended into this later Roman period and the additions to this are published together for the first time in Table 4.3.1. It is hoped this updated series will assist researchers working on Roman pottery from Southwark and the London area in general in conjunction with the London Archaeological Archive and Research Centre (LAARC) pottery codes.

In the last few years, our understanding of Roman Southwark has benefited from excavation and publication of several large-scale excavations undertaken in the 1970s–1990s (Drummond-Murray *et al* 2002; Taylor-Wilson 2002; Cowan 2003; Hammer 2003; Yule 2005). These coupled with the results from important recent excavations at Tabard Square and further investigations on Borough High Street have produced vast quantities of data on the supply, distribution and consumption of pottery in the Roman settlement. This therefore seems an appropriate point to assess our current understanding of pottery in Southwark and identify areas of research for the future.

On a general level, the recovery of substantial assemblages from Southwark has served to demonstrate that the settlement on the south bank of the Thames had access to, and made use of, much the same supply of pottery as the settlement on the north bank. This is not surprising given their close proximity but serves to emphasise that any differences in function and status do not appear to be reflected in the broad composition of the pottery assemblages. Some differences are apparent however, many of which are only now beginning to be recognised and still need to be explored further to ascertain their significance and the dynamics that may lie behind them. Detailed intra-settlement distribution and functional studies have not yet been explored and remain a major area for future study. Some possible themes and areas for study are outlined below.

Pottery in Southwark

Early Southwark

One of the most important discoveries impacting on our understanding of the origins of Southwark in general as well as pottery studies was the extensive pre-Boudican and Boudican fire horizon excavated at the Ticket Hall site on Borough High Street as part of the Jubilee Line Extension project (BGH95; Drummond-Murray *et al* 2002). Although hints at the presence of this fire horizon had been encountered on earlier small-scale excavations, the Borough High Street excavation provided positive evidence for large-scale destruction of the settlement south of the Thames (Drummond-Murray *et al* 2002, 46).

The assemblages recovered from the pre-fire activity and the fire horizon itself provided the first opportunity to study a large assemblage of this period from Southwark and, importantly, to compare them with the more extensively recovered Boudican groups from the City of London (Rayner and Seeley 2002, 162–74). These groups in conjunction with a small number of early groups from other sites such as 18 Park Street (PRK90; Cowan 2003) and 170–6 Grange Road on the Bermondsey eyot (GGW03; Rayner and Seeley forthcoming) are beginning to characterise the earliest Roman pottery in use in Southwark.

One potentially significant difference between the pre-Boudican assemblages examined from Southwark and those from the City of London is in the distribution of Sugar Loaf Court ware (SLOW). In the city this fabric is a key indicator of pre-Boudican activity although its occurrence in variable concentrations hints at a specialised manufacture or distribution. The largest groups recovered, aside from the possible manufacturing debris and wasters recovered from Sugar Loaf Court itself, are from the Fenchurch Street area and the ware is characterised by forms with continental parallels particularly from the region between the valleys of the Saône and the Aare (Chadburn and Tyers 1984; Richardson 2004; Davies *et al* 1994; Rayner forthcoming). This is not the place for a more general review of SLOW but it is notable that in the Ticket Hall site assemblage SLOW is absent in assemblages dated to *c* AD 55 and present in only very small quantities in the period *c* AD 55–61, at a

Table 4.3.1 Catalogue of additions to Southwark typology

The Southwark typology focused on the classification of coarse wares from the early Roman period (Marsh and Tyers 1978, 533). This has since been extended not only to include forms for the late Roman period but also to include those types not in the original type series: mortaria, amphorae and miscellaneous forms. The most common samian forms have also been added to the typology (not illustrated here), for example, Dragendorff form 37 bowl is referred to as a 4DR37. Additionally, the Roman numerals have been replaced by Arabic (eg IIA is now 2A). Where possible the vessels illustrated have been sourced from recently published or forthcoming Southwark sites. For full details of contexts and dating refer to publications. Where no existing illustrated vessel from Southwark was available examples from City sites were used.

Type	sub	Description	Date range	Fig ref
1 Flagons				
	1CX	**Later pinched/trefoil-mouthed flagon.** This type of flagon is rare in London. The example illustrated is from a late 4th-century group at BGH95 and is in the imported fabric, Mayen ware (MAYEN) (Rayner and Seeley 2002, 144, fig 102, no <P215>). However, most examples from London occur in Alice Holt Farnham ware (AHFA)	AD 200–400	4.3.1, 1
	1DX	**Later disc-mouthed flagon.** The illustrated example is in Nene Valley colour-coated ware (NVCC) from burial 17 at GDV96 (Seeley 2000, 40, fig 30, no <P19>). The burial is dated to the mid-2nd century. However, NVCC is uncommon in London before the early 3rd century and it is possible that this vessel (and the burial) is later in date. This type is also found in Much Hadham oxidised ware (MHAD)	AD 150–400	4.3.1, 2
	1L	**Disc-necked flagon.** The illustrated example is in an unsourced oxidised ware (OXID) and is from a well dated to AD 250–70/300 at 107BHS81 (Rayner and Seeley forthcoming, no <P159>)	AD 250–400	4.3.1, 3
	1N	**Flask/bottle.** This code refers to liquid holders without handles. The illustrated example is from a pre-Flavian group beneath Road 1 at AB78 (Rayner and Seeley forthcoming, no <P31>). The fabric is OXID	AD 50–400	4.3.1, 4
2 Jars				
	2FACE	**Jar with face applied decoration.** There is considerable variation within the decoration. Most commonly found in London in 2nd-century contexts and in the fabrics Verulamium region white ware (VRW) and Verulamium coarse white-slipped ware (VCWS), although imported examples are known. The illustrated vessel is in VRW (Davies *et al* 1994, fig 37, no 183)	AD 50–400	4.3.1, 5
	2F13	**Black-burnished-type cavetto-rim jar.** The majority of these vessels are decorated with narrow bands of obtuse lattice, AD 180–400. The illustrated example is from Leadenhall Court (LCT84) and is in BB1 (Symonds and Tomber 1991, 73, fig 9, no 65)	AD 180–400	4.3.1, 6
	2FX	**Later version of the everted-rimmed jar.** This code is used for all later examples of the everted-rimmed jar where the rim is not a true cavetto rim. Fabrics include black burnished ware one (BB1), black burnished style ware (BBS) and AHFA. The illustrated example is from a well at 107BHS81 dated AD 250–70/300 and is in the fabric BBS (Rayner and Seeley forthcoming, no <P165>)	AD 250–400	4.3.1, 7
	2T	**Otherwise indistinguishable necked jar.** This code is used for necked jars where there is no further defining feature. No illustration	AD 50–400	–
	2U	**Narrow-necked globular jar.** This form is the Alice Holt form 1A (Lyne and Jefferies 1979, 24, fig 9, nos 1A.1–5; 39, fig 23, nos 1A.6–20). Most examples are in AHFA such as the vessel illustrated from a late 4th-century group at GDV96 (Seeley 2000, 53–7, fig 40, no <P47>)	AD 50–400	4.3.1, 8
	2V	**Storage jar (other than 2M).** This code is used for large storage vessels other than those defined as 2L and 2M (Marsh and Tyers 1979, 564–5, fig 237, nos IIL and IIM). The pre-Flavian example from AB78 (Fig 4.3.1, 9a) is in an unsourced grog-tempered ware (GROG) (Rayner and Seeley forthcoming, no <P37>). Later storage jars are most commonly found in AHFA such as the illustrated example (Fig 4.3.1, 9b) from a late 4th-century assemblage at GDV96 (Seeley 2000, 53–7, fig 40, no <P48>)	AD 50–400	4.3.1, 9a & b
	2W	**Hooked-rimmed jar.** This form is most commonly found in London in the fabric Portchester ware D (PORD). The body of the vessel is usually rilled as shown in the illustrated example from a late 4th-century group at Lloyd's Register, 71 Fenchurch Street (FCC95; Seeley 2006, 111, fig 69, no <P50>)	AD 300–400	4.3.2, 10
	2X	**Lid-seated jar.** This code is used for lid-seated jars from all periods. The illustrated example is in MAYEN and from a well group at 4STS88 dated to AD 300–400 (Rayner and Seeley forthcoming, no <P188>)	AD 50–400	4.3.2, 11
	2Z	**Alice Holt Surrey flat-rimmed jar.** This form is the Alice Holt form 3A.1–15 (Lyne and Jefferies 1979, 25–7, fig 12). The illustrated example is from a well group at BGH95 dated AD 120–40 and is in Alice Holt Surrey ware (AHSU) (Rayner and Seeley 2002, 111, fig 88, no <P147>)	AD 50–270	4.3.2, 12
3 Beakers				
	3J	**Bag-shaped beaker.** This is a common form in the 2nd and early 3rd centuries and is present in all of the major fine wares common in London during this period including Cologne colour-coated ware (KOLN), Colchester colour-coated ware (COLCC) and NVCC. The illustrated example is in an unsourced colour-coated ware (CC) from a 3rd-century burial at GDV96 (Seeley 2000, 45, fig 37, no <P56>). Types of decorative techniques used on this form include barbotine decoration and, as with the illustrated example, clay pellet rough cast decoration	AD 100–250	4.3.2, 13

Table 4.3.1 Continued

Type	sub	Description	Date range	Fig ref
3J1 (formerly 3JP)		**Bag-shaped beaker with pedestal base** (Symonds 1992, fig 10, 203–12). This form is most commonly found in imported wares from central and eastern Gaul. The example here is in central Gaulish/Lezoux black colour-coated ware (CGBL) and is from a well at USB88 dated to AD 250–70/300 (Rayner and Seeley forthcoming, no <P122>)	AD 150–250	4.3.2, 14
3K		**Necked globular beaker.** There is a notable variety within this form as demonstrated by the two illustrated vessels. The example from the well at USB88 (Fig 4.3.2, 15a) is dated AD 250–70/300 and is in Moselkeramik (MOSL) (Rayner and Seeley forthcoming, no <P123>). The vessel in NVCC from a burial at GDV96 (Fig 4.3.2, 15b) has elongated indentations and three lines of rouletted decoration, and is considered to be mid- to late 3rd-century in date (Seeley 2000, 47, fig 36, no <P24>)	AD 180–400	4.3.2, 15a & b
3L		**Pentice beaker.** This form is developed from the 1st-century butt beaker. The majority of examples found in London are in NVCC as is the example illustrated here from the well group at 107BHS81 dated to AD 250–70/300 (Rayner and Seeley forthcoming no <P169>)	AD 180–400	4.3.2, 16
3N		**Later short-necked globular beaker.** This form is less common than the other late beaker forms. The example illustrated here is in AHFA and from a well at USB88 dated AD 250–70/300 (Rayner and Seeley forthcoming, no <P132>) It has four elongated indentations	AD 200–400	4.3.2, 17
4 Bowls				
4C306		**Camulodunum type 306 bowl with 'D-shaped' rim** (Hull 1963b, 186, fig 105, no 306). This vessel type is characterised by its poor manufacture. The vessel illustrated is from a well group at 107BHS81 dated to AD 250–70/300 where at least 25 examples of this form were found (Rayner and Seeley forthcoming, no <P149>)	AD 200–400	4.3.2, 18
4G226		**Bowl with incipient flange.** Gillam form 226 (Gillam 1970). This form is almost exclusively found in BB1. The illustrated vessel is from a well at USB88 dated c AD 250–70/300 (Rayner and Seeley forthcoming, no <P140>)	AD 160–300	4.3.3, 19
4M		**Black-burnished type flanged bowl.** This form mainly occurs in the fabrics BB1, AHFA and BBS. The flange varies in shape and size. The latest development of this form (4M4) has a vestigial flange and is more common in 4th-century assemblages and there are also indications that the form 4M3 is possibly later than the dates given. Lyne and Jefferies date this example to AD 270–420 (1979, 46, fig 32, no 5B.10). Forthcoming research on late Roman pottery from London will examine the development of this form. All the examples from the Lloyd's Register site (FCC95) are from late 4th-century contexts		
	4M1	**Long flange.** BB1. From well group at 107BHS81 dated to AD 250–70/300 (Rayner and Seeley forthcoming, no <P124>)	AD 250–400	4.3.3, 20a
	4M2	**Rounded flange.** AHFA. Lloyd's Register, 71 Fenchurch Street (FCC95; Seeley 2006, 112, fig 71, no <P73>)	AD 250–400	4.3.3, 20b
	4M3	**Rounded flange. Internal burnished decoration.** AHFA. From Lloyd's Register, 71 Fenchurch Street (FCC95; Seeley 2006, 112, fig 71, no <P72>)	AD 250–400	4.3.3, 20c
	4M4	**With vestigial flange.** AHFA. From Lloyd's Register, 71 Fenchurch Street (Seeley 2006, 117, fig 75, no <P121>)	AD 300–400	4.3.3, 20d
4MX		**Other flanged bowl.** This code is used for flanged bowls other than those in the black-burnished tradition. No illustration	AD 50–400	–
4N		**Necked bowl.** This code is used for the variants of the Oxfordshire necked bowl form C75 and the variants of the form, C76–80 (Young 1977, 164–6, figs 62–3) where it is dated from c AD 325. The majority of examples are in Oxfordshire red/brown colour-coated ware (OXRC). The example illustrated is from a late 4th-century group at GDV96 (Seeley 2000, 53, fig 39, no <P32>)	AD 240–400	4.3.3, 21
4Q		**Tripod bowl.** There is great variety within the rim forms of these vessels. The type occurs in a number of different fabrics in London, but the majority of these vessels are in mica-dusted wares. However, the example here is in OXID from an assemblage from a building at STU92 dated c AD 50–55 (Rayner and Seeley 2002, 39, fig 32, no <P60>)	AD 50–400	4.3.3, 22
6 Cups				
6H		**Hemispherical cup.** This form is usually found only in fine wares, in particular imported fine wares. The example here is in Lyon ware (LYON) and has scale decoration. It is from a dump in REW92 Open Area 2 dated AD 70–80/90 (Rayner and Seeley 2002, 80, fig 66, no <P108>)	AD 50–100	4.3.3, 23
7 Mortaria		Mortaria were not included in the original Southwark type series and their typology was developed separately. The two key types for the early period are the hooked flange mortarium (7HOF) and the bead and flange mortarium (7BEF). The majority of these vessels are from the Verulamium region industry. For the later period, the main supplier of mortaria to London is the Oxfordshire region. The Young (1977) form codes for the most commonly occurring mortarium forms for this industry have been incorporated into the Southwark typology eg 7M18 = Young type M18. Illustrations of these forms have not been reproduced here		
7BEF		**Bead and flange mortarium.** This form is characterised by a bead that is raised above the level of the flange. The illustrated example is in VRW and is from the kiln site at 20–28 Moorgate (MRG95; Seeley and Drummond-Murray 2005, 96, fig 125, no <P201>)	AD 140–400	4.3.4, 24
7EWAL		**Early wall-sided mortarium.** Two examples are illustrated to show the variety within this type. The first example (Fig 4.3.3, 25a) is in Colchester white ware (COLWW) and is similar to Symonds and Wade type 33 (1999, 165). The second vessel (Fig 4.3.3, 25b) has a triangular-sectioned wall and is unsourced. Both examples are from a pre-Boudican group at BGH95 (Rayner and Seeley 2002, 20, fig 20, nos <P18>–<P19>)	AD 50–70	4.3.4, 25a & b
7HAM		**Hammerhead mortarium.** The example illustrated is in a Rhineland white ware RHWW and is from the USB88 well dated AD 250–70/300 (Rayner and Seeley forthcoming, no <P112>)	AD 200–300	4.3.4, 26

Table 4.3.1 Continued

Type	sub	Description	Date range	Fig ref
7HOF		**Hooked flange mortarium.** The development of this form in the Verulamium region industry is discussed by Davies *et al* (1994, 47). The form does occur in the earliest assemblages in Southwark such as those in an unsourced shell-tempered ware (SHEL) at BGH95 (Rayner and Seeley 2002, 33–4, fig 30, no <P44>). The example illustrated here is typical of the Flavian period and is in VRW (Davies *et al* 1994, 47, fig 39, no 208)	AD 50–140	4.3.4, 27
7LWAL		**Late wall-sided mortarium.** The example illustrated is in OXID from a late 4th-century group at Lloyd's Register, 71 Fenchurch Street dated AD 350–400 (FCC95; Seeley 2006, 112, fig 70, no <P65>)	AD 180–250	4.3.4, 28
8 Amphorae		Amphorae were not included in the original Southwark type series. Form codes from existing amphorae classifications and typologies such as Dressel (1899) have been incorporated into the Southwark typology, eg 8DR20. Illustrations of these forms have not been reproduced here		–
9 Other forms				
9A		**Lid.** There is little variety within this form. Most commonly found in reduced wares or London oxidised ware (LOXI). This form has a raised handle, occasionally with an impression in the middle. It is rarely well finished. Some examples have a 'lip' as is shown on LOXI vessel (Fig 4.3.5, 29a) from a dump in LBI95 dated AD 90–110 (Rayner and Seeley 2002, 73–5, fig 62, no <P103>). This type of lid is most common in the late 1st and 2nd centuries. A second form of lid (Fig 4.3.5, 29b) comes almost exclusively in Pompeian red ware (PRW). This form has a shallow domed profile and no handle. The example illustrated here is from a late Flavian group at BGH95 (Rayner and Seeley 2002, 90, fig 73, no <P129>)	AD 50–400	4.3.5, 29a & b
9B		**Amphora seal.** Not illustrated	AD 50–400	–
9C		**Tazza.** This form is most commonly found in oxidised wares, in particular those produced by the Verulamium region industry. The two examples here are in VRW and are from a *bustum* at GDV96 (Seeley 2000, 37, fig 24, nos <P10> and <P13>). Both have frilled decoration on their rims and girths	AD 50–250	4.3.5, 30a & b
9D		**Dolium/seria.** In London this form is most commonly found in the (?)local coarse white-slipped ware (LCWS). A fabric that was possibly produced at the Moorgate kilns (Seeley and Drummond-Murray 2005, 131). The example illustrated is from the kiln site at 20–28 Moorgate (MRG95; Seeley and Drummond-Murray 2005, fig163, no <P10>). Smaller vessels which appear to copy this form are made in the Verulamium region, such as the example from a mid- to late Flavian group from BGH95 (Rayner and Seeley 2002, 90, fig 73, no <P131>)	AD 50–400	4.3.5, 31
9E		**Triple vase.** This rare form is almost invariably found in oxidised wares. The example illustrated is in VCWS (Davies *et al* 1994, 59, fig 48, no 277)	AD 50–250.	4.3.5, 32
9F		**Tettina/feeding bottle.** This enigmatic form is rare and can vary in detail. This example is in VRW (Davies *et al* 1994, 51, fig 40, no 221)	AD 50–400	4.3.5, 33
9G		**Castor box.** See below		
9GB		**Castor box base.** More commonly found in the late colour-coated wares such as NVCC, the illustrated example from Shadwell is in OXID. This is from a ditch dated to AD 250–70/300 (LD76; Seeley 2002, 18, fig 15, no <P33>)	AD 200–400	4.3.5, 34
9GL		**Castor box lid.** The illustrated example is in NVCC and from a 3rd-century context at Governor's House (SUF94; Symonds 2001, 39, fig 42, no <P35>)	AD 200–400	4.3.5, 35
9H		**Colander.** This form varies considerably but the defining feature is multiple small pre-firing holes in the base of the bowl. The example illustrated is from a late 4th-century group at Billingsgate Bath and is in MHAD (Symonds and Tomber 1991, 80, fig 15, no 161)	AD 50–400	4.3.5, 36
9J		**Patera.** These are uncommon forms in London. The majority are in local fine wares. The illustrated example is in London mica-dusted ware (LOMI) and from 201 Bishopsgate in a context dated AD 170+ where it is probably residual (BGB98; Seeley 2003, 10–11, fig 10, no <P2>)	AD 50–400	4.3.5, 37
9K		**Cheese press.** Not illustrated	AD 50–400	
9LA		**Lamp.** Illustrated example is in VRW and from the kiln site at 20–28 Moorgate in a late 2nd-century context where it is probably residual (MRG95; Seeley and Drummond-Murray 2005, 76, fig 116, no <S22>)	AD 50–400	4.3.6, 38
9LB		**Lamp holder.** The majority of these vessels are in VRW as is the illustrated example from the kiln site at 20–28 Moorgate (MRG95; Seeley and Drummond-Murray 2005, 96, fig 125, no <S23>)	AD 50–400	4.3.6, 39
9N		**Unguentarium (small 2J type).** Small flat-based unguentarium (previously 2J1). This example is in VRW and is residual in a late 4th-century context at Lloyd's Register, 71 Fenchurch Street (FCC95; Seeley 2006, 117–18, fig 75 & fig 76, no <P134>)	AD 50–400	4.3.6, 40
9NP		**Unguentarium with pedestal base/amphora stopper.** These unguentaria vary in size and form. Two examples are illustrated from the kiln site at 20–28 Moorgate, in the fabrics LOXI and VRW (MRG95; Seeley and Drummond-Murray 2005, 119, fig 149, no <P185>; 96, fig 125, no <P180>). The latter form in VRW is not self-supporting	AD 50–400	4.3.6, 41a & b
9P		**Counter** (can be from reused sherd). Not illustrated	AD 50–400	
9T		**Crucible.** The majority of examples in London are in VRW. This example is from a Hadrianic context from 2–3 Cross Keys Court, Copthall Avenue (OPT81; Davies *et al* 1994, 51, fig 41, no 225)	AD 50–400	4.3.6, 42
9U		**Bucket.** This form occurs in South Essex shell-tempered ware (SESH). This example is from a late 1st- to early 2nd-century context at Billingsgate Buildings, 101–10 Lower Thames Street (TR74; Davies *et al* 1994, 105, fig 91, no 589)	AD 50–400	4.3.6, 43

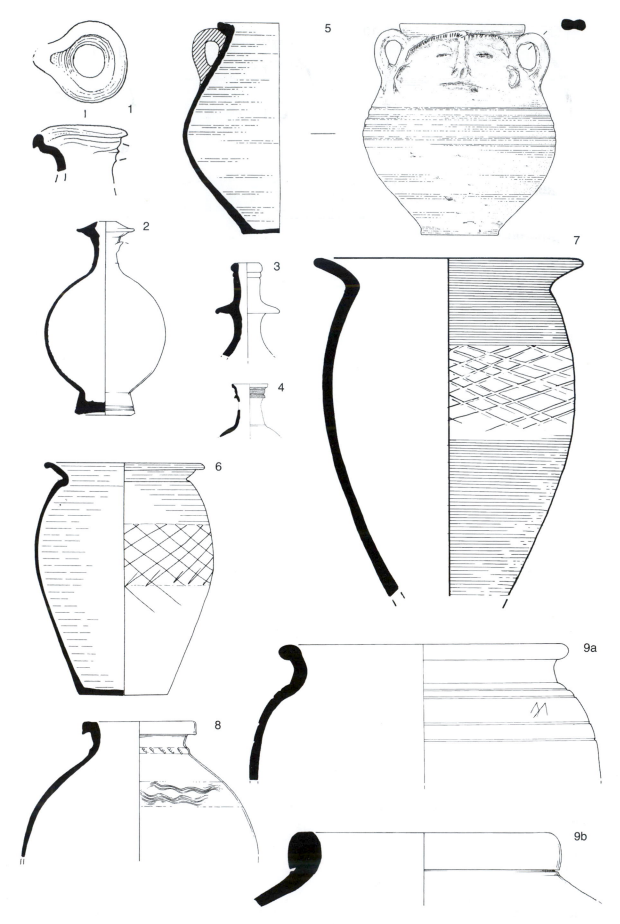

Fig 4.3.1 Additions to Southwark typology 1–9, flagons and jars

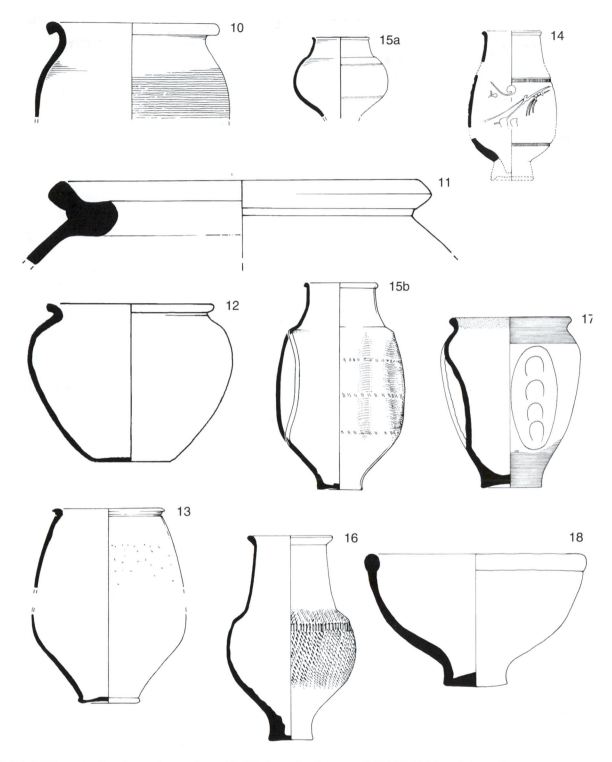

Fig 4.3.2 Additions to Southwark typology 10–18, jars, beakers and CAM 306 bowl (no 18)

time when it is at the height of its circulation north of the Thames. The ware is present in pre-Flavian groups from Park Street (Groves 2003) and Lant Street (LTU03; Lyne 2005) although also in small quantities. Other typically pre-Boudican and Boudican wares such as the imported Lyon colour-coated fine wares are also poorly represented in the Southwark assemblage suggesting that differences in the ceramic assemblages between the north and south bank settlements may be at their greatest in this early period.

Commercial and industrial Southwark

Evidence for the commercial and industrial nature of Southwark has been found at many excavations, most importantly those at the site of the Courage Brewery bottling plant (COSE84; Cowan 2003), and the Ticket Hall site on Borough High Street (Drummond-Murray *et al* 2002). Much of the evidence for these draw on datasets other than the ceramic assemblages but a number of aspects are worth highlighting, although many of these

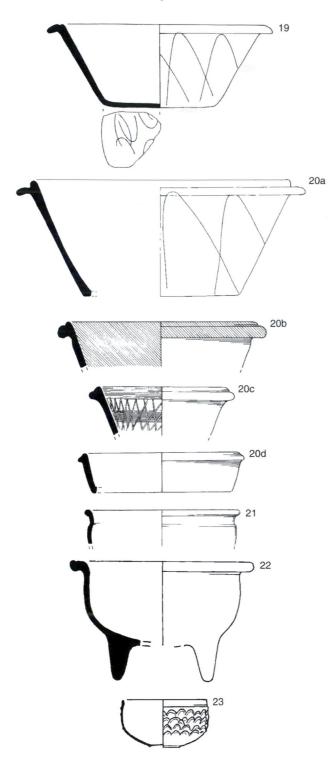

Fig 4.3.3 Additions to Southwark typology 19–23, bowls and hemispherical cup (no 23)

currently relate to negative evidence when compared with the north bank.

One of the most striking absences is the lack of warehouse dumps and assemblages of supposed shop or stall stock such as have been found in the city, both *in situ* and redeposited, including most recently the *in situ* contents of a Boudican shop at 1 Poultry (ONE94; Rayner forthcoming). No such deposits have been recovered in Southwark and the pottery evidence is exclusively derived from non-commercial assemblages. One possible exception to this is the excavation of a timber tank at Hunt's House, Guy's Hospital, which was constructed in the second half of the 3rd century (HHO97; Taylor-Wilson 2002, 23). From a fill representing 'rapid and deliberate infilling of the base of the structure following its abandonment and collapse or demolition' 322 sherds were recovered (Taylor-Wilson 2002, 26). Of these 113 (70% by weight) are amphorae, predominately Gauloise 4 with smaller quantities of Dressel 20 and including large fresh pieces (Williams 2002, 50). This tank has been interpreted as a storage facility for amphorae (Williams 2002, 26), possibly associated with trading activities taking place on the revetted channels (Williams 2002, 47). The evidence for this is not straightforward, however, due to the poorly refined dating of these amphorae types and issues surrounding vessel quantification for amphorae in comparison with other pottery types, which were also present in the tank fill (Williams 2002, 26). Similar tanks elsewhere in Southwark have been interpreted as storage for oysters, eels or fish (Cowan *et al* forthcoming). Whatever the correct interpretation for these tanks and in spite of the lack of evidence for other warehouse dumps and assemblages the range of amphorae in use in Southwark is comparable to those in the city.

The other industrial aspect worth mentioning here is the continued absence of strong evidence for pottery production in the settlement, which with the recent discoveries at Moorgate (mentioned below) contrasts strongly with the city. Possible wasters of the bowl form Camulodunum 306 (CAM 306; see also Haynes, this volume) from a number of sites including 107 Borough High Street (107BHS81; Rayner and Seeley forthcoming) and Hunt's House, Guy's Hospital (Lyne 2002, 27) remain the only candidates for vessel production in Southwark. As the number of groups recovered increases, whilst still lacking direct evidence for associated manufacture as opposed to vessels with a poor standard of production, the likelihood of these vessels actually being of Southwark origin is arguably increasingly unlikely.

Religion and ritual in Southwark

The recent excavations of a temple complex at Tabard Square (LLS02) have served to emphasise the importance of aspects of religion and ritual in Roman Southwark. The publication of this important site and its pottery assemblage is eagerly anticipated but the use and deposition of pottery vessels in ritual contexts in Southwark is already well evidenced from the presence of *tazze* in the *bustum* at the cemetery site at Great Dover Street (GDV96; Seeley 2000; Bateman, this volume) and the series of unusual well deposits which appear to be particularly characteristic of Southwark. These contain combinations of pottery vessels, faunal

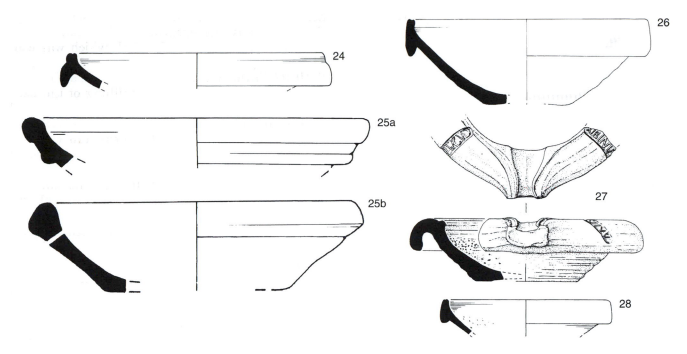

Fig 4.3.4 Additions to Southwark typology 24–28, mortaria

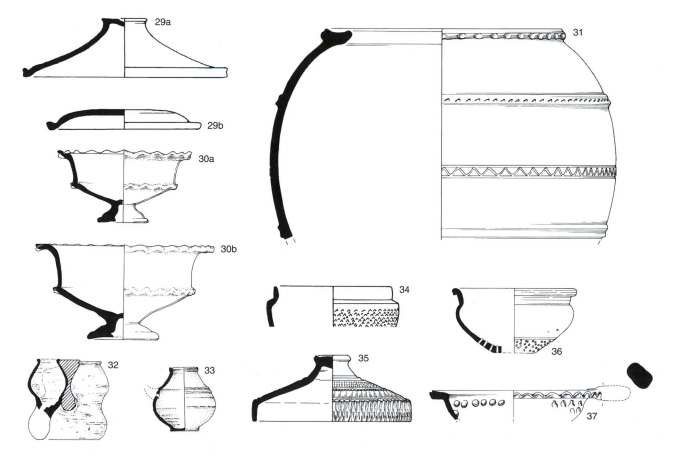

Fig 4.3.5 Additions to Southwark typology 29–37, other forms

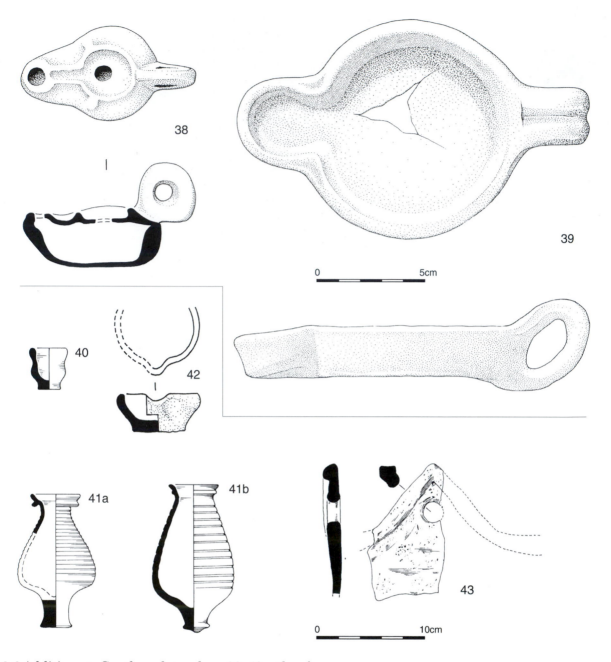

Fig 4.3.6 Additions to Southwark typology 38–43, other forms

remains, including intact and less common species, and occasionally other finds. Most recently a series of wells and shafts excavated at The Old Sorting Office site, Swan Street (SWN98), has confirmed the deposition of complete flagons that appear to have been purposefully damaged and include some unusual examples of vessels with red-painted motifs and 'solar rays' (Lyne 2000). One shaft included a human skeleton, deposited head down with evidence for 'ritual manipulation' prior to deposition (Beasley 2000). The vessels recovered from these wells, both in terms of their decoration and modification, are new and important additions to the Southwark repertoire. Whether they will inspire further extension to the Southwark typology is awaited with anticipation.

Although clearly and necessarily selective, it is hoped that the aspects highlighted above serve to

demonstrate the importance and continuing potential of further work on the Roman pottery from Southwark. Little of this would have been possible without the firm foundation provided by the Marsh and Tyers type-series and it is clear that this will serve the future study of vessel typology for many more years to come.

The updated type-series

Early pottery industries update – Verulamium region potteries

The discovery in 1999 of kilns at Northgate House, 20–28 Moorgate, confirmed the existence of pottery production in the City of London in the early to mid-2nd century (MRG95; Seeley and

Drummond-Murray 2005). The most significant finding was that the kilns were linked to the Verulamium region potteries in that they were producing the same fabrics, notably Verulamium white ware (VRW) and Verulamium coarse white-slipped ware (VCWS) in a similar range of forms to those at Brockley Hill and the other Verulamium potteries (Seeley and Drummond-Murray 2005, 142). The Moorgate kilns were also producing a range of reduced and oxidised fine wares and coarse wares that were not produced at the other Verulamium kiln sites. These included London ware (LONW), fine micaceous reduced ware (FMIC), London mica-dusted ware (LOMI), London eggshell ware (LOEG), London marbled ware (LOMA), London oxidised ware (LOXI) and Copthall Close grey ware (CCGW). The report on the kiln site suggests that the Northgate kilns are evidence of a trend within the Verulamium region industry to bring production closer to the main urban markets in the early to mid-2nd century (Seeley and Drummond-Murray 2005, 143). Two main phases of production have been identified at Moorgate, dated to AD 110/120–40 and AD 140–160/170. The end of this industry also marked the end of the early period of Roman pottery in London as traditionally defined by ceramicists working in the region (Davies *et al* 1994, 2; Symonds *et al* 1991, 59).

Pottery supply in the later Roman period

With the decline of the Verulamium region and Highgate Wood industries in the later 2nd century, the Southwark market is supplied by industries outside the immediate region. Notably, the black burnished ware industry in Dorset supplies reduced wares (BB1) which first appear in London around AD 120 (Davies *et al* 1994, 107). These are overtaken during the mid- to later 2nd century by the wheel-made black burnished ware 2 (BB2) from Kent and Essex. However, by the 3rd century, BB1 increases in quantity and becomes one of the more significant

suppliers of reduced wares to London. This continues into the latter half of the 3rd century, but by the mid-4th century it has been all but eclipsed by the products of the later Alice Holt industry. Current research suggests that Alice Holt Farnham ware (AHFA) is the most common sourced reduced ware in London in the 4th century (Seeley in preparation).

Oxidised wares, in particular mortaria, are supplied by the large Oxfordshire region industry. These are particularly common in the 3rd and 4th centuries. The Oxfordshire region also supplies the red/brown colour-coated wares (OXRC) which occur in forms derivative of the samian industry. OXRC appears in the London area in the latter half of the 3rd century, a period when imports of samian into the region appear to be in decline or have ceased. The Nene Valley industry supplies mortaria and parchment wares from *c* AD 200 but it is the colour-coated wares from this industry which are the most common fine wares in Southwark especially in the 3rd century when the colour-coated beakers reach their peak in popularity.

Acknowledgements

For many years Harvey Sheldon has been a dear friend and important colleague. This paper is offered with much affection and thanks for the endless support, advice and encouragement dispensed over numerous cups of tea.

The work of many colleagues is drawn upon here and gratefully acknowledged, in particular past and present Roman pottery specialists at the Museum of London. Special mention should be made of Jo Groves, Robin Symonds and Roberta Tomber for their involvement in the development of the type-series and the codes being added to the MoLAS Oracle database. We are grateful to Pre-Construct Archaeology Ltd for access to their unpublished assessment reports on their excavations at Lant Street and Swan Street.

4.4 Imagining health-care in Roman London
Ralph Jackson

Greek and Roman medical treatises were written by and for a literate elite. In consequence they shed light on disease theory and on the medicine and practices available to the leisured rich but far less on doctoring for the masses. With how much confidence, therefore, may we believe that the etiquette, book-learnt healing and drug therapies practised by 'society' doctors in Rome, and to some extent preserved in surviving texts, were transmitted to other parts of the Roman Empire and to people lower down the social scale, and with how much success (Nutton 2004)? And how might 'Roman' medicine of that kind, and its practitioners, have interfaced with other healing traditions and their mediators elsewhere in the expanding Roman world?

In the case of Britain, the rapid conquest of the south-east in AD 43 evidently would have brought about some profound changes to the lives of many native Britons in those parts, not least the introduction of Latin as the language of power and authority. But the extent to which existing British institutions and customs were eclipsed, modified or replaced, and the timescale for those changes, is by no means clearly understood. Prominent within this area of uncertainty are the strategies for maintaining and restoring health. What were the means of transmission, accommodation to and intermingling of 'Roman' and native British healing systems? It must be accepted that we cannot answer these fundamentally important questions with authority, having neither written nor archaeological evidence sufficient to do so. Nevertheless, if the restricted current evidence prevents an accurate assessment, it permits, at least, cautious speculation on the process of transition from British to Romano-British medicine, as it does on the nature of healers and healing in Britannia and, for present purposes, in Londinium and its hinterland.

In Londinium, native British healers and healers from Roman Italy might easily have mingled with Roman military medical personnel and with healers from as far afield as the Roman provinces in Hungary, Syria, North Africa and Spain. In fact, while variation undoubtedly occurred, it is likely, too, that there was a strong commonality, for the healing traditions of many early European cultures were rooted in herbal cures and religious rites. Thus, for example, the full panoply of health-preserving and health-restoring methods in 'Roman' medicine included amulets, charms, incantations, prayers and propitiatory acts in addition to dietetic and drug therapies. It is, therefore, improbable that the healers who arrived in Britain with or in the wake of the Roman army were unduly surprised by the indigenous healing practices they encountered.

Indeed, it is hardly to be doubted that they already knew much of those practices, since there had been a century of increased contact between Britain and the Roman world following Julius Caesar's British campaigns of 55 and 54 BC. To add to the mix, although minor wounds, injuries and day-to-day illness are likely to have been treated within the home or extended family, drug lore and healing appear to have also come within the ambit of druids, at least by the 1st century AD. As religious officiants, supervisors and interpreters, druids were the mediators of religious therapies, just as the priests of Aesculapius instructed and interceded on behalf of supplicants at healing sanctuaries in the Graeco-Roman world. In the absence of written testimony such divine-inspired healing is unlikely to be discerned in surviving material remains.

More readily identifiable is the paraphernalia of mortal medicine, above all surgery. Unlike other aspects of healing, which are more specifically driven by theory and are subject to geographical variation or change over time, surgery is an essentially practical response to disease, disorders and defects of the human body, the anatomy of which has hardly changed over thousands of years. In consequence there is a high degree of continuity of surgical practice as well as a marked similarity in the form of many purpose-made surgical tools over the ages. Even for the simplest surgical intervention skin and flesh have to be cut or punctured, incision or wound edges must be held apart and tissue, structures or foreign bodies need to be fixed, moved or excised, requiring blades, needles, retractors and forceps (though fingers, nails and teeth might serve for some purposes – eg Celsus *de medicina* 7, 5, 2C and 4B; 7, 12, 1B). The problem is that while some surgical applications required a specific and distinctive instrument – as, for example, catheterisation of the urinary tract – others did not, and they could be performed using 'loan' tools (such as craft, household or personal items) or implements whose form was not completely distinctive (for example, simple uneyed needles). In fact, a considerable part of ancient surgery potentially could be performed without any identifiably 'surgical' instruments. Because in antiquity healing, including surgery, might be done by 'part-time' practitioners – perhaps only occasionally by 'full-time' healers or medical personnel – such 'loan' tools may have been the norm, so that the surviving identifiable surgical instruments are very likely to represent only one end of a broad spectrum of surgical activity.

Roman London's surviving identifiable surgical instrumentation (Figs 4.4.1–4.4.2 show a selection) comprises examples of all the essential tools of basic ancient surgery – scalpels, sharp and blunt hooks,

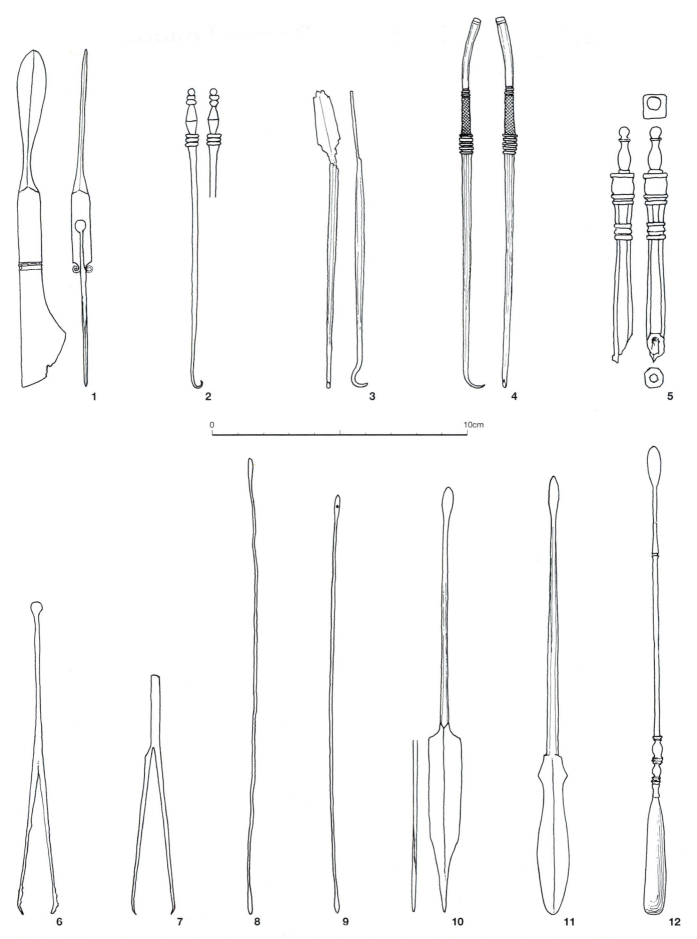

Fig 4.4.1 Surgical tools from London, various collections. 1: scalpel; 2–5: hooks and needles; 6–7: forceps; 8–9: dipyrenes; 10–12: probes. Copper alloy, except blade of 1, iron. Scale 2:3

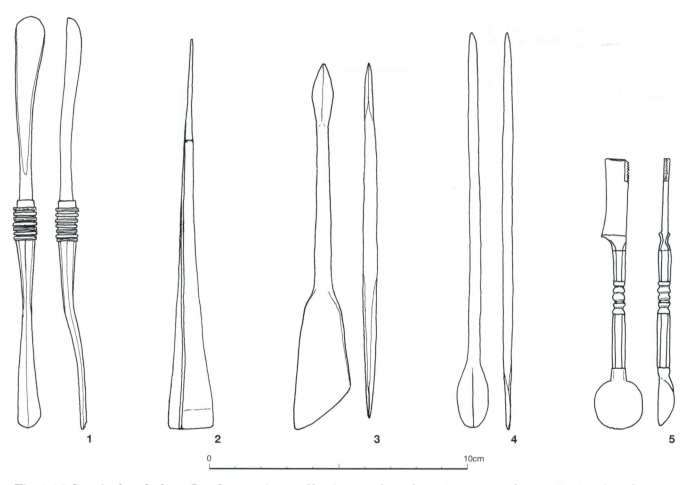

Fig 4.4.2 Surgical tools from London, various collections. 1: bone lever/curette; 2: forceps/pointed probe; 3: scalpel; 4: spatula probe; 5: saw-knife/spoon. Iron. Scale 2:3

surgical needles, spring forceps and probes – though not in particularly great numbers, few from known and dated contexts and none of those with an overtly medical setting. The instruments have been found as single objects, never as sets, which is in accord with finds from Roman Britain generally: only at Stanway, in the mid-1st-century 'Doctor's Grave', has an identifiable set of instruments been found (Jackson 1997; Jackson 2007), the claimed examples from Cramond (Gilson 1983) and from Corbridge (Gilson 1981, 5) both being problematic, the one probably a set or part-set but probably not from Britain, the other now lost and unverifiable. Similarly, London, like the rest of Britain, has yet to yield a single cupping vessel, though that is not to say that the ancient predilection for venesection (vein cutting) did not take place, simply that if it did so it appears on present evidence to have been done without the assistance of a recognisable suction cup (Jackson 1993a, 94; 1994, 182–4; 2002, 92).

The London surgical finds at present include very few specialised instruments. One, an instrument of bone surgery, from the Walbrook at the Bank of England site (Fig 4.4.2, 1), is a finely made single-piece iron tool which combines an elevator with a sharp spoon (curette), one at either end of a stout centrally moulded shank (Jackson 2005a, 103–4, fig 5.2, no 6). Another single-piece iron instrument, also

from the bed of the Walbrook (Fig 4.4.2, 3), appears to be a British version of the characteristic Roman scalpel, with blade and blunt dissector at either end of a central grip (probably not a modelling tool as suggested in Manning (1985, 32, pl 13, C10)). Other iron instruments include a smooth-jawed fixation forceps combined with a needle-probe (Fig 4.4.2, 2) and a variant spatula probe (Fig 4.4.2, 4), both from Angel Court (Wheeler 1930, pl 33, 6 and pl 37, 5).

There are also a number of objects of uncertain medical status (eg Fig 4.4.2, 5) – a combined saw-knife and spoon, tweezers stamped by Agathangelus (Gostenčnik 2002, 251, nos 6–8, fig 9, nos 1, 2, 5) and razors/knives by Olondus (Manning 1985, 111, type 6A, pl 53, Q11). Additionally, there are large numbers of undiagnostic, quasi-medical, multi-purpose implements, the spatula probes, scoop probes and ligulae which had medical uses (both in pharmacy and surgery) as well as toilet, cosmetic and other applications (Jackson 2002, 87–8); there are collyrium-stamps ('oculists' stamps'), used for marking sticks of eye-ointment, from Upper Thames Street and from Staines, as well as an unengraved blank from Coleman Street (Fig 4.4.3, 1–3) and a stamp on a samian vessel from Moorgate Street (Fig 4.4.3, 4) (Jackson 1996a, figs 21.2–3, 21.5–6); there are stone mixing palettes (Fig 4.4.3, 5), fine bronze balances, glass unguent bottles, jars and

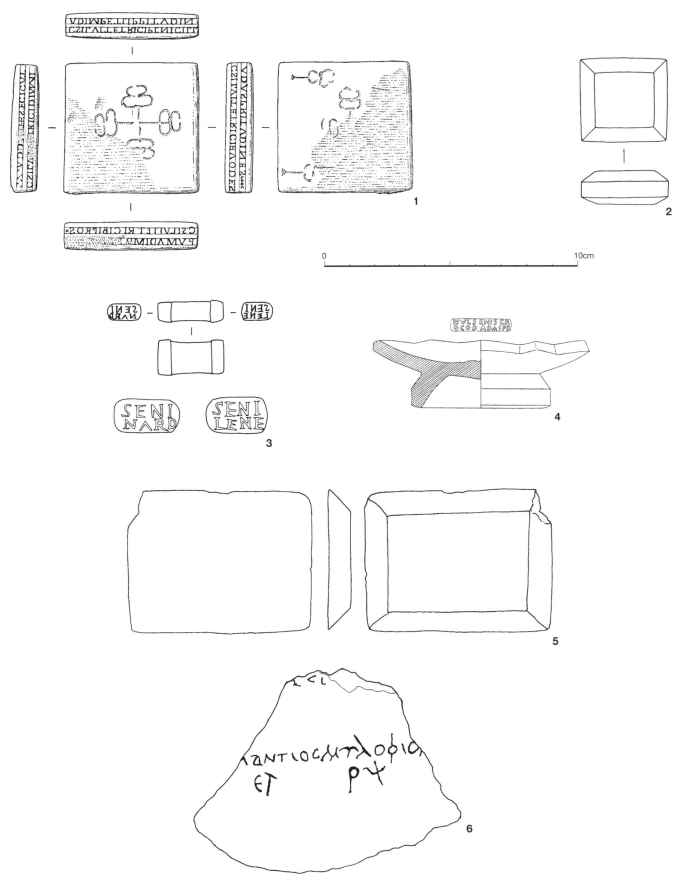

Fig 4.4.3 Medical implements from London and region. 1, 3: collyrium-stamps, C. Silvius Tetricus and Seni(or); 2: uninscribed collyrium-stamp; 4: samian vessel marked with collyrium-stamp, L. Julius Senex; 5: stone palette; 6: sherd with graffito attesting a 'mule-physician' (Jmantios mulophysi[kos])

both the legions and auxiliary units. Indeed, the army was probably the single most effective instrument of diffusion of the concepts of Roman medicine to Britain, as to other newly acquired provinces. The military *medici* appear to have been mostly of relatively low status and therefore amongst those veterans likely to retire locally. Their experience in treating the illnesses and wounds of a large body of men over a long period of time in different locations would have been of great value and we can imagine that some will not only have set up as private practitioners but perhaps will have opened premises as treatment centres, having been accustomed to practising in the military *valetudinaria*.

As well as entrepreneurs, personal physicians and retired military healers there may have been potential for civic appointments. In Rome Vespasian released doctors from taxation, and some towns employed public physicians, their salary fixed by the *ordo*. That system reached, for example, *Aventicum* in Gallia Belgica and may even have extended as far as Britain, and, by the later 2nd century, assuming that Londinium had by that stage acquired official status, it is possible that one or more civic doctors was resident, and that the town was subject to the statute of Antoninus Pius regulating the appointment of doctors to public service.

If these were some of the possible sources of healers where did they practise in Londinium and what might have been their numbers? The location of healers' premises is not feasible on the strength of their architecture or ground plan alone, which did not differ in any identifiable way from that of other houses, as is clear from known medical premises at Pompeii, Marcianopolis and Rimini (Bliquez 1994; Ortalli 2000; Jackson 2003; Jackson 2005b, 209–12). An identification is usually only possible through the *in situ* discovery of numbers of distinctive medical instruments and implements, something which, while we may remain hopeful, has not yet occurred in London with sufficient certainty (Jackson 1996a, 185–6). Looking especially to Pompeii, the settings are likely to be houses or houses with shop-fronts and thus might cut across the residential/commercial/industrial division of 1st- to 2nd-century Londinium discerned by Perring (1991a, 94) or the zoning of activities defined by Hall (2005, 140–1). Pompeian evidence also suggests, perhaps unsurprisingly, a relatively even distribution throughout the town with a position on one of the main streets as a favoured location.

By the standards of the city of Rome numbers of healers in Londinium will have been tiny (though that was not necessarily bad for health), but they may have compared more favourably with those of other towns in the western provinces. London, at 130 hectares, was, after all, large in area even if not always – or ever – densely occupied. Its population included, by the 2nd century, the governor, provincial administrators and wealthy merchants,

at least some of whom are likely to have had personal physicians (together with their books, drugs and instruments) in their household – to say nothing of those in the retinue of visiting emperors and officials; the governor's military *officium* and his bodyguard, the *pedites* and *equites singulares*, together numbering perhaps as many as 1500 men and including medical personnel; the office of the *classis Britannica*; military veterans and many resident craftsmen, traders and shopkeepers, as well as a more transient population of merchants and sailors.

While it is unlikely that the number of healers in Londinium was as great as that calculated for the 63ha town of Pompeii – somewhere between 20 and 40 for a population, including the *territorium*, of about 20,000 (Bliquez 1994; Künzl 1998; Künzl 2002, 68; Jackson 2003, 313; but see also Swain and Williams, this volume) – we may imagine that Londinium with its exceptional mix of population and an amphitheatre seating perhaps 7000 people would at times have been home to as many as five to ten healers, though not all permanent residents or full-time practitioners or healers available to all sectors of the community. Just a few would have practised surgery, some will have specialised, notably in eye medicine and bone surgery, and there would very likely have been female healers, both for women's diseases and childbirth. Above all we may imagine that in Londinium, cosmopolitan from the start, the healers were as culturally diverse as their patients.

Acknowledgements

When, as a callow youth, I spent weekends digging – and occasionally weeding the Roman wall – in the City of London, with a dedicated band of City of London Excavation Group (COLEG) volunteers, on important but woefully under-resourced excavations led by Peter Marsden, Nick Farrant and others, I was vaguely aware of an equally intrepid band across the river in Southwark (*terra incognita*) led by one Harvey Sheldon. Our groups even met occasionally, as I recall, for joint post-excavation finds processing – although we didn't call it that in those days. Harvey was already excavating sites across London and was involved in adult education. He has combined a flair for excavation with a talent for motivating others, vision with friendly enthusiasm and the linking of amateur and professional in a joint discovery and sharing of London's Roman past. It is a unique and enduring combination and it is a great pleasure to join in this celebration of Harvey's tremendous achievement.

For information, assistance and useful discussion I am grateful to Jenny Hall, Angela Wardle, Stephen Crummy and Nick Griffiths (Fig 4.4.3, 1).

4.5 *Bene lava:* bathing in Roman London
Angela Wardle

Introduction

Bathing is synonymous in the public imagination with Roman culture. Communal bathing establishments are some of the most impressive monuments of the classical world and there is a wealth of evidence for their existence in Britain, on the fringes of the Roman empire. The social and cultural aspects of Roman bathing have been addressed in recent studies (eg DeLaine and Johnston 1999). This study reviews the evidence for the equipment used by the individual bather in Londinium, examining its distribution in relation to the known bath house sites in an attempt to assess its importance in the daily life of the Roman Londoner.

The Roman bath was an elaborate affair, a progression of cold, warm and hot rooms, although the order in which these were taken could vary. The mechanics of the process demanded buildings of specific form, and the architecture and technology was introduced from the Roman Mediterranean. Londinium is known to have possessed a number of baths, conveniently summarised by Rowsome (1999, 273–6) and shown here on Figure 4.5.8. Of these only Huggin Hill, in use from the late 1st century and demolished by the mid-2nd century, is thought to have been a public bath and is the largest yet known from London. Other early baths are known at Cheapside (GM37) and there are possible sites at 15–18 Lime Street and perhaps at Cannon Street Station, on the site originally thought to be the governor's palace (Perring 1991a, 34). Later Roman bath houses were located at Pudding Lane (PDN81; Milne 1985, 140; Perring 1991a, 127), Billingsgate (GM111; Rowsome 1996) and 1 Poultry (ONE94; Hill and Rowsome forthcoming), all of moderate size and thought to belong to private houses, although small-scale commercial use cannot be ruled out. More tenuous evidence, based principally on antiquarian observations, exists for other bath suites. In Southwark, a large bath house dating from the mid-2nd to the 4th century was excavated at Winchester Palace in what is believed to be an official building (Yule 2005, 65–72).

Equipment for bathing

Roman bathing required specialised and distinctive equipment including oil flasks (*aryballoi*) and strigils (*strigiles*) (Fig 4.5.1). Oil, traditionally olive oil, was used to anoint the body and was scraped off, with the dirt, by the strigil after the progression to increasingly hot temperatures, prior to the final cold plunge. Glass oil flasks are sometimes found in or near bath houses, most strikingly at Caerleon (Allen 1986, 104–7) where the drain contained over 50 rims and handles and over 100 body fragments.

Fig 4.5.1 Glass bath flask (Cat no 1) and iron strigil (Cat no 65)

The *aryballos* is a standard form found throughout the empire. It appeared during the 1st century AD and was found at Pompeii and Herculaneum (Scatozza Höricht 1986, 55, nos 112–20). The basic form has a globular body with thickened base, a short neck with an out-turned rim and two loop 'dolphin' handles used for suspension. Flasks are generally 50–100mm high but there is considerable variation within this, as seen in continental collections (for example Musée de Picardie, Dilly and Mahéo 1997, 106, pl 14, nos 247–56), where they range from under 50mm (no 250) to nearly 110mm (no 247). A similar variation can be seen at Caerleon (Allen 1986, 104–7 nos 32–42, fig 41; nos 52–6, fig 42). The generally small size of the vessels reinforces the facts that oil, which could vary in quality and perfume, was expensive and that the flasks were for personal use.

The glass flasks, which were mass produced after the general introduction of glass-blowing, copied a metal form, which presumably remained the more expensive option. The range of copper-alloy vessels used for bathing, which included *ampullae* and vessels for carrying water, is described by Nenova-Merdjanova (1999), where it is noted that they are sometimes found in sets. The most easily identified vessels are small anthropomorphic flasks, only one of which has been found in London (Cat no 63; Fig 4.5.5). The other vital piece of equipment, the strigil, is also seen throughout the empire, from basic forms in iron (eg Fig 4.5.7), to highly decorative implements, as seen at Caerleon (Boon 1986).

Catalogue

All bath flasks and other equipment held in the Museum of London's permanent collections have been included where there is a reasonable assumption that they were found in the town, but the exact provenance is frequently unknown. All identified excavated material has been included, using as a basis for examination published data and the digitised records held in the London Archaeological Archive and Research Centre (LAARC) and the Museum of London Archaeology Service (MoLAS), the latter including some unpublished artefacts from current excavations. For sites excavated before 1992 the archive records were taken as the basis for selection and examination. The glass from many of the sites has previously been examined and recorded in digitised format by John Shepherd, but several large assemblages excavated in the late 1980s remain unrecorded and it has only been possible to examine these in a very cursory way for this study. Despite a potential underestimation it was felt that the sites for which data are readily available represent a sufficiently wide geographical spread within London for any spatial trends to be observed.

The full assemblage (62 glass flasks plus their fittings, two metal flasks and thirteen strigils) is summarised in Table 4.5.1. For the glass flasks complete vessels are listed first, followed by rim and handle fragments, then body sherds. The glass vessels are followed by copper-alloy fittings and vessels, and finally by the strigils. Details of the glass vessels held in the Museum of London's permanent collections are available from the Ceramics and Glass online catalogue (Museum of London 2006) and a full archive catalogue, prepared for this study, is available from the Museum of London. References to the glass forms are given in Isings (1957). In all cases provenance and context dates have been given where available, using either published data or spot dates, which have to be treated with some caution. Expansion of the site codes, with site addresses and National Grid References, are given in the site lists (Tables 1 and 2) and further information can be found in the published site summaries (Schofield and Maloney 1998; Thompson *et al* 1998; LAARC 2006).

Discussion

Where vessels are sufficiently well preserved, the range of sizes of the London *aryballoi* falls generally within that recorded elsewhere. The largest regular flask in the Museum of London collection (Cat no 2; Fig 4.5.2) is over 100mm; one from Southwark (Cat no 1; Fig 4.5.1) around 90mm; two of the incomplete excavated examples (Cat nos 8 and 17; Fig 4.5.4) are of approximately the same size. Flasks can be dated from their handle shape. In the 1st century handles are thicker and more circular, while in the 2nd–3rd century they are trailed up and doubled over outwards, creating a longer thinner handle loop (Price and Cottam 1998, 188). Some flasks, all from 3rd- or 4th-century contexts, are quite small and very thin walled, with thin handles (as Cat nos 14–16;

Fig 4.5.4), a trait that Allen (1986, 104) suggests is a 2nd-century development. One small fragment (Cat no 58) has trailed decoration, also a characteristic of flasks dating from the 2nd century and later, and a body fragment from the bath site at Huggin Hill has decorative ribbing (Cat no 57). A very small dark blue vessel from the cemetery area of Spital Square (Cat no 5; Fig 4.5.3) is a miniature, unlikely to have been intended for practical use.

The regular glass *aryballos* had copper-alloy handles, typically triple chains with connecting rings, as can be seen on Cat no 1 (Fig 4.5.1) and fragments of such chains have been identified without the accompanying flask (Cat no 61).

There are some variant forms of oil flask; two (Cat nos 22 and 23, identified by John Shepherd) have no handles, and it is possible that a small hexagonal unguent bottle (Cat no 60; Wardle forthcoming a) paralleled at Caerleon (Allen 1986, 105, fig 41, no 9) was also used in the bath. One flask (Cat no 59), a 19th-century discovery reconstructed from many fragments, is a standard *aryballos* shape, but is exceptionally large. It may either have functioned as a bulk container, from which smaller flasks were filled or, given its location east of the city in the Minories, may have been a funerary vessel.

The glass *aryballos* bears the same name as its metal counterpart (Nenova-Merdjanova 1999, 130, fig 2). No metal vessels of this form have been excavated, but Cat no 63 (see Fig 4.5.5) falls into a distinctive class of oil flask that became popular in the 2nd century (Nenova-Merdjanova 1999, 132). *Balsamaria*, which are found throughout the Roman empire, have in the past been described as incense containers (Hutchinson 1986, 226–9; Webster 1973), but their use as oil flasks has been convincingly argued by Nenova-Merdjanova (1997). The numerous examples from the Balkans include flasks from graves in Thrace and Moesia found with strigils (Nenova-Merdjanova 1997, 104) thus suggesting a connection between the two types of object. Their use as bath flasks, perhaps containing expensively perfumed oil, might help to explain the great variety of images found on the flasks, which include, as here, busts with Ethiopian features, perhaps representing black slaves or bath attendants. In similar vein, a flask from Aldborough shows the familiar figure of a watchman or lantern-bearer waiting to accompany his master home (Bishop 1996, 10). The calyx on the Bishopsgate flask is also a Bacchic reference and representations of the *thiasos* are sometimes found on anthropomorphic flasks. The convex-bodied flask (Cat no 64; Fig 4.5.6) found with the bust is equally unparalleled in London but is of similar capacity and is likely to have had an identical function.

Unusually, all the identified London strigils are made of iron, although as Manning (1985, 79) points out, they are usually found in copper alloy (see also Guildhall Museum 1908, 27, no 357, pl 22). Only one strigil (Cat no 65, Figs 4.5.1 and 4.5.7), was found on an excavation, in a silted channel and due to the

Table 4.5.1 Catalogue of bathing equipment from Londinium

For details of site codes see Table 2; for explanation of zones (column 2) see Figure 4.0.1; accession numbers are Museum of London unless otherwise stated. Standard glass colours as follows: NB = Natural blue glass; NGB = Natural greenish-blue glass; NG = Natural green glass

Nos: Cat (Fig)	Zone	Acc no; findspot (for reserve collection material)	Date: context; form	Object name	Material	Dimensions (mm)	Description	Reference
1 (4.5.1)	6: Sk	A16055; Southwark	—; 2nd–3rd C	bath flask; handle	glass; copper alloy	H 90; RD 28; L (cord) c 60	NB; good quality. Complete flask. Flat rim, edge folded in; each handle formed from a trail applied to shoulder, trailed up neck and folded back. Suspension chain made from a twisted two-strand plaited cord, cf Price & Cottam 1998, 188–9	
2 (4.5.2)	—	2258; London	—; 2nd C	bath flask; handle	glass; copper alloy	H 105; RD 50	NB, good quality with numerous small round bubbles; slight internal weathering. Complete flask reconstructed from fragments. Rim folded in with an angled down profile; each handle applied to shoulder, trailed up the neck, bent out and down into a 'dolphin' form; flattened, slightly concave base	Guildhall Museum 1908, 76, no 17, pl 8 no 4
3 (4.5.3)	—	2262; London	—; 1st C	bath flask	glass	H 70; RD 30	NB; numerous bubbles; unweathered. Complete flask. Rim edge folded in and bent out; flattened base. Each handle applied low on the shoulder, drawn up to form ring and looped back, cf Price & Cottam 1998, 188	
4 (4.5.3)	—	2257; London	—; 2nd–3rd C	bath flask	glass	H 49; RD 35	NGB; thick glass, few bubbles; slight weathering. Complete, with truncated pear-shaped body. Flat wide rim; each handle applied to the shoulder, trailed up the rim and folded back. Copper-alloy wire ring inserted through handle, cf Price & Cottam 1998, 188	
5 (4.5.3)	7: Cem N	35.118/25; 6–13 Spital Square	—; —	bath flask	glass	H 21; RD18	Dark blue, good-quality glass. Complete miniature flask from cemetery. Rim edge turned in and flattened; the aperture, which is only 3mm in diameter, suggests that the vessel was ornamental, used as an unguentarium or, given the funerary context, symbolic, rather than intended for practical use	
6	—	2261; London	—; —	bath flask	glass	H 70; RD 15	NB. Complete, Isings 61; 2nd century; wire handle loop	
7	7: Cem W	2259; Smithfield	—; 2nd C	bath flask	glass	H 50; RD25	NGB. Complete, Isings 61; sub-conical body	
8 (4.5.4)	6: Sk	179BHS89[307]<586>	1st–2nd C; 1st C	bath flask	glass	RD 38	NGB. Rim, neck and two handles. Folded rim with triangular profile; handles attached to shoulder, folded to form loops and attached to neck, with a trail continuing down the centre of the handle	
9	6: Sk	CO87[2378]<884>	70–120; —	bath flask	glass	L 27 ; RD 23	NGB; handle, body	
10	5: West	GHT00[6276]<1718>	1st C; —	bath flask	glass	RD 33	NGB; rim, neck, handles	
11	2: EoW	IME83[228]<220>	3rd C; 1st C	bath flask	glass	RD 30	NGB; rim, handle	
12	2: EoW	ORG86[1034]<129>	late 1st C;	bath flask	glass	L 28	NGB; loop handle	
13	2: EoW	LCT84[4308]<2742>	late 1st C; —	bath flask	glass	L 30	NGB; handle	Shepherd 1993, 112, fig 67, 258
14 (4.5.4)	7: Cem E	SCS83[144]<317>	3rd–4th C; 2nd–3rd C	bath flask	glass	H 21; RD 31	NGB glass. Rim neck and handles from a thin-walled flask of 2nd/3rd century type. Rim folded inwards to form a hollow tube, then folded outwards, very short squat neck; small loop 'dolphin' handles applied to shoulder trailed up the neck to touch the rim, bent out and down; thickened convex base. The body of the vessel is very thin, a development which Allen (1986, 104) dates to the 2nd century	Shepherd 2000, 145, B4.3

Table 4.5.1 Continued

Nos: Cat (Fig)	Zone	Acc no; findspot (for reserve collection material)	Date: context; form	Object name	Material	Dimensions (mm)	Description	Reference
15 (4.5.4)	1: Wal Up	LOW88[312]<515>	–; 2nd C	bath flask	glass	H 21; RD 27	NGB glass. Rim and one handle from a small thin-walled flask. Rim bent out, up and flattened; the small thin ring handle applied to shoulder, trailed out and down and also attached by a trail to the rim	
16 (4.5.4)	2: EoW	PDN81[1475]<2024>]	mid- to late 4th C; –	bath flask	glass	H 17; RD 31.5	NGB glass. Rim folded inward and flattened horizontally. Looped 'dolphin' handles, applied to shoulder, trailed up neck to underside of rim, folded back, with a thin trail running upwards; short neck	
17 (4.5.4)	1: Wal Up	TGM99[851]<62>	250–400; 2nd–3rd C	bath flask	glass	H 57; RD 44	NG. Upper part, rim, neck handles and shoulders of vessel surviving. Folded rim, the top flattened; short neck. The ring handles, which have thick lower terminals are applied to the shoulder and trailed up the neck, cf Price & Cottam 1998, 188	
18	–	78.106/8; London	–; –	bath flask	glass	H 22; RD 29	NG, rim, handles	
19	1: Wal Up	MOG86[63]<20>	1st–2nd C; 2nd C	bath flask	glass		NGB; rim, handle	
20	6: Sk	93BHS74[8]<135>	late 1st–2nd C; –	bath flask	glass	RD 28	NGB; rim, neck, handle	Sheldon & Townend 1978, 462, fig 207, no. 135
21	5: West	GHT00[5580]<1275>	–; 3rd–4th C	bath flask	glass	L 30	NGB; handle and neck	
22	2: EoW	LCT84[9819]<2303>	late 1st C; –	flask	glass	L 40	NGB; rim and neck	Shepherd 1993, 112, 256
23	6: Sk	CO87[1248]<201>	150–200; –	bath flask	glass	L 22; RD 37	NB; rim and neck, no handle	
24	2: EoW	IME83[739]<278>	late 1st C; –	bath flask	glass	H 25	NGB; loop handle	
25	2: EoW	FEN83[2190]<624>	early–mid-2nd C; 1st C	bath flask	glass	H 36	NG; handle	
26	2: EoW	PDN81[756]<294>	late 2nd–early 3rd C; –	bath flask	glass	L 14	NGB; loop handle	
27	1: Wal Mid	BUC87[278]<205>	post-Roman; –	bath flask	glass	L 14	NGB; loop handle	
28	5: West	GYE92[122197]<790>	200+; –	bath flask	glass	H 15	NGB; dolphin handle	
29	5: West	GSM97[2338]<609>	200+; –	bath flask	glass	H 24	NGB; dolphin handle	
30	5: West	GSM97[5611]<295>	150+; –	bath flask	glass	H 28	NGB; dolphin handle	
31	5: West	GSM97[8637]<1492>	150+; –	bath flask	glass	H 24	NGB; dolphin handle	
32	5: West	GHT00[2292]<494>	3rd C; –	bath flask	glass	L 250	NGB; dolphin handle	
33	5: West	GHT00[5757]<1494>	2nd C; –	bath flask	glass	L 26	NGB; handle	
34	5: West	GHT00[5766]<1903>	2nd C; –	bath flask	glass	L 32	NGB; handle	
35	2: EoW	KNG85[533]<165>	late 1st C; –	bath flask	glass	L 45	NGB; body fragment	
36	5: West	FOT01[1025]<9>	–; –	bath flask	glass	RD 41	NGB; rim, handle	Shepherd 1993, 112, 252
37	2: EoW	LCT84[4331]<1823>	late 1st C; –	bath flask	glass	L 57	NGB; body fragment	
38	2: EoW	LCT84[4418]<2722>	late 1st C; –	bath flask	glass	L 81	NGB; body fragment	Shepherd 1993, 112, 253
39	2: EoW	LCT84[6507]<2484>	late 1st C; –	bath flask	glass	L 50	NGB; body fragment	Shepherd 1993, 112, 254
40	2: EoW	LCT84[9577]<2128>	late 1st C; –	bath flask	glass	L 39	NGB; body fragment	Shepherd 1993, 112, 255

Table 4.5.1 Continued

Nos: Cat (Fig)	Zone	Acc no; findspot (for reserve collection material)	Date: context; form	Object name	Material	Dimensions (mm)	Description	Reference
41	2: EoW	LCT84[4459]<2684>	late 1st C; –	bath flask	glass	L 54	NGB; body fragment	
42	7: Cem N	BOS87[229]<193>	late 1st C; –	bath flask	glass	L 26	NB; body fragment	
43	2: EoW	FEN83[2551]<802>	early 2nd C; –	bath flask	glass	L 53	NG; body fragment	
44	1: Wal Up	OPT81[613]<960>	late 1st–early 2nd C; –	bath flask	glass	L 37	NB; body fragment	
45	3: WoW	WAT78[4308]<762>	120–160; –	bath flask	glass	L 31	NG; body fragment	
46	2: EoW	IME83[291]<223>	2nd–3rd C; –	bath flask	glass	L 56	NGB; body fragment	
47	2: EoW	PDN81[1710]<1542>	4th C; –	bath flask	glass	L 36	NGB; body fragment	
48	2: EoW	PDN81[1813]<1631>	4th C; –	bath flask	glass	L 33	NG; body fragment	
49	1: Wal Up	MOG86[6]<258>	post-Roman; –	bath flask	glass	L 40	NG; body fragment	
50	1: Wal Up	LOW88[1300]<591>	–; –	bath flask	glass	L 39	NGB; base	
51	2: EoW	FCC95[588]<204>	post-Roman; –	bath flask	glass	L 58	NGB; base	
52	6: Sk	2530; London	–; –	bath flask	glass	L 34	NG; body fragment	
53	6: Sk	179BHS89[302]<902>	1st C; –	bath flask	glass	L 80	NGB; body fragment	
54	6: Sk	CO88[6018]<1611>	70–120; –	bath flask	glass	L 34	NB; body fragment	
55	6: Sk	COSE84[1284]<409>	70–120; –	bath flask	glass	L 59	NG; body fragment	
56	6: Sk	CO88[6296]<1203>	70–160; –	bath flask	glass	L 39	NG; body fragment	
57	3: WoW	DMT88[3078]<517>	late 1st–2nd C; –	bath flask	glass	L 56	NB; body fragment, ribbed	
58	5: West	BAZ05[771]<869>	–; 2nd–3rd C	bath flask	glass	L 30	NB; body, trail decoration,	
59	7: Cem E	2260; Minories	–; –	bath flask	glass	H 250	NG; almost complete	
60	2: EoW	FER97[1680]<847>	250+; –	flask	glass	H 32	NGB; hexagonal, base, see text	
61	6: Sk	BGH95[2011]<975>	early 2nd C; –	handle	copper alloy	DM (rings) 25	chain and loop handle; 2 rings with chain attached	Wardle 2002b, 224, <R117>
62	6: Sk	201BHS73[54]<7>	late 1st C; –	handle	copper alloy	–	chain and loop handle; fragments only	Townend & Hinton 1978, 156, fig 62, no 7
63 (4.5.5)	2: EoW	ETA89[484]<196a>	2nd C; –	flask	copper alloy	H 64	Almost complete; found with Cat no 64. Anthropomorphic balsamarium, fashioned as the bust of a youth with Ethiopian features, rising from a calyx. The head is well modelled, the hair falling in stylised tiers of curls. The facial features are clearly defined, with full lips, prominent eyes and strongly marked eyelids. A faint line around the neck may be a string for an amuletic pendant seen on Balkan examples (Nenova-Merdjanova 1997, 106). Suspension hook for a swinging handle on each side of the head and a hinge for a tightly fitting lid, now lost. Lower part broken, but on analogy with other examples the flask is likely to have had a pedestal base, cf Faider-Feytmans 1979, no 220, pl 88	

Table 4.5.1 Continued

Nos: Cat (Fig)	Zone	Acc no; findspot (for reserve collection material)	Date: context; form	Object name	Material	Dimensions (mm)	Description	Reference
64 (4.5.6)	2: EoW	ETA89[484]<196b>	2nd C; –	flask	copper alloy	H 64	Almost complete, found with Cat no 63. Biconical flask, now dented and distorted in shape. The narrow neck on which there are two suspension loops expands regularly into the convex body, with linear engraving just above the widest point. Concentric circles are engraved on the underside of the circular base, but only traces of a foot ring survive. There is trace of a small upright collar at the neck, but the lid is lost	
65 (4.5.1, 4.5.7)	6: Sk	170BHS79[49]<18>	1st C; –	strigil	iron	L 215; W 20	Plain rectangular-section handle with narrow slot; U-shaped blade	
66 (4.5.7)	1: Wal Mid	13640; Bank of England	–; –	strigil	iron	L 175	Plain rectangular-section handle, with narrow slot; U-shaped tapering blade.	
67 (4.5.7)	1: Wal Mid	18650; St Swithin's House	1st–2nd C; –	strigil	iron	L 220; W 24	The handle is circular in section, slotted at the sides; semi-circular curved blade	Wilmott 1991, 114, no 295
68	1: Wal Mid	787a; Walbrook	–; –	strigil	iron	L 250	Almost complete, plain rectangular handle	
69	1: Wal Mid	787b; Walbrook	–; –	strigil	iron	L 165	Incomplete, loop handle	
70	1: Wal Mid	3547; Walbrook	–; –	strigil	iron	L 225	Incomplete, long handle loop	
71	1: Wal Mid	3450; Walbrook	–; –	strigil	iron	L 165	Incomplete, narrow slotted handle	
72	–	29.94/14a	–; –	strigil	iron	L 120	Incomplete, curved blade	
73	1: Wal Mid	A14415; Walbrook	–; –	strigil	iron/ iron/ copper alloy	L 125	Incomplete, handle with copper-alloy bands, cross-hatched	
74	–	786	–; –	strigil	iron	L 130	Incomplete, slotted handle	
75	1: Wal Mid	A29.94/14b; Walbrook	–; –	strigil	iron	L 150	Incomplete, slotted handle, line decoration, inscribed X, blade broken	
76	1: Wal Mid	2469; Walbrook	–; –	strigil	iron	L 130	Incomplete, rectangular handle	
77	1: Wal Mid	BM P&EE 1883,0404.13; Walbrook	–; –	strigil	iron	L 210	Complete; handle loop	Manning 1985, 79, K1

Fig 4.5.2 Bath flask (Cat no 2) in the Museum of London's collections (height 105mm)

perishable material it is unsurprising that most of the examples in the Museum's permanent collection are from the waterlogged deposits of the Walbrook valley. All are plain and functional forms with minimal decoration, but several show the diagnostic handle loop.

Discussion – distribution

This survey has identified some 62 glass flasks and metal fittings, two copper-alloy flasks and thirteen strigils; of these 77 objects, 66 can be ascribed to a relatively close find spot. For convenience and to permit comparison with the accompanying papers (Crummy, Shepherd and Henig, all this volume) the sites have been assigned to zones identified by the topographic areas and progressive development of Londinium (Fig 4.0.1). The locations of the bath houses or bath suites are shown in Figure 4.5.8.

Clearly there are no groups of flasks from bath house drains as seen at Caerleon and the only fragments from known bath house sites are one from the early bath at Huggin Hill (Cat no 57) and three

Fig 4.5.3 Bath flasks (Cat nos 3, 4, 5) in the Museum of London's collections (height of tallest flask 70mm)

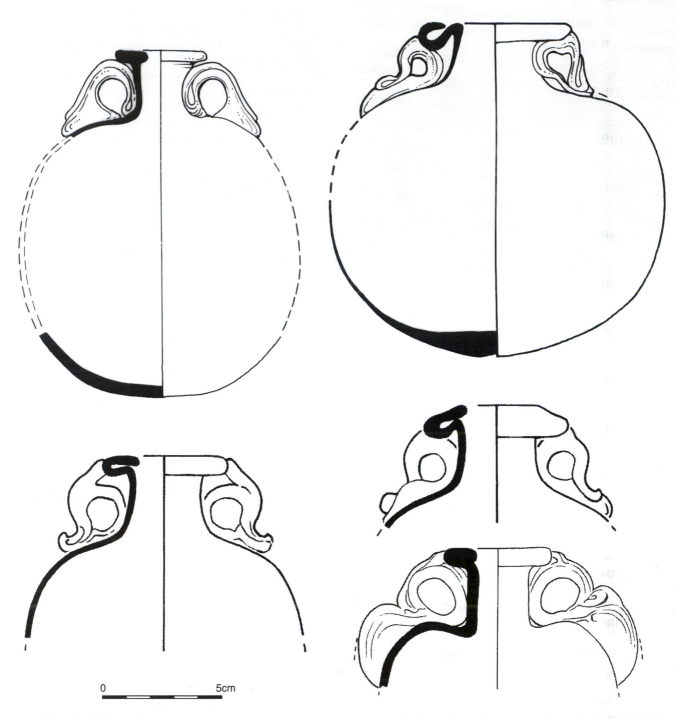

0   5cm

Fig 4.5.4 Bath flasks from excavated contexts (Cat nos, top row: 8, 14; bottom left: 15; bottom right: 16, 17)

from the 4th-century bath at Pudding Lane (Cat nos 26, 47 and 48), thought to be a private suite. There is an apparent cluster in the area of the Cheapside baths and larger numbers generally from sites east of the Walbrook than on the western side of the town. In absolute numbers (and the map shows findspots only) there are twenty fragments from seven sites east of the Walbrook, seven from five sites in the Walbrook valley, and thirteen from eight sites in the western side of the city. Where the fragments can be dated typologically, and most are undiagnostic body sherds, they appear to correlate with the dates of the nearest structures, with early

forms in the Forum area (Lime Street) and in the Cheapside area, and later vessels at Pudding Lane. In Southwark the eleven fragments come from nine sites, but six of these are in the area of Borough High Street. An additional fragment has been tentatively identified from the York Clinic site at 117 Borough High Street (BHB00; Cool forthcoming, cat no 90) and there is a flask of unusual form from a cemetery in nearby Lant Street (John Shepherd pers comm).

The picture is therefore of a fairly wide scatter, some in the general vicinity of bath houses, but there are factors which affect the deposition of glass

Fig 4.5.5 *Copper-alloy flask in the form of bust (Cat no 63) (height 64mm)*

Fig 4.5.6 *Copper-alloy flask (Cat no 64) (height 64mm)*

in London which may account for some of the concentrations seen in Figure 4.5.8. There are seven fragments from the 1st-century groups at Leadenhall Court (LCT84). These are closely associated with the buildings on the site and in discussing the well-preserved assemblage, which contains many large vessel fragments, John Shepherd has suggested that the glass was thrown away when the buildings were demolished for the construction of the basilica, at a time when there were no recycling facilities in the town (Shepherd 1993, 100). The practice of recycling vessel and window glass as cullet has been well demonstrated by the discovery of the massive early 2nd-century dump at Guildhall Yard (GYE92; Pérez-Sala Rodés and Shepherd forthcoming) and there is increasing evidence for glass-blowing workshops at various times.

Nevertheless the distribution may have some significance. The flasks at Leadenhall Court were found in private domestic contexts – the 1st-century inhabitants were clearly accustomed to Roman ways of bathing and the nearest bath house at this time may have been at Lime Street. It is possible the higher number of fragments from east of the Walbrook, particularly at this early period, might suggest a greater degree of 'Romanisation' than in the west, but the numbers are too small to be statistically viable.

There is a cluster in the western area from a limited number of sites and while they are quite close to the Cheapside baths, they are also close to the Guildhall Yard cullet dump, and there are fragments of production waste also on a site in Gresham Street (GHT00). It is worth noting that the Guildhall assemblage contains waste fragments, which might, according to a modern glass-blower (John Shepherd pers comm) be from the production of short-necked flasks such as *aryballoi*, so it is possible that this essential commodity was being manufactured (and recycled) in the town.

The group of flasks in the Borough High Street area of Southwark and the only excavated strigil are of interest as recent work on the building material assemblages from sites in the area (Pringle in Cowan *et al* forthcoming) has identified ceramic water pipes, box-flue tiles and elongated stone *tesserae*, suggestive of a bath house in the vicinity, although all the material is dumped in 2nd-century contexts. It is possible therefore that an early bath house existed in this part of Southwark, although its size and status is unknown.

The presence of twelve of the iron strigils on sites in and around the Walbrook raises the question of ritual deposition as opposed to rubbish disposal (Wilmott 1991; Merrifield 1995), the arguments for which are summarised by Nina Crummy (this volume; see also Merrifield and Hall, this volume). While it is certain that flasks and strigils sometimes appear as grave goods, and at least three of the London flasks are from cemeteries, the absence of iron strigils in other parts of the town may be due to the soil conditions. It may be significant that the

Fig 4.5.7 Iron strigils (Cat nos from top to bottom: 67, 65, 66) (length of top strigil 220mm)

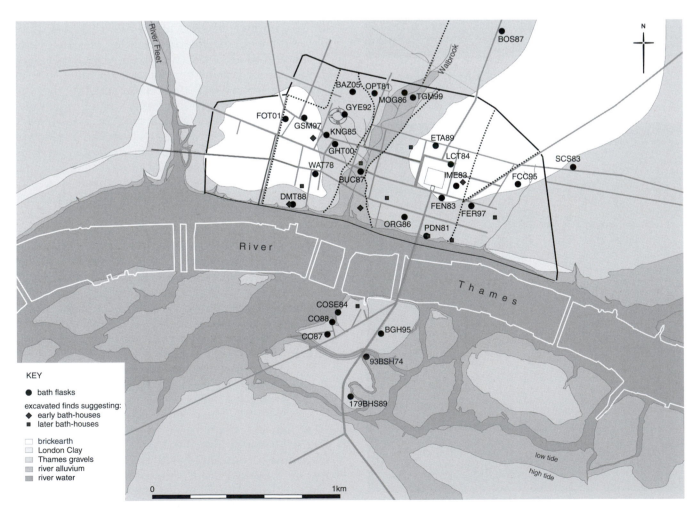

Fig 4.5.8 Distribution of bath flask fragments and location of known bath houses in London and Southwark

only excavated strigil from Southwark (Cat no 65) was also found in a waterlogged channel backfill, but with domestic rubbish. The Walbrook strigils are not accompanied by a significant number of bath flasks, but it must again be asked why so many apparently serviceable complete iron implements have been discarded in and around the stream.

Conclusion

The provision of baths in Londinium was dependent upon Roman technology, and the use of olive oil and method of bathing was not a local tradition. Their introduction can be seen as part of the process of 'Romanisation' in the province, but the question of the identity of those using the baths is more complex. In London, although the evidence is not extensive, baths are known to have existed at all periods and the distribution of glass bath flasks, again not numerous, is widespread both spatially and through time. The 1st-century concentration of flasks in the eastern part of the town, notably in the area around the forum and later basilica, and in early dumps in Southwark suggests that Roman bathing was an important part of everyday life from the very beginning of the town's development.

Acknowledgements

This paper aims to shed a little more light on the social history and meaning of artefacts in context (Nixon *et al* 2002, 37), thereby contributing another small building block in the history of Londinium which has always been of such importance to Harvey Sheldon.

Research for this paper was generously funded by a grant from the City of London Archaeological Trust. The author is also grateful to Francis Grew, Jenny Hall, John Shepherd and Roy Stephenson for help in compilation of the dataset and to Sue Pringle for discussions on the building materials.

4.6 Small toilet instruments from London: a review of the evidence *Nina Crummy with Christie Pohl*

Introduction

Small metal toilet sets of the Roman period in Britain usually consisted of tweezers, an earscoop, and a bifid nail-cleaner linked together on a ring or a shackle loop, though a few sets were more elaborate. Many instruments were disassociated in antiquity and are now individual finds, but some with no suspension loop were never linked. Part of a set was found in close association with a cosmetic set in a late 1st- to 2nd-century building at Blossom's Inn, Lawrence Lane, London, a pairing also seen in graves at Chichester and Verulamium (Table 4.6.1, Cat no 1; Jackson 1985; 1993b; Down and Rule 1971, 87, fig 5.18, 228u–z; Stead and Rigby 1989, 104, fig 126, 203/2–5).

Recent work has identified several characteristics of toilet sets in general and nail-cleaners in particular. In the La Tène period in Britain toilet sets are rare and their use was restricted to a social elite, but the creation of the new province in the mid-1st century triggered a surge in production that allowed them to be acquired by a wider segment of society. The bifid nail-cleaner is an insular survival from the earlier La Tène tradition; it is common in Britain from the mid-1st to the late 4th/early 5th century but is rarely found in Roman contexts on the Continent. Some nail-cleaner types have distributions conforming to tribal or *civitas* areas, pointing to regional manufacture and marketing. Nail-cleaners are most often found in small towns and minor nucleated settlements, with only comparatively low numbers recorded from large towns. Finally, toilet instruments are often found as *ex votos* at temples and shrines in both town and country (Crummy and Eckardt 2004; Eckardt 2005).

These results come from a dataset compiled from published excavation reports and have been confirmed by further work (Crummy 2004; Eckardt and Crummy forthcoming). However, the bias in the social context towards small settlements is open to question when there is a backlog in the publication of Roman small finds from excavations in several large towns, including London. This paper therefore reviews a group of toilet instruments from London, only 28% of which have already been published, setting them against the backdrop of the characteristics of production, distribution and deposition outlined above. A limited programme of metallurgical analysis introduces new data to the study.

Catalogue

Only toilet instruments with secure provenances in the walled Roman city and its immediate suburbs have been used. Grave finds, châtelaine brooches and surgical forceps have been excluded (but for forceps see Jackson, this volume), but a detached brooch implement has been included and a small number of tweezers found singly cannot be unequivocally defined as either toilet or medical instruments. Two published items have also been omitted as they cannot be identified among the museum collection and the accession numbers cited for them belong to different instruments (Wilmott 1991, fig 84, 345–6). The final assemblage numbers 86 items, with linked sets numbered as one piece; there are 105 instruments in total. Two further points need to be raised: first, corrosion often obscures any surface decoration on unconserved items, and second, the context details of objects from unpublished excavations are not always available, though broad date ranges are usually implicit in the site summaries (to be found in Schofield and Maloney 1998; Thompson *et al* 1998; LAARC 2006).

Table 4.6.1 catalogues each instrument in the sample and gives the relevant figure number if an instrument is illustrated. Sets and part sets are listed first, followed by single finds by instrument type. The address and National Grid Reference for each site are given in the site list, Table 2.

Date and distribution

Many of the instruments are associated with 1st- or 2nd-century buildings but there are none from bath buildings and their practical use seems to have been confined to the home. The proximity of the Blossom's Inn toilet set and cosmetic grinder to the Cheapside baths (Jackson 1993b, 166) must be coincidental, and emphasis should instead be laid upon their context within an early Roman timber building. Only one diagnostically late Roman piece is catalogued, a highly decorated tubular nail-cleaner from Bermondsey Abbey (Cat no 36; Fig 4.6.3), a site beyond the study area but included here to make the point of absence within it, intriguingly matched by a similar absence of late Roman nail-cleaner strap-ends (Eckardt and Crummy 2006). A dearth of late Roman nail-cleaners from Southwark is expected, given its decline in that period, while a similar absence within the walled town might be the result of several factors, such as a reduced population or the truncation of the late Roman levels, but there is a strong possibility that 4th-century Londoners did not engage with this particular aspect of Romano-British material culture.

The distribution of the London toilet instruments is illustrated in Figure 4.6.1 and summarised in Table 4.6.1, column 2. Each item is assigned to

Table 4.6.1 Catalogue of small toilet implements from London

For details of site codes see Table 2; for explanation of zones (column 2) see Figure 4.0.1; accession numbers are Museum of London unless otherwise stated. Type/Group (column 6) and EC cat no (column 11) refer to the dataset of toilet instruments compiled by Eckardt and Crummy (forthcoming; Crummy and Eckardt 2004).

Nos: Cat (Fig)	Zone	Acc no; site	Set	Instrument/ method of suspension	Type/Group	Material	Length (mm)	Description	Reference	EC cat no
1	3: WoW	94.111/3; (WFG41[63]<51>)	part set	nail-cleaner	Baldock	leaded bronze	37.5	Nail-cleaner damaged; with marginal grooves; tweezers straight-sided, ?plain	Jackson 1993b	301
				tweezers	—		36			578
2 (4.6.4, 7)	1: Wal Mid	21732; King's Arms Yard	set	nail-cleaner	wire loop	leaded brass	56	Nail-cleaner and earscoop have seven coils around the top of shaft	—	—
				earscoop	—		55			—
				tweezers	—		55.5			—
				shackle	shackle		—			—
3 (4.6.2)	1: Wal Mid	13859; Bank of England	part set	earscoop	—	iron	—	Tweezers have one horizontal and four diagonal incised lines on the top of the blades	—	—
				tweezers	penannular		54			—
				suspension ring	—		59.5			
4 (4.6.4, 6)	1: Wal Mid	19602; Bucklersbury House	set	nail-cleaner	penannular	leaded gunmetal	55	Nail-cleaner has a long neck with diagonal incised lines on one side only, and the blade has a median groove; tweezers have a marginal groove on one blade only	Merrifield 1965, pl 137, 3, shows earscoop with set, but this is now absent. de la Bédoyère (1989, fig 70, b–e) also shows an earscoop, but this is a rogue compilation as scoop has pointed shaft that could not be suspended	98
				earscoop	—		missing			607
				tweezers	—		54			606
				suspension ring	penannular		—			—
5 (4.6.2)	1: Wal Mid	19787; Bucklersbury House	part set	earscoop	—	copper alloy	60	Unusually, the earscoop is longer than the tweezers	—	—
				tweezers	—		50.5			—
6	1: Wal Mid	20089; Bucklersbury House	part set	nail-cleaner	penannular narrow leaf-shape with latticed neck	copper alloy	54	Nail-cleaner is as Cat nos 10 and 8 with marginal grooves and lattice decoration on one side of neck only. The earscoop has incised crosses on shaft	parallel: Trow 1988, fig 25, 19	—
				earscoop	—		missing			—
				suspension ring	—		missing			
7 (4.6.2)	—	A20136; London Wall	set	nail-cleaner	?penannular	leaded bronze	55	Originally with two nail-cleaners (one missing since at least 1974). All the instruments apart from the tweezers have bead-and-reel mouldings; the beads are grooved. The plate is decorated with enamel panels and knurling, and its suspension loop sits on a central knob	Wheeler 1930, pl 39. Compare similar set from Castleford, Cool and Philo 1998, 86, fig 31, 363	168
				nail-cleaner	—		missing			644
				earscoop	—		54			643
				tweezers	—		52.5			640
				file	—		54.5			642
				mini-scalpel	—		54			641
				suspension plate	bar and plate		32			—
8 (4.6.4, 4)	1: Wal Up	BM P&E 2005,0402.72, Moorgate	set	nail-cleaner	narrow leaf-shape with decorated neck	copper alloy	51	Nail-cleaner has long narrow straight shaft with slight shoulders, and small lip below a latticed neck; tweezers have flared blades with marginal grooves	Paralleled by Cat no 6, and by Trow 1988, fig 25, 19, from Puckeridge-Braughing	—
				earscoop	—		44			—
				tweezers	—		51			—
				suspension ring	penannular		—			

Table 4.6.1 Continued

Nos: Cat (Fig)	Zone	Acc no; site	Set	Instrument/method of suspension	Type/Group	Material	Length (mm)	Description	Reference	EC cat no
9 (4.6.4, 5)	6: Sk	A12018; Swan Street, Borough	set	nail-cleaner	grooved shoulder	leaded brass	45	Nail-cleaner has large suspension loop, no neck, incised grooves on the shoulders, and marginal grooves	Compare Crummy 1992, 212, fig 6.8, 96 from Colchester; Essex CC Field Archaeology Unit, HYEF94 SF 2742 [4000] from Heybridge, Essex	–
				earscoop			60			–
				tweezers	penannular		33			–
				suspension ring			–			–
10	6: Sk	15SKS80[148]<2724>	set	nail-cleaner	Baldock variant plain	copper alloy	47	Nail-cleaner has mouldings on neck, marginal grooves; suspension loop damaged; earscoop has round-section shaft; tweezers have flared blades and marginal grooves. From 2nd- or 3rd-C demolition debris	Stevenson 1992, 89, fig 23, 42	198
				earscoop			53			587
				tweezers			51			588
11	8: Fleet	VAL88[12533]<4989>	–	nail-cleaner	Baldock	leaded bronze	45	Marginal grooves, shoulders very rounded. From southern eyot near jetty	–	–
12	8: Fleet	VAL88[12533]<4990>	–	nail-cleaner	Baldock	copper alloy	35? (missing)	Length from accession card. From southern eyot near jetty	–	–
13	2: EoW	LCT84[9843]<2019>	–	nail-cleaner	Baldock	leaded gunmetal	22	Fragment, top of blade and part of loop only. From Period 4 midden, c AD 80–90	Milne and Wardle 1993, no 55	200
14 (4.6.4, 1)	4: East Up	LEA84[928]<96>	–	nail-cleaner	Baldock	leaded bronze	39	Marginal grooves. From post-Roman dump	Crummy and Eckardt 2004, 51–2	–
15	6: Sk	COSE84[1334]<411>	–	nail-cleaner	Baldock	copper alloy	51	Marginal grooves, one point missing; in 2 fragments. From 4th-C robbing	Wardle 2003, <S43>	1049
16	6: Sk	BGH95[3057]<691>	–	nail-cleaner	Baldock	copper alloy	44	From 2nd-C occupation	Wardle 2002b, 224, fig 110 <R114>	1044
17	2: EoW	SUF94[623]<101>	–	nail-cleaner	Baldock	copper alloy	39.5	Marginal grooves. From early 2nd-C dump behind waterfront	Wardle 2001, 05, fig 23, <S9>	–
18	4: East Low	PUB80[535]<7>	–	nail-cleaner	?Baldock	copper alloy	34	In fragments, distintegrating. From a Roman gravel surface	–	–
19	3: WoW	IRO80[558]<137>	–	nail-cleaner	Baldock variant	leaded bronze	29 approx	Cast mouldings on neck; grooved neck, blade very corroded	–	–
20	1: Wal	LYD88[2172]<796>	–	nail-cleaner	Baldock variant	copper alloy	47?	Marginal grooves, grooved neck; object on loan, length from accession card	–	–
21 (4.6.4, 2)	–	81.556/6; ?Walbrook or waterfront	–	nail-cleaner	Baldock variant	copper alloy	40.5	Grooved neck. Found on the corporation fly-tipping site, but probably from Walbrook or waterfront	Crummy and Eckardt 2004, 52	–
22 (4.6.4, 3)	4: East Up	26389	–	nail-cleaner	Baldock variant	leaded bronze	50	Grooved neck	Chapman and Johnson 1973, 46, fig 21, 4	194
23	6: Sk	207BHS72[T2, F6, L13]<36>	–	nail-cleaner	Baldock variant	copper alloy	22	Marginal grooves, grooved neck, lower part of blade missing. From pre-Flavian channel fill	SLAEC 1978, 57, 82, 156, fig 62, 2	169
24	4: East Low	PEP89[33]<395>	–	nail-cleaner	?Baldock	copper alloy	22	Lower part only; marginal grooves on both faces; file marks on surface. From late Roman dark earth	–	–

Table 4.6.1 Continued

Nos: Cat (Fig)	Zone	Acc no; site	Set	Instrument/ method of suspension	Type/Group	Material	Length (mm)	Description	Reference	EC cat no
25 (4.6.3)	1: Wal	19574; Bucklersbury House	–	nail-cleaner	–	leaded brass	60	Long narrow shaft and incised grooves on the twisted neck	–	–
26 (4.6.3)	1: Wal	20375; Bucklersbury House	–	nail-cleaner	–	leaded bronze	65	Slight shoulders, incised cross on both sides of the top of the blade and another between transverse grooves on only one side of the neck. Not part of a well-defined group	Similar from Monkton, Kent (Perkins 1985, fig 7, 20), and Colchester (mid-1st C) (Hawkes and Hull 1947, pl 100, 36)	–
27 (4.6.3)	1: Wal Mid	20771; Bucklersbury House	–	nail-cleaner	châtelaine brooch	copper alloy	59.5	From a châtelaine brooch, with typical enamel motif. Such brooches have not been included here, but detached instruments may have been used individually	Crummy 2001, 5; Hattatt 1985, fig 69, 603	–
28 (4.6.3)	1: Wal Up	COV87[151]<92>	–	nail-cleaner	–	copper alloy	50	Long plain neck and grooves across the shoulders on both sides of the blade	–	–
29	1: Wal Up	OPT81[450]<462>	–	nail-cleaner	–	copper alloy	28	Fragment, lower part of blade with marginal grooves. From early–mid-2nd-C occupation	–	–
30 (4.6.3)	2: EoW	LCT84[4229]<1150>	–	nail-cleaner	lugged neck	leaded gunmetal	39	Angular lugs at neck; blade leaf-shaped; points missing. A second example from London with a straight-sided blade is not catalogued as it is not closely provenanced	Smith 1859, 129, pl 33, 8; Ward 1911, 262, fig 70, D	–
31	2: EoW	LCT84[4485]<1459>	–	nail-cleaner	cast neck	copper alloy	14	Fragment, neck with small part of loop and shoulders; 3 reels on the neck. From midden, pre-dating AD 75	Milne and Wardle 1993, fig 42, 54	199
32	2: EoW	LCT84[3482]<173>	–	nail-cleaner	–	copper alloy	43 (as straight)	Plain, flared blade, like tweezers; bent. From road north of basilica	–	–
33	6: Sk	106BHS73[C36]<19>	–	nail-cleaner	swollen blade	copper alloy	40	Blade swells to centre. From Claudian-Neronian layer	SLAEC 1978, 178, 181, 191, 216, fig 94, 80	170
34	6: Sk	1STS74[T8 14]<298>	–	nail-cleaner	hunchback	copper alloy	58	Median groove on one side; shoulders damaged. From pit, with late 1st-C pottery	SLAEC 1978, 390, fig 177, 122	171
35	6: Sk	199BHS74[207]<30>	–	nail-cleaner	other straight-sided	copper alloy	41	Upper shaft square in section with rounded corners, lower flattened. From 2nd- to 4th-C layer	Hinton 1988, 111–12, 387, fig 175, 54	172
36 (4.6.3)	6: Sk	BA84[1]<361>	–	nail-cleaner	late Roman tubular	copper alloy	56	Highly decorated late Roman tubular form. Unstratified	cf close parallels from Verulamium (Kenyon 1934, fig 12, 17–18), Kelvedon (Rodwell 1988, fig 48, 45), Wanborough (Hooley 2001, fig 45, 206), and Caernarfon (Allason-Jones 1993, fig 10.5, 72)	–
37	2: EoW	LCT84[9868]<2212>	–	?nail-cleaner	–	copper alloy	22	Fragment; identification doubtful. From midden, c AD 80–90	Milne and Wardle 1993, no 56	201

Table 4.6.1 Continued

Nos: Cat (Fig)	Zone	Acc no; site	Set	Instrument/ method of suspension	Type/Group	Material	Length (mm)	Description	Reference	EC cat no
38	8: Fleet	VAL88[12533]<4992>	—	earscoop	—	copper alloy	64	Shaft tapers from square at top to rectangular above scoop; loop at right angles to scoop. From southern eyot near jetty	—	—
39	1: Wal Mid	19453; Bucklersbury House	—	earscoop	—	copper alloy	54	—	—	—
40	1: Wal Mid	20342; Bucklersbury House	—	earscoop	—	copper alloy	54	Not suspensible	—	—
41	1: Wal Mid	19133; Bucklersbury House	—	earscoop	—	copper alloy	44.5	Not suspensible	—	—
42	2: EoW	LDL88[1651]<302>	—	earscoop	—	copper alloy	36	Upper terminal missing; oval scoop	—	—
43	—	762; London Wall	—	earscoop	—	copper alloy	55	—	—	—
44	—	750; London Wall	—	earscoop	—	copper alloy	65	Not suspensible	—	—
45 (4.6.3)	8: Fleet	VAL88[0]<5071>	—	tweezers	—	copper alloy	38	Groups of transverse grooves on each blade. Unstratified	—	—
46	8: Fleet	VAL88[0]<1666>	—	tweezers	—	copper alloy	57	Blades flared, grips either missing or not formed. Unstratified	—	—
47	5: West	GPO75[9190]<3461>	—	tweezers	—	copper alloy	42	Blades flared	—	—
48	5: West	GPO75[9259]<3460>	—	tweezers	—	copper alloy	35	Blades flared, in fragments	—	—
49	5: West	GPO75[10642]<4293>	—	tweezers	—	copper alloy	—	In fragments	—	—
50	5: West	GPO75[11553]<2197>	—	tweezers	—	copper alloy	32	Part of one flared blade	—	—
51	5: West	POM79[2126]<268>	—	tweezers	—	copper alloy	65	Blades flared, with sliding loop	—	—
52	3: WoW	14547; Queen Street	—	tweezers	—	copper alloy	63	Blades straight	—	—
53	3: WoW	ABS86[191]<14>	—	tweezers	—	copper alloy	48	In fragments; flared blades	—	—
54	1: Wal Mid	19178; Bucklersbury House	—	tweezers	—	copper alloy	59	Blades flared	—	862
55	1: Wal Mid	19878; Bucklersbury House	?part set	tweezers; suspension ring	penannular	copper alloy	54; —	Blades flared; —	—	—
56	1: Wal Up	A238; Copthall Court	—	tweezers	—	copper alloy	38	Marginal grooves on blades	—	—
57	1: Wal Up	59.94/9; Copthall Court	?part set	tweezers; suspension ring	—	copper alloy	53	Fragment only	—	—
58	1: Wal	18184; Walbrook	—	tweezers	—	copper alloy	71	Marginal grooves on blades	Shepherd 1998, fig 167, 48	328
59	1: Wal	18246; Walbrook	—	tweezers	—	copper alloy	47.5	—	Shepherd 1998, fig 170, 51	329
60	1: Wal Up	AST87[186]<71>	—	tweezers	—	copper alloy	57 (as straight)	Blades flared, bent at right angles, corroded	—	—
61	1: Wal Up	LOW88[2303]<809>	—	tweezers	—	copper alloy	50 (bent)	Blades flare slightly just above grip. From 1st- to early 2nd-C waterlain deposit and dump	—	—
62	1: Wal Up	MGT87[385]<9>	—	tweezers	—	copper alloy	42	In fragments; narrow flared blades	—	—
63	1: Wal Up	OPT81[641]<850>	—	tweezers	—	copper alloy	55	Blades slightly flared. From late 1st- to 2nd-C dump	—	—
64	7: Cem N	ELD88[39]<10>	—	tweezers	—	copper alloy	49?	Heavily corroded	—	—
65	2: EoW	LCT84[3482]<172>	—	tweezers	—	copper alloy	50	Blades flared, ?mouldings below spring loop; corroded. From road north of basilica	—	—
66	2: EoW	LEN89[866]<145>	—	?tweezers	—	copper alloy	53	In fragments, very corroded, identification doubtful	—	—

Table 4.6.1 Continued

Nos: Cat (Fig)	Zone	Acc no; site	Set	Instrument/ method of suspension	Type/Group	Material	Length (mm)	Description	Reference	EC cat no
67	2: EoW	LDL88[1750]<297>	–	tweezers	–	copper alloy	49?	Object on loan, length taken from accession card; possibly small medical forceps	–	–
68	2: EoW	BIP88[468]<89>	–	tweezers	–	copper alloy	46	In fragments; blades straight-sided	–	–
69	2: EoW	81.556/7; ?Miles Lane (Peninsula House)	–	tweezers	–	copper alloy	46	Marginal grooves on blades; most of one blade missing, the other bent outwards	–	–
70	4: East Up	FCS87[929]<132>	–	tweezers	–	copper alloy	44	In fragments, very corroded	–	–
71	4: East Low	RAG82[1595]<742>	–	tweezers	–	copper alloy	43	Blades flared, corroded. From silt over pit, early–mid-2nd C	–	–
72	4: East Low	RAG82[1500]<40>	–	tweezers	–	copper alloy	56	Straight blades. From ditch fill, early–mid-2nd C	–	–
73	4: East Low	THL78(b)[33]<6>	–	tweezers	–	copper alloy	60	Straight blades	Whipp 1980, 65, fig 11, 1	583
74	7: Cem N	A17950; Moorfields	–	tweezers	–	copper alloy	57	Blades slightly flared	–	–
75	7: Cem N	ISH88[369]<14>	–	tweezers	–	copper alloy	40	Part of one blade missing; bent	–	–
76	–	773; London Wall	–	tweezers	–	copper alloy	77	–	–	–
77	–	A23805; 'Thames Street'	–	tweezers	–	copper alloy	54	Flared; moulded loop (an LIA/ early Roman feature)	–	–
78	–	87.122/17; ?Billings-gate excavation (BIG82)	?part set	tweezers suspension ring	–	copper alloy	54 –	Blades slightly flared; fragment only of suspension ring. From Hackney Road spoil heap, possibly from BIG82	–	–
79	6: Sk	207BHS72[T3 L3]<19>	–	tweezers	–	copper alloy	46	Straight blades, jaws ?missing. From Flavian layer	SLAEC 1978, 65, 85, 156, fig 62, 10	–
80	6: Sk	COSE84[1746]<588>	–	tweezers	–	copper alloy	51	Marginal grooves; in 3 fragments. From late Roman robbing	Wardle 2003, 157, <S41>	1047
81	6: Sk	CO87[2076]<472>	–	tweezers	–	copper alloy	33	Flared blades, lower part missing; in 2 fragments. 3rd–early 4th C	–	–
82	6: Sk	52SOS89[1]<25>	–	tweezers	–	copper alloy	45	Flared blades, most of one blade missing. Unstratified	–	–
83	6: Sk	15–23SKS[128]<4035>	–	tweezers	–	copper alloy	–	Fragment. From 2nd-C make-up containing 1st-C material	Stevenson 1992, 89, no 48	584
84	6: Sk	BGH95 [698]<664>	–	tweezers	–	copper alloy	49	In fragments. From a 2nd-C alley	Wardle 2002b, 224, <R115>	1045
85	6: Sk	BGH95[43]<51>	–	tweezers	–	copper alloy	54	From a drain, robbed in 4th C	Wardle 2002b, 224, <R116>	1046
86	2: EoW	SUF94[689]<124>	–	tweezers	–	copper alloy	42.5	Flared blades with marginal grooves. From an early 2nd-C dump behind waterfront	Wardle 2001, 95, <S10>	–

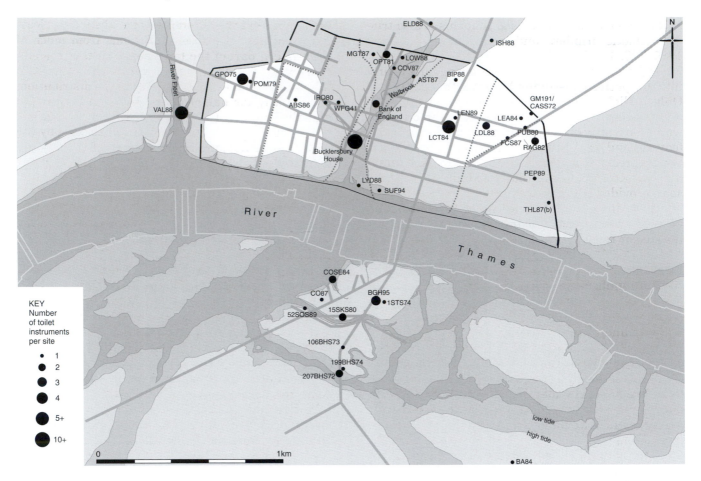

Fig 4.6.1 Distribution map of toilet implements in London

a topographic/settlement zone, as defined by dotted lines on Figure 4.6.1. The differences in the street grid in the zones west and east of the Walbrook may reflect the status of the inhabitants, with a military area in the west, a *conventus civium Romanorum* in the east, and perhaps a settlement of non-citizens in Southwark (Millett 1994, 433–4; Rowsome 1998, 38), therefore the British character of the bifid nail-cleaner may provide some matching differences in toilet instrument distribution.

The most noticeable characteristic of the distribution is the high number of items, particularly sets and part sets, in the Walbrook zone, with a marked concentration in the middle Walbrook valley. Merrifield (1965, 93; 1987, 26–7; 1995, 27–44) has argued convincingly that the middle Walbrook material is an assemblage of votive offerings (see also Merrifield and Hall, this volume), equivalent to similar concentrations in watery contexts both in Britain and on the Continent, but Wilmott (1991, 61–7) has instead suggested that they derived from rubbish dumped to assist in land reclamation. Maloney (1991), reviewing Wilmott, stressed that votive artefacts need not be overtly religious in form or function and that apposite assemblage comparison, particularly with waterfront sites with dump deposits, might clarify the controversy.

Figure 4.6.1 provides such a comparison, and clearly shows that the concentration of toilet

instruments in the middle Walbrook valley is wholly remarkable within *Londinium*, and even within the Walbrook valley. The numbers plotted could be further reinforced by those found at 1 Poultry in 1994 (ONE94) and by other finds of votive character from the same site (Wardle 1998, 83–6). The middle Walbrook assemblage may be flawed in its methods of retrieval and recording, but it clearly represents a genuine anomaly within the general distribution of controlled finds recovery in London, even more so if it is incomplete (Wilmott 1991, 66–7; Merrifield 1995, 27). The condition of the objects (as opposed to the preservation of the metal) is a major factor that also needs to be taken into consideration, and is best demonstrated by comparing the many complete sets and intact instruments from the middle Walbrook with the three nail-cleaners from the middens at Leadenhall Court (LCT84), all of them damaged single instruments and clearly more reasonably interpreted as discarded rubbish (Cat nos 13, 31, 37). The intact condition of the Walbrook items also militates against their representing the clearance of debris after the Boudican fire: none is scorched or deformed by contact with fire.

Turning to Maloney's first point, the practice of using toilet instruments and other small *personalia* as *ex votos* has often been noted (eg Mackreth 1986; Bagnall Smith 1995; 1998; Johns 1996b; Simpson and Blance 1998), and in the context of the present study it should be emphasised that this is also true for cosmetic grinders and nail-cleaners (Jackson 1985, 172; 1993b, 167; Crummy and Eckardt 2004, 60–1). The middle Walbrook assemblage fits neatly into this pattern, justifying Merrifield's conclusions. Only a slight change of emphasis is required, as offerings could be deposited not only directly into water but also on adjacent wetland, or in open features and small scrapes in the soil within or near temple precincts and shrines on dry sites, the unifying characteristic being that proximity to a sacred spot provided the liminal context necessary for effective interaction between the earth-bound devotee and the divine being whose aid was being invoked or repaid (see also Merrifield and Hall, this volume).

Merrifield's interpretation is further supported by the low number of toilet instruments from Thames waterfront sites. (An object from a post-Roman context on the waterfront Custom House site is not a nail-cleaner; Tatton-Brown 1974, 188, fig 36, 20.) An important exception is a cluster of five found around the jetty on the southern eyot in the mouth of the River Fleet. Though this group is too small to be unequivocally identified as votive, it is worth noting that a large octagonal structure, tentatively identified as a Romano-Celtic temple, built in the later Roman period on a hilltop overlooking the Fleet, may parallel the construction of the Mithraeum in the middle Walbrook valley (Spence *et al* 1989, 16–17; Shepherd 1998), suggesting that the lower Fleet valley might also have been a traditional focus of ritual activity.

In terms of social context, only tweezers were found in the western suburb and the Cripplegate fort, a style of toilet instrument consumption and use matched on military sites elsewhere in Britain and supported by the low number of nail-cleaners from military establishments in general (Crummy and Eckardt 2004, 49). The fort itself post-dates the initial surge in toilet instrument production. No items come from the grid of streets lying between the fort and the Thames, making the set from Blossom's Inn unusual in both its location and its almost intact condition. Some of the instruments west of the upper Walbrook are likely to be from dump deposits, others may be votives. East of the Walbrook the picture is different. Though large areas have no finds there are several pieces, many of them nail-cleaners, in the eastern part of the orthogonally gridded area, including some from timber buildings pre-dating the construction of the forum-basilica, and several in the eastern suburb, particularly from timber buildings pre-dating the town wall and close to the main north-east road. In Southwark the spread appears little different to that in the eastern part of the town and the eastern suburb.

The distinction in distribution between east and west of the Walbrook provides evidence for a military/civilian dichotomy, though the Blossom's Inn set and the influence of the Walbrook valley both show that the difference is not absolutely clear-cut. Similarly, the absence of items from much of the eastern part of the town supports the idea of a *conventus civium Romanorum* with non-native inhabitants, while the similarity in the distribution, particularly for nail-cleaners, between Southwark and the most easterly parts of the town suggests that such a community was closely encircled by the dwellings of Romano-Britons, some of whom were displaced when the forum-basilica was constructed (Milne 1992, 16).

The number of nail-cleaners from London is certainly low, supporting the bias in social context towards small towns and settlements noted by Crummy and Eckardt (2004). Direct inter-excavation comparison is always bound to be affected by differences in area and volume of soil removed, but, discounting the one from the Bermondsey Abbey site which lies well outside Roman Southwark, Table 4.6.1 records only 21 individual nail-cleaners from sixteen controlled excavations dug in London between 1974 and 1984 (a small proportion of the total number of interventions carried out over eleven years of continuous excavation), while thirteen came from five seasons of work at Baldock, Hertfordshire, and six from two seasons of fieldwalking and limited trenching at Hacheston, Suffolk (Stead and Rigby 1986, 130; Seeley 2004, 116, 121).

Typology in context

An exceptional item within the London assemblage is a decorated set made of iron (Cat no 3; Fig 4.6.2) and there is a second, unprovenanced, iron set in the MoL collections (MoL O1838), suggesting that iron toilet instruments were more common than they may appear from the archaeological record.

Tweezers and earscoops offer little scope for typological comparison, but the nail-cleaners and some sets show that in general the London objects are stylistically linked to types or broad morphological groups found north of the Thames. A set from Southwark (Cat no 9; Fig 4.6.4, 5) parallels one from Colchester, and there is a nail-cleaner of the same form from Heybridge, Essex, suggesting that the type is Trinovantian. Two London nail-cleaners with a long latticed neck (Cat no 6; Cat no 8; Fig 4.6.4, 4) are direct parallels for one from Puckeridge-Braughing, and, though three is too small a number to establish a discrete type, a connection with the Catuvellauni can be proposed. Another example (Cat no 4; Fig 4.6.4, 6) can also be associated with these three, as all four belong to a more broadly defined group with a distribution reaching from Hertfordshire down to Kent. A nail-cleaner fragment with moulded neck and narrow shoulders (Cat no 31) compares closely with a complete example from an early Roman context on the Fisons Way site at Thetford (Gregory 1991, fig 116, 11), and to others in the same broadly defined group from Spong Hill (Cool 1995, fig 96, 28), Stonea Grange (Jackson

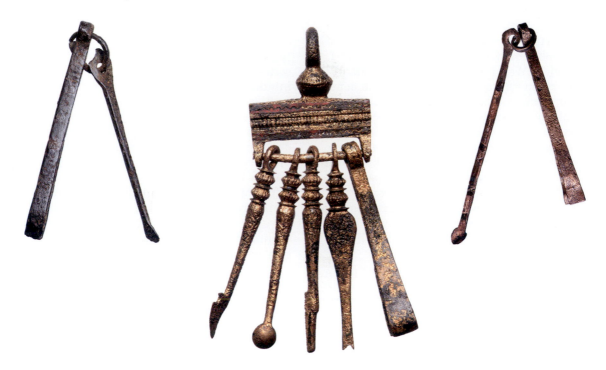

Fig 4.6.2 Toilet implements from London (Cat nos, from left to right: 3, 7, 5). Scale 1:1

1996b, 353 and fig 114, no 111), Hacheston (Seeley 2004, 1331–3) and Stansted (Major 2004, fig 134, 12/C). A positive link to the Iceni and/or Trinovantes is uncertain, but further finds may confirm this supposition.

Wider contacts are indicated by two sets. The nail-cleaner and earscoop with a wire suspension loop (Cat no 2; Fig 4.6.4, 7) belong to a group found across southern Britain, perhaps divisible by the position of the coil (see Alloys below). The only match for the elaborate châtelaine from London Wall (Cat no 7; Fig 4.6.2) is one from Castleford, West Yorkshire (Cool and Philo 1998, 86); both are so similar that they must be the product of one bronze-smith, but they differ in several details and are best seen as special commissions rather than common stock-in-trade.

The form of nail-cleaner that occurs most frequently in the London assemblage is the Baldock type, which dates from the mid-1st century into the 2nd and is found in the tribal or *civitas* areas of the Catuvellauni and Trinovantes (Crummy and Eckardt 2004, 51–6). Its distinguishing characteristic is the way in which the upper terminal sweeps round sharply at right angles to the blade, expands and thus defines a neck. The standard form is either plain or has marginal grooves on the blade, but some have grooves or mouldings on the neck (eg Fig 4.6.4, 1–3). Both varieties were in production by the pre-Flavian period (Webster 1987, 91, fig 23, 32; Stead and Rigby 1986, fig 56, 277). Of the fifteen certain Baldock-type nail-cleaners from London (Cat nos 1, 10–23), six have a grooved/moulded neck,

and there are other examples of the variant form from sites in the current MoLAS publication programme (Angela Wardle pers comm). These variants come only from sites west of the River Lea (Crummy and Eckardt 2004, 63; the Billericay example cited there can be discounted as idiosyncratic).

The numbers involved here are small, but at the least they raise questions in terms of production, supply and identity. For example, as plain Baldock types occur over a wider area than the variant form with decorated neck, was there any difference in the identity of the people choosing to own the latter, or were they simply the products of different workshops? In other words, were the decorated neck variants made in London and the plain examples elsewhere, perhaps at Baldock, Verulamium or Colchester? To investigate these points, a modest programme of metallurgical analysis was carried out on some of the London nail-cleaners and on a group from Colchester. The programme was not limited to the Baldock type, as the general range of alloys used needs to be established in order to highlight any variation or clustering. The results are outlined below.

Alloys and types *with Christie Pohl*

Thirteen nail-cleaners from London and eight from a site in Colchester were analysed using non-destructive X-ray fluorescence in order to establish the copper alloys used in their manufacture. A summary of the project is presented in Appendix 1

Fig 4.6.3 Toilet implements from London (Cat nos, from left to right: top row: 25, 26, 27; middle row: 28, 30, 36; bottom row: 45). Scale 1:1

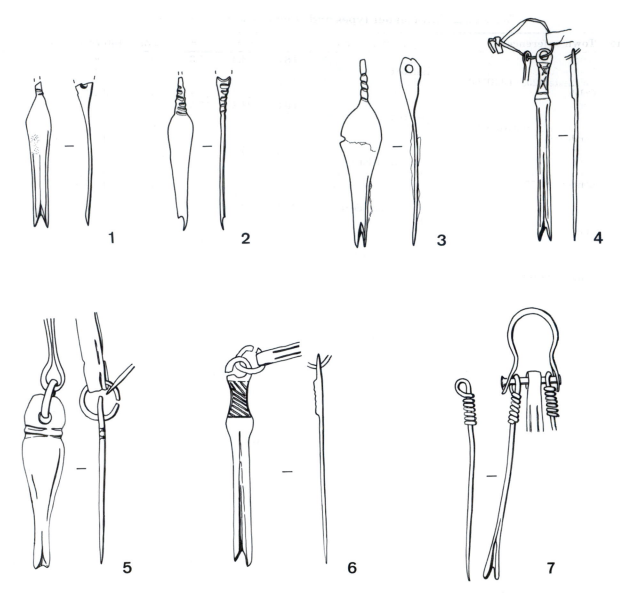

Fig 4.6.4 Nail-cleaners from London (where the cleaner is part of a set, an indication of the other instruments is included): 1–3, Baldock type and Baldock variants (Cat nos 14, 21, 22); 4, decorated neck type (Cat no 8); 5, grooved shoulder type (Cat no 9); 6, decorated neck type (Cat no 4); 7, wire loop type (Cat no 2). Scale 1:1

and a copy of the full report is deposited in the Museum of London.

Table 4.6.2 presents the results by nail-cleaner type, alloy XRF data and interpretation; the Colchester objects have been given an identifying letter to allow each item to be located on Figure 4.6.5, a ternary diagram for the three elements that characterise the alloys. The study sample was small, but some distinctions between the London and Colchester objects point to further lines of enquiry. In terms of the alloys present, for example, the leaded gunmetal of the London objects is tin-rich while that of the Colchester pieces is zinc-rich. A large proportion of the objects from both places were of leaded bronze, but items of leaded brass were only noted in the London assemblage, though, as

one of the latter (Cat no 9; Fig 4.6.4, 5) has a close typological parallel from Colchester that was not analysed, the absence of leaded brass in the Colchester group may be a result of the small size of the sample.

Matching alloy to morphological type, eight standard Baldock nail-cleaners (four from each place) and two decorated-neck Baldock variants from London were included in the sample and all but one proved to be of leaded bronze, with no clear distinction discernible between the three groups. It is important to note that the same alloy was used for many contemporary British-made brooches, including Colchester derivatives, which have a similar distribution pattern (Bayley and Butcher 2004, fig 122).

Table 4.6.2 Nail-cleaner types and copper alloys (and see Fig 4.6.5)

Cat no	Town; reference	Type/description	% Cu	% Sn	% Pb	% Zn	Interpretation
a	Colchester; 2001.64 SF 33	Baldock	58.4	14.3	27.3	0	leaded bronze
b	Colchester; 2001.64 SF 89	Baldock	76.9	10.3	12.8	0	leaded bronze
c	Colchester; 2001.64 SF 96	Baldock	66.3	14.0	19.7	0	leaded bronze
d	Colchester; 2001.64 SF 110	Baldock	67	21.3	11.7	0	leaded bronze
1	London; 94.111/3	Baldock	58.6	23.8	17.6	0	leaded bronze
11	London; VAL88[12533]<4989>	Baldock	73.2	13.8	13	0	leaded bronze
13	London; LCT84[9843]<2019>	Baldock	34.2	39.8	21.1	4.9	leaded gunmetal (tin-rich)
14	London; LEA84[928]<96>	Baldock	29.2	24.8	46	0	leaded bronze
19	London; IRO80[558]<137>	Baldock variant	71.6	19.1	9.3	0	leaded bronze
22	London; 26389	Baldock variant	52.8	26.2	21	0	leaded bronze
25	London; 19574	twisted decorated neck	75.1	0	5.2	19.7	leaded brass
26	London; 20375	slight shoulders, incised cross	92	5.6	2.4	0	leaded bronze
g	Colchester; 2001.64 SF 1872	angular shoulders, incised cross	73.6	6.4	7.1	12.9	leaded gunmetal (zinc-rich)
f	Colchester; 2001.64 SF 201	wire loop	71.6	21.4	7	0	leaded bronze
2	London; 21732	wire loop	81	0	1.2	17.8	leaded brass
9	London; A12018	grooved shoulder	73.3	0	11.2	15.5	leaded brass
e	Colchester; 2001.64 SF 271	early large loop	62	7.9	30.1	0	leaded bronze
7	London; A20136	enamelled set	90	6.8	3.2	0	leaded bronze
h	Colchester; 2001.64 SF 208	plain straight shaft	77.7	4.3	3.2	14.8	leaded gunmetal (zinc-rich)
4	London; 19602	decorated neck	82.1	7.1	7.5	3.3	leaded gunmetal (tin-rich)
30	London; LCT84[4229]<1150>	lugged neck	53.6	17.1	23.9	5.4	leaded gunmetal (tin-rich)

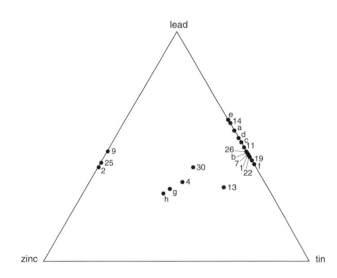

Fig 4.6.5 Ternary diagram of copper alloys used for toilet implements

One standard Baldock (Cat no 13) is made from leaded gunmetal (or bronze/gunmetal), perhaps produced by recycling mixed brass and bronze scrap objects but possibly the preferred alloy of a particular smith (Dungworth 1997, §6.7; Bayley and Butcher 2004, 15 and appendix 1). In either case, the presence of this piece implies that it could be a product of a different maker to the main run of Baldock nail-cleaners.

The analysis allowed one unparalleled London nail-cleaner (Cat no 25; Fig 4.6.3) to be discounted as a direct derivative of the Baldock type. It has a swept-round terminal and a grooved neck, but the sweep turns through 180° not 90° and the blade is very thin, long and shoulderless. Its manufacture from leaded brass reinforces its distinction from Baldock types and implies a common pool of

decorative techniques rather than a common source. Similarly, although nail-cleaners Cat no 26 (Fig 4.6.3) and Cat no g both make use of an incised cross as a decorative motif, their differences of both form and alloy show that they are not members of a discrete type. Nail-cleaners with a wire suspension loop secured by twisting the end around the shaft are a stylistic group rather than a true type as the twist may lie anywhere from the centre to the top of the shaft, and the number of coils varies. Here the London example (Cat no 2; Fig 4.6.4, 7) has the twist at the top and that from Colchester (Cat no f) has it at the centre. These differences of provenance and form are continued by the alloys, leaded brass (Cat no 2) and leaded bronze (Cat no f).

Conclusion

Within the Roman town the distribution of toilet instruments points to a characteristically military/continental style of consumption of these items in the western area and immediately east of the Walbrook, but a Romano-British one further east and in Southwark. This pattern serves to highlight the concentration of votive offerings in the middle Walbrook valley. The lower Fleet valley may also have been a focus of ritual activity. The early Romano-British population of Londinium (as distinct from any non-British element(s)) is closest in consumption to the Catuvellauni and Trinovantes, rather than to *civitates* to the south and west of the Thames, an important, if predictable, characteristic in terms of the identity of some of the early Romano-British inhabitants of the town. Londinium was probably a production and marketing centre for a particular variant of the Baldock nail-cleaner, but not necessarily the dominant one for the standard type. In the late Roman period there is no evidence for the use of nail-cleaners within the study area, implying a population that no longer participated in this aspect of Romano-British material culture.

The results of the metallurgical study further highlight the potential of toilet instruments for this kind of inter/intra-site and inter/intra-type or group study and the value of continuing to build up a dataset of alloy analyses matched to morphology, as a recommended element of Roman London's research priorities (Nixon *et al* 2002).

Acknowledgements

Harvey Sheldon has always aimed to set Roman London in the wider context of the province and its people. This paper uses small objects to offer him a peephole onto those vistas.

Nina Crummy is grateful to Adam Corsini, Jenny Hall, Catherine Maloney, Roy Stephenson and Angela Wardle of the Museum of London, Hella Eckardt of the University of Reading, and Ralph Jackson of the British Museum for their help in the compilation of the dataset, and to Stephen Benfield, Colchester Archaeological Trust, who permitted the analysis of the Colchester nail-cleaners. Mark Atkinson, Field Archaeology Unit, Essex County Council, gave permission on behalf of English Heritage for the nail-cleaner from Elms Farm to be cited in advance of publication. Angela Wardle, Hella Eckardt and Ralph Jackson kindly commented on a draft of the text, and Jon Cotton supplied Fig 4.6.4.

Christie Pohl would like to thank Marcos Martinón-Torres of the Institute of Archaeology, University College London, for his help and advice with the metallurgical study.

Appendix: The metallurgical data *by Christie Pohl*

The study of the London and Colchester toilet instruments was carried out at the Institute of Archaeology, University College London, under the supervision of Marcos Martinón-Torres. The objects were analysed using energy dispersive X-ray fluorescence (XRF); the primary radiation source was an X-ray tube with a rhodium target run at 35 KeV and the fluorescent X-rays were detected by a Si(Li) detector. The method analyses the surface composition and is non-destructive. The elemental composition of each item was evaluated to allow close examination of the base metal alloys (see archived report).

The most significant elements detected were copper (Cu), tin (Sn), lead (Pb) and zinc (Zn); lesser amounts of iron, aluminium, silicon and sulphur representing the corrosion products were also detected but were eliminated from the data, which was then manipulated and recalculated to total

100% (Table 4.6.3). To produce the ternary diagram (Fig 4.6.5), copper was then eliminated, and the data again manipulated and recalculated to total 100% (Table 4.6.3). This approach is consistent with that used by Bayley for Roman brooches (Bayley and Butcher 2004). It should be stressed that this type of XRF analysis is qualitative rather than definitively quantitative and certain results, such as for lead and tin, may be skewed to appear higher than the actual amounts within the alloy. Lead levels above 20% are atypical of the Roman period and cannot be interpreted as absolute in the XRF results; it is therefore better to state that an element exists in the alloy rather than to rely on the elemental percentage generated by the analysis. Regardless, this method can provide a sense of the overall elemental composition and the ratios of these elements within the London and Colchester groups.

Three alloys are present in the London sample, leaded brass, leaded bronze, and leaded gunmetal (Table 4.6.2). Only leaded bronze and leaded gunmetal are present in the Colchester sample. The copper alloys used during the Roman period in Britain are fully documented elsewhere, and it is sufficient to note here that brass has a zinc content greater than or equal to 8%, the tin content of bronze is greater than or equal to 3%, and gunmetal is an

Table 4.6.3 XRF data with copper eliminated. Zn, zinc; Pb, lead; Sn, tin

Cat no	Town; reference	Zn	Pb	Sn	Total (%)
1	London; 94.111/3	0	46.9	53.1	100
2	London; 21732	58.3	41.7	0	100
4	London; 19602	30.7	34.8	34.5	100
7	London; A20136	0	48.2	51.8	100
9	London; A12018	52.2	47.8	0	100
11	London; VAL88[12533]<4989>	0	49.6	50.4	100
13	London; LCT84[9843]<2019>	16.3	32.5	51.2	100
14	London; LEA84[928]<96>	0	60.6	39.4	100
19	London; IRO80[558]<137>	0	45.1	54.9	100
22	London; 26389	0	47.4	52.6	100
25	London; 19574	57.3	42.7	0	100
26	London; 20375	0	48.4	51.6	100
30	London; LCT84[4229]<1150>	23.3	41.7	35.0	100
a	Colchester; 2001.64 SF 33	0	56.5	43.5	100
b	Colchester; 2001.64 SF 89	0	45.2	54.8	100
c	Colchester; 2001.64 SF 96	0	51.3	48.7	100
d	Colchester; 2001.64 SF 110	0	52.9	47.1	100
e	Colchester; 2001.64 SF 271	0	61.1	38.9	100
f	Colchester; 2001.64 SF 201	0	42.8	57.2	100
g	Colchester; 2001.64 SF 1872	37.4	31.6	31.0	100
h	Colchester; 2001.64 SF 208	40.7	29.1	30.2	100

alloy of copper, tin and zinc, again with a minimum of 3% tin (Bayley and Butcher 2004, table 5). If lead was added to an alloy it is then described as 'leaded'. The recycling of scrap metal is thought to produce gunmetal and this can result in a different proportion of zinc to tin. The leaded gunmetals from London are tin-rich as opposed to those from Colchester which are zinc-rich.

Table 4.7.1 Continued

Nos: Cat (Fig)	Zone	Acc no; site	Date	Material; Shape	Size (mm)	Description	References
14	4: East Low	Tower of London TOL79[39]<14>, (AML791785.00); Tower of London	2nd C	jasper (red); oval; F1	L 17, W 13, Th 2	Minerva standing front, facing right, helmeted, supporting spear and shield with right hand, and with victory on outstretched left hand. Serpent in front. Parthenos type. Found in a post-Roman deposit near the riverside wall	Henig 1978a, 303 no App 126, pl 29; Henig 1978c, 114–15 fig 5; Parnell 1985, 66–7 & fig 34, 40
15	—	BM P&E 1855,0804.65; London	2nd C	cornelian; oval	L 15, W 10.5	Winged Minerva in profile right, holding steering oar and rudder of Fortuna. Set in massive silver ring type V. Intaglio damaged. Purchased with other London material (lot 267, Chaffers sale)	Henig 1978a, 303 no App 129, pl 29; Henig 1978b, 114 no 3
16	1: Wal Mid	19234; Bucklersbury House	2nd C	cornelian; oval; F2	L 9, W 7	Ceres standing front, facing left, wearing long *chiton* and mantle. Dish of fruit in right hand and two corn ears in left. Set in an iron ring. From eastern edge of Walbrook stream	Henig 1978a, no 259, pl 9
17	—	96.58/1; Thames foreshore	2nd C	chrome chalcedony or emerald; oval; F	L 10, W 7	Ceres standing front(?), facing left. Dish of fruit in right hand; her left is lowered and probably clasped corn ears. Badly chipped. Set in a gold ring, type V	
18 (4.7.1)	2: EoW	EST83[399]<58>	mid-1st C	nicolo (pale blue on dark ground); oval; F4	L 16, W 14, Th 3	Head of Dea Roma, wearing Attic helmet, left	Henig 1984a, 11–15 no 1; Murdoch 1991, 81 no 57, pl 14; cf Zienkiewicz 1986a, 135 no 41 for bust on cornelian from Caerleon
B		**COMPANIONS OF DEITIES**					
19	5: West	WFG9[9]<24>	1st C (from 3rd C context)	amethyst (low quality); oval; B1	L 7, W 5, Th 3	Cupid standing right, probably burning butterfly. From site of Cripplegate fort	Henig 1978a, 301, no App 118, pl 28
20 (4.7.1)	3: WoW	29.201/4; Moorgate Street	2nd C	jasper (red); oval; F1	L 18, W 14, Th 3	Head of youthful satyr in profile to the left. His hair is tightly plaited and he wears a *nebris* around his shoulders. *Lagabolon* projects behind his shoulder	Henig 1978a, 216 no 252, pl 8, 39
21	3: WoW	Private possession; Thames foreshore, west of Queenhithe	2nd C	nicolo; oval; F4	L 11, W 8, Th 3	Satyr prancing right. He holds a hare in left hand	Henig 1987a, 299 no App 103; Henig 1978b, 115 no 6
22	—	BM P&E 1856,0701.806; London	1st–2nd C	chalcedony (bleached); oval; F	L 10, W 8	Youthful satyr left with bag in left hand and *lagobolon* over right shoulder. Set in iron ring, type III. Ex Charles Roach Smith collection	Smith 1854, 60 no 269; Henig 1978a, 204 no 143 (not lost as stated); Henig 1978b, 114 no 2; Manning 1985, 77, J1
23	7: Cem E	WTN84[675]<903>	2nd C	cornelian or onyx; oval; F4	L 14.5, W 10	Youthful satyr seated on rock in profile right. He holds *pedum* in right hand, bunch of grapes in left hand. Set in iron ring, type V. Burnt	Whytehead 1986, 94–5 no 903, fig 41; Barber & Bowsher 2000, 118–19, fig 85
C		**PERSONIFICATIONS**					
24	—	833; London Wall (now lost)	2nd C	jasper (red); oval	–	Genius standing left, holding *cornucopia* in left hand and a *patera* in right hand. Set in an iron ring	Guildhall Museum 1908, 29 no 403, pl 86, 14; Henig 1978a, 199 no 108
25 (4.7.1)	5: West	GSM97[690]<1655>	?mid-2nd C	cornelian (black inclusions); oval; A4	L 14.5, W 11.5, Th 3.5	Bonus Eventus (the bearer of good things), standing front, facing right, holding corn ears in right hand and a *patera* in left. The figure is nude; the scratches down his left side which look a little like an attempt to depict a cloak (*chlamys*) draped over his shoulder may well be a mistake by a hasty gem-cutter, judging from comparanda	cf especially Johns 1997, nos 113–33, Snettisham jeweller's hoard dated to the mid-2nd C
26	—	BM P&E 1856,0701.804; London	2nd C	heliotrope; oval; A4	L 12, W 9.5	Bonus Eventus, standing front, facing right, holding corn ears and *patera* as cat no 25. Ex Charles Roach Smith Collection	Smith 1854, 60 no 267; British Museum 1926, no 1309; Henig 1978a, 211, pl 7

Table 4.7.1 Continued

Nos: Cat (Fig)	Zone	Acc no; site	Date	Material; Shape	Size (mm)	Description	References
27	–	826; London Wall	2nd C	nicolo glass; oval; ?	L 13, W 11	Bonus Eventus, standing front, possibly holding corn ears in right hand and *patera* in left hand. Type as cat no 25. Set in an iron ring	Guildhall Museum 1908, 29 no 396; Henig 1978a, 212 no 217, pl 7
28	7: Cem W	OBL97[230]<69>	late 2nd C	nicolo glass; oval; F2	ring 19 x 16	Bonus Eventus in profile, standing on right leg. A *chlamys* hangs from his shoulders behind him. In left hand he holds an object in front of him and would have held another object in right hand. Set in a copper-alloy ring	cf Henig 1978a, nos 193, 194 & App 111
29	1: Wal	835; Barge Yard, 1 Queen Victoria Street	2nd C	nicolo; oval; F4	L 13, W 10, Th 2.5	Fortuna/Concordia, standing, facing right. *Patera* in left hand, *cornucopia* in right	Guildhall Museum 1908, 29 no 405; Henig 1978a, 226 no 334, pl 11
30	–	A8005; London Wall	uncertain	glass (green); oval; F	L 14, W 11	Fortuna/Concordia. Type as cat no 29, left arm missing, in right a *cornucopia*. On her head is a *calathus*. Set in copper-alloy ring	Wheeler 1930, 100–1 fig 30.9; Henig 1978a, 226 no 338, pl 11
31	3: WoW	CID90[362]<358>	2nd C	cornelian; oval; F1	L 7, W 8, Th 2	Fortuna draped in a *chiton* and mantle, standing on ground line. Rudder on her right side. Only lower part of gem remains, dimensions for extant stone	Hill & Woodger 1999, 24 & 54
32	6: Sk	1STS74[59]<304>	late 2nd C	cornelian; ?; A5	L 11, W 7, Th 2	Spes, female figure personifying Hope, in profile to left, wearing long *chiton*, which she hitches up with her hand, and holds a flower in right hand	Henig 1978a, 306 no App 145, pl 30; Dennis 1978, 402–3 no 168
33 (4.7.1)	1: Wal Mid	ONE94[18089] <4687>	1st C	onyx; oval; F4	L 7, W 5	Thalia, the muse of Comedy; draped in *chiton* and *himation*, and seated on chair to left, holding mask in right hand. Set in an iron ring. The gem stands 1.5mm proud of the bezel	Henig 2000a, 74–5 fig 5.12
34	5: West	WFG9[10]<58>; site of Cripplegate fort	3rd C	nicolo glass; oval; F2	L 8, W 6, Th 1.5	Victory walking left shouldering a palm and holding a wreath. In a copper-alloy ring with engraved decoration on hoop	Henig 1978a, 306, no App 143, pl 29
D **HEROES**							
35	–	BM P&E 1855,0804.66; London 1846	Republican gem 2nd–1st C BC; ring 1st C AD	chalcedony (bleached); oval; F	L 12, W 10	Achilles, mortally wounded falling back upon his shield. An arrow has pierced his left ankle. Cable border. Set in an iron ring	Henig 1978a, 308 no App 153, pl 30, 79; Henig 1978b, 113 no.1
36	3: WoW	A24467; Miles Lane, Upper Thames Street	1st C	glass (brownish-red); oval; F1 or F6	L 14, W 11	Hercules nude, depicted to left, wrestling with anguiped giant; moulded. Set in an iron ring, type II	Wheeler 1930, 100 & fig 30, no 16; Henig 1978a, 240 no 434, pl 14
37	3: WoW	TEX88[1714]<1305>	2nd C	cornelian/sard; oval; F1	L 17, W 14, Th 2	Hercules walking left holding a club in left hand and an animal(?) slung over right shoulder. Chipped on top left edge	Murdoch 1991, 81 no 61, pl 14
38 (4.7.1)	1: Wal Mid	21568; Bank of England site, Threadneedle Street	1st/2nd C	jasper (red); oval; F1	L 16, W 12, Th 2.5	Theseus, nude standing left, right leg bent behind left, holding sword of his father Aegeus	Henig 1970, 250–1 no 1a, pl 23 a, b; Henig 1978a, 243 no 455, pl 14; Henig 1978c, 115 fig 6
E **DAILY LIFE**							
39	–	BM P&E 1856,0701.805; London	2nd–3rd C	onyx (white on dark); octagonal, bevelled edges; F	L 17, W 16	Hunting scene. Huntsman on horse galloping left; holding spear in left hand. Below hound chases a quadruped, probably a deer. Ex Charles Roach Smith Collection	Smith 1854, 60 no 268; British Museum 1926, no 2118; Henig 1978a, 250–1 no 507, pl 16
40	2: EoW or 6: Sk	82.347; Thames foreshore at London Bridge	3rd C	nicolo glass; ?; F2/F4	L 15, W 11	Hunting scene. Huntsman riding left. What is possibly an incipient wing might suggest Pegasus; however the animal below, its body to left, regardant, is a panther rather than the chimera so this is probably a hunting scene. Set in tin-alloy ring with everted shoulders; the intaglio stands proud of the hoop	cf Henig 1978a, 230 no 362 for Bellerophon slaying the chimera on a glass intaglio from Havering atte Bower, Essex.

Table 4.7.1 Continued

Nos: Cat (Fig)	Zone	Acc no; site	Date	Material; Shape	Size (mm)	Description	References
41	2: EoW	EST83[399]<61>	mid-1st C	nicolo; oval; F4	L 12, W 11, Th 3	Athlete (*discobolus*) walking right, looking over shoulder. Discus in left hand, and palm of victory in right	Henig 1984a, 11–15 no 4; Murdoch 1991, 176 no 499 (2); compare Henig 1988, 31 no 16
42	1: Wal Mid	3456; National Safe Deposit Company Ltd, 1 Queen Victoria Street	1st–2nd C	jasper (grey-brown); rectangular, rounded corners; F	L 12, W 9.5	War-galley with prominent ram to left. In it are four marines and standing figure, perhaps intended for Victory. Set in an iron ring, type II	Guildhall Museum 1908, 109 no 39; Henig 1978a, 254 no 535, pl 17
43 (4.7.1)	6: Sk	96.101; King's Reach, Winchester Wharf, Southwark	3rd C	cornelian; oval slightly convex; A6	L 17, W 12, Th 3.5	Warship containing four marines. The ship has a swan figurehead on the bow	Henig & Ross 1998
F	**ANIMALS**						
44 (4.7.2)	3: WoW	MLK76[429]<397>	2nd C	cornelian; oval; A4	L 13, W 9, Th 3	Lion walking left, holding head of a bull in his mouth; ground line; rather worn	Murdoch 1991, 81 no 59
45 (4.7.2)	7: Cem N	A14751; Eldon Street, Moorfields	2nd C	red jasper; oval; F1	L 14, W 11, Th 3	Boar charging left. Tree behind. Ground line	Wheeler 1930, 102, fig 30, 23; Henig 1972, 219 & pl 13 B; Henig 1978a, 261–2 no 620, pl 19; Henig 1978c, 110 fig 2
46	3: WoW	A27084; Coleman Street	3rd C	cornelian; oval; F	L 10, W 7	Stag in profile left, crouching beneath tree. Set in hexagonal copper-alloy bezel	Wheeler 1930, 100 no 8, fig 30; Henig 1978a, 261 no 617, pl 19; for style see Henig & Wilkins 1999, 55 no 37 (Wroxeter)
47	7: Cem E	MSL87[252]<562>	1st C	chrome chalcedony; oval; C4	L 6, W 4, Th 3	Cow or bull grazing, in profile left. Ground line. From a jewel box associated with an inhumation grave, outside city wall	Murdoch 1991, 71–2 no 5(6); Barber & Bowsher 2000, 66–7, no B 291.2.5 & 319 fig 110; compare Henig 1978a, 259 no 597 from Stanmore, Middlesex
48 (4.7.2)	–	LEK95[341]<173>	3rd C	stone (blue); oval; F3	L 10, W 14, Th 3	Two mice, nose to nose. Set in a gold ring, type VIII	
49	6: Sk	CH75[4238]<542>	?1st C	glass (green); oval; convex	L 12, W 9, Th 2	Two facing animals	
50		Private possession in USA; ?London	2nd C	onyx; oval; F	L 8, W 5	Eagle in profile to the right; holds wreath in its beak; cracked. Set in silver ring, type V	Henig 1978a, 314 no App 188, pl 31, 71; Henig 1978b 114–15 no 4
51	5: West	GPO75[1387]<913>	1st C	glass (light blue on dark blue); ?; F	L 11, W 9, Th 1.75	Eagle standing in profile right, wing raised above its body, attacking a serpent on the ground in front of it	Henig 1978a, 314 no App 191, pl 31
52 (4.7.2)	2: EoW	ILA79[597]<889>	mid-2nd C	cornelian; oval; B4	L 8, W 6, Th 2	Stork to left. Ground line. Chip on left side of stone; diminutive	Henig & Jones 1992, cf Johns 1997, no 200 (Snettisham Roman jeweller's hoard)
53	1: Wal Mid	3452; National Safe Deposit Company Ltd, 1 Queen Victoria Street	1st C	glass (opaque light blue); oval; F1 or F5	L 10.5, W 9	Indian parrot standing on a branch and facing left. Set in a copper-alloy ring, type III	Puleston & Price 1873, pl 8 no 12; Guildhall Museum 1908, 109 no 35; Henig 1978a, 269 no 686, pl 31, 49
54	6: Sk	AB78[134]<391>	1st C	glass (brown); oval; F	L 11, W 10, Th 1.5	Dolphin, swimming left, with D-shaped body and arched tail; moulded. Left side of intaglio chipped	

Table 4.7.1 Continued

Nos: Cat (Fig)	Zone	Acc no; site	Date	Material; Shape	Size (mm)	Description	References
55 (4.7.2)	2: EoW	EST83[399]<60>	mid-1st C	banded agate (black & white); oval; F1	L 13.5, W 11.5, Th 2	Pegasus walking left. Ground line	Henig 1984a, 11–15 no 3; Murdoch 1991, 81 no 58, pl 14
56	1: Wal Low	LYD88[1600]<266>	late 1st C	cornelian; circular; F	L 10, W 10, Th 2.5	Hippocamp swimming left; below a dolphin, likewise swimming left. Behind the dolphin is a trident, emblematic of Neptune	Murdoch 1991, 81–2 no 62, pl 14
57 (4.7.2)	6: Sk	1STS74[12]<161>	mid- to late 2nd C	cornelian (cloudy orange); oval; B4	L 14, W 11, Th 3.5	Eagle and standards. Eagle to right, looking left between *maniple* standards	Henig 1975, 243; Henig 1978a, 313 no App 186, pl 31; Dennis 1978, 402–3 no 167; Murdoch 1991, 129 no 299, pl 14, cf recent example from Drapers' Gardens DGT06 [403] <202>
58 (4.7.2)	6: Sk	BGG01[233]<80>	1st C	nicolo onyx; oval; F2	L 12, W 11, Th 2	Two Indian parrots perching on the edge of a *skyphos* (wine cup); sides bevelled outwards. Chip on underside	Henig 1978a, 235 no 397 pl 13
59	1: Wal Mid	20794; Bucklersbury House	1st C	chalcedony (mottled); oval; B	L 8, W 6	Bird (parrot?) standing on *cornucopia* facing cup containing corn ears and poppies. Set in an iron ring	cf Henig 1988, 33 no 32
G ATTRIBUTES							
60	–	81.282/8; ?Walbrook or waterfront (from dump in E2)	1st–early 2nd C	onyx (white on brown); oval, flat	L 7, W 6,	Corn-measure (*modius*) containing two ears of corn. Set in an iron ring, type II. Found in a dump in Bethnal Green, probably from a City site, waterfront or Walbrook	
61 (4.7.2)	2: EoW	EST83[399]<59>	mid-1st C	onyx (blue-grey on dark); oval; F4	L 14, W 13, Th 1.5	Clasped hands (*dextrarum iunctio*), set within olive wreath tied with ribbons. The name *ALBA* has been scratched (retrograde) below the hands, subsequently obliterated and again scratched more clearly above. However, the name was never properly engraved	Henig 1984a, 11–15 no 2; Murdoch 1991, 176 no 499(1), pl 14
62	7: Cem N	SRP98[5763]<2350>	1st C	cornelian; oval; A	L 6, W 4.5	Lyre, with three strings. Slightly chipped. Set in the remains of an iron ring	cf Johns 1997 no 219 (Snettisham Roman jeweller's hoard) for type
63 (4.7.2)	–	A1620; Royal Aquarium (site of), Tothill Street, SW1	1st–2nd C	sardonyx; oval; F3	L 10, W 8, Th 4	*Fulmen* (Jupiter's thunderbolt); set in an iron ring, type II	Wheeler 1930, 100 & fig 30, 18; Henig 1978a, 238 no 415, pl 13
H COMBINATIONS							
64	6: Sk	BAQ90[255]<251>	2nd C	red jasper; oval; F1	L 10, W 6	Combination, *hippalectryon*. Cupid rides a composite creature left. The front of its body is a bearded satyr's head surmounted by the head and neck of a horse; the back of the body is comprised of a small ram's head with ears of corn in its mouth. The creature has the legs and feet of a cockerel; chipped on left side (not available for study)	Rogers 1990, front cover & 231; for type of Henig 1978a, 233 no 382; Henig & Whiting 1987, nos 304–11
65 (4.7.2)	1: Wal Mid	20795; Bucklersbury House	1st–2nd C	nicolo; oval; F2 or F4	L 14, W 11,	Combination. Three conjoined bearded heads, a pair back-to-back and one above. A ram's head seems to be incorporated in the composition. There is a star below. Set in an iron ring	Guildhall Museum 1955, 6 pl 2, 10; Henig 1978a, 233 no 381, pl 12, 43
66	1: Wal Low	DGH86[277]<148>	1st–2nd C	glass; oval	L 8, W 6	Grotesque. Animal-like creature left holding stick over shoulder, left. Chipped on right edge. Set in iron ring, type III	Murdoch 1991, 129 no 298
I MISCELLANEOUS							
67	6: Sk	A8004; Southwark	3rd C	glass (green); circular; F2 or F4	DM 10	Romano-British imitation intaglio; figure of uncertain type. In a copper-alloy ring with everted shoulders, type VIIIa	Wheeler 1930, 100 & fig 30, 10; Henig 1978a, 257 no 574
68	7: Cem E	MSL87[599]<278>	3rd C	glass (green); oval; F3	L 14, W 12	Romano-British imitation intaglio; standing figure. In a copper-alloy ring with keeled shoulders, type VIII	Murdoch 1991, 74 no 12

Table 4.7.1 Continued

Nos: Cat (Fig)	Zone	Acc no; site	Date	Material; Shape	Size (mm)	Description	References
69	5: West	NHG98[731]<93>	2nd–3rd C	cornelian; circular; A	DM 6	Stone with single lap wheel slash set in copper-alloy ring with flattened hoop expanding towards bezel; late development of Henig type III looking towards the forms characteristic of late Antonine times and beyond. From area outside Cripplegate fort	Lyon 2004, 165, fig 13
70	6: Sk	179BHS89[0]<232>	2nd C	red jasper; oval; F1	L 15, W 12, Th 3.5	Stone. Not engraved. Uncut gems were sometimes mounted in rings worn as jewellery	
J **ALL METAL BEZELS**							
71	7: Cem N	STE95[894]<325>	?2nd C	silver	L 10, W 7	Apollo, nude, standing front, lyre in left hand and laurel in right hand. Base silver bezel. Only the bezel remains	
72	1: Wal Mid	19200; Bucklersbury House	2nd C	iron	DM (int) 23	Head of Serapis in profile, left, above an eagle flanked by semeion standards. Cut on the bezel of an iron ring type III	Henig 1974, p 51, no 357, passim
73	–	A13212: Railway Approach, London Bridge (now lost)	2nd C	gold	L 9, W 6	Cupid standing, right facing front, leaning on a reversed torch in attitude of mourning. Gold ring type V	Wheeler 1930, 98 & fig 30, 1; Henig 1978a, 277 no 762
74	5: West	GYE92[11879]<334>	4th–5th C	silver; square bezel	L 9, W 8.5	Silver ring bezel. Lion standing left, regardant. These square bezels, Henig type XV or Johns' (1996c, 53–5) 'Brancaster type', are late in date and should be assigned to the 4th–5th centuries. From the infilling of the amphitheatre in the late Roman period	For another stepped ring cf gold ring from Corbridge showing an animal (Henig 1974, no 782; Charlesworth 1961, p 28 no 55, pl 3, 10)
75	2: EoW	A23405; St Clement's Churchyard, Clement's Lane	1st–2nd C	gold	L 8, W 5	Parrot holding ?two cherries in its beak, shown in profile to the left. Incised on gold ring, type III (now lost)	Wheeler 1930, 98 & fig 30, 3; Henig 1978a, 279 no 779
76	2: EoW	A24748; Nicholas Lane	1st–2nd C	gold	L 7, W 4	Dolphin in profile, left. Incised on gold ring, type III (now lost)	Wheeler 1930, 98 & fig 30, 4; Henig 1978a, 279 no 783
77	2: EoW	A22180; near All Hallows Church, Lombard Street	1st–2nd C	gold	L 7, W 4	Palm-branch. Incised on gold ring, type III (now lost)	Wheeler 1930, 98 & fig 30, 2; Henig 1978a, 278 no 770
78	6: Sk	Museum of London acquisition pending Winchester Wharf, Southwark	1st–2nd C	silver	L 11, W 8	Branch, perhaps of wild olive. Incised on silver ring, type III	Henig 1976a; Henig 1978a, 317 no App 210; for wreath of wild olive see above Cat no 61
K **IMPRESSIONS ON POTTERY**							
79	1: Wal Up	76.119; 1–4 Copthall Close	mid-1st–mid-2nd C	ceramic oval	L 7, W 10	Impression of standing nude male figure on the base of a micaceous grey ware vessel	Henig 1976b, fig 11; Henig 1978a, 318 no App 212
80	2: EoW	12092; Talbot Court, Gracechurch Street	pot 1st C	ceramic oval	L 10, W 9	Impression of protome of Pegasus, on the base of a Belgic eggshell beaker	Henig 1978a, 281–2 no 806 (with wrong provenance)
L **ROMAN GEMS FROM LATER CONTEXTS, PROVENANCE UNCERTAIN**							
81	–	84.434; Thames foreshore, Cannon Street Railway Bridge, south side	13th-C context	chalcedony; circular; A	L 14, W 12.5	Two peacocks, one standing on globe. Set in silver seal inscribed in Lombardic lettering + *DVLCIS:AMORIS: ODOR*	Spencer 1984, 377–9 no 6; Henig 2000b, 4–5 fig. 8; Murdoch 1991, 83 no 72, pl 5
82	–	A14271; Cheapside, Friday Street (corner of)	early 17th-C context; gem late Hellenistic 1st C BC	sardonyx (3 layers); oval	L 27, W 21, Th 4	Cameo portrait of Ptolemaic queen or Isis, profile right	Wheeler 1928, 30, pl.9, 2; Plantzos 1996, 55 no B6; Plantzos 1999, 102, pl 87, 4; Forsyth 2003, 44–5

Table 4.7.1 Continued

Nos: Cat (Fig)	Zone	Acc no; site	Date	Material; Shape	Size (mm)	Description	References
83	—	A14267; Cheapside, Friday Street (corner of)	early 17th-C context; Republican gem early 1st C BC	cornelian (yellowish, mottled) oval	L 24, W 18, Th 2.3	Silenus standing left, partially draped in mantle, holding *thyrsus* in right hand. In front is a boy satyr, nude, holding wine cup and pedum. Ground line. From Cheapside hoard,1912	Wheeler 1928, 28, pl 9, 1; compare Vollenweider 1984, 52–3 no 73; Furtwängler 1896, 67–8 & pl 12 no 1014a
84	—	A14021; Cheapside, Friday Street (corner of)	early 17th-C context; gem late 2nd-early 3rd C	amethyst; oval; slightly convex	L 19.5, W 16.5, Th 6	Eagle standing with wings displayed, body towards right but head turned left. The bird has a wreath in its bill; gem crazed. From Cheapside hoard,1912	Wheeler 1928, 28, pl 9 (wrongly captioned A14020); Forsyth 2003, 44–5
85	—	A14241; Cheapside, Friday Street (corner of)	early 17th-C context; gem 1st C	nicolo; oval; F4	L 10, W 8	Plucked and trussed chicken between knife with looped handle and fish. Set in early 17th-century gold ring. From Cheapside hoard,1912	Wheeler 1928, 17–18, fig 2 & pl 3; Forsyth 2003, 46–7; compare Henig 1978a, 267–8 no 675, pl 21, 48
86	—	A14242; Cheapside, Friday Street (corner of)	early 17th-C context; gem 1st C	nicolo; oval; F4	ring DM 21	Hippocamp swimming left. Set in a gold ring. From Cheapside hoard,1912	Wheeler 1928, 18, fig 2 & pl 3
87	—	unknown; ?London	?17th-C context	rock crystal	–	Clasped hands holding corn ears. Most of Conyers' collection was acquired from money made from rebuilding London after the Great Fire	cf Henig 1978a, 292 no App 59 (chalcedony ring from Hayling Island)
88	—	A7996; Smithfield	4th C BC	copper alloy	L 17, W 10	Lion-griffin in profile left. Metal intaglio on copper-alloy ring. The shape of the ring, with its leaf-shaped bezel, and the subject are characteristic of rings of the late Classical period (4th century BC) so this must most probably be judged as *aliena*	Wheeler 1930, 98–9 & fig 30, 6; cf Boardman & Vollenweider 1978, 36, shape as no 156 (showing a sphinx)
M		**LATER GEMS IN ANTIQUE STYLE**					
89	—	BM P&E 1856.0701.803; Thames, London	?16th C	cornelian; oval; A4	L 15, W 11	Head of Julius Caesar left, laureate. Although previously published as Roman, stylistically it belongs with Renaissance gems figuring portraits of the 'Twelve Caesars'. Ex Charles Roach Smith collection	Cullum 1854, 74; Smith 1854, 60 no 266; Richter 1971, no 461; Henig 1978a, 247 no 481, pl 15
90	—	A14257; Cheapside, Friday Street (corner of)	early 17th-C context; gem 16th C	amethyst; oval; F7	L 20, W 15	Laureate head of clean-shaven emperor left, probably Domitian. Letters VIIX cut in front. From Cheapside hoard, 1912	Wheeler 1928, 28, pl 11, 1; Forsyth 2003, 46–7
91	—	CAP86[560]<11>	16th–17th C	cornelian; oval; F	L 14, W 12	Draped bearded male bust right. Perhaps intended for the Emperor Hadrian; set in a gold ring	Henig 1986, 192; Murdoch 1991, 177 no 508
92	—	A14269; Cheapside, Friday Street (corner of)	early 17th-C context; gem 16th C	cornelian; oval; F7	L 12, W 8	Bearded male head left. From Cheapside hoard, 1912	Wheeler 1928, 28, pl 11, 1
93	—	A14270; Cheapside, Friday Street (corner of)	early 17th-C context; gem 16th C	cornelian; oval; F1	L 32, W 22	Female figure, left; draped, holding branch in left hand. Shield and helmet in front. Base line. There is a star below. From Cheapside hoard, 1912	Wheeler 1928, 28, pl 11, 1
N		**MOULDED CAMEO**					
94	3: WoW	BBB05[1354]<280>	1st C	glass	L 31.5, W 23.5	Moulded glass setting depicting two figures in relief. The more prominent figure is a nude Hercules holding club in right hand. A smaller, helmeted, but nude, male figure, probably Iolaos, gazes up in admiration. Set in a corroded thin copper-alloy frame with no obvious trace of suspension loop for the pendant	

Some intaglios may have been intended to denote a military rank. In a gem depicting an eagle and standards (Cat no 57) we surely have a seal of a legionary. It was found in Southwark, which has also yielded a fine intaglio depicting a quarter-length figure of Mars or a hero (Cat no 2), and there was surely a military presence there. A recent city discovery from Drapers' Gardens (DGT06), also depicting an eagle and standards, may prove after further research to be the finest example from Roman Britain (James Gerrard, Pre-Construct Archaeology, pers comm). Other intaglios from Londinium proper, figuring Mars (Cat nos 3–5) and Theseus (Cat no 38), were very probably likewise intended to be worn by soldiers. Two gems show warships (Cat nos 42 and 43), the latter (also from Southwark) a 3rd-century vessel, such as those displayed on coins of Allectus or on the famous Arras Medallion.

The gods portrayed on the gems, such as Jupiter (Cat no 1) or his attribute, a thunderbolt (Cat no 63, from Tothill Street, Westminster), Mars (Cat nos 2–5), Mercury (Cat nos 6 and 7), Apollo (Cat no 71 and note his lyre, Cat no 62), Sol (Cat nos 8–11), Minerva (Cat nos 13–15) and Dea Roma (Cat no 18) are not unexpected in the context of a provincial capital and bear witness to the official importance of Londinium. All of them are to be seen on gems from the Second Legion fortress at Caerleon, for example (Zienkiewicz 1986a). They provide something of a corrective for the evidence from sculpture (Henig 1996) and inscriptions from Londinium in which local Romano-Celtic deities (the Hunter-God, the Matres and Mars Camulus (see Grew, this volume)) or exotic oriental deities (Mithras, Isis, Attis and Cybele) are what most strike the viewer's imagination. Londinium was, after all, a Roman capital city in which people of diverse culture congregated. By contrast, for what it is worth, Mars, Sol and heroic scenes are all lacking from gems so far found in the *civitas* capital at Wroxeter (Henig and Wilkins 1999, 51). Heroes are represented by two intaglios depicting Hercules (Cat nos 36 and 37) and together with other depictions (see J Bird this volume) illustrate local knowledge of mythology. One image of Mars (Cat no 2) is derived from representations of heroic youths who were perhaps regarded in antiquity as portraying Achilles or Alexander the Great (cf Henig 1970, 264–5).

Off-duty in Britain and elsewhere, people frequently turned to the saviour god Bacchus (Cat no 12), who also presided at banquets. His satyrs have been mentioned above. It may be noted that parrots (Cat nos 53, 58, 59 and 75) were closely associated with him and were believed to enjoy drinking wine! One example (Cat no 58) is similar, although not identical, to a cornelian from Wroxeter where parrots perch on pedestals either side of the cup (Henig 1978a, no 398; Henig and Wilkins 1999, 56 no 46). Confronted parrots associated with wine vessels appear also on a banded agate from Gadara, Jordan, where a pair of parrots perch on either side of a *cantharus* containing a *caduceus* and corn ears

(Henig and Whiting 1987, no 317). On a rock crystal from a late 1st-century deposit from the bath house drain of the fortress baths at Caerleon, two parrots, each standing on a cornucopia, face a cup (Zienkiewicz 1986a, 199 no 4). Another Caerleon gem, an amethyst, the colour of wine and a specific against inebriation, shows parrots on a cornucopia and a *calathus* (Zienkiewicz 1986a, 199 no 5). On one of two cornelian gems in Berlin there are two parrots on a *cantharus* and, on the other, two parrots on separate *canthari* (Furtwängler 1896, nos 7915–16). The symbolism of the gem is Bacchic, evoking prosperity and happiness.

One of the most interesting gems from London displays clasped hands surrounded by a bridal wreath of wild olive (Cat no 61). At the time of the Boudican revolt it was being prepared as a gift to a woman called Alba, but in the circumstances of the disaster it never reached its destination. A sprig of wild olive on a silver seal-ring (Cat no 78) may also have been a marriage gift.

A fine, elaborate gold ring holds an intaglio showing two mice confronting each other (Cat no 48). The device evokes the well-known fable in the *Satires* of Horace (2.6.77–117) where a town mouse visits his friend, the country mouse, only to be disgusted by the simplicity of the fare, and then entertains the country mouse right royally in town, only to be disturbed by the barking of a Molossian hound. The mice on the London gem are sharing a morsel of food, in contrast to the only other pair of confronted mice on a gem (from Cologne) known to the author, which are fighting (Zwierlein-Diehl 1998, 263 no 143; and compare a pair of fighting tortoises on a nicolo in Oxford, Henig and MacGregor 2004, 91 no 9.52). Single mice are fairly common subjects, normally nibbling a fruit or piece of bread, for example two gems in the Dutch Royal collection (Maaskant-Kleibrink 1978, 240 and pl 109, nos 616–17), both nicolos ascribed to the 2nd century, and three gems in Vienna, two of sardonyx and one of nicolo, which may be 3rd century and are certainly of the same shape as the London gem (Zwierlein-Diehl 1991, 101 and pl 46, nos 1906–8). Sometimes two mice are shown on tables or lamps, as though cleaning up the scraps after a banquet (eg Henig and MacGregor 2004, 90, no 9.37).

More general interests include hunting in the forests surrounding London, as is best represented by a hunting scene (Cat no 39) and a lively study of a boar (Cat no 45). Satyrs (Cat nos 20–3) came to be closely associated with Bacchus but originally were denizens of wild places, and their ubiquity on gems perhaps emphasises the need people felt for protection in a hostile world, a theme to which we will return under the heading of religion and superstition. The countryside was never far away and a grazing bovine (Cat no 47) represents pastoral life, while out in Middlesex, at Sulloniacae (Brockley Hill), we find a similar subject on a gem (Henig 1978a, 259 no 597). A corn measure or *modius* (Cat no 60) represents agriculture as do Bonus Eventus

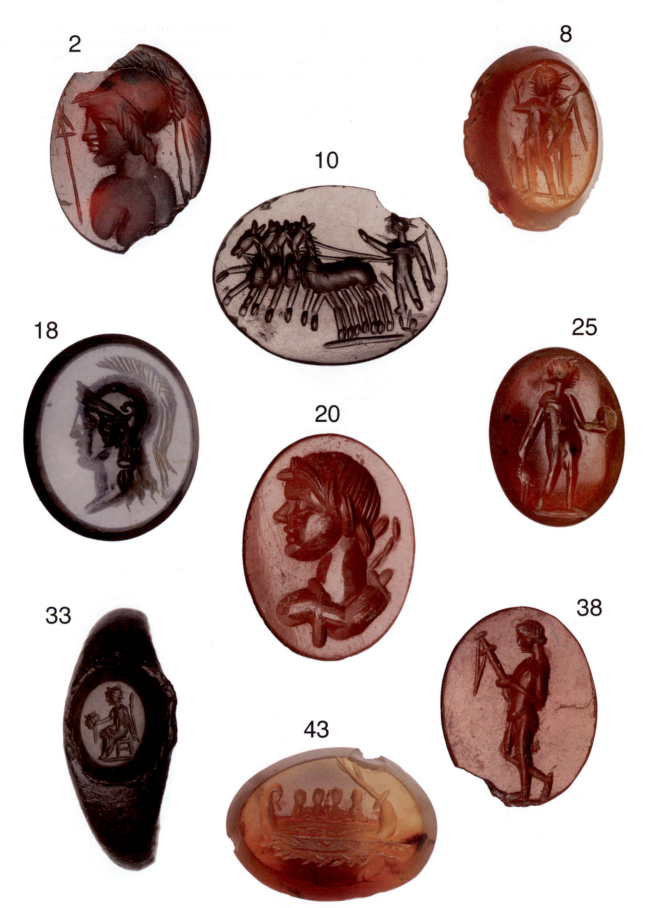

Fig 4.7.1 *A selection of intaglios showing examples of deities, heroes and aspects of daily life. The numbers refer to those in the Catalogue. Scale 4:1*

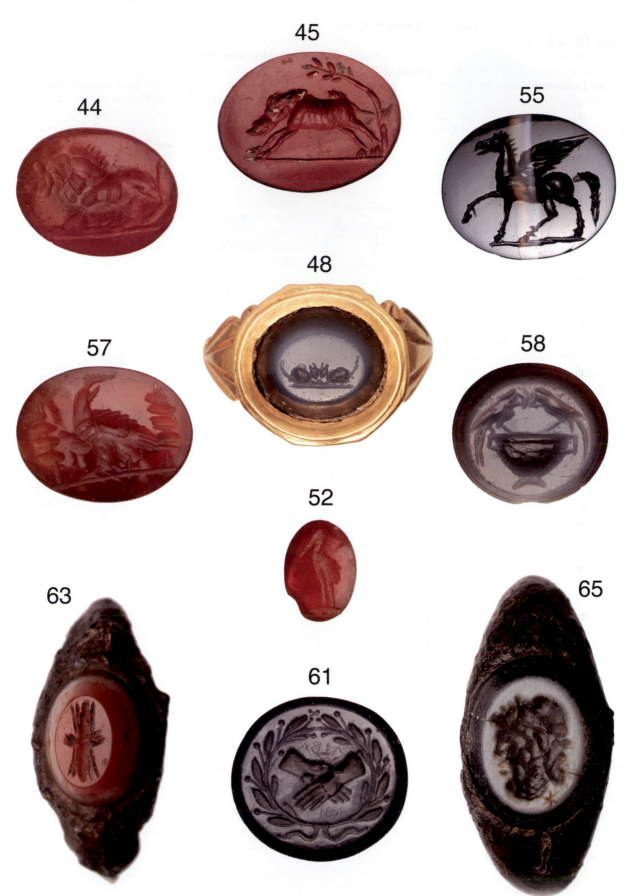

Fig 4.7.2 Intaglios depicting a variety of animals and birds, clasped hands, a thunderbolt and a three-headed combination. The numbers refer to those in the Catalogue. Scale 4:1

(Cat nos 25–8) and his female counterpart Ceres (Cat nos 16 and 17), both shown with their attributes of corn ears. It is probable that these standard types were adapted from a statue group of Triptolemos and Demeter made by Praxiteles (4th century BC) for display in the Gardens of Servilius in Rome (Pliny, *Naturalis Historia* 36, 23). One moulded nicolo glass intaglio of Bonus Eventus (Cat no 28) is paralleled by examples from Godmanchester, Cambridgeshire (also set in a similar copper-alloy ring and excavated in association with Antonine samian), Chesterton, Warwickshire, and Lincoln (Henig 1978a, 209 no13; 210 no 194; 300 app 3 respectively). Amongst leisure activities, Greek athletics (Cat no 41) and the theatre (Cat no 33) are represented on intaglios.

Various animals were endowed with symbolic otherworldly significance: lions, so often to be seen on tomb monuments (Cat no 44), and dolphins and hippocamps (Cat nos 54, 56 and 76) which represent the journey of the soul to the felicity of the afterlife. One silver ring portrays a lion (Cat no 74) which may have signified the astrological sign Leo, the personification of strength and manly qualities, or even, conceivably, symbolised the Lion of Judah in a Jewish or Christian context. Two silver rings from Amesbury, probably 5th century and distinctively Romano-British in style, portray such animals looking over their shoulders (Henig 1978a, nos 801, 802) but the London bezel is far more conventionally Roman than these. Most of the silver rings of the type from Britain (eg Henig 1978a, nos 795, 798, 799, 400) portray birds and one is combined with a Christogram. The votive use of gem-rings or gems by themselves remains a possibility worth considering; some of the gems and rings found in the Walbrook may have been thrown in as votive offerings (see Merrifield and Hall, this volume), and also in the Thames where, for example, a yellow jasper intaglio depicting a scorpion, found at Blackfriars (not included in this catalogue but see Henig 1980), may have been such a deposit. This seems to have been the case with gems recovered in the 19th century from the outlet of the sacred spring at Bath (Henig 1988).

The superstitions of Roman Londoners are above all attested by gems depicting grotesques or combinations (Cat nos 64–6); these are also very much the sort of devices to be found in Italy and throughout the Roman world. Symbols of prosperity, which as we have seen are associated with deities, birds on drinking vessels (Cat nos 58 and 59), the corn measure (Cat no 60) and lyre (Cat no 62) are likewise comparable with the devices on gems from the Mediterranean. Archaeological context can sometimes provide further evidence, and of interest is a small group of intaglios deliberately placed in a grave in the eastern cemetery, presumably for protective reasons, portraying Sol (Cat no 8) with his connotation of celestial apotheosis, Mercury (Cat no 7), the guide of souls, and a bovine (Cat no 47).

The artistic quality of the gems varies but the best of them are very fine artworks indeed, almost comparable with the famous marbles from the Walbrook Mithraeum, works of metropolitan quality. The Pegasus from Eastcheap (Cat no 55) or the Moorfields boar (Cat no 45) are surely worthy of inclusion in any general handbook of Roman art. I hope the illustrations to this article make this judgement: that although small we are dealing with very lovely jewels (although that would be true of a fair proportion of the gems from Britain). The question of workshops in Londinium is not yet fully resolved. Indeed, it is possible, as the writer suggested in dealing with the intaglios showing the military eagle and standards (Cat no 57) and the figure of *Spes* (Cat no 32) from St Thomas' Street Southwark, and again with the much finer and earlier gems from Eastcheap (Cat nos 18, 41, 55 and 61), that there were gem-cutting studios in Londinium. A jewellery workshop certainly existed in the Suffolk Lane area in the 1st century (Marsden 1975, 100–2, pl 7), making gold jewellery, and London with its large population, which included wealthy merchants, civil servants and military personnel, would have provided ready markets for such goods. It is to be hoped that more single finds and with luck debris from one or more gem-cutting workshops in Londinium will transform our understanding.

The last section of the catalogue is a reminder of the gems used and produced in the modern period, in particular the 16th and 17th centuries, when ancient gems reset in modern settings bear witness to a continuing link with Rome. One example of a seal-ring made completely of rock crystal (Cat no 87) from the collection amassed by John Conyers, a late 17th-century collector, was described thus by John Aubrey in his *Monumenta Britannica*: 'Mr Jo Conyers the Apothecary hath an antique crystal Ring. In the seale whereof is engraven hand in hand the [ears] of wheat, and heads of poppy, wch seems to shewe, that the ancients did use this wild poppy to take off ye acrimony of hunger' (Aubrey 1980, 432–3). The ancient gems, too, found in the large and splendid Elizabethan and Jacobean Cheapside hoard include a Hellenistic cameo (Cat no 82) and a large Roman republican intaglio (Cat no 83); here the likelihood is that they were acquired in Rome or further east in the Mediterranean, the latter being suggested by the presence of two Byzantine cameos depicting respectively Saints George and Demetrios and the Incredulity of St Thomas (Forsyth 2003, 44–7). Such a trade had existed in the medieval period and probably accounts for the single intaglio in a medieval setting listed here (Cat no 81), which evidently served an amuletic purpose. Tudor and Stuart versions or copies of Roman gems, which attest the general Renaissance desire to return to the world of ancient Rome, could have been made in London, together with other gems, both intaglios and cameos, depicting Tudor and Stuart monarchs (cf Forsyth 2003, 37).

This review of intaglios from Londinium clearly demonstrates the skill of the gemstone cutters but the choice of subject matter was gradually overtaken by the material from which the gemstones were fashioned. From the end of 2nd century and increasingly through the 3rd century colour and texture became the qualities admired by owners rather than intricacy in gem engraving (Henig 1981). One Roman gem (Cat no 69) was clearly designed to look like an engraved signet when worn and its colour and translucency were clearly of more importance to the owner than the possession of a real signet. An interesting comparison can be made with an 'intaglio' from South Shields, published as showing a possible chalice (Henig 1978a, no 421) but which was probably merely a random cut. In Roman times, as in the Elizabethan and Jacobean age, gemstones were prized as reflections not only of taste but of one's consequence in society.

Acknowledgements

Harvey Sheldon and I both came from north-west Middlesex, which I think provided a special perspective on London. One was conscious, even in a generation or so following massive pre-World War One suburban development, of a rural county distanced from the capital city still with remaining areas of historic woodland such as Park Wood, Ruislip, and retaining a number of unspoilt country churches like those of Pinner, Ruislip and Ickenham. This was a landscape in which the imaginative child could think her/himself back to at least medieval times. The only earlier field antiquity of which I, at any rate, was conscious was, however, the Pinner Grim's Dyke, plausibly built, or at least used, in late antiquity to divide the swathe of country which looked to London from that which looked to Verulamium, chief city of the Catuvellauni. That is another story, discussed in this volume by Colin Bowlt. You had to go north or north-east, to the area of Stanmore, before Roman sites began to appear in the landscape.

There are many ways of approaching the past, one of them clearly through landscape, and the normal archaeological processes of excavation, and Harvey Sheldon's achievement both practical and academic has been to pull so much together appertaining both to London and to Middlesex. Briefly I worked at the Guildhall Museum, coming under the influence of the late Ralph Merrifield for whose memory both Harvey Sheldon and I retain a lasting affection. He taught us that archaeology was about people, whatever evidence one used. He also showed us that London was a very special place, something which even those rather empty acres of Middlesex served to emphasise.

Although my academic path and Harvey Sheldon's have diverged, we have both continued to think of ourselves as Londoners by *origo* concerned with understanding London in its widest context, not forgetting the countryside beyond. Thus, not long ago, he and I found ourselves part of a campaign to protect *Verulamium* from agricultural damage, and we have both contributed to two survey volumes on London which were meticulously edited by, amongst others, Harvey Sheldon himself (Bird *et al* 1996; Haynes *et al* 2000).

4.8 Luxury colourless glass vessels in Flavian London *John Shepherd*

Maximus tamen honos in candido tralucentibus, quam proxima crystalli similitudine. Usus eorum ad potandum argenti metalla et auri pepulit.

However, the highest value is set upon glass that is entirely colourless and transparent, as nearly as possible resembling crystal in fact. For drinking-vessels, glass has quite superseded the use of silver and gold.

Pliny *Naturalis Historia* 36, 198–9

Introduction

In the middle of the 1st century, around the time when the first merchants, traders and settlers began to take advantage of the raised, dry land alongside the Thames at the place that was to become Londinium, the technique of glass-blowing was less than a century old. In those 100 years it had spread from its place of origin, probably in the provinces of the eastern Mediterranean, via Italy into the Celtic provinces north of the Alps. Indeed, by the middle of the 1st century artisans skilled in the craft of glass-blowing and the technology of high-temperature furnace design were just beginning to establish their workshops in these northern provinces (Foy and Nenna 2001, 44) and, by *c* AD 70, a glass-worker had set up a workshop in a warehouse alongside the recently constructed port facilities of Londinium (KWS94: Regis House). This person, perhaps travelling to Londinium with his family, should be identified as one of the first glass-blowers ever to set foot in the province, with such well-developed skills that we can only assume that he learnt them from others working across the channel.

From that time onwards until, at least, the late 2nd century, there was a succession of glass blowers working in Londinium – each setting up their workshops in different areas, as time progressed, on the margins of the built-up area of the town. This industry, and its relationship to other crafts and industries in Londinium, has been the subject of much research in the last fifteen years (Bailey and Shepherd 1985; Shepherd and Heyworth 1991; Keily and Shepherd 2005; Pérez- Sala Rodés 2001; Pérez-Sala Rodés and Shepherd forthcoming) and has demonstrated that the traditional view of glass supply to Londinium – that much of it was imported – is no longer tenable. Making use of recycled broken vessels and window glass, these glass-workers were capable of making a large number of different vessel types, for the table as well as for storage and transportation. It is evident, though, that the glass being produced was for practical use

– none of it was of the very highest quality. Furthermore, apart from the hot working of glass to make stirring rods, such as at the early Flavian workshop at Regis House and, possibly, window glass at Basinghall Street (BAZ05, Mark Taylor pers comm), only the technique of glass-blowing was practised in the Londinium workshops.

In candido tralucentibus – Flavian colourless glass

By the Flavian period, therefore, glassware had become generally cheap and commonplace. However, there were still certain vessels that, by their quality, skilful finishing and uniformity, demonstrate that centres for the production of some higher-quality products continued to exist. It may be significant that these vessels, produced in strong monochrome colours or good-quality colourless glass, were produced by techniques involving the use of a rotating wheel or lathe. Pliny (*Naturalis Historia* 36, 66) makes reference to such a technique, along with blowing and engraving (*aliud flatu figuratur, aliud torno teritur, aliud argenti modo coelatur* – . . . blown into various forms, ground on a lathe or engraved like silver . . .). The interpretation of this phrase, along with a detailed re-examination of many vessels made during this period, has led to a heated debate among glass specialists about the precise techniques used to make these vessels. On the one hand, there is the contention that they were made using a rotating wheel on which was fixed a former or mould (ie the glass pottery technique, see Lierke 1993) – the hot glass being dropped onto or forced into the former or mould resulting in the fine horizontal scratch marks seen on such vessels. On the other hand, there is the previously universally held belief that such vessels were made by a combination of slumping and/or casting, with the vessel being finished, that is, the surface was smoothed and polished, through the use of abrasives and lathes. Such would be a less enigmatic translation of Pliny's Latin, since *terere* means to rub, rub away, whet or grind. There is not the space to expand upon this debate here but there can be little doubt that the vessels under consideration here were created with a wheel of some sort and were the vessels being considered by Pliny. It is also very important to note that Pliny differentiates between 'blowing' and 'lathe-grinding' and it is more than possible that the two techniques were being carried out by two quite distinct groups of artisans.

The subject of this paper, therefore, is just one of the main examples of this quality glass production – namely cast cups, dishes and bowls in a colourless glass that have been decorated and finished by grinding and polishing. Such vessels are very well known and have been discussed widely (eg Grose 1991; Price 1987; Oliver 1984). The aim of this short paper is certainly not to attempt a revision of our understanding of this class of vessel; in any case, it is doubtful that a study from just one site, such as London, would be a valid approach. Rather, the purpose of this paper is simply to bring to the attention of the reader the wealth of glass awaiting further study in the Museum of London collections, and the existence of such luxury glassware among London's fragmentary assemblages. This will complement the recent research into glass-working in the North-West provinces of the Empire, which has emphasised that much glass vessel production could have been local, and generally to increase awareness of the rich opportunities for further study of glass from Londinium and its region.

As stated above, therefore, such vessels are well known and Grose's succinct description of them and their significance can be repeated here:

[This category of vessel is] characterized by angular, lathe-turned forms ... and the highest standards of craftsmanship. [They] dramatize the shift away from intentionally coloured to decolourized tablewares under the Flavians. This class is one of several 'international' styles, which is well documented in both the western and eastern Mediterranean. It is also the last of Roman glass to have been manufactured in quantity by casting methods as Imperial glassmakers progressively adopted free- and mould-blowing techniques during the course of the first century AD (Grose 1991, 1).

Appearing towards the end of the third quarter of the 1st century, these vessels are found most frequently in dated contexts from the late Flavian to the Hadrianic periods (Grose 1991, 15). The finds from Londinium demonstrate this very well. Apart from a few pieces that come from poorly dated contexts or are obviously residual, the majority of the fragments come from late 1st- or early 2nd-century contexts.

When this class of vessel was first recognised as a separate type by Harden (1936, 50), few examples were then known outside of Egypt and so he proposed an Alexandrian place of manufacture. However, the large body of evidence that is now available for study suggests that the production of these vessels need not be restricted to the eastern Mediterranean, but they could equally be the products of western glasshouses (eg in Spain, Southern France and Italy). Price has suggested that blanks may have been traded to be finished off and/or decorated with wheel-cutting at other places closer to the place of sale (Price 1987, 79) and Grose has suggested that they may be the products of peripatetic glass-workers (Grose 1991, 16). Whatever their places of manufacture, and there could have been many, they fit comfortably with Pliny's statement quoted at the beginning of this paper. These vessels were highly valued items.

Flavian colourless glass in Londinium

The examples from Londinium demonstrate all of the main categories of form and decoration for this class of vessel. Table 4.8.2 and Fig 4.8.6 contain

Fig 4.8.1 Glass dish (Cat no 6) and handled skyphos (Cat no 55)

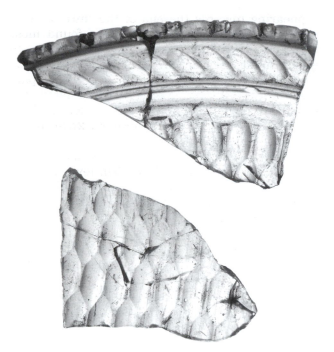

Fig 4.8.2 Fragments from a relief-cut bowl with facets (Cat no 37)

the results of a brief, initial search through the Museum of London's reserve collection and Archaeological Archive (LAARC). A total of 128 fragments of colourless vessels, finished and decorated with ground and polished methods, were identified, not including undiagnostic and indeterminate body fragments. The identifiable fragments, therefore, can be divided into broad groups according to their basic shapes, which reflect the lack of variation and standardisation remarked upon by Grose and emphasise his comment that these probably represent mass-produced vessels. Only in the decoration of the conical beakers (see Group IV) is there some variation – but even these varieties can be grouped into just a few basic categories of design.

In general, the forms represent examples of tableware – coasters, cups, bowls, dishes and, possibly, small ewers or flagons (although none of these closed forms are certain here). Exactly how such vessels were procured by their owners is difficult to deduce. The regularity of size and forms suggests that they were not specially designed, individual commissions. Perhaps sets could have been commissioned or perhaps they could be purchased 'off the shelf'. It is hoped that new research into batch analyses might cast more light on this subject (Ian Freestone and Hilary Cool pers comm). The large number of examples in Southwark, with concentrations at, especially, Tabard Square (LLS02; 27 examples), should be highlighted in regard to this new groundbreaking research. The comments associated below with each group are intended to give a guide only to the individual forms.

The Londinium groups can be described, briefly, as follows (see also Fig 4.8.4).

I Coaster or tablet (Cat no 1)

This coaster fragment, from Southwark Street (Calvert's Buildings) is an exceptional item of glass. It comes from a small circular stand with three legs carved into the shape of stylised animal legs, in imitation of real-sized tables. It must have functioned in much the same way as coasters or centre-plates do today – namely for placing under drinking vessels or serving dishes. Metal examples are well known, for example two circular silver ones from Pompeii (Ward Perkins and Claridge, 1976, nos 320–1). Glass examples are not common, however. Circular colourless glass stands come from Pompeii (unpublished, Naples Museum) and Baden, *Aquae Helveitica* (Fünfschilling 1986, 144 no 397, pl 21). Colourless rectangular stands are also known, for example one from Rome, now in the Corning Museum (Goldstein 1979, 152–3, no 326, acc no 66.1.211), and another, represented by just the leg and part of the flat plate, from a 2nd-century context at *Nicopolis ad Istrum*, Bulgaria (Shepherd 1999, 312, no 1).

II Shallow cup, bowl and dish forms (Cat nos 2–53)

Small cups, bowls and dishes make up the largest single category of the catalogue (52 examples, categorised as 'bowl'). No doubt many of the small vessels, with simple flared rims, would have served conveniently as drinking cups or side bowls, the small vessels with overhanging rims being less useful for drinking. The larger dishes and bowls would be more appropriate as serving dishes or centrepieces. It is more than likely that the vessels with wheel-cut decoration around the bodies would have been used in such a way that the facet-cutting would have enhanced, or been enhanced by, their contents. It is simple speculation, but it is tempting to suggest that such bowls would have been used for the serving of transparent or translucent liquid or semi-viscous foods.

Parallels for the plain bowls, with flared or overhanging rim forms, are numerous. For example Dura-Europos, Syria (Clairmont 1963, 18f, no 90), Karanis, Egypt (Harden 1936, Class IB I, 49–50, pl 12, no 166), four from a 2nd-century grave in Nieuwenhagen, Holland (Isings 1971, 77–8, nos 136–9) and Conimbriga, Portugal (Alarcão and Alarcão 1965, 76). In Britain examples are known from Lullingstone (Cool and Price 1987, 111, nos 325 and 326), New Market Hall site, Gloucester (Charlesworth 1974, fig 29, no 4), Caerwent (Boon 1973, fig 2, no 19), Fishbourne (Harden and Price 1971, fig 138, no 26) and Caerleon (Boon 1973, 116). See also Harden and Price (1971, 331) for examples from Belgium and Portugal, and Grose (1991) for numerous examples from Egypt, Germany, Hungary, Italy, Spain, Sudan, Syria and Tunisia.

The overhanging edge on a wide rim decorated with egg-and-dart motif is a distinctive feature of, especially, some larger dishes. Only a relatively small number of dishes empire-wide are decorated with both egg-and-dart motifs on the lip edge and facet-cut with circular or oval facets on the rim and/or body. However, the latter predominate in Londinium – indeed, it has not been possible to identify a vessel decorated with just relief cutting around the rim. All of the fragments with such decoration also have decoration on the flatter parts of the rim and on the bodies. Perhaps the best examples of such vessels are the three complete bowls from the Cave of Letters in Nahal Hever in the Judaean Desert (Yadin 1963, fig 40), hidden away during the Bar Kokhba revolt, AD 132–35. Price (1987, 72–3) notes that these bowls were evidently regarded as treasured possessions, and may not have been in current use at the time of their deposition, but some fragments from a nearby and contemporary deposit (in the Cave of Horrors) suggests that they were still used at least during the first third of the 2nd century. This can be corroborated by the evidence from Londinium which shows that fragments from many such bowls come from early to mid-2nd-century contexts (for example Cat nos 37, 39, 41, 44 and 45). Others come from Cosa, Italy (Grose 1991, fig 4), and Fishbourne (Harden and Price 1971, 336 and nos 33–4, pl 26). Price (1987, 72–8) also gives numerous examples and parallels from other sites in the western Empire, especially Spain and Portugal.

III Bowls or cups with handles (Cat nos 54–64)

Two forms are represented by the Londinium material. The first (Cat no 54), an antiquarian find from the Cornhill end of Old Broad Street, is from a wide, shallow dish with just the lower fixing part of a worked handle extant. The upper part of the fragment slopes slightly outwards, suggesting that the lip of the vessel is missing. The base is represented by a very low foot-ring and the shape of the vessel is very similar to two highly decorated bowls. One, in a monochrome, translucent green glass, formerly in the Sangiorgi Collection and now in the Corning Museum of Glass (Goldstein 1979, 151, no 320), is dated on stylistic grounds to the late 1st century BC or early 1st century AD. The other, in colourless glass similar to the Old Broad Street vessel, is from Siphnos and was found with a coin of Vespasian (Brock and Young 1949, 90–1, pls 33–4, tomb no 20, no 13; see also Harden 1970, 48 and 72, pl 1g and Massabo 2000, 70–1, fig 4). Isings (1957, 39), when discussing her form 25, notes a pair of two-handled colourless cups from Pompeii, both with relief ornament.

The second form is the more easily recognisable *skyphos,* a straight-sided, two-handled cup (Isings 1957, form 39) that has many parallels among the repertoires of metal-workers. These cups are known in the Mediterranean region during the Hellenistic period before the late 1st century BC but reappear in the colourless glass repertoires of the final quarter of the 1st century AD. The near complete example from St Swithin's House (Cat no 55), in the middle Walbrook zone, has been the subject of a detailed study by Jenny Price (1991, 159, no 610) who notes other examples similar to the Walbrook vessel from Mérida, Spain (Price 1974, 75–6, fig 2.2), Vindonissa (Berger 1960, 83, pl 14.215) and an unpublished fragment from a 1st-century context at the unexplored mansion site at Knossos, Crete. This form is depicted on a wall painting at Pompeii (Maiuri 1957, xxii) and also appears in the catacombs at Rome (Fremersdorf 1975, 82, no 800, pl 42) and at Köln (Fremersdorf 1967, 62, pl 21) but it is probable that these were made during the 3rd century. A number of *skyphoi* decorated with relief-cut foliage and lettered designs come from late 3rd- or 4th-century graves at Zülpich-Enzen (Heimberg 1980, 35–6), Rheinbach-Flerzheim (Follmann-Schulz 1988, 23–4) and Köln-Lindethal (La Baume and Nüber 1971, 80, pl 4.16; Harden 1987, 189, no 99).

IV Squat and tall conical beakers (Cat nos 65–128)

The facet-cut conical beaker (Isings 1957, form 21) is a distinctive vessel among Roman glass assemblages and easy to recognise. In fact, its distinctive attributes have led to it being the subject of a detailed study (Oliver 1984). This type of cup is dated to the Flavian and Trajanic periods and is widely distributed throughout the Empire. Oliver (1984, 46–58) lists just 105 examples from findspots as widespread as Britain to Begram in Afghanistan. Both categories of cup are recognisable in London, those without ridges above or below the zone of facets (Cat nos 66–9) and those with ridges (Cat nos 70–85). There are also numerous body fragments for which the precise category cannot be identified (Cat nos 86–97). It is evident, however, that the form with ridges appears to predominate here. Precisely what this means, assuming that there is any meaning to it other than simply a larger number being in circulation in Londinium, is not clear.

Also present are a number of vessels decorated not with a zone of overlapping, regularly shaped facets but with a decoration consisting of sinuous grooves formed by many overlapping facets with alternating oval facets orientated vertically (Cat nos 98–106) and beakers with diagonal grooves (Cat nos 107–11). All the London examples appear to come from the taller form of this vessel. A complete example of a conical beaker decorated in a similar manner comes from Pompeii (Harden 1987, 192). Harden notes that this type of decoration is rare and cites a low, wide footless cup in the Naples Museum (see also Arveiller-Dulong and Ziviello 2005, 109, fig

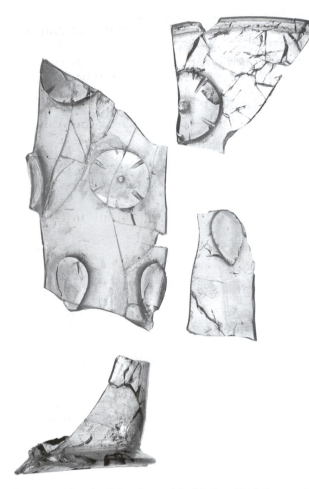

Fig 4.8.3 Conical beaker with high-relief decoration (Cat no 112)

1). In his study on eastern Mediterranean glass in Scandinavia, Ekholm (1956, 64, fig 1) made this his first category and Harden suggests that, owing to the Bay of Naples evidence, this tall form was the first of the late 1st-century conical beakers. Only three fragments of sinuous facet-decorated glass came from Vindonissa (Berger 1960, 68, nos 165–7).

To these can be added a number of vessels decorated with high-relief motifs, such as shells and oval elements (Cat nos 112–21). In a short article on relief-cut vessels of this type, von Saldern (1985) illustrated a complete conical beaker decorated with relief ovals and shells from Köln dated to the late 1st century. Three similar examples are known from London. One, decorated with relief-cut ovals and rosettes or flower motifs from Ironmonger Lane (Cat no 112) was associated with late 1st- and 2nd-century ceramics (London Museum 1970, 8, no 18). However, the other two, one decorated with just one zone extant (Cat no 113) from Leadenhall Street and the other from Southwark Street (Cat no 114) were evidently residual amongst 3rd- and 4th-century material. Other fragments from Londinium

with foliage decoration (Cat nos 115–16) come from late 1st- or early 2nd-century contexts.

The fragment from Guildhall Yard (Cat no 115), decorated with a high-relief ivy or vine leaf, was found among the large early 2nd-century cullet dump, discovered in the backfilled drains to the amphitheatre. Similarly dated examples include a narrow, conical beaker decorated with an ivy leaf from Fishbourne (AD 75–100) and one from Begram, Afghanistan (Harden and Price 1971, 333–6, no 30, fig 38, pl 26). Another example comes from Blake Street, York (Hilary Cool pers comm).

Finally, the Londinium assemblage includes five fragments from vessels, which appear to be hybrids of facet-cut Isings form 21 and indented forms such as Isings forms 32, 33 and 35. One (Cat no 124) comes from a context securely dated to AD 60–80 and another (Cat no 123) to AD 75–80. These are very fine vessels and the fact that the body has been indented suggests that the blanks for these were probably free-blown before cutting. It is possible that many of the forms described above could have had blanks created by some form of casting, slumping or sagging – evidence perhaps that they could be regarded as the products of a non-glass-blowing tradition. However, with these indented vessels we have a form that amalgamates the skills of colourless glass manufacture, glass-blowing and glass-cutting. Perhaps they represent the crossover of an older tradition into the younger but increasingly more predominant practice of glass-blowing.

Further study

This brief study has focused attention upon over 120 fragments of glass from late 1st-century vessels. These, however, would have been among the most valuable glass vessels being produced in the Empire at that time and, as Pliny says, would have been cherished more than vessels of silver or gold. Their presence in London, in such quantities, emphasises the cosmopolitan composition of Londinium's population. However, how they arrived here is a subject for debate and further research. There is the possibility that these expensive vessels were items of trade and exchange. It is also likely, however, that they travelled with their owners from one city to another, perhaps from one posting to another.

There is still much to learn about these vessels from London, their significance in their respective glass assemblages and their association with other material from their findspots. This short study has merely created a catalogue – the context of each fragment has yet to be analysed in detail. However, just a cursory examination of this catalogue shows that the simple distribution of these fragments (Table 4.8.1 and Fig 4.8.5) demonstrates a most interesting picture that is worthy of further study.

Of the 128 fragments in the catalogue, 20% come from the two zones west of the Walbrook, 37% from

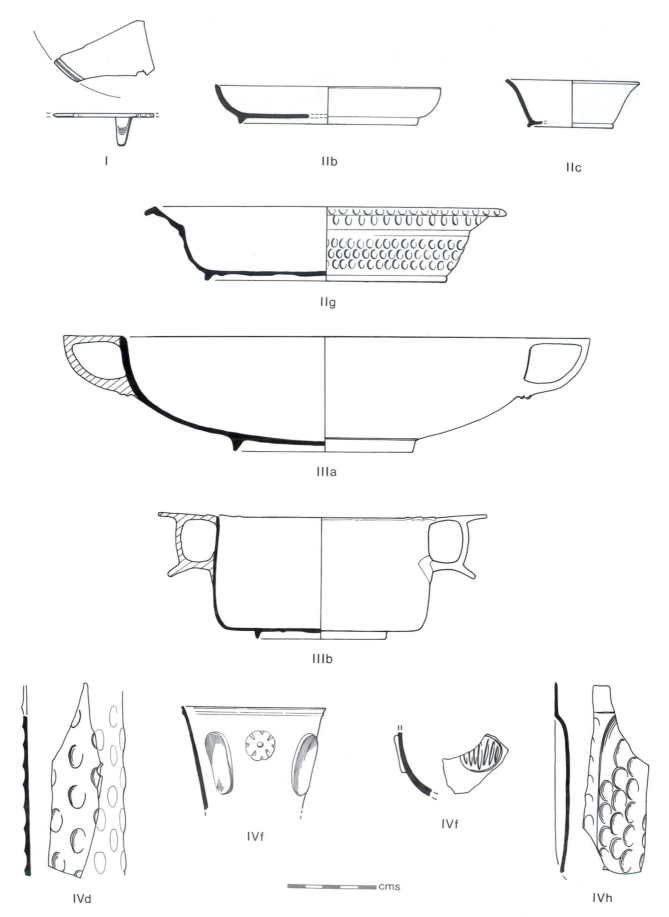

Fig 4.8.4 A selection of types of colourless glass from London:
Type I – Cat no 1   Type IIb – Cat no 6   Type IIc – Cat no 7   Type IIg   Type IIIa   Type IIIb – Cat no 55
Type IVd – Cat no 98   Type IVf – Cat nos 113 and 114   Type IVh – Cat no 123

Table 4.8.1 Summary of overall distribution of catalogued fragments, and comparison with some groups and subgroups

Type	Total	W of Walbrook		E of Walbrook		Southwark		Unknown
All fragments	128	26	**20%**	47	**37%**	52	**41%**	3
Group II	52	4	**7%**	13	**25%**	34	**65%**	1
Group II, f–g (elaborate facet-cut dishes)	11	1	**9%**	1	**9%**	8	**73%**	1
Group IV, a–c (facet-cut beakers)	33	11	**33%**	13	**39%**	9	**27%**	

zones east of the Walbrook and 41% from Southwark (2% are unprovenanced). Furthermore, of the 52 fragments of Group II vessels, only 7% come from zones west of the Walbrook, while 25% are from zones east of the Walbrook and 65% come from Southwark. There is an obvious weighting towards the sites south of the Thames for these fine vessels, especially the highly decorated, facet-cut dishes with all-over decoration (Group II, f and g: eight of the ten provenanced vessels come from Southwark, with just one apiece from zones east and west of the Walbrook). The distribution of the facet-cut beakers (Group IV, a–c), however, would appear to be reasonably equal throughout the town: 39% come from zones east of the Walbrook, 33% from the west and 27% from Southwark.

Of course, these statements and calculations are based upon a sample that is unlikely to be statistically valid. However, that there is a concentration of high-quality glassware south of the Thames is more than evident. Indeed, the only fragment of cameo glass from London, in fact from Britain, also came from Southwark. It is worth exploring further. The presence of these vessels throughout Londinium only emphasises the fact that there is still much work to be done in examining the contents of households throughout the different regions of the settlement.

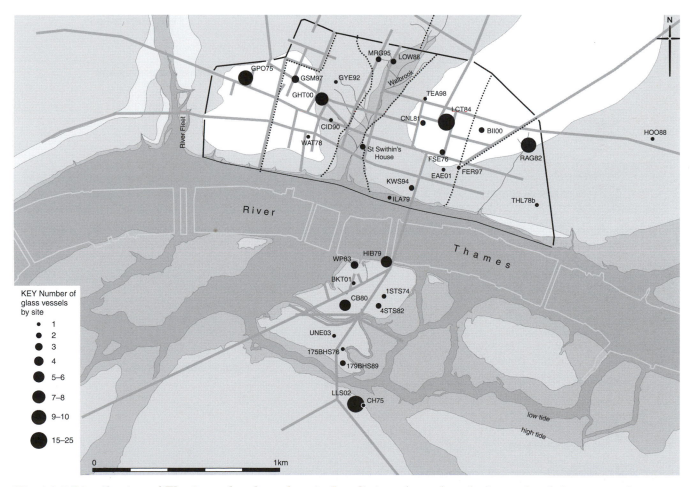

Fig 4.8.5 Distribution of Flavian colourless glass in Londinium (note that the later city defences are shown for purposes of orientation)

Fig 4.8.6 Chronological development of colourless glass vessels from Flavian London (by catalogue number)

Table 4.8.2 Catalogue of colourless glass vessels from Flavian London

For details of site codes see Table 2; for explanation of zones (column 2) see Figure 4.0.1; accession numbers are Museum of London unless otherwise stated.

Nos: Cat (Fig)	Zone	Acc no; site	Context date	Rim diameter (mm)	Base diameter (mm)	Description details	Reference
I Coaster or tablet							
1 (4.8.4, 1)	6: Sk	CB80[0]<918>	post-Roman				Shepherd 1992, 136, a
II Bowl							
						a) wide, with straight rim	
2	2: EoW	EAE01[1064]<212>	90–100	216			
3	6: Sk	LLS02[8378]	70–130	c 200			
4	6: Sk	LLS02[7236]	70–120	c 220			
						b) shallow bowl or dish	
5	6: Sk	BKT01[419]<106>	120–400	105			
6 (4.8.1, 4.8.4)	1: Wal Mid	18544 (GM158; St Swithin's House)	75–90	128	100		Price 1991, 159, no 611, fig 113
						c) with slightly flared, straight rim	
7 (4.8.4)	4: East Low	RAG82[1252]<881>	120–140	78			
						d) with flared rim	
8	4: East Up	BII00[230]<29>	50–150	84			
9	4: East Up	BII00[90]<9>	post-Roman	152	100		
10	6: Sk	HIB79[17]<192>	350–400	164			
11	2: EoW	LCT84[4246]<1886>	75–100	165			Shepherd 1993, 104, no 65, fig 63
12	6: Sk	HIB79[46]<298> and HIB79[48]<299>	70–100	174	140		
13	4: East Low	RAG82[1109]<898>	post-Roman	178			
14	5: West	GPO75[8944]<3877>; GPO75[9025]<3777>	70–100				
15	4: East Low	RAG82[1252]<870>	120–140				
16	4: East Low	RAG82[1243]<910>	120–140				
						e) with plain, overhanging rim	
17	6: Sk	LLS02[9986]	50–90	84			
18	6: Sk	LLS02[5218]	200–270	92			
19	6: Sk	LLS02[5452]	70–100	102			
20	6: Sk	1STS74[T8 11]<123>	–	124			
21	2: EoW	LCT84[4275]<1915>	95–100	c 150			
22	6: Sk	LLS02[8378]	70–130	164	130	profile	Shepherd 1993, 106, no 79
23	6: Sk	LLS02[11523]	late 4th–early 5th C	164			
24	6: Sk	LLS02[11672]	Roman	164			
25	1: Wal Up	MRG95[743]<340>	120–160	164			
26	6: Sk	CB80[2079]<2096>	late or post-Roman	172			Shepherd 1992, 125, no 62, fig 38
27	6: Sk	179BHS89[161]<344>	270–400	184			
28	6: Sk	LLS02[8378]	70–130	192			
29	4: East Low	THL78b[145]	100–200	204			Shepherd 1980, 63, no 3, fig 3
30	6: Sk	4STS82[893]<421>	120–160	c 250			
31	1: Wal Up	LOW88[1654]<165>	–	252			
32	7: Cem S	CB80[997]<1668a>	residual in late Roman burial	260			Shepherd 1992, 125, no 61, fig 38
						body fragment **f) with rounded, overhanging rim and facets on body**	
33	6: Sk	CH75[83]<381>	–				
34	6: Sk	LLS02[8378]	70–130				
35	6: Sk	LLS02[5933]	–	132			

Table 4.8.2 Continued

Nos: Cat (Fig)	Zone	Acc no; site	Context date	Rim diameter (mm)	Base diameter (mm)	Description details	Reference
(4.8.4)						**g) with overhanging rim, decorated with relief-cut moulding and facets on the body and base**	
36	–	23309; London	—				
37 (4.8.2)	6: Sk	HIB79[21]<203>; HIB79[31]<223>	[21] 140–250 [31] 120–140				Price 1991, 159, no 610, fig 113
38	6: Sk	LLS02[8457]	—	176			Shepherd 1993, 104, no 66, fig 63
39	6: Sk	LLS02[1172]	120–150	370		body and part of rim; probably part of Cat no 39	
40	6: Sk	LLS02[+]<2217>	unstratified				
41	6: Sk	LLS02[10511] & [10255]	70–120		120	possibly part of Cat no 39	
42	6: Sk	LLS02[765]	post-Roman			body fragment	
43	6: Sk	4STS82[555]<364>	180–250		160	base fragment	
44	5: West	GPO75[7464]<1580>	120–200			body fragment	
45	4: East Low	RAG82[1526]<585>	120–160			body fragment	
						h) decorated with oval facets and sinuous grooves base fragment	
						a–h) base fragment	
46	5: West	GHT00[8156]<2556>	50–160		c 100		
47	6: Sk	LLS02[8378]	70–130		c 120	low base ring at edge of base	
48	6: Sk	HIB79[35]<238>	70–100		170	low base ring at edge of base	
49	6: Sk	LLS02[4809]	post-Roman		68	high base ring	
50	6: Sk	LLS02[11665]	200–400		c 140	high base ring	
51	6: Sk	LLS02[5327]	180–250		148	high base ring	
52	6: Sk	179BHS89[305]<474>	post-Roman		150	high base ring	
53	6: Sk	LLS02[11463]			68	low base ring	
III Bowl with handles						**a) rounded**	
54	2: EoW	A27485; Old Broad Street	—				
						b) skyphos	
55 (4.8.1, 4.8.4)	1: Wal Mid	18542 (GM158); St Swithin's House	75–90	120	70		
56	2: EoW	LCT84[4331]<1821>	75–100	90			
57	6: Sk	CB80[971]<1623>	4th C			body fragment with handle attachment	
58	5: West	GPO75[836]<3856>	—			low base ring with 2 relief concentric rings (eg the Walbrook *skyphos* Cat no 55)	
59	5: West	GHT00[909]<209>	70–100		64		
60	5: West	GSM97[2468]<553>	120–140				
61	2: EoW	A27452: Old Broad Street	—			small frag from centre of base	
62	3: WoW	WAT78[2548]	850–1000				
63	2: EoW	FER97[3131]<1942>	100–120				
64	2: EoW	TEA98[1280]<279>	50–80				
IV Conical beaker						**a) plain**	
65	7: Cem E	HOO88[1417]<515>	180–300			lower part	
						b) without ridges above or below the zone of facets	
66	6: Sk	UNE03 [131] <209>	350–400			lower part	
67	2: EoW	LCT84[4337]<1934>	65–80			lower part	
68	6: Sk	LLS02[11737]	—			lower part	
69	6: Sk	WP83[751]<1005>	90–120			lower part	Shepherd 2005, 152, G17

Table 4.8.2 Continued

Nos: Cat (Fig)	Zone	Acc no; site	Context date	Rim diameter (mm)	Base diameter (mm)	Description details	Reference
						c) with ridges above and below the zone of facets	
70	3: WoW	CID90[852]<953>	70–120	c 100		tall beaker, rim missing	Hill and Woodger 1999, 15
71	4: East Low	RAG82[1516]<357>	70–120	88			
72	2: EoW	LCT84[4117]<1607>	70–100			upper part	
73	6: Sk	CB80[971]<1623>	4th C			upper part	
74	2: EoW	FSE76[71]<103>	55–70			small fragment from upper part of body	
75	6: Sk	LLS02[1547]				fragment from lower part of body	
76	2: EoW	KWS94[3474]<1768>	120–140			small fragment from lower part of body	
77	2: EoW	KWS94[2442]<805>	—			upper part	
78	4: East Low	RAG82[1516]<357>	70–120.			lower part	
79	6: Sk	LLS02[5555]	—		44	lower part	
80	6: Sk	LLS02[10608]			50	lower part	
81	5: West	GHT00[2864]<596>	70–130			lower part	
82	5: West	GPO75[7012]<1572>	100–120			lower part	
83	4: East Low	RAG82[1515]<356>	70–100			lower part	
84	4: East Low	RAG82[1537]<884>	120–200			lower part	
85	4: East Low	RAG82[1515]<356>	120–160			lower part	
			120–200			**b–c) body fragment with facets**	
86	5: West	GHT00[10735]<3201>	50–100				
87	5: West	GHT00[1159]<216>	70–100				
88	5: West	GPO75[4016]<4747>	—			base fragment	
89	5: West	GPO75[5857]<2965>	70–100				
90	5: West	GPO75[7745]<2876>	70–160				
91	5: West	GPO75[8112]<4255>	70–100				
92	5: West	GPO75[8982]<4379>	50–100				
93	5: West	GSM97[9527]<2064>	70–100				
94	2: EoW	ILA79[382]	100–200				
95	2: EoW	LCT84[4172]<1647>	40–100				
96	6: Sk	LLS02[6237]	10–120				
97	6: Sk	LLS02[8378]	70–130				
						d) with oval facets and/or sinuous grooves	
98 (4.8.4)	2: EoW	LCT84[9819]<2301>	75–80			body fragment	Shepherd 1993, 104, no 67, figs. 60 and 63
99	2: EoW	LCT84[4100]<1566>	95–100			body fragment	Shepherd 1993, 105, no 69
100	2: EoW	LCT84[4313]<1807>	85–95			body fragment	Shepherd 1993, 105, no 70
101	2: EoW	LCT84[4392]<1860>	85–95			body fragment	Shepherd 1993, 105, no 71
102	2: EoW	LCT84[9867]<2333>	65–75			body fragment	Shepherd 1993, 105, no 72
103	2: EoW	LCT84[4338]<2610>	55–80			body fragment	
104	2: EoW	LCT84[6432]<2445>	70–100			body fragment	
105	1: Wal Up	LOW88[841]<595>	—			body fragment	
106	6: Sk	WP83[4006]<1545>	80–100			body fragment	
						e) with diagonal grooves	
107	1: Wal Up	MRG95[1710]<285>	—	c 84		upper part	
108	2: EoW	CNL81[219]<46a>	70–120			upper part, rim missing	
109	2: EoW	CNL81[219]<46b>	70–120			body fragment, different vessel to Cat no 108	
110	6: Sk	HIB79[52]<324>	50–80			body fragment, probably same vessel as Cat no 110	
						f) with high-relief decoration	
111	6: Sk	HIB79[51]<323>	50–80				

Table 4.8.2 Continued

Nos: Cat (Fig)	Zone	Acc no; site	Context date	Rim diameter (mm)	Base diameter (mm)	Description details	Reference
112 (4.8.3)	3: WoW	21667; Ironmonger Lane	–	80	40	profile, decorated with 3 zones of flower and oval elements; H c 140 mm	
113 (4.8.4)	–	A21046; Leadenhall Street	–			upper part, decorated with hollowed out ovals and flowers, each with 8 slashes and a central pellet	Wheeler 1930, 122, no 7, fig 42
114 (4.8.4)	6: Sk	CB80[971]<1623a>	4th C			2 body fragments decorated with shells	Shepherd 1992, 125, no 59, fig 38
115	5: West	GYE92[14319]<*>	100–120			3 body fragments with leaf and stalks	
116	5: West	GHT00[8879]<2669>	70–100			body fragment with a horizontal ridge and a possible tendril or leaf stalk	
117	2: EoW	18029 (GM96); Lime Street	–			body fragment with probable leaves and stalks	
118	2: EoW	KWS94[1401]<2512>	–			body fragment with part of a high-relief oval and lozenge with a raised bar below	
119	2: EoW	LCT84[9598]<2155>	70–100			2 body fragments with a high-relief, broad and sinuous ribs with oval or circular motifs between	
120	5: West	GHT00[1327]<170>	90–100			body fragment with a large relief oval	
121	6: Sk	175BHS76[1156]<116>	60–100			body fragment with a relief lozenge(?) on a low-relief band	
						g) plain with indented body	
122	6: Sk	HIB79[48]<300>	50–120			body fragment	
						h) with indented body and facet decoration	
123 (4.8.4)	2: EoW	LCT84[9577]<2112>; LCT84[9760]<2263>	75–80			lower part	Shepherd 1993, 105, no 73, fig 63, pl 59
124	2: EoW	FSE76[48]<102>	60–80		66	body fragment	
125	5: West	GSM97[9358]<1987>	90–140			body fragment	Shepherd 2005, 151, G2, fig 10
126	6: Sk	WP83[3184]<1689>	80–120			body fragment	
127	–	23122; London	–				
						a–h) base fragment	
128	5: West	GHT00[10459]<2772>	60–160		32	a–h) base fragment	

5 Harvey Sheldon

Harvey puzzling out the stratigraphy of north Southwark. At this date (early 1970s) his pipe and trowel were never far away

5.1 Harvey Sheldon *Laura Schaaf with Nicholas Bateson, David Beard, George Dennis, Robin Densem, Fiona MacDonell, Derek Seeley and Rosemary Yeaxlee*

It is fitting that this volume of essays on Roman London is dedicated to Harvey Sheldon. Since the late 1960s Harvey has campaigned for the protection and study of London's rich buried archaeology and historic buildings. One of the key themes throughout Harvey's career has been the development of archaeology as a public service by leading local and regional archaeological units, teaching and publishing, and encouraging students and volunteers from a variety of backgrounds to enter the profession. Harvey's interest in history led him to attend his first archaeology adult education class in 1961 after graduating in Economics at Southampton, and starting work in market research in Holborn. It was in Holborn that Harvey conducted one of his earliest archaeological investigations when he observed work at the Holborn Post Office following a visit to a local pub.

His first excavation experience came in 1962 at Winchester Palace, Southwark, with Francis Celoria of the London Museum. Harvey completed his Diploma in Archaeology and, in 1966, with A E Brown commenced trial excavation of the Roman pottery kilns site at Highgate Wood. The first season of full excavation was in 1967 with 35 volunteers on site every day for six weeks and there was an annual training excavation into the 1970s. Many members of Harvey's developing team were recruited through this project. Finds were studied in evening classes and Harvey started teaching adult education archaeology courses in the mid-1960s, beginning a long association with the University of London Department of Extra-Mural Studies (later part of Birkbeck College). At this time he also worked on excavations in *Verulamium* and with John Alexander, a Lecturer in Archaeology at University of London and Cambridge extra-mural departments, allegedly leading a walkout on one of the sites.

Harvey and his team of part-time excavators undertook a programme of archaeological excavations from late 1969. The staff took casual employment between excavations and worked at weekends, enabling a team of experienced volunteers to develop alongside them. Work was commissioned through the London and Middlesex Archaeological Society (LAMAS) or the Southwark Archaeological Excavation Committee (SAEC, established in 1962, with funding provided by the Department of the Environment, other public authorities and landowners) to excavate sites at Clapham, Beddington, Old Ford and, in 1971, Topping's and Sun Wharves in Southwark. This last site was a turning point as the landowner was Hay's Wharf, an old-established company in the Pool of London, with headquarters overlooking the site. Soon a warehouse for finds processing and storage, and an office, were provided, an early example of corporate sponsorship that gave impetus and focus to the emerging team. The London Docks had largely been abandoned and the office next to Southwark Cathedral was surrounded by derelict warehouses. A sign on the door warned 'Close Door to Keep Rats Out'.

This period of consolidation was confirmed in 1972 when SAEC employed Harvey as Southwark Field Officer and he established a team of five full-time archaeologists. The 1970s saw the beginnings of a state-funded archaeology service as advocated at the Barford Conference in 1970. In the early 1970s the trust Rescue and the Council for British Archaeology campaigned for publicly funded regional archaeological units (*Rescue News* 1973 and Council for British Archaeology and RESCUE 1974). Many units were established across the country, often based in local museums and councils, and this expansive period was marked by research and rescue excavations and rapid development of techniques. Harvey's involvement in the development of publicly funded archaeological coverage for the boroughs around the city dates from this period. The Southwark unit began working in Lambeth in 1973, changing its name to Southwark and Lambeth Archaeological Excavation Committee (SLAEC), and Harvey had a major involvement in the establishment by LAMAS in 1974 of the Inner London Archaeological Unit, funded by the boroughs of Camden, Hackney, Hammersmith and Fulham, Islington, Kensington and Chelsea, Tower Hamlets and the City of Westminster. Other units working in Greater London in the 1970s included the South West London Archaeological Unit established by the Surrey Archaeological Society in 1974, the Passmore Edwards Museum team working in Newham and the Kent Archaeological Rescue Unit. In 1965 legislation was passed to join the London Museum and the Guildhall Museum to form the new Museum of London, and two teams were subsequently based there: the West London team in Brentford established in the mid-1960s and the new Department of Urban Archaeology (DUA) established in 1974. In 1975, Harvey was appointed a Field Officer in the Museum of London and assumed responsibility for the West London team, whilst continuing his role as head of the Southwark team.

In Southwark the work became more structured and a continuous programme of urban excavation on development sites ran throughout the 1970s. Excavations along Borough High Street and beneath old Thameside warehouses and wharves provided

Fig 5.1.1 Harvey and team at Lefevre Road, Bow, 1969/1970 (photo: John Warbis)

significant advances in understanding the Roman extra-mural settlement, its buildings, cemeteries, road system, chronological development and underlying topography, reflecting Harvey's enduring research interests. Prehistoric, Saxon and medieval discoveries were also plentiful. Members of the original Southwark team recall (in addition to the ruler for predicting Roman road alignments) Harvey's piece of string scaled to the length of hypothetical defences of the Saxon *burgh* of Southwark as given in the Burghal Hidage which could be overlaid on maps to test theories of the elusive Saxon settlement. For an irreverent flavour of those times, see the tribute to Harvey's 40th birthday, *Roman Southwark: my part in its downfall* (Barford *et al* 1979).

During the 1970s, Harvey was involved in new archaeological initiatives including a 1976 LAMAS working party investigating improvements to the funding and employment of archaeologists (Gromaticus 1978) and advocacy for the promotion of environmental archaeology by developing

London-wide policies and establishing a professional team (Keeley and Sheldon 1976).

The political, organisational and financial implications of drawing 32 London boroughs into a co-ordinated archaeological service were daunting. It is a mark of Harvey's and other leading London archaeologists' perseverance that this was eventually achieved. In 1983 Harvey became head of the Museum of London's new Department of Greater London Archaeology (DGLA), established with funding from the Greater London Council (GLC) and incorporating the Southwark and Lambeth, South West, West and Inner London teams. DGLA, the Passmore Edwards Museum and the Kent Archaeological Rescue Unit together provided archaeological coverage for the whole of Greater London. The GLC also funded London's first central database of excavations and finds, with a Sites and Monuments team. The epic inaugural celebration for DGLA at County Hall is fondly remembered, particularly for a red-coated master of ceremonies announcing each archaeologist in turn to the line of

Fig 5.1.2 For many years Harvey was rarely seen without his pipe. When he sent a 'customer's suggestion' form requesting a particular tobacco to the Harrod's smoke shop he was amused to receive a reply from the food halls expressing regret that they could not supply 'Sliced Condor' because it was a protected species

formally robed worthies greeting the guests. To their great credit, none appeared to notice that staff had come straight from the excavations in site clothing.

Rather like medieval city-states though, the cultures of the local units, often developed in tough inner city areas, remained strong within the larger whole. Rivalries were evidenced by lively debates over recording systems and highly competitive darts matches, first played on Harvey's initiative in the early 1970s. A Southwark stalwart was suitably impressed when visiting the West London office, within a council estate in Brentford, and being shown repairs to the walls where local youths had tried to break in using a concrete bollard mounted on a shopping trolley for a battering ram.

One of the authors, who like so many started as a volunteer and progressed to full-time work, remembers her first meeting with Harvey:

I came as a raw, completely overwhelmed volunteer to work on a site in Southwark towards the end of 1984. Totally bemused by levels, northings and southings, the site staff allowed this nutcase to find her feet and she began to realise that one name was often mentioned: Harvey Sheldon. The name became manifest late one afternoon when he visited the site and we werc all ready with finds trays on parade. It soon became apparent to me that Harvey's role in the formation of the unit was linked to the inroads he had made into the

Fig 5.1.3 Harvey, as immortalised by Old Ford and Southwark illustrator Eddie Jeffreys

attitudes of developers towards archaeology when he got them to appreciate not only the importance of the work but to pay for it. Then there was the personal side of becoming acquainted with Harvey. I discovered his kindness and concern when he learned of my father's death. Over the years I have known him as a class tutor, President of the Extra-Mural Archaeological Society and a person who has never ceased in his concern for London's archaeology. I have always thought of him as 'Mr London Archaeology'. Regrettably, not all volunteers' experiences were so positive. One new recruit was puzzled to be told that 'our boss ate your lunch', not realising that Boss was Harvey's eccentric Southwark terrier, well known for raiding bags left in the site office. She did not return after lunch.

But even at this moment of triumph, times and ideologies were changing. Margaret Thatcher had become Prime Minister in 1979 and the gradual move in British archaeology from regional trusts and units towards privatisation and site-specific developer funding was already under way. The GLC opposed the government and was abolished in 1986. Following a lengthy campaign by Harvey and others its financial responsibilities for DGLA were transferred to the Historic Buildings and Monuments Commission (later English Heritage) but it was becoming obvious that public sources alone would no longer sustain the service.

Typically, Harvey was at the forefront of the next phase in the evolution of London archaeology, its move into development planning. With the opportunity for co-ordinated initiatives via the GLC gone, in 1987 DGLA established a planning and negotiations team to work with individual local authorities and developers. The aim was to ensure that archaeological sites in Greater London affected by development were recognised, safeguarded and excavated in a systematic manner. Its success in establishing local archaeological policies through the London Unitary Development Plans and in generating developer funding during the 1980s development boom provided stability and helped offset the erosion of public sources. As a result, the mid- to late 1980s were again a confident, expansionary period, with a series of major excavations by DGLA. The individual sites are too numerous to list here but exciting discoveries included:

- prehistoric settlements and landscapes at Sipson Lane, Holloway Lane and Stockley Park on the gravel deposits of West London;
- nationally important Late Upper Palaeolithic and Early Mesolithic flint and faunal assemblages at Three Ways Wharf, Uxbridge;
- new information about Roman Southwark including rich stone-built complexes in Southwark Street and beneath Winchester Palace and a timber warehouse (rarely preserved) at the former Courage Brewery site;
- the eastern cemetery of Roman London at various sites in Tower Hamlets;
- Roman roadside settlements in Old Ford and Brentford;
- the 'lost' Middle Saxon trading port *Lundenwic* in the Covent Garden area;
- the important urban and rural medieval religious houses Bermondsey Abbey, Merton Priory, Charterhouse, the Priory of St John of Jerusalem and St Mary's nunnery in Clerkenwell, the Abbey of St Clare, Abbey of St Mary Graces and the Priory and Hospital of St Mary Spital;
- medieval Winchester Palace and Edward III's residence at Rotherhithe;
- London's medieval market towns Kingston and Uxbridge;
- medieval bridges at Kingston and London;
- Tudor playhouses the Rose and the Globe.

The immeasurable increase in the knowledge of Greater London's archaeology gained during the years of Harvey's leadership is documented in *Archaeology in Greater London 1965–90* (Thompson *et al* 1998) and *The archaeology of Greater London* (MoLAS 2000).

The 1980s model for archaeology, however, reflecting the free enterprise property world of the time, was heavily dependent on voluntary co-operation (British Archaeologists and Developers Liaison Group 1986). Although DGLA had great success in encouraging London boroughs to take a more formal responsibility for their own heritage (notably by seeking archaeological excavations in advance of development) government guidance was ambiguous and lagged behind professional practice. A Department of the Environment planning circular in 1985 recommended allowing archaeologists limited site access during construction (DoE Circular 1/85). Another in 1987 established the validity of preserving unscheduled remains, but implied that it was not reasonable to expect developers to pay for archaeological works (DoE Circular 8/87). The more successful DGLA was in generating commercial sponsorship, the more likely it became that the remaining core public service funding would be withdrawn. Combining these two functions became increasingly difficult and, without a clear regulatory framework, open to accusations of conflicts of interest.

These inherent tensions were dramatically exposed in 1989/1990. At the Queen's Hotel in York, Huggin Hill in the City of London and Southbridge House in Southwark, high-value urban developments coincided with high-profile, well-preserved remains of national importance. The first two sites contained important Roman buildings and the third the Tudor Rose Theatre. Although conventional excavations were feasible, this still implied removal of the physical remains and Museum of London archaeologists faced an unfamiliar dilemma. The public perception was clear – that structures of such quality should be retained *in situ* for posterity, preferably with public access. In the case of the Rose they included foundations of the stage on which Shakespeare's players performed. Prominent actors led a public blockade of the site and the newly formed Rose Theatre Trust sought a judicial review of the Secretary of State's refusal to Schedule the site but planning consents had been granted and could not be revoked without paying substantial compensation. Redesign to incorporate and display the remains could only be sought on a voluntary basis. This 1980s mechanism (based heavily on negotiation and to some extent bluff) had proved surprisingly successful in securing archaeological excavations but was inadequate to the new challenge and the design solutions did not resolve the issue of public access. The resulting furore reverberated at a national level, as reflected in the debates of the House of Commons and other contemporary accounts (discussed in detail in Eccles 1990,

147–237). Concerns within the archaeological profession about commercial pressures and the lack of regulation were reflected in a Rescue conference of 1990 (Swain 1991). The conference was organised while Harvey was Chair of Rescue, a post he held between 1986 and 1991 and again in 1999–2004 during a long association with the trust.

These events led, in 1990, to new government guidance which places archaeological decision making within the planning process, secures preservation *in situ* as the first option for nationally significant remains and emphasises the need for assessment and investigation prior to development (DoE 1990). But there were inevitably repercussions and London archaeology was heavily restructured in 1991. The establishment funding for the DGLA and both DUA and DGLA were abolished in favour of a new unified commercial structure, the Museum of London Archaeology Service, with the SMR and Greater London archaeological planning advice largely transferred to English Heritage. Harvey who characteristically had fought an uncompromising rearguard action for the public archaeology side in the debate lost his job.

Since then Harvey has not so much sought a new direction in his career as continued with the old one. Throughout and following the two decades when he did so much to establish and develop professional archaeological teams he has maintained close contacts with non-professionals by teaching and by an active involvement in archaeological and historical societies including serving as President of the West Essex Archaeological Group, the Enfield Archaeological Society, the Hendon and District Archaeological Society, the Extra-Mural Archaeological Society, the Southwark and Lambeth Archaeological Society, and notably the London and Middlesex Archaeological Society of which he is both a past President and for many years Chair of the Archaeological Research Committee (now Archaeology Committee). From the 1970s onwards Harvey has taught Certificate and Diploma of Archaeology students as well as leading lecture series, weekend courses, day courses and guided walks for the general public. In 1992 he increased his teaching commitments and in 1998, with Tony Legge, founded the MA in Archaeology at Birkbeck College where he is currently Associate Lecturer for the Archaeology MA.

In the 1990s he also re-established a summer training excavation for students and the general public, following on from the training digs held in Southwark in the 1970s and 1980s. Since 1995 the courses have been held in Havering, Hounslow, Lewisham and Southwark, proving very popular, with over 100 people taking part each year. In 2004 the training excavation moved to Syon Park, Isleworth, where each summer participants have investigated the remains of England's only Bridgettine Abbey, which preceded the present

Fig 5.1.4 Harvey on the roof of Syon House, 2006, during a break in the Birkbeck training excavations. Note that the pipe and trowel have now been replaced by a mobile phone! (photo: Jane Sidell)

stately home. Harvey also continues to work for the eventual display of the Rose Theatre as a founder member of the Rose Theatre Trust. Harvey's achievements have been recognised by his election as a Fellow of the Society of Antiquaries of London, a Fellow of the Royal Society of Arts and an invitation to become a Trustee of Borough Market.

Several of Harvey's attributes can be seen in the early days of his archaeological career. His charisma and belief that archaeology should be carried out as a team activity meant that volunteers and full-time excavators congregated around him. His belief that archaeology is a public activity led to him giving many lectures to local archaeological societies and to other audiences, gaining support for the endeavours and foreshadowing the current enthusiasm for promoting public access to archaeology. The fact that his projects were promptly published in the *London Archaeologist* and the *Transactions of the London and Middlesex Archaeological Society* encouraged public authorities to provide grants to Harvey and his burgeoning team to carry out excavations throughout London. Finally, his integrity and commitment were recognised by Hay's Wharf and the Southwark Archaeological Excavation Committee, providing him with premises and employment for his first full-time team. The rest is history – and he is still making it!

5.2 Harvey Sheldon: Bibliography
Compiled by Fiona MacDonell and Robin Densem

1966

Brown, A E, & Sheldon, H L, 1966 A note on observations in Holborn, Thames Valley Archaeological Observers Group

1968

Brown, A E, & Sheldon, H L, 1968 A Roman kiln site in Highgate Wood, *Camden J*, **3**(5)

1969

Brown, A E, & Sheldon, H L, 1969 Early Roman pottery factory in N London, *London Archaeol*, **1**(2), 38–44

Brown, A E, & Sheldon, H L, 1969 Post-excavation work on the pottery from Highgate, *London Archaeol*, **1**(3), 60–5

1970

Brown, A E, & Sheldon, H L, 1970 Highgate, 1969, *London Archaeol*, **1**(7), 150–4

Sheldon, H, 1970 Current dig at Old Ford, *London Archaeol*, **1**(6), 136–9

1971

Brown, A E, & Sheldon, H L, 1971 Highgate Wood 1970–71, *London Archaeol*, **1**(13), 300–3

Sheldon, H, 1971 Excavations at Lefevre Road, Old Ford E3, September 1969–June 1970, *Trans London Middlesex Archaeol Soc*, **23**(1), 42–77

Sheldon, H, 1971 Excavations at Toppings Wharf, Tooley Street, Southwark, *London Archaeol*, **1**(11), 252–4

1972

Barrett, J, Sheldon, H, & Symberlist, R, 1972 Roman Pottery found at 37, Southwood Lawn Road, Highgate Village, *Trans London Middlesex Archaeol Soc*, **23**(2), 171–3

Sheldon, H, 1972 A Roman burial from Armagh Road, Old Ford, *London Archaeol*, **1**(15), 348–53

Sheldon, H, 1972 Excavations at Parnell Road and Appian Road, Old Ford E3, February–April 1971, *Trans London Middlesex Archaeol Soc*, **23**(2), 101–47

1973

Evans, P, Sheldon, H, Walker, S, & Edwards, R, 1973 Excavations at New Hibernia Wharf, *London Archaeol*, **2**(5), 99–103

Farrant, N, & Sheldon, H, 1973 Rescue archaeology in the city – the future of London's past, *London Archaeol*, **2**(4), 87–9

Owen, W, Schwab, I, & Sheldon, H, 1973 Roman burials from Old Ford E3, February and May 1972, *Trans London Middlesex Archaeol Soc*, **24**, 135–45

Sheldon, H, 1973 Further excavations at no 31, Clapham Common, South Side, *Trans London Middlesex Archaeol Soc*, **24**, 151–4

1974

Brown, A E, & Sheldon, H L, 1974 Highgate Wood: The pottery and its production, *London Archaeol*, **2**(9), 222–31

Merrifield, R, & Sheldon, H, 1974 Roman London Bridge: A view from both banks, *London Archaeol*, **2**(8), 183–91

Sheldon, H, 1974 Excavations at Toppings and Sun Wharves, Southwark, 1970–72, *Trans London Middlesex Archaeol Soc*, **25**, 1–116

Sheldon, H, 1974 Letter: Excavations at New Hibernia Wharf, *London Archaeol*, **2**(7), 179

1975

Sheldon, H, 1975 A decline in the London settlement AD 150–250?, *London Archaeol*, **2**(11), 278–83

Sheldon, H, 1975 Reply: London's Decline AD 150–250, *London Archaeol*, **2**(13), 344

Sheldon, H, 1975 Review: *The Archaeology of London*, by Ralph Merrifield (1975), *London Archaeol*, **2**(11), 291

1976

Keeley, H, & Sheldon, H, 1976 Environmental Archaeology: A policy for London?, *London Archaeol*, **2**(16), 415–16

Sheldon, H, 1976 Principles of publication in Rescue Archaeology, *London Archaeol*, **2**(16), 414

Sheldon, H, 1976 Recent developments in the archaeology of Greater London, *J Royal Soc Arts*, **123**, 411–25

1978

Sheldon, H, 1978 The 1972–74 excavations: Their contribution to Southwark's history, in Southwark & Lambeth Archaeological Excavation Committee 1978, *Southwark Excavations 1972–1974*, LAMAS/SAS Joint Publ **1** (2 vols). London: London and Middlesex Archaeological Society, Surrey Archaeological Society, 11–49

Sheldon, H, 1978 93–95 Borough High Street, in Southwark & Lambeth Archaeological Excavation Committee 1978, *Southwark Excavations 1972–1974*, LAMAS/SAS Joint Publ **1** (2 vols). London: London and Middlesex Archaeological Society, Surrey Archaeological Society, 423–68

Sheldon, H, 1978 Ralph Merrifield retires, *London Archaeol*, **3**(8), 205

Sheldon, H, 1978 Review: Techniques of Archaeological Excavation by Philip Barker (1977), *London Archaeol*, **3** (6), 164–5

Sheldon, H, & Schaaf, L, 1978 A survey of Roman sites in Greater London, in J Bird, H Chapman & J Clark (eds), *Collectanea Londiniensia. Studies in London archaeology and history presented to Ralph Merrifield,* LAMAS Special Paper **2**.

London: London and Middlesex Archaeological Society, 59–88

1979

Ferretti, E, Sheldon, H, & Yule, B, 1979 Roman buildings in Greenwich Park, 1978, *Kent Archaeol Review*, **56**, 132

McIsaac, W, Schwab, I, & Sheldon, H L, 1979 Excavations at Old Ford, 1972–1975, *Trans London Middlesex Archaeol Soc*, **30**, 39–96

Sheldon, H, & Yule, B, 1979 Excavations in Greenwich Park, 1978–79, *London Archaeol*, **3**(12), 311–17

1981

Sheldon, H, 1981 London and South East Britain, in A King & M Henig (eds), *The Roman West in the Third Century: Contributions from archaeology and history*, BAR Int Ser **109**. Oxford: British Archaeological Reports, 363–82

1983

Sheldon, H, & Tyers, I, 1983 Recent dendrochronological work in Southwark and its implications, *London Archaeol*, **4**(13), 355–61

1984

Sheldon, H, & Schaaf, L, 1984 More light on Roman London, *Illustrated London News*, **272**, 56–7

Sheldon, H, & Schaaf, L, 1984 *Rescuing the past in Southwark*. London: Southwark and Lambeth Archaeological Excavation Committee

1985

Milne, G, & Sheldon, H, 1985 Where has all the funding gone?, *Rescue News*, **37**, 1

1986

Chitty, G, Clubb, N, Greenwood, P, Hammerson, M, Mills, J, Mills, P, Orton, C, & Sheldon, H, 1986 Greater London's Rescue Archaeology Service: A *Rescue News* special report, *Rescue News*, **38**

1988

Hobley, B, Sheldon, H, & Maloney, J, 1988 Big bang unearths London's rich past, *Illustrated London News*, **276**, 40–9

Sheldon, H, 1988 Crisis in maritime archaeology, *Rescue News*, **45**, 1–2

Sheldon, H, 1988 Foreword, in P Hinton (ed), *Excavations in Southwark 1973–76 and Lambeth 1973–79*, LAMAS/SAS Joint Pub **3**. London: London and Middlesex Archaeological Society & Surrey Archaeological Society, 1–2

1989

Sheldon, H, 1989 The curious case of the Queen's Hotel, *Rescue News*, **47**, 1

1990

Blackmore, L, Cotton, J, & Sheldon, H, 1990 *Recent Archaeological Excavations in Greater London: The work of the Department of Greater London Archaeology*, Museum of London 1986 Annual Archaeology Lecture. London: Museum of London

Hammerson, M, & Sheldon, H, 1990 Rescue archaeology in Greater London, *London Environmental Bulletin (Greater London Council)*, **6**(1), 17–19

Heard, K, Sheldon, H, & Thompson, P, 1990 Mapping Roman Southwark, *Antiquity*, **64**(244), 608–19

Sheldon, H, 1990 The Museum of London and the Rose, *Antiquity*, **64**(243), 286–8

1992

Sheldon, H, 1992 Hugh Chapman, *British Archaeological News*, **7**(5), 65

1993

Sheldon, H, 1993 Obituary: Eddie Jeffreys, *London Archaeol*, **7**(2), 46

Sheldon, H, 1993 Obituary: John Earp (d 1993), *London Archaeol*, **7**(4), 111

Sheldon, H, Corti, G, Green, D, & Tyers, P, 1993 The distribution of villas in Kent, Surrey and Sussex: some preliminary findings from a survey, *London Archaeol*, **7**(2), 40–5

1995

Corti, G, & Sheldon, H, 1995 Roman villas in south east England – an addendum, *London Archaeol*, **7**(14), 383

Sheldon, H, 1995 Hereward the unknown: a tale of a lost opportunity, *Rescue News*, **67**, 1

Sheldon, H, 1995 London and the Saxon Shore – the 1994 LAMAS Presidential Address, delivered in February 1994, *Trans London Middlesex Archaeol Soc*, **46**, 59–68

Sheldon, H, 1995 Obituary: Ralph Merrifield, *London Archaeol*, **7**(11), 298

1996

Bird, J, Hassall, M, & Sheldon, H, (eds) 1996 *Interpreting Roman London: papers in memory of Hugh Chapman*, Oxbow Monogr **58**. Oxford: Oxbow Books

Sheldon, H, 1996 Brief encounter I, *Rescue News*, **68**, 3

Sheldon, H, 1996 Eric S Wood, *London Archaeol*, **8**(3), 75

Sheldon, H, 1996 In Search of *Sulloniacis* in J Bird *et al* (eds) 1996, 233–42

Sheldon, H, 1996 Southwark and London – the 1995 LAMAS Presidential Address, delivered February 1995, *Trans London Middlesex Archaeol Soc*, **47**, 79–85

1997

Green, D, Sheldon, H, Hacker, M, Woon, C, & Rowlinson, H, 1997 The distribution of villas in some south eastern counties: Some preliminary findings from a survey, *London Archaeol*, **8**(7), 187–95

1998

Densem, R, & Sheldon, H, 1998 Popular archaeology: recent training digs in Southwark, London, *Rescue News*, **76**, 4

2000

Haynes, I, Sheldon, H, & Hannigan, L, 2000 *London Under Ground: The archaeology of a city*. Oxford: Oxbow Books

Sheldon, H, 2000 Roman Southwark, in I Haynes *et al* (eds) 2000, 121–50

Sheldon, H, & Haynes, I, 2000 Introduction: Twenty-five years of London archaeology, in I Haynes *et al* (eds) 2000, 1–8

2004

Sheldon, H, 2004 Review Article: Recording Roman London, *Antiquity,* **78**(300), 442–9

2006

Cotton, J and Sheldon, H, 2006 Archaeological work at Hatch Furlong, Ewell 2006: Interim report, *Surrey Archaeol Soc Bull,* **397**, 1–5

Sheldon, H, 2006 *The Lost Abbey of Syon*. London: Birkbeck, University of London

2007

Cotton, J and Sheldon, H, 2007 Archaeology at Hatch Furlong, Ewell, 2007: Second interim report, *Surrey Archaeol Soc Bull,* **405**, 1–6

Sheldon, H, 2007 Verlamio(n), Verulamium and St Albans: A Tale of Three Cities?, *Britannia,* **38**, 370–2

Bibliography

Adams, J N, 1990 The *forfex* of the *veterinarius* Virilis (Vindolanda Inv No 86/470) and ancient methods of castrating horses, *Britannia,* **21**, 267–71

Adams, J N, 2003 The word *moritix* in a new inscription from London, *Zeitschrift für Papyrologie und Epigraphik,* **143**, 275–6

Alarcão, J, & Alarcão, A, 1965 *Vidros romanos de Conimbriga.* Lisbon: Ministério da Educação Nacional

Alexander, M, & Stephenson, A, 2004 A post-excavation assessment report on archaeological evaluation and excavation work carried out at Crown Iron Works, Borough of Tower Hamlets, London E3. Unpubl report for AOC Archaeology, Site Code DAC03

Allason-Jones, L, 1993 Small finds in P J Casey & J L Davies, *Excavations at Segontium (Caernarfon) Roman Fort 1975–1979,* CBA Res Rep, **90**. London: Council for British Archaeology, 165–210

Allen, D, 1986 The glass vessels, in J D Zienkiewicz 1986b, 98–116

Allen, M J, Scaife, R, Cameron, N, & Stevens, C J, 2005 Excavations at 211 Long Lane; prehistoric neckinger-side environment in Southwark and its implications for prehistoric communities, *London Archaeol,* **11**(3), 73–81

Alston, R, 2002 *The City in Roman and Byzantine Egypt.* New York: Routledge

Amand, M, 1984 *Vases à Bustes, Vases à Décor Zoomorphe et Vases Cultuels aux Serpents dans les Anciennes Provinces de Belgiques et de Germanie.* Brussels: Palais des académies

Anon, 1923 Course of the Grimsdyke, *Antiq J,* **3**, 66

Anon, 1992 St Neot's Sport Ground, An Archaeological Evaluation. Unpubl report for Newham Museum Services, Site Code RO-SN92

Anon, 2003a 69 Main Road, Gidea Park Romford, Archaeological Report. Unpubl report for Essex County Council Field Archaeology Unit, Site Code MNF03

Anon, 2003b Roman baths at trading settlement by Thames, *Brit Archaeol,* **69**, 4

Anon, 2004 The 'Babe Ruth' bath-house: Londinium's lost port?, *Current Archaeol,* **193**, 20–7

Armitage, P, Davis, A, Straker, V, & West, B, 1983 Underground London. Bugs, bones and botany, *Popular Archaeol,* **4**(9), 24–34

Arveiller-Dulong, V, & Ziviello, C, 2005 Quelques verres à décor grave du Musée Archéologique National de Naples in *Annales du 16e Congrès de l'Association Internationale pour l'histoire du Verre.* Nottingham: L'Association Internationale pour l'Histoire du Verre, 109–12

Atkinson, D, 1942 *Report on Excavations at Wroxeter (the Roman City of Viroconium) in the County of Salop 1923–1927,* Birmingham Archaeol Soc. Oxford: Oxford University Press

Aubrey, J, 1980 *Monumenta Britannica, or, a miscellany of British antiquities: Parts One and Two,* eds J Fowles & R Legg. Sherborne: Dorset Publishing Co

Auguet, R, 1972 *Cruelty and Civilization: The Roman Games.* London: Allen & Unwin

Baatz, D, 1993 *Der Römische Limes. Archaölogische Ausflüge zwischen Rhein und Donau.* Berlin: Gebr. Mann Verlag

BADLG, 1986: British Archaeologists & Developers Liaison Group, 1986 *Code of Practice*

[Bagford, J], 1710 An Account of several Antiquities, supposed to buried by the Romans, and also of the most Remarkable Structures, Rarities, &c. in the City of London, in *A Compleat Volume of the Memoirs for the Curious, from January 1707, to December 1708,* 2 vols. London: A Morphew, J Woodward & D Leach, vol 2, 113–22, 149–51

Bagford, J, 1715 A Letter to the Publisher, written by the ingenious Mr. JOHN BAGFORD, in which are many curious Remarks relating to the City of LONDON, and some things about LELAND, in T Hearne (ed), *Johannis Lelandi Antiquarii de Rebus Britannicis Collectanea,* 2nd edn, 6 vols. Oxford: E Theatro Sheldoniano, vol 1 lviii–lxxxvi

Bagnall Smith, J, 1995 Interim report on the votive material from Romano-Celtic temple sites in Oxfordshire, *Oxoniensia,* **60**, 177–203

Bagnall Smith, J, 1998 More votive finds from Woodeaton, Oxfordshire, *Oxoniensia,* **63**, 147–85

Bailey, D, 1983 Terracotta revetments, figurines and lamps, in M Henig (ed) 1983, 191–204

Bailey, J, & Shepherd, J, 1985 The glass-working waste, in G Parnell 1985, 72–3

Bairoch, P, 1988 *Cities and Economic Development.* Chicago: University of Chicago Press

Barber, B, & Bowsher, D, 2000 *The Eastern Cemetery of Roman London: Excavations 1983–1990,* MoLAS Monogr Ser **4**. London: Museum of London Archaeology Service

Barber, B, Bowsher, J, & Whittaker, K, 1990 Recent excavations of a cemetery of Londinium, *Britannia,* **21**, 1–12

Barber, B, & Thomas, C, 2002 *The London Charterhouse,* London: MoLAS Monogr Ser, **10**. London: Museum of London Archaeology Service

Barford, S, Hammerson, M, Mackenna, S, & Schaaf, L (eds), 1979 *Roman Southwark; my part in its downfall or they only came for the archaeology. Essays presented to Harvey Sheldon FSA on the occasion of his 40th Birthday.* London: privately printed

Barker, B, 2004 63 Main Road, Gidea Park. Archaeological evaluation by trial trenching. Unpubl report for Essex County Council Field Archaeology Unit, Site Code MGK04

Barrett, A A, 1977 A Virgilian scene from Frampton Villa, Dorset, *Antiq J,* **57**, 312–13

Barrett, A A, 1978 Knowledge of the literary classics in Roman Britain, *Britannia,* **9**, 307–13

Barton, C A, 1989 The scandal of the arena, *Representations,* **27**, 1–36

Barton, N J, 1962 *The Lost Rivers of London.* London: Phoenix House, Leicester University Press

Bateman, N, 1997 The London amphitheatre: Excavations 1987–1996, *Britannia,* **28**, 51–85

Bateman, N, 2000 *Gladiators at the Guildhall. The story of London's Roman amphitheatre and medieval Guildhall.* London: Museum of London Archaeology Service

Bateman, N, Cowan, C, & Wroe-Brown, R, forthcoming *London's Roman Amphitheatre: Guildhall Yard East, City of London EC2,* MoLAS Monogr Ser. London: Museum of London Archaeology Service

Bateman, N, & Milne, G, 1983 A Roman harbour in London: Excavations and observations near Pudding Lane, City of London 1979–82, *Britannia,* **14**, 207–26

Bauman, R A, 1996 *Crime and Punishment in Ancient Rome.* London: Routledge

Bayley, J, & Butcher, S, 2004 *Roman Brooches in Britain: A technological and typological study based on the Richborough collection.* Soc Antiqs London Res Rep, **68**. London: Society of Antiquaries of London

Beard, M, North, J, & Price, S, 1998 *Religions of Rome,* 2 vols. Cambridge: Cambridge University Press

Beasley, M, 1993 Evaluation at Havering Council Technical Offices and Social Education Centre, Spilsby Road, Harold Hill. Unpubl report for Newham Museum Services, Site Code RO-TO93

Beasley, M, 2000 An archaeological excavation at The Old Sorting Office, Swan Street, London Borough of Southwark, Unpubl report for Pre-Construct Archaeology

Beasley, M, Armitage, P, & Lyne, M, 2006 Roman boundaries, roads and ritual: Excavations at the Old Sorting Office, Swan Street, Southwark, *Trans London Middlesex Archaeol Soc,* **57**, 23–68

Bedford, R, & Bowlt, C, 1977 Excavations of an earthwork at Manor Farm, Ruislip, *London Archaeol,* **3**(4), 87–9

Bentley, D, 1984 A recently identified valley in the City, *London Archaeol,* **5**(1), 13–16

Berger, L, 1960 *Römische Gläser aus Vindonissa,* Veröffentlichungen der Gesellschaft pro Vindonissa **4**. Basel: Birkhäuser Verlag

Bidder, H F, & Morris, J, 1959 The Anglo-Saxon cemetery at Mitcham, *Surrey Archaeol Collect,* **56**, 51–131

Biddle, M, 1967 Two Flavian burials from Grange Road, Winchester, *Antiq J,* **47**, 224–50

Biddle, M, Hudson, D, & Heighway, C, 1973 *The Future of London's Past. A survey of the archaeological implication of planning and development in the nation's capital,* Rescue Publ, **4**. Hertford: RESCUE

Bidwell, P, 1997 *Roman Forts in Britain.* London: Batsford/English Heritage

Bird, D G, 1994 The origins of Roman London, *London Archaeol,* **7**(10), 268–70

Bird, D G, 2004 *Roman Surrey.* Stroud: Tempus

Bird, J, 1993 Third-century samian ware in Britain, *J Roman Pottery Stud,* **6**, 1–14

Bird, J, 1996 Frogs from the Walbrook: A cult pot and its attribution, in J Bird *et al* (eds) 1996, 119–27

Bird, J, 1998 The samian, in J Shepherd 1998, 106–7 & *passim*

Bird, J, 2002 Samian wares, in D Lakin *et al* 2002, 31–48

Bird, J, forthcoming a The decorated samian, in N Bateman *et al* forthcoming

Bird, J, forthcoming b The decorated samian, in J Hill & P Rowsome forthcoming

Bird, J, Chapman, H, & Clark, J (eds), 1978 *Collectanea Londiniensia. Studies in London archaeology and history presented to Ralph Merrifield,* LAMAS Special Paper, **2**. London: London & Middlesex Archaeological Society

Bird, J, Hassall, M, & Sheldon, H (eds), 1996 *Interpreting Roman London: papers in memory of Hugh Chapman,* Oxbow Monogr, **58**. Oxford: Oxbow Books

Birley, A R, 2005 *The Roman Government of Britain.* Oxford: Oxford University Press

Bishop, M C, 1996 *Finds from Roman Aldborough,* Oxbow Monogr, **65**. Oxford: Oxbow Books

Black, E W, 1987 *The Roman Villas of South-East England,* BAR Brit Ser, **171**. Oxford: British Archaeological Reports

Black, E W, 1995 *Cursus Publicus. The infrastructure of government in Roman Britain,* BAR Brit Ser, **241**. Oxford: British Archaeological Reports

Blackmore, L, 1997 From beach to *burh:* new clues to the identity of 7th- to 9th-century London, in G de Boe & F Verhaeghe (eds) 1997, 123–32

Blackmore, L, 2008 Pottery, in R Cowie & L Blackmore 2008, 168–93

Blackmore, L, Vince, A, & Cowie, R, 2004 The origins of Lundenwic? Excavations at 8–9 Long Acre/16 Garrick Street WC2, *London Archaeol,* **10**(11), 301–5

Blackmore, L, with Williams, D, 1997 The fifth-century pottery, in G Milne, *St Bride's Church*

London: Archaeological research 1952–60 and 1992–5, EH Archaeol Rep, **11**. London: English Heritage, 54–9

Blagg, T, 1980 The sculptured stones, in C Hill *et al* 1980, 125–93

Blagg, T, Plouviez, J, & Tester, A, 2004 *Excavations at a Large Romano-British Settlement at Hacheston, Suffolk, 1973–74*, East Anglian Archaeol, **106**. Ipswich: Suffolk County Council

Blair, I, Spain, R, Swift, D, & Taylor, T, with Goodburn, D, forthcoming Wells and bucket chains: The unforeseen elements of water supply in early Roman London, *Britannia*

Bliquez, L J, 1994 *Roman surgical instruments and other minor objects in the National Archaeological Museum of Naples*. Mainz: Philipp von Zabern

Bluer, R, 2002 Romford Golf Course, Gidea Park, Romford. An archaeological excavation. Unpubl report for Museum of London Archaeology Service, Site Code RGC02

Bluer, R, & Brigham, T, with Nielsen, R, 2006 *Roman and Later Development East of the Forum and Cornhill: Excavations at Lloyd's Register, 71 Fenchurch Street, City of London*, MoLAS Monogr Ser, **30**. London: Museum of London Archaeology Service

Boardman, J, & Vollenweider, M-L, 1978 *Engraved Gems and Finger Rings in the Ashmolean Museum. I Greek and Etruscan*. Oxford: Clarendon Press

Böhme, H W, 1986 Das ende der Römerherrschaft in Britannien und die Angelsächsische Besiedlung Englands im 5 Jahrhundert, *Jahrbuch Römisch-Germanischen Zentralmuseums Mainz* **33**, 469–574

Bolindeţ, V, 1999 Considérations sur l'attribution des vases de Dacie romaine décorées de serpents appliqués, *Ephemeris Napocensis*, **3**, 129–33

Boon, G C, 1973 Roman glassware from Caerwent 1855–1925, *Monmouthshire Antiq*, **3**, 111–23

Boon, G C, 1986 A strigil inlaid with labours of Herakles, in J D Zienkiewicz 1986b, 157–66

Bowe, P, 2004 *Gardens of the Roman World*. Los Angeles: J Paul Getty Museum

Bowman, A K, 1991 Literacy in the Roman empire: Mass and mode, in J H Humphrey (ed), *Literacy in the Roman World*. JRA Suppl Ser **3**. Ann Arbor, Mi: Journal for Roman Archaeology, 119–31

Bowman, A K, 1994 The Roman imperial army: Letters and literacy on the northern frontier, in A K Bowman & G Woolf (eds), *Literacy and Power in the Ancient World*. Cambridge: Cambridge University Press, 109–25

Bowman A K, & Thomas, J D, 1994 *The Vindolanda Writing-Tablets: Tabulae Vindolandenses* **2**. London: British Museum Press

Bowman, A K, & Thomas, J D, 2003 *The Vindolanda Writing-Tablets: Tabulae Vindolandenses* **3**. London: British Museum Press

Bowsher, D, 1995 An evaluation of the Roman road at Brockley Hill, Middlesex, *Trans London Middlesex Archaeol Soc*, **46**, 45–57

Boyer, M N, 1976 *Medieval French Bridges*. Cambridge, Mass: Medieval Academy of America

Boyer, P, 2003 An archaeological investigation at 510–518 Roman Road, Bow, London Borough of Tower Hamlets, Unpubl report for Pre-Construct Archaeology Ltd, Site Code RBW03

Branch, N, no date Pollen analysis of the sediment and peat columns from Bricklayers Arms Southwark London, Unpubl archive report for Department of Greater London Archaeology, Site Code BLA87

Braun, H, 1933 Earliest Ruislip, *Trans London Middlesex Archaeol Soc*, **7**(1), 99–123

Braun, H, 1936 Some earthworks of North-West Middlesex, *Trans London Middlesex Archaeol Soc*, **7**(3), 379–88

Brayley, E W, 1829 *Londiniana: or, Reminiscences of the British Metropolis*, 4 vols. London: Hurst, Chance & Co

Brewer, R J, 1993 Venta Silurum: A civitas capital, in S Greep (ed), *Roman Towns: The Wheeler inheritance. A review of 50 years' research*, CBA Res Rep, **93**. York: Council for British Archaeology, 56–65

Brewer, R J, 1997 *Caerwent Roman Town*, 2nd edn. Cardiff: Cadw

Brigham, T, 1990a A reassessment of the second basilica in London, AD 100–400: excavations at Leadenhall Court, 1984–86, *Britannia*, **21**, 53–97

Brigham, T, 1990b The late Roman waterfront in London, *Britannia*, **21**, 99–183

Brigham, T, 1998 The port of Roman London, in B Watson (ed) 1998b, 23–34

Brigham, T, Goodburn, D, & Tyers, I, 1995 A Roman timber building on the Southwark waterfront, London, *Archaeol J*, **152**, 1–72

Brigham, T, & Watson, B, 1996 Current archaeological work at Regis House in the City of London (part 2), *London Archaeol*, **8**(3), 63–9

Brigham, T, Watson, B, & Tyers, I, with Bartkowiak, R, 1996 Current archaeological work at Regis House in the City of London (part 1), *London Archaeol*, **8**(2), 31–8

Brigham, T, & Woodger, A, 2001 *Roman and Medieval Townhouses on the London Waterfront: Excavations at Governor's House, City of London*, MoLAS Monogr Ser, **9**. London: Museum of London Archaeology Service

British Museum, 1926 *Catalogue of the Engraved Gems and Cameos, Greek, Etruscan and Roman, in the British Museum*, 2nd edn. London: British Museum

British Museum, 1964 *Guide to the Antiquities of Roman Britain*, 3rd edn. London: British Museum

Brock, J K, & Young, G M, 1949 Excavations in Siphnos, *Ann Brit School at Athens*, **44**, 1–92

Brooks, N, 2000 Rochester Bridge AD 43–1381, in N Brooks 2000, *Communities and Warfare 700–1400*. London: Hambledon Press, 219–65

Brown, A, E (ed), 1991 *Garden Archaeology: Papers presented to a conference at Knuston Hall, Northamptonshire, April 1988, CBA Res Rep,* **78**. York: Council for British Archaeology

Brown, G, 1988 First century horticultural activity close to the municipal boundaries of Londinium, Unpubl archive report for Museum of London Archaeology Service, WIV88

Brown, G, Douglas, A, Ridgeway, V, & Taylor-Wilson, R, forthcoming *Traffic Control to Development Control: Archaeology at the Lefevre Walk Estate and adjacent sites in Old Ford*, PCA Monogr. London: Pre-Construct Archaeology Ltd

Brown, R A, 1986 The Iron Age and Romano-British Settlement at Woodcock Hall, Saham Toney, Norfolk, *Britannia,* **17**, 1–58

Brown, S, 1992 Death as decoration: Scenes from the arena on Roman domestic mosaics, in A Richlin (ed), *Pornography and Representation in Greece and Rome*. Oxford: Oxford University Press, 180–211

Brulet, R, 1989 The continental Litus Saxonicum, in V Maxwell (ed), *The Saxon Shore: A handbook*, Exeter Studies in History, **25**. Exeter: University of Exeter, 45–77

Budd, P, 2002 *Combined O-, Sr- and Pb-isotope analysis of dental tissues from a Neolithic individual from Shepperton and an Iron Age individual from Southwark, London,* Archaeotrace Rep **106**. Halifax: Archaeotrace

Burdon, N, 2004 Hindu finds from the Thames, *London Archaeol,* **10**(10), 276–9

Burkert, W, 1983 *Homo Necans: The anthropology of ancient Greek sacrificial ritual and myth* (trans P Bing). Berkeley, Ca & London: University of California Press

Burn, A R, 1969 *The Romans in Britain: An anthology of inscriptions,* 2nd edn. Oxford: Blackwell

Burnham, B C, & Wacher, J, 1990 *The 'Small Towns' of Roman Britain*. London: Batsford

Burton, E, Corcoran, J, Halsey, C, Jamieson, D, Malt, R, & Spurr, G, 2004 Lea Valley mapping project, Unpubl report for Museum of London Archaeology Service & British Geological Survey

Butler, J, 2005 *Saxons, Templars and Lawyers in the Inner Temple: Archaeological excavations in Church Court and Hare Court*, PCA Monogr **4**. London: Pre-Construct Archaeology Ltd

Butterworth, P, 1969 Moving a Roman kiln, *London Archaeol,* **1**(4), 75–9

Camden, W, 1610 *Britain, or a Chorographicall Description of the Most Flourishing Kingdomes, England, Scotland, and Ireland, and the Islands Adjoyning, Out of the Depth of Antiquitie*, trans P Holland. London: George Bishop & John Norton

Cameron, K, 1980 The meaning and significance of Old English w*alh* in English place-names, *J English Place-Name Soc,* **12**, 1–53

Campbell, G, & Hall, A, 2004 Roman plant introductions, Unpubl report for English Heritage

Carcopino, J, 1941 Daily Life in Ancient Rome (trans E O Lorimer). Harmondsworth: Penguin

Carlin, M, 1996 *Medieval Southwark*. London: Hambledon Press

Carr, G, 2003 Creolisation, pidginisation and the interpretation of unique artefacts in early Roman Britain, in G Carr, E Swift & J Weekes (eds), *TRAC 2002: Proceedings of the Twelfth Annual Theoretical Roman Archaeology Conference*. Oxford: Oxbow Books, 113–25

Carruthers, W, 2002 The plant remains, in R Taylor-Wilson 2002, 61–3

Cary, M, Nock, A D, Rose, H J, Harvey, H P, & Souter, A (eds), 1949 *The Oxford Classical Dictionary*. Oxford: Clarendon Press

Casson, L, Drummond-Murray, J, & Francis, A, forthcoming *Excavations at 10 Gresham Street, City of London*, MoLAS Monogr Ser. London: Museum of London Archaeology Service

Castle, S, 1975 Excavations in Pear Wood, Brockley Hill, Middlesex, 1948–1973, *Trans London Middlesex Archaeol Soc,* **26**, 267–77

CBA Group 10, 1960 *The Archaeologist in Essex, Hertfordshire, London and Middlesex 1959*

CBA/RESCUE, 1974 *Archaeology and Government*. York: Council for British Archaeology

Celoria, F, & Spencer, B W, 1968 Eighteenth-century fieldwork in London and Middlesex: some unpublished drawings by William Stukeley, *Trans London Middlesex Archaeol Soc,* **22**, 23–31

Cepas, A, 1989 *The North of Britain and the Northwest of Hispania, an Epigraphic Comparison,* BAR Int Ser, **470**. Oxford: British Archaeological Reports

Chadburn, A, & Tyers, P, 1984 The Roman Ceramics from Fenchurch Street, Early Roman Pottery from the City of London: 5, Unpubl report for the DUA

Chaffers, W, 1847 Exhibitions at ballot, April 22, 1846, *J Brit Archaeol Assoc,* **2**, 199

Chapman, H, & Johnson, T, 1973 Excavations at Aldgate and Bush Lane House in the City of London, 1972, *Trans London Middlesex Archaeol Soc,* **24**, 1–84

Chapouthier, F, Seston, W, & Boyancé, P (eds), 1940 *Mélanges d'études anciennes offerts à Georges Radet, Directeur de la Revue des études anciennes*. Bordeaux: Feret & fils; Paris: C Klincksieck

Charlesworth, D, 1961 Roman jewellery found in Northumberland and Durham, *Archaeol Ael 4th Ser,* **39**,1–36

Charlesworth, D, 1974 Glass vessels, in M Hassall & J Rhodes, Excavations at the New Market Hall, Gloucester 1966–67, *Trans Bristol & Gloucestershire Archaeol Soc,* **93**, 75–6

Chenery, M, 2005 The small finds, in B Philp 2005, 162–81

Clairmont, C W, 1963 *The Excavations at Dura-Europos, Final Report IV, Part V: Glass vessels.* New Haven: Dura-Europos Publications

Clark, J, 1981 Trinovantum – the evolution of a legend, *J Medieval Hist*, **7**, 135–51

Clark, J, 1996 The Temple of Diana, in J Bird *et al* (eds) 1996, 1–9

Clark, J, 2000 Late Saxon and Norman London: Thirty years on, in I Haynes *et al* (eds) 2000, 206–22

Clarke, P A, 2004 *A History of Pinner.* Chichester: Phillimore

Clauss, M, 1990 *Mithras: Kult und Mysterien.* Munich: C H Beck'sche

Clavel-Lévêque, M, 1984 *L'Empire en Jeux: Espace symbolique et pratique sociale dans le monde romain.* Paris: CNRS

Coates, R, 1998 A new explanation of the name London, *Trans Philological Soc*, **96**(2), 203–29

Codrington, T, 1928: *Roman Roads in Britain,* 3rd edn. London: The Sheldon Press

Coleman, K, 1990 Fatal charades: Roman executions staged as mythological enactments, *J Roman Stud,* **80**, 44–73

Collingwood, R G, & Taylor, M V, 1931 Roman Britain in 1930, *J Roman Stud,* **21**, 215–50

Collingwood, R G, & Wright, R P, 1965 *The Roman Inscriptions of Britain, 1: Inscriptions in stone.* Oxford: Oxford University Press

Collingwood, R G, Wright, R P, & Tomlin, R S O, 1995 *The Roman Inscriptions of Britain* (new edn). Stroud: Alan Sutton Publishing

Collins-Clinton, J, 1977 *A Late Antique Shrine of Liber Pater at Cosa.* Leiden: Brill

Cook, N C, 1969 An Anglo-Saxon saucer brooch from Lower Thames Street, London, *Antiq J*, **49**, 395

Cool, H E M, 1995 Other Roman objects of copper alloy, in R Rickett *The Anglo-Saxon Cemetery at Spong Hill, North Elmham, 7: The Iron Age, Roman and early Saxon settlement,* East Anglian Archaeol, **73**. Dereham: Norfolk Museums Service, 72–4

Cool, H E M, 2004 *The Roman Cemetery at Brougham, Cumbria: Excavations 1966–67,* Britannia Monogr Ser **21**. London: Society for the Promotion of Roman Studies

Cool, H E M, forthcoming *The Roman Glass from the Wolfson Wing, King's College London*

Cool, H E M, & Philo, C (eds), 1998 *Roman Castleford, excavations 1974–85 I: The small finds.* Wakefield: Yorkshire Archaeology

Cool, H E M, & Price, J, 1987 The glass, in G W Meates, *The Roman Villa at Lullingstone, Kent: 2, The wall-paintings and finds,* Kent Archaeol Soc Monogr, **3**. Maidstone: Kent Archaeological Society, 110–42

Corcoran, S J J, Salway, R W B, & Salway, P, 2002 *Moritix Londiniensium, Brit Epigraphic Soc Newsletter New Ser,* **8**, Autumn 2002, 10–12

Cosh, S R & Neal, D S, 2005 Daphne at Dinnington, *MOSAIC,* **32,** 23–5

Cotterill, J, 1993 Saxon raiding and the role of the late Roman coastal forts of Britain, *Britannia,* **24**, 227–39

Coupland, S, 1991 The fortified bridges of Charles the Bald, *J Med Hist*, **17**, 1–12

Cowan, C, 1992 A possible *mansio* in Roman Southwark: Excavations at 15–23 Southwark Street, 1980–86, *Trans London Middlesex Archaeol Soc,* **43**, 3–191

Cowan, C, 2003 *Urban Development in North-West Roman Southwark: Excavations 1974–90,* MoLAS Monogr Ser **16**. London: Museum of London Archaeology Service

Cowan, C, Seeley, F, Wardle, A, Westman, A, & Wheeler, L, forthcoming *Roman Southwark: Origins, Settlement and Economy: Excavations in Southwark 1973–1991.* MoLAS Monogr Ser. London: Museum of London Archaeology Service

Cowie, R, 2000 Londinium to Lundenwic: Early and Middle Saxon archaeology in the London Region, in I Haynes *et al* (eds) 2000, 175–205

Cowie, R, 2001 Mercian London, in M Brown & C Farr (eds), *Mercia: An Anglo-Saxon kingdom in Europe.* Leicester: Leicester University Press, 194–209

Cowie, R, & Blackmore, L, 2008 *Early and Middle Saxon Rural Settlement in the London Region,* MoLAS Monogr Ser **41**. London: Museum of London Archaeology Service

Cowie, R, & Blackmore, L, forthcoming *Lundenwic: Excavations in Middle Saxon London, 1987–2000,* MoLAS Monogr Ser. London: Museum of London Archaeology Service

Cox, J E, 1876 *The Annals of St Helen's, Bishopsgate, London.* London: Tinsley Brothers

Creighton, J, 1990 The Humber frontier in the 1st century AD, in S Ellis & D R Crowther (eds), *Humber Perspectives: A Region through the Ages.* Hull: Hull University Press, 182–98

Creighton, J, 2000 *Coins and Power in Late Iron Age Britain,* New Studies in Archaeology. Cambridge: Cambridge University Press

Creighton, J, 2006 *Britannia: The creation of a Roman province.* London & New York: Routledge

Croxford, B, 2003 Iconoclasm in Roman Britain?, *Britannia,* **34**, 81–95

Crummy, N, 1992 The Roman small finds from the Gilberd School site, in P Crummy, *Excavations at Culver Street, the Gilberd School, and Other Sites in Colchester 1971–85,* Colchester Archaeol Rep **6**. Colchester: Colchester Archaeological Trust, 206–50

Crummy, N, 2001 Nail-cleaners: Regionality at the clean edge of Empire, *Lucerna, Roman Finds Group Newsletter,* **22**, 2–6

Crummy, N, 2004 Using the Portable Antiquities Scheme data for research, *Lucerna, Roman Finds Group Newsletter,* **28**, 23–7

Crummy, N, & Eckardt, H, 2004 Regional identities and technologies of the self: Nail-cleaners in Roman Britain, *Archaeol J,* **160**, 44–69

Cullum, J, 1854 Exhibitions at ballot, January 12, 1853, *J Brit Archaeol Assoc,* **9**, 74

Cunliffe, B (ed), 1968 *Fifth Report on the Excavations of the Roman Fort at Richborough, Kent.* Soc Antiq London Res Rep, **23**. Oxford: Society of Antiquaries of London

Cunliffe, B, 1971 *Excavations at Fishbourne 1961–1969: 1, The site,* Soc Antiq London Res Rep, **26**. London: Society of Antiquaries of London

Cunliffe, B, 1998 *Fishbourne Roman Palace.* Stroud: Tempus

Currie, C, 2005 *Garden Archaeology,* CBA Practical Handbook, **17**. York: Council for British Archaeology

Daremberg, C, & Saglio, E (eds), 1877–1919 *Dictionnaire des Antiquités Grecques et Romains,* 5 vols. Paris: Hachette

Davey, N, & Ling, R, 1982 *Wall-painting in Roman Britain.* Britannia Monogr Ser, **3**. London: Society for the Promotion of Roman Studies

Davies, B, 1991 Roman pottery assessment from Docklands Light Railway Shaft, Bucklersbury, 3 Queen Vic St (near), EC4 City, Unpubl report for Department of Urban Archaeology, Museum of London

Davies, B, Richardson, B, & Tomber, R, 1994 *The Archaeology of Roman London 5: A dated corpus of early Roman pottery from the City of London,* CBA Res Rep, **98**. York: Council for British Archaeology

Davies, H, 2002: *Roads in Roman Britain.* Stroud: Tempus Publishing Ltd

Davies, R W, 1970 Some Roman medicine, *Medical History,* **14**, 101–6

Davis, A, 1993 Plant remains, in G Milne & A Wardle 1993, 59–67

Davis, A, 2003 The plant remains, in C Cowan 2003, 182–91

Davis, A, forthcoming a The plant remains from 1 Poultry, in J Hill & P Rowsome forthcoming

Davis, A, forthcoming b *The Londinium plant remains*

Davis, A, forthcoming c The plant remains from Blossom's Inn, 30 Gresham Street, in I Blair & B Watson with J Taylor, *Excavations at 30 Gresham Street London, City of London.* MoLAS Monogr Ser. London: Museum of London Archaeology Service

Davis, A, forthcoming d The plant remains from Regis House, in T Brigham & B Watson, *Excavations at Regis House, City of London.* MoLAS Monogr Ser. London: Museum of London Archaeology Service

Davis, A, & de Moulins, D, 2000 The plant remains, in B Barber & D Bowsher 2000, 368–78

de Boe, G, & Verhaeghe, F (eds), 1997 *Urbanism in Medieval Europe: Papers of the 'Medieval Europe Brugge 1997 Conference'* **1**. Zellik: Institut vor het Archeologisch Patrimonium

de la Bédoyère, G, 1989 *The Finds of Roman Britain.* London: Batsford

de la Bédoyère, G, 1998 Carausius and the marks RSR and INPCDA, *Numismatic Chronicle,* **158**, 79–88

de Moulins, D, 1990, Environmental analysis, in C Maloney & D de Moulins 1990, 85–115

de Moulins, D, 2005 The plant remains, in I Howell 2005, 101–12

Dean, M, 1977 SLAEC Excavations at Harper Row, Southwark, *London Archaeol,* **3**(5), 122

Dean, M, 1980 Excavations at Arcadia Buildings, Southwark, *London Archaeol,* **3**(14), 367–73

Dean, M, & Hammerson, M, 1980 Three inhumation burials from Southwark, *London Archaeol,* **4**(1), 17–22

Déchelette, J, 1904 *Les vases céramiques ornés de la Gaule Romaine (Narbonnaise, Aquitaine et Lyonnaise),* 2 vols. Paris: Alphonse Picard et Fils

DeLaine, J, & Johnston, D E (eds), 1999 *Roman Baths and Bathing,* JRA Suppl Ser **37**. Portsmouth, Rhode Island: Journal for Roman Archaeology

Dennis, G, 1978 1–7 St Thomas Street, in SLAEC 1978, 291–422

Densem, R, 2004 22–24 Lincoln Road, Enfield, Middlesex, Unpubl report for Heritage Network Ltd, Archaeol Evaluation Report 228

Derks, T, 1995 The ritual of the vow in Gallo-Roman religion, in J Metzler, M Millett, N Roymans & J Slofstra (eds), *Integration in the early Roman West: The role of culture and ideology.* Luxembourg: Musée national d'histoire et d'art, 111–27

Derks, T, 1998 *Gods, Temples and Ritual Practices.* Amsterdam: Amsterdam University Press

Detsicas, A, 1974 Excavations at Eccles, 1973: Twelfth interim report, *Archaeol Cantiana,* **89**, 119–34

Detsicas, A, 1981 A group of pottery from Eccles, Kent, in A C Anderson & A S Anderson (eds), *Roman Pottery Research in Britian and North-West Europe: Papers presented to Graham Webster,* BAR Int Ser, **123**. Oxford: British Archaeological Reports, 441–5

Diaconescu, A, Haynes, I, & Schäfer, A, 2001 The Apulum project – Summary report of the 1998 and 1999 seasons, in S Altekamp & A Schäfer (eds), *The Impact of Rome on Settlement in the Northwestern and Danube Provinces,* BAR Int Ser, **921**. Oxford: Archaeopress, 115–28

Dickson, C, 1994 Macroscopic fossils of garden plants from British Roman and medieval deposits, in D Moe *et al* (eds) 1994, 47–72

Dilly, G, & Mahéo, N, 1997 *Verreries antiques du Musée de Picardie.* Amiens

Dingwall, H M, 1994 *Late Seventeenth-Century Edinburgh.* Aldershot: Scolar Press

Dodgson, J McN, 1996 A linguistic analysis of the place-names of the Burghal Hidage, in D Hill & A Rumble (eds) 1996, 98–121

DoE (Department of the Environment), 1990 *Planning Policy Guidance: Archaeology and Planning*, PPG 16. London: HMSO

Douglas, A, 2004 The lost port of Londinium, http://www.pre-construct.com/sites/highlights/lostport.htm

Down, A, & Rule, M, 1971 *Chichester Excavations 1*. Chichester: Chichester Civic Society Excavations Committee

Dressel, H, 1899 *Corpus Inscriptionum Latinarum*, XV, Pars 1. Berlin

Drucker, L, 1932 *Chartulary of the Hospital of St Thomas the Martyr, Southwark (1213 to 1525)*. London: privately printed for the Governors

Drummond-Murray, J, Thompson, P, with Cowan, C, 2002 *Settlement in Roman Southwark: Archaeological excavations (1991–98) for the London Underground Ltd Jubilee Line Extension Project*, MoLAS Monogr Ser, **12**. London: Museum of London Archaeology Service

Dungworth, D, 1997 Iron Age and Roman copper alloys from northern Britain, *Internet Archaeol*, **2**, http://www.intarch.ac.uk/journal/issue2

Dunwoodie, L, 2004 *Pre-Boudican and Later Activity on the Site of the Forum: Excavations at 168 Fenchurch Street, City of London*, MoLAS Archaeol Stud Ser, **13**. London: Museum of London Archaeology Service

Dunwoodie, L, Harward, C, & Pitt, K, forthcoming, *Military and Civil Development in Roman London East of the Walbrook: Excavations at Plantation Place*, MoLAS Monogr Ser. London: Museum of London Archaeology Service

Durrani, N, 2004 Tabard Square, *Current Archaeol*, **192**, 540–7

Dyson, T, 1980 London and Southwark in the seventh century and later. A neglected reference, *Trans London Middlesex Archaeol Soc*, **31**, 83–95

Dyson, T, 1990 King Alfred and the restoration of London, *London J*, **15**(2), 99–110

EAS 1959 *Enfield Archaeological Society Bulletin*, **2** & **3** (September & December 1959)

EAS 1967 *Enfield Archaeological Society Bulletin*, **26** (September 1967)

Eccles, C, 1990 *The Rose Theatre*. London: Hern

Eckardt, H, 2002 *Illuminating Roman Britain*. Monographies *Instrumentum*, **23**. Montagnac: Editions Monique Mergoil

Eckardt, H, 2005 The social distribution of Roman artefacts: The case of nail-cleaners and brooches in Britain, *J Roman Archaeol*, **18**(1), 139–60

Eckardt, H, with Crummy, N, 2006 'Roman' or 'native' bodies in Britain: The evidence of late Roman nail-cleaner strap-ends, *Oxford J Archaeol*, **25**(1), 83–103

Eckardt, H, & Crummy, N, forthcoming *Personal Grooming in Roman Britain*

Egan, G, 2007 Acessioned finds, in D Bowsher, N Holder & I Howell with T Dyson, *The London Guildhall: An archaeological history of a neighbourhood from early medieval to modern times. Part 2*, MoLAS Monogr Ser **36**. London: Museum of London Archaeology Service, 446–72

Ekholm, G, 1956 Orientalische Gläser in Skandinavien während der Kaiser- und frühen Merowingerzeit, *Acta Archaeologica*, **29**, 21–50

Ellis, R, 1982 Excavations at Grim's Dyke, Harrow *Trans London Middlesex Archaeol Soc*, **33**, 173–6

Ennodius, 1885 *Magni Felicis Ennodi Opera*, ed F Vogel. Monumenta Germaniae Historica: Auctores Antiquissimi **7**. Berlin: Wiedermann (reprinted Berlin: Hildebrand, 1961)

Esmonde Cleary, A S, 1996 Roman Britain in 1995, *Britannia*, **27**, 424–33

Esmonde Cleary, A S, 1997 Roman Britain in 1996, *Britannia*, **28**, 435–40

Esmonde Cleary, A S, 1998 Roman Britain in 1997, *Britannia*, **29**, 409–13

Esmonde Cleary, A S, 1999 Roman Britain in 1998, *Britannia*, **30**, 356–61

Evans, J G, no date Land and freshwater molluscs, New Palace Yard, Westminster. London, Unpubl report for Ancient Monuments Laboratory, no 1745

Evershed, R P, Berstan, R, Grew, F, Copley, M S, Charmant, A J H, Barham, E, Mottram, H R, & Brown, G, 2004 Formulation of a Roman cosmetic, *Nature*, **432**, 35–6

Faider-Feytmans, G, 1979 *Les bronzes romains de Belgique*. Mainz: von Zabern

Farrar, L, 1998 *Ancient Roman Gardens*. Stroud: Budding Books

Faulkner, N, with Reece, R, 2002 The debate about the end: a review of the evidence and methods, *Archaeol J*, **159**, 59–76

Fiedler, M, 2005 Kultgruben eines Liber Pater-Heligtums im römischen Apulum (Dakien), *Germania*, **83**, 95–125

Filtzinger, P, 1972 *Novaesium V. Die Römische Keramik aus dem Militärbereich von Novaesium (etwa 25 bis 50 n Chr)*, Limesforschungen **11**. Berlin: Mann

Finlay, R, 1981 *Population and Metropolis. The demography of London 1580–1650*. Cambridge: Cambridge University Press

Fisher, T, 1804 Notes on discovery of a tessellated pavement in Leadenhall Street, *Gentleman's Magazine*, **1**, 83

Fisher, T, 1807 Notes on discovery of a tessellated pavement at the Bank of England, *Gentleman's Magazine*, **1**, 415

Fishwick, D, 1994 *Numinibus Aug(ustorum)*, *Britannia*, **25**, 127–41

Fitzpatrick, A, 1984 The deposition of La Tene Iron Age metalwork in watery contexts in southern England, in B Cunliffe & D Miles (eds), *Aspects of the Iron Age in Britain*. Oxford University

Committee for Archaeology Monogr, **2**. Oxford: Oxford University Committee for Archaeology, 178–90

Fitzpatrick, A, 2002 Roman Britain in 2001, *Britannia*, **33**, 326–37

Fletcher, J, 1981 Roman and Saxon Dendro Dates, *Current Archaeol*, **7**(5), 150–2

Fletcher, J, 1982 The waterfront of Londinium: the date of the quays at the Custom House site reassessed, *Trans London Middlesex Archaeol Soc, 33*, 79–84

Flouest, J-L, & Stead, I M, 1979 *Iron Age Cemeteries in Champagne: The third interim report*, BM Occas Paper, **6**. London: British Museum

Follmann-Schulz, A-B, 1988 *Die römischen Gläser aus Bonn*, Köln: Rheinland-Verlag

Forsyth, H, 2003 *The Cheapside Hoard*. London: Museum of London

Foy, D, & Nenna, M-D, 2001 *Tout Feu Tout Sable. Mille ans de verre antique dans le Midi de la France*. Aix en Provence: Musées de Marseille

Fremersdorf, F, 1967 *Die römischen Gläser mit Schliff, Bemalung und Goldauflagen aus Köln*, Die Denkmäler des römischen Köln, **8**. Köln

Fremersdorf, F, 1975 *Antikes, islamisches und mittelalterliches Glas: sowie kleinere Arbeiten aus Vatikanischen Sammlungen Roms*, Catalogo del Museo Sacro, **5**. Vatican City: Biblioteca Apostolica Vaticana

Frere, S S, 1971 The Forum and Baths at Caistor by Norwich, *Britannia, 2*, 1–26

Frere, S S, 1972 *Verulamium Excavations Vol 1*, Soc Antiq London Res Rep, **28**. Oxford: Society of Antiquaries of London

Frere, S S, 1984 *Verulamium Excavations Vol 3*, Oxford University Comm Archaeol Monogr **1**. Oxford: Oxford University Committee for Archaeology

Frere, S S, 1987, *Britannia. A History of Roman Britain*, 3rd edn. London: Guild Publishing

Frere, S S, Roxan, M, & Tomlin, R S O, 1990 *The Roman Inscriptions of Britain (2401–2411)*, **2.1**. Gloucester: Alan Sutton

Frere, S S, & Tomlin, R S O, 1991 *The Roman Inscriptions of Britain (2421–2441)*, **2.3**. Stroud: Alan Sutton

Frere, S S, & Tomlin, R S O, 1992 *The Roman Inscriptions of Britain (2442–2480)*, **2.4**. Stroud: Alan Sutton

Frere, S S, & Tomlin, R S O, 1993 *The Roman Inscriptions of Britain (2481–2491)*, **2.5**. Stroud: Alan Sutton

Fuentes, N, 1985 Of castles and elephants, *London Archaeol*, **5**(4), 90–4, 106–8

Fulford, M, Clarke, A, & Eckardt, H, 2006 *Life and Labour in Late Roman Silchester: Excavations in insula IX since 1997*, Britannia Monogr, **22**. London: Society for the Promotion of Roman Studies

Fulford, M, & Timby, J, 2000 *Late Iron Age and Roman Silchester. Excavations on the site of the Forum-Basilica 1977, 1980–86*, Britannia Monogr, **15**. London: Society for the Promotion of Roman Studies

Fulford, M, & Tyers, I, 1995 The date of Pevensey and the defence of an '*Imperium Britanniarum*', *Antiquity*, **69**, 1009–14

Fünfschilling, S, 1986 Römisches Gläser aus Baden-Aquae Helvetica (aus den Grabungen 1892–1911), in *Jahresbericht 1985, Gesellschaft pro Vindonissa* 1986, 81–160

Furtwängler, A, 1896 *Beschreibung der Geschnittenen Steine im Antiquarium*. Berlin: Verlag von W Spemann

Gadd, D, 1998 Land adjacent to 63 Main Road, Gidea Park. Archaeological report. Unpubl report for Essex County Council Field Archaeology Unit, Site Code MGP98

Galley, C, 1998 *The Demography of Early Modern Towns: York in the sixteenth and seventeenth centuries*. Liverpool: Liverpool University Press

Garmondsway, G N (ed), 1953 *The Anglo-Saxon Chronicle*. London: J M Dent & Sons

Garwood, P, 1989 Social transformation and relations of power in Britain in the late fourth to sixth centuries AD, *Scot Archaeol Rev*, **6**, 90–106

Gassner, V, 1990 Schlangengefäße aus Carnuntum, in H Vetters & M Kandler (eds), *Akten des 14. Internationalen Limeskongresses 1986 in Carnuntum*. Vienna: Österreichische Akademie der Wissenschaften, 651–6

Gatch, M McC, 1986 John Bagford, bookseller and antiquary, *Brit Library J*, **12**, 150–71

Gelling, M, 1953 The boundaries of the Westminster charters, *Trans London Middlesex Archaeol Soc New Ser*, **11**(2), 101–4

Gelling, M, 1977 Latin loan-words in Old English place-names, *Anglo-Saxon England*, **6**, 1–13

Gentry, A, Ivens, J, & McClean, H, 1977 Excavations at Lincoln Road, London Borough of Enfield, November 1974–March 1976, *Trans London Middlesex Archaeol Soc*, **28**, 101–89

Geoffrey of Monmouth, 1966 *The History of the Kings of Britain*, trans L Thorpe. Harmondsworth: Penguin

Gervase of Tilbury, 2002 *Otia Imperialia: Recreation for an Emperor*, ed & trans S E Banks & J W Binns, Oxford Medieval Texts. Oxford: Clarendon Press

Gifford, E, & Gifford, J, 2002, *Anglo-Saxon sailing ships*, 2nd edn, reprinted from *Mariner's Mirror*, **82**(2), 1996. Sutton Hoo: Greenside Publishing for the Sutton Hoo Society

Gillam, G R, 1953 *A Romano-British Site at Edmonton, Middlesex: An account of the excavations carried out at Churchfield during 1951*. London: Privately printed

Gillam, G R, 1973 *Prehistoric and Roman Enfield*, Enfield Archaeol Soc Res Rep, **3**. Enfield: Enfield Archaeological Society

Gillam, J P, 1970 *Types of Roman coarse pottery vessels in Northern Britain* (3rd edn). Newcastle-upon-Tyne: Oriel Press

Gillmor, C, 1989 The logistics of fortified bridge building on the Seine under Charles the Bald, in R A Brown (ed), *Anglo-Norman Studies XI: Proceedings of the Battle conference 1988.* Woodbridge: Boydell Press, 87–105

Gillmor, C, 1997 Charles the Bald and the small free farmers 862–869, in A Norgard-Jorgensen & B Chausen (eds), *Military Aspects of Scandinavian Society in a European Perspective AD 1–1300,* Studies in Archaeology & History, **2**. Copenhagen: Papers from an International Research Seminar at the Danish National Museum, 38–46

Gilson, A G, 1981 A group of Roman surgical and medical instruments from Corbridge, *Saalburg Jahrbuch,* **37**, 5–9

Gilson, A G, 1983 A group of Roman surgical and medical instruments from Cramond, Scotland, *Medizinhistorisches Journal,* **18**, 384–93

Giorgi, J, 2000 The plant remains, in A Mackinder 2000, 12, 65

Giorgi, J, 2005 The plant remains, in B Yule 2005, 169–76

Giorgi, J, forthcoming The plant remains, in C Cowan *et al* forthcoming

Goffin, R, 1995 The accessioned finds, in P Mills 1995, 87–90

Going, C J, 1987 *The mansio and other sites in the south-eastern sector of Caesaromagus: the Roman pottery,* CBA Res Rep, **62**, Chelmsford Archaeol Trust Rep, **3.2**. York: Council for British Archaeology

Goldstein, S M, 1979 *Pre-Roman and Early Roman Glass in the Corning Museum of Glass,* New York State: Corning Museum of Glass

Goodburn, D, forthcoming The wood, in J Hill & P Rowsome forthcoming

Gostenčnik, K, 2002 Agathangelus the bronzesmith: the British finds in their Continental context, *Britannia,* **33**, 227–56

[Gough, R], 1780 *British Topography; or, an historical account of what has been done for illustrating the topographical antiquities of Great Britain and Ireland,* 2 vols. London: T Payne, W Brown *et al*

Gough, R, 1787 Account of the discoveries in digging a sewer in Lombard-street and Birchin-lane 1786; in a letter to Mr Gough and communicated by him, *Archaeologia,* **8**, 116–32

Gover, J E B, Mawer, A, & Stenton, F M, 1934 *The Place-Names of Surrey,* Eng Place-Name Soc, **11**. Cambridge: Cambridge University Press

Gover, J E B, Mawer, A, & Stenton, F M, 1942 *The Place-Names of Middlesex, apart from the City of London,* Eng Place-Name Soc, **18**. Cambridge: Cambridge University Press

Graham, A H, 1978 The geology of north Southwark and its topographical development in the post-Pleistocene period, in SLAEC 1978, 501–17

Grant, M, 1967 *Gladiators.* New York: Barnes & Noble

Graves, R, 1960 *The Greek myths* (2 vols). Harmondsworth: Penguin Books

Gray-Rees, L, 2001 The Roman plant remains, in T Brigham & A Woodger 2001, 110–15

Green, A, 2001 Safeway project. The Grove, Stratford, London E15. Archaeology final report. Unpubl report for Museum of London Archaeology Service, Site Code SFG98

Green, M J, 1976 *A Corpus of Religious Material from the Civilian Areas of Roman Britain,* BAR Brit Ser, **24**. Oxford: British Archaeological Reports

Greenidge, A H J, 1894 (repr 1977) *Infamia: Its place in Roman public and private law.* Oxford: Clarendon Press; repr Aalen: Scientia, 1977

Greenwood, P, & Maloney, C, 1995 London Fieldwork and Publication Round-up 1994, *London Archaeol,* **7**(13), 333–56

Gregory, A K, 1991 *Excavations in Thetford 1980–82, Fison Way,* East Anglian Archaeol, **53**. Dereham: Norfolk Museums Service

Greig, J R A, 1992 The deforestation of London, *Review of Palaeobotany and Palynology,* **73**, 71–86

Grenier, A, 1940 Hercule et les théâtres gallo-romains, in Chapouthier, Seston & Boyancé (eds) 1940, 636–44

Grimes, W F, 1968 *The Excavations of Roman and Mediaeval London.* London: Routledge & Kegan Paul

Gromaticus, 1978 Commentary, *London Archaeol,* **3**(8), 198

Grose, D F, 1991 Early Imperial Roman cast glass: The translucent coloured and colourless fine wares, in M Newby & K Painter, *Roman Glass: Two centuries of art and invention,* Soc Antiq London Occas Paper, **13**. London: Society of Antiquaries of London, 1–18

Groves, J, 1990 Summary finds report, in C Maloney & D de Moulins 1990, 82–4

Groves, J, 2003 The dating of early groups at site S in C Cowan 2003, 124–5

Guildhall Museum, 1908 *Catalogue of the Collection of London Antiquities in the Guildhall Museum,* 2nd edn. London: Corporation of London

Guildhall Museum, 1955 *Small Finds from Walbrook (1954–55).* London: Corporation of London

Gurney, D, 1986 *Settlement, Religion and Industry on the Fen-edge. Three Romano-British sites in Norfolk,* East Anglian Archaeol, **31**. Dereham: Norfolk Museums Service

Haarhoff, T, 1920 *The Schools of Gaul: A study of pagan and Christian education.* London: Oxford University Press

Hagland, J R, & Watson, B, 2005 Fact or folklore: the Viking attack on London Bridge, *London Archaeol,* **10**(12), 328–33

Hall, A F, 1942 A three-tracked Roman road at Colchester, *J Brit Archaeol Soc 3rd Ser,* **7**, 53–70

Hall, J, 1996 The cemeteries of Roman London: A review, in J Bird *et al* (eds) 1996, 57–84

Hall, J, 2005 The shopkeepers and craftworkers of Roman London, in A MacMahon & J Price (eds) 2005, 125–44

Hall, J, & Conheeney, J, 1998, Roman Bodies: The stresses and strains of life in Roman London, in A Werner (ed), *London Bodies: The changing shape of Londoners from prehistoric times to the present day*. London: Museum of London, 34–49

Hall, J, & Swain, H, 2000 *High Street Londinium*. London: Museum of London

Halsall, G, 1999 Review article. Movers and shakers: The barbarians and the fall of Rome, *Early Medieval Europe*, 8(1), 131–45

Hamerow, H, 1993 *Excavations at Mucking. Volume 2: The Anglo-Saxon settlement*, EH Archaeol Rep **21**. London: English Heritage

Hammer, F, 2003 *Industry in North-West Roman Southwark. Excavations 1984–1988*. MoLAS Monogr Ser **17**. London: Museum of London Archaeology Service

Hammerson, M, 1978 The coins, in SLAEC 1978, 587–601

Hammerson, M, 2002 Roman coins, in D Lakin *et al* 2002, 53–7

Hammerson, M, & Coxshall, R, 1977 The coins, in A Gentry *et al* 1977, 161–8

Hanson, W S, & Conolly, R, 2002 Language and literacy in Roman Britain: Some archaeological considerations, in A E Cooley (ed), *Becoming Roman, Writing Latin? Literacy and epigraphy in the Roman West*. JRA Suppl Ser, **48**. Int Roman Archaeol Conference Ser. Portsmouth, Rhode Island: Journal of Roman Archaeology, 151–64

Harden, D B, 1936 *Roman glass from Karanis found by the University of Michigan archaeological expedition in Egypt 1924–29*, Univ of Michigan Stud, Humanistic Ser, **4**

Harden, D B, 1970 Ancient glass II: Roman, *Archaeol J*, **126**, 44–77

Harden, D B, 1987 *Glass of the Caesars*. Milan: Olivetti

Harden, D B, & Price, J, 1971 The glass, in B Cunliffe, *Excavations at Fishbourne, 1961–1969: 2, The finds*, Soc Antiq London Res Rep, **27**. Leeds: Society of Antiquaries of London, 317–68

Harris, E, & Harris, J R, 1965 *The Oriental Cults in Roman Britain*, Études Préliminaires aux Religions Orientales dans l'Empire Romain, **6**. Leiden: E J Brill

Hart, F A, 1984 Excavation of a Saxon *grubenhaus* and Roman ditch at Kent Road, St Mary Cray, *Archaeol Cantiana*, **101**, 187–216

Hartley, B R, & Dickinson, B M (eds), forthcoming *Names on Terra Sigillata: An index of makers' stamps and signatures on Gallo-Roman terra sigillata (samian ware)*. London: Institute of Classical Studies

Hassall, J M, & Hill, D, 1970 Pont de l'Arche: Frankish influence on the West Saxon *burh*?, *Archaeol J*, **127**, 188–95

Hassall, M W C, 1976 Britain and the Notitia Dignitatum, in R Goodburn & P Bartholomew (eds), *Aspects of the Notitia Dignitatum: Papers presented to the conference in Oxford, December 13 to 15, 1974*, BAR Suppl Ser, **15**. Oxford: British Archaeological Reports, 103–17

Hassall, M W C, 1980 The inscribed altars, in C Hill *et al* 1980, 195–8

Hassall, M W C, 1996 London as a provincial capital, in J Bird *et al* (eds) 1996, 19–26

Hassall, M W C, & Tomlin, R S O, 1978 Inscriptions in Roman Britain in 1977, *Britannia*, **9**, 473–85

Hassall, M W C, & Tomlin, R S O, 2003 Inscriptions in Roman Britain in 2002, *Britannia*, **34**, 361–82

Hassan, F A, 1981 *Demographic Archaeology*. New York: Academic Press

Hatchwell, R, 2005 *Art in Wiltshire: from the Wiltshire Archaeological and Natural History Society Collection*. Devizes: Wiltshire Archaeological & Natural History Society

Hatchwell, R, & Burl, A, 1998 The Commonplace Book of William Stukeley, *Wiltshire Archaeol Natur Hist Mag*, **91**, 65–75

Hattatt, R, 1985 *Iron Age and Roman Brooches*. Oxford: Oxbow Books

Haverfield, F, 1902 Quarterly notes on Roman Britain, *Antiquary*, **38**, 175–6

Haverfield, F, 1911 Roman London, *J Roman Stud*, **1**, 141–72

Hawkes, C F C, & Hull, M R, 1947 *Camulodunum: First report on the excavations at Colchester 1930–1939*, Soc Antiq London Res Rep, **14**. London: Society of Antiquaries of London

Hawkins, N, Brown, G, & Butler, J, 2008 Drapers Gardens, *Brit Archaeol*, **98**, 12–17

Haynes, I, 2000 Religion in Roman London, in I Haynes *et al* (eds) 2000, 85–101

Haynes, I, 2006 The *favissae* project homepage, http://www.bbk.ac.uk/hca/staff/haynes/favissae.htm

Haynes, I, Diaconescu, A, & Schäfer, A, forthcoming *The Sanctuary of Liber Pater in Colonia Aurelia Apulensis (Alba Iulia, Romania)*, JRA Suppl Ser. Portsmouth, Rhode Island: Journal of Roman Archaeology

Haynes, I, Sheldon, H, & Hannigan, L (eds), 2000 *London Under Ground: The archaeology of a city*. Oxford: Oxbow Books

Haywood, J, 2005, Anglo-Saxon sailors, in litt, *Brit Archaeol*, **82**, 31

Heard, K, Sheldon, H, & Thompson, P, 1990 Mapping Roman Southwark, *Antiquity*, **64**(244), 608–19

Hedan, E, & Vernhet, A, 1977 Representations d'Hercule sur les sigillées de La Graufesenque, in Congrès national des sociétés savantes *Archéologie franc-comtoise: archéologie funéraire*, Actes du 99e congrès national des sociétés savantes (Besançon 1974), Section d'archéologie et d'histoire de l'art, 287–301. Paris: Bibliothèque Nationale

Heimberg, V, 1980 Vielleicht heiss sie Nonnula. Ein spätrömischer Sarkopharg aus Zülpich-Enzen, in *Das Rheinische Landesmuseums Bonn. Berichte aus der Arbeit des Museums,* 24–6

Henig, M, 1970 The veneration of heroes in the Roman Army, *Britannia,* **1**, 249–65

Henig, M, 1972 The origin of some ancient British coin types, *Britannia,* **3**, 209–23

Henig, M, 1974 *A Corpus of Roman Engraved Gemstones from British Sites,* BAR Brit Ser, **8** (2 vols). Oxford: British Archaeological Reports

Henig, M, 1975 'Eagle and standards' intaglio from St Thomas's Street, Southwark, *London Archaeol,* **2**(10), 243

Henig, M, 1976a A silver finger-ring from Winchester Wharf, Southwark, *Trans London Middlesex Archaeol Soc,* **27**, 256

Henig, M, 1976b A stamped sherd from Copthall Close, *Trans London Middlesex Archaeol Soc,* **27**, 239, 241

Henig, M, 1978a *A Corpus of Roman Engraved Gemstones from British Sites,* BAR Brit Ser, **8**, 2nd edn. Oxford: British Archaeological Reports

Henig, M, 1978b Signet rings from Roman London, *Trans London Middlesex Archaeol Soc,* **29**, 113–16

Henig, M, 1978c Some reflections of Greek sculpture and painting in Roman art from London, in J Bird *et al* (eds) 1978,109–23

Henig, M, 1980 An intaglio and sealing from Blackfriars, London, *Antiq J,* **60**, 331–2

Henig, M, 1981 Continuity and change in the design of Roman jewellery, in A King & M Henig (eds) 1981, 127–43

Henig, M (ed), 1983 *A Handbook of Roman Art: A survey of the visual arts of the Roman world.* Oxford: Phaidon Press

Henig, M, 1984a A cache of Roman intaglios from Eastcheap, *Trans London Middlesex Archaeol Soc,* **35**, 11–15

Henig, M, 1984b *Religion in Roman Britain.* London: Batsford

Henig, M, 1986 An intaglio ring from the City Ditch, London, *London Archaeol,* **5**(7), 192

Henig, M, 1988 The gemstone, in B Cunliffe, *The Temple of Sulis Minerva at Bath: 2. The finds from the sacred spring.* Oxford: Oxford University Committee for Archaeology, 27–33

Henig, M, 1993 *Corpus Signorum Imperii Romani, Great Britain I.7: Roman sculpture from the Cotswold region with Devon and Cornwall.* Oxford: Oxford University Press

Henig, M, 1995 *The Art of Roman Britain.* London: Batsford

Henig, M, 1996 Sculptors from the west in Roman London, in J Bird *et al* (eds) 1996, 97–103

Henig, M, 1998 The temple as a *bacchium* or *sacrarium* in the fourth century, in J Shepherd 1998, 230–2

Henig, M, 2000a Art in Roman London, in I Haynes *et al* (eds) 2000, 62–84

Henig, M, 2000b *English Gem-set Seals,* Datasheet **27**. Finds Research Group 700–1700

Henig, M, 2002 Intaglio, in J Drummond-Murray *et al* 2002, 221

Henig, M, 2005 The intaglio, in B Philp 2005, 182

Henig, M, & Jones, C E E, 1986 A Roman intaglio from London, *Trans London Middlesex Archaeol Soc,* **37**, 145

Henig, M, & Jones, C E E, 1992 A cornelian intaglio from Miles Lane, City of London, *Trans London Middlesex Archaeol Soc,* **43**, 1–2

Henig, M, & MacGregor, A, 2004 *Catalogue of the Engraved Gems and Finger-Rings in the Ashmolean Museum 2: Roman,* BAR Int Ser, **1332**. Oxford: Archaeopress

Henig, M, & Ross, A, 1998 A Roman intaglio depicting a warship from the foreshore at King's Reach, Winchester Wharf, Southwark, *Britannia,* **29**, 325–7

Henig, M, & Whiting, M, 1987 *Engraved Gems from Gadara in Jordan: The Sa'd collection of intaglios and cameos.* Oxford: Oxford University Committee for Archaeology

Henig, M, & Wilkins, R, 1999 One hundred and fifty years of Wroxeter gems, in M Henig & D Plantzos (eds), *Classicism to Neo-Classicism: Essays dedicated to Gertrud Seidmann.* BAR Int Ser, **793**. Oxford: Archaeopress, 49–66

Henry of Huntingdon, 1996, *Historia Anglorum: The History of the English People,* ed & trans D Greenway, Oxford Medieval Texts. Oxford: Clarendon Press

Hermet, F, 1934 *La Graufesenque (Condatomago).* Paris: Librairie Ernest Leroux

Heyob, S K, 1975 *The Cult of Isis among Women in the Graeco-Roman World.* Leiden: Brill

Higham, N, 1992 *Rome, Britain and the Anglo-Saxons.* London: Seaby

Hill, C, Millett, M, & Blagg, T, 1980 *The Roman Riverside Wall and Monumental Arch in London: Excavations at Baynard's Castle, Upper Thames Street, London, 1974–76,* LAMAS Special Paper **3**. London: London & Middlesex Archaeological Society

Hill, D, & Rumble, A (eds), 1996 *The Defence of Wessex. The burghal hidage and Anglo-Saxon fortifications.* Manchester: Manchester University Press

Hill, J, & Rowsome, P, forthcoming *Roman London and the Walbrook Stream Crossing: Excavations at 1 Poultry and vicinity 1985–96,* MoLAS Monogr Ser. London: Museum of London Archaeology Service

Hill, J, & Woodger, A, 1999 *Excavations at 72–75 Cheapside/83–93 Queen Street, City of London,* MoLAS Archaeol Stud Ser **2**. London: Museum of London Archaeology Service

Hill, J D, 2001 Romanisation, gender and class: Recent approaches to identity in Britain and their possible consequences, in S James & M Millett (eds), *Britons and Romans: Advancing an archaeological agenda,* CBA Res Rep, **125**. York: Council for British Archaeology, 12–18

Hillam, J, 1990 The dendrochronology of the late Roman waterfront at Billingsgate Lorry Park and other sites in the City of London, in T Brigham 1990b, 164–70

Hillam, J, 1993 Tree-ring dating of oak timbers from Peter's Hill and Sunlight Wharf, in T Williams 1993, 95–9

Hillam, J, & Morgan, R A, 1981 Dendro dates from Sheffield, *Current Archaeol,* **7**(9), 286–7

Hillam, J, & Morgan, R A, 1986 Tree-ring analysis of the Roman timbers, in L Miller, J Schofield & M Rhodes 1986, *The Roman Quay at St Magnus House, London,* LAMAS Special Paper **8**. London: London & Middlesex Archaeological Society, 75–85

Hills, C, 2003 *Origins of the English.* London: Duckworth

Hind, J G F, 1989 The invasion of Britain in AD 43 – an alternative strategy for Aulus Plautius, *Britannia,* **20**, 1–21

Hind, J G F, 2005 The watchtowers and fortlets on the North Yorkshire coast (*Turres et Castra*), *Yorkshire Archaeol J,* **77**, 17–24

Hines, J, 2004 *Sūpre-gē* – the foundations of Surrey, in J Cotton, G Crocker & A Graham (eds), *Aspects of Archaeology and History in Surrey: Towards a research framework for the county.* Guildford: Surrey Archaeological Society, 91–102

Hingley, R, 1989 *Rural Settlement in Roman Britain.* London: Seaby

Hinton, P (ed), 1988 *Excavations in Southwark 1973–76 and Lambeth 1973–79,* LAMAS/SAS Joint Pub **3**. London: London & Middlesex Archaeological Society & Surrey Archaeological Society

Hoadley, M, 1996, *The Roman Garden: Plants and gardens in Roman Britain.* Newcastle upon Tyne: Frank Graham

Hobson, D W, 1985 *House and Household in Roman Egypt.* Cambridge: Cambridge University Press

Holban, M, forthcoming Favissae: *A problem of interpretation*

Holbrook, N (ed), 1998 *Cirencester: The Roman town defences, public buildings and shops,* Cirencester Excavations **5**. Cirencester: Cotswold Archaeological Trust

Holden, S, 2002 An Archaeological evaluation at 417 Wick Lane, Old Ford, London Borough of Tower Hamlets, Unpubl report for Pre-Construct Archaeology Ltd

Holder, P A, 1980 *Studies in the Auxilia of the Roman Army from Augustus to Trajan,* BAR Int Ser **70**. Oxford: British Archaeological Reports

Home, G, 1925 *Roman London.* London: Benn

Home, G, 1948 *Roman London, AD 43–457,* 2nd revised & enlarged edn. London: Eyre & Spottiswoode

Hooley, D, 2001 Copper-alloy and silver objects, in A S Anderson, J S Wacher & A P Fitzpatrick, *The Romano-British Small Town at Wanborough,*

Wiltshire, Britannia Monogr Ser, **19**. London: Society for the Promotion of Roman Studies, 75–116

Höpken, C, 2004 Die Funde aus Keramik und Glas aus einem Liber Pater-Bezirk in Apulum, in M Martens & G de Boe (eds) 2004, 239–58

Hopkins, K, 1983 *Death and Renewal: Sociological studies in Roman History,* **2**. Cambridge: Cambridge University Press

Horn, H G (ed), 1987 *Die Römer in Nordrhein-Westfalen.* Stuttgart: K Theiss

Horsman, V, Milne, C, & Milne, G, 1988 *Aspects of Saxo-Norman London: I Building and street development,* LAMAS Special Paper, **11**. London: London & Middlesex Archaeological Society

Howe, E, 1998 A Romano-British farmstead at St Mary Abbot's Hospital, Marloes Road, Kensington, *Trans London Middlesex Archaeol Soc,* **49**, 15–30

Howe, E, 2002 *Roman Defences and Medieval Industry: Excavations at Baltic House, City of London.* MoLAS Monogr Ser **7**. London: Museum of London Archaeology Service

Howe, E, & Lakin, D, 2004 *Roman and Medieval Cripplegate, City of London: Archaeological excavations 1992–8.* MoLAS Monogr Ser **21**. London: Museum of London Archaeology Service

Howell, I (ed), 2005 *Prehistoric Landscape to Roman Villa. Excavations at Beddington, Surrey 1981–87,* MoLAS Monogr Ser **26**. London: Museum of London Archaeology Service

Hull, M R, 1958 *Roman Colchester,* Soc Antiq London Res Rep, **20**. Oxford: Society of Antiquaries and the Corporation of the Borough of Colchester

Hull, M R, 1963a Roman Roads, in W R Powell (ed), *Victoria History of the Counties of England: Essex* **3***: Roman Essex.* Oxford: Oxford University Press, 24–5

Hull, M R, 1963b *The Roman Potters' Kilns of Colchester,* Soc Antiq London Res Rep, **21**, Oxford: Oxford University Press

Hunter, M, 1975 *John Aubrey and the Realm of Learning.* London: Duckworth

Hutchinson, V J, 1986 *Bacchus in Roman Britain: The evidence for his cult,* BAR Brit Ser **151**. Oxford: British Archaeological Reports

Isings, C, 1957 *Roman Glass from Dated Finds.* Groningen: J B Wolters

Isings, C, 1971 *Roman glass from Limburg,* Archaeologica Traiectina, **9**. Groningen: Wolters-Noordhoff

Jackson, R P J, 1985 Cosmetic sets from Late Iron Age and Roman Britain, *Britannia,* **16**, 165–92

Jackson, R P J, 1986 A set of Roman medical instruments from Italy, *Britannia,* **17**, 119–67

Jackson, R P J, 1988 *Doctors and diseases in the Roman Empire.* London: British Museum Press

Jackson, R P J, 1993a Roman medicine: the practitioners and their practices, in W Haase &

H Temporini (eds), *Aufstieg und Niedergang der römischen Welt (ANRW)* **2**, 37.1. Berlin/New York: Walter de Gruyter, 79–101

Jackson, R P J, 1993b The function and manufacture of Romano-British cosmetic grinders: two important new finds from London, *Antiq J,* **73**, 165–9

Jackson, R P J, 1994 The surgical instruments, appliances and equipment in Celsus' *De medicina*, in G Sabbah & P Mudry (eds), *La medicine de Celse. Aspects historiques, scientifiques et littéraires*, Mémoires **13**. St Étienne: Centre Jean Palerne, 167–209

Jackson, R P J, 1995 The composition of Roman medical *instrumentaria* as an indicator of medical practice: a provisional assessment, in Ph J van der Eijk, H F J Horstmanshoff & P H Schrijvers (eds), *Ancient Medicine in its Socio-cultural Context,* vol 1, *Clio Medica*, **27**, 189–207

Jackson, R P J, 1996a A new collyrium-stamp from Staines and some thoughts on eye medicine in Roman London and Britannia, in J Bird *et al* (eds) 1996, 177–87

Jackson, R P J, 1996b Other copper-alloy objects, in R P J Jackson & T Potter 1996, 339–59

Jackson, R P J, 1997 An ancient British medical kit from Stanway, Essex, *The Lancet,* **350**, 1471–3

Jackson, R P J, 2002 Roman surgery: the evidence of the instruments, in R Arnott (ed), *The archaeology of medicine*, BAR Int Ser **1046**. Oxford: British Archaeological Reports, 87–94

Jackson, R P J, 2003 The *domus* 'del chirurgo' at Rimini: an interim account of the medical assemblage, *J Roman Archaeol,* **16**, 312–21

Jackson, R P J, 2005a Holding on to health? Bone surgery and instrumentation in the Roman Empire, in H King (ed), *Health in Antiquity.* London: Routledge, 97–119

Jackson, R P J, 2005b The role of doctors in the city, in A MacMahon & J Price (eds) 2005, 202–20

Jackson, R P J, 2007 The surgical instruments, in P Crummy, S Benfield, N Crummy, V Rigby & D Shimmin, *Stanway: an élite burial site at Camulodunum*, Britannia Monogr **24**. London: Society for the Promotion of Roman Studies, 236–52

Jackson, R P J, & Potter, T, 1996 *Excavations at Stonea Cambridgeshire 1980–85.* London: British Museum Press

Jamieson, D, 2002 An assessment of the feasibility of the modelling of sub-surface deposits beneath the City of London, Unpubl MSc dissertation for University College London

Jarrett, C, 2001 The post-Roman pottery, in J Butler, The City defences at Aldersgate, *Trans London Middlesex Archaeol Soc,* **52**, 65–70

Jarrett, M G, 1994 Non-legionary troops in Roman Britain, Part One: the units, *Britannia,* **25**, 35–77

Jashemski, W F, 1979 *The Gardens of Pompeii, Herculaneum and the Villas Destroyed by Vesuvius.* New Rochelle, New York: Caratzas Bros

Jashemski, W F, 1981 Campania peristyle gardens, in E B MacDougall & W F Jashemski (eds), *Ancient Roman Gardens,* Dumbarton Oaks Colloquium on the History of Landscape Architecture: Papers. Washington, DC: Dumbarton Oaks Trustees for Harvard University, 29–48

Jashemski, W F, 1994 Archaeological evidence for plants in ancient Vesuvian Gardens, in D Moe *et al* (eds), 1994, 15–18

Johns, C, 1996a Isis, not Cybele: A bone hairpin from London, in J Bird *et al* (eds) 1996, 115–18

Johns, C, 1996b Mounted men and sitting ducks: The iconography of Romano-British plate brooches, in B Rafferty (ed), *Sites and Sights of the Iron Age: Essays of fieldwork and museum research presented to I M Stead.* Oxford: Oxbow Books, 103–9

Johns, C, 1996c *The Jewellery of Roman Britain. Celtic and classical traditions.* London: University College London Press

Johns, C, 1997 *The Snettisham Roman Jeweller's Hoard.* London: British Museum Press

Johnson, J, 1970 The date of the construction of the Saxon Shore fort at Richborough, *Britannia,* **1**, 240–8

Johnson, S, 1976, *The Roman Forts of the Saxon Shore.* London: Elek Books

Johnson, S, 1983 *Late Roman Fortifications.* London: Batsford

Johnson, T, 1975, A Roman signal tower at Shadwell E1, *Trans London Middlesex Archaeol Soc,* **26**, 278–80

Jones, C E E, 1983 A review of Roman lead-alloy material recovered from the Walbrook Valley in the City of London, *Trans London Middlesex Archaeol Soc*, **34**, 49–59

Jones, J, 1986 Broad Street Station, London 1985, Unpubl environmental archive report

Jones, M U, 1968, Crop mark sites at Mucking, Essex, *Antiq J,* **48**, 210–30

Jope, E M, 2000, *Early Celtic Art in the British Isles.* Oxford: Clarendon Press

Keeley, H, & Sheldon, H, 1976 Environmental Archaeology: a policy for London?, *London Archaeol,* **2**(16), 415–6

Keene, D, 1989 Medieval London and its region, *London J,* **14**(2), 97–111

Keene, D, 2000 London in the post-Roman period, in D M Palliser (ed), *The Cambridge Urban History of Britain 1: 600–1540.* Cambridge: Cambridge University Press, 187–216

Keene, D, 2003 Alfred and London, in T Reuter (ed), *Alfred the Great.* Aldershot: Ashgate Publishing, 235–50

Keily, J, 2004 The non-ceramic finds, in E Howe & D Lakin 2004, 118–22

Keily, J, & Shepherd, J, 2005 Glass working in the Upper Walbrook Valley, in F Seeley & J Drummond-Murray 2005, 147–55

Kempe, A J, 1836 Discovery of Roman antiquities in Deveril Street, Southwark, *Archaeologia,* **26**, 466–70

Kent, J, 1977 The coin hoard, in A Gentry *et al* 1977, 168–9

Kenyon, K, 1934 The Roman theatre at Verulamium, St Albans, *Archaeologia,* **84**, 213–61

Keppie, L, 1998 *Roman Inscribed and Sculptured Stones in the Hunterian Museum University of Glasgow,* Britannia Monogr, **13**. London: Society for the Promotion of Roman Studies

Keynes, S, 1998 King Alfred and the Mercians, in M A S Blackburn & D N Dumville (eds), *Kings, Currency and Alliances. History and Coinage of Southern England in the Ninth Century.* Woodbridge: Boydell Press, 1–43

Keynes, S, & Lapidge, M, 1983 *Asser's Life of Alfred and Other Contemporary Sources.* London: Penguin Books

Kightly, C, 1982 *Folk Heroes of Britain.* London: Thames & Hudson

King, A, & Henig, M (eds), 1981 *The Roman West in the Third Century. Contributions from archaeology and history,* BAR Int Ser **109**. Oxford: British Archaeological Reports

Knight, J K, 1998 Late Roman and post-Roman Caerwent, some evidence from metalwork, *Archaeol Cambrensis,* **145**, 35–66

Köhne, E, & Ewigleben, C, 2000 *Gladiators and Caesars: The power of spectacle in ancient Rome* (English version ed R Jackson). London: British Museum Press

Kolling, A, 1973 Römische Kastrierzange, *Archäologisches Korrespondenzblatt* **3**, 353–7

Körber, K, 1911 Die in den Jahren 1909 und 1910 gefundenen römischen und frühchristlichen Inschriften und Skulpturen, *Mainzer Zeitschrift,* **6**, 121–41

Kostof, S, 1991 *The City Shaped: Urban patterns and meanings through history.* London: Thames & Hudson

Kühnen, H-P, 2000 *Morituri: Menschenopfer, Todtgeweihte, Strafgerichte,* Schriftenreihe des Rheinischen Landesmuseum Trier **117**. Trier: Rheinischen Landesmuseum Trier

Künzl, E, 1998 L J Bliquez und die medizinischen Instrumente aus Pompeji: die medizinische Versorgung einer römischen Stadt im 1 Jh n Chr, *J Roman Arch,* **12**, 575–92

Künzl, E, 2002 *Medizin in der Antike. Aus einer Welt ohne Narkose und Aspirin.* Stuttgart: Theiss

Kyle, D, 1998 *Spectacles of Death in Ancient Rome.* London: Routledge

L'année épigraphique, Revue des publications épigraphiques relatives à l'antiquité romaine. Paris: Ernest Leroux

La Baume, P, & Nüber, E, 1971 Das Achatgefäss von Köln, *Kölner Jahrbuch,* **12**, 80–93

LAARC 2006 London Archaeological Archive & Research Centre, http://www.museumoflondon.org.uk/laarc

Lactantius, 2003 *Divine Institutes,* trans A Bowen & P Garnsey, Translated Texts for Historians **40**. Liverpool: Liverpool University Press

Lakin, D, Seeley, F, & Rielly, K, 2002 *The Roman Tower at Shadwell, London: A reappraisal,* MoLAS Archaeol Stud Ser, **8**. London: Museum of London Archaeology Service

Lakin, D, Symonds, R P, Gray-Rees, L, Rielly, K, Sidell, E J, & Betts, I, 1999 A Romano-British site at Summerton Way, Thamesmead, London Borough of Bexley, *Archaeol Cantiana,* **119**, 311–41

le Glay, M, 1990 Les amphithéâtres: loci religiosi, in C Domergue, C Landes & J-M Pailler (eds), *Spectacula. 1: Gladiateurs et amphithéâtres. Actes du colloque tenu à Toulouse et à Lattes les 26, 27, 28 et 29 Mai 1987.* Lattes: Imago, 217–30

Lierke, R, 1993 It was the turning wheel, and not the lathe. Mold pressing and mold turning of hot glass in ancient glass vessel production, *Glastechnische Berichte,* **66**, 321–9

Ling, R, 1991 *Roman Painting.* Cambridge: Cambridge University Press

Ling, R, 2005 *Pompeii: History, life and afterlife.* Stroud: Tempus

Lloyd-Morgan, G, 1981 *Description of the Collections in the Rijksmuseum G M Kam at Nijmegen. IX The Mirrors, including a description of the Roman mirrors found in the Netherlands, in other Dutch Museums.* Rijswijk: Ministry of Culture Recreation & Social Welfare

London Museum, 1970 *Glass in London.* London: Museum of London

Longley, D, & Poulton, R, 1982 The Saxon cemetery at Upper West Field, Shepperton, *Trans London Middlesex Archaeol Soc,* **33**, 177–85

Lyne, M, 2000 Pottery Assessment, in M Beasley 2000

Lyne, M, 2002 Roman Pottery, in R Taylor-Wilson 2002, 49–52 and *passim*

Lyne, M, 2005 Pottery Assessment, in K Sayer, An assessment of an archaeological excavation at 52–56 Lant Street, London Borough of Southwark, Unpubl report for Pre-Construct Archaeology (site code LTU03)

Lyne, M A B, & Jefferies, R S, 1979 *The Alice Holt/Farnham Roman Pottery Industry,* CBA Res Rep, **30**, London: Council for British Archaeology

Lyon, J, 2004 New work on Cripplegate Fort: Excavations at 25 Gresham Street, 2000–2001, *Trans London Middlesex Archaeol Soc,* **55**, 153–82

Lyon, J, forthcoming *Within these Walls: Roman and medieval defences north of Newgate, at the Merrill Lynch Financial Centre, City of London,* MoLAS Monogr Ser **33**. London: Museum of London Archaeology Service

Maaskant-Kleibrink, M, 1978 *Catalogue of the Engraved Gems in the Royal Coin Cabinet, The Hague: The Greek, Etruscan and Roman collections.* The Hague: Government Publishing Office

McCann, W A, & Orton, C R, 1989 The Fleet Valley Project, *London Archaeol,* **6**(4), 102–7

MacDonald, W L, 1986 *The Architecture of the Roman Empire II: An urban appraisal.* New Haven: Yale University Press

McIsaac, W, Schwab, I, & Sheldon, H L, 1979 Excavations at Old Ford, 1972–1975, *Trans London Middlesex Archaeol Soc*, **30**, 39–96

Mackinder, A, 2000 *A Romano-British Cemetery on Watling Street: Excavations at 165 Great Dover Street, Southwark, London,* MoLAS Archaeol Stud Ser, **4**. London: Museum of London Archaeology Service

McKinley, J I, 2003 The Early Saxon cemetery at Park Lane, Croydon, *Surrey Archaeol Collect*, **90**, 1–116

Mackreth, D, 1981 The brooches, in C Partridge, *Skeleton Green A Late Iron Age and Romano-British Site,* Britannia Monogr Ser, **2**. London: Society for the Promotion of Roman Studies, 130–51, 324–6

Mackreth, D, 1986 The brooches, in D Gurney 1986, 61–7

Mackreth, D, 1991 Brooches of copper alloy and of iron, in A K Gregory 1991, 120–9

Mackreth, D, 1996 Brooches, in R P J Jackson & T Potter 1996, 296–327

MacMahon, A, & Price, J (eds), 2005 *Roman Working Lives and Urban Living.* Oxford: Oxbow Books

Macphail, R I, 1988a Soil report on the Middle Saxon floor and 'dark earth' at Jubilee Hall, in R Cowie & R L Whytehead with L Blackmore 1988, Two Middle Saxon occupation sites: Excavations at Jubilee Hall and 21–22 Maiden Lane WC2, *Trans London Middlesex Archaeol Soc*, **39**, 156–9

Macphail, R I, 1988b Soil micromorphology, in G Brown, First-century horticultural activity close to the municipal boundaries of Londinium, Unpubl archive report for Museum of London Archaeology Service, WIV88

Macphail, R I, 2003 Soil microstratigraphy: a micromorphological and chemical approach, in C Cowan 2003, 89–105

Macphail, R I, 2005 Soil micromorphology, in B Yule 2005, 88–90

Maitland, F W, 1897 *Domesday Book and Beyond.* Cambridge: Cambridge University Press

Maiuri, B, 1957 *Museo Nazionale di Napoli.* Naples: Novara

Major, H, 2004 Metal objects, in R Havis & H Brooks, *Excavations at Stansted Airport, 1986–91 1: Prehistoric and Romano British,* E Anglian Archaeol **107**. Chelmsford: Essex County Council, *passim*

Maloney, C, 1991 Review of Wilmott 1991, *Trans London Middlesex Archaeol Soc*, **42**, 122–3

Maloney, C, & de Moulins, D, 1990 *The Archaeology of Roman London 1: The upper Walbrook Valley in the Roman period*, CBA Res Rep, **69**. London: Council for British Archaeology

Maloney, C, & Gostick, T, 1998 London fieldwork and publication round-up 1997, *London Archaeol*, **8** (suppl 3)

Maloney, C, & Holroyd, I, 1999 London fieldwork and publication round-up 1998, *London Archaeol*, **9** (suppl 1)

Maloney, C, & Holroyd, I, 2000 London fieldwork and publication round-up 1999, *London Archaeol*, **9** (suppl 2)

Maloney, C, & Holroyd, I, 2001 London fieldwork and publication round-up 2000, *London Archaeol*, **9** (suppl 3)

Maloney, C, & Holroyd, I, 2002 London fieldwork and publication round-up 2001, *London Archaeol*, **10** (suppl 1)

Maloney, J, 1983 Recent work on London's defences, in J Maloney and B Hobley (eds), *Roman Urban Defences in the West*, CBA Res Rep, **51**. London: Council for British Archaeology, 96–117

Manning, W H, 1985 *Catalogue of the Romano-British Iron Tools, Fittings and Weapons in the British Museum.* London: British Museum Publications

Margary, I D, 1973 *Roman Roads in Britain,* 3rd edn. London: John Baker

Marsden, P, 1969 Guildhall Museum 1969–70: Archaeological finds in the City of London, 1966–9: Central Criminal Court Site, Warwick Square, *Trans London Middlesex Archaeol Soc*, **22**(2), 1–9

Marsden, P, 1975 The excavation of a Roman palace site in London, 1961–1972, *Trans London Middlesex Archaeol Soc*, **26**, 1–102

Marsden, P, 1976 Two Roman public baths in London, *Trans London Middlesex Archaeol Soc*, **27**, 2–70

Marsden, P, 1980 *Roman London.* London: Thames & Hudson

Marsden, P, 1987 *The Roman Forum Site in London, Discoveries before 1985.* London: HMSO

Marsden, P, 1994 *Ships of the Port of London: First to eleventh centuries AD,* EH Archaeol Rep, **3**. London: English Heritage

Marsden, P, & West, B, 1992 Population change in Roman London, *Britannia*, **23**, 133–40

Marsh, G, & Tyers, P, 1978 The Roman pottery from Southwark, in SLAEC 1978, 533–82

Marshall, K, 1964 Ancient roads at Stratford E15, *Essex Naturalist*, **31**, 208–13

Martens, M, 2004 Re-thinking sacred 'rubbish': The ritual deposits of the temple of Mithras at Tienen (Belgium), *J Roman Archaeol*, **17**, 333–53

Martens, M, & de Boe, G (eds), 2004 *Roman Mithraism: The evidence of the small finds. Papers of the international conference Tienen 2001.* Brussels: Museum Het Toreke

Mason, D J P, 2003 *Roman Britain and the Roman Navy.* Stroud: Tempus Publishing

Massabo, B, 2000 La più produzione di vetri figurati ad incisione e ad ingalio di età romana, in *Annales du 14e Congrés de l'Association Internationale pour l'Histoire du Verre.* Lochem: Association Internationale pour l'Histoire du Verre, 68–75

Maurin, J, 1984 Les Barbares aux arènes, *Ktema*, **9**, 103–11

Meeks, N, 1988 A technical study of Roman bronze mirrors, in J E Jones (ed), *Aspects of Ancient Mining and Metallurgy: Acta of a British School*

at Athens Centenary Conference at Bangor, 1986.
Bangor: Department of Classics, University
College of North Wales, 66–79

Mees, A W, 1995 *Modelsignierte Dekorationen
auf südgallischer Terra Sigillata*, Forschungen
und Berichte zur Vor- und Frühgeschichte
in Baden-Württemberg, **54**. Stuttgart: Konrad
Theiss Verlag for Landesdenkmalamt Baden-
Württemberg

Merrifield, R, 1962 Coins from the bed of the
Walbrook and their significance, *Antiq J*, **42**,
38–52

Merrifield, R, 1965 *The Roman City of London*.
London: Ernest Benn Ltd

Merrifield, R, 1969 *Roman London*. London:
Cassell

Merrifield, R, 1983 *London: City of the Romans*.
London: Batsford

Merrifield, R, 1987 *The Archaeology of Ritual and
Magic*. London: Batsford

Merrifield, R, 1995 Roman metalwork from the
Walbrook – rubbish, ritual or redundancy?,
Trans London Middlesex Archaeol Soc, **46**,
27–44

Merrifield, R, & Perring, D, 1997 The Roman city
of London, in S Bradley & N Pevsner, *The
Buildings of England. London 1: The City of
London* (new edn). London: Penguin, 27–43

Metcalf, D M, 1978 The ranking of boroughs:
Numismatic evidence from the reign of Aethelred II, in D Hill (ed), *Ethelred the Unready:
papers from the millenary conference*, BAR Brit
Ser **59**. Oxford: British Archaeological Reports,
159–213

Millett, M, 1980 The Thames Street section: 1974,
in C Hill *et al* 1980, 14–27

Millett, M, 1990 *The Romanization of Britain:
An essay in archaeological interpretation*.
Cambridge: Cambridge University Press

Millett, M, 1994 Evaluating Roman London,
Archaeol J, **151**, 427–35

Millett, M, 1996 Characterizing Roman London, in
J Bird *et al* (eds) 1996, 33–7

Millett, M, 1998 Introduction: London as capital?, in
B Watson (ed) 1998b, 7–12

Millett, M, & Graham, D, 1986 *Excavations on
the Romano-British Small Town at Neatham,
Hampshire, 1969–1979*, Hampshire Field Club
Monogr, **3**. Winchester: Hampshire Field Club

Mills, A D, 2001 *A Dictionary of London Place
Names*. Oxford: Oxford University Press

Mills, P, 1984 Excavations at Roman Road/Parnell
Road, Old Ford, London E3, *Trans London
Middlesex Archaeol Soc*, **35**, 25–36

Mills, P, 1995 Excavations at the dorter undercroft,
Westminster Abbey, *Trans London Middlesex
Archaeol Soc*, **46**, 69–124

Mills, P, 1996 The battle of London 1066, *London
Archaeol*, **8**(3), 59–62

Milne, G, 1985 *The Port of Roman London*. London:
Batsford

Milne, G (ed), 1992 *From Roman Basilica to
Medieval Market*. London: HMSO

Milne, G, 1995 *Roman London*. London: Batsford/
English Heritage

Milne, G, 1996 A palace disproved: Reassessing the
provincial governor's presence in 1st-century
London, in J Bird *et al* (eds) 1996, 49–55

Milne, G, Battarbee, R W, Straker, V, & Yule,
B, 1983 The London Thames in the mid-first
century AD, *Trans London Middlesex Archaeol
Soc*, **34**, 19–30

Milne, G, & Wardle, A, 1993 Early Roman development at Leadenhall Court, London and related
research, *Trans London Middlesex Archaeol
Soc*, **44**, 23–169

Moe, D, Dickson, J H, & Jorgensen, P M (eds), 1994
*Garden History: Garden plants, species, forms
and varieties from Pompeii to 1800*, European
Symposium: Papers. Belgium: Council of
Europe, PACT, Rixensart

MoLAS, 2000 *The Archaeology of Greater London:
An assessment of archaeological evidence for
human presence in the area now covered by
Greater London*. London: Museum of London

Monteil, G, 2005 Samian in Roman London. Unpubl
PhD thesis, University of London

Morgan, P, 1978 *Domesday Book, Cheshire*.
Chichester: Phillimore

Morgan, R, 1980a The carbon 14 and dendrochronology, in C Hill *et al* 1980, 88–94

Morgan, R, 1980b Tree-ring analysis of timber, in D
M Jones, *Excavations at Billingsgate Buildings
'Triangle', Lower Thames Street, London, 1974*,
LAMAS Special Paper, **4**. London: London and
Middlesex Archaeological Society, 28–32

Morris, J, 1959 Anglo-Saxon Surrey, *Surrey
Archaeol Collect*, **56**, 132–58

Morris, J, 1975 *Domesday Book: Middlesex*. London
& Chichester: Phillimore

Morris, J, 1978 *Oxford;* revised edn. Oxford: Oxford
University Press

Morris, J, 1982 *Londinium: London in the Roman
Empire*. London: Weidenfeld and Nicholson

Murail, P, & Girard, L, 2000 Biology and burial
practices from the end of the 1st century AD to
the beginning of the 5th century AD: the rural
cemetery of Chantambre (Essonne, France),
in J Pearce *et al* (eds), 2000, 105–11

Murdoch, T (ed), 1991 *Tresures and Trinkets:
Jewellery in London from pre-Roman times to
the 1930s*. London: Museum of London

Murphy, P, & Scaife, R G, 1991 The environmental
archaeology of gardens, in A E Brown (ed) 1991,
83–99

Museum of London, 1983 *Londinium: A descriptive
map and guide to Roman London*, 2nd edn.
Southampton: Ordnance Survey

Museum of London, 2006 Ceramics and Glass online
http://www.museumoflondon.org.uk/ceramics/
last accessed 21/01/08

Myres, J N L, 1968 The Anglo-Saxon pottery from
Mucking, in M U Jones 1968, 222–8

Nayling, N, 1991 An identification of sweet chestnut (*Castanea sativa*) from Roman London, *Wetlands Archaeol Res Project (WARP)*, **10**, 12

Nearing, H, Jr, 1948 Julius Caesar and the Tower of London, *Modern Language Notes*, **63**, 228–33

Nenova-Merdjanova, R, 1997 Gods, youths and slaves: On the bronze bust-vessels from the Roman period, *Archaeology in Bulgaria*, **1**(1), 103–12

Nenova-Merdjanova, R, 1999 Roman bronze vessels as part of *instrumentum balnei*, in J DeLaine & D E Johnston (eds) 1999, 131–4

Nixon, T, McAdam, E, Tomber, R, & Swain, H (eds), 2002 *A Research Framework for London Archaeology 2002*. London: Museum of London

Noël Hume, I, 1978 Into the jaws of death . . . walked one, in J Bird *et al* (eds) 1978, 7–22

North, J J, 1963 *English Hammered Coinage*. London: Spink & Son

Nutton, V, 2004 *Ancient Medicine*. London: Routledge

Oliver, A, 1984 Early Roman faceted glass, *J Glass Stud*, **26**, 35–58

Ortalli, J, 2000 Rimini: la città, in M M Calvani (ed), *Aemilia: la cultura romana in Emilia Romagna dal III secolo a.C. all'età constantiniana*. Venice: Marsilio, 501–6

Oswald, F, 1936–37 *Index of Figure-types on Terra Sigillata (Samian ware)*, Annals of Archaeol & Anthropol Suppl **23**: 1–4; **24**: 1–4. Liverpool: Liverpool University Press

Owen, W, Schwab, I, & Sheldon, H, 1973 Roman burials from Old Ford E3, February and May 1972, *Trans London Middlesex Archaeol Soc*, **24**, 135–45

Page, W (ed), 1909 *Victoria History the Counties of England: A history of London*, **1**. London: Constable & Co

Parnell, G, 1985 The Roman and medieval defences and the later development of the inmost Ward, Tower of London: Excavations 1955–77, *Trans London Middlesex Archaeol Soc*, **36**, 1–79

Parnum, A, & Cotton, J, 1983 Recent work in Brentford: Excavations and observations 1974–82, *London Archaeol*, **4**(12), 318–25, 336

Pasciuti, D, 2002 *Part II. A measurement error model for estimating the population sizes of preindustrial cities*. Riverside: Institute for Research on World-Systems, University of California

Paul of Aegina, 1844–47 *The Seven Books of Paulus Aegineta*, trans T Adams, 3 vols. London: Sydenham Society

Pavels, A, 1984 *Abbo von Saint-Germain-des Pres, Bella Parisiacae Urbis*. Frankfurt am Main: Verlag Peter Lang

Pre-Construct Archaeology, 2003 The Tabard Square excavations, http://www.pre-construct.com/sites/highlights/tabard.htm

Pearce, J, 2000 Burial, society and context in the provincial Roman World, in J Pearce *et al* (eds) 2000, 1–12

Pearce, J, Millett, M, & Struck, M (eds), 2000 *Burial, Society and Context in the Roman World*. Oxford: Oxbow Books

Pearson, A, 2002 *The Roman Shore Forts. Coastal Defences of Southern Britain*. Stroud: Tempus

Pearson, J, 1973 *Arena. The Story of the Colosseum*. London: Thames & Hudson

Peddie, J, 1999 *Alfred the Good Soldier: His life and campaigns*. Stroud: Alan Sutton

Pérez-Sala Rodés, M, 2001 El estudio del reciclaje del vidrio en el mundo romano: el caso de Guildhall Yard, Londres, in T Carreras Rossell (ed), *I Jornades Hispàniques d'Historia del Vidre: Actes* (Sitges 2000). Barcelona: Museu d'Arqueologia de Catalunya, 65–72

Pérez-Sala Rodés, M, & Shepherd, J, forthcoming The Cullet Dump and Evidence of Glass-working at Guildhall Yard, London, in N Bateman *et al* forthcoming. London: Musuem of London Archaeology Service

Perkins, D R J, 1985 The Monkton Gas pipeline: phases III and IV, 1983–84, *Archaeol Cantiana*, **102**, 43–69

Perring, D, 1991a *Roman London*, The Archaeology of London. London: Seaby

Perring, D, 1991b Spatial organisation and social change in Roman towns, in J Rich & A Wallace-Hadrill (eds), *City and Country in the Ancient World*. London: Routledge, 273–93

Perring, D, 2002 *The Roman House in Britain*. London, Routledge

Perring, D, Roskams, S, with Allen, P, 1991 *The Archaeology of Roman London 2: The early development of Roman London west of the Walbrook*, CBA Res Rep, **70**, London: Council for British Archaeology

Petronius Arbiter, 1953 *The Satyricon*, trans P Dinnage. London: Spearman & Calder

Pharr, C, with Davidson T S & Pharr, M B (trans) 1952 *The Theodosian Code and Novels; and the Sirmondian Constitutions*. Princeton NJ: Princeton University Press

Phillips, E J, 1977 *Corpus Signorum Imperii Romani, Great Britain 1.1: Corbridge, Hadrian's Wall east of the North Tyne*. Oxford: Oxford University Press

Philp, B, 1981 *The Excavation of the Roman Forts of the Classis Britannica at Dover, 1970–1977*, Kent Monogr Ser Res Rep, **3**. Dover: Kent Archaeological Rescue Unit

Philp, B, 2005 *The Excavation of the Roman Fort at Reculver, Kent*, Kent Monogr Ser Res Rep, **10**. Dover: Kent Archaeological Rescue Unit

Philpott, R, 1991 *Burial Practices in Roman Britain: A survey of grave treatement and furnishing AD 43–410*, BAR Brit Ser, **219**. Oxford: British Archaeological Reports

Piercey Fox, N, 1969 Caesar's Camp, Keston, *Archaeol Cantiana*, **84**, 185–99

Piggott, S, 1950 *William Stukeley: an eighteenth-century antiquary*. Oxford: Clarendon Press

Pilcher, J R, Baillie, M G L, Schmidt, B, & Becker, B, 1984 A 7272-year tree-ring chronology for western Europe, *Nature*, **312**, 150–2

Pitt, K, 1990 Preliminary report on the archaeological excavations at 72a Armagh Road and 91–93 Parnell Road, London E3, Unpubl report for Department of Greater London Archaeology, Museum of London, Site Code AGH90

Pitt, K, 1991 A report on archaeological excavations in Area M of the DICE project, Ranwell East Estate, Bow E3, Unpubl report for Department of Greater London Archaeology, Museum of London, Site Code BOD91

Pitt, K, 1995 An archaeological evaluation, 91–93 Parnell Road, Bow, London Borough of Tower Hamlets E3, Unpubl report for Museum of London Archaeology Service, Site Code PRB95

Plantzos, D, 1996 Ptolemaic cameos of the second and first centuries BC, *Oxford J Archaeol*, **15**, 39–61

Plantzos, D, 1999 *Hellenistic Engraved Gems*, Oxford Monogr on Classical Archaeol. Oxford: Clarendon

Plass, P, 1995 *The Game of Death in Ancient Rome*. Madison, Wis: University of Wisconsin

Plouviez, J, 2004 Brooches, in T Blagg *et al* 2004, 87–108

Plutarch, 1958 *The Fall of the Roman Republic. Six Lives by Plutarch: Marius, Sulla, Crassus, Pompey, Caesar, Cicero*, trans R Warner, Penguin Classics L84. Harmondsworth: Penguin

Poole, H, 1870 Some account of the discovery of the Roman coffin in the north green at Westminster Abbey, *Archaeol J*, **27**, 119–28

Porter, G, 1997 An early medieval settlement at Guildhall, City of London, in G de Boe & F Verhaeghe (eds) 1997, 147–52

Poulton, R, 1987 Saxon Surrey, in J Bird & D G Bird (eds), *The Archaeology of Surrey to 1540*. Guildford: Surrey Archaeological Society, 197–222

Price, J, 1974 The glass, in G D B Jones, *Roman Manchester*. Altrincham: Sherratt & Manchester Excavation Committee, 131–4

Price, J, 1977 The Roman glass, in A Gentry *et al* 1977, 154–61

Price, J, 1987 Late Hellenistic and Early Imperial cast vessel glass in Spain, in *Annales du 10e Congrés de l'Association Internationale pour l'Histoire du Verre*. Amsterdam: Association Internationale pour l'Histoire du Verre, 61–80

Price, J, 1991 Glass, in T Wilmott 1991, 153–67

Price, J, & Cottam, S, 1998 *Romano-British Glass Vessels: A handbook*, Practical Handbooks in Archaeol, **14**. York: Council for British Archaeology

Pringle, S, forthcoming Building materials, in C Cowan *et al* forthcoming

Puleston, J H, & Price, J E, 1873 *Roman Antiquities Recently Discovered on the Site of the National Safe Deposit Company's Premises, Mansion House*. London: Nichols & Sons

Ramage, N H, & Ramage, A, 1995 *Roman Art: Romulus to Constantine*, 2nd edn. London: Laurence King Publishing

Rayner, L, forthcoming The Roman Pottery, in J Hill & P Rowsome forthcoming

Rayner, L, & Seeley, F, 2002 The Roman Pottery, in J Drummond-Murray *et al* 2002, 162–212 & passim

Rayner, L, & Seeley, F, forthcoming The Roman pottery, in C Cowan *et al* forthcoming

RCHM(E) 1928 Royal Commission on Historical Monuments (England), *An Inventory of the Historical Monuments in London 3: Roman London*. London: HMSO

RCHM(E) 1976 Royal Commission on Historical Monuments (England), *Ancient and Historical Monuments in the County of Gloucester 1: Iron Age and Romano-British monuments in the Gloucestershire Cotswolds*. London: HMSO

Redknap, M, 1987 Recent work at Stratford E15, 30 Romford Road, *London Archaeol*, **5**(11) 291–7

Reece, R, 1983 Coins and medals, in M Henig (ed) 1983, 166–78

Reece, R, 1991 *Roman Coins from 140 sites in Britain*, Cotswold Studies, **4**. Cirencester: Cotswold Studies

Reece, R, 2002, *The Coinage of Roman Britain*. Stroud: Tempus Publishing

Reece, R, 2005 The coins, in B Philp 2005, 103–13

Rescue News 1973 Worcester: Trust for British Archaeology

Reynolds, A, 1999, *Later Anglo-Saxon England. Life and landscape*. Stroud: Tempus Publishing

Reynolds, J, 2000 A bronze figurine of Hercules from St Paul's Churchyard, London, *Britannia*, **31**, 363–5

Rhodes, M, 1991a The hoard of iron nails, in T Wilmott 1991, 132–8

Rhodes, M, 1991b The Roman coinage from London Bridge and the development of the City and Southwark, *Britannia*, **22**, 179–90

Richardson, B, 1978 Excavation round-up 1977, *London Archaeol*, **3**(6), 159–63

Richardson, B, 1980 Excavation round-up 1979, *London Archaeol*, **3**(14), 384–9

Richardson, B, 1981 Excavation round-up 1980, *London Archaeol*, **4**(2), 44–50

Richardson, B, 1991 Billingsgate bath house (GM111/ER), 100 Lower Thames Street EC3, in R Symonds *et al* 1991, 61–2

Richardson, B, 2004 Roman Pottery in L Dunwoodie 2004, 44–50 and *passim*

Richmond, I A, 1953 Three Roman writing-tablets from London, *Antiq J*, **33**, 206–8

Richter, G M A, 1971 *Engraved Gems of the Greeks, Etruscans and Romans, part 2*. London: Phaidon Press

Rielly, K, & Ainsley, C, 2002 Animal bone, in D Lakin *et al* 2002, 60–3

Riley, H T, 1863 *Chronicles of the Mayors and Sheriffs of London*. London: Trubner and Co

Riley, H T, 1868 *Memorials of London and London Life in the XIIIth, XIVth and XVth Centuries.* London: Longman, Green & Co

Riley, W, & Gomme, L, 1912 *Ship of the Roman Period Discovered on the Site of the New County Hall.* London: London County Council

Rivet, A L F, & Smith, C, 1979 *The Place-names of Roman Britain.* London: Batsford

Roberts, K, forthcoming The plant remains from 12 Arthur Street (AUT01), MoLAS Monogr Ser. London: Museum of London Archaeology Service

Robinson, J A, 1910 The church of Edward the Confessor, *Archaeologia,* **62**, 81–100

Robinson, W, 1823 *History and Antiquities of Enfield I.* London

Rodríguez-Salgado, M J, & staff of National Maritime Museum, 1988, *Armada 1588–1988. An international exhibition to commemorate the Spanish Armada.* Harmondsworth: Penguin/National Maritime Museum

Rodwell, K A, 1988 *The Prehistoric and Roman Settlement at Kelvedon, Essex,* Chelmsford Archaeol Trust Rep, **6**, CBA Res Rep, **63**. London: Chelmsford Archaeological Trust & Council for British Archaeology

Rogers, W, 1990 Mesolithic and Neolithic flint tool manufacturing areas buried beneath Roman Watling Street in Southwark, *London Archaeol,* **6**(9), 227–31

Rogge, M, Vermeulen, V & Moens, L, 1995 Ein bemerkenswerter Fund römischer Bronzestatuetten aus Kruishoutem (Ostflandern), *Archäologisches Korrespondenzblatt,* **25**, 193–207

Roskams, S P, 1991 The dark earth, in D Perring *et al* 1991, 64–5

Roueché, C, 1993 *Performers and Partisans at Aphrodisias in the Roman and Later Roman Periods,* J Roman Stud Monogr, **6**. London: Society for the Promotion of Roman Studies

Rous, J, 1745 *Historum regum Angliae,* ed Thomas Hearne. Oxford

Rowsome, P, 1996 The Billingsgate Roman house and bath – conservation and assessment, *London Archaeol,* **7**(16), 415–23

Rowsome, P, 1998 The development of the town plan of early Roman London, in B Watson (ed) 1998b, 35–46

Rowsome, P, 1999 The Huggin Hill baths and bathing in London: barometer of the town's changing circumstances, in J DeLaine & D E Johnston (eds) 1999, 262–77

Rowsome, P, 2000 *Heart of the City: Roman, medieval and modern London revealed by archaeology at 1 Poultry.* London: Museum of London/English Heritage

Rüger, C B, 1981 *Vindex cum inermi provincia?* Zu einer weiteren neronischen Marsinschrift vom Rhein, *Zeitschrift für Papyrologie und Epigraphik,* **43**, 329–35

Rumble, A R, 1996 An edition and translation of the Burghal Hidage, together with Recension C of the Tribal Hidage, in D Hill & A Rumble (eds) 1996, 14–35

Ryley, C, 1998 *Roman Gardens and their Plants.* Lewes: Sussex Archaeological Society

Salway, P, 1981 *Roman Britain.* Oxford: Oxford University Press

Salway, P, 1993 *The Oxford Illustrated History of Roman Britain.* Oxford: Oxford University Press

Sankey, D, 1998 Cathedrals, granaries and urban vitality in late Roman London, in B Watson (ed) 1998b, 78–82

Sankey, D, 2005 Sutton's Wharf South, Palmers Road, London E2. An archaeological Evaluation Report. Unpubl report for Museum of London Archaeology Service, Site Code SNM05

Sauer, E, 2000 Alchester, a Claudian 'vexillation fortress' near the western boundary of the Catuvellauni, new light on the Roman invasion of Britain, *Archaeol J,* **157**, 1–78

Saulnier, C, 1984 Laurens Lauinas: quelques remarques à propos d'un sacerdoce équestre à Rome, *Latomus,* **43**, 517–33

Scaife, R G, 1982 Pollen analysis of Roman peats underlying the Temple of Mithras, London, Unpubl report for Ancient Monuments Laboratory, no 3502

Scaife, R G, 1998 Point Pleasant; Pollen analysis of early Holocene peats, Unpubl report for Southampton, Palaeopol

Scaife, R G, 2001a Chelsea Bridge Wharf (QST 01): Pollen analysis, Unpubl report for Southampton, Palaeopol

Scaife, R G, 2001b Pollen analysis and stratigraphy of sediments from 51–53 Leroy Street. London SE1, Unpubl report for Southampton, Palaeopol

Scaife, R G, 2003a Arthur Street (AUT01): Pollen assessment analysis, Unpubl report for Southampton, Palaeopol

Scaife, R G, 2003b Fenchurch Street, London (FNE01): Pollen assessment analysis, Unpubl report for Southampton, Palaeopol

Scaife, R G, 2003c White Hart Triangle, Thamesmead: Pollen assessment analysis, Unpubl report for Southampton, Palaeopol

Scaife, R G, 2004, Blossom's Inn Fields (GHT00): Pollen analysis, Unpubl report for Southampton, Palaeopol

Scaife, R G, no date The Arndale Centre, Garrett Lane, Wandsworth (GLW01). Pollen analysis, Unpubl report for Southampton, Palaeopol

Scaife, R G, forthcoming The pollen, in J Hill & P Rowsome forthcoming

Scatozza Höricht, L A, 1986 *I Vetri Romana di Ercolano,* Cataloghi 1. Rome: Ministero per i beni culturali ed ambientali soprintendenza archeologica di Pompei

Schäfer, A, 2004 Relgiöse Erkennungszeichen, in C Roman & C. Gazdac (eds), *Orbis Antiquus: Studia in honorem Ioannis Pisonis.* Cluj: Fortuna, 125–31

Schäfer, A, & Diaconescu, A, 1997 Das Liber Pater Heligtum von Apulum (Dakien), in H Cancik & J Rüpke (eds), *Römische Reichsreligion und Provinzial Religion*. Tübingen: Mohr Siebeck, 195–218

Scheid, J, 1991 Sanctuaires et territoire dans la *colonia Augusta Treverorum*, in J-L Brunaux (ed), *Les sanctuaires celtiques et leurs rapports avec le monde méditerranéen*, Actes du colloque de St-Riquier (8 au 11 novembre 1990). Paris: Errance, 42–57

Schmid, D, 1991 *Die Römischen Schlangentöpfe aus Augst und Kaiseraugst*, Forschungen in Augst **11**. Augst: Römermuseum, Augst

Schofield, J, 1994 Saxon and medieval parish churches in the City of London, *Trans London Middlesex Archaeol Soc*, **45**, 23–145

Schofield, J, & Maloney, C (eds), 1998 *Archaeology in the City of London 1907–1991: A guide to records of excavations by the Museum of London and its predecessors,* Archaeol Gazetteer Ser, **1**. London: Museum of London

Seeley, F, 2000 The Roman pottery, in A Mackinder 2000, 53–7 & passim

Seeley, F, 2002 Roman (non-samian) pottery, in D Lakin *et al* 2002, 30–1

Seeley, F, 2003 The Roman Pottery, in D Swift 2003, 68–9 & passim

Seeley, F, 2004 Chapter 4: The small finds, in T Blagg *et al* 2004, 86–149

Seeley, F, 2006 The Roman Pottery, in R Bluer *et al* 2006, 105–23

Seeley, F, forthcoming Late Roman pottery in London

Seeley, F, & Drummond-Murray, J, 2005 *Roman Pottery Production in the Walbrook Valley: Excavations at 20–28 Moorgate, City of London*, MoLAS Monogr Ser, **25**. London: Museum of London Archaeology Service

Sharpe, M, 1932 *Middlesex in British, Roman and Saxon Times* (2nd edn). London: Methuen & Co

Sheldon, H, 1970 Current dig at Old Ford, *London Archaeol*, **1**(6), 136–9

Sheldon, H, 1971 Excavations at Lefevre Road. Old Ford E3, Sept 1969–June 1970, *Trans London Middlesex Archaeol Soc*, **23**(1), 42–77

Sheldon, H, 1972 Excavations at Parnell Road and Appian Road Old Ford E3, February–April 1971, *Trans London Middlesex Archaeol Soc*, **23**(2), 101–47

Sheldon, H, 1974 Excavations at Topping's and Sun Wharves, Southwark, 1970–2, *Trans London Middlesex Archaeol Soc*, **25**, 1–116

Sheldon, H, 1978 The 1972–74 excavations: Their contribution to Southwark's history, in SLAEC 1978, 11–49

Sheldon, H, 1981 London and South East Britain, in A King & M Henig (eds) 1981, 363–82

Sheldon, H, 1996 Southwark and London, *Trans London Middlesex Archaeol Soc*, **47**, 79–85

Sheldon, H, 2000 Roman Southwark, in I Haynes *et al* (eds) 2000, 121–50

Sheldon, H, & Schaaf, L, 1978 A survey of Roman sites in Greater London, in J Bird *et al* (eds) 1978, 59–88

Sheldon, H, & Townend, P, 1978 93–95, Borough High Street, in SLAEC 1978, 423–68

Sheldon, H, & Tyers, I, 1983 Recent dendrochronological work in Southwark and its implications, *London Archaeol*, **4**(13), 355–61

Shepherd, J, 1980 The glass, in D Whipp 1980, 63–6

Shepherd, J, 1992 The glass, in C Cowan 1992, 120–36

Shepherd, J, 1993 The glass, in G Milne & A Wardle 1993, 99–114

Shepherd, J, 1998 *The Temple of Mithras, London: Excavations by W F Grimes and A Williams at the Walbrook*, EH Archaeol Rep, **12**. London: English Heritage

Shepherd, J, 1999 The Glass, in A G Poulter with R K Falkner & J Shepherd 1999 *Nicopolis ad Istrum: A Roman to Early Byzantine City – The Pottery and Glass*, Soc Antiq London Res Rep, **57**. London: Leicester University Press, 297–378

Shepherd, J, 2000 Glass, in B Barber & D Bowsher 2000, 125–30

Shepherd, J, 2002 Glass, in D Lakin *et al* 2002, 49–51

Shepherd, J, with Brehm, B, & Yule, B, 2005 Glass, in B Yule 2005, 151–5

Shepherd, J, & Heyworth, M, 1991 Le travail du verre dans Londres, romain (Londinium): un état de la question, in D Foy and G Sennequier (eds), *Ateliers de Verriers de l'Antiquité à la Période Pré-industrielle*, Actes des 4ème Rencontres – Rouen 24–25 Nov 1989. Rouen: Association Française pour l'Arcéologie du Verre, 13–22

Shotter, D, 2004 Vespasian, *auctoritas* and Britain, *Britannia,* **35**, 1–8

Sidell, E J, 2001 The prehistoric marsh, in T Brigham, & A Woodger (eds) 2001, 73–7

Sidell, E J, 2003 Archaeology and relative sea level change in the inner Thames estuary, London, UK, Unpubl PhD thesis, Department of Geography, University of Durham

Sidell, J, & Rielly, K, 1998 New evidence for the ritual use of animals in Roman London, in B Watson (ed) 1998b, 95–9

Sidell, E J, Wilkinson, K N, Scaife, R G, & Cameron, N G, 2000 *The Holocene Evolution of the London Thames: Archaeological investigations (1991–1998) for the London Underground Ltd Jubilee Line Extension project*, MoLAS Monogr Ser, **5**. London, Museum of London Archaeology Service

Simpson, G, & Blance, B, 1998 Do brooches have ritual associations?, in J Bird (ed), *Form and Fabric: Studies in Rome's material past in honour of B R Hartley*. Oxford: Oxbow Books, 267–79

Simpson, G, Crummy, N, & Blance, B (eds), forthcoming *Pre-Roman and Roman Brooches* (M R Hull catalogue)

Sims-Williams, P, 1983 The settlement of England in Bede and the Chronicle, *Anglo-Saxon England*, **12**, 1–41

SLAEC 1978 Southwark & Lambeth Archaeological Excavation Committee, *Southwark Excavations 1972–1974*, LAMAS/SAS Joint Publ **1**, 2 vols. London: London and Middlesex Archaeological Society, Surrey Archaeological Society

Sloane, B, & Malcolm, G, 2004 *Excavations at the Priory of the Order of the Hospital of St John of Jerusalem, Clerkenwell, London*, MoLAS Monogr Ser, **20**. London: Museum of London Archaeology Service

Sloane, B, Swain, H, & Thomas, C, 1995 The Roman Road and the River Regime, *London Archaeol*, **7**(14), 359–70

Smith, A, 1979 Lucius of Britain: Alleged king and church founder, *Folklore*, **90**(1), 29–36

Smith, C R, 1854 *Catalogue of the Museum of London Antiquities collected by and the property of C R Smith*. London

Smith, C R, 1859 *Illustrations of Roman London*. London: privately printed

Smith, R, 1902–3 Roman interments at Enfield, *Proc Soc Antiq London*, **19**, 206–10

Smith, R, 1909–11 A stone coffin and other Roman burials found at Old Ford in East London, *Proc Soc Antiq London*, **23**, 230–8

Smith, W, 2002 A review of archaeological wood analyses in southern England, Unpubl report for English Heritage; CFA report 75/2002

Snape, M E, 1993 *Roman Brooches from North Britain*, BAR Brit Ser, **235**. Oxford: British Archaeological Reports

Sole, B, 1993 Metropolis in Mayfair, *London Archaeol*, **7**(5), 122–6

Spence, C, Schofield, J, & Shepherd, L (eds), 1989 *Digging in the City: The annual review 1988*. London: Museum of London

Spencer, B, 1984 Medieval seal-dies recently found at London, *Antiq J*, **64**, 376–82

Staehelin, F, 1948 *Die Schweiz in Römischer Zeit*, 3rd edn. Basel: Schwabe

Stanfield, J A, & Simpson, G, 1958 *Central Gaulish Potters*. London: Oxford University Press for the University of Durham

Stead, I M, 1991 The Snettisham Treasure: Excavations in 1990, *Antiquity*, **65**, 447–60

Stead, I M, & Rigby, V, 1986 *Baldock: The excavation of a Roman and pre-Roman Settlement, 1968–72*, Britannia Monogr Ser, **7**. London: Society for the Promotion of Roman Studies

Stead, I M, & Rigby, V, 1989 *Verulamium: The King Harry Lane site*, HBMC(E)/English Heritage Archaeol Rep, **12**. London: Historic Buildings and Monuments Commission for England

Stephenson, A, 2006 A London Crannog?, *Archaeology Matters*, **22** (Museum of London leaflet)

Stevenson, J, 1992 Copper-alloy objects, in C Cowan 1992, 82–97

Stone, H J W, 1935 The Pinner Grims Dyke, *Trans London Middlesex Archaeol Soc*, **7**, 284–301

Stow, J, 1720 *A Survey of the Cities of London and Westminster ... corrected, improved, and very much enlarged ... by John Strype*, 2 vols. London: A Churchill *et al*

Stow, J, 1908 *A Survey of London ... reprinted from the text of 1603*, intro and notes by C L Kingsford, 2 vols. Oxford: Clarendon Press; repr 1976, Oxford University Press

Straker, V, 1984 First and second century carbonised grain from Roman London in W Van Zeist & W A Casparie (eds) 1984, 323–9

Strong, D, 1968 The monument, in B Cunliffe (ed) 1968, 40–73

Strong, D, 1976 *Roman Art*. Harmondsworth: Penguin Books

Struck, M, 1993a Busta in Britannien und ihre Verbindungen zum Kontinent: allgemeine Überlegungen zur Herleitung der Bestattungssitte, in M. Struck (ed) 1993b, 81–94

Struck, M (ed), 1993b *Römerzeitliche Gräber als Quellen zu Religion, Bevolkerungsstruktur und Sozialgeschichte*, Archäologische Schriften des Instituts für Vor- und Frühgeschichte der Johannes Gutenburg-Universität Mainz, **3**. Mainz: Instituts für Vor- und Frühgeschichte der Johannes Gutenburg-Universität

Stukeley, W, [1717–] Commonplace Book, MS volume, Wiltshire Archaeological and Natural History Society Library, Wiltshire Heritage Museum, Devizes

Stukeley, W, 1724 *Itinerarium Curiosum: or, an Account of the Antiquitys and remarkable Curiositys in Nature or Art ... Centuria I*. London: printed for the author

Stukeley, W, 1776 *Itinerarium Curiosum: or, an Account of the Antiquities and remarkable Curiosities in Nature or Art ...* 2nd edn, 2 vols. London: Baker and Leigh

Sturges, G W, 1938 *Edmonton Past and Present I*. Edmonton: Montagu School Press

Suetonius, 1957 *The Twelve Caesars*, trans R Graves, Penguin Classics. Harmondsworth: Penguin

Sutherland, C H V, 1967 *Roman Imperial Coinage 6: From Diocletian's reform (AD 294) to the death of Maximinus (AD 313)*. London: Spink & Son Ltd

Swain, H (ed), 1991 *Competitive Tendering in Archaeology: papers presented at a one-day conference held in June 1990*. Hertford: Rescue

Swann, V G, & Macbridge, R, 2002 A Rhineland potter at the legionary fortress of York, in M Aldhouse-Green & P Webster (eds), *Artefacts and Archaeology: Aspects of the Celtic and Roman world*. Cardiff: University of Wales Press, 190–234

Swanton, M, 1996 *The Anglo-Saxon Chronicle*. London: J M Dent

Swift, D, 2003 *Roman Burials, Medieval Tenements and Suburban Growth: 201 Bishopsgate, City of London* MoLAS Archaeol Stud Ser, **10**. London: Museum of London Archaeology Service

Swoboda, E, 1937 Die Schlange im Mithraskult, *Jahreshefte des Österreichischen Archäologischen Institutes in Wien*, **30**, 1–27

Symonds, R P, 1992 *Rhenish wares: fine dark-coloured pottery from Gaul and Germany*, Oxford University Committee for Archaeology Monogr **23**. Oxford: Oxford University Committee for Archaeology

Symonds, R P, 1998 Quelques aperçus sur le port romain de Londres provoqués par les travaux du projet César, in L Rivet (ed), *SFECAG, Actes du Congrès d'Istres*. Marseille: Société Française d'Etude de la Céramique Antique en Gaule, 339–48

Symonds, R P, 2001 The Roman pottery, in T Brigham & A Woodger 2001, 85–92

Symonds, R P, & Fiedler, M, 2004 From Cantharos to Camulodunum form 306: Some unusual vessels found in the Western and Eastern Provinces, Unpubl paper presented at Res Cretariae Romanae Fautores, 2004, Namur, Belgium

Symonds, R P, & Tomber, R S, with Lakin, D, & Richardson, B, 1991 Late Roman London: an assessment of the ceramic evidence from the City of London, *Trans London Middlesex Archaeol Soc*, **42**, 59–99

Symonds, R P & Wade, S, 1999 *Roman pottery from excavations in Colchester, 1971–86*, Colchester Archaeol Rep **10**. Colchester: Colchester Archaeological Trust

Tanner, C E, & Clapham, A W, 1933 Recent discoveries in the nave of Westminster Abbey, *Archaeologia*, **83**, 227–36

Tatlock, J S P, 1950 *The Legendary History of Britain: Geoffrey of Monmouth's* Historia Regum Britanniae *and its early vernacular versions*. Berkeley: University of California Press; repr New York: Gordian Press 1974

Tatton-Brown, T, 1974 Excavations at the Custom House site, City of London 1973, *Trans London Middlesex Archaeol Soc*, **25**, 117–219

Taylor, J, 2004 Cannon Place, City of London EC4, Unpubl evaluation report for Museum of London Archaeology Service

Taylor-Wilson, R, 2002 *Excavations at Hunt's House, Guy's Hospital, London Borough of Southwark*, PCA Monogr, **1**. London: Pre-Construct Archaeology Ltd

Tester, P J, 1968 An Anglo-Saxon cemetery at Orpington: first interim report, *Archaeol Cantiana*, **83**, 125–50

Tester, P J, 1970 Excavations at Fordcroft, Orpington: concluding report, *Archaeol Cantiana*, **84**, 39–77

Thomas, C, Cowie, R, & Sidell, J, 2006 *The Royal Palace, Abbey and Town of Westminster on Thorney Island: Archaeological excavations (1991–8) for the London Underground Limited Jubilee Line Excension Project*, MoLAS Monogr Ser, **22**. London: Museum of London Archaeology Service

Thomas, C, & Rackham, D J, 1996 Bramcote Green, Bermondsey: A Bronze Age trackway and palaeoenvironmental sequence, *Proc Prehist Soc*, **61**, 221–53

Thompson, A, Westman, A, & Dyson, T (eds), 1998 *Archaeology in Greater London 1965–1990: A guide to records of excavations by the Museum of London*, Archaeol Gazetteer Ser, **2**. London: Museum of London

Tipper, J, 2004 *The Grubenhaus in Anglo-Saxon England: An analysis and interpretation of the evidence from a most distincitive building type*. Yedingham: Landscape Research Centre

Tomlin, R S O, 1979 Graffiti on Roman bricks and tiles found in Britain, in A McWhirr (ed), *Roman Brick and Tile*, BAR Internat Ser, **68**. Oxford: British Archaeological Reports, 231–51

Tomlin, R S O, 1996 A five-acre wood in Roman Kent, in J Bird *et al* (eds) 1996, 209–15

Tomlin, R S O, 2003 'The girl in question': a New Text from Roman London, *Britannia*, **34**, 41–51

Tomlin, R S O, & Hassall, M W C, 2003 Roman Britain in 2002: 2 Inscriptions, *Britannia*, **34**, 361–82

Tomlinson, P, & Hall, A R, 1996 A review of the archaeological evidence for food plants in the British Isles: an example of the use of the Archaeobotanical Computer Database (ABCD), *Internet Archaeol*, **1**, http://intarch.ac.uk/journal/issue1/index.html

Townend, P, & Hinton, P, 1978 Small finds, 201–211 Borough High Street, in SLAEC 1978, 156–63

Toynbee, J M C, 1962 *Art in Roman Britain*. London: Phaidon

Toynbee, J M C, 1964 *Art in Britain under the Romans*. Oxford: Clarendon Press

Toynbee, J M C, 1973 *Animals in Roman Life and Art*. London: Thames & Hudson

Toynbee, J M C, 1986 *The Roman Art Treasures from the Temple of Mithras*, LAMAS Special Paper, **7**. London: London and Middlesex Archaeological Society

Trow, S D, 1988 The copper-alloy objects, in T W Potter & S D Trow, *Puckeridge-Braughing, Hertfordshire: The Ermine Street excavations 1971–72*, Hertfordshire Archaeol **10**. Hertford: St Albans & Hertfordshire Architectural & Archaeological Society, 58–67

Turcan, R, 1996 *The Cults of the Roman Empire* (trans A Neville). Oxford: Blackwell

Turner, E C, & Skutsch, O, 1960 A Roman writing-tablet from London, *J Roman Stud*, **50**, 108–11

Tyers, I, 1988, Environmental evidence from Southwark and Lambeth, in P Hinton (ed) 1988, 5–12

Tyers, I, 1994 Appendix 6. Dendrochronology of Roman and early medieval ships, in P Marsden 1994, 201–9

Tyers, I, 2001 Appendix 2. Tree-ring analysis of the Roman and medieval timbers from medieval London Bridge and its environs, in B Watson *et al* 2001, 180–90

Tyers, I, Hillam, J, & Groves, C, 1994 Trees and woodland in the Saxon period: the dendrochronological evidence, in J Rackham (ed), *Environment and Economy in Anglo-Saxon England: A review of recent work on the environmental archaeology of rural and urban Anglo-Saxon settlements in England*, CBA Res Rep, **89**. York: Council for British Archaeology, 12–22

Tyson, M, 1925 The annals of Southwark and Merton, *Surrey Archaeol Collect*, **36**, 24–57

Urban Task Force, 1999 *Towards an urban renaissance: the report of the Urban Task Force*. London: Department of Environment

van Andringa, W, 2002 *La religion en Gaule romaine*. Paris: Errance

Van Zeist, W, & Casparie, W A (eds), 1984 *Plants and ancient man* Rotterdam: Balkema

Veyne, P, 1990 Bread and Circuses: Historical sociology and political pluralism (trans B Pearce). London: Allen Lane

Vince, A, 1990 *Saxon London: An archaeological investigation*. London: Seaby

Vince, A, & Jenner, A, 1991 The Saxon and early medieval pottery of London, in A Vince (ed), *Aspects of Saxo-Norman London II: Finds and environmental evidence*, LAMAS Special Paper, **12**. London: London and Middlesex Archaeological Society, 19–119

Vollenweider, M-L, 1984 Deliciae Leonis: *Antike geschnittene Steine und Ringe aus einer Privatsammlung*. Mainz: Verlag Philipp von Zabern

von Saldern, A, 1985 Römischer Hochschliffgläser, *Sonderdruck aus den Jahrbuch des Museums für Kunst und Gewerbe Hamburg*, **4**, 27–42

Vuolteenaho, J, 2005 568A Roman Road, Bow, London. An archaeological evaluation report. Unpubl report for Museum of London Archaeology Service, Site Code ROB05

Wacher, J, 1995 *The Towns of Roman Britain*. London: Batsford

Wakeford, J, 1984 Two *wahl* names in the fields of Kingston, *Surrey Archaeol Collect*, **75**, 251–6

Wallace-Hadrill, A, 1994 *Houses and Society in Pompeii and Herculaneum*. Princeton: Princeton University Press

Ward, J, 1911 *The Roman Era in Britain*. London: Methuen & Co Ltd

Wardle, A, 1998 Roman London: recent finds and research, in B Watson (ed) 1998b, 83–9

Wardle, A, 2000 Funerary rites, burial practice and belief, in A Mackinder 2000, 27–30

Wardle, A, 2001 The Roman finds, in T Brigham & A Woodger 2001, 92–9

Wardle, A, 2002a Accessioned finds, in D Lakin *et al* 2002, 51–3

Wardle, A, 2002b The accessioned finds, in J Drummond-Murray *et al* 2002, 212–30

Wardle, A, 2003 The accessioned finds, in C Cowan 2003, 150–75

Wardle, A (ed), 2005 Londinium: An assessment of resources, Unpubl report for English Heritage

Wardle, A, forthcoming a The accessioned finds and glass, in L Dunwoodie *et al* forthcoming

Wardle, A, forthcoming b The finds from 1 Poultry, in J Hill & P Rowsome forthcoming

Ward-Perkins, J, & Claridge, A, 1976 *Pompeii AD79*. Bristol: Imperial Tobacco Ltd

Watson, B, 1998a Dark earth and urban decline in late Roman London, in B Watson (ed) 1998b, 100–6

Watson, B (ed), 1998b *Roman London: Recent archaeological work*, JRA Suppl Ser, **24**. Portsmouth, Rhode Island: Journal of Roman Archaeology

Watson, B, Brigham, T, & Dyson, T, 2001 *London Bridge: 2000 years of a river crossing*, MoLAS Monogr Ser, **8**. London: Museum of London Archaeology Service

Watson, S, 2003 *An Excavation in the Western Cemetery of Roman London: Atlantic House, City of London*, MoLAS Archaeol Stud Ser, **7**. London: Museum of London Archaeology Service

Webb, P H, 1933 *Roman Imperial Coinage 5.2: Probus to Amandus*. London: Spink & Son Ltd

Webster, G A, 1987 Other objects of bronze, in G B Dannell & J P Wild, *Longthorpe II*, Britannia Monogr Ser, **8**. London: Society for the Promotion of Roman Studies, 87–95

Webster, J, 1973 A bronze incense container in the form of Bacchus from Carlisle, *Trans Cumberland Westmorland Archaeol Soc*, **73**, 90–3

Webster, J, 1995 *Interpretatio*: Roman word power and the Celtic gods, *Britannia*, **26**, 153–61

Webster, L E, & Cherry, J (eds), 1980 Medieval Britain in 1979, *Medieval Archaeol*, **24**, 218–64

Welch, M G, 1975 Mitcham Grave 205 and the chronology of applied brooches with floriate cross decoration, *Antiq J*, **55**, 86–95

Welch, M, 1997 The Anglo-Saxon cemetery at 82–90 Park Lane, Croydon, Surrey: excavation or preservation?, *London Archaeol*, 8(4), 94–7

Wells, C, 1986 *The Roman Empire*. Stanford, Ca: Stanford University Press

Westlake, H, 1923 *Westminster Abbey*. London: P Allen & Co

Westman, A, 1998 Publishing Roman Southwark: New evidence from the archive, in B Watson (ed) 1998b, 61–6

Wheeler, R E M, 1928 *The Cheapside Hoard of Elizabethan and Jacobean Jewellery,* London Museum Cat, **2**. London: London Museum

Wheeler, R E M, 1930 *London in Roman Times,* London Museum Cat, **3**. London: London Museum

Wheeler, R E M, 1934 The topography of Saxon London, *Antiquity*, 8, 290–303

Wheeler, R E M, 1935 *London and the Saxons,* London Museum Cat, **6**. London: London Museum

Whimster, R, 1981 *Burial Practices in Iron Age Britain: A discussion and gazetteer of the evidence c. 700 BC–AD 43*, (2 vols), BAR Brit Ser, **90**. Oxford: British Archaeological Reports

Whipp, D, 1980 Excavations at Tower Hill, 1978, *Trans London Middlesex Archaeol Soc*, **31**, 47–67

Whittaker, C, 1911 *An Illustrated Statistical and Topographical Account of the History of Enfield.* London: George Bell & Sons

Whytehead, R, 1986 The excavation of an area within a Roman cemetery at West Tenter Street, London E1, *Trans London Middlesex Archaeol Soc,* **37**, 23–124

Whytehead, R, Cowie, R & Blackmore, L, 1989 Excavations at the Peabody site, Chandos Place, and the National Gallery, *Trans London Middlesex Archaeol Soc,* **40**, 35–176

Wiedemann, T, 1992 *Emperors and Gladiators.* London: Routledge

Wightman, E M, 1970 *Roman Trier and the Treveri.* London: Rupert Hart-Davis

Wilkes, J, 1996 The status of *Londinium,* in J Bird *et al* (eds) 1996, 27–31

Wilkinson, D R P, 1994 Excavations on the White Cliffs Experience site, Dover 1988–91, *Archaeol Cantiana,* **114**, 51–148

Wilkinson, K N, 1998 An investigation into the geoarchaeology of foreshore deposits at Bull Wharf, Unpubl report for King Alfred's College, Winchester

Wilkinson, K N, Scaife, R G, & Sidell, E J, 2000 Environmental and sea level changes in London from 10,500 BP to the present: a case study from Silvertown, *Proc Geologists' Assoc,* **111**, 41–54

Willcox, G H, 1977 Exotic plants from Roman water-logged sites in London, *J Archaeol Science,* **4**, 269–82

Willcox, G H, 1978 Seeds from the late-2nd-century pit F28, in SLAEC 1978, 411–14

Williams, D, 2002 Amphorae, in R Taylor-Wilson 2002, 50

Williams, H P G, 2004 *Carausius. A consideration of the historical, archaeological and numismatic aspects of his reign,* BAR Brit Ser, **378**. Oxford: British Archaeological Reports

Williams, T, 1993 *The Archaeology of Roman London 3: Public Buildings in the South-West Quarter of Roman London,* CBA Res Rep, **88**. London: Council for British Archaeology

Williams, T, forthcoming *The Archaeology of Roman London 4: Roman London east of the Walbrook.* CBA Res Rep

Willis, S, 1998 Samian pottery in Britain: Exploring its distribution and archaeological potential, *Archaeol J,* **155**, 82–133

Willis, S, 2005 The context of writing and written records in ink: The archaeology of samian inkwells in Roman Britain, *Archaeol J,* **162**, 96–145

Wilmott, T, 1991 *Excavations in the Middle Walbrook Valley, City of London 1927–1960,* LAMAS Special Paper, **13**. London: London and Middlesex Archaeological Society

Wilson, R J A, & Creighton, J D, 1999 Introduction: recent research on Roman Germany, in J D Creighton & R J A Wilson (eds), *Roman Germany. Studies in cultural interaction,* J Roman Archaeol Suppl Ser, **32**. Portsmouth, Rhode Island: Journal of Roman Archaeology, 9–34

Witt, P, 2005 *Mosaics in Roman Britain: Stories in stone.* Stroud: Tempus

Witt, R E, 1971 *Isis in the Graeco-Roman World.* London: Thames & Hudson

Woodward, J, 1723 *Remarks upon the antient and present state of London, occasioned by some Roman urns, coins, and other antiquities, lately discovered,* 3rd edn. London: A Bettesworth, W Taylor, R Gosling & J Clarke

Woolf, G, 1998 *Becoming Roman.* Cambridge: Cambridge University Press

Woolliscroft, D J, 2001 *Roman Military Signalling.* Stroud: Tempus Publishing

Worrell, S, 2005 Roman Britain in 2004 II. Finds reported under the Portable Antiquities Scheme, *Britannia,* **36**, 447–72

Wren, C (ed), 1750 *Parentalia: or, Memoirs of the Family of the Wrens ...* London: T Osborn *et al*; repr (facsimile) Farnborough: Gregg 1965

Wright, R P, 1956 Roman Britain in 1955: II Inscriptions, *J Roman Stud,* **46**, 146–52

Wright, R P, 1977 A Roman veterinary physician from the Thames valley, *Britannia,* **8**, 279–82

Wuilleumier, P, 1963 *Inscriptions Latines des Trois Gaules,* Gallia suppl, **17**. Paris: Gallia

Yadin, Y, 1963 *The Finds from the Bar Kokhbar period in the cave of Letters.* Jerusalem: Israel Exploration Society

York, J, 2002 The life cycle of Bronze Age metalwork from the Thames, *Oxford J Archaeol,* **21**(1), 77–92

Young, C J, 1977 *The Roman pottery industry of the Oxford region,* BAR Brit Ser, **43**, Oxford: British Archaeological Reports

Youngs, S M, Clark, J, & Barry, T (eds), 1986 Medieval Britain and Ireland in 1985, *Medieval Archaeol,* **30**, 114–98

Yule, B, 1982 A third century well group and later Roman settlement in Southwark, *London Archaeol,* **4**(9), 243–9

Yule, B, 1988 The natural topography of north Southwark, in P Hinton (ed) 1988, 13–18

Yule, B, 1990 The 'dark earth' and late Roman London, *Antiquity,* **64**, 620–8

Yule, B, 2005 *A Prestigious Roman Building Complex on the Southwark Waterfront: Excavations at Winchester Palace, London, 1983–90,* MoLAS Monogr Ser, **23**. London: Museum of London Archaeology Service

Zeepvat, R J, 1991 Roman gardens in Britain, in A E Brown (ed) 1991, 53–9

Zienkiewicz, J D, 1986a The engraved gemstones, in J D Zienkiewicz 1986b, 117–41

Zienkiewicz, J D, 1986b *The Legionary Fortress Baths at Caerleon; II The Finds.* Cardiff: Cadw

Zwierlein-Diehl, E, 1991 *Die antiken Gemmen des Kunsthistorishen Museums in Wien 3.* Munich: Prestel Verlag

Zwierlein-Diehl, E, 1998 *Die Gemmen und Kameen des Dreikönigenschreines.* Cologne: Verlag Kölner Dom

Suggested editions for classical sources cited

Annales Vedastini Available at http://www. thelatinlibrary.com/annalesvedastini.html last accessed 21/01/08

Aphthonius Προγυμνασματα, in L Spengel ed 1854 *Rhetores Graeci* **2**. Leipzig

Apuleius *Metamorphoses*, 2 vols, Loeb Classical Library **453**, 1989

Augustine *Confessions*, 2 vols, Loeb Classical Library **26**, 1912

Ausonius *The Poems*, 2 vols, Loeb Classical Library **115**, 1919–21

Bede *Ecclesiastical History of the English People*, Oxford Medieval Texts, 1969

Caesar **1** *The Gallic War*, Loeb Classical Library **72**, 1917

Cato, *de Agricultura*, in Cato & Varro *On Agriculture*, Loeb Classical Library **283**, 1934

Celsus *On Medicine*, 3 vols, Loeb Classical Library **292, 304, 336**, 1935–38

Cicero **18** *Tusculan Disputations*, 2nd edn, Loeb Classical Library, **141**, 1945

Dio, Cassius *Roman History*, 9 vols, Loeb Classical Library **32 etc,** 191415027

Galen *On the Natural Faculties*, Loeb Classical Library **71**, 1916

Gellius *Noctes Atticae*, 2nd edn, Oxford Classical Texts, 1969

Horace *Satires,* in Horace **2** *Satires, Epistles, The Art of Poetry* Loeb Classical Library **194**, 1926

Juvenal, in *Juvenal and Persius*, Loeb Classical Library, **91N**, 2004

Livy *History of Rome*, 14 vols, Loeb Classical Library **114 etc**, 1919–67

Martial *Epigrams*, 3 vols, Loeb Classical Library **94, 95, 480**, 1993

Martial *Spectacles*, in *Epigrams* 1, Loeb Classical Library **94**, 1993

Ovid **3-4** *Metamorphoses*, 2 vols, Loeb Classical Library **42, 43**, 1916

XII Panegyrici Latini, Oxford Classical Texts, 1964

Petronius *Satyricon*, in Petronius & Seneca *Satyricon and Apocolocyntosis,* Loeb Classical Library **15**, 1913

Pliny *Natural History*, 10 vols, Loeb Classical Library **330 etc**, 1938–63

Pliny *Panegyricus,* in Pliny the Younger **2** *Letters (books 8–10), Panegyricus,* Loeb Classical Library **59**, 1969

Plutarch *The Obsolescence of Oracles,* in Plutarch *Moralia* **5**, Loeb Classical Library **306**, 1936

Plutarch *Isis and Osiris,* in Plutarch *Moralia* **5**, Loeb Classical Library **306**, 1936

Plutarch *Sulla,* in Plutarch *Parallel Lives 4: Alcibiades and Coriolanus, Lysander and Sulla,* Loeb Classical Edition 80, 1916

Scriptores Historiae Augustae **2**, Loeb Classical Library **140**, 1924

Scriptores Historiae Augustae **3**, Loeb Classical Library **263**, 1932

Suetonius *The Lives of the Caesars*, 2nd edn, 2 vols, Loeb Classical Library **31, 38**, 1998, 1997

Tacitus *Agricola* in Tacitus **1**, 2nd edn, Loeb Classical Library **35**, 1970

Tacitus *Annals,* Tacitus **3-5**, Loeb Classical Library **249, 312, 322**, 1931, 1937, 1937

Tacitus *Historiae,* Tacitus **2-3**, Loeb Classical Library **111, 249**, 1925, 1931

Tertullian *ad Nationes* Available via http:// www.tertullian.org/works/ad_nationes.htm last accessed 21/01/08

Tertullian *Apology*, in Tertullian *Apology and de Spectaculis* & Minucius Felix *Octavius,* Loeb Classical Library **250**, 1937

Tertullian *De Spectaculis*, in Tertullian *Apology and de Spectaculis* & Minucius Felix *Octavius,* Loeb Classical Library **250**, 1937

Varro *Rerum Rusticarum*, in Cato & Varro *On Agriculture*, Loeb Classical Library **283**, 1934

Virgil, *Aeneid* 2 vols, 2nd edn, Loeb Classical Library **63–4**, 1999, 2000

Virgil *Eclogues,* in Virgil **1** *Eclogues, Georgics, Aeneid books 1–6*, 2nd edn, Loeb Classical Library **63**, 1999

Index

Entries in bold refer to the illustrations